THE BEST PLAYS OF 1943-44

"WINGED VICTORY"

Pvt. Mark Daniels, Pvt. Don Taylor, Pfc. Edmond O'Brien, Pvt. Peter Lind Hayes, Pvt. George Petrie, Pvt. Alfred Ryder, Pvt. Karl Malden, and Pvt. Martin Ritt, of the "Winged Victory" detail, take time out to relax at a rehearsal of the soldier show.

THE BEST PLAYS
OF 1943-44

AND THE
YEAR BOOK OF THE DRAMA
IN AMERICA

EDITED BY
BURNS MANTLE

With Illustrations

DODD, MEAD AND COMPANY
NEW YORK - - - 1944

COPYRIGHT, 1944,

BY DODD, MEAD AND COMPANY, INC.

★   ★   ★   ★

569208

INTRODUCTION

WHILE the theatre season of 1943-44, our third war year, may reasonably be listed with other war casualties, it had its points. Men must work and women must weep through such emergencies; inspirations falter and routines fail, but some good is bound to come out of the overall adventure.

The greatest disappointment strangely was in the quality of the war plays themselves. They were still full of bombs and heroics. None, save perhaps Howard Rigsby and Dorothy Heyward's "South Pacific," added much to the philosophical or psychological acceptance and understanding of war that could help a groping and confused people. "South Pacific" did pose the interesting problem of a Negro's reaction to the freedom for which a world is fighting, and also striving variously to commit every form of material and spiritual destruction made known to man through the centuries of his climb out of the primordial ooze.

The two war plays I have selected are Moss Hart's "Winged Victory" and Maxwell Anderson's "Storm Operation." These two, to me, have qualities of actuality and immediacy that lift them above the others.

"Winged Victory" was confessedly propaganda drama. It was deliberately conceived and written to do honor and credit to that blessed American Army Air Force for which millions of prayers have gone into the "wild blue yonder" about which they sing so lustily in their Army Air Corps song.

If you want to believe that the Hart story is told by idealized boys hand-picked from forty-eight states and put through certain glamorized war pictures, all right. But remember that not a day passes without one or another first page proudly blaring forth the news of just such boys completing gloriously just such missions. Take a moment out to be proud and grateful.

Anderson's "Storm Operation," like Anderson's "Candle in the Wind," mixed realistic war and theatrical romance unevenly and unimpressively, but it happens to have been the one play of the year that, in its better moments, did bring a particular phase of this war home to the American public, which needed to be told about it.

Lillian Hellman's "The Searching Wind" and Edward Chodorov's "Decision" are more impressive in character than they are convincing in story, but each was honestly written and with a purpose. Miss Hellman was, of course, advantaged by that factor of hindsight which is not only common to all humanity but of quite universal application. But it also should be strongly stressed that for years, antedating the so-called Spanish Civil War and the dealings of both appeasers and sympathizers with the Franco Government, this author was of the one mind that sweeps through "The Searching Wind."

Mr. Chodorov's "Decision" may overstress, through a prejudiced conviction, both racial injustice and the viciousness of high-standing politicians, but there is enough sound and moving drama in his exaggerations and enough truth in his better character studies, to give the play a good deal of force.

Rose Franken, it seems to me, overgenerously rather than exaggeratedly, peopled her stage with a household of unhappy and slightly abnormal humans in "Outrageous Fortune." She thereby weakened the general appeal of her play by limiting it to the more intelligently analytical type of playgoer. Elsa Shelley (or her directors) similarly overstressed the sordidness and misery that lead to social disease and human catastrophe in "Pick-up Girl." But as this over-emphasis does not defeat either the timeliness or sociological importance of the "Pick-up Girl" exposures, neither does it obscure completely the truth and honesty of Miss Franken's characters and their respective reactions in "Outrageous Fortune."

Let us be grateful for the lighter plays. There have not been many of them, but they literally have saved the season by proving that the art of writing sane and stimulating human comedy has not been lost.

John Van Druten's "The Voice of the Turtle" is an extraordinarily human story of sinning with the sophisticates. It was made acceptable and appealing by the wisdom of its casting and the basic decencies that shone through the performances of its original players—Margaret Sullavan, Elliott Nugent and Audrey Christie.

Miss Gordon's "Over 21" was plainly written in the hope that it would amuse the Ruth Gordon following, which is large, and add a public represented by her soldier husband, Garson Kanin, whose adventures as a service man it doubtless reflects. It turned out to be a sample of keenly observant playwriting and character creation, and this augurs well for the comedienne's writing future.

The Theatre Guild, properly puffed with pride because of its success with "Oklahoma!" and the Paul Robeson "Othello," made two happy comedy selections with the Behrman-Werfel "Jacobowsky and the Colonel" and the Osborn-Hughes "The Innocent Voyage," but only the first of them paid a profit.

"Jacobowsky," a good character comedy, makes a strong war-time racial and refugee appeal, and is smartly played. "The Innocent Voyage" seemed to fall between two publics—the one that had read the Richard Hughes novel, "A High Wind in Jamaica," and liked the book better than the play, and the typical Broadway public that is never very deeply interested in plays touching upon the fantastic and calling for the support of finer imaginations.

A casualty list these 1943-44 best plays may be, but it is a list that fits consistently into the theatre record of a nation at war. Historians of the future, contrasting it with earlier war-time seasons, and linking it to those that are to follow, will, I hope, be able to extract from it significant trends and interesting analogies.

CONTENTS

	PAGE
INTRODUCTION	V
THE SEASON IN NEW YORK	3
THE SEASON IN CHICAGO	17
THE SEASON IN SAN FRANCISCO	22
THE SEASON IN SOUTHERN CALIFORNIA	27
WINGED VICTORY, BY MOSS HART	32
THE SEARCHING WIND, BY LILLIAN HELLMAN	69
THE VOICE OF THE TURTLE, BY JOHN VAN DRUTEN	104
DECISION, BY EDWARD CHODOROV	133
OVER 21, BY RUTH GORDON	164
OUTRAGEOUS FORTUNE, BY ROSE FRANKEN	198
JACOBOWSKY AND THE COLONEL, BY S. N. BEHRMAN	236
STORM OPERATION, BY MAXWELL ANDERSON	277
PICK-UP GIRL, BY ELSA SHELLEY	315
THE INNOCENT VOYAGE, BY PAUL OSBORN	355
THE PLAYS AND THEIR AUTHORS	394
PLAYS PRODUCED IN NEW YORK, 1943-44	400
DANCE DRAMA	485
OFF BROADWAY	488
STATISTICAL SUMMARY	491
LONG RUNS ON BROADWAY	492
NEW YORK DRAMA CRITICS' CIRCLE AWARD	494
PULITZER PRIZE WINNERS	496

x CONTENTS

	PAGE
PREVIOUS VOLUMES OF BEST PLAYS	498
WHERE AND WHEN THEY WERE BORN	512
NECROLOGY	523
THE DECADES' TOLL	530
INDEX OF AUTHORS	533
INDEX OF PLAYS AND CASTS	538
INDEX OF PRODUCERS, DIRECTORS AND DESIGNERS	544

ILLUSTRATIONS

WINGED VICTORY . . . . *Frontispiece*

FACING PAGE

THE SEARCHING WIND 84

THE VOICE OF THE TURTLE 116

DECISION 148

OVER 21 180

OUTRAGEOUS FORTUNE 212

JACOBOWSKY AND THE COLONEL 244

STORM OPERATION 308

PICK-UP GIRL 340

THE INNOCENT VOYAGE 372

THE BEST PLAYS OF 1943-44

THE BEST PLAYS OF 1943-44

THE SEASON IN NEW YORK

FROM the showman's point of view, which is naturally that of the box office, this third war season in the theatre will doubtless be counted one of the best. More poor plays sold for more good money than were ever before recorded. Many merely good plays were fairly consistent box office successes and, of course, the legitimately successful plays were sensational money makers.

However, the generally current impression that there were practically no box office failures was not borne out by the facts. That commercially biased, but generally honest compiler of theatre statistics, *Variety*, counted only fourteen real hits and six moderate hits against fifty failures. As all *Variety* statisticians know but one yard stick—the money in the till—this estimate added up to a quite average season, so far as the new offerings were concerned.

To be entirely fair such holdover successes as "Oklahoma!," "Arsenic and Old Lace," "The Doughgirls," "Life with Father," "Angel Street," "Kiss and Tell," "Three's a Family," "Tomorrow the World" and "Ziegfeld Follies" should be listed as legitimately successful shows. And certainly two outstanding revivals, the Paul Robeson "Othello" and the Kiepura-Eggerth "Merry Widow," should be included. Both proved happy surprises to their producers, their stars and their new-found publics.

In years to come the season of 1943-44 will be listed as one more slightly abnormal play-producing period when neither the New York Drama Critics' Circle nor the Pulitzer Prize Committee could agree upon a single play of American authorship worthy of their respective accolades. The critics recorded six of thirteen votes for Lillian Hellman's "The Searching Wind," but the Pulitzers came no closer to a selection than to vote a special citation of excellence and $500 to the long-running and still popular "Oklahoma!"

There was during the Winter quite a rush of Hollywood writers back to Broadway with such scripts as they couldn't sell in story conferences out West. Few of them won more than a patronizing nod from either reviewers or audiences, but several of them did do well in that successful box office group before mentioned.

It was a wonderful season for angels. There was probably more "outside" money invested in show business in 1943-44 than in any previous theatre season on record. Much of it came in small lots from friends and relatives of playwrights and play producers. Groups of backers ranging in number from ten to thirty were common. There were, by report, twenty-three backers of "Arsenic and Old Lace" and each of them according to the *Times*, realized something like a $7,400 return on every $583.34 invested for a 5/6th of 1 per cent interest.

There was not even a mythical dividing line between theatre seasons the Summer of 1943. Taking June 15 as an arbitrary closing date for the purpose of keeping the record straight we ended the last issue of "Best Plays" with the production of a soldier show—"The Army Play-by-Play"—which John Golden and Lt.-Col. William R. Bolton of the Second Service Command jointly sponsored on June 14, 1943. And we started the new season with a wartime love romance called "Those Endearing Young Charms" two evenings later. Edward Chodorov was the author, Max Gordon the producer. Mr. Gordon selected the players carefully, giving the ingénue lead to pretty Virginia Gilmore of the movies and adding the capable Zachary Scott, Dean Harens and Blanche Sweet to make up a four-character cast. The play was politely, though not enthusiastically received, and was reluctantly withdrawn by Mr. Gordon after 61 performances.

The following night Richard Kollmar, taking a flier in play production with a rowdy musical, "Early to Bed," and singing the baritone lead himself, struck the season's first jackpot. The popular colored composer, Thomas ("Fats") Waller, who died last Winter, had written the score for this one, and George Marion, Jr., the book. "Early to Bed" kept service men and vacation visitors to Broadway excited the Summer through and made a subway circuit tour after that. According to the Broadway gossips, Producer Kollmar was generously backed by a group of successful night club proprietors.

July was barren of Summer productions, but early August found the producers active. Because of the one-night succcess of "The Army Play-by-Play," that soldier show was brought back and continued for a run of 40 performances, after which it went touring and added goodly sums to the Army Relief charities. Elizabeth Bergner, a popular continental comedienne and a popular Berlin favorite before the war, was started on a starring engagement in a slightly shivery melodrama called "The Two Mrs. Carrolls." The author, programmed as Martin Vale, turned out to be the widow of the late Bayard Veiller. The producer was Miss Bergner's husband, Paul Czinner, working in association with Robert Reud. The result was a popular success, traceable quite obviously to the personal charms of Miss Bergner, a pert and pleasing ingénue with definite dramatic gifts.

Two Summer revivals were "The Vagabond King," which did not do so well, and "The Merry Widow," which did much better than expected. In "The Vagabond King" the François Villon role, with which Dennis King had earned a great personal success in 1925, was sung by John Brownlee of the Metropolitan. In "The Merry Widow" two former Continental favorites, Jan Kiepura and Marta Eggerth, sang the roles of Sonia and Prince Danilo. Backed by a handsome production, they brought the old-time favorite to life again, and kept it in favor for many months.

Because the Negro play, "Run Little Chillun," had proved much more popular west of New York than it had in New York, even though it did run for 126 performances in 1933, Lew Cooper, Meyer Davis and George Jessel decided to revive it in August. However, though the reviews were favorable, and even a little exciting, the weather was neither and 16 performances were all that were given.

A revival of the Russian "Chauve Souris," which had been a sensation when Morris Gest brought it to America from Paris just after the First World War, suffered a similar public reaction. Revived competently, with a new group of Russian specialists assembled by Leon Greanin, by an arrangement with Mme. Nikita Balieff, widow of the original leader and popular conferencier, its petered out in two weeks.

A group of experienced theatre folk, including Bretaigne Windust, the director, thought to try for a Summer run with a murder mystery called "Murder Without Crime." Young Mr. Windust played a harassed hero who was about to lose his mind. He was made to believe he had murdered the woman with whom he had been having an affair. Again the reviewers were not unfriendly, but the public was. Thirty-seven performances and "Murder Without Crime" became a failure without dishonor.

By September it had become increasingly apparent that New York was to be crowded with vacationers and war workers, probably for the duration of the war. Broadway blossomed with play producers who were burdened with boom-time ambitions. Jack Kirkland revived his fabulous "Tobacco Road," to give it a new boost toward an eighth year on the road. The Shuberts brought "Blossom Time" back with Alexander Gray and Barbara Scully singing the leads. Noel Coward's highly successful "Blithe Spirit," which had been withdrawn for the summer to give the cast a rest, was resumed, preliminary to taking to the road. A vaudeville combination headed by Ethel Waters, Frank Fay and Bert Wheeler, quickly found a public and ran on for 126 performances. "Porgy and Bess," also headed for the touring country, was given a three-week start in 44th Street.

A new revue, Irving Caesar's "My Dear Public," which had been threatened with production for months, was finally exhibited. It proved to be still a threat rather than an achievement. Another, "Bright Lights of 1944," with Smith and Dale, Jim Barton and Frances Williams, among many others, lasted no more than 4 performances.

The first serious drama of the season was Elmer Rice's "A New Life," with the author's gifted wife, Betty Field, playing the heroine. Some little stir, and a slight embarrassment, was caused when the reviewers discovered that Mr. Rice had staged one scene in the delivery room of a maternity hospital at the climax of the heroine's accouchement. Following this scene the protagonists of "A New Life" argued earnestly for and against the American way of living and thinking. The heroine (a radio actress) contended that she had every right to direct the upbringing of her own offspring. Her husband's capitalistically-conscious family insisted that the child should be turned over to those who could give it proper social and financial advantages. The heroine won, but the play had a struggle. It quit after 69 performances.

A second serious September effort was "Land of Fame," which in a way repeated the story of the little people's part in the war that Dan James had told in "Winter Soldiers." Albert and Mary Bein wrote it, and there was support from a small but loyal public. However, the bankroll was weak and the play closed at the end of its first week.

"All for All," a fairly crude revival of the older "Give and Take," with comedians Harry Green and Jack Pearl playing the Potash-Perlmutter leads, hung around for eleven weeks, a little to its backers' surprise. Something called "Hairpin Harmony," with a score, book and bankroll by Harold Orlob, was out in two performances, following a terrible drubbing by the press.

Mary Martin, who had made a reputation singing "My Heart Belongs to Daddy" in "Let's Face It," helped a good deal in carrying "One Touch of Venus" through a season's run. Frederick Lonsdale's "Another Love Story" also surprised those reviewers who did not care for it by playing 103 performances, when they had figured that it would be all through in a week or two. The popularity of Roland Young and Margaret Lindsay, he a popular comedian, she a picture favorite, was credited with the run.

The Theatre Guild's revival of "Othello," which had been waiting a year to permit Paul Robeson to clear his concert engagements, was a mid-October event of first importance. The colored actor's reception created an enthusiasm verging on the rapturous. His personal success mounted as the engagement continued and his reading and performance gained in resonance and poise. José Ferrer was the Iago and Uta Hagan (Mrs. Ferrer) the Desdemona.

Eddie Dowling found a part in a play Roy Walling had written and called "Manhattan Nocturne" that pleased him. It was that of a novelist who, during a temporary frustration, agrees to divorce his disappointed wife. To provide the necessary legal evidence he visits a call house and engages a companion with whom to be surprised by the wife and her lawyer. Later, becoming interested in the case of the girl who has helped him, the novelist defends her in court and helps her gain her release from the panderers who had been holding her captive. Three uncertain weeks was as long as "Manhattan Nocturne" could last, although many thought it deserved better than that.

A farce comedy, "Victory Belles," written by Alice Gerstenberg, brought Barbara Bennett on from Hollywood. The critics thought it was pretty poor entertainment, but audiences laughed and the engagement was extended several times. Mary Elizabeth Sherwood, a theatre-conscious Californian, decided that New York was ready for a popular-priced stock company, and engaged the roof theatre atop the New Amsterdam for purposes of experiment. Her first week she revived Robert Sherwood's "The Petrified Forest." The second week she revived the Allan Scott-George Haight "Good-by Again." The third week she flirted with the idea of trying an original play, "Crosstown Bus." The fourth week she called it a season and quit. A courageous venture, but New York just doesn't like popular-priced stock companies. It will pay outrageous prices for new hits, but old hits, even of better plays, leave it cold.

The most controversial, and the most intelligently written, of the early season plays, was Rose Franken's "Outrageous Fortune." The play was brought to production by its author and her husband, William Brown Meloney, after having been tried out with Gilbert Miller as a co-producer. Mr. Miller withdrew when the Meloneys objected to taking the play off the stage while Miss Franken rewrote it in part. The press reception of "Outrageous Fortune" was surprisingly friendly. Even those reviewers who could not generously approve of it admitted its interest-exciting qualities and the excellence of the performance given it. The company was headed by Elsie Ferguson, returned to the stage after a thirteen year retirement, and included Mme. Ouspenskaya, Margalo Gillmore and Frederic Tozere. For ten weeks arguments for and against the drama's statements and conclusions were freely spoken. When by that time a paying response on the part of the public had not developed, "Outrageous Fortune" was withdrawn.

An October item was a farce called "Naked Genius." Gypsy Rose Lee, famed as a stripteuse, wrote it; George Kaufman staged it; Michael Todd produced it and Joan Blondell came on from Hollywood to play its leading character. This heroine was a strip-tease girl with social and literary ambitions who sold tickets to her own wedding and gave a floor show for the guests. The reports from out of town were that Miss Lee and Mr. Kaufman both begged Mr. Todd not to risk "Naked Genius" in New York, but Mr. Todd would not listen. The box office reception on Broadway was lively, but after the film rights had been made secure Todd voluntarily withdrew the play.

"I'll Take the High Road" proved a weak comedy, interesting principally because it introduced Jimmy Cagney's younger sister, Jeanne, as its heroine. "What's Up" turned out to be a musical comedy of slight appeal, though it had Jimmy Savo as its star and a troupe of promising youngsters in its cast.

The Theatre Guild tried Paul Osborn's dramatization of a Richard Hughes novel, "The Innocent Voyage"—an amusing story of a group of English children who find themselves on a pirate ship in 1860 and proceed to reorganize temporarily the pirates' routine, as more fully appears in later pages.

Richard Rodgers, looking for work to employ his idle hands and active inspirations, following the success of "Oklahoma!", for which he wrote the score, decided to revive his own and

Lorenz Hart's sixteen-year-old "A Connecticut Yankee" with a refurbished score and a modernized libretto. It turned out to be as good as ever and even better than expected.

Moss Hart, who had been flying around the country collecting material for a stage show that would represent the popular Air Force, brought "Winged Victory" to Broadway in mid-November. A success duplicating that enjoyed by Irving Berlin's "This Is the Army" the summer before followed, as more fully appears in other pages of this record.

William Saroyan's memories, happy and unhappy, of his experience with the motion picture autocrats of Hollywood, which he embodied in a comedy called "Get Away Old Man," did not live up to expectations. It was withdrawn after thirteen performances. Katharine Cornell's selection of Dodie Smith's "Lovers and Friends" was also a bit of a disappointment, but the Cornell-McClintic production saved it for the season.

Oscar Hammerstein 2d's Harlem version of "Carmen," for which the original Bizet music was retained, proved a mid-Winter sensation. The all-colored cast covered itself with the glory that attracts fine press notices. The Broadway Theatre, where Billy Rose, the producer, had established it, was sold out literally months in advance.

Nunnally Johnson's first play, "The World's Full of Girls," did not do that story writer justice, closing after two weeks. "The Voice of the Turtle" brought John Van Druten back into the Broadway spotlight with a rush. With but one set and three characters, played by Margaret Sullavan, Elliott Nugent and Audrey Christie, the new play proved the first real comedy success of the season.

At this juncture, which would be the middle of December, Mayor La Guardia and the City of New York took a hand in show business. An auditorium, the Mecca Temple, a roomy place with a stage, an auditorium seating 2,800 (with two balconies) and considerable stage equipment, reverted to the control of the city through unpaid back taxes. The situation was discouraging to the tax collectors, but to Mayor La Guardia it was the fulfillment of a dream. He had always wanted a City Center of Music and Drama and here it was.

Entering into a sort of civic partnership with Newbold Morris, President of the City Council, the Mayor proceeded to organize his City Center on a practical shownmanship basis. "We couldn't sell it, we couldn't rent it," Mr. Morris explained later, "so then and there we hit upon the idea of using the place as a center where music and drama lovers could come at reasonable prices. It was our plan to run a non-profit corporation very much like the Planetarium, the New York Public Library, the Metropolitan Museum and the Museum of Natural History."

Just like commercial showmen, the first thing the Messrs. La Guardia and Morris had to do was to raise a little capital. In no time the City Center enterprise had been underwritten for $75,000 by a group of citizens interested in music, drama and art, the underwriters and incorporators ranging from the Amalgamated Clothing Workers of America to John D. Rockefeller, Jr., and from the International Ladies' Garment Workers' Union to Marshall Field, John Golden, Mrs. Lytle Hull, Howard Cullman, the Dramatists' League, Mrs. Myron Taylor, the Jewish Labor Commission, the Workman's Circle and the Negro Labor Committee. Here was the democratic impulse in full flower.

On July 22, 1943, the first meeting of the Board of Directors was held. Mayor La Guardia was elected president, Gerald Warburg vice-president, Almerindo Portfolio treasurer, Mrs. Arthur M. Reis secretary. Mr. Morris was chosen Chairman of the Board and also of the Executive Committee.

Immediately thereafter the old Mecca Temple, now the new City Center, was thoroughly washed down. Six weeks later the auditorium, a huge ballroom, a huge banquet hall and two large lodge rooms, two stories high, were spick, span and ready to rent. The theatre was opened for business in early December. As the opening attraction the New York Philharmonic-Symphony Orchestra, conducted by Dr. Artur Rodzinski, gave a concert that was promptly over-subscribed. The prices ranged from 55 cents to $1.65. The Mayor made the dedicatory address in which he spoke optimistically of the directors' hopes and plans for the new Center and promised as much as a Mayor could, or should. "Not so long ago in Europe," said the Mayor, "only the nobility and the church were privileged to listen to the great works of music and opera. Now, in this country, more people can hear Beethoven in one day than in the lifetime of the composer."

Speaking of future attractions the Mayor said: "No performances will be given just to fill in a vacant date. We must have the best and there will be no compromise." The first drama to be produced at the Center was a revival of Rachel Crothers' "Susan and God," with Gertrude Lawrence the star, as she had been when the play was first produced. The second theatrical showing was that of Sidney Kingsley's "The Patriots," with a cast headed by Walter Hampden. This was followed by entertainments varied in character but of an even excellence in quality. Paul Draper, dancer, and Larry Adler, harmonica virtuoso, were highly successful in recital. Thornton Wilder's "Our Town," with Marc Connelly substituting for Frank Craven as the Stage Manager, had three fine weeks. The DuBose Heyward-George Gershwin "Porgy and Bess" played two extremely successful engagements.

In February a City Center Opera Company was organized for the production of "La Tosca," "Martha" and "Carmen," under the direction of Iaszlo Halasz. "Tosca" was given in Italian, "Carmen" in French and "Martha" in English, with a revised book by Vicki Baum. The response of the people was immediate.

Two pleasant comedies, produced just before Christmas, were Pauline Jameson and Reginald Lawrence's "Feathers in a Gale" and a Russian work adapted from the original of Alexander Afinegenov called "Listen, Professor!" The first was a story of three maiden ladies who were, by the working of a New England law in 1804, about to be put up for sale to the highest bidder as available housekeepers. One finds a husband, one is bought in for $3 and one is still hoping at the end of the play.

"Listen, Professor" was the story of a crusty scientist at work on a study of the Fourth Century who is suddenly brought back to living in the Twentieth Century by the arrival of a 15-year-old granddaughter. She, introducing her grandfather to the young collectivists of her group, so changes the old man's outlook that he sends for her mother and reorganizes all his routines. Both comedies were pleasantly received but neither prospered, "Feathers" lasting but 7 performances and "Professor" 19.

William Brown Meloney, emboldened by the experience he had had backing his wife's, Rose Franken's, "Outrageous Fortune," decided to try again with a Franken opus in the writing of which he also had had a hand. This was a comedy called "Doctors Disagree," reviving the slightly dated theme of a progressive heroine who sought to rule love out of her life in favor of a career as a surgeon. Love won. So also did surgery. But the play failed, being withdrawn at the end of its third week.

A thoughtful drama by Howard Rigsby and Dorothy Heyward called "South Pacific" brought Canada Lee, the popular colored actor, back to the stage two years after his first great success in "Native Son." Mr. Lee's performance as a black seaman thrown into the sea by the torpedoing of a merchant ship was highly praised. He floats on a raft with a white Army Captain to a Jap-controlled island near Bougainville. There for the first time in his life he finds he holds an advantage over the white race and is so impressed by the experience that he refuses to join the white men in their war against the Japs. His conscience finally redeems him.

Two highly personalized performances were those of Ruth Gordon in her own comedy, "Over 21," and Zasu Pitts in a melodramatic farce by George Batson, "Ramshackle Inn." Miss Gordon carried her comedy to a quick success and played it through the season. Miss Pitts, thanks to the loyalty of her motion picture following, also gained a run for her farce, for all it was soundly blasted by the reviewers.

Much had been hoped for when announcement was made that Maxwell Anderson, with the sanction of the higher-ups of the Army, was writing the story of the invasion of North Africa and of Sicily for the stage. "Storm Operation" was the play. It arrived in January, was given competent staging by the Playwrights' Company and a good cast of actors. The reviewers "praised it with faint damns," however, and it was withdrawn after 23 performances.

Jack Kirkland, "Tobacco Road" author, got a play out of a novel written by Mary Lasswell entitled "Suds in Your Eye." Jane Darwell of the movies came on from the Coast to play its lead, that of a Mrs. Feeley who inherits a junk yard from her husband and a taste for beer from her forbears. She was joined by Brenda Forbes, eccentric comedienne, and Kasia Orgazewski, as well as a numerous cast, but they could not save "Suds." Five weeks and it was gone.

"Jackpot," a musical comedy with an array of authors and librettists and a cast headed by Allan Jones, Nanette Fabray, Jerry Lester and Kenny Baker, richly produced by Vincent Youmans (with, it was rumored, Doris Duke money), took a grilling from the critics, but fought on for several weeks. Philip Merivale did what he could for a somewhat dated type of melodrama, "The Duke in Darkness," but could not get it past its third week. Sex and adolescence, boldly discussed, carried "Wallflower" into the success column, despite critical disapproval. Mary Orr and Reginald Denham were the authors.

Margaret Webster had a hand in the revival and staging of Chekhov's "The Cherry Orchard," with Eva Le Gallienne and Joseph Schildkraut featured. Here was a new and livelier version of the Russian classic, translated by Irina Skariatina, which pleased its early audiences and ran through till Spring.

Michael Todd had Bobby Clark, comedian, and a gorgeously staged and costumed production directed by Hassard Short, to thank for the success of a new musical called "Mexican Hayride." Cole Porter, who wrote the songs, and Dorothy and Herbert Fields, who tacked the plot together, were also valuable aids.

Edward Chodorov, who had failed earlier with "Those Endearing Young Charms," came forward again with a serious drama having to do with home-front fascists, called "Decision." The press decision was both for and against the play, but it won a certain deeply interested public, and is one of our chosen ten. John Emery and his wife, Tamara Geva, found a play called "Peepshow" in which they could generously exploit their individual talents. A comedy by Ernest Pascal, it had to do with "a wolf and his conscience," and served them variously for several weeks.

No one expected a comedy called "Take It As It Comes," written by a modest tyro who signed himself E. B. Morris, to last long, and it didn't. But it beat the estimates of the reviewers by two weeks at that. It was not a bad idea. A New Jersey family, having been given a press award of honor as the model family of the community, came into possession of $100,000 "hot" money, accumulated by a narcotics ring, and was tempted to keep it. After a struggle the family honor was upheld, but there was plenty of evidence that it might very easily slip again.

In February R. H. Burnside, in association with the Messrs. Shubert, brought the Gilbert and Sullivan Opera Company to the Ambassador Theatre and stayed there until early March. The company included Florenz Ames, Kathleen Roche, Bertram Peacock, Robert Pitkin and other veterans. The repertoire included all the standard Gilbert and Sullivan favorites.

The Blackfriars' Guild, interested in producing plays that will bring new dramatists to the attention of Broadway producers, and a healthier type of drama to the attention of Broadway audiences, produced a comedy written by the Rev. Thomas McGlynn that caused considerable comment. "Caukey" (short for Caucasion) was the title and the story reversed the problems of the black and white races—Negroes in this instance being in command of a community's destinies and inclined to be pretty hard on the struggling whites.

A string of comedy failures included "Mrs. Kimball Presents," "Thank You, Svoboda," with Sam Jaffee as the star; and "Bright Boy." In the midst of this depression the Theatre Guild brought in a comedy that had a Pacific Coast origin under the sponsorship of John Skirball. "Jacobowsky and the Colonel" was the title. Franz Werfel had written the first draft and later turned it over to S. N. Behrman who revised it. With Louis Calhern and Oscar Karlweis playing the name parts, those of a Polish colonel and a Jewish refugee, the comedy quickly achieved audience popularity and ran out the season.

Ludmilla Pitoeff, famed as a progressive and successful actress in Paris between wars, made her New York debut in a fairly startling drama called "The House in Paris." The debut was successful, so far as Mme. Pitoeff was concerned, but the play failed her and was shortly withdrawn.

Paired with Frank Craven, Billie Burke came back from Hollywood for another try at Broadway. The play this time was a comedy called "Mrs. January and Mr. X," by Zoe Akins, in which Billie played a wealthy nitwit widow who experiments with the Communistic way of life in a New England town in order to be ready for the coming revolution. Her next-door neighbor, and landlord as well, is a canny ex-President of the United States (Mr. Craven), who is finally charmed out of his shell and into matrimony by the ebullient one. Compliments for the co-stars but not for the comedy, which was withdrawn after 85 performances.

Philip Merivale and Ann Andrews tried to save another comedy about Hollywood extravagances, matrimonial and domestic, called "Public Relations." No go. A roomy theatre in upper Seventh Avenue that had been named for, and opened by, Al Jolson in the old theatre boom days, was recovered by the Messrs. Shubert and renamed the Century. It was reopened by Dave Wolper with a musical comedy called "Follow the Girls," in which Gertrude Niesen was successfully featured.

Harry Carey and Elizabeth Patterson also came back from Hollywood to play amusingly in a comedy called "—But Not Goodbye." The Carey part was that of an earth-bound family man who, after his death, tried desperately to protect his wife (Miss Patterson) and family from a sharper who would cheat them out of their rightful inheritance.

Interest in the late season was considerably stimulated by the production of Lillian Hellman's "The Searching Wind." One of the few thoughtful dramas of the season, this exposure of the appeasers and the politicians who may have had something to do with bringing on the Second World War came as close to being the prize-winning play of the year as any, receiving six of the

Drama Critics' Circle's thirteen votes.

Sidney Blackmer, another fugitive from the cinema, was featured with Stella Adler in "Pretty Little Parlor," a play by Claiborne Foster, who used to be an actress herself. Good performances; muddled drama.

Edmund Gwenn gave practically his all to a comedy Somerset Maugham wrote ten years ago called "Sheppey." Unhappily it was not enough. "Sheppey," the story of a London Bond Street barber who won a sweepstake prize and thought to give it away as Christ might have done, was more popular in London than here. Alfred Bloomingdale assembled a revue called "Allah Be Praised!" and tried to reclaim the Adelphi Theatre in Fifty-fifth Street with it. Twenty performances and Allah was out, despite an expensive cast and production.

Two experimental productions were those of "War President," done for two performances by the Experimental Theatre, Inc., and "Earth Journey," by the Blackfriars' Guild. "War President," by Nat Sherman, dramatized Gen. McClellan's effort to bring the Civil War to a stalemate. "Earth Journey," by Sheldon Davis, was a fantasy concerned with the reawakened love life of a Chinese idol long dead.

Still another ghost play was that of Margaret Curtis, called "A Highland Fling." This one told amusingly of a stubborn Scot who, dead a hundred and fifty years, had been denied room in heaven because of his attachments to certain earthly ladies. His ghost carries on numerous worldly adventures, being visible and articulate only to the town's "daftie," Silly Shalott, and a busy little 7-year-old. He finally makes heaven by saving the soul of the town's most persistent sinner. Miss Curtis, the author, played the daft one in her comedy.

Two social service dramas were Elsa Shelley's "Pick-up Girl" and Frederick Stephani and Murray Burnett's "Hickory Stick." "Pick-up Girl" considers the case of the endangered adolescents who have fallen victim to the war fever and their desire to do something to brighten the lives of service men. "Hickory Stick" visualized with depressing authenticity conditions prevailing in certain vocational schools to which problem students are sent. "Pick-up Girl," managed to sell itself to an interested and frankly curious public. "Hickory Stick" was set down as too free an exaggeration of selected situations.

Richard Kollmar, having been surprisingly successful with "Early to Bed," thought to pour another pot of gold into a fantastic dream piece called "Dream with Music." He had a stageful of known entertainers, headed by Vera Zorina, the ballerina, and carloads of beautiful scenery and costumes. But he didn't have enough entertainment. Twenty-eight performances and his bankroll was as completely deflated as his producer's ego. Father Murray's "Career Angel," the comedy that the Blackfriars' Guild had produced in the fall, was taken over by Broadway producers and presented professionally with Whitford Kane and Glenn Anders in the leading roles. The critics found that Broadway influences had cheapened both text and certain performances, and that the charm and simplicity of the original semi-amateur production had been lost in transit.

J. C. Nugent wrote himself a comedy called "That Old Devil," which, by report, Elliott Nugent, his son, helped him produce. It made sport of an amiable old man who gallantly assumed the paternity of a pretty refugee's expected infant, and found himself a favorite with all the widows who had previously ignored him. The belated appearance of the refugee's soldier-husband and the clearing of the scandal left the old devil a little older and much wiser. The Nugent performance was praised, but the Nugent comedy got only 16 performances.

The season fluttered to a June close with only one fairly promising summer entrant. This was F. Hugh Herbert's comedy called "For Keeps." Mr. Herbert, having won a fine success with his first adolescent comedy, "Kiss and Tell," sought to continue his study of the knowing and ambitious teen-age youngster in "For Keeps." She is 15, the daughter of divorced and neglectful parents, and pretends to be 18, if not 19. She is headed for a love adventure with a youth in his twenties when he luckily discovers her real age and quickly backs away. The heroine finds a home with her belatedly awakened father and the boy agrees to wait until she grows up.

There were twenty more plays produced the season of 1943-44 than there were the season before, carrying the theatre year from mid-June to mid-June, as we do in this record. But the percentage of hits and failures remained about the same, three flops to one success. No fewer than nine plays went through the season as holdovers from the season of 1942-43. Several of these threaten to continue on into next year, too.

THE SEASON IN CHICAGO

By CLAUDIA CASSIDY

Drama Editor of the *Chicago Tribune*

A YEAR ago Cecil Smith described the Chicago theatre season of 1942-43 as prosperous but uninteresting. The best I can say for the season of 1943-44 is that it was busier but no better. It was, in fact, so busy that Katharine Cornell had to cancel her spring booking in "Lovers and Friends" for want of a playhouse. True, had she been as clairvoyant as she is radiant, she might have guessed that just two weeks later the soaring thermometer would do exactly what the booking office had failed to accomplish. But the fact remains that in 1943-44 we had no theatre for Katharine Cornell, who has been faithful to us in her fashion—a fashion we wish more producers and stars would copy in the matter of keeping Chicago interested in playgoing. After all, it is possible to get up from a full table hungry, if you don't like the food.

But topnotch and tawdry, first-rate and floundering, from a brilliant "Oklahoma!" to a dreary "Maid in the Ozarks," Chicago achieved 306 weeks of playgoing in eight theatres from the first of June, 1943, until the end of May, 1944. This meant a steady climb in playing time over the last four years from 178 weeks in 1940-41 to 195 weeks in 1941-42 and 235 weeks in 1943-44. The gain of 71 weeks over last season was largely based on increased length of run, because we had just two more shows, a total of 31 productions. Twenty-two were plays, six of them held over from last season, five of them return engagements or revivals. Nine were musicals, four of them revivals, including the 10 Gilbert and Sullivan repertory productions considered here as a unit. So you see that of our 31 productions, exactly 16 were new, and if you saw the 16 you know that several of them came under the head of theatrical slumming and a mere handful achieved theatrical distinction. People went to the theatre last season literally in spite of it.

For the first time in Chicago history its twin theatres, the Selwyn and Harris, hit the jackpot. "Kiss and Tell" took care of the Harris single-handed, rolling out a full year in its second season and blithely clipping into the third. F. Hugh Herbert, the playwright, couldn't come to the birthday party, but he sent this wire, "Most men are known by the company they keep. I am known by the companies that keep me."

The next-door Selwyn rang up its 52 weeks with 16 for "The Doughgirls," a holdover from the previous season; six for "Dark Eyes," which came to town without Eugenie Leontovich, not very smart booking in the city that made her a star; 23 for "To-morrow the World," which won the season's honors in serious plays; and seven for Daphne du Maurier's dramatization of "Rebecca," which came to us in advance of New York. Florence Reed played Mrs. Danvers to the hilt in a curious combination of her roles in "The Shanghai Gesture" and "Mourning Becomes Electra," while Bramwell Fletcher was miscast but capable as the brooding master of Manderley, and Diana Barrymore, the daughter of John who looks like Aunt Ethel, played the nameless Mrs. de Winter with a hint that someday she may carry on the family reputation. Had that hint flamed up unmistakably or even vividly at the opening she would have been starred overnight. No producer could have resisted such temptation in the very theatre where John Barrymore made his last fabulous stand in "My Dear Children," particularly at a time when the national best seller was Gene Fowler's "Good Night, Sweet Prince."

The Great Northern, a roomy old theatre fallen on evil ways, managed 50 weeks' booking and an applauded comeback to the ranks of enjoyable playgoing. It had been operated for some time as subhuman theatre, with "Maid in the Ozarks" attracting so unaccustomed a cutrate audience it innocently paid 25 cents for playbills. If you couldn't tell a player without a score card you paid for the score card and got a couple of luridly inaccurate poses from the play thrown in. A hangover from the previous season, "Maid in the Ozarks" hung on for 24 more weeks, while "Unexpected Honeymoon," a cheap revision of Barry Connors' 12-year-old "Unexpected Husband," ran for 21. Then the management suddenly did an about face, cleaned up the house—it needed fumigating—and booked "Uncle Harry," with Luther Adler and Beth Merrill playing the roles created by Joseph Schildkraut and Eva Le Gallienne. It had five weeks before the season ended, and was putting the theatre back on the map while the management proudly polished its unaccustomed halo of praise from playgoers.

The Blackstone Theatre, which had been having everything its own way, first with the record-breaking "Life with Father," and then with the astounding "Good Night, Ladies," held its own pretty well with 49 weeks. It owed 40 of them to that same "Good Night, Ladies," which made the record goose hang high with a total of 100 weeks. This was the show every stranger who hit town made a beeline to see, then went away saying, "It's what Chicago likes." Whoever liked it, "Good Night, Ladies" left town in the face of capacity business, and the Blackstone finished its season with five weeks of a "Blossom Time" revival and four of Katherine Dunham's brilliant "Tropical Revue."

The Erlanger came next with 41 weeks, one of them a lapover for Cornell's unforgotten "The Three Sisters"; five for a return engagement of "Junior Miss"; three for "Without Love" without Katharine Hepburn and Elliott Nugent—the most remarkable thing about it was Constance Bennett's waistline; three for "The Student Prince," which never forsakes us; and 29, as of the end of May, for that blithe blessing in time of boredom, "Oklahoma!" This came to us with an irresistible cast, so everyone loved the Theatre Guild again, even when it stole our singing stars for New York. The Guild came through with good replacements and actually managed to give us all six plays this season. In addition to "Oklahoma!," which healed all wounds the way the Lunts used to, we got "Dark Eyes," "Without Love," "The Patriots," "Rebecca" and the revival of "A Connecticut Yankee." But the strain must have been fearful, because next season's American Theatre Society dividend has been cut to five plays.

The Studebaker had a crazy quilt season of 24 weeks, or 26½ if you count the Yiddish Art Theatre's "The Family Carnovsky," an interesting but specialized play omitted in this tabulation. One of those weeks went to the holdover of an unfortunate revival of "You Can't Take It with You," with Fred Stone miscast as Grandpa; three to the amusing GI one-acters known as "The Army Play-by-Play"; four to Ethel Barrymore's return in "The Corn Is Green," far too brief a booking for potential business; two to a return of "Blithe Spirit," this time with Clifton Webb, Peggy Wood and Mildred Natwick, but with Haila Stoddard replacing Leonora Corbett; four to "The Patriots," with Cecil Humphreys still making Washington come to life, but with Walter Hampden and Guy Sorel as replacements in the roles of Jefferson and Hamilton; two to Gilbert and Sullivan repertory offering "The Mikado," "Cox and Box," "The Pirates of Penzance," "Trial by Jury," "H.M.S. Pinafore," "Iolanthe," "Patience," "The Yeomen of the Guard," "The Gondoliers" and

"Ruddigore"; seven to a revival of "Abie's Irish Rose," which was just what we thought it was the first time; and one to the opening week of "A Connecticut Yankee." Jack Whiting had replaced Dick Foran, and Anita Alvarez made a hit dancing in Vera Ellen's shoes.

The Civic Theatre, a cozy house under the wing of the Civic Opera, achieved 21 weeks—not bad when you consider it did not enter the lists until mid-October. "Janie" was its first show, with Edith Fellows from the movies, and it lasted 9 weeks. There were 9 weeks, too, for the Chicago troupe of "3 Is a Family," and the best of it was Charles Burrows as the doddering old doctor. Mr. Burrows wore no makeup and wanted no dressing room. Content to hang his hat on a hatrack and rest beneath it between scenes, soaking up applause like sunshine, he was given the actors' accolade when the cast pasted a star over his hatrack.

Next on the Civic's list was "The Lady and the Clown," which defies description. A circus play of changelings, feuds and rhetoric, it was composed by Byron Taylor, whose real name is Edwin B. Self and who, when not writing plays, is engaged in the brewery business—successfully, no doubt, as he backed his own play. Perhaps even as a salesman, for how else did Estelle Winwood get mixed up in it, to spend two weeks flourishing plumed fans, velvet dust catchers and hauteur? Billy Bryant would have had a picnic without rewriting a line. Nor was this all. "School for Brides," an unlikely attempt to duplicate the prosperity of "Good Night, Ladies," got under the season's rope for one week, with Roscoe Karns playing a somewhat wrinkled matrimonial plum à la Tommy Manville.

The Civic Opera House, which has been stagestruck of late, added 17 weeks of playgoing to its usual schedule of opera, concert and ballet, plus an occasional weekend of Yiddish musicals. As it seats more than 3,500 it can pile up a lot of business if it gets a hit, and a lot of headaches if it gets a flop. When Billy Rose was trying desperately to put a roof over "Carmen Jones'" head, he wanted the opera house, but the choice went to a dismal piece called "The Waltz King." It was one of those Straussian affairs with Richard Bonelli, Ira Petina and Tatiana Riabouchinska mired up (for four weeks) in a book so appalling some of us felt we should apologize, however belatedly, to Moss Hart. Up to then we had suspected, quite unjustly, that Mr. Hart's book for "The Great Waltz" was the worst that could happen to Johann, junior or senior.

Rose velvet, gilt and Gargantuan mosaic fire curtain, the Civic Opera House was an odd place to find Olsen and Johnson, but there they were, or their counterparts, for eight weeks of "Sons o' Fun." Some of the stooges were so far away from the stage their lords and masters couldn't locate them with spy glasses. Mike Todd found the house sizable, too, when he brought Joan Blondell to town for five weeks of "Something for the Boys." Miss Blondell had the bouncing bloom of a ripe apricot, but in Ethel Merman's songs she needed wiring for sound.

So there is our season, for what it was, and fortunately it was more fascinating in prospect than in retrospect—a recurrent circumstance which keeps that glint in the eye of the stagestruck. Things always look better for Fall, and the looming season of 1944-45 is no exception. A lot of its prospects will die a-borning, some will expire in transit, and some will be less attractive on the stage than on paper. But at least no one has said lately that the theatre is dead, or even dying, though there have been complaints about what it does to deserve its exuberant state of box office health. But a dull season is better than a dead one—after all, it can always improve—and Chicago finds it pleasanter to have managers fighting for its theatres than to be tearing them down for parking lots.

THE SEASON IN SAN FRANCISCO

By Fred Johnson

Drama Editor of the San Francisco *Call-Bulletin*

IN taking stock of a year's best theatrical business since the depression and advent of talking pictures, San Francisco showmen made confession that its entertainment quality had not always been foremost as boomtown customers crowded through the turnstiles. One manager had this phrase for it: "All we do is open the doors—then get out of the way."

This busy war embarkation port, jammed with uniformed men, other transients and a vastly increased civilian population, was host to a record throng of hungry amusement-seekers, many of whom were witnessing their first stage performance.

There was evidence of San Francisco's living up to its old reputation as "a good show town," but stress no longer could be laid on its distinction as a metropolis of notably discriminating audiences. They took the bad with the good in their quest of "some place to go" and were equally eager for drama, comedy, "variety revues" and musicals.

The town's once boasted discrimination vanished with the heavy patronage given at least four new productions originating in Los Angeles or Hollywood for tryouts here in the hope of quick and easy money. Two of these had their demise at this waypoint, one went on to Broadway, despite profitable early business—to succumb after one week—and the fourth hastened to Chicago.

The latter was Howard Lang's "School for Brides," with which he visioned a repetition of his success with "Good Night, Ladies" (based on the old "Ladies' Night in a Turkish Bath"), a Chicago record-breaker in its run of more than one year. The "Brides" comedy, by Frank Gill and George Carleton Brown and directed by Hollywood's Joan Hathaway, showcased a bevy of comely girls in bedroom atmosphere, with Film Comedian Roscoe Karns as the featured principal.

With a like accent on sex, as suspected appeal to the uniformed forces, Film Producer Samuel Bischoff headed the sponsors of "Mother's Day," by Radio Writer Aleen Leslie, as a new comic slant on the idea of juvenile "expectancy." This was the offering that hurried on for its one week on Broadway, under the new title of "Slightly Married," after three weeks of capacity business at the Geary Theatre and prospects of indefinite lush returns.

Of the "six critics in search of a play" on its San Francisco première this reviewer was commiserated as the sole confessor of inability to discover one in the Leslie piece, or anything worthy of a place on the stage. His only consolation was the subsequent unanimous concurrence of the New York critical fraternity.

Not to be discouraged by this misadventure, Jack Linder and William B. David offered a comic version of "Lady Chatterley's Lover," a Thomas West dramatization of the D. H. Lawrence novel, staged and directed by Actor Ian Keith. Like "Mother's Day," its off-color treatment was without benefit of cleverness in dialogue, situation or acting. And yet its one week's stay was profitable, its closing mysterious.

Of similar stripe was "Sleep It Off," a farce comedy by Lyford Moore and Harlan Thompson, starring the former striptease artist and current film actress, Ann Corio. Her stage portrayal as entertainer at a university soirée proved exciting enough for a five weeks' run.

Paul Small, associated with Fred Finklehoffe in producing here the "Show Time" variety revue which later played successfully on Broadway and his own show, "Big Time," starring Ed Wynn, also premièred in San Francisco another vaudeville attraction, "Laugh Time," with Frank Fay, Bert Wheeler and Ethel Waters, for a moderate month's return. In midwinter, four months later, he was rewarded with better business for his "Curtain Time," featuring Chico Marx and Connie Boswell in a six weeks' run.

As in the previous season, New York successes on tour did well in return engagements. Although "Kiss and Tell" ran for ten weeks in the early Winter, it returned for another month's engagement in the Spring for an excellent box office take.

"Junior Miss" also came back for three weeks that were well worth while, and so did "Claudia," with similar profit. "Life with Father" made its third annual visit for an average run, with Harry Bannister and Nydia Westman as new principals here.

In addition to the annual San Francisco and Los Angeles Light Opera Associations' Spring season, musicals fared well.

A Coast version of "Die Fledermaus," titled "The Rose Masque," was produced under the direction of Reinhold Schunzel, with dialogue by Erich Weiler, lyrics by Weiler and Thomas Martin and with Marita Farell as the star. It was staged mainly by San Franciscans and was well supported for five weeks.

Hollywood Film Producer Boris Morros presented Richard Bonelli and Margot Bokor in "The Waltz King," based on the music and romance of Johann Strauss, with Tatiana Riabouchinska in new ballets by David Lichine. The light opera, which later was offered in New York, played to capacity for three weeks in its San Francisco debut.

The Shuberts sent out two operetta revivals in the Spring, which had previously played on Broadway. The first was "Blossom Time," with a company headed by Barbara Scully, Douglas Leavitt and Roy Barnes, which received good patronage, even during Holy Week, in its month's engagement. "Student Prince," the second light opera, which opened next door just before the first had ended, starred Everett Marshall for a fortnight of capacity business, whereas it had previously been more of a favorite in San Francisco than "Blossom Time." And there had been better companies here in both than were these latest consigned by the Shuberts.

Early in the season "The Doughgirls" recall the days of long runs in San Francisco when it ran up nine weeks of profitable receipts with an excellent touring company headed by Joy Hodges.

Film Actor John Carradine deserted his usual chores on the screen with fulfillment of his long dream of taking out his own Shakespearean repertoire company, with a first metropolitan engagement in San Francisco. His star performances in "Hamlet," "Merchant of Venice" and "Othello," playing to a fortnight's capacity houses, were marked by excellent readings if not distinguished portrayals. Business exceeded that achieved by Maurice Evans and the Stratford-upon-Avon Players in similar classics.

Sylvia Sidney and Jack Adler in "Jane Eyre" and Constance Bennett in "Without Love" were less fortunate in their early Winter engagements, but Ethel Barrymore played to capacity in her return visit with "The Corn Is Green," three nights of which were canceled by her illness.

What was termed "boners in booking" cut short the engagements of two attractions which played to crowded houses, in the face of which they were compelled to leave for imperative dates elsewhere.

One was "Blithe Spirit," with most of the Broadway cast, which might have run for eleven weeks, it was estimated, but was limited to three. The other was "Sons o' Fun," without Olsen and Johnson, playing the same period to turn-away crowds.

"Abie's Irish Rose," with Alfred White in his original role of Solomon Levy, returned after a score of years for a fortnight's run. And Brock Pemberton personally accompanied his production of "Janie," with satisfying results on its first visit here, and with a fatherly side interest also in the year-old Stage Door Canteen at this port.

The San Francisco and Los Angeles Light Opera Associations were rounding out in June the joint annual season, now regarded as the theatrical year's official closing event. The fifth series gave promise of being the most brilliant of all staged by an organization grown to national prominence due to the high caliber of artists attracted to its ranks.

Walter Cassel, new baritone of the Metropolitan Opera; Helena Bliss, from the Philadelphia operatic forces; Eric Mattson and other top-flight performers insured the success of a "New Moon" revival and crowded house at the season's start. In the ensuing "Show Boat" production appeared Film Actor Gene Lockhart as Cap'n Andy, Marthe Errolle, Todd Duncan, Lansing Hatfield, Carol Bruce, Collette Lyons and Comedian Sammy White.

Jane Deering, the Broadway dancing ingénue, was starred in a revival of Jerome Kern's "Sally," with the Lyons-White comedy team again featured. The final offering, scheduled for July, was "Song of Norway," the organization's first original operetta, based on the life and music of Edvard Grieg and story by Homer Curran, joint owner of the theatre in which it was to be staged. Several opera favorites and a section of the Ballet Russe de Monte Carlo were to be its performers. The producers had plans to take the operetta to New York following the Los Angeles and San Francisco engagements.

The Tivoli Theatre, of Tetrazzini and one-time comic opera fame, was reopened for five months of legitimate attractions by Joe Blumenfeld, a motion picture theatre operator. The venture was only partially successful, its demise being laid to the theatre's spaciousness and a seemingly common opinion the house was "jinxed." Bela Lugosi was starred in "Arsenic and Old Lace," Edward Everett Horton in "Springtime for Henry," C. Aubrey Smith in "Old English," Nancy Carroll in "Mr. and Mrs. North," Gladys George in "Personal Appearance" and Otto Kruger in "Correspondent Unknown."

Clifford C. Fischer, whose "Folies Bergère" was a hit attraction in engagements both years at the Golden Gate Exposition, conceived at that time the plan of staging later on a more elaborate extravaganza in the Winterland Rink in San Francisco. He had been so impressed by the spectacular "Ice Follies" in its use of the arena that he brought his augmented "Folies Bergère" into it for a successful winter run of four months and then took it on the western road for presentation in similar houses and auditoriums.

In the local rink Shipstads and Johnson brought back their "Ice Follies" for the annual Summer season, during which their next production is readied. Regarded for six years as a home institution, it has become the town's most popular attraction and required enlargement of its show spot.

Wartime stress and entertainment activities in behalf of the armed forces have reduced operations by San Francisco's little theatres, leaving Theatre Arts Colony almost alone in this field during the last year. Stanford and the University of California, however, have staged several productions. And in the city there have been such revival ventures as "The Drunkard" and even "Easy for Zee Zee," a risqué farce which had its first notoriety in the Little Italy section a dozen years ago.

THE SEASON IN SOUTHERN CALIFORNIA

By EDWIN SCHALLERT

Drama Editor of the *Los Angeles Times*

THE discerning eye viewing the 1943-44 theatrical season in Southern California in retrospect can find comparatively little evidence of either imagination or enterprise in the activities that composed its history. Even so-called war-time prosperity did not inspire any new and great creative impulses. Only in a few musical productions, and some little-theatre activities, was there any evidence of a spirit of daring and progress, and the extent of this considered, by and large, was at a minimum.

Naturally, the 1943-44 season can always be proclaimed as the one which brought forth "The Song of Norway" as the first original work presented under the auspices of the Los Angeles Civil Light Opera Association. This was premièred toward the close of the fiscal theatrical year, and proved a delight to its musical-minded audiences, exploiting as it did the music of Edvard Grieg, and essaying to relate a chapter out of his life in the semi-biographical manner of a "Blossom Time."

"The Song of Norway" ran three weeks in Los Angeles, and could have had a much longer engagement. It was lavishly produced with a cast of highly competent singers including at the outset Irra Petina, Helena Bliss, Walter Cassel and Robert Shafer. Excellent, too, for his comedy was Sig Arno, even as Miss Petina was also a colorful personage in this department. The Ballet Russe de Monte Carlo took part in the dances to the "Peer Gynt" suite and as arranged for the famous Grieg piano concerto. The musical arrangements made by Robert Wright and George Forrest, including the lyrics written for the adaptations, were most interesting, and the primary cause of success, along with the quality of the presentation itself.

Dramatic content of the operetta was being subjected to revisions during the run in Los Angeles and San Francisco, the aim being to overcome the story weaknesses. Researches of Homer Curran, credited with the basic narrative, were largely responsible for "The Song of Norway," while the showmanship of Edwin Lester, as producer of the light operas, brought it to full fruition. It was a test of the powers of the whole organization in synthesizing the various elements, including the rich treasures of the Grieg music, into a popular and worth-while entertainment.

The investment was the largest in any effort of this kind, it was estimated, since the Max Reinhardt production of "Midsummer Night's Dream" at the Hollywood Bowl ten years ago. Total cost was well over $100,000, and the undertaking had all the prospects of being highly profitable before it has fulfilled its destiny in New York and probably also on tour. While New York's judgment cannot at this time be recited, the Coast sponsors were hopeful of the outcome, and in any event a large stipend for this phase was practically assured in advance.

Peculiarly "Song of Norway" gives, perhaps, the keynote to the theatrical mood throughout the season—namely, reliance on what has been tested already, very little breaking of new ground. The operetta fundamentally depended on well-established appeal of the Grieg music—especially that which has been rendered familiar through jazz band adaptation, like the Concerto. In this case excellent use was made of the classical values, and they were the life of the attraction.

Otherwise dependence was put on the tried and true in much less impressive fashion, for one finds repeats of shows that had been observed before a heavy strand in the theatrical warp and woof. "Claudia," with Phyllis Thaxter in the lead, "Arsenic and Old Lace" in two different engagements, "Life with Father," "Personal Appearance" restarring Gladys George," "Junior Miss," "The Corn Is Green," and even "Abie's Irish Rose" were all back for a re-surveying. Bela Lugosi starred in the "Arsenic" revival, Harry Bannister and Nydia Westman were the Mr. and Mrs. in "Life with Father," which paid its third visit; Ethel Barrymore, of course, gleamed in "The Corn Is Green" and halted her tour temporarily to make her first motion picture appearance in more than a decade in "None But the Lonely Heart." The studio agreed, incidentally, to pay not only her salary for this engagement but took care of the losses occasioned by the deferment of the further traveling by the company. This is one of the most unusual instances of this sort, and pleased Miss Barrymore exceedingly. As a consequence she is likely to become more identified with the cinema in the future.

Resort to a tested formula in show-giving was revealed also during the year in "The New Meet the People," which over all had about a nine months' run at the Assistance League Playhouse and the Music Box. It was given new attributes once during that time, and utilized some numbers out of the previous creations of its authors, Henry Myers, Jay Gorney and Edward Eliscu. While it was not liked as well as the original "Meet the People," it nevertheless enjoyed a substantial popularity, and was one of the few fortunate efforts along original lines during the year.

Vying with it for about six months was the vaudeville revue, "Yours for Fun," headed by Billy House and Eddie Garr, which gravitated toward boisterous comedy and divertissements that held interest and were often "clever enough." With the two comedians keeping the entertainment moving, resemblances to the "Blackouts" of Ken Murray were also to be noted, but nothing can take away from the luster of this institution. Changed from time to time, due to the addition of new acts, this modern vaudeville thrives in its third year, due to Murray's own resourcefulness, aided now and again by the eccentric comedy of his valuable "stooge," the pleasing Marie Wilson. Miss Wilson had a record for never having missed a performance at the close of the second year. A few times Edgar Bergen has substituted for Murray, who was once lately injured by falling in the orchestra pit during an athletically demanding piece of stage business. "Blackouts" may go on forever, as does "The Drunkard" which has celebrated its 12th anniversary. No one will make a prediction nowadays as to when that will cease if ever.

Climbing, too, is the Turnabout with Forman Brown, Elsa Lanchester and the Yale Puppeteers, which has passed its third milestone. These long-lived affairs spread a sirenic spell to the minds of theatrical operators who feel that they also might find the magic sesame to similar victory. But you never can tell about Southern California!

The visiting productions that might be rated as "new" included "Janie," with cast headed by Edith Fellows; "Kiss and Tell," "Sons o' Fun," without Olsen and Johnson, except at one special performance, their places being taken by Marty May and Steve Olsen; and "Without Love," starring Constance Bennett, rather than Katharine Hepburn; "Jane Eyre" with Sylvia Sidney and Luther Adler; and the one very bright period during the year, which brought "Blithe Spirit," with Clifton Webb, Peggy Wood, Haila Stoddard and Mildred Natwick. One missed Leonora Corbett, though for those who had not seen the production in the East Miss Stoddard offered abundant compensation.

A word is also probably fitting at this point about the staging of "Night Must Fall" late in the season at the Musart, with the cast including Howard Johnson in the Emlyn Williams role, Lilian Fontaine, mother of Joan Fontaine and Olivia de Havilland, as his elderly patron; A. E. Gould-Porter, Renée Godfrey and Marjorie Bennett, with Barbara Vajda directing. At the season's close the allure of this offering seemed to demonstrate that the worth-while endeavor can always find a satisfying audience. The play had not been thus professionally produced in this area previously, and was welcomed.

Running through the diversified list one discovers the following events, mostly of minor impress, even though in some cases enjoying popularity: "Student Prince," with Everett Marshall; "Blossom Time," featuring Barbara Scully; "Sweet 'n Hot," a colored revue that had a run at the Mayan; "Silk Hat Harry," a weak show by Vincent Lawrence, though a première, at least; "The Face," concerning Leonardo da Vinci; Felix Young's "8:40 Revue," which cost plenty of money but failed to come off successfully; "Dream of Romance," another expensive musical that missed; "The Waltz King," with Richard Bonelli and Joan Petrie, plus the ballerina Tatiana Riabouchinska; "The Rose Masque," a version of "Die Fledermaus" by Richard Strauss; "That Old Devil" which starred J. C. Nugent and went to New York after some revisions, though it fared badly there. There were numerous other experiments in the theatre but these will suffice for a general perspective. Short engagements told the tale for most of them.

Orson Welles provided an individual diversion with his magical presentation, "The Mercury Wonder Show for Service Men," which was accomplished with humor, bombast and fanfare in a tent. He was assisted by Rita Hayworth, Joseph Cotten and Marlene Dietrich. "Laugh Time," starring Frank Fay, Ethel Waters and Bert Wheeler, added agreeably to the year's vaudeville. Earl Carroll's and the Florentine Gardens provided their customary entertainment.

The light opera season, which was prosperously enriched, brought "Showboat," "The New Moon" and "Sally" as the attractions, besides "Song of Norway." "The New Moon" met with the highest approval apart from the Grieg operetta. Gilbert and Sullivan were represented during the American Opera Association's staging of "Pinafore" and "Trial by Jury" on one bill, "Mikado" on another. "Two in a Bed" closed in its second year, and "Maid of the Ozarks" had a stay.

As always one arrives at a peak in reviewing the Pasadena Community Playhouse repertoire, which never fails to be comprehensive. Out of this cradle of aspiring purposes came during the year the John Carradine Shakespearean venture, which did well in San Francisco and unfortunately lost ground financially in Los Angeles. The well-known film actor appeared in "Othello," "The Merchant of Venice" and "Hamlet," and was especially effective in his interpretations of the two more somber tragedies.

The Saroyan event, "A Decent Birth, a Happy Funeral," was provocative, but in no sense as arresting as "Time of Your Life," needless to say. It had its points, but lacked cohesion and final convincing impact. The Midsummer Drama Festival of June to August, 1943, was dedicated to Booth Tarkington, while Sidney Howard received the tribute for 1944. Aurania Rouverol won the première distinction apart from William Saroyan with "Young Man of Today," which was typical and pleasing for the occasion. "The Damask Cheek," by John Van Druten and Lloyd Morris, a Burns Mantle selection, was given for the first time on the Coast. Ditto for "Those Endearing Young Charms" by Edward Chodorov; "Rebecca" by Daphne du Maurier; "Dark Eyes" by Elena Miramova and Eugene Leontovich. The other plays included "Personal Appearance," "A Christmas Carol," "Pursuit of Happiness," "Quiet Week-End," "Rope's End," "Ladies of the Jury," "It's a Wise Child," "My Sister Eileen" and "Murder in a Nunnery." One can only give praise to the Pasadena organization for the continued maintenance of its high standards and pioneering.

Theatrical experimenting within the confines of Los Angeles was also actively carried out by the Callboard, Geller, Bliss-Hayden, Little Wayside and various other workshops and centers that often essay the introduction of new plays and talent. With Hollywood so close at hand, these projects will go on determinedly and constantly, and have a value in this field.

What is really needed is more courage in the professional domain.

WINGED VICTORY

A Drama in Two Acts

BY MOSS HART

LAST Spring, so the story goes (and goes more truthfully than many similar stories related to sensational stage productions), last Spring Moss Hart, dramatist, was sitting in the Oak Room of the Hotel Plaza in New York when a young Air Forces Lieutenant stopped at his table and asked, casually, if he (Hart) would like to do a play about the Air Forces. He would, admitted Mr. Hart, and less than a fortnight later he was in Washington planning the detail of that assignment with Gen. H. H. Arnold, Commander of said Air Forces.

A few days after that Hart found himself aboard a bomber flying toward an Air Force training camp in Mississippi. In the next two months he visited camp after camp. The story also goes that during his research work he assumed both a fake name and a phony uniform, but the probability is strong that the playwright did not fool very many very much.

Hart traveled 28,000 miles in that bomber, though he is frankly allergic to flying. At the end of that time he wrote "Winged Victory" in a little more than three weeks and staged it in seventeen days. Applications were received from 7,000 service men who felt qualified by experience and talent to take part in the show. These were reduced finally to 350, including forty-one wives of soldiers in the show and nine professional actresses.

Mr. Hart has explained that he was able to handle so big a crowd, and get the results he did in seventeen days, because he had no actor temperaments to deal with. These were not professional actors, however much professional experience they may have had. They were soldiers on assignment. They did what they were told to do promptly and without question or debate. And that, according to their director, was swell.

"Winged Victory" opened in Boston and was, literally, a cheering success from the rise of the first curtain. Word spread to New York, and there were lines of people before the box office from the day it opened until all the seats for any allotted period were sold. Whenever a new batch of tickets was put in the racks new lines formed. Mr. Hart was prompt in waiving all royalties and the Army Emergency Relief will, it is estimated, be enriched in a sum approximating $10,000,000 before the play is withdrawn.

The anonymous play reviewer for *Time Magazine* summed up the case for "Winged Victory," as both show and drama, with fair completeness. "A salute to the Air Forces, it is simple, warm-hearted, big—and served up with a rousing Army Band," wrote he. "As a play it never once batters the mind. But as a show it often whops the emotions, as a spectacle often tingles the blood."

There is a pleasant sweep of lawn back of Allan Ross's home in Mapleton, Ohio, that being the opening scene of "Winged Victory." It stretches out from the back porch, with a tree in the middle of it. On the lawn Allan and his friend, Frankie Davis, are lazily trying to mend a broken lawn-mower and not making too good a job of it. As they work they are whistling the Air Corps song with enthusiasm. They break off when the roar of a plane is heard overhead. Now they are on their feet, eagerly following the flight of the plane across the sky.

"It's a B-24!" shouts Allan.

"Uh-uh! It's a B-17! Look at that tail!" insists Frankie.

"Nope! Listen to those engines! That's a B-24!"

"Maybe. Look at him bank her over, Allan. Is that sweet or isn't it?"

"Watch him bring her out! Boy!"

Their eyes are fixed on the plane until it disappears. Their mood grows fretful. "When the hell are they going to *send* for us?" demands Allan. "It's over four months now."

"Nearer five. Cripes, Allan, if *my* father was a Colonel in the Air Corps, I'd have wings by now."

"Oh, sure. You'd be General Arnold by now."

"Say, all we want is to be pilots and get a crack at them. That's not too much to ask, is it? Can't you get your father to hurry them up a little?"

"You know damn well I can't. We've just got to wait our turn. Come on, let's get this thing fixed."

They go back to the lawn-mower. But not for long. Presently another youthful voice floats in. Another lad is singing "Off we go into the wild blue yonder." A second later "Pinky" Scariano comes barging through the gate.

Pinky is giving an imitation of an airplane in flight. His arms are outstretched for wings, his body twists and spins and he is making a fine series of airplane noises in his throat. Presently he is down with what, to him, is a perfect three-point landing. Also he is ready for the coke that Allan's wife, Dorothy, brings from the house. Dorothy is pleased to be of service, but she wishes heartily that at least one of these brave young pilots knew how to fix a lawn-mower.

After Dorothy has gone, the boys sit for a little staring at the sky and silently drinking their cokes. Then they begin wondering what it is going to be like after they do get in the Air Corps. Pinky knows. Pinky is just going to take his little old P-38 and off he'll go "into the wild blue yonder." But neither Allan nor Frankie is sure. Allan had tried to get some idea from his father, the Colonel, but beyond the statement that it is likely to be "pretty rugged" he had got nothing.

Of course they expect to be scared—at first. At least Allan and Frankie expect to be scared. But Pinky, the barber's son—he knows—

"The day you get in they strap you in a plane, take you up nine thousand feet, put her into a tailspin—and (*He imitates a dive.*) if you burp—back to mama!" That's Pinky's idea.

A lot of fellows wash out. Allan knows that. Lots of good guys, too. "Remember Bailey? Graduated the year before we did. Track team. Football. Awful good guy. *He* washed out."

"Oh, this is fine—fine!" Pinky is disgusted. "We're not even *in* yet—and you're washing us out!"

"You know, it's funny if you think about it," muses Frankie. "All of us going through school together, and thinking about jobs, and girls and kind of getting started—and now suddenly everything disappears and it's just—flying. We never talk about anything else now. Just flying. Your whole life changed. Funny."

"What's wrong with it?" Pinky wants to know.

"Nothing's wrong with it. I think it's wonderful. Only . . ."

"I know what he means," says Allan. "It *is* kind of funny, too. I work in a bank, and Pinky's a barber, and Frankie's a chemist. . . ."

"Say," counters the undismayed Pinky, "where do you think Pilots come from? Warner Brothers? They're all guys just like me!"

Another plane roars overhead. They are all on their feet again, watching the flyer as he crosses the sky. It would be great, thinks Frankie, if they could all stay together after they get in. Might be. But Pinky has a feeling that he will get through a little ahead of the others. "They push us pursuit flyers through pretty fast, you know," ventures Pinky.

Mrs. Ross, Allan's mother, comes through the gate. She has had a hard day at the Red Cross, but refuses to admit that she is tired. And she has brought Allan a letter. Her hands aren't too steady as she opens her handbag and hands it to him.

Frankie and Pinky instinctively crowd around as Allan excitedly tears open the envelope and gulps down the contents.

"Report in thirty-six hours!" he shouts, throwing his arms about his mother. "This is it, Mom!"

With whoops of joy the boys grab eagerly for the letter. Dorothy comes wonderingly out on the porch, aware of what the news must be. Shouting that their letters must have come too, Frankie and Pinky rush pellmell through the gate.

"Hey, Dot—it's here!" Allan calls wildly. " 'Report in thirty-six hours!' This is it!" He takes his wife in his arms.

"Yes . . . I guess this is it," mutters Dorothy.

Mrs. Ross has gone into the house. Dorothy and Allan are sitting on the steps. There is a lot to talk about. First, Dorothy wants to go with Allan. She has been waiting for that letter, too. She knows what it means. For a year they will be teaching him to fly—and then he'll be off. She wants to be with him that year—

"I was afraid of this," admits Allan. "Baby, do you know what being a cadet's wife means? We don't take our training all in one place, you know. Every six weeks or so we move on. Sometimes the field is near a big town and if it is the town is jammed. Sometimes the field is smack out in the middle of the desert and the town is just a collection of shacks. You'd be living in tourist camps and flea-bitten hotels. You'd be alone all week—just sitting and waiting for those four hours we could have together—maybe. It's no good, Dot. It's a rotten life, believe me. I won't let you do it."

"It's my life from now on," says Dorothy, quietly. "I want those four hours."

Nor can Allan argue her out of that decision. Her mind is made up. Besides, as Mrs. Ross admits when she comes from the house, Dorothy is already packed. "Don't interfere with the Four Freedoms, Allan," advises Mother.

"Some damn family I've got!" announces Allan, kissing his

mother and throwing his arms about Dorothy. "Okay, you're a cadet's wife."

Dorothy has gone to put the supper on. Allan is assuring his mother that he certainly will be careful of those planes. Suddenly there is another joyous shout from the near distance. Pinky and Frankie are back, wildly waving their letters: "We're in! We got 'em! Lookit, Al!"

"Look out below! We're in the Air Corps!" yells Pinky, going into his repertoire of plane noises.

Out of the happy confusion Allan can be heard yelling: "Dot, how many lamb chops we got?"

"Four."

"Everyone stay to dinner! We're celebrating! I'll eat cornflakes."

Pinky has gone into another act. He is addressing himself: "Major Scariano, the citizens of Mapleton salute you and present you with a certified check of ten thousand bucks as the hero of Ohio!"

A third plane roars overhead. They are all staring at it and laughing at Pinky. "Don't worry, fellers!" Pinky has cupped his hands and is yelling at the plane. "Don't worry about a thing! We're in the Air Corps!"

Allan is saluting the "blue yonder" as the curtain falls.

The scene has shifted to a barracks street at an induction training field. "The barracks are what every soldier would recognize as pure G.I. Plain wooden structures built quickly right out in the middle of nowhere, and they look it. Right now, however, they are being taken care of as though each one were the Taj Mahal. Soldiers swarm all over them. It is the evening before the regular weekly inspection. . . . The boys are mostly in fatigues, and those who are not are in shorts and shirts, washing out socks, brushing shoes, and doing all the chores a soldier knows too well."

There is not much talking, but a good deal of singing as one lusty chorus follows another.

> "The biscuits in the Army they say are mighty fine,
> One rolled off the table and killed a pal of mine,
> Oh, I don't want no more of Army life,
> Gee, Mom, I want to go home!"

They ring the changes on that one and then there is a call for "When the War Is Over . . ."

"When the war is over, we will all enlist again,
When the war is over, we will all enlist again,
When the war is over, we will all enlist again,
We will like hell, we will."

There is only time for one verse of this before a soldier called
Whitey spies "a new batch" coming down the street, "all nice
and shiny." A moment later as a detail of rookies march in,
the soldiers go into their reception stuff. They break into shouts
of: "You'll be sorry!" "The first two weeks are the hardest!"
"Don't volunteer for anything!" "Wait 'til you get your first
K.P. Oh, boy!" "Don't get homesick—it won't do you any
good!" "Never trust a Sergeant!" "Wait 'til you taste the
food here!" "The mess hall's a mile and a half away!" "You'll
be sorry!"

"Into the street, led by a Sergeant, march about twenty green
rookies, just off the train, still in civilian clothes, still carrying
their valises, and still pretty bewildered by it all. Allan, Frankie
and Pinky are among them."

The Sergeant counts off the first six, leaves them at ease and
marches the rest of the rookies off down the street. The six who
are left set down their suitcases and look around uneasily. The
soldiers, evidently expecting this, go on with their hazing.
Finally they bring up the soldier Whitey to finish them off.
Whitey, "a small fellow in undershirt and shorts," stands on a
mop rack and addresses them all as though it were a congre-
gation:

WHITEY—Brethren, long, long ago we saw a poster. It was a
beautiful poster, was it not?

SOLDIERS (*yelling back*)—Yes!

WHITEY—What did it say?

SOLDIERS—Join the Air Corps!

WHITEY—Join the Air Corps! Be a Pilot, Bombardier, Navigator! Fly that Fortress! Fly that Liberator! Wear those
wings! Get those women! Did we join? (*A groan goes up
from the soldiers.*) Three months, four months, five months, six
months . . . Where's that letter? Talk flying, eat flying, sleep
flying—! Breathe flying—! Where's that letter? Will it ever
come?

SOLDIERS—Yes!

WHITEY—It comes! Report in thirty-six hours! Good-by,

Mom, good-by, Dad, good-by, Sis, good-by, kid! Don't worry!
I'll write you from Africa—I'll write you from Australia! Right?

SOLDIERS—Right!

WHITEY (sadly)—Join the Air Corps! And see the Garden
Spot—of Mississippi! To the right, gentlemen, is Pneumonia
Gulch—that is where we sleep. You fry by day, you freeze by
night. To the left—just a little ways—just a mile and a half—
is Ptomaine Tavern. That is where we eat. The wheat cakes
we leave are used as depth bombs by the Navy. And the planes,
you ask? Where are the planes? Ah, gentlemen—they can be
seen at night—in the movies! And how, then, do we become
Pilots, Bombardiers, Navigators?

SOLDIERS—Fall in! Fall out! Eyes right! Eyes left! Double time, hut! Wipe that smile off your face! Look proud—
you're in the Air Corps! Get on the ball! Stay on the ball!
Fall in! Fall out! Hut, two, three, four!

WHITEY—So what about that beautiful poster, with the beautiful pilot, in the beautiful Fortress? Gentlemen, we have a little
song here that tells it far better than any words of mine. It
goes: "We joined the Air Corps to fly machines, and all we do
is clean latrines!" But the hand that holds that mop will some
day run a Fortress. This is how it all starts. And that poster,
gentlemen, was a goddam lie. I thank you.

The soldiers give Whitey a big hand. Irving, from Brooklyn,
refuses to be let down. All this stuff don't scare Irving none. If
they don't like it, why don't they get out?

"Listen, Brooklyn, we like it fine," a soldier answers him.
"But we love to gripe. That's half the fun!"

A whistle blows twice. That's the mail call. With a rush
and shouts of glee the soldiers are off down the street. The six
recruits are left alone. It is a time for introductions now. There's
Irving, and Bobby, and Dave and Allan, and Frankie and Danny.
"They call me Pinky," admits Danny.

"Maybe I should have stood in Brooklyn," Irving is saying.
"At least if you wanted to see planes you could go to La Guardia
Field on Sunday. (He laughs.) Hell, they gotta let us at 'em
sometime. I can take all this—as long as they show us a plane
once in a while. I'm plane crazy. Don't ask me why. I'm in
the hardware business, see? And the hardware business don't
know nothing from flying, believe me. My whole family thinks
I'm nuts. So I'm nuts—I want to fly. Do me something. I

got the bug. Since I was a kid, I got it."

"I got it pretty early, too," says Bobby. "I used to stand in the cornfield and watch for planes till my eyes hurt me."

"You a farmer?"

"Yep. This is the furtherest I ever been away from home in my life."

"You see? It's a bug. What's a farmer know from flying?"

Down in Texas, Dave puts in, they had their own Flying Club. Sure, he's flown. Is he rich? Not for Texas. Dave's father only owns about six oil wells at the moment.

Frankie is worried. He had promised Jane he'd send her a wire the minute he got to camp. Now he's afraid to leave before the Sergeant gets back. Frankie, fishing for his wallet, would like them to see Jane's picture. Frankie is only a two-day groom, Allan explains. Only a one-day groom, really, Frankie corrects him.

The soldiers are coming back from the mail call and going into their barracks—"some with packages, some with home-town newspapers, all reading the letters from home as they walk."

Now there is more excitement down the street. A small contingent of WACS comes into view. Whitey is on the job again: "Hi, fellers. G.I. women!" Immediately the barracks bursts into song:

"The Girl on the right is quite all right, parley vous.
The Girl on the right is quite all right, parley vous.
The Girl on the right is quite all right,
But her uniform's a little tight,
Inky, dinky, parley vous!"

"The Girl on the right pulls her uniform down self-consciously, and gets out of step." That's a laugh. But the boys go right on singing.

A moment later a detail of twenty-five boys marches on. "They are not in fatigues but in uniform, and spruce as hell. They have gas masks slung over their shoulders, and are smartly singing 'Into the air, Army Air Corps.' . . ."

The detail disappears. "We're not gonna wash out!" shouts Allan, his face aglow.

"Are you kidding? That's *us* in six weeks!" says Pinky, slapping him on the back.

The Sergeant is back. "All right, you men," he barks. "Fall in! Get on the ball. Wipe that smile off your face! Straighten

up! Look proud! You're in the Air Corps! 'Tention! Hut,
two, three, four . . ."

They have started to march off. Pinky tentatively starts his
song: "Off we go, into the wild blue yonder . . ."

The Sergeant turns sharply. "Halt!" He is standing men-
acingly before Pinky. "Was that you, soldier?"

"Yes, sir."

"Don't whisper it, pilot—sing it!"

They don't have to be told twice. "They march off—six
very, very eager beavers!"

"You'll be sorry—you'll be sorry!" The soldiers are calling
after them, tauntingly, as the curtain falls.

The examination room is long and bare. Along one side is a
machine divided into sections. Before each section a chair; before each chair a boy stands at attention. There are ten of
them. They are being addressed by Major Halper. Standing
near the Major is the Examiner, fingering a sheaf of papers.

Major Halper explains to the boys that he is there as a Classification Officer, to give them an idea of the processing which
they will go through during the next two weeks.

"This processing will determine your classification into the
Aircrew, either as Pilots, Bombardiers or Navigators," the
Major is saying. "During the next fourteen days you are going
to be watched, tested and judged, and the method in which you
conduct yourself and the manner in which you accept the processing will be decisive factors in your classification."

The Major knows how hard the boys have worked, and what
they have been through to get where they are. "But remember
this," he concludes; "everything else was only the beginning;
everything else was the warmup. You've got to get through here.
And a lot of good men don't. So stay with it all the way. From
now on—it's up to you. Good luck!"

Major Halper retires and the Examiner takes over. He calls
the roll. The men respond smartly. He orders them to be
seated.

"When I say 'Ready' you will grasp the handle and withdraw
the rod two inches," he instructs them. "When I say 'Inhale'
take a normal breath and hold it. When I say 'Go' your trial
begins. Try to keep the metal rod free from the sides of the
hole. You will note that each time the metal rod comes in contact with the sides of the hole, the light flashes on. Each flash
of light indicates an error. You must at all times avoid contact

between the metal rod and the sides of the hole."

There is a slight pause. The Examiner's voice takes on a shade more intimacy. "Gentlemen," he says, "I want to be frank with you. Far too many aviation students are being washed out in Flying School who should never have been permitted to get that far. The man who becomes nervous and tense in critical situations—the man who gets rattled under fire —is not the man for aircrew training. We must stop him *here*. We shall now have the first trial."

The Examiner has stepped back and resumed his instructor's attitude. "Ready! Inhale! Go! Watch the stylus. See it hit the sides of the hole. Watch each flash of light. That's all. Just keep watching. You are counting your own errors. Each flash advances you a notch closer to failure. Stop! Write down the number of errors. You have ten seconds."

A half dozen times the exercise is repeated. The intoning of the Examiner can still be heard as the lights fade. The curtain falls.

Along the back wall of a washroom there is a long row of basins and above each basin a square mirror. Within hearing a shower is running and someone is singing. That would be Pinky. The others—Allan, Frankie, Dave, Bobby and Irving—their shirts off, are in various states of washing up or shaving. They are pretty well fagged. Another six days of what they've just been through would be more than Bobby could take. And Pinky is singing! Pinky just ain't got no nerves. That's Irving's opinion. "It was all fun to that bastard!" recalls Irv. "Even the thing with the lights. Boy, my legs wouldn't hold me up after that one, and I ain't ashamed to admit it. (*He mimics the* Examiner.) 'Watch the light. Count your errors. Every mistake is bringing you closer to failure. Watch the light. Count your errors.' What the hell did he think we were doing? Playing potsie?"

It will be another five days before they will know how they came out on their tests. They are all pretty anxious. Frankie shows signs of breaking. Allan sees that. Perhaps, he thinks, if he gets tough with Frankie he can pull him out of his worry. He tries it. But Frankie, hurt, only picks up his towel and stalks out of the room.

"I've tried to buck him up, but it's no good," Allan explains to the others. "Listen, be tough with him, will you, if he tries to talk to you guys? We've got to keep him on the beam until

Tuesday, in case— Well, let's not think about that."

Pinky is in from the shower with a towel wrapped about his middle. He's all for going to a movie. Betty Grable. And legs! Oh, boy!

The others are ready to sock Pinky. Especially Irving. That guy just ain't human—

"Irv, you bring around a good-looking dame and I'll show you how human I am and how tired I get, too. But those tests—why, they were fun, Pal!"

Allan is still worrying about Frankie. That makes Pinky sore, too. "Oh, come off it! Quit worrying, Allan!" snaps Pinky. "You fuss over him like an old hen!"

"Yes, I know—suppose he *doesn't* make it?"

"He'll make it. He's made it this far, hasn't he? And you worried all along the line, too. Didn't you?"

"Yeah."

"Oh, sure he'll make it." But the thought isn't too sure, even to Pinky. "Why, it wouldn't be the same thing at all without— all of us. Goddamit, there you go spoiling Betty Grable for me! I'll be seeing Frankie now instead of those legs! Why didn't you wait and tell me tomorrow?"

Frankie has come back. He goes quickly to Allan. "I'm sorry, Al," he says.

"Hell, it was me. I'm sorry, Frankie."

"What the hell is this?" roars Pinky. "I'm sorry Al, I'm sorry Frankie— For God's sake, you're like two old women."

He hasn't time to say any more. Allan and Frankie grab him. They are tossing him back into the shower as the curtain falls.

The new scene is a Faculty Board Meeting Room. Behind a long oak table six officers are sitting, each with a file of papers in front of him. Facing them are fifteen students. Major Halper, Chairman of the Board, is addressing this group.

They have been summoned, he tells them, to discuss their qualification or disqualification for aircrew training. If any of them has any objection to any officer member of the board let him speak. To this there is no reply. The Major continues:

"Gentlemen, it is my unpleasant duty to tell you that you have been recommended for disqualification from aircrew training because of an unsatisfactory Adaptability Rating for Military Aeronautics or because of some physical deficiency which has become apparent during your examination here."

It is the opinion of the Board, says Major Halper, that each of them could learn to fly a plane under peacetime conditions, but under war conditions the risk they individually present is too great. Every man in a bomber is responsible for nine other lives besides his own. Individual hearings will follow at which time the Board will answer any questions and give each man a chance to make any statement he may wish to make. They may now retire.

The boys march out. For a moment no one speaks. Then Major Halper releases a confession. "Jesus, how I hate this job!" says he, with feeling.

"Who doesn't?" demands Captain Speer of the Board. "I just can't look at their faces when the news first hits them. I have an idea of what's going on inside. My kid washed out, you know."

They get on with the job. The first boy called back is Peter Clark, a stalwart, handsome lad in his early twenties. He marches smartly to the table and salutes. They ask him to sit down.

Peter has failed to make a passing grade in any one of the aptitude tests. His grades in the pencil and paper tests were excellent. In fact, because his record as an aviation student up to now has been a particularly fine one the Board is admittedly reluctant to disqualify him. Is there anything that Peter Clark would like to say?

There is, Peter admits, hesitantly, but it is kind of personal. And, anyway, Peter hates a guy who makes excuses. Assured that the Board will respect his confidence, Peter admits that there is a girl. It is, he repeats, kind of personal.

"We understand, Mr. Clark," encourages Major Halper. "If you think you can tell us, I wish you would. I am aware that we may seem ancient to you, but we've all had girls ourselves."

PETER—Yes, sir. Well, the night before we were supposed to take the aptitude tests, I got a letter from my sister. She said my girl—we got engaged about five and a half months ago before I left—was running around with another guy and I ought to know about it.

MAJOR HALPER—I see.

PETER—It threw me for a loop. At first I couldn't believe it. I read the letter about a hundred times, I guess, and then I read all the letters my girl had written me. Finally, I couldn't stand it any more, so I tried to phone her.

MAJOR HALPER—Your sister?

PETER—No, sir. Cuddles—I mean my girl, sir. It took me about two hours before I could even get to the telephone, and then I waited another two hours while they tried to put the call through. She's from St. Louis. Anyway, by that time I didn't care about anything but *knowing,* so I just stayed there.

MAJOR HALPER—After lights out?

PETER—Yes, sir. I'm sorry, sir. But I just didn't care. I just walked up and down for the rest of the night.

MAJOR HALPER—And the next morning at seven you started the aptitude tests?

PETER—Yes, sir. I know it's no excuse, but all I kept seeing through every test was the face of that Navy guy she was running around with.

MAJOR HALPER—Oh, the Navy, eh? May—er—we ask what finally happened?

PETER—Yes, sir. My girl got here three days later, and on Saturday we were married. My cock-eyed sister didn't know this guy was her cousin. Why, he's a middle-aged man, sir!

MAJOR HALPER—Really. About thirty-three, I suppose?

PETER—Thirty-two, sir.

MAJOR HALPER—Mr. Clark, I think I speak for the rest of the Board when I say that we feel there was more than a little justification for your behavior—unmilitary though it was. Aptitude tests and—er—love never quite did mix successfully, and sometimes we wink a collective eye in the direction of love. Mr. Clark, do you expect to get a good night's sleep tonight?

PETER—Yes, sir.

MAJOR HALPER (*to his fellow officers*)—Will it be satisfactory to you gentlemen if Mr. Clark takes the Aptitude Tests over again tomorrow? (*The officers nod or murmur assent.*) Very well, Mr. Clark. We will advise your Section Leader accordingly.

PETER (*haltingly*)—Sir—I'd like to thank you—but I can't seem to get the words out.

MAJOR HALPER—You're very welcome, Clark. But if you don't pass with a very high mark tomorrow there are a couple of middle-aged men on this Board who will come after you with a baseball bat.

PETER—Yes, sir. (*All smiles, he salutes and goes out.*)

"Be nice if they were all like that," suggests a Captain at the end of the table. But they're not. The next one, promises Major Halper, is a tough one. This boy has made a fine record all the way through, but he just can't make the Depth Perception test. The Examiners have put him through twice; they gave him a double check, and still he can't make it. "Send in Danny Scariano," he calls into the inter-office phone.

Pinky reports smartly, but uneasily. The Major's tone becomes almost paternal as he explains the situation to him. Because of Pinky's fine record, the Major says, he had been given special consideration. Yet he had not been able to pass that one test. Is there anything he would like to say to the Board?

"Yes," snaps Pinky, bitterly. "Why did they let me come this far? Why didn't they kick me out before? I took a perception test when I first joined up. I took another one at Camp. And at college. Why didn't they tell me then? Why do they let me get this far and then wash me out?"

"Yes, Scariano, you're quite right," admits the Major. "That shouldn't be. We're doing all we can to avoid just that. But you see, those doctors are under great pressure. They're examining hundreds day in, day out. And they're human. They pass some quite obvious cases that should have been caught at the beginning. That's why we here have to be especially careful. This is the place we try and catch all the mistakes. You understand that, Scariano—don't you?"

But Pinky cannot answer. He is crying quite unashamedly. "I'm sorry, sir. I can't help it," he mutters, the tears rolling down his face.

"Sure. Go right ahead. Don't be ashamed, Scariano. Lots of fellows do it."

At Major Halper's suggestion the Board takes a five minute break for a cigarette and leave Pinky alone. Before the Major leaves he beckons Frankie and Allan to come in through a side door. They would comfort Pinky if they could, but there isn't much that they can say. Pinky would have them get back before they have to do a couple of days of K.P. for missing inspection. Who the hell cares about that, Frankie would know.

"Look, Pink—we know how you feel—and we know you don't want to talk about it right now. But stay on the ball, huh?" says Allan.

"Yeah."

"No, listen to me for just a minute—will you, Pink? There's really something in that guff they've been drumming into us about the whole crew being a team—it's not just the Pilot, Bombardier, Navigator and that's all."

"Sure, Pink," adds Frankie, "where would they be without the

Gunners and the Radio Men? Makes a lot of sense. Why, the ground crew is just as important as the Pilot. You know that."

"The thing is *you* didn't fail," Allan would point out. "Not personally. This is a tough, lousy break. But this is still for you. Any part of it. Maybe you don't feel that way now, but it's true, Pink. That's why I'd love to see you stay in there, pitching. All right—so you won't have wings. What the hell? This is bigger than that, isn't it? Isn't it, Pink?"

Pinky does not answer at first. Then he says, quite wearily: "I'll be shipping out tomorrow."

He doesn't want to talk any more about anything just then, he tells them. But he does agree to meet them in the bunk after mess. They'll get some beers and take them away somewheres— away from the crowd, Allan promises.

For a moment or two after they have gone Pinky stands quite motionless. "Then he takes out the handkerchief and blows his nose. He seems, suddenly, to be very, very, weary. He leans heavily against the table, twisting and untwisting the handkerchief in his hands. Then, slowly—disjointedly—he begins to whistle in a low key . . . The Air Corps Song." The lights fade and the curtain falls.

In the Lecture Hall Major Halper is again addressing the boys to whom he had spoken two weeks before. There has been a noticeable thinning of the ranks, but Allan, Frankie, Dave, Bobby and Irving are still present, obviously keyed to a high pitch. "This is the day they have been so anxiously awaiting."

Before the classifications are announced, Major Halper would like to say a few words to these future Pilots, Bombardiers and Navigators. Whatever their classification, let them determine to be the best. They've *got* to be.

"Remember," he says, "you train to save not only your own life but those of your comrades, too. So if you want to bring your sweet little neck back to that sweet little woman of yours— get every damn thing you can. Thank you and good luck."

Major Halper turns the meeting over to Lieut. McCarthy, who instructs the boys as to how they shall advance to receive their classifications. If they accept they will sign the card handed them and return to their places. If they do not accept they are to retire to the rear of the room and later state their objections to Major Halper. The Lieutenant calls the first name—

"Larsen. Henry Larsen."

Larsen comes smartly forward to the desk, stands and salutes.

"Pilot. Do you accept the classification?"

"Yes, sir."

"Sign here."

Larsen signs, salutes again, and returns to his place. His face is wreathed in happy smiles and he is met by the explosive but muffled congratulations of his pals.

"Simpson. Al Simpson."

Again the quick approach, the snappy salute, the happy acceptance and the return to the group. The first boy to be classified as a Bombardier is obviously disappointed, but he accepts. The first Navigator refuses the classification and starts the line of objectors at the rear.

Both Allan and Frankie are classified as pilots. Allan takes it calmly enough, but Frankie can't quite smother an exultant "I made it!" as he goes back to his place, and to a lot of handshaking and backslapping. Irving Miller, too, is so enthusiastic in his acceptance, so fervent in his "Yes, sir! I sure do!" that even the Lieutenant joins in the laughter.

The expression on each anxious student face reflects each boy's own little drama as the exercises proceed. The Pilots are aglow with pride and relief; the Bombardiers and Navigators are mostly downcast with disappoint, but most of them are firm with determination to see the adventure through.

The Lieutenant is still calling the names, and the airmen are still advancing and receiving their classifications as the lights slowly fade and the curtain falls.

The entrance gates at the Classification Center are of wrought iron and tall. There is a stone bench on either side of them. These are occupied at the moment by soldiers and their girls, the girls' heads usually on the boys' shoulders. It is Sunday evening. The week-end pass is over, and the boys are coming back to Camp. Some stroll back alone, some saunter slowly along with girls to linger and kiss for a moment in the shadows and then pass through the gates. Back of the gates the barracks glow softly with light, and the boys already back are lifting their voices in song.

A soldier has come in with his father and mother. They pause just outside the gate for their good-bys. The atmosphere is a little tense. The boy would break it by introducing Mom and Dad to the leader of his section, Lieut. Stevens. Dad is pleased

to state to Lieut. Stevens that he thinks Jimmy makes a pretty
good looking soldier. Mom is satisfied, too, though she isn't
quite used to the awful haircut the Army's given Jim. It has
taken all the wave out. The Lieutenant gracefully helps Jimmy
out of his embarrassment and goes on.

". . . I hate to go, but I'd better," Jim is saying.

"Good-by, darling. Take care, will you? And keep writing?
We love your letters so." Mother is in her son's arms.

"Good-by, Dad."

"Good-by, Jim. Got everything you need?"

"Everything. Take care of yourself."

"I will. Keep up the good work, Jim."

"You bet. Good-by."

Another quick kiss for Mom and Jim is gone. They watch
him until he disappears, then walk slowly, silently away.

The scene is ever changing and ever the same. Sally and Ed
have left each other's arms for the last time before she tells him
she has taken a job at Woolworth's. She had waited till then
so there wouldn't be any time for argument. She just had to do
it—she was so lonesome. Then she gives him the wrist watch
she has spent her first money for and is forgiven.

Allan and his wife, Dorothy, and Frankie and the Jane he
married two days before the boys left for Camp, stroll on, their
arms around each other's waists. It is the end of another week
and they are putting it off as long as possible.

A moment later, Irving, Dave and Bobby arrive, gaily singing
"Happy is the day, when the airman gets his pay—" These
three have had a grand time on leave. "We pooled our dough
and took a room at the hotel," Irving reports. "Went to bed
at 4 o'clock Saturday afternoon and didn't get up until just an
hour ago. We had all our meals served right in the room. And
the *waiter* did the K.P. . . ."

"I sat in a warm tub and read the funnies for about four hours.
Boy!" This from Dave.

"We woke up at 5:30, just to torture ourselves for a minute,
and then went right back to sleep," reports Bobby.

They wrote letters, and Irving spent $6 on long distance to
hear his kid say "da-da" and "ma-ma." It was wonderful!

Allan still thinks that Dorothy should go back to Mom. They
will be shipping him out pretty soon now, and when they do
it will probably be to some desert station where there's a flying
field. For Dorothy that will mean heat and dust and a rotten
little room—

Dorothy will go back if he wants her to, but she had rather stay. "It isn't fun—of course it isn't—but if it won't worry you too much, let me stay, Allan. I want to—terribly."

For answer, he takes her in his arms. "I'm afraid I want it, too, Dot," he says.

A last kiss, a last embrace and the boys are gone. And Jane hadn't told Frankie. Dorothy can see that. And Jane had promised—

"Oh, Dot, I just couldn't," protests Jane. "He'd be sure to worry and they're just going into the most important part of their training."

"Jane, he ought to know. He might want you to go home and stay with his folks. Having a baby under these conditions is pretty risky. You know that."

"But I don't want to go back, Dot. I want to stay with him. We'll be together. You'll always be there. I'll tell him later, Dot. Not now. I'm afraid he'll make me go back." . . . As they start for the last bus Jane adds cheerfully: "Maybe I'll tell him next week and we could announce it to all of them."

"Wonderful!" agrees Dorothy. "He'll be too confused in front of everybody to do much arguing."

"That's what I figured," admits Jane, and they both laugh.

In the near distance a bugler blows taps. "The singing ceases and the lights in the barracks begin to go out. The girls turn and watch until the Camp lies in darkness." The curtain falls.

This side of a hangar on the flying field is open. Against the wall of the closed side there is a series of blackboards, chalked with the names of students and their instructions. It is 10 o'clock of a moonlight night and everything is bustling with activity. There are students and instructors around the blackboards, and flyers are constantly arriving and leaving, goggled and helmeted, their parachutes dangling from their shoulders. "This is a far cry from the barracks and the Classification Center. This is it! The very air is different. They are no longer aviation students. They are cadets now—and don't they know it!"

The talk has a knowing technical flavor. "Coming in a little too hot, isn't he?" mutters one of a group of boys looking out over the runway. "No, he's all right. Throttle her back, brother! That's it! Cut the gun!" . . . "Did you see Bill Lewis make that 90 degree bank at the tree by the bridge?" "Yeah. He really reefed her in. He's hot, that boy." "Not any more. Old McIntyre chewed his can off when he got down."

Allan and Bobby are in. They have just done their first night solos and, boy, what a thrill! Irving, too. Allan and Bobby swarm on Irving when he comes in. Bobby gives Allan the nudge, and Allan takes over—

"Don't spill it all at once, Irv," cautions Allan. "Take plenty of time. Tell us all about the moon, and how close the stars seemed, and how the clouds looked like white velvet."

"Go jump in the lake, smart guys. I just had the biggest damn thrill of my life, and you muggs ain't gonna talk me out of it, either. I suppose it was just another flight to you jerks?"

"Bobby, did we say that? We want you to tell us, Irving, in your own original way. That's all. We want to get it hot off your lips, Irv."

"Oh, shut up. Listen, I wish I was a poet. I ain't fooling. I'd like to write it down for my kid. This first night solo does something to you—inside. I ain't over it yet. Gimme a cigarette."

"Wait till we get a load of Frankie!" promises Allan, laughing. "He gets romantic about a propeller blade! This will be a regular love story!"

"Well, goddamit, it *is* romantic! And you don't hate yourself in the morning, either!"

There is a letter from Pinky. Larsen brings it to Allan, and Allan reads it to the boys: "Dear Allan and Frankie and the rest. Well, I suppose by the time *this* letter reaches you, you'll all be Hot Pilots dangling those parachutes from your behinds like medals. As for myself, I am now at advanced gunnery school, and all I can say is, it shouldn't happen to a dog. The nearest town is 62 miles away and has a population of 300—all Indians. Makes it very nice for week-ends. The women all look like shoeleather, and *my* shape is better than any woman's I've seen since we got here. We have a swell bunch of officers and they are very nice to us. Last week a case of Coca-Cola arrived— the first one—and they let us watch them drink it. Movies arrive every three weeks by Pony Express, and the mail is flown in by Carrier Pigeons. Yesterday, a pigeon took a look at the camp and turned right around and went back. Why the hell don't you write? Well, keep 'em flying, you guys, and if you need the best damn turret gunner in the Air Corps, let me know a few days in advance. P.S. I also give haircuts on the side. Pinky."

The boys are still chortling, when there is a sudden stir at the back of the hangar. Several of the boys have snapped to attention. Capt. McIntyre is coming. He puts the men at ease and gathers them around him. He has bad news. A plane has crashed. A farmer had just telephoned. Col. Gibney and the search planes have already left. Which of the boys of Flight D haven't come back yet? It is one of that four.

There is a hurried count among the boys. Marshall isn't back. Nor Stevens. Nor Michaelson. Nor Davis. Allan reports for Frankie, and his face goes suddenly white. Capt. McIntyre is continuing—

"Okay. Now I came here myself because it's spreading over the field, and I wanted you to hear it from me. We don't know anything yet. Remember that. Maybe it's just a forced landing. When a farmer says he saw a plane dive you can't tell what the hell he means, so take it easy."

"Sir—was there—any fire?" Allan asks, anxiously.

"He didn't say. He just told us where it was and hung up. He was going out there himself. (*He looks off.*) There's one coming in. Don't crowd now. He'll get here in a minute."

Silently, grimly, the little group stands watching the runway. The lights of an incoming plane outline their faces. Presently the man who has landed comes into the group. Marshall is accounted for. He can't understand the excitement of his relieved friends. Another plane lands. It is Stevens. Then Michaelson comes—and they know.

"It's Davis," slowly announces Capt. McIntyre.

"Capt. McIntyre—can I go, please?" Allan pleads.

"I'm sorry, Ross. The Colonel left strict orders."

"But I can't just stand here, sir!"

Presently Col. Gibney appears. He dismisses the others and keeps Allan there. Allan has sunk to the bench and covered his face with his hands. The Colonel understands.

"Don't talk unless you want to, Ross. I'll just sit here with you for a while. Or I'll go if you'd rather."

"Did—did he have a chance, sir?"

"The nose was buried deep in the ground."

"I just can't make myself believe it yet. I can't. Poor guy. He was going to have a baby, sir."

"Oh. I didn't know that. His wife live in town?"

"Yes, sir. With my wife. Did you know him at all, sir? He was such a wonderful guy."

"I think I've spoken to him once or twice."

"Sir, may I have a pass for town?"

"You want to go to his wife?"

"Yes, sir."

"I'll take you over in my car."

"You're very kind, sir."

"Kind? The word 'kind' sounds a little foolish. Sure you're all right, Ross?"

"Yes, sir."

"All right. My car's in front of Headquarters."

They start slowly out. The lights fade. The curtain falls.

It is two days before graduation. The boys of the graduation group are holding star parties at which their instructors are the guests of honor. Under a gnarled and twisted cactus tree Allan's crowd is sprawled, beer mugs and sandwiches in hand. There are a keg of beer and a crate of fruit near by. One boy is playing a harmonica and another is tap dancing to the tune. There is much shouting and laughter, and occasionally from the near distance sounds of other parties blend in.

Presently there are calls for Lieut. Thompson and yells for a speech. Considerably confused the Lieutenant allows himself to be lifted onto a food crate. He can make a pretty good speech in a plane, the Lieutenant says, but he's no damned good on the ground. They know that, the boys call back. He "has chewed their cans off plenty." But let him go on.

Lieut. Thompson lets them have it. When they first came to the flying line they were awful, he tells them. "Are these the jerks I've got to learn to fly!" he thought. His stomach did a snap roll and his brain just ground-looped. But, to the Lieutenant's great surprise they made it.

"Just to get serious for a minute," the Lieutenant concludes, "I want to tell you that I'm mighty pleased. Y'see, we instructors have a lousy job. We're all dying to get over there, but the Army says 'no': your job is to stay here and instruct a lot of raunchy cadets. That's a bitter pill to swallow, fellows, and the only kick we get is when you guys make it. It means more than you think. Because *we* get mighty tired and discouraged, too. Yesterday I got a letter from a fellow who graduated four classes ago. He's in the South Pacific now, and he still remembers me. I got quite a kick out of that. Made me feel that I was kinda out there, too. Oh, hell—all I want to say is, it's been swell teaching you to fly—and I'm sorry to see you go. You're a swell bunch, and I'll miss you."

There is a storm of applause and much whistling and then Jerry Ellison replies for the boys. The first glimpse they got of their instructor that same first day, remembers Jerry, he had turned to Allan and said: "That guy ain't gonna teach us to fly—he's gonna teach us how to rhumba." And the first time the Lieutenant had taken them up they all went to Mass very early the next day. But, as it turned out, the Lieutenant came through, too. Jerry is speaking for all of them, he feels sure, when he says that they had the best damned instructor on the field.

Now, strangely enough, Lieut. Thompson finds a small box lying at his feet. When, at Jerry's suggestion, he picks it up he finds his name inscribed on it. And when he opens it he finds a gold identification bracelet inside. Of course, they must know that instructors are not permitted to accept any presents from cadets. They do, and they wouldn't dream of such a thing. But when this box was just lying there on the ground, and they simply called his attention to it, there can't be any damned rule against that!

The Lieutenant doesn't get very far with his thanks before he is drowned out with their singing "For he's a jolly good fellow."

Now Irving, who is a little drunk, thinks he will make a speech. Irving never had much of an education, he admits, but all he wants to say is that when a fellow meets guys like Bobby and Allan and the rest—why—that's *it*—it's the *stuff*—it's the McCoy —that's it—"

But the boys take care of Irving. Soon he is on his way to camp, with Henderson on one side of him and Marshall on the other.

Now the party has broken up. Bobby and Allan have drawn straws and lost, which leaves them behind to clean up. As they work their minds go back to the day they first met—and how far off their wings seemed that day! Yet, here it is—the day after tomorrow—Wings!

Most of the fellows will have their folks down to pin their Wings on. Or their girls. But Bobby won't. His folks just can't afford it. So, will Allan pin his Wings on for him? Bobby asks it as a favor.

"That's no favor, Bobby," Allan protests. "I'd have socked you if you had let anybody else do it."

And after that is attended to, Bobby is to come to the hotel, where Allan's folks are giving him and Dorothy a little blow-out.

They are about through now. There are just about two beers left in the keg. They pour it out into paper cups.

"What'll we drink to, Al?"

"To Frankie, Bob."

"To Frankie," murmurs Bob, softly, as they lift their cups. The curtain falls.

A platform has been erected for the graduation exercises. It is flag-draped and flower bedecked and on it sit Col. Gibney, the Commanding Officer, the Honor Guests and the Officers of the Field. At one side of the platform the lower classmen of the Field, with their parents, wives and sweethearts, are placed. The Band is seated below the platform, and a hollow square has been left for the cadets to march into. As the last man reaches his place, the band finishes a stirring march and the Chaplain arises to ask the Lord's blessing on these pilots of America, that they may be granted victory, "for they are freedom-loving men." "In granting them victory you fulfill their resolve that liberty, true and universal, shall not perish from this earth," prays the Chaplain.

As the prayer is ended to the swelling "Amens" of the assemblage, Col. Gibney arises to address the graduates. The Colonel is prepared to confess unblushingly that, though this is just another graduation to him, every graduation gives him a thrill—"a real kick—right down to my very toes—as though each graduation were the first I had ever seen. You see," the Colonel continues, "I am an old Air Force man, and I still cannot get over the miracle that has been wrought. . . . Do you realize, gentlemen, that in my day you had to have seven years' service and fifteen hundred hours of flying time before you could even step *inside* a B-17? And you didn't fly them for a full year after that, either. You fellows fly them in fifteen months! Fifteen months! Gentlemen, we graduate more pilots in a month from this field alone than the entire Air Force used to graduate in a year. I never will get over that. Never! . . . And maybe the biggest miracle of all, gentlemen, is that it came out of the people—it's a people's miracle. Because you are all of us. Gentlemen, the Flying Training Command salutes you, the people of our nation pray for you, and may God bless you."

Col. Gibney returns to his place. Capt. McIntyre steps forward to announce that Col. Charles Ross will present the trophy to the outstanding man of the class. Col. Ross takes his place. "Ladies and Gentlemen, I ask your indulgence," he begins. "I have here in my hand a copy of the speech I was to deliver. I find now that I cannot do it—for the simple reason that in awarding this trophy to my son I can find no words to express what I feel. It happens to be the proudest moment of my life. Allan . . ."

Allan emerges from the crowd. He faces and salutes his father. For a moment the two men smile uncertainly at each other. They shake hands, the trophy is presented and Allan returns to his place amid a good deal of applause.

Now Lieutenant Sperry administers the Oath of Office, the cadets standing with right hands raised, repeating after him the familiar words: "I do solemnly swear that I will support and defend the Constitution of the United States against all enemies, foreign and domestic. . . ."

"The Squadron Commanders will now present the Wings," announces Lieutenant Sperry. Four Squadron Commanders take their places below the platform. At a given signal the cadets, four at a time, come forward to receive their Wings. The crowds in the stands have broken into the Air Corps song.

"They sing it thrillingly—pouring all of their patriotism, all of their pent-up feelings of what this moment means—into the song. Each man about to receive his Wings, salutes, accepts the proffered Wings, salutes again, and turns. But as he turns to go back to his place, his face, which has been set sternly, breaks into an unearthly smile. Relief, achievement, and pride are all mirrored in that smile, and he clutches the Wings in his fist as though it were the key to Heaven. On and on they come, each face stern and military, then each face breaking into that grin as they receive their Wings and turn back."

It is over now and bedlam has broken loose. The crowds are streaming down, embracing their beloved kinfolk, many weeping unashamedly. Allan has left the crowd. He waves gleefully to his father and mother and Dorothy and then dashes madly about looking and calling for Bobby.

Allan finds Bobby presently. They look at each other for a moment and then Bobby hands over his precious Wings. Without a word Allan pins them on. And then the bars. They shake hands and Allan, throwing his arm across Bobby's shoulder, leads him across to Dorothy and the others.

The singing has suddenly switched from the Air Corps song to "Auld Lang Syne." Allan kisses his mother—then stands as she pins the wings on, and Dorothy the bars.

The curtain falls.

ACT II

It is Bobby Grills' wedding day, "and a festive occasion, not only for the Grills family, but for the entire town." On the lawn outside the Grills' farmhouse in Oregon an altar decked in apple blossoms has been erected under two peach trees in full bloom. The wedding guests are assembled. The farmers and their wives are in their Sunday best, and a proper military touch is given to the scene by Allan, Dave and Irving, "resplendent in their officers' uniforms."

The ceremony has just been concluded, and there is a good deal of embracing and congratulating going on. From the house there is a call for Lieut. Ross. Long Distance is calling.

The crowd mills about. Everybody is chatty and happy. The Mayor is recalling that it was he who had signed Bobby's birth certificate. He has been in office so long that he is thinking of issuing one of those personal statements that he is no longer a candidate, but is willing to talk things over.

"What's this fellow La Guardia like?" the Mayor wants to know of Irving.

"He's okay," admits Irving, cagily. "He's a hell of a fireman."

Allan is back from his call. Quietly he singles out Irving and Dave. The call, he tells them, was from Headquarters. All leaves have been canceled. They are to report at the Field Tuesday at 5 o'clock. That means they will have to be seeing about trains right away. Fortunately the Mayor, being the passenger agent as well, can help them with that.

"It's going to be tough on Bobby. Bobby's been dreaming about this for a year," recalls Allan. But there's nothing to be done. And here's the bride—

The new Helen Grills looks charming in her wedding finery. She has come in search of the best man and his best friends. They haven't even tried to kiss the bride. Why?

"We didn't want to be killed in the crush, that's all," cracks Irving. "When you're in the army, Helen, you tackle anything *but* a bunch of civilians after rationed goods."

After they have attended to the kissing matter Helen would have them confirm her impression that it has been a beautiful wedding. They admit it.

"You know, it is almost like standing off and watching a picture come to life," muses Helen. "Bobby and I planned it just like this ever since I can remember. The one thing we didn't plan was—you. (*She gestures toward the boys.*) And I don't think even you know how much it means to Bobby to have you here. And to me, too. His letters were so full of you, always."

"I'd have liked to see him get married without us," says Irving.

"And you gave up half of your leave to be here. I'll never forget that. Neither will Bobby."

Bobby has joined them, his face pretty well smeared with lipstick. Tactfully, after he has been cleaned up a bit, Bobby manages to suggest to his bride that they begin to think of getting away from there. There's not too much time—

Helen has gone to change her dress. Bobby is ready to follow. There is no waiting any longer. Bobby must be told.

"There's no way of breaking this to you easy," says Allan grimly. "I'll have to come right out with it. All leaves are canceled. That was the telephone call I got."

"You're kidding!"

"No, we're due at the Field at 5 on Tuesday. You'll have to leave today—right now."

"All I've got is three days—maybe that's all I'll have to remember. I want to do my job—sure. But I want to live just a little bit first. For just three days—three lousy days. This is our last leave. I might never see Helen again. Tell 'em I won't do it. Tell 'em I'm A.W.O.L. Let them take their Wings back. I won't do it."

"Look, Bobby—go right to the station. We'll get our tickets and yours and meet you there. At least you can have those last few minutes alone—just you and Helen. And nobody need know 'til afterwards. Don't you think that's better?"

"Yes—yes—I guess it is, Allan," Bobby admits, slowly. "It's the best way to handle it. Poor kid."

"Better get started, Bobby. There isn't much time."

"Okay. Thanks, Allan."

The boys watch Bobby until he disappears. Then they go into a huddle with the Mayor. On the lawn the guests are organizing a square dance. Presently Helen appears. She is wearing a traveling suit and carrying her bridal bouquet. With squeals of excitement the girls of the wedding party prepare for the throw.

Now Bobby and Helen have made their way through the crowd. Suddenly Bobby sets down his valises and runs back to hold his mother in his arms for a moment. He shakes hands with his father. Then he rushes back to Helen and soon they are out of sight. The square dance is resumed. The curtain falls.

On a California Flying Field a wing of a Fortress juts out across the foreground. Only one huge wheel and engine are visible. Shortly Barker, a flyer, arrives. He stands under the front of the Fortress and looks up at her nose. Satisfied, he calls out. "Hey, fellers—here she is, over here. Number 73."

Adams and Milhauser join him. And later, Pinky. They are all pleased with the ship. For no particularly sound reason they decide that 73 is a lucky number. Of course they can't tell what kind of a pilot they'll draw. "I hope we have a good guy," hopes Barker. "You know it ain't exactly unimportant. From today on—we're a crew. This is it."

"Yep," agrees Pinky. "This is the day, fellers! From now on we eat together, sleep together, fly together and maybe die together. It's a big day. Me—I'm glad it's here. This is it!"

It will probably be a month before they push off on "the big hop," thinks Pinky. They usually want a crew to fly together at least that long before they go over.

The talk turns to what they are going to do when they get back home. O'Brien thinks he will just sit in the sun for about a year and a half. What will he do for money? Well, he's figuring on coming back a hero and charging so much a look.

Pinky plans to do a bit of standing in front of his father's barber shop, gassing about the war; telling the natives a pack of lies about how he told off the C.O. and that sort of thing. After that he is going to try and get back in. "I couldn't stay on the ground after this," says Pinky. "I got Wings in my head, anyway. Maybe I can make it after combat flying is out. I'm gonna give it a helluva try."

Now Milhauser has caught sight of the pilot and co-pilot approaching. The men snap to their feet. The next moment Pinky has emitted an excited "My God!"

"It's Allan and Irv!" shouts Pinky. "Gee, boy—this is gonna be the best goddam crew in the world!"

Allan is quick to put his crew at ease and to ask to be excused while he says hello to an old buddy. "H'ya, Pink!"

"Al! You old sonova—!" He is shaking Allan's hand wildly. "And Irv! Boy, this is wonderful!"

"A little more respect, Sergeant. Get a load of this uniform," says Irv.

With that the formalities are over. Irv laughingly throws his arm around Pinky's shoulder and Allan resumes command. Let them all get to know each other. The men step up one by one: "Barker, sir. Engineer and Turret Gunner." . . . "Milhauser— Assistant Engineer and Turret Gunner." . . . "Adams—Radio Operator and Waist Gunner." . . . "O'Brien—Tail Gunner." . . . Gleason, sir—Waist Gunner"—

"And I suppose the best damn belly gunner in the Air Corps!" ventures Irving, when it comes Pinky's turn. "Yes, sir. Thank you, sir," responds Pinky, and that's a laugh for the men.

While the crew is inspecting the ship, Allan and Irving have a chance to bring Pinky up to date on the news. They tell him of Bobby's wedding and the missed honeymoon. But Bobby is in camp now and Helen's in town. Pretty soon Allan's Dorothy is going to join him. It all sounds like a dream to Pinky. It's too good!

Now the men have come back. The subject for a name for the ship is brought up. That honor is usually accorded the pilot, but Allan prefers to call for suggestions.

Pinky thinks perhaps "The Flying Eagle—" But that stinks, according to Irving. How about "The Vulgar Virgin?" Too romantic, decides Allan. What about "Out of the Blue?" No response. How about "Mr. America?" This from O'Brien, who, says Barker, has been seeing too many movies. "Well, should it be funny or serious?" Pinky wants to know. "We should decide."

"Doesn't matter," insists Allan. "If we hit it—we'll know it right away."

Irving tries again with "Big-Breasted Angel." That's what a Fortress means to Irv. Allan thinks Irv should see a doctor. " 'Big-Breasted Angel!' I'd like to hear you explain that if we got shot down some place."

"This Is It" is suggested. And "The Eagle Screams." And then Allan picks a winner: "Winged Victory!"

"That's it! Right on the nose! That's it!" The others are quick to chime in with their endorsements. "Winged Victory" it is.

"Well, I guess the ship's got a name," says Allan. "We'll paint it on tomorrow. And here's to good flying for all of us."

They toss back a collection of "Good flying, sirs" and Allan shocks them all into still more excitement when he says: "Well— shall we take her up? This is it, I guess!"

The boys leap to their feet with alacrity.

"Okay! Let's go."

They are swarming toward the plane as the curtain falls.

In their bedroom in barracks Allan and Irving are writing letters, Allan at a table in the center of the room, Irving stretched out on one of the two bunks. These are to be their last letters before the big hop, and, curiously, they find it difficult to think of something to say.

Funny, Irving has decided, what a fellow thinks of in moments like these. Probably it should be something important—"America, with a capital A. The Statue of Liberty. Democracy." Instead of which Irving can get no farther than the day he saw the Dodgers win a no-hit, no-run game. Or the day he took his kid to Prospect Park to watch the seals get fed.

As for Allan, he has been thinking a lot about coming home from the bank on a Saturday afternoon; fooling around the car; taking a bath and lying in the warm water until Dorothy and his mother called him to supper. "That smell of soap and fried chicken on a summer afternoon is the greatest perfume in the world," sighs Allan. ". . . It's only *now* we remember these things," Allan explains. "Because we're leaving 'em—and maybe for good."

They are still writing letters when Pinky comes. "Yep. The last word. The last word. Something to remember," muses Pinky. "Y'know you guys are driving me to marriage." Just now he is remembering his pals' wives, and how sweet and gay they were the other night though they knew this was the boys' last visit. "No bawling or nothing. They did a good job, those girls."

"Yeah," agrees Irving. "And they got the toughest part ahead—the waiting."

The girls, it appears, are still in Oakland. They're going back home tomorrow. "We didn't tell 'em, of course, but they kinda know we're kicking off tonight. Women always know those things."

Bobby and Dave are in, with cokes, a last drink together. They have been briefed. They're leaving about an hour before the others. But they're all going in the same direction. Maybe they'll meet up. No one wants to think of a toast, so they drink to what they are all thinking.

"Good-by, Allan," says Bobby, as they shake hands. "Something nice happened to me out of this war, anyway. You guys."

"Good flying, feller!"

Bobby and Dave have gone.

Irving has stuffed his letter into an envelope, sealed it and started for the door. At the window he stops. "Look at that sunset—will ya!" he calls to Allan and Pinky. "Old Lady Nature is giving us a fine send-off. Come here, Pink—take a look at it. Isn't that something? Our last American sunset!"

Pinky comes over to have a look. "I thought it was going to be red, white and blue by the way you were carrying on," says Pink.

"You got about as much sentiment as a cockroach. Take a good look, mugg. You won't be seeing another one for a long time. Good-by, Frisco, good-by."

Allan has shooed them out of the room and returned to his letter. For a moment he writes feverishly—"pouring the words onto the paper." Before he seals the letter he takes a picture from his wallet, staring at it for a long moment. He has turned out the light now and is standing at the window in the fading light of the sunset, "drinking in every detail of the distant shore. His face, sharply outlined in the afterglow, is the face of a man looking at something he loves and wants to remember always."

The room grows darker. The curtain falls.

In a hotel room in Oakland, Dorothy, Helen and Ruth, Irving's wife, are busy. It is obviously an old hotel. There is a double bed in the room, which is grim and tawdry, and a washstand in the corner. On a portable ironing board Dorothy is ironing out a slip. Helen is washing out stockings in the wash basin and Ruth, sitting on the bed, is sewing a collar and cuffs on a suit.

The talk is, at the moment, largely about New York. Helen, who never has been further than Seattle, Wash., wonders if she would like the big city. Ruth isn't sure. She might. She might not. As for Ruth, she hopes one day to live in the country, if she can ever pry Irving away from Brooklyn and Prospect Park.

Dorothy has an idea she'd die in New York. She and Allan have lived all their lives in Mapleton. Helen is a farm girl. After the war Bobby's father and her father are going to buy a farm for them.

"If we were home now, and had our farm," Helen is saying, "I'd be canning and Bobby would be just putting in the winter wheat. Instead of—this."

"You will, Helen," comforts Dorothy. "We'll all have homes, and babies, and good, peaceful lives. That's what this is all for. That's why they're leaving tonight." She stops, guiltily. "I'm sorry. I didn't mean to say it. It slipped out."

"I'm glad you said it," declares Helen, a shade of hysteria creeping into her voice. "I'm tired of pretending we don't know it—to myself and to each other. They're going tonight. They're getting ready now, across the bay."

The thought is too much for Helen. "Oh, God—if they don't come back!" she cries.

The others would comfort Helen if they could, but it isn't easy. She and Bobby have had so pitifully little of life compared with the others. Dorothy has had a year, and Ruth has her baby. But she has had so little—

"We're not alone," says Dorothy, sadly but firmly. "Somehow —I don't know why—that helps—and it will you, too, Helen, after a while. In this hotel, in every hotel in town, I guess, in a room just like this, there are girls like us—waiting—feeling the way we feel—thinking the same things tonight. All the way through training I sat in hotel lobbies and tourist camps— talking to other cadet wives—always about the same things, always with that same pain inside—and after a while—you begin to share the pain. It doesn't go—but it's helped, somehow. You'll see, Helen."

They fall silent for a moment. "What time do they go, do you think?" Helen asks.

"I don't know," answers Dorothy. "Sometimes it's early evening—sometimes very late. They all looked so sweet the other night, didn't they? Like little boys trying to put something over."

"Yes, and knowing they hadn't. They knew we knew it was the last pass, don't you think?"

"Yes, I think they did," admits Dorothy.

Suddenly from across the bay comes the muffled roar of a plane. Helen and Ruth have rushed to the window and stand, staring out. Dorothy, quite still for a moment, suddenly throws herself on the sofa and begins to sob.

"The roar of the planes comes regularly now—evenly spaced. Plane after plane is taking off. The girls at the window remain looking out into the night. There is only the roar of the planes

and Dorothy's gentle crying."
The curtain falls.

It is Christmas Day at an island base in the South Pacific.
In a bit of a clearing in a thick, tropical jungle, officers and men
are celebrating the day, opening letters and packages. They are
wearing tropic shorts, for the most part, or bathing trunks, or
pants and no shirt.

Alongside a stage improvised of oil drums, backed by huge
jungle palms, one big palm tree has been transformed, with the
help of bits of Red Cross gauze and cotton, into a sort of
Christmas tree. Under it is a huge pile of Christmas packages.

Irving has a new picture of his kid. That's fine. Pinky has
a sweater from his mother. Not so good for this climate. Allan
has a new shaving kit from Mother and a check from Dad.
What would he be buying with that? And a lot of things from
Dorothy.

They haven't much time to go through the mail. The Christmas Show is about to go on. "The Yuletide Follies," the M.C.
calls it. When the first act isn't quite ready the M.C. fills in
with the one about the 80-year-old Colonel who married a young
wife. A year later, when she presented him with a fine son and
heir, he called the entire squadron into the mess hall, got up on
the dais and said: "Boys, I am a happy man today. My wife
just gave birth to an 8-pound bouncing baby boy. Gentlemen,
I thank you." The boys shout with glee.

"And now for our first act, a lovely maiden whose skin has
the incomparable soft texture of a full blown peach—fuzz and
all. Direct from South America with her famous drummer, that
exciting and sex-citing 'Carmen Miranda.' "

The Soldier Carmen is elaborately made up. His Miranda
head-dress, in place of fruits and flowers, consists of all the
G.I. implements of eating and warfare he could stick together.
The boys find Miranda and her drummer very funny.

Now the M.C. is back to introduce the second number. "Ah,
those Latins are wonderful lovers," he pauses to inform the audience in his best Bob Hope manner. "All night long they make
passionate love and all day long they sit in the hot sun to cool
off."

The Andrews Sisters, direct from Hollywood, is his second
promise, and three husky soldiers, trying their darndest to look
and act like the Andrews Sisters, keep the stage rocking and the
crowd shouting approval for the next five minutes. They retire

in a perfect whirlwind of applause.

"And now I have the pleasure and the honor of presenting to you our Commanding Officer, Col. Robert Blakely," says the M.C.

The Colonel had been definitely impressed the night before, as he lay slapping at mosquitoes and pulling his mosquito netting about him, with the strangeness of this particular Christmas. Something of the same thought must also have occurred to them.

"But this afternoon, as I watched the show, and watched you, too," the Colonel goes on, "I must confess, it suddenly seemed to me like Christmas after all. For there is a kind of peace in comradeship and courage, and the very fact that we're spending Christmas here is a living proof that there are still men of good will abroad throughout the world. So this—and I didn't mean to make a speech at you—is not only to wish you a Merry Christmas, but to thank you all for making *my* Christmas one I shall always remember."

There is a burst of applause, and many of the men yell back "Merry Christmas to you, Colonel." There is one thing more. The Colonel has taken the liberty of asking Corporal Regan to sing "Holy Night" as the closing feature of the show.

The men in utter silence listen to Corporal Regan's singing. Just as he is finishing the song the alert sounds. With a rush the men jump to their feet and start for their stations.

The curtain falls.

Near a landing field in the South Pacific a place for a hospital tent has been hacked out of the jungle. A patchwork road leads to it. On the road a Red Cross ambulance has just come to a stop.

A Doctor comes from the tent, walks wearily to a rusty oil drum at the edge of the clearing and sinks down upon it.

A moment later the Doctor spies a Nurse entering the tent. He calls to ask if this ambulance is also full. It is. This has been the worst night yet, the Nurse tells him.

"Doctor—did that Bombardier make it?" the Nurse asks, as she starts again for the tent.

"No. Died a couple of minutes ago," he says. It is sad news for them both.

A Stretcher Bearer comes to grub a cigarette. He's been going since 2 in the afternoon. He, too, would know about the Bombardier. The Doctor shakes his head.

"Too bad. I sure was pulling for that kid," says the soldier.

"I think everyone was."

"I did my very best." The Doctor sighs heavily.

"Oh, sure you did, Doc." The Stretcher Bearer's sympathy is very real. "You mustn't feel that way. We all knew he didn't have a chance when we carried him in, but he was such a damn sweet kid we couldn't help hoping."

"Goddamit, they're all such sweet kids," the Doctor shouts, fiercely. Another ambulance screeches to a stop just out of sight. "And here's some more of 'em! Get going, Bert!"

A stretcher comes into sight. Allan and Irving are following closely. As the stretcher disappears into the tent Allan turns to the Doctor.

"Are you the Chief, sir?"

"Yes."

"That's our gunner. Name's Pinky. He's pretty badly shot up. Lost a good deal of blood before I could come down. Doctor—would you look at him yourself? I hate to ask favors, but he's from my town—and he's my friend."

"All right."

"Mind if we stick around for a few minutes, Doctor? I'm waiting for a replacement gunner before I go up again. Could you let us know, sir?"

"Yes. Wait right here. I'll come out as soon as I can."

For a moment or two Allan and Irving stand motionless. Then they walk over to the oil drums and sit down. They're worried about Pink. Allan is at the edge of a break. He remembers now, with a little hysterical laugh, how he and Pinky and Frankie had stood in his back yard in Mapleton and waved gaily to the B-17s. "That's us in a little while!" they had shouted. Now Frankie's gone and maybe Pink!

"Look, Al," protests Irving, "it doesn't do any good to think like that. It doesn't even help Pinky. This is his job, and our job and we've got to finish it."

ALLAN—Yes, you're right, Irv. If only—

IRVING—If only what?

ALLAN (savagely)—If only people learn something out of this. I don't want Frankie dead and Pinky blind for nothing. I couldn't stand that. It's the one thing I couldn't take.

IRVING—You know what I been thinking, Al? Don't laugh at me now—I'm no philosopher. But I got to thinking there's a meaning to all this. When this war is over everybody is going to have the biggest chance in history.

ALLAN—Chance?

IRVING—Yeah! To make the whole Goddam world over. Why not? Is it too much to ask after what we're doing?

ALLAN—No—no, it isn't, Irv. I'll tell you what I've been thinking—and don't laugh at me, either. I'm a different guy from the kid who sat in that back yard and waited for a letter a year ago. It's more than just growing up. I'm different inside. Why, think of it—me from Mapleton, Ohio, and you from Brooklyn—we've been in Australia and the South Pacific, and we have flown with English kids and French kids and Chinese kids and Russian kids and some of us have died right with them. I've got a different idea of the world than I had a year ago. All the guys have. I wonder if they realize that back home.

IRVING—Maybe—maybe not. But there's something different on the way. We got to believe that or I can't keep fighting. And I'm glad I'm young and alive and I'm gonna be part of it. Flying has done something to me, too, Allan. I don't know nothing from big words like International Law and Tariff Controls, but I do know that too many nice people in this world are ignorant and hungry. They're not just names to me now, they're people. And guys like us know how small the world really is. There ain't no boundaries in the sky!

ALLAN—That's it, Irv! That's it exactly. If it doesn't add up to that—Frankie died for nothing—Frankie died for nothing.

Allan has started a search of his pockets for cigarettes. Suddenly he comes on a letter from Dorothy that he had stuffed in there when the alert sounded. He tears it open, reads a few lines and sinks weakly down upon the drum.

Irving is worried. Is it bad news? No. It's great news.

"I've got a son!" says Allan, slowly, wonderingly. "She never said a word! Didn't want to worry me." And then, his excitement mounting: "I've got a kid, Irv! Seven pounds!" He laughs a little as he rereads the letter. "He looks just like me at a day old!"

"Hi'ya, Papa!" Irving is laughing, too, as he extends a hand in congratulation.

"Thanks, Irv." But Allan has turned quickly away. Irving doesn't understand.

"It just hit me, Irv. I'm afraid!" There's a new, serious light in Allan's eyes. "I was never afraid before but now I'm scared. I don't want to die, Irv. I want to see my kid."

"Listen, stupe. You ain't gonna die. All you're feeling right now is the regulation New Father miseries. I'll be calling on you when you're an old A.K. with three grandchildren."

The Doctor has come briskly from the tent. He brings them good news. Their friend is going to be all right. Yes, they can see him for a minute. They're shipping him back to the base hospital.

A stretcher with Pinky on it is carried out of the tent. Allan bends low to speak to him. "Hello, Pink. You had us worried."

Pink's lips move but no sound is heard. "Don't talk, Pink. Irving and I just wanted you to know how happy we are. And I've got to tell you a big piece of news. I'm a poppa! I've got a son! How about that, Pink?"

Again Pink's lips move and Allan bends close to hear. Then, at the Doctor's suggestion, the stretcher moves off toward the ambulance.

"So long, baby. We'll be seeing you tomorrow, maybe," calls Irving. Allan has turned to the Doctor.

ALLAN—Thanks a million, Doctor! You don't know what it means!

DOCTOR—Don't I though! You don't know what it means to *us* when we pull 'em through. I'm as pleased as you are. Good luck, fellows. (*He goes back into the tent.*)

IRVING—Whew! That's a load off our minds. What did Pinky say when you told him about the kid? I couldn't hear.

ALLAN (*smiling*)—He said: "Don't let anybody but my Pop give him the first haircut!"

SOLDIER (*approaching and saluting*)—We have a new gunner, sir. And the ship is ready.

ALLAN—Thanks, Milhauser. Okay, Irv?

IRVING—Okay! (*They start up—then:*) Well, come on. What's the matter?

ALLAN—Irv—wait a minute. (*He sits down on the log, pulls out the letter from Dorothy.*) Give me your pencil, will ya?

IRVING—What the hell do you want a pencil for, Daddy?

ALLAN—Shut up. I want to send a note to my kid.

IRVING (*handing him the pencil*)—Al—kids don't read till they're eight years old. You got time with that letter. (*He leans over ALLAN's shoulder and reads.*) Say, that's nice, Al. That's nice.

ALLAN—I'd like my kid to know how it was here tonight—the night I first knew he was born. The world'll be better for our kids, Irv—huh?

IRVING—At least we're trying, Al—we're trying like hell!

The Army Air Corps Song can be heard as

THE CURTAIN FALLS

THE SEARCHING WIND

A Drama in Two Acts

By Lillian Hellman

IT was not until April, 1944, that the New York theatre season produced a drama on which the reviewers could agree as one that was at least moderately satisfying. "The Searching Wind," they wrote, was certainly not Lillian Hellman's best play, citing her three successful dramas, "The Children's Hour," "The Little Foxes" and "Watch on the Rhine" in evidence, but it was much the best serious drama to be produced this particular season and they were correspondingly encouraged.

In point of fact the competition had been less than keen. Moss Hart's "Winged Victory" was in the nature of a special wartime event. Elmer Rice's "A New Life" had proved timely and of a certain pertinence, but not sufficiently weighty. Rose Franken's "Outrageous Fortune" had overstressed the unpleasantness of certain biological exhibits. Maxwell Anderson had spent months at the front in pre-invasion Africa and come back with no more than a readable correspondent's report, plus an unconvincing fox-hole romance, which he put into "Storm Operation." And Edward Chodorov, disappointed by the failure of "Those Endearing Young Charms," sat down and a little hurriedly wrote "Decision," which simmered with indignation and occasionally boiled over with prejudice.

It was a proper time for the appearance of a thoughtful play on a vital theme. The Hellman drama filled that bill. " 'The Searching Wind' is in no sense Shavian," wrote Louis Kronenberger in the New York newspaper *P.M.*, "but it does resemble Shaw in its incisive dialogue, its provocative ideas, its political awareness and its force of personality. On these grounds it greatly deserves success, and will have it."

Miss Hellman has been a fortunate dramatist to date, in that she has worked exclusively with one producer. Herman Shumlin, who has staged and directed all her plays, is the only man of the theatre to whom they have been submitted.

"If a Gallicism is permitted then Miss Hellman and Mr. Shumlin are *en rapport*," Richard Maney once wrote of them. "Neither of them wants any truck with escapist nonsense. Both

of them look upon the theatre as an adult institution rather than
one schemed to distract juveniles from their tops and blocks.
They are as one in thinking that in time of crisis the theatre
has a function that goes beyond coddling amatory neuroses."

As to the title of "The Searching Wind," Miss Hellman thinks
she got it from a colored maid who once worked for her. "Some
mornings when she came she'd say: 'It's a searching wind today,'" the author told Helen Ormsbee. "She meant one of
those winds that go right through you to your backbone. I suppose in my title I was thinking of the wind that's blowing
through the world."

It is about seven-thirty of a Spring evening in 1944. In the
drawing room of the Hazen house in Washington, D. C., Moses
Taney, a hearty, distinguished man of about seventy, is com-
fortably slumped in a large chair reading a newspaper. Near
him, sitting on a small couch with his right leg resting on a
chair, is Corp. Samuel Hazen, "a pleasant-looking young man
of twenty." Sam, too, is reading a newspaper with at least such
pretended interest that he does not wish to be bothered. Moses
Taney, however, is not one to be denied a bit of conversation if
he has something in mind he wants to talk about.

"What do you think of it, Sam?" asks Moses.

"I don't know, Grandpa," mutters Sam, without looking up.
"I don't read as fast as you do. I still have to spell out the
words."

"I know. Must be hard to learn to read in only one year at
Harvard. If your international mother and father hadn't taught
you so many other languages—I don't believe in teaching Americans other languages. We never really learn them. Only the
fancy words in which to gossip, or eat, or be malicious. Hey,
Sam, answer me."

"Shut up, Grandpa, and let me read."

For a second Moses is quiet. Then he yawns, turns again to
the paper and says: "Maybe it would be quicker if I read it to
you." And he begins to read: " 'This is the first of a series of
articles by former Ambassador Alexander Hazen. Mr. Hazen
has just returned from a tour of Africa and Southern Italy. Although Mr. Hazen has never before been willing to write his
impressions of the current scene, this newspaper convinced him
that although—' What in hell do they think although means?
People on newspapers write English as if a rat were caught in
the typewriter and they were trying to hit the keys which
wouldn't disturb it."

"All right, Grandpa. I'll read Father's article after you go to bed."

"Why do you have to read it twice? In three thousand words of diplomatic double talk it says that sometimes democracies have to deal with people they don't approve and sometimes, in order to save something or other, you have to do something else or other. It's simple."

It may be simple to Moses, but it is not simple to Sam. All he had seen in Italy were the little towns and the people and a bit of the country. But his father, being important, had met important people. No, Sam admits, just being a soldier had not made him any less capable of thinking for himself, but "Children of famous fathers and famous grandfathers learn to walk late," he adds.

Moses has turned again to the paper. "I can almost remember the words in which your father and I talked about this same Victor Emmanuel gentleman twenty-two years ago," he says: "the day Mussolini marched into Rome. I ran the paper then—"

There is a moment's interruption as Ponette, a tall Frenchman of about forty-five, wearing the uniform of a butler, but looking quite uncomfortable in it, crosses the room bearing a tray with bottles, glasses, soda, etc., on it.

"Why did you ever sell the paper, Grandpa?" Sam asks. "Everybody says it used to be so good, and now it's nothing. It's just wishy-washy when it's not downright bad."

"I didn't sell it. I never could have sold it. It was that way in my father's will. I leased it to them."

"How could you let them make it into anything like this? I'd always thought you sold it, needed the money or something—"

"I don't read it often. I advise you not to."

"Don't you care? How could you have given it up? Let it become this—"

"It's a long story, son. Like all former thinkers, I'm writing a book. Or rather I keep a book. It's meant for you to read."

Sam thinks he will soon be having plenty of time to read, when he's discharged. That suggestion worries Moses. Why should they discharge Sam? Hadn't they said that his leg would be all right?

Sam is quick to reassure his grandfather. But he still thinks he will be discharged. And what he will do with himself after two years in the Army he doesn't know. He smiles at Moses' suggestion that he sit in a library and read, seeing that he is going to be a serious man—

"If I'm wrong and you're not serious," adds Moses, "I'll give you the newspaper and you can spend the rest of your life acting important and misinforming folks. That would break my heart, Sam."

Emily Hazen has come briskly into the room. "She is a handsome woman of about forty-three or forty-four." Emily is wearing a dinner dress, and is plainly nervous. She would know from the servants, Ponette and Sophronia, the latter "a nicelooking Negro woman of about sixty-three," if everything is all right in the kitchen. It is. But, after telling Ponette to make martinis, Emily moves on to investigate the kitchen situation for herself. . . .

Back from the kitchen Emily is plainly disturbed to discover that both her father and her son are planning to have dinner at home. She had counted on their being out, as they had intimated they would be. Their change of mind is a little upsetting.

"You see, er—I—er—Catherine Bowman is coming. I haven't seen her in over twenty years and—"

"And you didn't want us here," interrupts Moses. "Then we shall certainly stay. Any dinner at which you are not wanted is always a little less dull than the one at which you are."

It would please Emily if her father would take an apartment at the Shoreham and come to them for Sunday tea, but Moses has no idea of doing that. "Your mother always forgets that this house belongs to me," he says to Sam. "And when I die it will belong to you."

Alexander Hazen, "a good-looking man of about fifty," has come into the room, and goes straight to his son. He has heard that Sam has been to the hospital and he is anxious. Sam denies the hospital rumor, and is firm in reassuring his mother that there is nothing new for her to worry about.

Alex would also like to know what Sam thought of his (Alexander's) newspaper piece. He gets little satisfaction. Sam is free to admit that he and his father undoubtedly did not see Italy the same way.

The sound of a taxi heralds the arrival of Cassie Bowman. Alex is a little upset by the announcement of Cassie's having been invited. Why? Emily directs her explanation at her son—

"Cassie's never seen you or Sarah," she reminds Sam; "which seems strange to me. Cassie and I grew up together, school and college, and down the street, and your grandfather used to take us to Europe in the summer— Your father used to take us both to dances and—"

"Why is Cassie coming?" repeats Alex, sharply.

"Why not?" demands Emily, a shade too lightly. "You've seen her—when was the last time?—but I haven't in twenty, twenty-one years. Well, it seems it's her sabbatical—(*Cheerily to* SAM *and* MOSES.) She's teaching girls the age we were when I last saw her. That makes me feel so old—(*To* ALEX.) She's visiting the Taylors. For a month or two. It seemed crazy, sort of, for Cassie to be living in Washington and not to have her here—"

"I saw her—last week," answers Alex, slowly.

"But *I* haven't seen her, Alex."

"You haven't wanted to. Neither has she. Why tonight?"

"Why didn't you see each other, if you were such good friends?" Sam asks his mother. "A fight?"

"No, no, no fight. I don't know why. Or maybe I—"

Moses is all for going on with the martinis. Certainly the coming meeting can't have the historic importance of the reconciliation of Gen. Grant and Gen. Lee. At which moment Catherine Bowman arrives. "She is a good-looking woman of about forty-four. She has on a simple dinner dress. Her movements are hesitant, cautious, as if she were unsure of herself."

The greetings are a little awkward and conscious, particularly on the part of both Cassie and Emily. It has also been a long time since Cassie has seen Mr. Taney, and this is her first meeting with Sam.

"I'm glad to know you," she says to Sam. "Your father has spoken of you so often. Does he tell you how proud he is of that?" she asks, pointing to the ribbon on Sam's chest. "Your father told me last night that your leg was getting better. I'm so glad to hear that."

"There's too much talk about my leg." Sam is smiling. "You'd think it was the only leg that had been in the war."

"Do give us a cocktail, Alex," Emily interrupts, nervously turning to Cassie. "Well, well! That seems to be all I can say after all these years. Let's have several cocktails quick. That'll help. Don't go away, Alex. We'll swallow this one and you stand by for another." And as Cassie gulps her cocktail Emily adds: "I'm not used to drinking much, are you?"

"No, but it might be a good idea tonight."

Presently Emily and Cassie have come to a recounting of their recent activities. Cassie hasn't much to relate. She is head of the English department of her school now, and as everybody has a specialty hers is poetry. She gets down to New York whenever she can. Otherwise she meets the same people, takes long vacations and so on.

Emily has more to tell than that, and tells it a little excitedly. "We've been abroad most of the time, as you know," says Emily. "I'm sorry I missed you that day in Paris—. Well, after '39 Alex stayed on in London as a kind of Ambassador without a country, or maybe with too many countries, the governments in exile, I mean—"

"I know, Em. I—" Cassie is looking toward Alex, uncomfortably.

"Although Biddle takes care of them, really, or he did. I came back home last year and Sam went into the Army, before that, I mean, and Alex stayed on for a while—"

"Emily—" Alex would stop her if he could.

"Then Alex went to Italy as an observer—Sam and Alex were there at the same time, but they didn't see each other— And then Sam came back wounded and Alex got back last month. I'm not talking English."

"Em, I've been trying to tell you that Cas knows all that. You've forgotten I've seen her."

"Oh, you mean at dinner last week, last night— Well, I wanted to bring her up to date. It's been so long—we have to start somewhere—"

Emily has stopped, a little helplessly. Moses takes over. He is concerned about the European situation. Who are we sending over, for example, "to take over those elderly clowns who call themselves governments-in-exile?" he asks Alex.

Alex doesn't know, but he is convinced that the men Moses refers to are not clowns. They are honest men who are doing the best they can, just as we are.

"Moses, you have to work with what there is to work with," insists Alex. "You accept the people you have to accept, and that doesn't mean you always like them or always trust them."

"Sometimes that's a dangerous game, Alex," puts in Cassie, laughing. "And it seems to me I've heard you say those words before. I remember you and Mr. Taney and Rome in 1922—" She stops suddenly, and the laughter dies on her lips.

"A very dangerous game," Moses goes on. "Mr. Wilson played it. It goes on the assumption that bad men are stupid and good men are smart, and all diplomats are both good *and* smart. Well, the last time, Mr. Clemenceau was both very bad and very smart. Why don't you people ever read a book?"

"Is it like old times, Cassie? Father and Alex—"

"Yes. It's as if I'd never been away from here."

Ponette has announced dinner and they have started toward the dining room. "Of course, my dear, I remember that day in Rome," Moses is saying to Cassie. "That was the time I duennaed you and Emily to Italy. And you and I and Sophronia came home alone and Emily stayed on to play the piano. That was the day I decided to retire and let the world go to hell without my help."

"Were you and father married then?" asks Sam.

"No, darling. That was 1922. You weren't born until '24, and you're legitimate."

Cassie and Emily are the last to reach the door. Cassie thinks martinis must be for remembrance, seeing they have talked so much of the past. But she has an idea, too, that that is the way Emily intended it.

"Why did you ask me here, why did I come?" Cassie demands, turning on Emily. "It's too difficult for us to meet again. Why did you ask me, why did I come?"

"Because we wanted to see each other again."

"I don't think that's the truth."

"I don't think so, either," answers Emily, pleasantly. "Come along to dinner, Cas."

As Cassie starts through the door she drops her evening bag. Both she and Emily stop to stare at it.

"Remember the tennis match and how you broke your racket and then you dropped your mother's best cut glass punch bowl; and at college, before exams, you always dropped everything?" remembers Emily. "Whenever you were frightened or nervous you'd always drop things."

"That's right, Em," admits Cassie, looking steadily at Emily. "Everybody does something when they get nervous; you speak more slowly. You always did. You're doing it now."

"I know. Come along now." Emily is speaking very slowly, as though on purpose. They go through the door. The curtain falls.

We have gone back to the Italy of October, 1922. In the living room of a suite in the Grand Hotel in Rome the furniture has been pushed back to make room for three large trunks which are open and partly packed. There are a couch and two chairs in the room, and a piano in the corner. Sophronia (20 years younger) is also there, ironing underwear on an ironing board. Outside there are the sounds of guns, which presently die out.

When the telephone rings Sophronia answers it. The call is from Alexander Hazen and Sophronia reports that though Mr. Taney had not been asleep at all, she doesn't think he will come to the phone. The girls are up, but they haven't come in for breakfast. If anybody is frightened they haven't showed it.

Sophronia puts down the receiver and knocks on Moses Taney's door. There is no answer. She opens the door and calls in— "Mr. Taney, it's Alex Hazen on the phone again. . . . He says the Ambassador told him to tell you, you and the girls and me should come and stay in the Embassy until our boat leaves. Mr. Hazen says he'll come down in an Embassy car and take us—"

"Tell Alex to tell the Ambassador to go to hell," mumbles a voice that is the voice of Moses. "Shut the door, Sophronia."

"Mr. Taney says to thank the Ambassador, but we'll stay here," Sophronia reports at the phone.

An elderly and a young waiter wheel a breakfast table into the room and arrange the dishes. The elderly one makes a report in Italian to Sophronia which the younger waiter translates, with an accent suggesting an Italian who has learned to speak English in London.

"He says the manager will call on all guests to tell them not to be frightened by guns. Nobody, he says, need be frightened in the city of Rome, Italy."

The elderly waiter has withdrawn. The younger waiter, remaining to serve the breakfast, is seized with a fit of coughing, which is plainly embarrassing to him. When Sophronia fetches him a glass of water he quickly explains that his trouble comes from a war experience; that he has had his job but two days, and that if he is reported as being sick he will lose it. Sophronia pours him a cup of coffee and when Moses (at 50) comes from the bedroom in his dressing gown tells him the young waiter is scared because he is afraid Moses will get mad at him for taking a cup of coffee.

"They're all scared. I'm sick of it," declares Sophronia. "Everybody's got the same look. You come to Europe next summer, you come without me."

"All right. All right. We're going home," Moses promises.

Again there is the sound of guns, more guns and steadier firing. "Those are the government guns," ventures Moses, with conviction. "They are not being answered. A child of six would conclude that they are not being fired at anything, and won't be. The bastards are putting on a fake show and they won't even spend the money for a good one. Well, that means Signor Mussolini should be in the city in a few hours."

YOUNG WAITER (*cautiously*)—I am told many foreigners here think it wise, sir.

MOSES—Yes, many foreigners. Are you a Fascist?

YOUNG WAITER—No, sir. I am not.

MOSES—You must feel out of place. Everybody else in the hotel is.

YOUNG WAITER (*smiling*)—In every hotel. They live to please those who give orders.

MOSES—How many men do you think Mussolini's got? I've heard everything from sixty thousand to six hundred.

YOUNG WAITER—Not sixty thousand. My brother-in-law is one of them. He laughs and says the government garrison could stop them, but the garrison will not. He says the King and the Government are with the Fascisti now, and want them to march in. What do you think, sir?

MOSES—Your brother-in-law is right. It's all finished now.

YOUNG WAITER—It has been finished for a long time.

MOSES—When was it finished for you?

YOUNG WAITER—It does not finish like a clock, or begin like one, either.

MOSES—No, but I guess all of us want to know when things happened. Or when we first should have realized they were happening. I've been awake all night. (*Motions toward the window.*) Not with this. I knew most of this a year ago. But I should have known before that, and I did. But I didn't know I did. All night I've been trying to find out when I should have known.

YOUNG WAITER (*softly*)—For me, for many Italians, it was there in 1919, three years ago. Your President Wilson came to speak to us, in the Piazza Venezia. It meant much to us. The great man would speak to us, tell us what to do, tell us how to make a free country. Fifty thousand people came. Many of them walked all night. They carried their children—(*Looks at* MOSES.) I speak too much. (MOSES *shakes his head.*) But our King and our Government did not wish President Wilson to speak. They were afraid of us. All day they keep him inside the palace, meeting the great names who came to call. All day the people waited. Until night time. Night time! It was too late. I waited with the last. I did not know it then, but that night it was finished for me.

Moses (*getting up*)—Wilson is a man who likes fancy words and fancy names. That's one of the things I didn't know in time. I am sorry for that. I might have saved you some of this.

Emily and Cassie (at 22) have arrived. They are in their dressing-gowns and their hair is down. Emily is a little frightened by the noise of the guns, but Cassie doesn't mind. Nor was anyone disturbed at Mrs. Hayworth's party the night before, Cassie reports. "Mrs. Hayworth has met Mussolini. She admires him. So did everybody there."

"Did the guns interfere with Mrs. Hayworth's chamber music?" Moses would know.

"No. Nobody seemed nervous," reports Emily. "Signor Orlando was very disappointed you didn't come to dinner. He said he hadn't seen you since the Peace Conference but that he always read your articles. He said you were a great liberal, a great man."

"Did you tell him I thought he was a son of a bitch?"

"I would have, father, if you had told me in time." Emily is laughing. "You were generally admired. A man called Perrone said he'd only come because he thought you might be there. He said he didn't think you understood the situation here and he had wanted to talk to you about it. He hoped Mussolini would take over the government. He said the Fascisti will mean a recovery for Italy—"

"He's an impartial judge. He put up the money for Mussolini."

"He didn't mention that. He said the Fascist leaders were true idealists—"

"And would return to Rome the glory of Caesar," adds Cassie.

"Is one allowed to spit at Mrs. Hayworth's table?" asks Moses.

"You always told me not to spit at dinner."

"I've changed my mind."

"Then it's just as well you weren't there. Alex didn't come, either, and Cassie came home early with a headache. I'll send flowers for you."

"You will not send flowers, you will not make an apology, and you will not go to the Hayworths' again." With this sharp announcement Moses retires to his room.

The morning mail is there and the girls sort out their letters. There is the usual home gossip. Cassie has word from the college that she has been approved by the trustees and may return to teach English at fifteen hundred a year.

Emily is surprised and a little hurt at that news. She had not known that Cassie was trying for the teaching job. She had expected her to come back to Washington with the Taneys and stay with them until she found a job that would be fun. But Cassie is firm. She had known for a long time that this was coming and now she plans to go through with it.

A moment later Emily is laughing over something she reads in Sarah Sturgis' letter. "She says she told George that she'd had a beau before him, and he didn't seem to mind much, and she says that settles all the arguments—" Emily is thoughtful for a moment. "My entire memory of college is a discussion as to whether you ought to have an affair before you marry and, if you do, should you tell your husband?" She laughs at that recollection. "Baby talk. None of us would ever have had the nerve —except Sarah, and then she had to get so drunk she couldn't remember a single interesting detail to tell us. Remember how daring we thought her?"

CASSIE (*after a second*)—I don't think even then I thought it daring. There's nothing daring about it.

EMILY (*smiling*)—How do you know, Cas?

CASSIE (*hesitates and then quickly*)—I did have a headache last night. But that isn't why I left the Hayworths'. I met Alex.

EMILY (*after a second*)—You mean you met him in the lobby downstairs or—

CASSIE—No. We had planned to meet.

EMILY (*slowly*)—How strange. Why should you and Alex *plan* to meet?

CASSIE—Why not?

EMILY—What do you mean "Why not"? We've grown up with Alex Hazen. We always saw him together. What— I understand. So it's not very daring. (*Very slowly.*) We've known each other all our lives. But sometimes I don't think we understand each other, Cas. I never thought you and Alex got along very well. You're so unlike. (*Quickly.*) And then, of course, I suppose I'd always thought I might marry him.

CASSIE (*quickly, sharply*)—I didn't know that. And I know

he doesn't know it. You made it up this minute—

EMILY—I didn't say he knew it. I said that sometimes I had thought that—

CASSIE (*slowly*)—Then it was a fantasy, Emily. And as dangerous as most.

EMILY—Yes. What plans have you got? The two of you, I mean?

CASSIE—None. I—

EMILY (*coming to her*)—Cassie, talk to me. Tell me things. Because otherwise we might get mixed up, or—

CASSIE (*carefully*)—We have nothing you would call plans. I suppose we said all the things people have always said to each other. (*Suddenly points to window.*) It's not a good time to talk about oneself. So much important happening to so many people—

EMILY—What high-faluting talk, Cas. You sound like Father, only he means it. You know that no matter what happens any place in the world, people go on talking about themselves, and always say they haven't because they think it sounds better that way.

Alexander Hazen (at 27) has pushed his way through the lobby crowded with excited Italians and a dozen newspaper men and finally reached the Taney apartment. Emily has gone back to her room but Cassie is there.

"The Ambassador wants all of you brought to the Embassy right away," Alex is saying, a little excitedly. "We have assurances that no American will be touched, but with that crew outside you can't tell. Where's Mr. Taney?"

"He won't go to the Embassy, and you know it," says Cassie.

"All right. But I want to talk to him about something else. The A.P., Reuters, Havas are downstairs. I want to ask him—"

"What will happen?"

"Second secretaries aren't told much. But I think they've decided to let Mussolini in. The government soldiers are really there to see that nobody stops him."

It's a dirty mess, as Cassie says, but Alex cannot see that the American Ambassador can do anything about it.

"We're an ignorant generation," says Cassie. "We see so much and know so little. Maybe because we think about ourselves so much. I just told Emily that, and she said I was faking: Everybody thought about themselves no matter what happened."

Neither is Cassie satisfied in her mind as to how she and Alex stand toward each other. That they do not always agree she knows, but half the time they can't tell what they are disagreeing about.

"A revolution is going on outside. And by this time next year it will be nothing more than dinner-table conversation. Things mean so little to us." Cassie is puzzled.

ALEX—They mean a lot to me. I've been trying hard to figure them out. People like me didn't have much time to think. A few years of college, then the Army—

CASSIE—And now three years of the Embassy. More than you know, you've come to think the way they think—

ALEX (*very sharply*)—For God's sake, Cassie, if you disapprove of me so much, why did you sleep with me? I don't believe people in love fight about things like this. They only use it as an excuse. It must be something else—(*Puts his arms around her.*) Are you in love with me?

CASSIE (*softly*)—I don't know. I think so. Are you, with me?

ALEX—Yes. Very much. Cassie, stay here. Stay in Rome with me. We'll find out here—

CASSIE (*very quickly, very nervously*)—No, no. I can't. I want to go home and think about us. I couldn't stay here and see these people and lead this life and still think straight. I'm mixed up about everything. I want to be alone and find out what I feel, what I want, what I want for you and me.

ALEX—All right, darling. I'll be coming back to Washington for Christmas. I know what I want. By then I want to know what you want.

CASSIE—Yes. Yes. In a few months maybe I'll make sense—(*Grips his arm.*) I told Emily about us. And she was upset. She said—(*Tensely.*) What's the difference what she said? This is a bad day. The guns outside seem to have come in here, and I don't want to think—

ALEX (*puzzled*)—All right, darling, all right.

Alex has leaned down to kiss Cassie. Moses Taney, coming into the room, is not surprised. People probably kissed during the French Revolution, too.

Outside there is a good deal of shouting, followed by three gunshots. That indicates to Moses that the people are getting on with the revolution. It's like an operation. "Just a few minutes more and the patient will be an invalid for life."

A moment later the manager of the hotel is propelled into the room by two Fascist soldiers. Everything is under control, the manager is quick to report. The soldiers are only there to check the guests.

From a ticker tape machine on the table Moses reads: "King Victor Emmanuel has asked Benito Mussolini to form a government. Proclamation to the people of Rome by the King of Italy reads: 'My people, I wish to ask you—' " Moses has thrown the tape down in disgust and turned to face the intruders—

"Get yourself and these swine out of here!" orders Moses. When the manager would caution him, Moses repeats the order in Italian: "I said—'volevo voiatri porci fuori di qua.' "

For a moment the soldiers are threatening, but when Alex also promises to take a hand, as one representing the American Embassy, they back away and retire to the hall, slamming the door after them.

Moses is quick to admit that he may have been wrong, and promises not to show off again. "Mr. Taney," says Alex, sharply, "we heard that you were about to give out a statement. The newspaper people are waiting downstairs. You are a powerful man at home and your paper is a powerful paper. Any statement you give will be dangerous to the relations between our country and Italy. The Ambassador feels that we cannot take sides in an internal uprising—"

Moses (*sharply*)—Stop that foolish talk. He long ago took sides. And so, I think, did you.

Alex (*softly*)—You've been ragging me for years, Mr. Taney. I don't usually mind it! I do today. (*Points to window.*) I can only speak for myself: I don't like this, and I don't like your thinking I do. But another few months of the kind of misery and starvation they've had, and there would have been a revolution. If Mussolini can put it down, that doesn't make me like him, or the money behind him, or the people. But somebody had to do it, and you don't pick gentlemen to do the job. You were at the Peace Conference and you know that wasn't wild talk about Communism in Italy. (*Slowly, carefully.*) And now I am going to tell you, Mr. Taney, that with all your liberal beliefs, I do not believe you wanted that. (*There is a pause, and he moves away.*)

Moses (*quietly*)—That's well said, and mostly true. (*Then sharply.*) But I didn't want this, and I have fought hard, in my way, to stop it. I like people, and I don't like to see them put down by gangsters who make a job of doing it for those who want it done. (*Very sharply.*) Don't worry, and tell your boss not to worry. I'll give no interviews and write no pieces. *I want no more of any of it. Anywhere.* I'm through with the paper. (*Slowly, wearily, he goes toward his room. Instinctively,* EMILY *follows him. He turns to look at them.*) I want to cry. And you should want to cry. You are young. This is a sad day, and you will pay for it. Whenever such things happen, the rest of the world some day pays for it. It's going to be over for me now, but it's just beginning for you. (*He goes into the room.* EMILY *stands at the door. Nobody speaks.*)

EMILY (*after a minute*)—Well.

ALEX (*uncomfortably*)—I think he's making too much of it all. They're only exchanging one bad lot for another. But I admire your father, even when I don't agree with him or know what he's talking about. Ach. Nobody knows what they're talking about. Least of all me. (*Picks up his hat.*) I'll see you later.

Cassie has gone to her room. As Alex reaches the door Emily speaks to him. She has been thinking, she says, and has decided that she will not go home with the others. She wants to go on with her music lessons. She will stay in Rome for a few months and Alex can beau her around. They have known each other so long there would not be any gossip about that. The idea fails to enthuse Alex. He thinks Emily had better change her mind.

Emily, alone, moves idly about the room. When she reaches the piano she sits down and begins to play. Outside, the guns have started again. Now they are louder and closer.

Cassie comes from the bedroom with an armful of things to be packed. The playing irritates Cassie. It does not go very well with the guns. Neither does Cassie answer when Emily suggests that she, too, stay on in Rome.

"I guess you don't want to talk to me," says Emily, pleasantly. "Now that I think back, there were so many times, even when we were little girls, when that was true. Maybe it's best that you and I should be away from each other for a little while. I've decided not to sail with you and Father. I'm going to stay here. I'll ask Aunt Sophie to come. We'll take a house, I think, for a few months—" Cassie drops the slippers she is holding. "What's the matter, Cassie? Why are you dropping things?

That means you're nervous or hiding something. What is there to be nervous about or to hide?"

As Cassie leans down to pick up the slippers, the curtain falls.

We are back in the Hazen drawing room in Washington in 1944. Sophronia and Ponette are straightening up the room against the return of the family from dinner. Ponette is free to admit that he did not enjoy the conversation at table. Two bottles of Chablis and two of Haut Brion should have produced something a bit lighter, with jokes.

Sophronia isn't interested in Ponette's observations until he speaks of young Sam Hazen. Ponette does not think the Corporal looks well. He happens to know, too, that John, the chauffeur, had driven Corp. Hazen to the hospital that day and that when he came out Sam had asked John not to tell anyone that they had been there. Sophronia is plainly worried about that report.

Emily and Cassie come from the dining room. Cassie reports a headache. Either there has been too much talk about the past or too much wine for one not used to drinking.

Shortly Emily and Cassie are followed by the men, led by Moses. "Filthy habit, leaving the men at the table," complains Moses. "Arrange to stop it, Emily."

"I didn't start it, Father. You've been doing it ever since I can remember."

MOSES (*sitting down*)—That's true enough. I used to want it because two hours of your mother at dinner were long enough. (*Turns to look at* EMILY.) Emily, you're old enough for me to tell you that I didn't like your mother.

EMILY (*quietly*)—I always knew it, Father. Children don't miss things like that.

MOSES—I felt sorry when she died, but all I remember now is that I said, to *myself* of course, "Really, my dear, you didn't have to go that far to accommodate me." It's a bad thing not to love the woman you live with. It tells on a man.

CASSIE—Tells on a woman, too, I should think.

MOSES (*nodding*)—Comes out in ways you don't recognize. Now you take your father, Alex. Same thing with him. He didn't like your stepmother. So what did he do? He fell in love with the State Department, and that's nothing to climb into bed with on a wintry night.

"THE SEARCHING WIND"

"Alexander Hazen, 'a good-looking man of about fifty,' has come into the room. He goes straight to his son. He has heard that Sam has been to the hospital and he is anxious. Sam denies the rumor."

(*Dennis King, Montgomery Clift, Cornelia Otis Skinner*)

EMILY (*looking at* SAM)—Stop frowning, Sam. It's bad for the young.

SAM (*smiling*)—I was thinking that you often know more about people in books than—than I've known about any of you, I guess. (*To* ALEX.) I didn't know that you had been in Italy when Fascism first started. There you were on such a big day and it was so important how you figured out that day. Or maybe I only think so because I was there and saw what it did— (*Lamely.*) I can't seem to say what I mean.

ALEX—You mean that if people like me had seen it straight, maybe you wouldn't have had to be there twenty-two years later.

EMILY (*softly*)—But most people don't see things straight on the day they happen. It takes years to understand—

SAM—If that were true then everybody would understand everything too late.

ALEX—There are men who see their own time as clearly as if it were history. But they're very rare, Sam. (*To* MOSES.) And before you speak, I want to say I don't think you're one of them.

MOSES (*laughing*)—I don't think so either. (*Gaily.*) Just because I understood things quicker than you did, didn't make me smart, if you know what I mean.

ALEX—I do.

SAM (*as if to himself*)—I'd like to learn how to put things together, see them when they come—

EMILY—Maybe you will, darling. (SOPHRONIA *appears with the coffee tray.*) It's what everybody wants to do. Don't let us discourage you. Our generation made quite a mess. Come and have coffee on the terrace.

As the others move out to the terrace Sophronia would have Sam go to bed, but he only smiles at her and chides her for fussing over him. His arm is around her and his cheek pressed against her hair as he goes out.

Inside the room Cassie has moved over to Alex. For a moment they talk softly together. Alex would know why Cassie has come.

"Remember? A long time ago I asked you if you were going to feel guilty. I told you then I didn't want it that way."

"And I told you then that it was between me and you, and me and Emily. I don't feel guilty, and you haven't answered me."

"Emily called me at the Taylors'. Twice. I didn't know what to say—"

"Simple to say you couldn't come, or didn't want to. What's the sense of sitting at a dinner table and talking about twenty-two years ago?"

"I didn't start that talk, Alex. And I didn't say anything that all of us didn't know."

Emily has come from the terrace and Cassie would make her adieux. Why? "Because it's late. And because I think it was wrong for us to meet again and because it's never a good idea to talk about the past. Let's remember by ourselves, Em, with the lights out."

Emily will not have it that way. She does not want Cassie to leave. "This has been coming for a good many years," she says. "We've started it. Let's finish it."

"Whatever you want to know, Em, I'll tell you," says Alex. "It's between you and me, and we can do it alone."

"I know what you would tell me. I've known for a long time. But there's a great deal that you don't know, and Cassie doesn't know, and I don't, either. It's time to find out."

Alex moves over to close the terrace doors, but Sam gets up and stands in the doorway.

"If you and Mother will let me, I'd rather stay," he says. "I don't know what's happening, but I've got a feeling it's got to do with me, too. Anyway, it's kind of an important night for me because—well, just because."

"You can stay, Sam," says Emily.

"Leave it alone, Em! Leave it alone!" Cassie has turned to Emily, as if to shut out the others. "It's no good for people to sit in a room and talk about what they were, or what they wanted, or what they might have—"

"Yes, it's hard," admits Emily, softly. "For all of us. It scares me, too."

"What is it you want?" Alex demands. "What are you doing?"

"I don't know, Alex. But maybe we'll find out." She turns to Cassie. "Sit down, Cassie. Please."

The curtain falls.

ACT II

Berlin. It is the Autumn of 1923. This is a corner of Herr Eppler's restaurant. At a table in a small room Alexander Hazen is having a cocktail and waiting for Emily. Back of the table a large window, partly open, looks out upon the street. Guests and waiters are moving toward other tables.

Eppler, taking Mr. Hazen's order, is eager to explain the

crisis which his country is facing, the mounting costs and all. "This morning I buy bread for one hundred and forty billion marks the loaf. You are lucky to have American money."

"I'm ashamed to use it with things as they are."

"There are not many such who are ashamed," says Herr Eppler, laughing and looking around at the other tables. "In all my years in business I have not seen so many American dollars and English pounds. Here now they buy a drink for more than a German can earn in a week. It is the fault of no one, but it causes bad feeling. You understand, Mr. Hazen. It is not wise to have rich tourists here now. You work in Berlin, you understand that."

"I understand, of course. But we can't keep them home. And your government seems to want them here."

"Ach, I know. It goes in a circle. I no longer know what it is. Bread for a hundred and forty billion marks! It is crazy—"

The noise of a large mob in action some distance away comes through the window. There is a good deal of shouting and running and occasionally out of the confusion words can be heard. "The Jews! The Uden . . . strasse! The Jews!"

Five or six men are running past the window. One stops and shouts in German: "Close the doors! Close the doors!" Another laughs and adds: "We're going for the Jews. If you've got any, bring them out to us!"

The waiter has closed the windows. People are crowding in the aisles, talking loudly and excitedly. Manager Eppler is back with renewed assurances that the police have everything under control. Anyway, the trouble is far from there. "The Freicorps, the Fascists, a bread riot and they went to the Jewish section."

The diners become more restless. Checks are called for. His guests will not listen to Eppler. They demand that the doors be opened. Finally Alex addresses them in English—

"I am Hazen of the American Embassy. Herr Eppler wishes me to tell you that there has been a disgraceful riot of hoodlums against the Jewish section. The police tell him that it is under control. In any case, it is not near here, but the doors must be kept closed until he is allowed to open them. Mr. Eppler asks you to go on with your lunch. There is nothing to be done now except by the police."

As the excitement is dying out Catherine Bowman comes quietly into the room. At first Alex does not see her. She is standing near him and speaking softly. "It is hard to believe that we should live to see a pogrom in the year 1923," she says, and, as he recognizes her she adds: "It scares me, Alex. It scares me."

He has gone to her now to express his surprise that she is in Berlin. Why hadn't she let them know? Who is she with? Will she have lunch?

Cassie had been in Paris for a month and in Berlin for a week. She knows that Alex had been changed from Rome soon after he married.

"But you didn't call us when you got here—"

"Look, Alex," she says, as she gently touches his hand. "You and I had a fight. It did bad things to me."

"It did bad things to me, too."

"I know. And I wanted to wait until I could see you, well, without feeling—"

"Yes, I understand."

They are still talking when Emily, in a state of considerable excitement, comes into the room, followed by a young man from the Embassy.

"Alex, Alex," Emily calls, without noticing Cassie. "The car had to cross the Jüdenstrasse. They were dragging a man through the streets. And they were beating an old lady on the head— We got out and tried to get through to help them, and the crowd began to scream at us and push us back. They screamed after us that we were dirty Americans and to mind our business—"

The young man from the Embassy, Halsey by name, adds to Emily's report. "The Freicorps people are in on it," says Halsey. "Today's leaders were well dressed. I think its real leaders came from the Young People's League, just as they did last week. There's no question now that it's tied up with the Bavarian trouble. The story around is that somebody from Thyssen put up the money for Ludendorff and for those clowns outside."

"That's hard to believe. He's a bad guy, but nobody's bad enough to put up the money for this—"

"Dear Alex. You haven't changed." Cassie is laughing. "Nobody's that bad, even when the proof is outside the door."

"I didn't say the proof wasn't outside the door," snaps Alex. "I said I didn't believe a man like Thyssen—"

"It's like old times. You and Cassie." Emily is smiling.

Suddenly Alex realizes that Emily and Cassie have not been at all surprised at seeing each other. That puzzles Alex, but it seems perfectly natural to the girls. In fact they had seen each other from a distance in that same restaurant the week before, but had made no attempt to meet.

Alex would send Halsey back with the car while he goes to the police. It is his plan to make a strong official protest, putting it on the grounds that many Americans are in Berlin—

"The Embassy couldn't put it on the grounds that it's a horror and disgrace," suggests Cassie. "That would be too simple, wouldn't it?"

"Dine with us tonight and I'll tell you about it," answers Alex, smiling. As he leaves them he leans down to kiss Emily. Cassie slightly turns her head.

When they are alone Emily and Cassie talk a little consciously of their recollections of this unhappy Berlin when they were there as girls; of Moses Taney, who had come over for Emily and Alex's wedding and then gone back; of the wedding itself, about which Emily had written Cassie, but had had no reply.

Cassie had written to Alex and wonders that he had not told Emily. "Don't you talk about things like that?" Cassie asks.

"Things like what?"

"Like me."

"You haven't been a problem, Cassie."

"I feel dismissed," says Cassie, laughing. "And I don't believe you."

Emily has decided again that she does not want to stay on in Berlin. She does not want her expected baby to be born here.

CASSIE—When are you going to have the baby?

EMILY—March.

CASSIE—You always said you didn't think people should have babies so soon after they were married. That they should wait and find out if the marriage was going to work out—

EMILY—This marriage has worked out very well.

CASSIE—You're very sure about it, aren't you? What did Alex tell you, when he came back from seeing me? When he came back to Rome where you were waiting for him?

EMILY—I didn't make you and Alex fight. I didn't even know you'd had a fight for months after he came back to Rome. Then all he ever told me was that you disagreed with what he thought and what he was, and that you'd both decided to quit. What good is this, Cassie? It's all over with now.

CASSIE—Is it, Em? Is it really? Your best friend marries your beau and a year after it's as if it never happened. You've always done that, Em. You've always made things as simple as you wanted them to be.

EMILY—Your best friend married your beau. But only after you'd given him up, and Alex told me it was finished for him. You won't make me feel guilty about that now or ever. You and Alex would have been very wrong for each other and I think you know it. Alex and I have a happy marriage and— Why are you in Berlin? Why are you here?

CASSIE (*shrugs*)—I worked hard at college last year and I wanted a vacation. (*Quickly.*) I wanted to see you and Alex. I wanted to find out if we could be—could be as good friends as we used to be. But all that was pretty fancy because I seemed to have been the only one who was disturbed. And now that's all right, I think, and we can—

EMILY—I don't believe it's all right now. Things are very wrong between us. Cassie, let's not dine tonight. Let's not—

CASSIE (*softly*)—Let's not see each other again. That's right. But it isn't easy to put away the people you've loved and been close to—

EMILY (*touching* CASSIE's *hand*)—It isn't easy for me, either. But it doesn't have to be for always. We'll forget after a while. You'll get married and have children and we'll rock on the porch of a summer hotel and watch our kids play together and laugh that it could have been any other way—

CASSIE (*sharply*)—Please. Please. Please stop talking that way.

EMILY (*stares at her, then after a second*)—Good-by, Cas.

As she begins to rise, the curtain falls.

It is Paris, 1938. In the living room of a large suite in the Hotel Meurice James Sears, "a thin, tired-looking man of fifty," secretary to Ambassador Alexander Hazen, is clipping items from a newspaper.

The telephone interrupts him. The call, which he later relays to the Ambassador through the door of his room, is from the German Embassy. The Count Max von Stammer, who just happens to be in Paris, would like to see the Ambassador.

Alex (at 43), coming into the room, decides that Sears should call the Count von Stammer and say that he (Alex) also just happens to be in Paris, and will be glad to receive the Count von Stammer informally. That attended to, he would have a report on what is happening—

"The children will be evacuated from Paris tomorrow," says Sears, taking up his clippings; "people who can afford it are leaving for the South of France, and the railroads are dangerously clogged; there are an estimated seventy-two anti-aircraft batteries around Paris, but Halsey says he doesn't believe it. Yesterday morning, Benes telephoned London. There's the report, supposedly compiled by the Poles, with figures on the Soviet Union war potential. The report says Russia is in no shape to fight Germany."

ALEX—That report is two months old. Why has it appeared again?

SEARS—I asked the same question and Halsey didn't know.

ALEX (*irritably*)—God knows, we're not a nation of spies. Usually that pleases me. But this month it doesn't. Halsey never knows anything until the French and English have decided to give it to the Roumanians, and that's the last stop on the road to misinformation. Get Halsey. Get him on the phone for me— (SEARS *picks up the phone. As he dials—*) Never mind. Never mind. I can't make sense out of any of it, and I'm trying to blame it on him.

SEARS—I've made you a calendar, sir—I don't think you'll need Halsey—

ALEX—Washington must think I'm dead. My report should have been sent five days ago—(*Looks up.*) All right. Let's hear the calendar. Dates, at least, are facts.

SEARS (*taking sheet of paper from desk*)—Two weeks ago Bonnet went to Geneva to see Litvinov. Halsey says it's true that Litvinov promised aid to Czechoslovakia and sent Bonnet to see if the Roumanians would consent to let the Russians cross the borders and go through. Bonnet, when he reported to the French Cabinet, said that Litvinov had *not* been definite. Halsey is positive Bonnet was lying because—

ALEX—That's bright of Halsey: the one fact we have, maybe the one fact in all of Europe, is that Bonnet has never yet told the truth.

SEARS—Four days ago, Litvinov told the League of Nations that Russia will support France if she goes to the aid of Czechoslovakia, and strongly hinted she may do so even if France not go to Czechoslovakia's aid—

ALEX—So once more out trots the supposed Polish report to discredit the quality of the Russian army. I understand. And so would a child of four.

Emily (at 37) has arrived in a tailored afternoon suit. She is trying to trace her children. Her daughter, Sarah, it appears,

is being taken to some art gallery by Mademoiselle and Sam has
gone with Moses Taney for a walk.

"We come to Paris every Summer to meet the children," says
Emily, laughing. "Then Father arrives and that is the last we
see of Sam."

Emily is concerned about Alex. He looks tired. She would
have him stop working and take advantage of his vacation. Why
can't they go to the opera and hear "Figaro."

"Cassie Bowman is coming for tea," she adds, quickly. "She's
here this Summer. I called her yesterday— Of course, you had
lunch with her last Summer, and I think the Summer before,
wasn't it? But I have seen her since 1923. I suppose—"

"I've seen her this trip. I saw her last week."

"I know. Maggie Taylor told me. I suppose you'd forgotten
to tell me—"

"She called here one evening. You were out somewhere, and
we had a late dinner together."

"Yes. I'm sure you forgot to tell me," says Emily pleasantly.

"Oh, only half-forgot, I suppose," admits Alex. "I've never
understood about you and Cassie. She's here every Summer,
usually when we are. I don't understand why you don't want
to see each other— Or, for that matter, why it's important
one way or the other."

"I don't know, either." Emily is speaking slowly, hesitantly.
"But I think after all these years, I'd like to see her alone."

"Of course."

Count Max von Stammer is ushered into the room. He is a
very old man and remembers Alex from a conference in Genoa in
1922. At that time Moses Taney was with Alex. What has
become of Mr. Taney? Is he still, in politics, a great liberal?

"Mr. Taney retired many years ago," Alex tells him.

"All liberals retired with the Versailles treaty," answers Von
Stammer.

Entering informally a confessional stage, Von Stammer is free
to admit that he has been sent to see Ambassador Hazen because
in Berlin the visit was considered important. Otherwise, Von
Ribbentrop would have come. Also he has been sent to influence Alex, though he has little faith in men influencing
other men. "Each of us goes the way he goes, and that way
is decided early in a man's life. . . . I come to influence you
about a war, and I come to *you* because you are about to send
back a report to your government."

"Your intelligence department is remarkable," says Alex. "My report is not yet written, and there are none who know about it."

A further exchange of diplomatic pleasantries and evasions, and then Von Stammer comes to the point—

"What I have to say is most simple: we would like to know that your government will not bring pressure on England or France to make war with us."

ALEX (*sharply*)—It is your country which is making the demands, it is your country which is trying to make war. Now, Count von Stammer, if you have come here to get assurances from me, your visit is wasted. I don't make the policy of my country. No one man makes it, thank God. And I am an unimportant man sending back an unimportant report.

VON STAMMER—No report is unimportant to my new bosses. (*As* ALEX *is about to speak.*) Let us go back, Your Excellency. You have said that my country wishes to make war. That is a large generality. Let us put it this way: What war, with whom —and when? Not over the Sudetenland. Hitler has promised that if the Sudetenland is ceded, there will be no further attempt—

ALEX (*repeating the words with the same intonation*)—What war, with whom—and when?

VON STAMMER—I speak unofficially, of course. But if we are given the proper freedom and co-operation we might be prepared, in time, to turn East. East to rid Europe of the menace of Russia. We realize you would wish such a promise to come from men more highly placed than I. So I have been instructed to suggest to you—

ALEX (*getting up*)—I am an old-fashioned man. After all these years in Europe, my roots are still deep in America. Therefore, I don't like such promises or such deals, and I do not believe they will be considered by *any* other democracy. I resent the deals of war, and I don't like your coming here with them.

VON STAMMER (*puzzled, amused*)—Well. Well. I have always admired Americans. If they eat dinner with a man, he must be honorable. If they ride with the Esterhazys in Hungary and the Potockis in Poland, they must be honorable men. How could men who dine out, or mount horses, be otherwise?

ALEX—I do not ride and I seldom dine out.

VON STAMMER (*rising*)—Ambassador Hazen, encourage the English and French not to make war. They are now willing to give us—

ALEX (*quickly*)—I know of nothing they are willing to give

you. I know of no decision they have made. (*Rings the bell on the desk.*) And now I hope you will excuse me. I have an appointment.

VON STAMMER—You know of no decision they have made? Is it possible? Well. By the end of this week I would guess that a journey will be made and a conference will be held. And if there is no meddling from your side of the world, all will be settled. And if your side of the world does meddle, I would guess that—(*Smiles.*) Well, it will still be settled.

Cassie has come. Emily had sent for her. Cassie is glad to see Alex; sorry to find him upset and irritable. But she doesn't think she wants to go to lunch with him or dinner, or for a drive in the country. True, it will be a whole year before they will be seeing each other again, and perhaps longer. The world is cracking up. Perhaps nobody will be coming to Europe another year.

Cassie is going to Fontainebleau for a week—to the little hotel they used to go to. as kids. No, she hasn't a beau. A half-beau, perhaps. And she has never married because—well, maybe she doesn't marry easy—or maybe— Suddenly the question has been asked—

"Are you in love with Emily?"

"I love Emily," answers Alex, simply. "Very much, I think. But I—" He has taken her arm. "Oh, Cassie, it has taken me fifteen years to say these words, even to myself. I was only in love once."

"Me, too," says Cassie, very softly.

"Let me come down to the country to see you. Please, Cas."

"I—er, I want to, Alex. The truth is, I've wanted to for a long time. I mean— But I don't want it to be wrong. I—I couldn't stand it if it worried you afterwards or you felt guilty, or Emily— Or I felt guilty—"

"I don't feel guilty. Emily's been a good wife. And I've been a good husband, too. I think I'll go on being. This has nothing to do with Emily. This has to do with you and me. From a long, long time ago. It's a strange day for us to come together again. Strange for me to be thinking about myself and you when— (*He puts his arms around her.*) Please, Cas. Let me come down."

Cassie is looking up at him and smiling. "All right, darling. It will make me happy. I hope it will make you happy, too." She touches his face and then moves away. "I'll go now. Tell

Em I couldn't wait. And tell her I don't want to come again."

When Emily arrives she is nervously excited. Everybody appears to be leaving Paris. She can't understand it. People shouldn't pack up and leave the minute their country's in trouble.

Alex has been looking over his secretary's newspaper clippings. Emily, it appears, has been seeing much too much of the Renaults, the Polignacs "and the fashionable society wash that runs with them." Emily's excuse is that she has been lonely for a long time. She sees such people as come along. She is sorry that he is not coming to the opera, but she knows the importance of the report he has been worrying about.

"You're a sound man and you will be listened to," says Emily. "It comes down to peace or war now, doesn't it? Last night at dinner Toni said the Czechs were acting like fools. He said if Hitler got what he wanted now, that would shut him up for good. And Baudouin said that if there is war, it means Russia in Europe and—"

"That's what I meant," says Alex sharply. "That kind of people and that kind of talk. Toni has been doing business with the Nazis for years and Baudouin's bank is tied up with the Japs."

"I have a lot of investments in his bank. They've been there since my grandfather."

"That's bad news. I've never known about your money. Why are you telling me now, Em?"

"You've made a great point of not knowing about my money, and not touching it. I wonder if you were scared to find out that we are rich; to find out that we are the people we are."

"You've never talked about your money before. I don't know what you mean now. But if I thought you were trying to tell me that what I think or believe or report should be influenced by it, I would be very angry, Em. Very angry with both of us."

Emily doesn't want to influence Alex. Neither does she want him to pretend that he has no connections and no prejudices and no world that influences him. He might profitably take count of these things. And there is also the matter of his son. If there is a war, Sam will soon be old enough to fight. Emily doesn't want that, or any part of it. "I don't like Nazis any better than you do," she says. *"But I don't want a war.* I love Sam and I want him to be happy in a peaceful world."

"I love Sam, too. But I'll report what I think is the truth.

And it will have nothing to do with my desire to keep Sam alive."

Suddenly they realize that this is the first time they have ever talked to each other like this. The thought is disturbing. It may stem from a mutual loneliness. Emily knows about Cassie. She had been waiting in the lobby until Cassie left. Someway Emily was kind of afraid to interrupt—

"Afraid to see Cassie? What are you talking about? You asked her here. I never thought of you afraid of anything."

"I'm going to tell you about me—some day when we're very old and you're so deaf you can't hear me. I'm afraid of a great many things. Including—"

Sears has come to warn them of a radio announcement. Alex turns on the radio in time for them to hear:

" 'The announcement has just been made that Prime Minister Chamberlain and Mr. Daladier will fly to Munich tomorrow morning. There are already hints of Cabinet resignations. Although no official statement, other than the announcement of an hour ago, has been forthcoming, a high official source said a few minutes ago that—' "

Alex has snapped off the radio. "Well, there's your peace," he says, a little bitterly.

That will mean that Hitler will get the Sudeten and Emily is sorry for that. But why *her* peace? She didn't want anyone to suffer.

"No, of course not," answers Alex, sharply. "Nobody wants anybody to suffer. Maybe even this decadent trash in the society columns doesn't want it."

"If it makes you feel better to make fun of those people, then do it. But don't tell yourself that having contempt for them puts you on the opposite side. Why are you attacking me, and unjustly, I think?"

"I suppose I am being unjust. I think I even know why. I don't know how to tell you, Em, but maybe it's a good day to get things straight—"

She comes to him quickly. "I think we've talked enough, Alex," she says. "Sometimes putting things in words makes them too definite, before one really means them to be." She has put her hand on his arm. "You're having a hard time. It's as if a machine were running us all down and we didn't know where to go or what to do or how to get away from it."

She has called Sears and left. Sears wheels up his typewriter and is ready to take the message. Alex begins to dictate—

" 'By the time this reaches you the results of the Munich meeting will be known. But there is no doubt here that the Sudeten will be given to Germany in return for the promise that it will be the last of Hitler's demands. That I do not believe. (*Pause. Begins to dictate again.*) I have been told by Count Max von Stammer that the agreement will probably carry a second promise: Hitler will talk of making war at some time in the future on the Soviet Union. That I do not believe, although it has long been a rumor here. It is my earnest recommendation— (*Gets up.*) It is my belief—' "

He pauses and is pacing the room nervously. The futility of the whole thing sweeps over him. What the hell difference does anything he says, or thinks, mean? But he goes on again—

" '—my earnest belief that we should protest against any further German aggressions or against any further concessions to them. But I am convinced that Mr. Chamberlain is working in the interests of peace and his actions must not be judged too sharply. If he can save his sons and our sons from war—' "

No. That last sentence must come out. Again the nervous hesitancy and again he resumes—

" 'It is difficult to give you a picture of a muddled situation. On the side of peace there are many selfish and unpatriotic men willing to sacrifice the honor of their country for their own private and dishonorable reasons, and of those who deplore the Munich meeting—and I am one of them—many see it as a complete capitulation and as the beginning of a world war. I think that is a harsh and unwarranted judgment based on inadequate facts. If a generation can be kept from war, if we can spare our sons—' "

No. That must come out, too. Back to "inadequate facts." Then let Sears code it and send it as a cable. After that they will go out and get drunk, and see if they can forget it for a few hours.

Moses Taney comes in. Mrs. Hazen is making him go to the opera, and he is looking for a tie. So the boys are going to Munich? Well, Moses will be glad to sail for home and get back to his chair in the library.

"We may be crooks at home," says Moses, "but we aren't elegant about it. I can't stand elegant crooks. They talk too pious for me."

"Whatever I feel about them, or you feel about them, maybe they're acting for the best," says Alex, wearily. "It can't be easy to throw your country into a war."

"What a simple way of putting it, and how understanding you are. I feel sorry for people who are as tolerant as you."

"Thank you. I find I'm sorry for myself." And Alex leaves.

Moses would, if he could, pry out of Sears some idea of what Alex has written in his report. He even takes a peek at the message when Sears goes for the tie.

"For God's sake, Mr. Taney!" exclaims the horrified confidential secretary, coming back into the room. "That's official. Since when do people read other people's—"

"Since when do people read other people's mail? Since always."

Moses waves Sears aside and goes to the door of Alex's room. "Difficult world, eh, Alex?" he calls in. "So many people doing so many strange things. All we can do is compromise. Compromise and compromise. There's nothing like a good compromise to cost a few million men their lives. Well, I'm glad I retired. I don't like having anything to do with the death of other people. Sad world, eh, Alex?"

The door slams. Moses smiles.

"Very sad," he concludes. The curtain falls.

We are back in the drawing room of the Hazen house. It is about an hour after Emily has insisted that she and Alex and Cassie talk things out, and Sam has asked to be allowed to stay. (2d Scene, Act I.)

Now the talk is nearing its end. Moses is on the terrace. Sam is sitting on a stool facing the terrace doors. The others are inside the room.

Emily is about finished. There are still one or two things she would like cleared. Why, for instance, did Cassie and Alex go back to that little hotel in Fontainebleau, where she and Cassie had played as children? The terrace door is slammed shut.

"For God's sake, Emily," Alex protests. "If you wanted to know about me and Cassie I would have told you. Did we have to go through all the fumblings, all the mistakes of years, to find it out? Like everybody else in the world, I don't want to look back on what was wrong—"

"None of us," agrees Cassie, with considerable force, turning to Emily. "None of us. It hasn't been a pretty picture. And not of you, either."

"That's true," admits Emily. "I haven't liked myself in it. I haven't liked myself for a long time, now." She turns to Alex.

"I knew about you and Cassie. I've known about you and Cassie for—"

"Then why did you do this? And why tonight?" demands Cassie.

"Tonight has been coming for a long time. When I found out that you were here in Washington I knew that now we'd have to meet and get it finished. Always it's been the three of us, all our lives. We can't go on that way."

Cassie is the first to attempt an explanation of her part in what has happened. She had never thought of what she did as being bad. Frankly, she had been haunted by Emily all her life. "I was angry when Emily married you," Cassie says to Alex. "I felt it had been done against me. I had no plans then to do anything about it, but—" Cassie is talking rapidly, desperately, now. "I wanted to take you away from Emily: there it is. It sounds as if I didn't care about you, but I did and I do. But I would never have done anything about you if I hadn't wanted, for so many years, to punish Emily—I didn't know that was true until tonight. (*Puts her hands to her face.*) That's a lie. I did know it. But I never wanted to see it, I don't want to see it now—I— (ALEX *takes her hands from her face, holds her hand.*) I think I used to be worth something. But this got in the way of everything! My work, other people. Well, I guess you pay for small purposes, and for bitterness. (*Turns to* ALEX, *touches his hand.*) I can't say I'm sorry. I can say I got mixed up and couldn't help myself. I've always envied you, Emily: your life seemed so full and your world so exciting. If I learned about myself tonight, I also learned about you. And you, Alex. It's too bad that all these years I saw it wrong. (*With deep feeling.*) Oh, I don't want to see another generation of people like us who didn't know what they were doing and why they did it. Tell your son to try— Good-by, my dear."

Alex kisses Cassie's hand and she smiles. "Somebody told me once that when something's been wrong with you and it gets cured, you miss it very much at first." She turns to them and adds, warmly: "I'm going to miss you, in a funny kind of way."

Emily presses her arm. "Good-by, Cas," she says, warmly. Cassie moves swiftly into the hall.

Emily and Alex are agreed that they will not talk about what has happened for a long time. They will just see how it works out. Emily has opened the terrace doors. Moses is sitting where he was. Sam is walking nervously about the terrace.

Emily goes to the piano and is playing when Sam comes into

the room. He hasn't heard his mother play for a long time. He listens for a moment and then starts for the hall. He seems embarrassed as he says his good nights.

Alex calls Sam back. There is no use his pretending that nothing has happened. If there is anything he would say, let him say it.

There was a lot, Sam admits, that he didn't understand. But he doesn't want to talk about it now.

Emily, too, adds her word. She and Alex have sensed that Sam had been worried for some time now. It hadn't been easy for them to have him hear what he has heard tonight. "You're not doing us a favor now by sparing us what you think," she says.

There have been some things that have troubled Sam. For one, in the report sent home the day before Munich, did his father recommend appeasement? Yes, Alex admits, that is what it came down to, though the word was unknown to him then.

"Look here," interrupts Moses. "There have been many times when I haven't agreed with your father. But you mustn't blame him too much. What he, or anybody else, recommended, wouldn't have made any difference."

Sam turns on his grandfather. He remembers that Moses had once written him that "History is made by the masses of the people. One man or ten men don't start the earthquakes and don't stop them, either." That is what Tolstoi meant in "War and Peace." Well, adds Sam, that is what Moses has made an excuse for sitting back and watching: nothing anybody can do makes any difference, so why do it!

"I think you mixed me up quite a lot, Grandpa," says Sam. "But one fine thing you taught me: That I belong here. I never liked that school in France or the one in Switzerland. I didn't like being there.

"You know," Sam goes on. "I never felt at home any place until I got in the Army. I never came across my kind of people until I met Leck and Davis. (Quickly.) I guess I never could have belonged to your world nor to Grandpa's, either—I still don't know where I belong. I guess that's what's been worrying me. But with only one leg you've got to start thinking faster—"

Emily and Alex, startled, move toward Sam. Moses turns sharply in his chair. Sam is himself a little panic-stricken by what he has said. He goes on hurriedly, to cover his embarrassment—

"I have to go back to the hospital tomorrow night. They've

decided it's something called traumatic sarcoma of the bone, and they can't avoid amputation any longer. I was going to tell you tomorrow."

Alex has covered his face with his hand. Emily is muttering her son's name over and over. Moses gets up slowly from his chair. "I guess I'll go to bed," he says. As he comes toward Sam he begins to cry. "I hope you won't laugh at me, but I would have given my life if I could have saved you any—" Without looking at Sam he touches his arm. "Well, son—" he says, and moves slowly to the hall door.

"I'm sorry I told you tonight," says Sam, softly.

ALEX (*with great feeling*)—Don't be sorry for us.

EMILY (*with great feeling*)—I hate pity for the relatives. It's your leg. It's your trouble and nobody else will ever know anything about it. (*Very loudly.*) We'll be walking all right. But you won't—(*She puts her hands over her face.*)

SAM (*sharply*)—All right, Mother. (*To* ALEX.) I was lucky. Out of nine men, four got killed. (*Nervously, talking as if he wants to make conversation.*) Did you tour around that part of Italy, Father? They call the place Bloody Basin now because it's a sort of basin between two hills and so many guys got killed there that we called it Bloody Basin. (ALEX *goes to* EMILY, *leans down, kisses her.* SAM *speaks chattily, as if for* EMILY.) I liked Leck, you know, the boy I've told you about who used to be a baker in Jersey City. We'd sit around and talk: why we were in the war, and what was going to happen afterwards, and all of us pretended we knew more than we did. But not Leck. He never pretended to anything because he really knew a lot. Sometimes they'd ask me about you, Father, and I'd tell them all the things you'd done. Then one day one of them handed me a clipping. His mother had sent it to him. (*As if it were painful.*) I don't think I ever in my life was really ashamed before. After all the fine talk I'd done about my family—God in Heaven, it did something to me—(*Stops abruptly.*)

EMILY—What is it?

SAM—Never mind.

ALEX (*tensely*)—Say it, Sam. Say it.

SAM—I was thinking Mother had had enough and—

EMILY—Stop being sorry for me.

SAM (*taking the newspaper clipping from his pocket*)—Well, this soldier wanted to make fun of me, I guess. It's from one of those women columnists. It's about a dinner party that she gave. Kind of international people were there, she says. A French novelist and a milliner who used to be a White Russian and a movie actress and a banker from Holland—(*Slowly begins to read from the clipping.*) "It was, if I say so myself, a brilliant gathering. The last to arrive was the handsome Mrs. Alexander Hazen. Her husband, Alex Hazen, used to be our Ambassador to—"

EMILY (*sharply*)—Your father wasn't at the dinner.

ALEX (*wearily*)—That doesn't matter. Go on, Sam.

SAM (*reading*)—"I looked around the table and I thought 'Europe isn't dead. These people will go home some day and once more make it the charming, careless, carefree place I knew so well.'" So the soldier who gave me the clipping says, "Glad to be sittin' in mud here, Sam, if it helps to make a carefree world for your folks." And Leck tells him to shut up. But when we're alone, Leck says to me, "Sam, that banker the piece talked about, he used to deal with the Germans before it got too hot. He's a no good guy. And the rest of those people: they're all old tripe who just live in our country now and pretend they are on the right side. When the trouble came in their countries they sold out their people and then beat it quick, and now they make believe they're all for everything good. My God, Sam," he said, "if you come from that you better get away from it fast, because they helped to get us where we are."

ALEX (*coming to* SAM)—Sometimes I was wrong because I didn't know any better. And sometimes I was wrong because I had reasons I didn't know about. But I never had anything to do with people like that.

EMILY (*to* SAM, *sadly*)—Maybe I've no right to ask you. But try not to be too hard on us, Sam.

SAM (*as if he hadn't heard her*)—Well, for a couple of days I thought about what Leck said and I was going to tell him something. But that afternoon we went down to Bloody Basin and he got blown to pieces and I got wounded. (*Looks up at* EMILY *as if he had just heard what she said.*) How do you say you love your country?

EMILY (*after a second*)—I don't know. We're frightened of saying things like that now because we might sound like the fakers who do say them.

SAM (*getting up*)—Well, I want to say it. I love this place. (*With great passion.*) And I don't want any more fancy fooling around with it. I don't want any more of Father's mistakes, for any reason, good or bad, or yours, Mother, because I think they do it harm. I was ashamed of that clipping. But I didn't really know why. I found out tonight. I am ashamed of both of you, and that's the truth. I don't want to be ashamed that way again. I don't like losing my leg, I don't like losing it at all, I'm scared—but everybody's welcome to it as long as it means a little something and helps to bring us out some place. All right. I've said enough. I love you both. Let's have a drink.

"As Emily moves toward the table, Alex moves toward Sam."

THE CURTAIN FALLS

THE VOICE OF THE TURTLE

A Comedy in Three Acts

By John Van Druten

THIS story is told by three characters, the shortest cast of the theatre season and one of the most satisfying. It is the second comedy John Van Druten has written calling for few players that has in turn promptly discovered huge groups of playgoing admirers, indicating that a proper concentration on simple romance is good box-office sense. Back in 1931-32 Herbert Marshall and Edna Best played Mr. Van Druten's "There's Always Juliet" for many months, with only two assisting players in their company, and "Juliet" afterward became a stock company favorite wherever there were stock companies to play it.

Nothing very exciting happened during the early career of "The Voice of the Turtle." Mr. Van Druten, spearing the idea, it may be, while en route to the Coast, wrote the play in three weeks at his California ranch. He sent the script to Alfred de Liagre, Jr., a New York producer who happened to be in Hollywood at the time. Mr. De Liagre read it and bought it within twenty-four hours and had it cast within the week. His first and last choice was Margaret Sullavan and Elliott Nugent for the leads, and Audrey Christie fitted in perfectly with them and with the author's intent as the third character of the trio.

The comedy's introduction to the East was equally simple and similarly unexciting. Tried first in New Haven, Boston and Philadelphia, critical receptions were all but perfect and audience receptions were frequently ecstatic. Here and there a moral force arose to protest certain liberties of word or action taken by author and director, but nothing ever came of these somewhat half-hearted objections. The Broadway crowd, experiencing at the time an artistically depressing, though financially successful theatre season, and adoring tastefully staged sophisticated comedy above all other types of dramatic entertainment, fairly leaped at the new play. "The Voice of the Turtle" was a runaway success from the rising of its first curtain.

The apartment that Sally Middleton rented from a friend, which is the scene of the week-end we spend with her in the Van

Druten comedy, is located in the East Sixties in New York, near Third Avenue. It is a smallish apartment, three rooms and bath, and, excepting for the bath we see it all. Looking toward the stage, the bedroom with double bed, is at the left, the living room occupies the stage center and a fully equipped kitchen is at the right. Bedroom and living room are smartly but not extravagantly furnished. There is a day bed under a window at the back of the living room and a telephone and reading lamp on a small table at the head of the bed.

In the kitchen a modern ice-box, sink and stove, with considerable wall space given to shelf covers for dishes, are appropriately distributed. It is in the kitchen that we now find Sally working one Friday afternoon in April. She is carrying a tray bearing highball glasses, Scotch and soda into the living room and rehearsing the potion scene from "Romeo and Juliet" at the same time.

" 'Oh, look! Methinks I see my cousin's ghost seeking out Romeo, that did spit his body on a rapier's point!' " recites Sally, with feeling, as she deposits the tray on top of a nest of tables. " 'Stay, Tybalt, stay! Romeo, I come! This do I drink to thee—' " And she is back in the kitchen for the ice.

Sally is an attractive young actress in her middle twenties. She is pleased at having at least conquered the potion speech. She is still going over it as she arranges the drinkables when the doorbell rings. At the door is Olive Lashbrooke. Olive is about 28, "smart and attractive without being good looking, and rather gay."

With mingled "Darlings!" the girls are in each other's arms. The history of Sally's renting the apartment from Claire Henley, who is on the road with the Lunts, is told with enthusiasm. Olive herself is just back from a tour of split weeks and one-night stands. Sally, less fortunate, only got five nights with her most recent flop.

"Darling, it's the cutest place I ever saw in all my life," Olive is saying, as she pulls aside the curtains at the living room window. "Where do you look out?"

"Onto the Summer garden of the 'Bonne Chanson.' That French restaurant next door."

"What's that like?"

"Lovely. But terribly expensive. You know, no menu. The man comes and *suggests*."

This would be living next door to temptation, thinks Olive, whose wonder grows that Sally can afford all that she is showing.

No job. Summer coming on. What's the answer?

Simple. Sally still has something left from her last radio serial. And she feels it is when a person isn't working that she needs a nice place to live. Besides, there are other reasons. But —more about those later. Right now they must have a drink and Olive must tell of her tour.

It was a pleasant enough tour. However, there wasn't the kick being in a company with Henry Atherton that Sally was sure there would be. "Henry," reports Olive, "isn't interested in anything a day over twenty." Which reminds her that she has asked someone to call for her at Sally's. A man named Bill Page who is in the Army now.

"He's at Camp Something-or-other up the Hudson. Got a week-end pass, starting this afternoon. I left a message at my hotel telling him to come on here and pick me up."

"What's he like?"

"He's sweet. And he's mine."

"I didn't mean . . ."

"I know, darling, but I thought I'd tell you. I've known him for ages. He used to live in Pittsburgh, and whenever I played there we always had a gay little something. Though when I say 'whenever,' I think actually it was only twice. Yes, that's all it was. I'd lost sight of him for years, and then when we were in Detroit about six weeks ago, he turned up again. He was stationed somewhere near, and came to see the show. Now he's moved up here."

"And are you still having a gay little something?" Sally is smiling.

"Well, we did in Detroit."

"Are you in love with him?"

"No, darling, not a bit. But he's attractive. Only he's sort of the . . . reserved kind, you know. You never know what he's thinking or get any further with him."

"It doesn't sound as though there was much further left for you to get."

And what about Olive's former passion, the Commander? What about Ned Burling? Well, it appears that Olive is still fondly smitten with Ned, but— Well, Ned has been away a long time and he isn't the writing kind. "Besides, that was one of those . . . 'Lovely things that isn't meant to last. A wild, brief intermezzo,'" quotes Olive.

"'One of those lovely things that isn't meant to last,'" repeats Sally. A trace of sadness has come into her voice, which

Olive is quick to note.

"Sally, what's the matter?" demands Olive. "You're unhappy about something. What is it? Is it . . . love?"

"I guess so. If you can call it that."

"You can always call it that. Come on. Tell Aunty Olive all about it. Well?"

And Sally tells Olive the story of her friendship with Kenneth Bartlett, the producer, who confines himself mostly to musical comedies, and has just produced a smash hit. They had met at a cocktail party. Kenneth was young and attractive, or seemed young. They had gone on to dinner. That was Sally's introduction to the "Bonne Chanson" next door.

That was two months ago. "He told me all about the show," reports Sally. "It was in rehearsal then . . . sang me some of the songs . . . he made me feel wonderful. Like being starred and getting the star dressing room. You know?"

"I know."

"Well, then I found that Claire was going away, and had this place right next door to . . ."

"Your place . . ."

"So I took it. You know it was funny . . . when I came to see it, Claire had the radio on, and it was playing the London-derry Air . . . and that's always been my lucky tune . . . I thought it meant the apartment would be lucky . . ."

"So you let her soak you a hundred and a quarter."

"Well, it was nice to have. And just occasionally he stayed all night . . . and I got breakfast, and . . . oh, I don't know . . . but it was nice, and . . . I love having someone to do for."

Sally's romance didn't last long after that. Kenneth was insistent that they should keep their friendship gay, and not get serious about it. Sally couldn't quite do that. Kenneth accused her of making scenes—and perhaps she did. Little scenes. And he, being married— Did Sally know he was married?

"Yes, he told me that first evening," admits Sally. "But they don't get on, and she's a lot older than he is. Oh, he didn't tell me that. He didn't say anything about her, except to let me know he had a wife. And they've two children, so you see, it couldn't be anything serious for him. Oh, he was very sweet about it . . . really he was. Only he said that it couldn't go on like that . . . for my sake. So, it's all over. We said good-by a month ago." Sally has risen and is pacing the room. "I've been so miserable," she goes on. "We've had the most awful weather. I don't think Spring's ever coming this year. I've just stayed home and studied Juliet and read Dorothy Parker's poems. I never used to mind being by myself, but now . . . since Ken . . . it's the first time I've had an apartment of my own, and it seems much waste."

"I know. I feel the same way whenever I go to a hotel, and they give me a big double room all to myself."

Of one thing Sally is certain. It's not going to happen again. Not till she's thirty at least. If she had only stayed in Joplin nothing of this kind would have happened. This whole sex business is puzzling to Sally.

"Olive, tell me something. Something I want to know," says Sally, quite seriously.

"What?"

SALLY—Well, *do* ordinary girls? I was raised to think they didn't. Didn't even want to. And what I want to know is— don't they? They don't in movies. Oh, I know that's censorship . . . but . . . the people who go and *see* the movies . . . Well, are they like that, too? Or else don't they notice that it's all false?

OLIVE (*rising*)—I've wondered about that, myself.

SALLY—Even in Shakespeare, his heroines don't. Ever. Juliet carries on like crazy about *not*. I don't know whether what Mother and Father taught me was right, or true or anything. Were you raised like that?

OLIVE—Oh, sure. And I wasn't even legitimate. But Mama raised me just as strict as if I was.

SALLY—Did you have qualms when you started?

OLIVE—Never.

SALLY—What did you feel?

OLIVE—I just felt—"So this is it. I like it." (*Then, kindly. Crossing to* SALLY.)—Sally, darling, you're not starting a conscience, or thinking you're promiscuous, because you've had one affair, are you?

SALLY—I've had two. There was that boy from the company at Skowhegan last summer that I was so unhappy about. I told you.

OLIVE—Well, two, then.

SALLY (*reflectively*)—No, I . . . don't think I'm promiscuous . . . yet. Though I don't imagine anyone ever does think that about themselves. Do . . . (*She stops.*)

OLIVE—Do I . . . were you going to say?

SALLY—Well, I was, only I suddenly realized how awful it sounded.

OLIVE—No, I don't. Maybe you're right, and no one does, but I just think for a gal with a funny face I've really done rather well. *You're* pretty. You can afford to be choosey.

Olive thinks she had better call her hotel and find out what has happened to Bill Page. She does. Bill had called, got her note and is on his way over. There is also a message for Olive from Commander Burling. The Commander is in town and has left his phone number. Olive is in a stew. "Wouldn't you know it would happen like this?" she explodes.

Olive gets the Commander on the wire. He, too, has only the week-end and is terribly, terribly anxious to see Olive. But she just can't. She— Oh, hell, she will! She doesn't know how, but she will! She'll be at her hotel at 8—

Now, what's to be done with Bill Page? What can she tell him? How can she convince him that there is someone she can't possibly ditch? Suddenly Olive has an idea. She'll tell Bill that she's married; that her husband has appeared unexpectedly; that it is his last leave; that she must be with him—

"Oh, darling," she wails, "I know it's awful of me, but you've not seen Ned. It's nearly a year since I have, and he's so divine."

Of course Sally will have to help her out with the husband story. Sally isn't sure she should—or can—but— And then Bill arrives.

Bill "is about 32, adult, quiet and attractive. He wears a Sergeant's stripes, and carries an evening paper and a tiny week-end toilet case." A moment later he has thrown his arms around Olive.

Bill is full of plans. He thought for his first night he and Olive would go to dinner and sort of concentrate on good food, good drinks and a good time. The next night they would take in a theatre and—

Then Bill has to be told. Sally manages to slip into the bedroom, despite Olive's protests, so she isn't much help. Olive hadn't told Bill about her marriage before, she explains, because, well, it didn't take. But, just today her husband called her up. He is in the Navy and this is his last leave. They're not divorced, and she feels she must go back to him. Probably not permanently—but for this week-end anyway.

Bill is disappointed. Not mad—no. He understands. Still

it is a disappointment. Olive has begun to gather her things. If she meets Ned at 8 she will have to hurry. No, she wouldn't have Bill take her back to her hotel. Bill should stay there and finish his drink in peace.

Sally is back to report that it has started to rain. Olive will have to find a taxi. "Good-by, Bill—and do forgive me," she says, kissing the Sergeant on the cheek. "I'll call you. Where are you staying?"

"I don't know yet. I went straight from the station to your hotel. I asked if they had a room there, but they were all full up. So I just came on here."

With Olive gone, Bill is a little let down, but he brightens, politely, as he turns to Sally. He will give Olive a minute to get clear, and then he will be going on, he says. There's no hurry, Sally assures him. She's not going out. Still, Bill thinks— Could he use her telephone? Certainly.

Sally shows him where it is—in the bedroom. She shuts the door that he may have privacy for his calls, and goes about straightening up the living room. Finished with that she props herself up on the couch with Bill's evening paper.

In the bedroom Bill takes out a small notebook, looks up a number, dials it and waits. He is sitting on the edge of the bed and has lighted a cigarette. He has no luck with the call. Joan Westbury has moved, and whoever has answered the call doesn't know the new address.

Bill thumbs through the book and calls another number. No luck again. Miss Van Huysen is out of town for the week-end. "Well, just tell her Monday that Mr. Page called Friday," he says. "Mr. Bill Page of Pittsburgh."

He does get Frank Archer, but it doesn't do him much good. Joan Westbury, Frank tells him, is now a Wac or a Wave or something in uniform. And Alice Hopewell got married. As for Frank himself, he's got a dinner date. Bill thumbs through the book again, hesitates at one name, and then gives the whole thing up. "Oh, the hell with it," he mutters. "She's probably dead."

He is back in the living room now. Sally suggests that he have another drink and he agrees. He would talk a little about Sally's friendship with Olive. It's been going on ever since her first play, Sally explains. Olive was in that, too. No, Sally is not a well-known actress. Her longest run was only three weeks.

"What do actresses do between jobs?" Bill would know.

"Well," confesses Sally, "I just sit and think about how I'm

going to act all the parts I'll never get a chance to act—like
Juliet or Nina in 'The Seagull.' "

Bill can't quite understand why Sally should want to keep on
with so discouraging a business, and Sally tries to explain that
it is just that impelling something that won't let artists of any
kind quit. "All of us . . . actors and authors, too . . . we
aren't really living in the real world at all," she says. "We're
giving our whole lives to . . . make-believe."

It may be "That one talent which is death to hide" of which
Milton wrote, Bill thinks. Sally agrees perhaps it may be. Then
they get around to Bill. What did he do before the war?

Bill hadn't done much of anything until he was twenty-five.
His people had money. He just played around—and appreciated
things. Then things happened and he had to buckle down and
learn something about real life. Then came the Army. And
afterwards?

"I haven't any plans for afterwards," he says. "I just hope
there'll still be things left to appreciate."

"There'll always be . . . So long as there are people. Free
people. That's what it's all about, isn't it? The war, I mean."

"You mustn't ask a soldier what the war's about."

" 'That one talent which is death to hide . . .' " Sally is
savoring the phrase.

"That sums you up, does it?"

"Oh, no. Milton could say that. I'm not that conceited. But
it's what it feels like, when you're out of work, or doing something second-rate. It's like having something *entrusted* to you
. . . for the benefit of others . . . that you're wasting. (*Breaking off.*) Oh, no . . . that sounds awful. Phoney and arty, like
Madame Pushkin."

"Who's she?"

Mme. Pushkin, Sally explains, is a character she and Olive
invented. An old Russian actress who runs a school where she
teaches the Pushkin method. It is an amusing recital, with imi-
tations, and Bill is quite impressed. The next minute he is asking her to go to dinner with him. No, Sally decides, after a
second's pause, though she thanks him sweetly. Why not? Bill
wants to know.

SALLY—You don't have to ask me.
BILL—I know I don't. But will you?
SALLY—Well . . . we go Dutch.
BILL—No, I asked you.

SALLY—Only because Olive let you down.

BILL—Only because if she hadn't, I wouldn't have had the chance.

SALLY (*embarrassed by the compliment*)—Well, thank you very much, then.

BILL—Where shall we go?

SALLY—Wherever you say.

BILL—What's the place next door like?

SALLY (*after a half-second's pause, with an echo in her ears*)—Very expensive.

BILL—But good?

SALLY—Yes, but . . .

BILL—Let's go there. (*Noticing her hesitation.*) Have you anything against it?

SALLY—N . . . no . . . But it's . . . *very* expensive.

BILLL—All the same. Besides, it's raining quite hard now, so *let's* go next door.

SALLY—All right.

BILL—There was a restaurant of the same name in Paris that I used to go to quite a lot, once upon a time. Did you know Paris?

SALLY (*by the bedroom door*)—No. I never went to Europe. I was only eighteen when the war broke out.

BILL—My God. That hurts.

SALLY—What?

BILL—That that's possible already. (*He looks at her.*)

SALLY (*after a pause*)—I'll just get my coat.

As she goes towards the bedroom the curtain falls.

It is 10:30 that evening when they return to Sally's apartment. It is still raining and Bill comes in for a moment. It has been a lovely evening, they are agreed, and an excellent dinner. A better dinner than usual Sally thinks. Due probably to the fact that Bill and the proprietor had remembered each other from Paris days. In Paris, this same fellow had run a tiny place where Bill used to go a good deal with a certain American girl with whom he thought he was in love. The restaurant, the proprietor and all had rather brought things back to Bill.

Sally, too, had had her moments of fleeting memories that were a little distressful. The "Bonne Chanson" wasn't a very happy choice for either of them. But— That's over. And, save for the fact that he's terribly sleepy, Bill is having a grand time. He tries to stifle a yawn. "That wasn't misery . . . or boredom," he explains. "It was too much dinner and not enough sleep."

"Don't you get enough?"

"I haven't had enough for months. Tomorrow morning I shall stay in bed till lunchtime. Sunday I probably shan't get up at all . . . till it's time to go back."

No, Bill admits, that isn't the way he wants to spend his leave, but there are worse ways. The thought recalls Olive. He wonders if Sally thought he believed that story of Olive's? He didn't. If she had been married she would have told him six weeks ago in Detroit.

"I'm not the least in love with her," says Bill, "so don't worry. I guess I *am* a little sore at her for letting me down. I'll get over it. By tomorrow."

Another yawn, another apology, and Bill is sure he must be going. But . . . it is still raining, even harder than before. So he agrees to wait a little. While he waits this time he would have Sally tell him more about Mme. Pushkin, which she does, with her best dialect. And that's fun. . . .

Now Sally, a little self-consciously, has brought Olive into the conversation again, and again Bill is at pains to assure her that Olive has not broken his heart, or anything like it. Had the girl in Paris? He doesn't answer that one, but it seems to him that love is a subject pretty constantly in Sally's thoughts.

"Because I'm a fool, I guess," says Sally. "I always think that everyone ought to be in love with *someone.*"

"Are *you?*"

"I . . . think I am."

"Not sure? Have you been in love often?"

Sally gives the question a moment's serious thought. "No . . . not often," she says.

"I suppose actresses need to fall in love a lot . . . to be good actresses?" suggests Bill, with a smile.

"Oh, yes, Meester Pache," quickly answers Sally, going immediately into her Madame Pushkin act. "Always ven I play a role I must be in lof. Sometimes I valk de streets for hours to find someone to fall in lof wiz. (*The telephone rings. She continues in the accent.*) De telephone. Excuse please. I go."

Sally skips gaily into the bedroom, turns on the light and answers the phone, still using the Pushkin accent. Bill sits alone for a moment and then has another look at the weather out of the window. Turning the radio on softly, he lights a cigarette and sinks back in great comfort on the couch.

In the bedroom Sally continues her telephone conversation, though she has dropped Mme. Pushkin. The caller is Olive, and Olive is obviously curious about what has happened and is happening to Bill. "Olive, you don't mind our having gone to dinner, do you?" Sally asks. "It's just that he asked me, and he hadn't any other place to go . . . No, I don't think he has. I don't think he's tried. Well, it's raining. Hard. . . . Of course he's all right. Why not? I won't tell him if you don't want me to. Good-by, Olive."

Sally comes back into the living room but stops at the door. Bill has fallen fast asleep. His cigarette is burning in his hand. She tiptoes over and takes it from his fingers and he wakes with a start. Now he is convinced that he must be getting on.

But the hotels are all full up, Sally reports. The friend who just called had told her. And it is still raining hard.

"Well, I'll dig up something," says Bill, walking over to shake hands with her. "This is liable to keep up all night. So . . ."

SALLY—Would you want to stay here? That's a day bed. It's quite comfortable.

BILL—I know it is. But . . . I don't think I should do that.

SALLY—I can give you a toothbrush.

BILL—I've got that with me.

SALLY—It seems silly to go out in all that rain. You'll get so wet looking for a taxi, you haven't any change of clothes. You're tired. I'll give you breakfast in the morning.

BILL—Oh, you needn't do that.

SALLY—Oh, I'd like it.

BILL—Well, it's very good of you.

SALLY—Then will you?

BILL—Yes, thank you. (*Yawns again.*) Oh . . .

SALLY—Look at you. Why don't you go to bed right away? It's all made up. I've only got to take the cover off.

BILL—Let me help you.

SALLY—Oh, thank you. (*They strip off the covers.*) Would you like some pajamas?

BILL—I couldn't wear your pajamas.

SALLY—They aren't mine. They're men's pajamas. My . . . brother stays here sometimes.

BILL—Thank you very much. That would be a luxury.

SALLY—I'll get them for you.

Sally goes into the bedroom, gets the pajamas and a pair of slippers. Bill takes off his coat and hangs it over a chair back. There is a trace of embarrassment, but they overcome this gradually. The radio is now playing the "Londonderry Air." That, announces Sally, is her lucky tune. "It's silly," she admits, "but whenever I hear that, nice things always happen to me."

She is gathering up the ash trays now. "The bathroom's through there," she indicates, as she starts for the kitchen.

While Bill is in the bathroom Sally continues to set the house in order for the night. Empties the ash trays into the garbage pail; gets a thermos bottle of ice water from the frigidaire and a glass, which she puts beside the couch; adds match box and cigarettes to these; beats up the cushions of the couch and straightens them; folds down the blankets, etc.

While she is taking the cover off her own bed she calls to Bill to ask if he has everything he wants. Bill comes to the door, toothbrush in hand, to report that he has. She is back in the living room when he reappears in pajamas, his own clothes carefully folded over his arm. He lays them neatly on the chair and goes to the couch. "You don't know how good that looks . . . and feels . . . and is!" he adds, progressively as he sinks contentedly upon it.

Sally has gone to shut off the radio. As she turns she notices that Bill is sitting at the edge of the couch and smiling.

SALLY—What are you smiling at?

BILL—I was just remembering a novel I once read about life in 1910 . . . where the heroine was compromised because she was seen coming out of a man's apartment after dark.

SALLY—I guess things *have* changed.

BILL—You're not kidding.

SALLY (*dubiously*)—Although I don't know that my mother would . . . *quite* understand this. It's silly, because it couldn't be more sensible. But there are a lot of people still who wouldn't believe in it.

BILL—Well, don't tell them.

SALLY—I don't intend to. (*Pause.*) Well . . . good night.

BILL—Good night, Sally. (*He switches out the lamp on desk.*)

SALLY—Good night, Cousin Bill. (*Starts into bedroom.*)

BILL—Huh?

SALLY—Nothing. Oh, I left the kitchen light on. (*Goes to kitchen.*) I'll just leave a note for Verona, to tell her not to disturb you, if she comes. She's the colored maid. I don't expect she'll show up, but I'll be on the safe side. (*She scribbles note, leaves it and switches off the light. The only remaining light is now in the bedroom. She returns to the living room.*) Are you all right?

"There is no answer. Bill is asleep. She goes on into the bedroom. As she opens the door, the light hits him, asleep on the daybed. She closes the door very quietly, sits on bed, takes off her shoes and starts to take off her stockings."

The curtain falls.

ACT II

By noon the next day Sally's apartment has been tidied up, with both beds made, and Bill fussing with a coffee percolator in the kitchen. When Sally lets herself in the door, her arms full of bundles, it is told that she has been out since 9:30, having been called by telephone. She had left a note for Bill. She hasn't had any breakfast, either. Only a cocktail. And there's a story goes with that.

Sally's phone call was from a manager, and she has a job. Everything is looking up, even the weather. It's a glorious Spring day. And Sally is very happy.

Bill has nothing much to report. The phone had rung—twice—while Sally was out, but he had not answered. Didn't think it would sound very well to have a man's voice answering Sally's phone. Sally would never have thought of that. Phone calls fascinate her. Any call might mean something lovely—like a long-lost uncle with money, or a party, or a job like she got this morning.

It's a good job, Sally thinks. A friend of hers had it, but this being the fifth day she was fired. That's Equity. A producer either has to keep the actors he hires or pay them two weeks' salary after the fifth day of rehearsal.

"I feel sort of badly about that," Sally admits. "Getting her part I mean . . . though, actually, she couldn't have been in it very long, if it had run, because she's going to have a baby, only she didn't tell them that. And I don't think it was quite honorable. I mean, it may be an Act of God, but not if it's already started, I should think."

Photo by Vandamm Studio.

"THE VOICE OF THE TURTLE"

Bill—I want you to let yourself love me . . . if you can. I think you've a great talent for love, Sally, and that you're trying to fritter it and dissipate it . . . because it's been trodden on before."

(Elliott Nugent, Margaret Sullavan)

Bill is properly impressed and understanding about the baby, but he doesn't seem quite so understanding about Sally's report that there is a chance of her manager's getting Henry Atherton for the lead. Bill had heard about Henry from Olive. Just the same, it would be a great chance for her, Sally insists.

It is a great part she has, too, Sally reports. In one act she has to go mad, not very mad, just a little mad.

"I'm glad of that," registers Bill, with a relieved smile. "I don't like plays where people go *very* mad."

"Nor do I—though they're fun to do. What other kinds of plays don't you like?"

"Plays about men who are paralyzed from the waist down. Plays where a lot of people all get caught together in a catastrophe. A flood, or an earthquake, or an air-raid, and all face death in a lump. There's always a prostitute in those plays, have you noticed? Usually a clergyman too. That's what's called 'taking a cross-section of humanity.' I don't like plays about prostitutes."

"They're lovely to act. Olive's played lots. I haven't been one since I was in high school."

"I bet you were immense."

Bill has lighted a cigarette and is full of contentment when a new idea hits him. Sally is clearing off the table and taking the things into the kitchen.

"Well, things are looking up for you," Bill observes, as Sally moves back and forth. "The weather has changed. The rain is over, the winter is past, and the voice of the turtle is heard in our land."

"What did you say?" Sally has stopped in the kitchen door.

"I was quoting from the Bible."

"Turtles don't have voices, do they?"

"Turtle doves."

"I never could understand the Bible," Sally flings back at him as she goes on into the kitchen. "I don't see why they give it to children to read."

"You know we ought to do something to celebrate this job of yours," Bill calls after her. "Will you have dinner with me?"

"You took me to dinner last night." Sally has come back to the couch and taken off her jacket.

"So what?"

"So you shouldn't do it again."

"But I want to do it again. Very much. And what do you say we go to a theatre? That new musical. Do you like musicals?"

"I adore them. If they're good."

This being a good musical comedy, according to reports, it will probably be hard to get seats. Even at the brokers'. Bill had thought perhaps Olive would have some influence. She might, but Sally wouldn't like to ask her even if she had. And why?

"Well, you're her friend, and Olive is rather hot against that sort of thing," says Sally. "Beau-snatching. I don't know that I really ought to come at all."

Bill has come around to the front of the sofa to sit beside her. "Now, you listen to me," says he, a little sternly. "In the first place, you haven't snatched me. Any snatching that's been going on, *I've* been doing. And in the second, I'm not her beau . . . any more. She gave me the good, old-fashioned gate last night, even though I did suspect she was trying to leave it on the latch. The point is, we're going to that musical."

But how to get the seats? Sally explains that there is a way that works sometimes. There are what are known as "house seats." These are certain seats held out by the management for emergencies—for friends and influential people. It happens that Kenneth Bartlett is the producer of this hit. Sally knows Kenneth. But—

No buts for Bill. Let her phone Mr. Bartlett, tell him she has a friend in town for the week-end—a service man—and can he buy two seats for the show? She might add that this is her friend's last furlough. That will make it a better story.

Still Sally hesitates. It is a question of pride with her. She puts the question to Bill rhetorically: "Suppose someone had . . . not treated you badly, it's not that . . . suppose you had behaved badly to someone . . . do you think you ought to ask them for a favor?"

"I should hardly think so. What's this about? The theatre tickets?"

"No. Oh, no. Just general principles," Sally is quick to answer.

She is still pondering the thought when Billy suggests that they quit all abstract speculation and get lunch. He has come close to her and reached for both her hands.

"Sally, you're very sweet," he says. She looks up at him with surprise. "I haven't the faintest idea what goes on in that funny little head of yours, but you're very sweet."

He holds her hands and then kisses her gently, a kiss they hold for a moment. Then he releases her.

"Oh . . . that was a surprise," says Sally.

"Do you mind?"

"No, it was nice."

"I thought so, too. Come and show me where the things are."

Sally is a little more disturbed than before, as she follows Bill into the kitchen. She finds herself agreeing with him that scrambled eggs cooked in the double boiler are a lot nicer than they are cooked in a frying pan. Then she excuses herself and dashes into the bedroom, closing the door after her. She hesitates a moment as she starts to lift the telephone from its hook, but only for a moment. Soon she is in the midst of a lightly excited conversation with Kenneth Bartlett.

She explains to Kenneth the predicament of her soldier friend, who wanted terribly to see Kenneth's show. Yes, she was going with him. Told that the tickets will be at the box office in Sergt. Page's name, she is terribly thankful. And, of course, they will be ever so glad to have a drink with Kenneth during the intermission. "Ken, I read the notices," she says, sweetly. "I'm so glad it's such a hit. Well, thank you again . . . so much. Good-by, Ken."

She is a little bit exhausted from the strain as she hangs up, but the next minute she has flown back to the kitchen, arriving just as Bill is about to break the first egg into the double boiler. Just in time, too, to find him the egg beater. Scrambled eggs are always better if they are beaten.

"Bill . . ." she interrupts.

"What?"

SALLY—It's all right about tonight. I've got the tickets.

BILL—You have? How?

SALLY—I called up Kenneth Bartlett. They're at the theatre, in your name. You're to pick them up by seven o'clock. He wants us to have a drink with him in the intermission.

BILL—Good. What is he like?

SALLY—He's nice. Very.

BILL—What made you suddenly change your mind?

SALLY—I don't know. Yes, I do.

BILL—What was it?

SALLY—Your kissing me.

BILL—I don't quite see the connection.

SALLY—I don't think I could explain.

BILL—May I kiss you again for getting them?

SALLY—If you want to.

BILL—I do. (*He kisses her.*)   Thank you.
SALLY (*smiling*)—Thank *you.*
BILL—We're going to have a nice evening.   Now then . . .

He starts beating eggs in bowl as the curtain falls.

It is two o'clock in the morning when Sally and Bill arrive back at the apartment.   The living room is dark, but the radio is still on and the telephone is ringing.   As they let themselves in it is Sally's impulse to run to the phone, but Bill is quick to stop her.   Undoubtedly it is Olive who is calling, and Sally surely doesn't want to talk to Olive now.   Sally doesn't, but she has a hard time not doing it.   Fortunately the phone stops ringing about the time she is ready to weaken.

Sally suggests a drink.   Bill thinks he might do with a night-cap, but they both settle for milk and some cookies that Sally's mother had sent her from Joplin.   Sally likes her family, but she must confess she finds it hard to stand them for more than two weeks at a time any more.   "I hate myself for it," admits Sally.   "But it's no good trying.   I guess a family's really only good when you're sick . . . once you're grown up.   And I'm never sick.   So . . ."

Sally can't forget Olive and the telephone.   It is too bad, she thinks, that she and Bill had to run into Olive and her Ned at the theatre.   And worse that they had not seen them afterward.   But, they had had a drink with Kenneth at intermission, and had joined Kenneth's party at the Plaza after the show.   They had no chance to see anybody.   But Olive is sure to think they were avoiding her.

It has been an evening of adventures.   Bill had met Kenneth and liked him.   And agreed with Kenneth, too, when he said he thought Sally was a grand kid and a good little actress.   That pleases Sally.   For Bill it has been a grand evening and a grand day, except that he hasn't seen much of Sally.

"You've seen me steadily for the last thirty hours," Sally reminds him.

"I haven't.   I slept ten of them, damn it.   Spent three alone this afternoon getting a hotel room . . . sat beside you in a crowded theatre all evening, and shared you with a party of ten ever since.   Will you spend tomorrow with me, to make up?"

"I'd love to."

"Good."

Then Bill has a small confession to make.   The girl he had

gone across the Persian Room to speak to at the Plaza was the girl from Paris. It was the first time he had seen her in seven years.

"Were you engaged or anything?" Sally wants to know.

"We were engaged and everything," admits Bill. "We were going to be married that summer, but that was the summer things busted up for me. She couldn't see herself living in Pittsburgh with no money."

"Was it awful . . . seeing her again?"

"No. Not after the first moment. And that was funny, because . . . last night at the restaurant it did get me down, remembering it all. And then the minute we'd said hello, the corner of my mouth suddenly stopped twitching, and I found myself looking at her and wondering what the hell it had all been about. I don't know when I stopped loving her—I just stopped thinking of her, I guess, and didn't realize I had . . . until tonight. Last night must have been just a . . . sort of reflex action."

No, Bill hasn't been in love since, nor wanted to be. He doesn't believe in being unhappily in love, and he's not taking any chances. Sally understands. But she has learned tonight it does not feel good to be over being in love. She had been dreading meeting Kenneth Bartlett at the theatre. But the minute she had seen him everything was all right. She just thought how nice he was.

"It's a good feeling. But you're right. It is a little shocking," she says.

"I think it's only one's vanity that is shocked," suggests Bill. "One likes to think one's the kind that *doesn't* get over things."

SALLY—But you do think one *ought* to . . . get over them, I mean?

BILL—Good God, yes.

SALLY (*after a pause*)—It's funny our being in the same boat.

BILL (*moving to couch and taking her hand*)—It's a good boat, Sally.

SALLY—What?

BILL—Do you think . . . *my* coming along had anything to do with helping to set you free?

SALLY—I . . . don't know.

BILL—I'd like to think it did.

SALLY—I think it did.

BILL—I'm glad.

SALLY—So am I . . . Did—(*She stops.*)   No, I won't ask that.

BILL—Why not?

SALLY—No, I won't.

BILL—Were you going to ask whether *your* coming along helped to set *me* free?

SALLY—You don't have to answer that.   And I *didn't* ask it.

BILL—If I say I think I was free already . . . let me say, too, that I think it was your coming along that helped me to *know* I was, and that I'm very grateful.

SALLY—I'm glad.

BILL—So am I.   (*He draws her to him and kisses her.*) You're very sweet.

SALLY—You're very nice.

BILL—I couldn't have imagined . . . possibly . . . having so nice a time as this.

SALLY—Me, too.   I've had such awful week-ends here alone. (*Silence for a moment.   He continues to fondle her, his lips against her hair and cheek moving towards her lips again.   Again they kiss.   Then, suddenly, she thrusts him aside.*)

BILL—What's the matter?

SALLY—We mustn't go on like this.

BILL—Why not?

SALLY—Because I've given it up!

BILL—What?

SALLY—That sort of thing.

BILL—For Lent?

SALLY—No . . . permanently.

BILL (*protesting, laughing*)—Oh, Sally . . . darling . . .

SALLY—I have.   I'm sorry, but I have.

BILL—Why have you?

SALLY—I *can't* go on doing it with every man I meet.

BILL (*amused*)—Do you?

SALLY—I *did*.   No, I didn't, *really*, but . . . I've got to draw the line somewhere.

BILL—So you draw it at me?

SALLY—There's nothing personal about it.   I do *like* you, but . . . we mustn't go on like that.

BILL—I'm sorry.   Do you want me to go?

SALLY—No, but well, maybe you'd rather.

BILL—Because you won't let me make love to you?

SALLY—Yes.

BILL—Is this another of your theories about "men"?

SALLY—It's a true one. If you start something like that . . .
well, you've no right to start it, if you don't mean to go through
with it. And I *don't* mean to . . . and I shouldn't have started
it. And you've every right to be mad at me.

Bill's not mad. He may think she is a little absurd, but he
isn't mad—so long as she likes him and will let him come tomorrow. He will come early, if she will let him. They can have
breakfast and then perhaps, as Sally suggests, they can go for
a walk in the park, or to the Zoo, or take a bus ride as far as
The Cloisters, so long as they have the day together.

Who's going to call who in the morning, and at what time?
As for that, why shouldn't Bill stay there another night, even
if he has found a room outside? Then he can sleep as late as
he wants to, and they will do whatever they want to with the
rest of the day. Agreed.

Tonight, says Bill, it is his turn to tidy up. Sally should go
to bed first, having been up longest. After further persuasion
Sally agrees. In the bedroom she turns down her bed and starts
getting out of her dress. That stops her because the zipper
sticks. She pulls and hauls, but it still sticks. Finally she has
to call Bill from the kitchen. Bill also pulls this way and that,
but the zipper beats him, too.

Bill thinks if he had a pair of pliers he could do something.
Sally sends him to the tool-box in the kitchen. He's back in a
minute and the next instant with Sally holding her breath, the
zipper unzips its full length and Sally's dress falls to the floor.
She is left standing in her slip for an embarrassed second. She
reaches for her dress and is about to make a dash for the bedroom when Bill grabs her.

"Girls who wear zippers shouldn't live alone. Modern prov-
erb," says Bill.

Sally starts again for the bedroom, but now Bill holds her and
kisses her warmly. For a second she responds, but suddenly she
pulls herself away. "Don't, Bill, don't . . . please don't."

He lets her go and she goes back to the bedroom. Sitting on
the bed Sally takes off her shoes, hangs up her dress and goes
into the bathroom.

Bill, in the living room, is thoughtful and worried. He turns
down the bed, puts out the light in the kitchen and is sitting on
the couch starting to take off his shoes when suddenly he changes
his mind. "No, this is all too god-damned silly!' he murmurs.

He goes to the desk, takes paper and pencil and starts to write a note.

In the bedroom Sally comes from the bathroom in her pajamas, looking very small and young. Also very melancholy. She is near to tears as she turns out the bedlight and gets into bed.

Bill has finished his note and put it on the pillow of the day-bed, with a paper cutter on it. He turns out the desk light and is about to leave when Sally calls.

"Bathroom's all clear." Her voice is muffled. "Bill! I said the bathroom's all clear."

BILL (*coming into the room, cap in hand*)—Sally, I'm not staying.

SALLY—Why not?

BILL—Because it's silly.

SALLY—Why?

BILL—Well, because . . . as they'd say in one of those plays we both hate . . . because I'm a man, and you're a woman.

SALLY (*after a tiny pause—gravely, but with quote marks*)— And I . . . rouse the beast in you?

BILL—Exactly . . . So . . . I'll see you tomorrow. (*He starts to go.*)

SALLY (*in a small voice*)—Bill . . . there's a beast in me, too. (*He stands looking at her and then comes slowly to the bed.*) I'm sorry, Bill, for being such a fool.

BILL (*tenderly*)—Sally . . . (*He sits on the bed and takes her in his arms. She melts into him.*) Oh, Sally, sweet . . .

SALLY—Oh, Bill . . . (*The telephone rings. She starts, disengages herself, stretching out her hand.*)

BILL (*slapping her hand*)—Uh, huh. No.

SALLY (*looking stricken*)—Oh . . . (*He draws her into his arms again. She remains pressed against him, her cheek against his, looking at the telephone with scared eyes. Whispering.*) You shouldn't be here.

BILL—Ssh!

SALLY—She'll come around in the morning.

BILL—Let the morning look after itself. (*He kisses her again, and without breaking the embrace, switches out the bedlight, and lifts himself onto the bed. The telephone goes on ringing.*) I love you, Sally.

SALLY—No. No, don't say that. You mustn't. We must keep this gay.

BILL (*as telephone goes on ringing*)—Don't talk.
The curtain falls.

ACT III

It is around noon Sunday morning. In the living room a card table has been set for breakfast. In the bedroom Sally's bed has been made. The divan bed is still open and unslept in.

In the kitchen Sally has poured two glasses of orange juice. She puts one on the table and takes the other to the bathroom door for Bill. When Bill is ready and Sally would go on cooking the eggs, Bill won't let her. Let them at least have their coffee in peace, without a lot of hopping up and down.

It is going to be a grand day. It is Bill's idea that they should go out and get all the Sunday papers and really mess up the apartment. "I must have my funnies," confesses Bill. "It wouldn't be Sunday without Dick Tracy," admits Sally.

"This is so pleasant, Sally *dear*. Our second breakfast together. Quite an old married couple. You're nice to have breakfast with."

"So are you." Then after a pause: "Have you . . . have you had breakfast with a lot of girls?"

"Sally dear, that's not a question to ask *now*. If ever."

"I wasn't being curious . . . about your life, I mean. I was just wondering whether there was a lot of difference between girls at breakfast."

"Yes. A lot."

Sally would be quite inquisitive if Bill would let her, but he is firm. Let her be herself and not worry about things. Then the bell rings.

"Olive!" mutters Sally in a stricken whisper.

"Don't answer it!" orders Bill.

But that doesn't settle anything. In excited whispers they decide the best thing to do is for Bill to take the breakfast table and himself into the kitchen. In a furious scramble they manage to get all such telltale evidence as Bill's coat out of the room. Then Sally goes to the door and greets Olive with creditable surprise.

"I've been ringing and ringing," announces Olive with a show of spirit.

"I'm sorry. I was in the bathroom," calmly answers Sally. "I *thought* I heard the buzzer."

There is a good deal of fencing after that, Sally pacing the floor and straightening up things while Olive plies her with questions. In the kitchen Bill has poured himself another cup of coffee and is sitting by the sink listening.

Olive would like to know why Sally was out until after 3 o'clock the night before, and where? They had gone to the Persian Room with Ken, Sally reports. They had met Ken at the theatre. She and Bill were also with Ken having a drink at intermission. It was Ken who had managed to get tickets for them.

Sally suddenly remembers Bill's cap in the bedroom. By pretending to hear the telephone she manages to get into the bedroom and hide the cap in the drawer of the night table. Then she comes hurriedly back.

"You and Bill have certainly been seeing a lot of each other," quizzically observes Olive.

"Well, I don't think he knows many people in New York," blandly answers Sally.

"So you thought you'd be kind to him." Olive's tone takes on a sarcastic edge.

"It wasn't a question of being kind to him," snaps Sally, with a glance toward the kitchen. "He's very nice. Very nice indeed."

"I know he is. I introduced him to you. Where did he finally end up staying?"

"He got a room at the Hotel . . . Taft."

"Is he there now, do you know?"

"How should I know?"

"Would you mind if I called him up?"

"No, of course not."

Olive goes into the bedroom to phone, and drags Sally with her for company. Good thing, too, because the first thing Olive does is to start to look in the drawer of the night table for the phone book. Sally, remembering Bill's hat, is quick to interrupt her. Bill, sneaking out from the kitchen, is also looking for his cap, but finally goes without it.

Olive gets the Hotel Taft, but the clerk can't find Mr. Page. This naturally adds to Olive's peevishness. Altogether it has been a bad week-end for her. She didn't like Kenneth's show; she was terribly disappointed in Ned Burling, who decided he wanted to spend most of his leave playing gin rummy, and she isn't at all pleased with Sally's taking over Bill Page.

"You know, I'm a fool," Olive concludes. "That's what's the matter with me. Trusting everyone. Gullible Gertie. You . . . who were so worried about yourself the other afternoon . . .

who were going to 'give it all up.' "

"Well, I meant that."

"Only Bill came along, and, you couldn't keep your hands off him."

"Olive . . . I think you'd better go!"

Sally is angry. Also agonized imagining that Bill is hearing. Before Olive can leave, as she is quite prepared to do, the phone rings. Even Olive can hear it this time.

Sally dashes into the bedroom. The call is from Bill. "Yes . . . yes . . . of course you can come around. Olive's here," says Sally sweetly. "She's just been calling you at the Taft."

"Let me talk to him," calls Olive, barging into the bedroom. And she does. Bill, Olive reports, is at a drugstore near by and will be right over. She will wait and just say hello to him. She has already forgotten Sally's anger. And so has Sally.

Suddenly Sally remembers something she has to give the elevator man. As tactfully as she can she gets Olive out of the bedroom, covers Bill's cap with a copy of *Vogue* magazine and manages to get it past Olive and into the hall. It's the elevator man's wife who likes *Vogue*, she explains.

Sally is obviously so pleased with what she has done that Olive is a shade suspicious. Olive hopes Sally isn't getting silly and sentimental about Bill. If she is she is in for a big disappointment.

"I've no intention of getting sentimental," affirms Sally.

"No, darling—no intention—but you're the kind who can't sew a button on for a man without thinking it's for life. And Bill told me, over and over again, that he'd no place for sentiment in his scheme of things."

"Well, I've told you before, neither have I . . . any more. So that's fine."

Bill is at the door. He is carrying a morning paper and a bunch of daffodils for Sally.

Olive would fix things with Bill, if she could. Her husband's train goes at four and Bill will have until ten. Perhaps they could have dinner together. Or at least a cocktail. Bill is already dated for both hours.

Then the telephone rings and Sally discovers that she is wanted right away for a rehearsal. The leading man of her show has been fired and Henry Atherton has been hired. They want her to run through the part with Atherton. No, she won't have time to lunch with Bill first, but perhaps he can take her there. She'll go and change.

Olive is worried about Sally—and Henry Atherton, but Bill is sure Sally can take care of herself.

"Oh, yes, she can . . . if she wants to," agrees Olive. "But a star's a star. And she's always had a crush on him, you know. By the way, can you still not manage cocktails?"

"I'm afraid I can't, Olive."

"Well, let me know next time you're coming, won't you? And I won't let anything interfere."

"Olive, I'm afraid I don't play around with married women."

"Oh, but that's all over. We talked it out thoroughly. I'm not seeing him again."

"You mean—you're divorcing?"

"Yes."

"Do you think it looks well—to divorce a service man?"

"What are you trying to say?"

"Just . . . very tactfully, and with no hard feelings, that I think we'd better . . . leave things as they are."

"Well, I guess I bought that! I've got a lunch with my ex. Good-by, Bill."

"Good-by, Olive."

And that, as Bill tells Sally a moment later, is what he fears is the end of a beautiful friendship. For her, too, Sally suspects.

Bill is not altogether pleased to discover that Sally is to re-hearse with Henry Atherton at his apartment, even if the prac-tice is quite common with stars. How long will it take? All afternoon? Bill doesn't like that, either. What's he going to do? He can come back to the apartment, if he likes. She will give him the key. Yes, she will have dinner with him.

"Sally, I don't see anything of you . . . at all." He has stopped and is holding her. "I want to talk to you . . . about so many things."

"No—why?" answers Sally, shyly. "We don't need to talk. There's nothing to talk about. We've had a lovely time . . . We don't want to get . . . sentimental about it. Do we?"

"I guess not." Bill's disappointment is plain.

"Well, then. Come along. I'm late." She picks up her script and starts out. He is standing still. "Aren't you coming?"

"Sure."

"I'll ring for the elevator."

She has gone. Bill is staring after her. He puts out his ciga-rette, his face puzzled and unhappy, picks up his hat, shrugs and follows after. The curtain falls.

About six-thirty that evening Bill is back in Sally's apartment.

He has set up the card table, put the daffodils in a bowl in the center of it, brought out champagne glasses and all the attractive silver and dishes he can find.   The room is abloom with Spring flowers.

At the moment Bill is kneeling on the divan, looking anxiously out the window for Sally.   Presently he catches sight of her and rushes into the kitchen for the champagne.

Sally is properly surprised at the preparations for her home-coming and greatly pleased, especially with the floral decorations.   Bill's a darling and she kisses him lightly as a reward. But she thinks they will be having something of a scratch dinner. No.   Bill has seen to that, too.   Everything's arranged for. Everything's lovely.   Now they can have their drink to the Spring.

Sally is excited about her reherasal.   That had gone fine and Henry Atherton was good.   Sally has an idea that this engagement may prove to be the very thing she has been waiting for. Which brings a bit of a frown to Bill's face.

"Sally, this is our Spring, isn't it?" he asks, coming to sit beside her on the sofa.   "We'll have it together?"

"Of course . . . if you're going to be here."

"I think I am.   I think I can count on the Spring and Summer . . . if I'm lucky.   I've been thinking of it all afternoon. Things that we can do. . . ."

Suddenly Sally is busying herself hunting for a cigarette.   Bill senses an effort to discourage him.   He had planned the dinner so that he might have a chance to talk to her.

"I wish you wouldn't," she says, moving away from him.

BILL—Sally . . . if I told you that . . . given the littlest possible encouragement from you . . . I think I could be . . . very much in love with you . . . what would you say?

SALLY (*after a second*)—I wouldn't give it to you.

BILL—Why not?

SALLY—Because I don't want you to be in love with me . . . or think you are.

BILL—Why don't you?

SALLY—Because that isn't how we started this.

BILL—Sally, you don't go into a love affair *deliberately* . . .

SALLY—I know, but . . . I don't want it to *be* like that.   This is . . . fun.

BILL—Will it be any less fun if I'm in love with you?

SALLY (*positively*)—Oh . . . yes.   Bill, we don't have to talk about it. It has been fun . . . it *is* fun . . . it can go on being fun, if you don't spoil it.

BILL—That is a remark I seem to have heard before . . . but not from anyone like you.

SALLY—What do you mean?

BILL—It's the kind of thing old-fashioned women used to say . . . the older, married women . . . when they wanted to keep you hanging around.

SALLY—But I do want to keep you . . . well, not *hanging* around . . . but *around* . . . if you want to be.

BILL—I do.

SALLY—Well, then . . .

BILL (*after a moment*)—I can't be so crazy as to have got you *all* wrong, but . . . you baffle me, Sally.

SALLY—I don't see why.

BILL—I guess it's the times.

SALLY (*puzzled*)—The *Times?*

BILL—I don't mean the newspaper. I mean . . . the times . . . the war, or something. Or perhaps it's the theatre.

SALLY—I don't know what you're talking about.

BILL (*going to her*)—Sally, you're not the kind of girl who has affairs . . . promiscuously . . . Or are you?

SALLY—I don't know.

BILL—What do you mean by that?

SALLY—I don't know what constitutes "promiscuously." I have affairs. I mean, I've had affairs.

BILL (*quietly*)—Many affairs?

SALLY—You told me that was a question that one shouldn't ask.

BILL—I was quite right. One shouldn't. Sally, if I said that rather than keep this . . . just an affair . . . I'd sooner . . . call the whole thing off—what would you say?

SALLY (*slowly*)—I think I'd say . . . we'd better call it off.

Sally frankly is afraid of being hurt. She has been before—twice—and she is determined not to be hurt again. Bill is not pleased that Sally has had two previous experiences. Two is not a great number, but it is two too many for Sally. He does think, too, that affairs are different for a man. At least he thinks "the permissible number is different for a man." Of course he had guessed about Sally. He had not really believed the pajama story. But now he seriously wants their meeting to *mean* something to her. If it doesn't Bill will feel as though a door had been slammed right bang in his face.

"As if the Spring had suddenly turned around and said, 'That's all there is. Now you can go back to Winter.'"

"Not Winter," protests Sally, her voice a little uncertain. "We can keep it Spring."

BILL—Nothing *stays* Spring. I wouldn't want it to be. There'd be something stultified and horrible about the Spring, if it always stayed like that. It's *got* to become Summer, and Fall, and . . .

SALLY (*bitterly*)—Winter.

BILL—Yes, one day. But for both of us . . . at the same time. Sally, I am in love with you. There's still time to turn back . . . for me to turn back, I mean . . . without it's hurting too much. I told you I didn't believe in being unhappily in love. I don't. And I'm not going to be. I'm not having an awfully happy time right now. None of us are. That's not a bid for pity. It's just telling you why I feel this way. I gave up looking forward to anything seven years ago, and I've got along all right that way. With . . . Olive . . . and taking what came. That's how I wanted it. And I can go on like that. But I can't begin again . . . hoping . . . and wanting . . . and planning . . . unless there is *some* chance of those plans working out. *You're* scared of getting hurt again. Well, so am I. *Bitterly* scared.

SALLY (*almost in tears*)—What do you *want?*

BILL (*sitting beside her*)—I want you to let yourself love me . . . if you *can*. Because I think you can. I think you've a great talent for love, Sally, and that you're trying to fritter it and dissipate it . . . because it's been trodden on before. And if you go like that, you'll kill it. And . . . (*Slowly.*) I think that's one talent that *is* death to hide. (SALLY *bursts into tears.*) Yes, cry, if you want to. Please, please cry. Only . . . don't shut me out . . . and don't shut yourself out.

SALLY (*sobbing*)—Oh, Bill . . .

BILL—I'm not asking such a great deal. I want to marry you. But we won't talk of *that,* yet. I want you to love me . . . *terribly*. But I'm not even asking that of you, yet . . .

SALLY (*between tears*)—I *do* love you. I love you terribly. That's the hell of it. (*Scrambling to her knees on the couch, beside him.*) I won't make scenes, Bill. I won't be troublesome . . . I won't . . .

BILL—Ssh. You've said all I wanted you to say now. (*Kissing her lightly.*) Drink up your cocktail. It's getting warm.

SALLY (*gulping it and tears at the same time*)—I shall be tight again. I haven't had any food.

BILL—What—not all day? You must have dinner right away. Come and sit down.

SALLY—It'll take a little while to fix.

BILL—It's all fixed. They're sending it up from next door. From . . . "our place." It's coming up at seven. And the first course is in the icebox. Vichysoisse. I'll get it right now.

SALLY—Bill . . .

BILL (*at kitchen door*)—You pour yourself another drink and sit down. Pour me one, too. (*He goes to the kitchen. SALLY, moving a little as if in a dream, pours two more drinks. BILL returns with the soup.*) There. (*He bends and kisses her, lightly again. Then, standing waiter-like, with his napkin over his arm.*) Madame est servie.

SALLY (*still blinking away the tears, dips a spoon and tastes*) —Oh, Bill, this is heaven.

BILL (*who hasn't touched his—looking at her*)—Isn't it?

"He puts out his hand, and holds hers. They look at each other and smile, and then, still holding hands, dip their spoons and begin to eat."

THE CURTAIN FALLS

DECISION

A Drama in Three Acts

By Edward Chodorov

EDWARD CHODOROV is one of the younger American dramatists who is whole-heartedly devoted to the theatre and to the profession of writing for the theatre. He will write, and has written, for the producers of motion pictures if and when an assignment interests him, and when its indulgence seems practical. But, goodness, how he hates it.

Mr. Chodorov happens to have been the first American playwright in the field this season. It was mid-June when Max Gordon offered his war-time romance, "Those Endearing Young Charms," on Broadway. This comedy was generally endorsed by the play reviewers on its merits as a written work, but as generously condemned as a story that was obviously vacillating in "coming to grips with reality." It was, in effect, the same story that was later told in John Van Druten's "The Voice of the Turtle," but missed the charm of that sensational success in the personnel of its cast and the skill of its staging.

Following the failure of "Those Endearing Young Charms," which was withdrawn after fifty-three performances, Mr. Chodorov accepted one of those Hollywood assignments he so frankly resents. He was on the Coast for five weeks, and during that time he wrote "Decision." This in addition to his picture chores. "Decision," he believed strongly, was a play that should be written and a subject that should be seriously treated in the theatre.

After five weeks he brought his manuscript to Broadway and offered it to every manager of outstanding prominence in New York. None of them would assume the responsibilities of production. People, they said, were not interested in, nor would they endorse, a play dealing with the threat of Fascism on the home front. In the end, Mr. Chodorov, in association with Edward Choate and a few other friends, backed his own play.

Neither audience nor critical response was enthusiastic or immediate, but "Decision" grew steadily in favor with serious-minded playgoers. It was, by the record, the first serious drama

133

of the year to give signs of achieving success on its merits as drama and its timeliness of theme.

The scene of Mr. Chodorov's play is "an American city in the present." The action begins in the office of Superintendent Riggs of the High School. In a conference room adjoining the Riggs office a citizens' meeting is being held. In the office Miss Baines is at work at the filing cabinets, trying a little wearily to find the proper places for a stack of cards. "Miss Baines is a spinster of thirty-odd, wears clutch-nose glasses . . . though of a naturally sweet disposition, many years of exposure to the infinite deviltries of adolescence have given her a protective acidity."

Miss Baines' temper at the moment is not greatly helped by the appearance of an inquisitive redhead, name of Felix, who has many pestering questions to ask. Nor by the coming of Harriet Howard, one of the younger teachers, "a pretty, intelligent-looking girl of twenty-two, dressed for the street." Harriet is pale and tense and definitely worried, managing to look, as Miss Baines suggests, a little "like Saint Joan in the flames."

Through worrying Harriet has managed to acquire a touch of stomach trouble—"butterflies, with bayonets"—and is frank to confess it. Tommy Riggs, the Superintendent's son, is expected home at seven-thirty. It has been two years, a week, three days —and ten hours—since Tommy went to war. And Harriet's convinced he must have changed.

"He's been wounded," she reminds Miss Baines; "but he's all right. . . . And he's killed men . . . I don't see how he could be the same—any more than *I'm* the girl I was two years ago."

It is hard for Harriet to explain just why she is scared to death. "You keep writing letters," she says, "and once in a while you get some back. And though you keep *writing* to each other in the same way—you keep wondering—what he's really like now—and what he thinks about you. . . . When you haven't seen someone for so long—even if there wasn't a way . . . it's like a stranger coming back . . . I'm so afraid he might have outgrown me . . . he might think I'm very small town."

"Small town?"

"Comparatively—"

MISS BAINES—God knows I'd sooner be found dead than defending this miserable little city. The best thing they could do with it is wipe it out and start all over again! But I know, if they did, we'd wind up with Masters—and his *Free Press*—God save the name—and his Fuhrer—Senator Dufresne. I saw the great man today—

HARRIET—Dufresne?—Did you—?

MISS BAINES—Mm. Riding around town with Masters, in an open car. Inspecting the—holocaust, no doubt. I hope they were very pleased.

HARRIET—Explain something to me? (MISS BAINES *inclines her head.*) Senator Dufresne *is* a Senator—and an American—an old American family. . . . *How* can he let Masters use his newspaper to start a riot—in a *war* plant?

MISS BAINES—Harriet, you're a fool. Masters is a very patriotic man—and Dufresne saves the country every day of his life.

HARRIET—There isn't a human being in this town over the age of twelve who doesn't know the truth about Dufresne and Masters and the *Free Press!*

MISS BAINES—Do they buy it and read it?

HARRIET—They don't believe it.

MISS BAINES—Did they elect Dufresne? Girly, you just worry about Tommy for a while, will you? Now go home and take a nice hot bath and relax. Then go down to the station and get your boy.

HARRIET—I want to take Mr. Riggs with me—

MISS BAINES—He'll be there. He's just as excited as you are, believe me.

HARRIET—*Please* tell him I'm waiting for him? Please?

MISS BAINES—Honey, I can't. They've got the President and Vice-President of the Business Men's group in there—showing them the affidavits—

HARRIET—Did they *get*—the business men? That's good!

MISS BAINES—I don't know if they've *got* them—but if they don't *get* them, they may as well throw their whole citizen's committee in the ashcan—

HARRIET—Why do you say "affidavits"? Are there more?

MISS BAINES—One more—but a good one, from the man that did the actual *hiring* of the gangsters that walked into the Anderson plant that night. This one got his orders from Masters, direct—

HARRIET—That's wonderful!

Harriet has just started for the door when the meeting breaks up and those attending come into the office. They include, in addition to Superintendent Riggs, Anderson, who owns the plant;

his lawyer, Bennett; a colored delegate, Jim; a woman delegate, Mrs. Bowen, and Fitzgerald, a union foreman who has favorably impressed Miss Baines as "quite a figure of a man."

Echoes of the meeting come through the conversation. "In the long run we will accomplish very little by running to Washington and the Attorney General with a complaint about a hired man," Riggs is saying. "But we'll do our community—and perhaps the whole country—a service by pinning those affidavits where they belong—on the honorable chest of Senator Dufresne."

The others are agreed that Riggs is right, but are also convinced that he has chosen a hard way in deciding to attack "in the place where victory will mean 'unconditional surrender' of the whole reactionary clique here in the State."

BENNETT—Dufresne can be a very dangerous man for much less reason.

RIGGS (*quietly*)—Good. Excellent. I am certainly not in the least afraid of him myself, Mr. Bennett. (*Looks at his watch.*) But I *am* afraid I must leave you—

BROWN—Just one more word, Mr. Riggs, if you please. Axton and I have promised you that our people will go along with you, personally, whatever you decide to do. But we hope that you *will* keep this a real "Citizens' Committee"—and not a front for any special interest—whether it's your plant, Mr. Anderson, important as that is—or the labor unions—or the organized Negro.

RIGGS—I can promise you that because *without* your people— the average citizen, which I myself am—I'd have no place on this committee.

FITZGERALD—Well, let's not kid ourselves, Mr. Riggs! There wouldn't *be* any committee without you!

BROWN—Exactly. With all due respect—a lot of our people hate the unions, especially the organized Negro, just as much as Masters and the *Free Press* do. A lot more of 'em are Washington-haters from way back, and never got over it. But we'll bring 'em all in on the basis of your leadership and your integrity, Mr. Riggs—because they know you're honest.

RIGGS—I hope not. (*They look at him.*) I hope they come along with us for a much better reason than that. My own reason—(*Takes* Mrs. BOWEN *by the arm.*) Mrs. Bowen's face—as she looked at her husband that night of the riot . . . (*Touches the colored boy's shoulder.*) Jim Morgan holding his father in his arms . . . and those other dead and wounded men and women lying on the ground—for no reason—except the insanity of lunatics in high places. They *must* be opposed. They must be *licked*. If I can serve you to that end, I will, very gratefully and with all my heart.

Riggs and Harriet have gone to meet Tommy. The others linger for a moment, congratulating themselves upon gaining the leadership of such a man as Riggs. They've got a fine, clean leader, Anderson agrees, and they should back him up with everything they have. "If we can match his guts we won't be beat," says Mrs. Bowen.

They have left now, all except Fitzgerald. Miss Baines would hold him to suggest that if there is anything she can do nights—in the way of secretarial work, for instance—she'd like to offer it as her bit. As it happens Fitzgerald has five daughters—all secretaries—so he doesn't think he will be needing more help than he can get at home.

"If—anything happens to all five of 'em some night, I'll call on you," promises Fitzgerald.

"Thank you," snaps Miss Baines, exhaling sharply as she stares after him. The curtain falls.

The living room of the Riggs home is modestly furnished, immaculately clean and well kept. There is a fireplace, with bookshelves on the upper side of it, windows looking out across a porch and another window disclosing a small garden. A large oval table is evidently used frequently as a work desk, and a smaller low table holds a humidor and pipes. A comfortable couch and a small armchair are near the fireplace.

Tommy Riggs, Father Riggs and Harriet Howard are just coming in the front door. Harriet sends Tommy, carrying a bag, on ahead and for a moment he stands in the center of the room looking slowly, fondly around at familiar objects. Tommy "is a boy of twenty-three or four wearing the uniform and insignia of a Sergeant in the Engineers."

"Well—I'm home," Tommy exclaims, after a moment. He takes off his hat, tosses it carefully at the hatrack in the hall, admits with a chuckle that he can still miss it, and turns to throw his arms around his father, putting his face affectionately against the older man's cheek.

He turns now to grab Harriet and kiss her violently on the lips. "Harrie, you look like a bloody angel, as the Tommies say. And you smell—like the Garden of Eden."

Tommy looks like a bloody angel to them, too, Riggs and

Harriet agree. And he smells of iodoform. Tommy is all right, he is quick to assure them. He had checked in at a base hospital in New York and they had given him a once-over. He can't bend over far enough to touch the floor, but who the hell wants to do that, anyway? Tommy, it appears, had caught a small slug in his back the time a bloody jerk had kicked a mine when they were throwing a tank track across a stream. "No matter how much you teach some guys they *never* learn," he explains.

He feels a little conscious, holding his father's hand, but he's afraid to let go, he says, for fear he'll wake up. And now he has pulled Harriet down to the couch on the other side of him and has his arms around the two of them.

"I'm beginning to loosen up," Tommy says, with a heavy sigh. "Hey, when I got off the train and saw the poolroom still shining across the street from the station I wanted to bust out crying. I couldn't see the trees in the park, but I could hear 'em! . . ."

Tommy is all set for the greatest week of his life. A *week?* That's right. "They're switching me to the Quartermaster Corps and sending me to school in New Jersey," he explains. "That'll be a few months anyway, if I last."

He'll be wanting them to come to New York to see him. And will Harrie marry him, right away? She will. And how, really, is his father? He looks tired. Hasn't been sick or anything? No, Pop's all right. And whatever has happened to Virgie? Virgie is working in the Anderson plant they tell him. And the plant! He wouldn't know it now. It's spread out all over the North Side. Fifteen thousand employees now.

Tommy is wandering through the house now; across the hall into the dining room and on into the kitchen. The kitchen faucet, he reports when he comes wandering back, is leaking again. He'll bet he has fixed that one a hundred times. . . .

Then Virgie comes. Virgie "is a stout colored woman of about sixty, with a mobile face and alert eyes, who shakes from top to toe when she laughs." And is Virgie glad to see Tommy! She has clasped him to her ample bosom with a hearty hug. "Look at you, Tommy! Just look at you!" . . .

Five minutes later the toot of an automobile horn has taken Virgie away. That would be her share-the-ride car. Virgie hasn't got a car to pool with the other workers, but she hasn't told them yet, so she's riding free. . . . She's gone now—to brag about her boy who's come back—with ribbons.

Harriet's Aunt May pops in. Aunt May is an attractive, fussy little woman and she, too, is awfully glad to see Tommy and to find him looking so fine. Supper? Of course Tommy is invited to supper—with or without a ration book. "God never sends the mouth but he sends the meat," quotes Aunt May like a true optimist. Then she pops out again.

Tommy, Harriet and Father settle back to recollections and to hopes Tommy's furlough has inspired. Tommy is serious in thinking that he and Harriet better be making up their minds about their marriage arrangements. Harriet is ready to do anything Tommy suggests, but isn't a week a pretty short leave after a year and a half? It is, but there had also been leaves on the other side, which explains that.

Tommy is full of reminiscences about his adventures in Sicily. He went looking for movie gangsters there. Nice folks in Sicily. They threw flowers at the boys. Some of the flowers weighed as much as five pounds. And when you caught one of these dropped from a three-story window—boy! No, he didn't find any movie gangsters, but he did come on a bunch of kids in a classroom—

"And what do you think they were doing? Yeah—practicing a verb altogether—like poor little suckers everyplace—'Io mi amazzo—tu se amazzi—Egli si amazza'—and what do you think *that* means? 'I assassinate myself—you assassinate him—he assassinates me'— No kidding! Sicily!"

They laugh at this, but Tommy is pretty serious. He thinks suddenly of the contrasting emotions he had when he got home. "I left a few nice guys in Sicily—with flowers growing on 'em," he says, and then quickly adds: "I'll tell you one thing I learned. I *didn't* forget . . . when we slipped into New York, in a fog . . . You couldn't see a bloody thing . . . and then it was on top of you . . . I could hear a streetcar, and I got a chill up my back . . . and I kept thinking—'breathes there the man with soul so dead, Who never to himself hath said, This is my own, my native land . . .' You know . . ." Now he has paused, a little irritatedly. "Now, what the hell! I swore I wouldn't talk about it—and that's all I've been doing!"

Harriet has taken his hand, and Pop has moved over to be nearer him. "Talk away, son. We want to hear."

"I can't, Pop. I'm getting it now. You know, after all New York wasn't home to me. And this is. And, brother, how . . ."

Pop Riggs is glad that Tommy remembered the Scott poem

about his native land. There are other excellent lines in that
poem worth remembering, too. For instance—

> " 'In peace, love tunes the shepherd's reed;
>   In war, he mounts the warrior's steed;
>   In halls, in gay attire is seen;
>   In hamlets, dances on the green.
>   Love rules the court, the camp, the grove,
>   And men below and saints above;
>   For love is heaven, and heaven is love.' "

Harriet and Tommy are alone. Pop has gone to bed. They
have come to talking about themselves and the immediacy of
their own affairs, *officially*, as it were. "Honey, there is something I have been saving up for two years to ask you," Tommy
is saying.

"What, Tommy?"

TOMMY—Harrie, when did you first think you could go for
me? That's a screwy question, isn't it? Well, when you're laying around over there—especially when that mud begins creeping through your clothes, and your skin—you pull the blanket
over your head and think of the damndest things—you know—
what am I going to do when I get home? How's Harrie—?
What's she doing right now—this minute? Is that gym teacher
—the guy with the muscles and the bad eyes—is he blinking
those glasses at her . . . ?

HARRIET (*putting her arms around his head*)—Dearest—

TOMMY—Is Pop sitting at his desk—this minute—still rubbing
his head like he does? That's what you think. And I began to
wonder—how did it start with us? I never bought you a soda—
or carried your books in my life! I didn't even like you. I
thought you were too skinny. And your mouth was funny—
crooked—and you always had that—you know—"put 'em up"
look! (*Puts up his fists.*)

HARRIET—Suspicious.

TOMMY—Yeah. Then one day—I'm sitting under a tree with
you, in the Park—and there was a look on your face . . . I
thought if I didn't grab hold of you then . . . you know?

HARRIET (*stroking his face*)—Yes, Tommy.

TOMMY—How did that happen?

HARRIET—If I tell you—you won't have anything to think
about—in New Jersey.

Tommy—I don't have to think in New Jersey! Come on, Harrie.

Harriet—Well . . . (*Stops.*) I don't know that I *should* tell you—

Tommy—Oh, yes, you've got to!

Harriet—All right. Do you remember the day—Thanksgiving Day—the game where you caught a long forward pass . . . ? About fifty yards, I think . . .

Tommy—Yeah . . . ?

Harriet—Well, when you caught that pass—on the tips of your fingers—running down the field without stopping—and everyone gasped and then they yelled and yelled—and you curved behind the goal posts like a race horse . . .

Tommy—You mean that was it?

Harriet—That was it.

Tommy (*incredulously*)—Catching that pass?

Harriet—Mm—hm. I said to myself, That's my man.

Tommy isn't quite sure that Harriet isn't kidding him. The idea of a girl's falling in love with a man for a thing like catching a forward pass! What about his personality?

Well, Harriet admits, there was something else, too. "Watching you in class . . . and the way you became just another pupil instead of the principal's son," she explains. "And the way you made the teachers explain what they meant when they said something you didn't understand—and still nobody thought you were showing off—because you weren't—and the way that big bully Michael Baldwin used to ride you—and you used to kid him—and the day you really got mad—and put your sandwich down—and hit him—and then picked him up—and then sat down and finished your sandwich—and, oh, millions of things I could never remember—except that little by little I knew you were the boy all right . . . And then you caught that pass . . ."

"Harrie, I'm so nutty about you—"

They are just reaching for each other when the doorbell rings. It isn't a welcome interruption. The caller is Ed Masters, an aggressive, self-satisfied fellow. The information that Mr. Riggs has gone to bed does not stop him. He comes in anyway. He is glad to meet Tommy, glad to congratulate him on his overseas mission—

The elder Riggs is coming down the stairs now in his shirt sleeves. He is plainly more resentful than curious about the Masters call, but submits to the five-minute talk in private that

Masters suggests. Tommy and Harriet promptly make themselves scarce.

When Riggs and Masters are alone, Masters is as gentle and persuasive as may be in explaining that he has come only for a friendly chat. This Citizens' Committee that Riggs is fostering —does Riggs consider that a good thing in these days of conflict and confusion?

Mr. Riggs does. As he sees it such conflict and confusion as exists has been largely created by Mr. Masters' newspaper, the *Free Press*. He (Riggs) is acting as an individual, and not as tool of any interest or of any group. As for the Citizens' Committee, it certainly must mean a great deal to Mr. Masters or he would not be there in protest against it. "Our committee represents the vast majority of our citizens who have waked up, at last, to the danger of a corrupt, reactionary political group which has brought terror and murder to us," declares Riggs. "You've gone too far, Masters. They will not tolerate it any longer."

"Mr. Riggs, I edit a newspaper," answers Masters. "I say what I believe to be true and for the benefit of the community. You may not agree with me, but do you think I should be persecuted for my opinion?"

"I believe you have no opinion."

"What?"

"If I had the money and the inclination I believe I could establish a newspaper here and pay you well to print opinions directly opposed to those you now hold—" Masters would stop the attack, but Riggs continues to ride over him; "which is precisely why we will not 'persecute' you—only insofar as you are an employee of Senator Dufresne."

Now the fat is completely in the fire and Masters is livid with anger. Riggs, however, has no intention of withdrawing a single charge. He would rather add a few. It is Senator Dufresne who owns the *Free Press*, and it is the Senator who was criminally responsible for the race riot in the Anderson plant two months before. Of that the Citizens' Committee has documentary proof, which it has taken out of the hands of a corrupt city administration and will present directly to the Attorney General of the United States. Furthermore Mr. Masters is at liberty to inform his employer that it is the intention of the Citizens' Committee to make every effort to involve Senator Dufresne personally, holding that he and the *Free Press*, which he owns, have consistently played on the theme of race hatred and race discrimination—

"Now wait," interrupts Masters, with a smile. "Let's get me straight. I was born here, in a white, native Protestant community—and I intend to restore it to that position before I'm through. I'm going to get rid of this army of niggers and trash that Anderson has presented us—along with the rape and disease which he and Washington gave us for nothing."

"Have you tried to correct these conditions?"

"Correct? I'm no 'idealistic reformer,' man! You high-flying Hottentot Missionaries want to 'Win the war and reform the world!' Bunk! We won't win any war if we keep giving in to these damn socialist slogans—or what we win won't be worth winning!"

"I disagree with you completely, Masters. I believe we will win only if we extend democracy to its fullest extent everywhere —and now—so that all men understand exactly why we fight. Especially our many millions of colored citizens."

"Now look, Riggs—on the level—who do you think you are? Abe Lincoln? Going to free the nigger all over again? Well, he's not going to be free—not to stand up and work as an equal with the decent white man—and certainly not to draw the same pay—not permanently—not around here—not while I'm around. I don't want you to make any mistake about my personal opinion."

"I realize, Masters, that I have made no mistake."

It is his war contracts that have induced Anderson to open his plant to colored workmen, Masters charges; it may also have been in response to government decisions, but weren't these decisions made by "a bunch of communistic New Dealers and labor racketeers?" "Kowtowing to Washington bureaucrats doesn't spell patriotism to me!" shouts Masters.

Furthermore he would remind Riggs that he (Riggs) is an employee of the city; that he had no right to hold school meetings of disaffected elements with the purpose of disturbing the peace "in time of war"; that the Riggs job is education and that he should leave politics to practical men.

It is because many practical men are deeply worried that they are joining such organizations as the Citizens' Committee, Riggs is quick to point out, but the argument is not convincing to Masters—

"A bunch of frightened rats who make their money selling to the Anderson plant," he sneers. "Joining up with a lot of lousy labor leaders and nigger radicals because some screwy bastards in

Washington tell 'em it's okay—!"

"Stop! There are ways of criticizing your government . . ."

MASTERS—Yes, and I use 'em all! I have my newspaper, thank God, and I'm not telling you anything you can't read on every page of my paper every day of the week.

RIGGS—We believe you have used other means. We have sworn affidavits that show you have used paid assassins.

MASTERS—That's a filthy lie! Anderson and Bennett can bribe all the bums in Christendom to sign all the affidavits on God's green earth! They're a tissue of lies from start to finish— and that's why they're trying to put 'em out through a "Citizens' Committee." But they wouldn't *have* any citizens if they didn't have you—and that's why you're getting *off* that committee, Riggs, just as fast as you got on!

RIGGS (*losing his control fast*)—I shall do nothing of the sort —*nothing* of the sort—

MASTERS—Listen, you damn fool, do you think you're going to be allowed to attack the Senator with a charge like that—right here in his home town? Have you any idea who stands behind Dufresne in the state?

RIGGS (*almost trembling*)—No, I have not. I should like to hear. For whom does he speak? Certainly not his own people— whom he must regard with the contempt you so ably express on his behalf, every day of the week—

MASTERS—Now, listen—

RIGGS—No. No, sir—it is your turn to listen. Since you speak for the "city"—I apologize to you for my unwarranted use of public property to conduct a meeting. That will not happen again. I wish, sincerely, that you would make use of your school —yes, I do . . . because the education which seems to you so remote from "practical" life, Mr. Masters, even a most super-ficial education, would remind you, if your own newspaper does not—that there is no future in a hatred for common humanity . . . none!

MASTERS—I'd like to remind *you*—

RIGGS—No—no, you may not. We have nothing more to say to each other. Will you leave my house, at once, please.

MASTERS (*picking up his hat and going to the door*)—You're the one man that has nothing to gain by persecuting me *or* the Senator. And you're holding the bag. Now, we've got nothing against you personally, and we wouldn't like you to get hurt, for no reason. You think it over before you go running to the Attorney General with a lot of fake affidavits.

Riggs—It isn't the affidavits that you and Mr. Dufresne fear. Whether they are true or false, Senator Dufresne knows he will never explain away the spectacle of a united people rising to accuse their elected representative of criminal treason. I am right, am I not, Mr. Masters?

Masters—That depends on whether your Citizens' Committee stands up.

Riggs—It will.

Masters (*winking*)—Let's see.

He is stamping out of the room as the curtain falls.

ACT II

Several hours later Miss Baines is again working industriously with her cards in Superintendent Riggs' office. This time she has them scattered over several pieces of furniture, including the couch. Frequently she is forced to crawl about on her hands and knees in search of a card or its particular alphabetical location. Attorney Bennett is standing near by watching Miss Baines, and wondering impatiently how long a faculty meeting that is now in progress in the inner office is likely to continue.

It is not easy to hold Miss Baines' attention at the moment. The job that she is working upon takes all her thought. When you try to juggle six thousand "hot little bodies" into a space made for six hundred it becomes something of a strain. Sometimes she finds herself wondering if the founder of the school, looking down from his painting on the wall, is still wearing his natural expression or is just leering at her.

Mr. Bennett decides not to wait. Let Miss Baines tell Mr. Riggs that he (Bennett) has reserved accommodations for Washington for Saturday on the 1 o'clock train. He is just leaving when Harriet Howard appears. He must stop long enough to tell her that he had seen her and young Riggs leaving the movies the other evening, and heard them laughing happily. That was a demonstration unfamiliar on the streets these days, and it had pleased him. One reason for Tommy's happiness, Harriet suspects, may be that she and Mr. Riggs have not told him anything of the trouble at the school. Just let him have a wonderful time getting acquainted with the town again. Tommy will be leaving for camp Sunday.

The boy Felix drops in to report that a photographer is taking pictures of the school. He's from the *Free Press*. What he wants the pictures for Miss Baines can't guess. Harriet thinks it may be a story about Tommy.

By judicious probing on Miss Baines' part it is revealed that Harriet had taken time at her lunch hour to go shopping; that she had selected a suit to get married in; that Tommy was highly elated at the prospect of such a bloody fine wedding and that she was not going to hang around an army camp to be near him, but was going to stay right where she was. Certainly this was no time for her to be leaving.

A Mr. Allen, a fairly impressive fat man, and a Mr. Peters, a sallow, furtive rat type, have arrived. They have, Mr. Allen says, an appointment with Mr. Riggs. A moment later Riggs has come from the faculty meeting and is ready to talk with Mr. Allen, who has left his friend Peters in the other room. Mr. Allen would like to have Harriet present, but Miss Baines, he thinks, had better withdraw. The fewer people acquainted with the nature of his errand the better.

It is Mr. Allen's hope that, reasoning together, he and Mr. Riggs may be able to avoid an extremely unpleasant situation for the school and for Mr. Riggs personally. His friend, Mr. Peters, reports Mr. Allen, is in an extremely bad way. He has a child, a girl of fifteen or so, who has been a pupil of the school. Frances Peters. Harriet knows her well. She is the girl Mr. Riggs had suggested transferring to the State Vocational School some weeks before. Mr. Riggs recalls the incident vaguely.

Frances Peters, it appears, had disappeared from her home some days before. This morning the police had found her living in a cheap hotel near the Anderson plant, unharmed. "Frances looks a little older than her age," admits Mr. Allen.

"Yes, she does!" Harriet quickly agrees. "About five years older! She's a tall, thin girl, with reddish-straw hair. (*To* RIGGS.) After our talk with her you asked me what was the matter with her hair, and I told you she had probably tried to dye it herself."

Regretting Harriet's attitude toward his client, Mr. Allen comes quickly to the most difficult part of his story. When her father questioned Frances about her disappearance, continues Allen, he discovered to his surprise that she had been expelled from Mr. Riggs' school some time before, a fact of which he (Allen) had never been informed.

Of course, as Harriet reports to Mr. Riggs, Miss Baines had written Mr. Peters several times about Frances, but had had no reply. It was Frances' report that her father had told her to do as she liked. According to Frances' story, continues Mr. Allen, she had long been unhappy in school; she had always felt Miss Howard's antagonism toward her, and it was Miss Howard who had taken her to Superintendent Riggs and suggested that she be dropped as a bad influence. Thereupon, according to Frances, Superintendent Riggs had suggested that she be sent to a reformatory.

Mr. Riggs is quick to deny the suggestion. He would never think of sending any child to a reform school. The State Vocational School is one of the finest in the country. What the Peters girl needed was the utmost care and treatment, probably by a psychiatrist—

"Yes. Well, it seems, Mr. Riggs," continues Allen, "that when you proposed the idea of a reformatory—as she thought of it— the child begged you to give her another chance—and you did." He leans forward insinuatingly. "You even made her a kind of 'monitor'? In charge of this office?"

Mr. Riggs, puzzled, turns a little helplessly to Harriet.

HARRIET (*tensely; to* RIGGS)—Yes, Miss Baines and I did that. We tried a little amateur psychiatry of our own—by giving Frances some responsibility. It meant that she came in for a few minutes, before school, prepared your mail and fixed the desk. . . . It was a little silly because we didn't realize we were trying to treat someone as a "child"—who was a lot tougher and more sophisticated than we were.

ALLEN—As I say, Mr. Riggs, she was put in charge of your office, which I see consists of two offices—the one outside, with the couch, being a kind of reception room.

RIGGS—Yes, sir?

ALLEN—The child's story is that she was told to report back to your office one evening, and when she arrived she found you here. You locked the door, she says—

HARRIET—Oh, my God—

RIGGS (*cuts her off with a fierce gesture, bends toward* ALLEN, *the veins standing out on his forehead*)—Go on?

ALLEN—The child told her father, Mr. Riggs, that you attempted to molest her—that you did in fact molest her—

HARRIET—I—!

ALLEN (*rapidly*)—When you were interrupted by someone attempting to enter the office. The child said she recognized your voice, Miss Howard. (*Turns to her abruptly.*) Is that correct?

HARRIET (*after a moment*)—Yes. (RIGGS *stares at her.*)

ALLEN—Then you do recall the incident?

HARRIET—Yes . . . I never told you this, Mr. Riggs, but I came back here one night for some papers I wanted, and on my way out I heard a noise in the reception room, and a man's voice. I listened for a minute, and then I heard a girl talking. The Peters girl. The door was locked, but I got in by way of the conference room. They'd heard me and they were gone—but there was a man's cigarette—one of those square leather cases with a navy insignia on it. I never told you about it—but the next day I pleaded with you to transfer her. (*With bitter contempt.*) You see, Mr. Allen, practically every pupil in school knew all about your client before I discovered her bringing men in here.

ALLEN—May I ask—why didn't you report the child, Miss Howard?

HARRIET (*with angry contempt*)—I realized that "the child" was a very *sick* child—and there wasn't anything we could do about her—

ALLEN (*calmly interrupting; to* RIGGS)—I hope I did you a service by coming here, Mr. Riggs. Whatever we think, Peters is convinced his daughter told the truth. On the face of it, of course, her story does not jibe with what is known of your long and honorable career. Still, such things do happen. I hoped that you and Peters could thrash this out quietly. You might show him what evidence you have—(*Looks at* HARRIET.) The—cigarette case might help . . . (RIGGS *starts to get up, sits back, touches his hair.*)

HARRIET (*to* ALLEN)—What do you want? What is it you want? You know this is a horrible lie—!

ALLEN—If you would like to see Peters now, Mr. Riggs—Miss Howard seems so upset—I wonder if we might excuse her . . . ?

RIGGS—Send him in, Harriet. And wait outside, please.

Peters "is a little man with a sullen look. His sparse hair is plastered down on the sides of a prominent skull. He wears a dark shirt held together by an unaccustomed tie."

Prompted by Allen, Peters awkwardly tells Mr. Riggs the story as Frances had told it to him. It was Mr. Riggs who had locked her in the office and made her—

"Peters," interrupts Riggs, "I should like to see your daughter."

"Ain't nobody goin' to see her till the court," mumbles Peters.

"Have you sent her away?" prompts Allen.

"Yeah, I sent her away till the court. I'm goin' to—I'm goin'

"DECISION"

"The doorbell has rung and a moment later Harriet has appeared with a folded newspaper. She is deathly pale. She hands the paper to Riggs. Tommy reads it over her shoulder—
" 'Principal Accused . . .' "

(*Larry Hugo, Gwen Anderson, Raymond Greenleaf*)

to sue you for rape!"

There is a pause and then Riggs asks, quietly: "Peters, why are you doing this? Whether or not this poor girl is your flesh and blood, and I find that difficult to believe, you are taking a criminal advantage of a human life. You must not—must not do it."

"I don't think we'll get anywhere that way, Mr. Riggs," interrupts Allen. "I think Peters wants to be fair, under the circumstances, if we give him a chance." He looks at Peters.

"Yeah. I ought to put a bullet through your head," explodes Peters, as though on cue. "Maybe I will before we get to court. I ought to kill you with my bare hands for what you done. I wonder how many more innercent kids—afraid to talk about it— you locked up in here."

"Peters, I beg you to think what you are doing—"

"Shut up. I don't want to hear nothin' you got to say—"

"All right, Fred. You can go." Allen is satisfied. Peters shuffles out. "Well, Mr. Riggs, we're up against something there. . . ."

It is a bad situation but Mr. Allen has a plan. It happens that Mr. Peters has been working as a night watchman at the *Free Press* plant. It is just possible that they might be able to get someone, like Masters, for example, to reason with Peters. Then, if Mr. Riggs were to resign from the Citizens' Committee to investigate this fantastic charge, no one would blame him and everyone would understand. Fishing in his brief case Allen has found a statement which he now pushes toward Riggs—

"It is my impression, Mr. Riggs," he is saying, as he unscrews his fountain pen, "that if you agree to resign— In the unmistakable language of this statement—the Peters girl will confess she lied. The entire affair will blow over. You have a son and, we hope, a long and honorable career still ahead of you. . . ."

There are, continues Allen, issues involved in this case that are far more important than Mr. Riggs realizes. Furthermore, has Mr. Riggs considered what will happen, even if he should present his affidavits to the Attorney General? "Long before you reach him every affidavit you have will be nullified by new confessions by the same individuals," promises Mr. Allen. "That process is now in work."

Beyond that, what if they do succeed in getting Mr. Masters indicted and are satisfied with the smearing they administer to Senator Dufresne. What will be the end result? "A long and involved legal battle which will drag on for years, with an almost positive dismissal of the entire matter at the finish," predicts Allen. "Against that you stake your future and the future of your son. You must resign, Mr. Riggs."

"Get out!"

"Mr. Riggs, you are making a bad mistake. Will you resign?"

"No—there is no power on earth that can stop me from showing up Dufresne for what he is—a blackmailer—a murderer—and a traitor. Tell that to him. Tell him that men like him have been found out and punished before and I intend to do my part in adding him to that company. Do you understand? Now, get out!"

Without looking at Riggs again, Allen closes his brief case and goes. Harriet and Miss Baines can't understand. They are answered by the one word, "Masters." But Mr. Riggs can't give up—Harriet feels that, though she thinks perhaps he should—he has already done so much. Riggs does not answer them. The bell has rung to indicate the end of the rest period. It is time for his class—English Four. He goes slowly out the door.

The boy Felix is in again. "He's in the back!" Felix announces. "The photo-grapher!"

"Go to your class!" shouts Miss Baines and Felix vanishes. The curtain falls.

It is early evening a few days later. Tommy is in the Riggs living room. In place of his uniform he is wearing an athletic sweater and carrying a wrench. Whatever he has been fixing he has left the job to talk with Virgie, who is making one of her periodical family checkups. "I been nursing this furniture thirty years and I ain't goin' to let it fall apart now—job or no job," announces Virgie.

About her job—Virgie is willing to confess to Tommy, but to no one else, that it isn't quite as secret as she has let on. Some people she's told she was making widgets. Some she has insisted they were gidgets. But what she is really doing in the room they have given her at the plant is making sandwiches and coffee for the bosses. "They hang around a lot at night, and 'long about eleven-twelve o'clock they yelling at each other and throwing papers around—and somebody say, 'I'm hungry!' Then I get busy with the sandwiches. Ain't that a job?"

"That's a *big* job," agrees Tommy.

It is a good old-fashioned visit Virgie and Tommy have. She can remember the first day he started to school and didn't want to go. And when he came home at night he cried because he hated it. So Virgie baked him up some cookies to take with him next day, and that helped. And now Tommy is askin' her to his wedding! Time certainly has "flew by" for Virgie.

Their talk has turned to Pop Riggs. Tommy is worried a little and Virgie is worried a lot. Mr. Riggs isn't just tired—he's wore out. Anybody can see that. And Tommy ought to know why. Surely his father has told him about the fuss at the plant? No, Tommy assures her, he hasn't.

VIRGIE—Ain't that just like him? If he elected President of the U—nited States, you have to find out in the paper!

TOMMY—Well, what, what did Pop do?

VIRGIE—I'll tell you what! If he didn't git smack in the middle of that shambles at the plant, we don't know how far it go. He stop it by hisself, that's all he do!

TOMMY—Virgie, what are you talking about? What did *Pop* have to do with the plant?

VIRGIE—*I'll* tell you. There was a riot start there one night, last month, between the white and black. It begin in the weldin' plant with a fist fight. But in a minute they is shootin' and stabbin'—it was bad. We call the police, but *they* never get there—and *that* was no accident. Then Mr. Bennett think to send for your father—and he come a-runnin'.

TOMMY—They sent for Pop. Why?

VIRGIE—Because they know them boys know him—and even them that don't know he a good man, and he tell them the truth. They know he treat their kids, rich and poor, black and white, just the same, and he got always time for them—you know, Tommy—

TOMMY—Well, what did Pop do?

VIRGIE—He go around and talk to the men—right in the middle of it . . . and, Tommy, that was a *bad* night. Three good boys get it for good that night. He git in there and yell at them to stop—and he tell them—when you see a knife or gun—you grab that boy because he is a spy! And that work! The knives and guns disappear fast—but, Tommy, they left a *lot* of blood on the floor that night. When it all over, your father speak to them, and he speak to them again the next day—and he explain to them how the fight start—how they send troublemakers in— and there ain't been no trouble since. How come Miss Harrie didn't tell you?

TOMMY—Holy cats . . . (*Gets up and walks around.*)

VIRGIE—But your father don't stop them neither, Tommy. He

talk every night—in the colored neighborhoods—and the union meetings—and all over—gettin' everyone together so that don't never happen again. He a real man, Tommy—as if you don't know.

TOMMY—I sure didn't know that Pop . . .

The door has opened and Riggs, pale and distracted, comes into the room. He is all right, he assures them, when they demand anxiously to know. Nor will he say anything more until Virgie confesses that she has told the whole story to Tommy. It is good that Tommy should know, Pop is agreed, because Tommy will be coming back one day—

"Never mind one day!" snaps Tommy, excitedly. "I'm not going away now thinking you might get your head knocked off any minute! You pull out of this, Pop—and pull out of it right away."

"That isn't possible, Tom—"

"Oh, yes, it is! Who are you fighting anyway?"

"Masters—the editor of the *Free Press*—but mainly Senator Dufresne."

"Whew!" Tommy emits a long whistle. "You've got your nerve, haven't you? Holy Mackerel, Pop—have a heart! That Dufresne is a bad sonofabitch."

"You know that, son?"

"Sure, I know it! We hear what he says. We aren't as dumb over there as you think. We know plenty! But, Pop, what are you *worrying* about it for? Hey—let me do the fighting for this family, will you? That's why they gave me a uniform and a gun!"

"And do you quit, Tommy?" demands Virgie, with some force.

"Huh?"

"You're tellin' him to quit. When the goin' git tough, do you quit?"

"Quiet, Virgie!"

"Don't tell me quiet, boy!" Virgie's tone is impassioned. "You know what happen if your father quit? You throw a stick of dynamite in the plant, that's what you do!" With profound feeling she turns to Riggs. "Mr. Riggs, don't quit! Don't ever quit! You know them poor people learn to trust your word. They ain't dumb. They know you fightin' for them and tryin' to send Mr. Dufresne to jail. But if *you* scared out, all the dirty bugs crawl around laughin', and that makes more trouble, and worse trouble—you know."

Virgie is still protesting as Riggs goes to comfort her, and still pleading with him not to quit the fight, and with Tommy not to ask his father to quit. "Your pa don't wear no uniform, maybe —but he been fightin' just the same—and with *no* gun."

Virgie has gone, her best wishes for Tommy and Harriet's wedding trailing back after her. The doorbell has rung and a moment later Harriet has appeared with a folded newspaper. She is deathly pale. She hands the paper to Riggs. Tommy reads it over his shoulder—

"Principal Accused . . ."

For a second they are stunned. Then Riggs sinks helplessly onto the couch. Tommy's anger flares hysterically, though he tries to control it. Who is—where is this Masters? Tommy would make him eat every word printed; he would shove that paper down his throat. *"Where is he? . . . I'll find him!"*

Harriet is clinging desperately to Tommy, trying to hold him back, trying to convince him that anything he does will just add to the trouble. If he tries to kill Masters they will put him in prison, and what good will that do? But Tommy has broken away from both of them and started for the door when Attorney Bennett arrives.

He, too, offers arguments. Tommy will not have to worry about personal revenge. The court will attend to that. "This isn't only the dirtiest trick I've seen in twenty-five years of law —but the stupidest," says Bennett. He can't understand it. "Allen is too shrewd a lawyer to give Dufresne this kind of advice. He knows that when I get Peters and the girl up there I'll tear their story to shreds before the case is a day old. He knows I am going to tie them up with Masters. . . . Allen must have warned him about that. Why is Dufresne taking the risk?"

Tommy is sitting by his father as Bennett continues to search for a logical explanation of the Allen-Dufresne plotting. They are hoping to break up the Citizens' Committee, of course, but with the publication of the rape story they know they must go to trial.

"Dufresne's whole power might be at stake here—at the worst possible time for him," reasons the attorney. "Why does he take that gamble? On the theory that a half-crazy girl will make this yarn stand up? It's wonderful—but I don't understand it."

Suddenly Tommy's anger flares again. "Yeah! It must be great to be a lawyer and prove that what looks like mud—and tastes like it—is chocolate ice cream. . . . What are you so happy about, mister? Don't you know what this means to my father?" He is on his feet now, and refusing to be quieted by his father's argument that getting angry will not help. "I know one thing that'll help!" says Tommy, fiercely. "Pop, let me at this guy Masters! You want to get rid of him, don't you?"

"Getting rid of Masters, Tom—as one gets rid of a cockroach —while it might satisfy all of us for the moment—will not wipe out the plague—and would be a very empty victory. It might even defeat our end. It is not the prostitute, Masters, but Dufresne and his whole power and position that are at stake."

There is a ring at the door. A Police Sergeant appears. He has a warrant calling Riggs to headquarters. Riggs will have to appear, but Bennett will be there with a writ and see about bail. Tommy will get dressed and go with his father.

The Police Sergeant is friendly. His son had played on the same school team with Tommy. And he would warn Mr. Riggs not to figure too much on bail or a writ of habeas corpus. "I think they're going to keep you in custody for your own protection," warns the Sergeant. "I don't get it neither, Mr. Riggs. But all you got to do is take it easy, the way you're doing, and you're going to be all right. You might be surprised to find out how many you got behind you that don't say anything."

There is a thump on the window, followed by a clod of dirt and gravel. Outside a couple of piercing whistles are heard. The Sergeant dashes out the door. Tommy comes running down the stairs. "What was that, Pop?"

"That, son, was the establishment of a reason for protective custody. Tom, there is nothing harder to bear than senseless humiliation. I would be lying to you if I told you that I am calm. I am not. But I am trying as hard as I can to seem calm, with as much grace as possible. Will you do the same, son?"

"I don't know. Pop, can I ask you something? I know what you're fighting for. But is it worth all this to you?"

"Yes, son."

"They got you in the middle—knocked you down, and they're stepping all over you! Is it worth that?"

"What price would you put on the freedom to speak and act, Tom?"

"I'd give anything to get you out of this," says Tommy, avoiding a direct answer.

The Police Sergeant is back. He had expected to find it was kids that had thrown the dirt, but it was a couple of grown men.

They are starting for the Sergeant's car. Pop has put out the

lights. Tommy is waiting for him in the shadowed doorway.
As his father starts through Tommy clasps him in his arms.
"I'm sorry with all my heart you had to come home to this,"
says Riggs.

TOMMY—No—no, Virgie wasn't kidding . . . I did get back
just in time . . . But I don't know whether to be sore at you
or not, Pop! I don't! You're not a politician. You're a teacher.
Sure I can see why Anderson and Bennett—and Virgie—want to
put the kibosh on Dufresne . . . but I don't see—what do you
get out of it? How does he bother you?

RIGGS—Tom, many times in the past two years I lay awake at
night and wondered about you . . . the chance that you might
not come back . . . thank God you have. But I satisfied myself
that I had made a loan of your very precious life, to me, for a
good reason: I respect the fundamental law of our country—justice and equality for all—and I believed you were fighting to preserve it. At the same time, son, I saw it violated, every day,
here before my eyes . . . I realized that I had watched it violated all my life. I think you will understand—that when I
was given the chance to join you in the line of battle—(*Smiles.*)
—even in this small way—I could not resist taking that chance—
hoping that I could make good at last on my lip service of so
long to simple democracy. I have that feeling now, son—at this
moment—more strongly than ever. You see, I have become a
fanatic, son, as great a fanatic as Dufresne and those who plan
a fascist-minded future for us all.

TOMMY—Fascist? Pop, you must be kidding! Do you think
we'd let Dufresne—or a thousand Dufresnes—get away with anything like that? Is that what you mean? Fascist? Pop—!

RIGGS—Yes, yes, son—

TOMMY—But you *know* there isn't a chance of that—!

RIGGS—I think you are mistaken, Tom. I think there is an excellent chance. To my mind an *excellent* chance. I believe we
are living, now, in the midst of a very real civil war—a war that
must be decided before you come home for good—or you will
come home to the ashes of the cause for which you fought. And
now, come, son.

TOMMY (*stopping him*)—Pop . . . You know you're a hell of
a . . . of an excellent guy?

RIGGS—I'm glad you think so, son. I thank you.

They go out as the curtain falls.

ACT III

It is very early—about 6 o'clock—next morning. The Riggs living room is still in shadow. Tommy comes downstairs to answer the doorbell. Harriet and Aunt May have come to get his breakfast. They are both anxious and sympathetic, but Tommy is harsh and not too responsive. The memory of what has been done to his father is still strong with him and his bitterness is apparent.

Aunt May can't understand all that has happened. After Harriet has explained to her that Mr. Bennett couldn't get Mr. Riggs released with a writ of habeas corpus because none of the judges left in town would sign it, she still doesn't understand. Anyway, Mr. Riggs didn't have to stay in a—jail—did he?

"Oh, no! It was swell!" sardonically reports Tommy. "A kind of crummy back room—with the police garage behind it. The cars coming in and out all night must have made it nice!"

All night long people stood in front of the City Hall, Harriet tells him. They were people from the plant who had just got off the day shift. All night they stood in the street—just waiting.

"If that doesn't frighten Mr. Masters, nothing can," adds Harriet. "These people—waiting there—he can't stand that. What he wants is a good riot."

All night long Harriet had been awake, too, watching the light in Tommy's room come on and go off; watching him pace back and forth before the window. "Dearest, may I tell you something?" she pleads. "You're going to camp school—but you won't do very well if you keep thinking about this all the time. You've got to let us worry about it—and you work hard and—graduate with honors— That's what you've got to do."

"You're crazy! I've got to pray for the end of the war—that's what I've got to do! And then you—and me—and Pop—and your aunt have got to get the hell out of here. I *hate* this place! I never want to see it again!"

Harriet can't understand that. Nor does she think that Tommy's father will agree to leaving. True, he is lying over there in a dirty back room, because he's a hero. It is the best men who always take the punishment. . . .

Tommy and Harriet have gone over to Aunt May's to get some breakfast rolls when Mr. Bennett arrives. He is "taut and very grave," and he has come to see Tommy.

"Mr. Bennett . . . how do you account for a thing like this," Mrs. Howard is asking; "this Peters man accusing Mr. Riggs—

his own child—why on earth would he do such a dreadful thing?"

"I don't know." Bennett has sat down and is holding a hand over his eyes.

"The child might be ruined for life," Mrs. Howard prattles on. "You understand. Harriet says it is Mr. Dufresne's doing—but I keep thinking of that father . . . Mr. Bennett, could it all be a terrible mistake? Could Mr. Riggs have unconsciously said something—completely unconsciously, of course—some ridiculous thing that would have made the child imagine . . . ? I ask you, Mr. Bennett, because you are a lawyer."

She pauses for an answer. Mr. Bennett continues to sit with his hand over his eyes. "Is something wrong . . . ?"

"Mrs. Howard, Mr. Riggs is dead."

It is a moment before Mrs. Howard can speak. Her mouth opens, but there are no words. Bennett has gone to the window, and is staring out at the garden.

"Dead?"

"He apparently hung himself—with his braces—suspenders—some time in the night."

"Oh, dear . . . Oh, why . . . why did he . . . ?" Mrs. Howard is weeping.

"Ask Dufresne. He'll tell you."

When she has quieted her tears Mrs. Howard is troubled by the thought of Tommy's facing the shock, and of what people will think. "If he—if he was innocent—you know what I mean . . ." she suggests, haltingly.

"Yes, I know what you mean," answers Bennett, with spirit. "That's the diabolical part of it. Nothing else would have been so good. Peters might have shot him. But this . . . this takes care of everything, doesn't it?"

"I don't understand."

"Don't you? They lynched him in that back room last night. Killed him in cold blood. Do you understand that, Mrs. Howard?"

"Oh, I—I can't believe that . . . !"

"Can't you. (*Grimly.*) But you can believe he hung himself because he was guilty, can't you?"

"No! I never said that . . . !"

"I'm afraid you did. And you're a good woman—and a good friend of the family . . . Now you know why they did it." He is pacing the room. "And I wondered why Dufresne was willing to gamble on a trial! He knew there wasn't going to be any trial, damn his soul!"

Tommy and Harriet are back. Tommy is eager to get breakfast over with so he can go with Bennett to see his father. He
has been thinking about those tough fellows, Masters and
Dufresne—they're worse than the Fritzes. You see a Fritz and
you can shoot him, but these other guys walk around, own newspapers, get elected and put honest men like Pop in jail. If
Tommy only had one good sapper from his outfit there he would
dig a tunnel under Masters and Dufresne and blow hell out
of them.

But now Tommy knows. He has read the dread news in
their blanched faces. He has jumped up and faced them, holding Harriet's arms and demanding, quietly at first, then with a
shout: *"What's the matter?* What did they do? What did they
do to Pop? What did they do to him?"

"He . . . he was found . . . hung!"

Tommy stands, stunned for a moment. He sinks slowly onto
the couch, his hands across his stomach. He turns to Bennett:
"How did they do it? . . . Why did they do that? He . . ."

Tommy is sobbing convulsively now. The others stand helplessly around him. When Harriet can speak she asks Bennett
please not to let any one think that Mr. Riggs—

Bennett knows what she would say, but can promise nothing.
"I spoke to the medical examiner," he says, with a quick glance
at Tommy. "There are no marks—nothing . . ."

"But you must—tell everyone."

Harriet goes to Tommy, comfortingly, but he pushes her away,
almost violently. His tears flow again before he can turn to
her. He hears Bennett saying— "I want to make arrangements
now."

"Yeah. Go on. You arranged it . . . Didn't I tell you?"
Hysteria has come again to Tommy's voice. *"Didn't I tell you
I didn't want to leave him alone?* Didn't I tell you that? You
wise, silly bastards! You silly, silly bastards! Leaving him
alone in that lousy hole! Go on, tell 'em! Tell 'em my old
man—who never did a thing—not a thing—tell 'em . . ." His
tone has quieted. He is pleading now, like a boy— "Can I go
get him now?"

"I want to make arrangements for that," says Bennett.

"Yeah. Do it, will you?"

"I will. I will let you know."

Again Harriet tries to come close to Tommy. She would like
to stay with him, if he will let her. She will not say a word, she
promises. "Do you hate me, Tommy? Is it my fault?"

"No. It's my fault," he says, shaking his head. "I had a hunch . . . but I let him talk me out of it. I let you all talk me out of it. Even Virgie . . . pushing him around . . . Everybody hiding behind one poor guy."

Again Harriet would plead with Tommy, first to let her stay near him, and then that he will promise her please not to try to do anything to Masters. That wouldn't do any good—would it? Tommy isn't too sure. A bullet—right through the belly—that might be good!

There is someone at the door. It is Mr. Anderson, "a short, wiry, little middle-aged man." He has come to express his sympathy and to offer to do anything that he can do—

"You're a little late, aren't you, mister?" There is bitterness in Tommy's voice, but Anderson passes it over. He had tried to see Masters the night before, he tells Tommy. He had hoped to call the whole thing off. But Masters had left town—

TOMMY—Oh, that yellow—yellow—yellow . . . Okay . . . I'll catch up with him—sooner or later. They killed Pop without leaving a mark, huh? Wait and see the marks I leave! You learn how, over there.

HARRIET—Mr. Anderson, do you think people will believe that Mr. Riggs really did—did—?

ANDERSON—Yes. Many will. We'll prove differently. I think in a way, it was Dufresne who killed himself last night. Because I think the truth about this will have to come out—and not only the people but the gentlemen who have been supporting him will drop him soon. They won't trust him.

TOMMY—Who's that?

ANDERSON—The gentlemen for whom Dufresne speaks—because he himself is only an employee of the boys who lay awake nights figuring ways to push back the clock. I'm an old line manufacturer myself, and I've always believed in a man's right to make a fair profit on his brains and his investment. But these people aren't satisfied with that. They want the whole damned hog—head, hooves and heels. Your father was no fool. He wanted to know where I stood before he agreed to help me, and I told him what I've told the never-give-up gang again and again—I'll take anything that comes before I go along with the boys that keep trying to turn the country back to—

TOMMY—Oh, I get it. *Your* conscience is clear, huh? It isn't your fault! It's a lot of big shots back there some place!

HARRIET—Tommy, dear—

ANDERSON—I don't absolve myself. But I do think, that with your help, young man—

TOMMY—*My* help?

ANDERSON—We must have your help-—to justify your father, and to make sure this never happens again. I think you ought to ask for a leave of absence to investigate his death. As his son, you can make demands, legally, that we cannot. And of course your presence here will mean a great deal to all of us.

HARRIET (*eagerly*)—Would they let you do that, Tommy?

TOMMY—Yeah . . . They'd let me. What do you think they're switching me to, Harrie? A desk supply job. I'm going to learn how to fill out forms so I can send supplies to my old outfit . . . And I had to beg for that . . . Well, now you know . . .

HARRIET—Dearest—

TOMMY—They'd let me . . .

ANDERSON—In that case, young man, I think—

TOMMY—Yeah! You told me. Now let me tell you. You can take your plant and all the rest of it and—! (*Turns away.*) We're getting out of here.

ANDERSON—I'm sorry to hear that. While I agree that what I think may be unimportant—I'm afraid you'll have to consider even your own feelings as unimportant now. (TOMMY *jerks his head to him.*) I know that's a harsh, cruel thing to say to you. But these are cruel days, and there is very little time to waste. I believe that in a sense we are living in a kind of civil war, as real as the other. I'm sorry you feel that you have no part in our fight. I hope you change your mind. You know where to find me, Miss Howard, if you need me for anything at all.

Anderson is right. Harriet is sure of that. Something tells her going away isn't the answer. She and Tommy would never agree about what has happened. That is the most important thing in their lives. It wouldn't be right for Tommy to try to forget about his father. There are thousands of other people who won't—the people at the plant. They'll remember—

"You don't want to understand," Harriet is saying. "And you should. You should! You know better than any of us what it means to fight side by side with people who depend on you— for their lives. And that's what happening here—but you won't see it. In back of you, and me, and Mr. Anderson—are all these people—who are just like an army! . . . but with eighty different generals shouting at them—trying to make them go this way

—or that . . . and what your father did was give them a feel-ing of unity, because they trusted him—and now all that might be wasted—because you won't help . . . because you think they're only 'dumb slugs.' Are you a dumb slug, Tommy, be-cause you don't give the orders, but just obey them?"

"I can't argue with you, Harrie. I feel like I did when that mine exploded under me. I can hear you all right—but I can't feel anything."

He has reached out for her hand and is holding it as he ex-plains that he will be going on now. He will be putting the house up for sale. There is nothing in it he will be wanting to take— except his mother's picture and—perhaps—Pop's old pipe. He is fighting back the tears again, thinking of what has happened to this homecoming of his—to his dream of Paradise he was go-ing to find—

"Tommy—I know it is hard to forget a horrible memory—like seeing your father for the last time in that room. But you have so many other things to remember about him—so many— How really fine he was . . . and how much he believed in everything he said, and did . . . You're very lucky. When my father died I prayed every night, 'Oh, God, let me forget him—please let me forget him . . .' I did. Because he was a man—like Mas-ters. He was. I saw him plan—and kill—because the people who owned him told him to! And he was so hated—we never went anywhere from the time I was born that a man with a gun didn't go with us . . ."

Harriet is crying now, sobbing out the rest of the sorry story of her childhood. When Tommy would comfort her she pleads again with him a little desperately.

"Tommy—I know that nothing I can say will bring your father back. But if you leave now, hating everyone, you'll only prove that Dufresne was right. If you won't fight to prove it was him —that it was *always* him—you'll take the heart out of everyone —and he'll go on . . . and, dearest . . . I . . . I don't want to lose you . . . !"

Suddenly she is in his arms. For a moment neither of them pay any heed to the doorbell. Then Tommy puts Harriet on the couch and opens the door to Virgie. Virgie is devastated with grief, her hands clasped before her, and she is worried for fear she may have done wrong in letting some people from the plant come with her. But they had asked to come—

"Mr. Riggs, we didn't come to express our sympathy—we don't have to tell you about that," says a man named Fitzgerald, who steps into the room. "But Mrs. Bowen here—and Jim—wanted to meet you and we'd like to ask you something."

With Tommy's consent they have come in—Mrs. Bowen, a wholesome, buxom woman, and Jim, a young Negro.

"We won't stay but a minute," continues Fitzgerald. "I'll tell you—Mrs. Bowen lost her husband in the riot—and Jim, here, lost his dad. They picked both men out because they were strong men—and they carried a lot of weight at the plant. That's what happened to your father. Do you mind my talking like this?"

"No."

"As I said, we don't have to tell you how we feel about it. I worked pretty close with your father, and I never met a more sensible and a more modest man. He wasn't well known outside of here, maybe, but every working man and woman in the United States is going to know his name, and what he stood for. They're going to know all about him. We held a meeting this morning, the day shift and the night shift both, and we want your permission for the fifteen thousand of us to come to your father's funeral. We'll be very grateful if you'll let us do that."

"Yeah . . . I guess so. Sure."

"Thank you. Well, that's all." He turns to Mrs. Bowen.

"I only wanted to say there isn't hardly a family in the plant hasn't got someone in the service," says Mrs. Bowen. "So we all knew how your pa felt about your coming home. And we know how you feel now. Jim and me, especially. Well—I was glad to be able to take my husband's place—and we hope you'll take your pa's place, the same way."

"Thank you—but you see I'm—(To Fitzgerald.) I'm going away . . . and I don't think I'll ever be back here again."

It is hard for them to take that, but they can understand how he feels. They thank him again and wish him luck.

"I didn't feel any worse about my own dad than I do about Mr. Riggs," says the boy, Jim. "But don't you worry. We won't let him down."

"You don't remember me, young feller," Mrs. Bowen adds, as she puts out her hand. "But I remember you when you were knee high to Virgie over there. I did a lot of sewing for your ma when I was a young girl—right here in this room. Made these drapes, didn't I, Virgie?"

VIRGIE—Yes, Mrs. Bowen . . .

MRS. BOWEN—I sewed most of your ma's trousseau too . . .

that was before your time. Well, if you're not coming back
. . . you tell 'em out there, will you . . . wherever you do go.
You tell 'em for your pa and for us. Tell 'em what they've done
here—and what they're aiming to do. (*Hitches her coat around
her.*) And then you tell 'em we're not going to let them *do* it!

TOMMY (*turning away, his eyes blinded with tears*)—Yeah,
I'll tell 'em.

FITZGERALD—We'd better go, folks.

TOMMY—Yeah—I'll tell 'em. You're bloody right I'll tell
'em! (*They look at him.*) You don't have to do any fighting
for me! I won't let Pop down! Don't you worry about *that!*
(HARRIET *rises.*) And I won't let you or anyone else down either
—if that's what you mean! Okay, Harrie—you're right! This
is my home, goddamnit—and no Masters or Dufresne or anyone
else is going to run me out of it! I'll see them in hell first! Do
you hear that? (*To* FITZGERALD.) Okay, Mister! You all
think my Pop was a terrific guy? You all think he died for
something? Well, let's find out! Let's go!

HARRIET (*going to him*)—Tommy . . .

TOMMY (*turning to the window to hide the tears pouring down
his face, grasping the drapes*)—Let's go . . . !

THE CURTAIN FALLS

OVER 21

A Comedy in Three Acts

BY RUTH GORDON

IF you were to ask the author of "Over 21" how she happened to write that comedy she would probably tell you that it was because she had nothing better to do at the time, and it seemed like a good idea. Also I have no doubt she would insist that her husband, the director, Garson Kanin, be credited with an assist. Ruth Gordon had been recently married the summer of 1942 and was keeping house for her husband in Washington, D. C., where he was in service. Being a smart housekeeper she found she had a lot of spare time on her hands. She had, like most stage folk, always wanted to write a play; probably had started two or three and abandoned them when they reached the problem stage.

She began work on "Over 21" and found the writing fun. She was surrounded by Army people, and that was a help. She had the service experiences of her husband to draw upon, and these were an inspiration. And she had troops of highly individualized friends on whom to model her characters. So the comedy was written.

As it turned out, "Over 21" was as much an actress' success as it was an author's success. Miss Gordon, having a chance at last to indulge herself in the sort of comedy scene in which presumably she takes the greatest relish, had a grand time playing her own heroine. Or, as Lewis Nichols explained it in his *New York Times* review: " 'Over 21' is in the class of wisecrack comedy, which dashes along from joke to pun to situation. After a quiet sort of start Miss Gordon, the author, begins taking down her hair, scattering the pins about and making a brilliant commotion. Jokes of all sorts, to be delivered rapidly or slowly, never have fazed Miss Gordon, the actress, and she is obviously having a whale of a time with her own show."

The Gordon comedy was the first hit of the new year, having been brought to Broadway January 3, 1944, after pleasant adventures in New Haven, Philadelphia and Washington. The reviewers, for the most part, were a bit stingy with their praise, but playgoers were enthused in sufficient number to carry the play through the season, greatly, as may be readily believed, to Miss Gordon's satisfaction.

"Across the road from the main gate of an Army Air Force Training Command near Miami, Florida, is a place called Palmetto Court," writes the author of "Over 21." "It is composed of a group of thirty or forty almost identical bungalows. In the old days they used to be rented sort of by the hour, but the war has brought them a new respectability. They are rented now by the week to a lucky few: officers, instructors, officers' wives and miscellaneous members of that hardy group who are somehow related to the Army. This story is concerned with the happenings in Bungalow 26-D, Palmetto Court, over a six-week period in the summer of 1943."

The arrangement of 26-D places a front door leading to a tiny vine-trellised porch at one side of the living room, and a door leading to bedroom and bath at the other side. At the back there are double Dutch doors which, when opened, reveal "what the owners call a kitchenette"—a series of shelves with a small refrigerator and a two-burner electric plate. The furnishings include a large sofa, covered with a faded flowered cretonne slip-cover. There are chairs, a standing lamp and a small table with a telephone on it. It is a worn and shabby room.

As we are shown in, the sole occupant of this room is a highly decorative Jan Lupton, "very John Held, Jr., if you can remember that far back." Jan apparently is about ready to leave. Her hat, purse and gloves are handy, and so are an officer's khaki duck folding bag, an army duffle bag, filled to the top, and a lady's suitcase and blue cosmetic box-like bag.

Presently Jan is joined by her husband, Roy Lupton, young, handsome, energetic and "a one-day-old Second Lieutenant." Roy is excitedly waving a large kraft paper envelope. It contains the Lieutenant's assignment orders, but he has not opened it because he thought he and Jan should get this news together. Now Jan has the order and is solemnly unfolding it. And now she is about to swoon. Of all the places to be ordered! "Roy, go and talk to them! Tell them you're married! Tell them I just couldn't live there!" protests Jan.

"Gosh—Crocker Field, Arkansas!" mournfully reads Roy. "Arkansas—"

"Darling, please go talk to them."

"Sweetheart, I would. You know I would. But in the Army,

baby, you *can't* talk to them. You just have to do it."

"Even a Second Lieutenant?"

"Yeah."

"Oh, dear."

Roy is sympathetic, and very sweet, but there just isn't anything that can be done about it. None of the wives go to Crocker. "It's twenty miles through a swamp before you get to the place *you'd* have to live at—Muscalong, remember?" prompts Roy. "Twenty-two hundred population—and where would you find a place to stay? There's only one hotel, and that's packed full of wives that are permanent . . . I mean they're *there* permanently."

Suddenly Jan remembers that right after his training at Crocker Roy will be going overseas. She may not see him again. That, too, is a distressing thought and calls for a lot of comforting.

"That's why I've *got* to get you safe and settled—so I won't have that worry on my mind," explains Roy, taking Jan's chin in his hand and turning her face up to him. "Honey—please—"

Jan decides to be helpful. Anyway, she can go on the train with him as far as Kansas City, where her mother lives. That will be something. And Roy promises to get the war over quick. With a final embrace Roy goes to arrange about the tickets and Jan phones a wire to her mother. By cutting out "Dear Mama" she keeps it down to ten words.

Jan has just collected her hand baggage and is about to go into the bedroom when a "well-traveled, much-labeled Vuitton suitcase" slides in the front door, obviously assisted by a foot. The suitcase is shortly followed by Paula Wharton, "known to her friends as Polly." "Polly is strikingly dressed and is detailed with the accessories of wealth and good taste." She thought she was in 26-D and is about to withdraw, with apologies, when Jan recognizes her as Paula Wharton, famous author of "Fellow Americans," and one of her favorite novelists. What a coincidence! Jan should have known when Max Wharton was in that afternoon with some of his baggage—

"Max Wharton!" There's another name that gives Jan pause. Of course! Max Wharton, the famous editor! "He runs that newspaper Roy is so crazy about!" And he must be awfully unusual. "You hardly *ever* hear of anyone like an editor getting to be only a *private*," muses Jan.

"And what's more, he didn't use any pull," boasts Polly.

Now their respective stories are matched: Jan's husband has

just been assigned to Crocker Field, Arkansas, which is a terrible place. And Polly is just coming in from California, where she has been adapting her own "Fellow Americans" for the screen.

Then Max Wharton arrives—an attractive, youngish, late-thirties fellow. Max is wearing the summer uniform of the Officers' Candidate School, tortoise shell glasses and an overseas cap.

With surprised exclamations of "Angel" and "Darling!" Max and Polly are in each other's arms. But Max can't stay. "I have to go back again right away, darling," he explains. "I only came to change my socks."

"Oh, isn't it good my train was on time?" coos Polly. "I wouldn't want to miss *that.*"

Max will have to go back to sign the payroll and then he hopes to be off until 11. Now Jan has excused herself and the Whartons are repeating the enthused greetings inspired by their reunion. They check on things that have happened. Polly has, she thinks, done a pretty good script for her Coast producer. Max is fine, but still a little worried about "the paper." He has been purposely avoiding a look at it for fear it may be worse than he expected. It is, Polly assures him. It has lost all the independent spirit it had under Max's editorship—but why worry about that? He's in the Army now.

"But I *am* worried about it," insists Max, pulling on his left sock. "The paper's important. It's what I'm fighting for, in a way. When it all boils down to it, the thing you fight for is your *own.* Every guy I've met since I've been in this thing has a personal reason for being in it." He reflectively reaches for his left shoe. "There's a fellow sleeps on my left—name's Levine—he used to own a gas station. So here we are. First thing you know I'm helping him fight for his gas station, and he's helping me fight for my idea of what a newspaper ought to be . . . So—"

"I know, darling, and don't worry. I'm sure the paper will be all right."

"I certainly thought Kennedy would be able to—"

"What about Gow? What does he think?"

"Gow, he doesn't have to think. He's the publisher. He keeps writing me long inter-office communications. 'Memo from Mr. Robert Drexel Gow.' He thinks I'm still working for him."

"Well, he's not your boss any longer. Don't you answer him."

"Answer him? Why, I'm so busy down here—"

From across the field come the notes of a bugle. It is the "Pay Call." Max leaps to his feet, grabs his right shoe and rushes through the door.

"I guess he had to go, all right," mutters the astounded Polly, as Jan appears in the bedroom doorway.

"Oh, yes," explains Jan. "Signing the payroll is the same as standing a formation and it's ten demerits if you don't—"

"You sound as though you've graduated, too."

"Oh, you get to know a lot, all right. You know, it's awfully hard down here. They just work all the time. Of course, if you're young it isn't so bad, but it was terrible for Roy. He's *twenty-five.*"

"Oh."

"A friend of Roy's in the Surgeon-General's department said that the Army has proved that over twenty-one you don't absorb any more. He said they'd proved it scientifically. You simply don't absorb a thing."

"Well, mercy. What about Max, then? He's going on forty."

"He is? Oh, well, he's special."

Things being as they are Jan thinks perhaps Polly would like a drink. She would. This brings out the peroxide bottle into which Jan has put the Scotch for traveling, and a milk bottle which they will have to use for a water jug. Not forgetting the lily cups that can be had at the five-and-ten. "Better take two. It soaks right through."

There is a long-distance call from New York for Mr. Wharton, but it is delayed while the operator discovers whether the Mr. Gow who is calling will talk with Mrs. Wharton.

Meantime Polly's introduction to 26-D is continued. It is, insists Jan, the best bungalow in Palmetto Court, but still there are some curious things about it. For example, there is no sink in the kitchenette. All water has to be brought from the bathroom. Then the refrigerator (which is now performing with a slight bronchial effect) does make a noise. However, that's an advantage. When it's noisy you at least know it is working.

There was a time, too, when the roof leaked. But Roy fixed that. Of course a person has to be careful about moths. And there isn't any shower. Polly isn't too surprised at these features, but the lighting plans are a trifle confusing, as Jan explains—

"The one in the bedroom doesn't work from the bedroom. You have to turn it on and off out here," and she gives a demonstration at the switch. "The lights in here are peculiar, too.

You have to step outside to turn them on and off." She goes outside for this demonstration, but is right back to explain about the casement window. "The only way you can open it is—"

Jan is stamping her foot on the floor. She tries several places, searching for the right spot, and finally finds it. The window flies open.

"Does it close the same way?"

"No, you just—" Again Jan demonstrates by reaching out and pulling the window shut.

"Well!" exclaims Polly. "And where is the place your skirts blow up?"

There is no answer to this one. Roy Lupton at that moment comes bursting into the room with glad tidings. Jake has agreed to loan him and Honey his car to get to the station, and they can go on the same train, which, as Polly agrees, after she has been somewhat confusedly introduced to the excited Roy, is certainly *something*.

The Luptons' train goes at 9, which means that they had better be starting. They are busy collecting their bags and tucking in the few things that have not been packed, like the peroxide bottle, when Max Wharton rushes in. He, too, is a little flustered, finding the room practically crowded, but recovers his poise quickly when Jan introduces him to her lieutenant.

"Gee, it is sure great to get to meet you and your wife," explodes Roy, taking off his hat and shaking hands with Max.

"Thank you, sir," answers Max.

This is a little too much for Jan, who gasps audibly and then excuses herself. "That's the first time I ever heard anyone call Roy 'sir,' " she explains.

"Shouldn't he have saluted?" Polly asks Roy.

"Oh, no. Only when we meet outside. Indoors he isn't required to."

"Well, we'll go out to the car with you and then he can." Which is a good laugh for Roy and Jan.

"Can I give you a hand with your bags, sir?" inquires Max.

"Thanks," answers Roy, quickly pushing over the blue suitcase and the khaki folding bag. "That's very nice of you." And he picks up the small blue cosmetic bag, stopping above the door to let Max go out before him. In a moment they are back for the other things, and enjoying a lively discussion regarding such things as the "techniques of zone reconnaissances" as they work. Roy picks up the heavy duffle bag and swings it onto Max's shoulder. "There are a lot of things that can bog you down," he warns, as Max staggers out with the duffle bag. Roy walks carefully behind with his fingertips under the end of the bag, ready to catch it if it should fall.

Everything is in the car now, and the Luptons are calling their good-bys. The roar of their motor has barely faded before Polly is back in the house, setting the catch on the door and closing it tight. The next minute she is in Max's arms—

MAX—Darling, darling, where have you been?

POLLY—Oh, angel, am I really here? Or are we writing all this in a letter?

MAX—Darling, I know I promised I wouldn't argue any more, but now I see you here— What's this kind of a place going to be like for you? *I'm* here because I can't see myself doing anything else— But that's no reason why it should uproot your life, too. Angel, *how* are you going to live here?

POLLY—With you, darling. That makes it my best place to live in this world.

MAX—Summer in Miami—in an overnight bungalow—

POLLY (*turning to him*)—But, darling, I'm not the only one. All the way across the country, what do you see? Soldiers coming along, girls tracking right along with them. Mink coats arm in arm with Privates. Polo coats and week-end bags and Second Lieutenants in and out of Greyhound buses and day coaches and transcontinentals, and they're holding on to what they love just as long as they can. And that's the way I am, too.

MAX—No, you're not. You're different.

POLLY—No, no. I don't want to be different—I want to be like those other girls, following their fellers around.

MAX—All right then, come here. (*Takes her in his arms and kisses her.*) And please don't ever leave me again. Until you have to.

POLLY (*her arms around him*)—Baby, I'll *never* have to.

MAX—I doubt if they'll let you go overseas with me.

POLLY—When's that, darling?

MAX—Well, if I graduate—then there's six weeks' advanced training somewhere—and then—over.

POLLY—Uh-huh.

MAX—*If* I graduate. Don't bet.

POLLY (*with a touch of impatience*)—Max!

MAX—It's tougher than I thought.

POLLY—It is?

MAX (*nodding*)—Yeah! There's a chance that—I may not—

POLLY—What?

MAX—Sweetheart, you didn't get here a minute too soon. To-day was end-of-the-rope day for me.

POLLY—Aw . . . (*Bugle warning.*)

MAX—First thing this morning, inspection. I had a spot on my shirt—I didn't even see it—five demerits. Then we had a quiz. You have to get seventy-eight to pass. You know what I got? (POLLY *shakes her head.*) Seventy-eight.

POLLY—Well, that's good, isn't it?

MAX—No, it isn't. I *always* get seventy-eight, no more, no less. It's nerve-wracking. I'd almost rather flunk once in a while . . . Then we had regimental review. I stood at atten-tion for an hour and fifteen minutes.

POLLY—Oh, darling.

MAX—Sounds simple, but try it.

POLLY—Right now?

MAX—I spent the whole time asking myself questions. What *is* this? Is this what you should be doing? Are you ever going to be any good to the Army? Shouldn't you have stayed with the paper? Aren't you just being a Boy Scout?

POLLY—And what'd you get on that quiz—seventy-eight?

MAX—I don't know. (*He rises.*) I only know that my best doesn't seem to be good enough. I thought doing all this was sort of a formality. I was wrong. This is a profession. I haven't said this to anyone, not even myself. But at my age . . . I don't know—Polly, I can't wash out.

POLLY (*crossing to* MAX)—You're not going to. Because I don't care what you say, you are the smartest, handsomest, blue-eyedest-sexiest . . . You are the best ballroom-dancerest sol-dier in this whole Army.

Polly has started to unfasten her shoulder straps and Max is taking off his tie when there is another bugle call sounded from the near distance. Max listens anxiously. And Polly, too.

"What is it, darling? Do you have to go?"

"No," says Max, reassuringly. "Only I'm not sure whether that's 'Lights out' or 'Dismount.'"

"I'm sure it's lights out," says Polly, as she turns to him to unsnap her dress.

She is in his arms again when he asks, with a shade of serious concern: "Angel, will you love me even if I don't graduate?"

"Oh, no," she protests. "I've got my heart set on a Second Lieutenant—and you'd better see that he turns out to be you.

Darling, what a wonderful thing it is to be in love! When you think of all the people out there just flapping around." She has picked up her hat box and started for the bedroom. Outside the wind is beginning to blow.

"Where are you going?" demands Max.

" 'The sky is falling, the sky is falling, and I'm running to tell the king,' " she chirrups and disappears.

Left alone, Max continues to undress, but suddenly he glimpses his Army Manual. He picks it up, reads for a moment and begins mumbling—"Airplane chemical bombs are used to disperse agents of varying persistency . . . and require protective measures . . . Ha-Ha—" He has at least got that much. He sits in the wing chair, takes off a shoe, goes back to the Manual, reads a little and starts again: "White phosphorus is used as standard filling in the 75-millimeter, 105-millimeter and—145— no—155-millimeter artillery shell, and—"

His difficulties increase. He peeks at the book, then quickly covers the page again before he starts over. Some minutes of this when a mate call is heard from the bedroom—

"An-gel. . . ."

"Yeah?"

"If you're lost, follow the pieces of my petticoat I tore up."

"Oh, darling—"

Contritely Max gathers up his shoes and rushes into the bedroom, closing the door after him. Outside the wind has risen to a howl. A moment of silence and then the phone begins ringing. No response. A moment later there is a light knock on the front door. Another moment, another knock. Finally a solid bang-bang. A brief pause and then "the bedroom door flies open and Polly, in negligee, comes sailing through, goes to the front door and opens it as though she intended to tell someone what for. There stand the Luptons, tired and disheveled. The wind howls."

The Luptons' train is eight hours late. Not until 5 in the morning can they hope to get away. Of course they have no intention of staying there, but they had come back to the Court thinking perhaps there would be another bungalow they could use just for the night. There isn't. Roy thinks perhaps, if they could use the telephone— Sure, they can.

Max appears "like a sunrise in the door." He calls a cheery greeting and blinks a friendly blink at them. Now the Luptons realize that the Whartons had really gone to bed and are deeply chagrined. "It's kinda like a cartoon in Captain Billy's Whiz

Bang," ventures Polly.

Roy continues to call up various places, but without any luck. It soon becomes apparent to all four what will have to be done to meet the situation, but none of them cares to be the first to make a suggestion. A good deal of expressive pantomime goes on, "the whole effect being that of a discussion taking place, except that not a word is spoken."

Finally Max takes the situation in hand and makes some headway. "Now, look," says Max; "I've got to get back to the field pretty soon, anyway—so—"

Both Jan and Roy are on their feet. "Oh, no—". "No, honest, we couldn't—"

"But, for heaven's sake," interjects Polly, with the air of a born salesman, "now where are you going to find a place like this? It's away from it all, and at the same time it's in touch with everything—"

The Luptons continue their protests, but in the end it is decided that they will stay. They can have the bedroom and Polly will make out with the couch. The boys go out to bring in the bags. The wind is still howling. Shortly Max reappears with the duffle bag on his shoulder and the khaki folding bag in his other hand. Roy is right at his heels, carrying nothing but talking earnestly—

"Yeah, but if you take Aircraft Structures, Terminology and Theory of Flight—you don't have to take Elementary Aero-Dynamics—"

Max drops the bags and they are out again, still talking. It's Army talk, Jan explains to a mystified Polly. Candidates talk it all the time. They have to in order to learn it.

Now the boys are back again, Max carrying the blue suitcase, followed by Roy, empty-handed but still talking. Presently Max has gone into the bedroom to dress and Roy has followed him in, still harping on the best way to whip the course.

Jan and Polly have, at Polly's suggestion, broken out the peroxide bottle and are discussing the available stores. There's Hutchinson's, says Jan, where they have everything, but you have to stand in line for hours and they don't deliver. Then there's Martin's, where they deliver, but they don't have anything.

Now Max is dressed and has departed for the field and the Luptons have retired, still apologetically, to the bedroom. Polly sits quietly for a moment and then goes resignedly about the business of getting herself ready for a night on the couch.

First she takes off the slip cover and disposes of that. Then she gingerly lifts off the patched army blanket and deposits it on the wing chair. In her Vuitton suitcase she finds a pale blue Asprey shawl and a lacy round pillow which she deposits on the sofa. Next she gets together her black eye-shade and her pink cotton to stuff in her ears. Now she has her tooth paste, tooth brush and sponge bag and would invade the bathroom if she did not suddenly realize that this might not be a good time to disturb the Luptons. She listens discreetly and decides it isn't.

Going back to where there should be a sink, Polly proceeds to spread the tooth paste on her brush and brush her teeth vigorously. But when it comes to rinsing her mouth there is no water. The milk bottle is empty. There's nothing but the peroxide bottle and the Scotch. "With a what-the-hell feeling she takes the bottle up to the kitchenette, pours it into the lily cup, takes a mouthful, sloshes it around and stops abruptly as she wonders what to do with it next."

She spies the window, but the window is closed. She remembers the rules, stamps on the floor once, twice, three times and, when the window doesn't open, jumps up and down hard with both feet. The window flies open and the wind spreads out the curtains. Polly, free of the mouth wash, is back at the sofa, unbuttoning her negligee. The bugler blows Taps. "All right! All right! Don't rush me!" Polly calls back.

She has thrown off her negligee and crawled into bed in a dainty nightgown. Suddenly the refrigerator sets up a clatter. Out comes the pink cotton. As she stuffs it in her ears the noise stops. Now she turns out the stand lamp and then realizes the ceiling lights are still on. With a sigh she gets up, goes to the door and tries to reach the switch around the corner. No good. She opens the door, goes out, and, as the lights go out, a gust of wind blows both door and window shut with a bang. From outside comes a muffled "Oooooooo! Dammit!" followed by a knock on the door.

The lights go off and on as a signal, but there is no one to see the signal. A group of passing soldiers are singing. "Off we go into the wide blue yonder, Climbing high into the sun—" There is an abrupt silence, followed by the "Army sex whistle" and a friendly "Hi'ya, kid—yoo-hoo!"

The Luptons finally hear the knocking and Roy, his tunic off and shirttails out, rushes to Polly's rescue. Glimpsing her nightgown he scurries as quickly back into the bedroom.

Jan appears in a white negligee to sympathize with Polly. "I got locked out once," she says.

POLLY—They ought to have a couch out there, just in case.

JAN—Yes—well, good night—again.

POLLY—Good night (*Gets cotton, plugs her ears and tests for audibility.*)   Hello?

ROY (*sticking his head out of bedroom*)—Did you say something, Mrs. Wharton? (POLLY *shakes her head and smiles, then waves her hand, a sort of good night with her fingertips.*)

POLLY (*putting out light*)—God bless Mommy and Daddy— (*Instantly the phone rings, two short rings.* POLLY *answers.*) Hello? . . . What? . . . Well, speak up— (*Realizes she has cotton in ears, takes it out.*) Yes? . . . Oh, . . . er . . . well . . . Is Mr. Gow really on the line? . . . Robert? . . . It's me . . . Polly . . . Max had to go back to the field . . . No, lamby, no telling when he'll be back. He's in and out like a morning glory, so you stop bothering him . . . Uh-huh . . . Max isn't going to be a bit of use to you from now on . . . Listen, Robert, I don't care what troubles you've got. Max is not going back on that newspaper . . . Will you stop trading on my lovable disposition and get the hell off this phone . . .

ROY (*coming from bedroom, his legs bare, an army blanket around him*)—Excuse me. The lights—

POLLY (*resuming her phone conversation*)—If you had the proper respect for what Max is doing, you'd leave him alone without being told . . . No! Don't you dare come down here, you parasitic son of a . . . (*She hangs up with a bang, puts out the stand lamp.*)   God bless Mommy and Daddy and make me a good girl!

She cuddles up on the sofa as the curtain falls.

ACT II

It is three weeks later, and the living room of 26-D has a somewhat changed appearance. There is a new tailored slip cover on the couch and a new cover on the wing chair. Polly's Vuitton wardrobe trunk is conspicuously present, and so is Polly's typewriter. The trunk bears many labels, showing its foreign travels.

There is an open ironing board, and on the smaller table there is a framed picture of Alexander Woollcott and a bowl of yellow roses. Scattered about the tables are a variety of Army Manuals and questionnaires.

There is a knock at the door, followed first by a call for "Polly" and then by the entrance of Robert Drexel Gow, "a tall, well-fed, handsome man nearing sixty. The world has been kind to him, and he acknowledges this by constantly giving it a grateful smile. He is wearing a blue flannel suit and a Panama hat and has a white carnation in his buttonhole."

Gow strides across the room and at the bedroom door again calls for Polly. There being no answer he starts back across the room. The telephone rings. Putting the several papers he is carrying under his arm on the sofa he answers the phone.

"Yes? . . . She's not here just now. Who wants her? . . . The *Miami News?*" This information puts Mr. Gow right in his element. He clears his throat and proceeds: "Why, this is Robert Drexel Gow . . . Yes, it is . . . Well, that's very complimentary . . . No, no . . . I'm just down here looking at some property . . ."

Mr. Gow is pleased to learn who is running the *Miami News* now and he would also like to have the racing man tell him who came in in the sixth at Jamaica. "If it isn't Wingfoot don't tell me—just hang up," says Gow. A moment later he has slammed the receiver back in its cradle.

When Polly arrives she "is dressed in a Mainbocher creation for shopping. She is wearing Eduard shoes, has on a pair of gloves and is carrying a string shopping bag which might have been designed by Mainbocher, too.' The bag is full of groceries.

Polly meets Gow with a friendly embrace and the information that she has never seen anyone less welcome in her whole life. When he repeats that he had to come down to look at some property she is quick to assure him that she understands: "Some property named Max," she snaps.

When Gow would know how she is, Polly's answer is free and complete. "Well, look at me!" she says. "For the last three weeks I have been living here at 26-D Palmetto Court, Miami, Florida—where it is—if I may say so—very hot for July." As she talks Polly distributes the groceries into various sections of the refrigerator. "And I stand on a street corner every day with my arms full of Uneeda Biscuits and White Rock and Rinso, watching my husband march by with a lot of other fellows, all singing 'Wait Till the Sun Shines, Nelly,' just because a guy went nuts in Berlin."

The trouble with Polly, Gow decides, is love. And love, Polly has been told, is what makes the world go round. "You know what I think?" adds Polly. "I think the world's going around with some very peculiar people."

Gow can understand that. He's got some of them on his paper —"Katzenjammer Kids and Foxy Grandpas," says he. "Only they're not in the funnies any more. They're on the city desk."

"I don't care how cleverly you cue into the conversation," Polly warns him; "Max isn't going back on the paper."

Max, Polly admits, is having a tough time with his training. That is probably because, as scientists have proved, that after twenty-one you simply don't absorb a thing. And look at the stuff Max is expected to absorb. For example—and Polly reads from one of Max's books:

" 'Theory of Flight.' Yes, this will do. 'Resultant. The resultant of two vectors is defined as the single vector which will produce the same effect upon a body as is produced by the joint action of the two vectors.' "

"What's a vector?"

"I don't know. And this is simply *nothing*. That's only one tiny, unimportant little thing he has to learn. He has to learn everything in this whole book. And I don't know how many more."

"Why, that's a terrible thing to put a man through," blurts Gow, taking the Manual from her. "Does Stimson know about this?"

"Of course he knows about it. This is an Army Manual. They're not training on McGuffey's Reader. People simply don't realize *what* it takes to make even a Second Lieutenant. They're heroes. They are terrific. They know things you and I couldn't possibly learn."

"Damned if I see how they do it."

"They're all young, Robert, that's how. They're all twenty or so. Max is thirty-nine."

"So what? So he can get a discharge and come back to the paper."

Polly will have none of that. Let Gow understand that Max and the paper have parted company for the duration. Whatever Gow may think about it, Max is convinced that his war effort is more important than saving a paper. "Because, if we lose there won't be any paper."

Now Max has arrived, loaded down with bottles of ginger ale and Seven-up and bursting with great news. Col. Foley is coming to see them. So important is this social item that Max practically overlooks Robert Drexel Gow. After a hurried greeting he admits that Gow will be a definite addition to the party when the Foleys arrive.

And how did Max manage to get the Foleys? Polly would know. Well, it seems that, quite unexpectedly, Col. Foley had sent for Max and was very cordial. "How are you getting along?" Max reports the Colonel as having askèd. "And I says, 'Oh, fine, sir.' So he says, 'Why, Mrs. Foley happens to be a great admirer of your wife, Wharton. She's calling for me in a little while and we thought we might just drop around and pay you and her a call!' "

That, admits Polly, is simply wonderful. It is probably the greatest thing that has happened since Spearmint, sneers Gow. Naturally there is a good deal of flustery excitement when the Whartons start getting ready for the Foleys. There's the room to straighten up and Polly must change into something appropriate. Happily, a huge basket of flowers has arrived for Mrs. Wharton. The order for them has been telephoned all the way from Hollywood, which makes it pretty impressive to the messenger, an elderly gent in a seersucker suit.

The flowers are from Joel I. Nixon and his card to Polly reads: "For you, for your Art, for your lofty spirit that lifts the screen to a new height." The tone of the greeting convinces Polly that they must be having a terrible time with the picture. . . .

It is while Max is changing his shirt that Gow presses the business that has really brought him to Florida. He needs an editor. Most of all he needs Max—"Certainly never thought you'd lose interest in the paper," Gow is saying.

MAX (*putting on his tie*)—Lost interest? That paper is part of my life. But it happens to be this is the way I can best preserve it.

GOW—You can preserve it best back of your desk.

MAX—I'm trying to earn the right to have my say later on. Kennedy could do a good job there if you'd only give him a chance.

GOW—He can't write. He writes editorials like—an editorial writer.

MAX—You just don't like him, that's all.

GOW—No, I don't. He eats too loud.

MAX—All right, then. Get someone else.

GOW—Try it. Try running a business today. You can't only

not *get* anybody else but even the ones you've *got* won't stay put! Crowell's the best man we got in Italy. He's coming *back*. Don't even discuss it with me—just cables he can do a better job on the home front. I'd like to have seen old man Pulitzer's face if anyone had cabled *him* that.

Max—Get onto things, boy. These days a boss watches his *employees'* faces.

Gow—How the hell can he? They aren't with him long enough.

Max—Why don't you go to work *yourself?*

Gow—I *am* working. I'm working on *you.*

Max—That's not work, that's just a bad habit. (*From the field comes a bugle call.*)

Polly—What's that?

Max—I think that's the one that doesn't mean anything.

Polly—Angel, have we got stuff?

Max—I brought some Seven-up and ginger ale and we've got White Rock and Gin and Scotch and Bourbon. That ought to cover it, don't you think?

Gow—It ought to unless they're awfully thirsty.

The sound of an approaching automobile indicates the arrival of the Foleys. The bustle to receive them is increased. Polly's first impulse is to be caught playing cards with Robert Drexel Gow, as though they had been interrupted, but on second thought she decides it will be better if Robert is permitted to sit down and nonchalantly appear as much like a millionaire—a millionaire with class—as possible.

Now Max has rushed onto the porch and is excitedly receiving the visitors. Presently they begin to filter into the living room to be formally greeted by Polly. The first is a Mrs. Gates, "a woman on the elderly side. She is wearing her best clothes and under her arm she is carrying the familiar red book, 'Fellow Americans.' "

Polly a little gushingly greets Mrs. Gates as Mrs. Foley, but the correction is soon made. Then Col. Foley appears. "He is every inch a military man, and his uniform, bedecked as it is with overseas stripes, wound stripes and campaign ribbons, attests to the fact that he is a Regular Army Officer."

Polly sweetly introduces Col. Foley as Col. Gates, but that, too, is soon corrected. Lest there be any mistake, Robert Drexel Gow is quick to supply his own name.

When the company is seated and properly plied with cigarettes (cigars for the Colonel), Polly is ready to serve the drinks, if Publisher Gow will fetch the ginger ale. The Publisher will, if he can find it. His first search ends with his opening the kitchenette doors with a great clatter.

Now Mrs. Gates is staring at Polly with apparent admiration. "Oh, Mrs. Wharton," she finally finds words to exclaim. "I just think I will have to pinch myself."

"Well, you go right ahead," agrees Polly.

"I told Daddy, and you can ask him if it isn't just exactly what I said. I told him driving over here, I said, 'Daddy, I'm going to drive the carefullest I've ever driven, because I could not positively stand it if anything should happen now when I'm just about to meet Paula Wharton.' "

"That's just what she said."

"You see, you're around with famous people all the time, but we aren't ever seeing anyone like you. Once we saw Mae West up in Boston. And Fritz Kreisler—but not together."

"Why, you just don't realize who you are," adds Mrs. Gates. "I don't guess there isn't anyone at the Field that hasn't written home to someone that Paula Wharton is right here in Miami."

"Yes, everyone's terribly excited about it."

Robert Gow has got the doors to the refrigerator open, but he is having trouble with the ice trays. Grabbing a small frying pan he gives the tray several lusty whacks. No ice. That's the way the Foley refrigerator acts, according to Mrs. Foley, so the Colonel offers to lend a hand. Taking the frying pan from Gow the Colonel clears a good free arm space and then whams the resisting ice tray so hard that the two middle drawers spill their fruit and vegetables out into the room. The Colonel politely stands aside while the rest of the company have some little trouble collecting the spill. Then he arms himself with a large sauce pan and is prepared to resume the bombardment when Polly decides she had better take the rest of the things out of the ice chest before the attack. Deftly she recovers a large platter holding a raw mackerel, then a head of cauliflower and one of lettuce, and finally a box of strawberries. These she passes among the company to hold. The Colonel is about to resume his assault upon the refrigerator when he suddenly thinks of a different strategy. Quietly he approaches the ice box and carefully manipulates the ice tray. In a second he has lifted the tray out quite easily. "All you need is—just a little common sense," says the Colonel, an observation that causes Robert Drexel Gow considerable pain.

"OVER 21"

Polly—You come down here and you circle around like an old crow.

Max—A vulture!

Gow—Damndest thing I ever heard—I'm a bum 'cause I'm not in the army. A bum!

(*Ruth Gordon, Harvey Stephens, Loring Smith*)

Gow, under further prompting by Polly, serves the company with Bourbon and ginger ale, while Max is busy getting the icebox contents where they belong. Meantime Polly is holding the fort conversationally.

"You've just come back from Hollywood, haven't you, Mrs. Wharton?" Mrs. Foley is asking.

Polly nods and Mrs. Gates sighs impressively.

MRS. FOLEY—Do you like Hollywood, or do you prefer it back East?

POLLY—Oh, I love Hollywood. It's fine.

MRS. GATES—What's that Clark Gable like? He was down here, you know.

POLLY—Yes, it was in the paper. Oh, he's terribly nice.

MRS. GATES—Is he really? I'm glad to hear that.

POLLY—Why, did you hear anything different?

MRS. GATES—Oh, heavens, no. No, indeed. But it's just his being such a success, of course, it's nice to know he kept his head.

MRS. FOLEY—Tell me, when a star like Betty Grable gets married, now doesn't that upset a lot of people?

POLLY—It didn't upset *me*.

MRS. FOLEY—No, I mean all those boys that pin her up.

POLLY—Oh!

MRS. GATES—Betty Grable— Oh, yes—she sleeps in just the top of her pajamas.

MRS. FOLEY—Tell me, Mrs. Wharton, what kind of a person is that Bob Hope? (*Knowing this will please the* COLONEL.)

COLONEL FOLEY (*laughing loudly at the thought of Bob Hope*) —Bob Hope—

MRS. FOLEY (*laughing apologetically*)—Daddy likes him.

MAX (*adding his laugh*)—He's a great guy, all right. Isn't he, Polly?

POLLY (*laughing heartily to* COLONEL FOLEY)—Oh, *yes*, indeed.

MRS. FOLEY—What *I* want to know is— Oh, Daddy, you're going to be furious with me—what happens when—well, if an actress has a baby in the middle of a picture?

POLLY—Oh, she wouldn't do that.

MRS. FOLEY—No, I mean what do they do about it?

MRS. GATES—Yes—do they have their babies in between the *pictures* or do they make the pictures in between the *babies?*

COLONEL FOLEY—I don't think Mrs. Wharton's interested in that.

POLLY—Oh, yes, I am interested.

MRS. GATES—You know, I don't like that *Hays Office*. You take, in "Gone With the Wind," when Clark Gable carried her upstairs, and locked the door—and then you saw just a picture of the sky. (*She makes a wry face, turning up her nose in disgust.*)

MRS. FOLEY—Mrs. Wharton, who's going to be in *your* picture?

POLLY (*putting her glass down*)—Well, Gary Cooper—

MRS. FOLEY (*with great delight*)—OO-oh—

POLLY—And Irene Dunne—

MRS. FOLEY (*still greater delight*)—Oo-oh—

POLLY—And Orson Welles—

MRS. FOLEY (*a great letdown to her*)—Ugh—oo—

MRS. GATES—What's *he* like?

POLLY—Well, Orson is Orson. Either you do—or you don't.

After Mrs. Gates has succeeded in telling the story of her nephew's sitting in the seat next to that of Rochelle Hudson in a Massillon, Ohio, high school, Polly remembers something that she wants to ask Col. Foley: "Do all the men, when they're graduated from here, get sent to Crocker Field, Arkansas?"

Before the Colonel can answer Mrs. Foley answers for him. No, the men are sent all over, she explains. "Of course, there is no way of knowing what the assignments will be. It's, uh—security, of course, until they cut the orders. The men get them the day they're graduated."

A moment later Mrs. Foley has looked up smilingly at the Colonel and added: "Wasn't that cute, Daddy, asking if they all went to Crocker?" She laughs heartily at Polly's naïveté.

It is Mrs. Foley, too, who pops in with all the answers when Polly is asking Col. Foley about his decorations and his service stripes. It is a record that covers twenty-eight years' service and is greatly to the Colonel's credit, but it is Mrs. Foley's story when it comes to the recital. Col. Foley does finally have a chance to sum up—

"Great life in those days," he says, with some enthusiasm. "Lots of fighting all the time."

"Then came the Good Neighbor policy and shot the hell out of it," snaps Mrs. Gates.

"What are you going to do when the war's *over*, Colonel?"

Publisher Gow asks. "There's not going to be another, y'know."

"The war isn't over yet, Mister Gow," says the Colonel.

"You just see to it you get Wharton here—in with you and it'll be a matter of days," continues Gow, laughing politely. "Yes, sir, you're getting a fine man—very progressive—full of ideas— you happen to read his piece called 'The Backward Military Mind?'"

Max has risen hurriedly and would stop this line of talk. Polly is quick to intervene with: "Max has always been crazy about the Army."

But Gow is not to be stopped. "You see," he goes on, "it was his notion that the trouble with our military men—"

"Robert! Is there any ice?" Polly tries again.

"No, there isn't." Gow turns to the Colonel. "Surprised you didn't see it—we ran it on page one!"

"I don't think the Colonel will be interested." Max is plainly worried.

"The brass hats sure raised Old Ned about it," chuckles Gow. "I'll send you a copy."

"Robert, will you kindly get on a subject you know something about?" snaps Polly. "After all, who knows more about the Army than Col. Foley?"

The Colonel has risen quickly and flashed the family departure signal to Mrs. Foley. Mrs. Gates is reluctant to leave until she has heard one of Mrs. Wharton's celebrated quips. Polly is perfectly willing to oblige if she only knew which quip Mrs. Gates would like to hear. And she is, of course, perfectly delighted to autograph their copies of "Fellow Americans."

They file out, through a barrage of affectionate farewells and Polly does think of something pretty original to fling after them: "Well, now that you've found us, I hope you'll come here often," she calls.

The sound of the Foleys' motor no sooner dies out in the distance than Max turns furiously on the publisher. "What the hell are you trying to do—get me thrown out of here?" he demands.

Gow—Sure. You don't belong in this thing—even if you think you do.

Max—I'll decide that.

Gow—I'm trying to do you and the Army a good turn.

Max—Well, you send him that editorial and I'll—

Polly (*coming back*)—Darling, don't worry. It's all fixed.

We're having dinner with them on Tuesday.

Gow—Aren't you ashamed of yourselves—toadying to a hick like that?

Max—The rest of your life is in the hands of hicks like that.

Gow—Aah!

Max—Who the hell are *you?* You're just a crummy millionaire. That doesn't mean a thing these days.

Polly—You *are* kind of dated, come to think of it.

Max—Having you around is like entertaining a buffalo.

Polly—You're extinct. You belong in the Smithsonian.

Max—Anybody takes a look at Colonel Foley—they know who he is. And that he's doing a job. He's got a record of service to his country right on his coat—what have you got on yours?—A sixty-five cent carnation.

Gow—Oh, I get it. I'm just a civilian. I don't do anything. Publishing a newspaper, that's a hobby, I suppose. That doesn't take brains, skill, work.

Max—You don't know what work is—

Polly—No!

Max—Unless it's working on other people. What are you down here *now* for? You said so yourself— You're down here working on me . . . like some lousy ambulance chaser, waiting to pick me up if I don't pass my exams.

Polly—You come down here and you circle around like an old crow.

Max—A vulture!

Polly—A vulture!

Gow (*flabbergasted*)—Damndest thing I ever heard—I'm a bum 'cause I'm not in the Army. A bum!

In his anger Gow stamps his foot vigorously. This makes little impression on the Whartons, but it does open the window. Overcoming his surprise at this happening, and being suddenly possessed of a new thought, Gow jumps quickly back into the fray. He was in the last war, wasn't he? He was, Max admits, but that wasn't a war anyone should boast about. Sure, we won it. But what did we win? Why did it have to be fought all over again?

"All your life you've put yourself and your own interests before anything else," shouts Max. "Even now, when it's been proven to you—over and *over* again—that *your* life and *your* interests are bound up with everybody else's you're still concerned with nothing but Robert Drexel Gow."

"What about you? You're just down here engaged in a willful piece of self-indulgence at the expense of your paper, because you haven't got any more chance of passing that examination and getting to be a Second Lieutenant than I have."

On that proposition Gow is willing to lay Max odds of two to one. Polly is for taking the bet quick, but Max hesitates. Even when Gow raises the odds to five to one Max doesn't want to take his money. Why? Because, shouts Gow, he knows he is going to lose. Why lose? "You'll find out, brother, when they say to you: 'Sorry, but you're forty and it's showing.'" With this final fling the wrathy publisher stomps out of the room.

It is peaceful for a moment after Gow leaves. Polly is quick to notice that. But she is terribly worried about Max. Something is troubling him. She can see that. But he won't tell her what it is. Mechanically Max goes about getting ready to press his pants before he returns to the field. When Polly cautions him to be careful that his false tooth is in his mouth and not in his pants pocket, as it was the time before, he is plainly peeved. Even this doesn't clear his mind for long. Finally he admits what it is. Gow was probably right. "I don't think I'm going to make it," admits Max.

Polly could cry, but she doesn't. She's too good an actress. Instead she picks up the questionnaire containing the questions that Max will be asked in the next day's quiz. Softly she calls to him:

"Lovey . . . Define me directional control."

Max looks up from his pressing. Then his eyes fall again. "No. It's no good, darling. I'm too old for all this."

"Define me directional control," orders Polly. "And holler it out so loud that even Gow can hear you."

"Oh, God." Max sighs, takes a deep breath and starts to rattle off the answer wearily. "Directional control is effected by the rudder-fin combination, the same considerations in general governing the distribution of the total area as in the case of the stabilizer-elevator combination."

POLLY—Angel! That's it. You got it.

MAX—But that's only the first one. I don't know the others.

POLLY—Oh, Max, don't sit there and tell me you don't know a simple thing like question number two: What is meant by terminal velocity?

MAX (*wearily*)—Honey, say I am too old. I don't mean I

want to be. Just say that I am—I've learned a lot down here, and that isn't going to be lost.

POLLY—Did you learn about terminal velocity? You're going to be furious with me, Daddy, but tell me about terminal velocity. (MAX *just stands there.* POLLY *pleads.*) Darling, please, you got this first one just absolutely perfect. Wouldn't you please just try this?

MAX (*puts his hand over his eyes, screws up his face, and takes off*)—Terminal velocity is the hypothetical maximum speed that an airplane could attain along a specified straight flight path under given conditions of weight and propeller operation if diving an unlimited distance in air of specified uniform density. If the term is not qualified, a vertical flight path angle, normal gross weight, zero thrust and standard sea level air density are assumed.

POLLY (*whispering*)—My God.

MAX (*dully*)—What?

POLLY (*on her knees beside him*)—Oh, Angel!

MAX (*dully*)—Did I get that right, too?

POLLY—Yes. You see, darling? You're so wonderful. Oh, darling, it was just absolutely perfect.

MAX (*brightening a little*)—All right. What's the next? You sure you want to?

POLLY (*rising ecstatically*)—Want to? Oh— Question number three. Define Azimuth and cite the standard example.

MAX—Azimuth is the measurement of direction in degrees by the clock method. Example: Using twelve o'clock as either True or Magnetic North, the direction of three o'clock reading clockwise is—the direction of three o'clock reading clockwise is—uh—uh—

POLLY (*troubled*)—What street did we used to live on?

MAX (*without altering his pose*)—East ninetieth. Oh, Ninety —the direction of three o'clock reading clockwise is ninety degrees; of nine o'clock is two hundred seventy degrees; of ten o'clock is three hundred degrees.

POLLY—Wonderful!

MAX—How many is that?

POLLY—Er—three. Practically half. All right, here we go. Question number four.

Max has found a telegram in his coat pocket. It had come for Polly the day before and he had forgotten. He would use it as an excuse to halt the quiz, but Polly won't have that. She knows. Joel I. Nixon. That picture can wait. "Come on, darling. Question number four: 'Describe the performance of the V-G recorder.' "

Max does pretty well with the V-G recorder. When at one place he sticks, Polly helps him out. He once had a music teacher named—what? Poynter. That's it, "pointer." Still Max is not happy. A man either knows a thing or he doesn't know it, so what's the use? "I don't know it and that's what you get graded on," protests Max; "not on how you play twenty questions with your wife."

Polly will not give up. He can do it, with a little coaching, if he will, and he's just got to do it. On they go to question five: "Summarize the Radar Chart Am-4." That, Max suddenly remembers, belongs to last week's quiz: They have had the wrong paper all the time! To Max the whole thing is silly. He can't even remember the examinations he has already passed! But Polly is still firm. Hundreds of others have passed it—

"What man can do, man can do! Darling, we've gotten this far, please let's graduate. Where is this week's paper?"

Max would keep that one from her, but she finds it and renews her hammering ruthlessly. "Question number one: 'What is Longitudinal Stability?' "

He twists and squirms, stutters and protests, but she will not let him go. "What is Longitudinal Stability?" When he does not answer she begins prompting. "Come on— 'Longitudinal Stability is—' " He starts to repeat after her—" 'Stability with influence.'

"—'is stability with influence'—"

POLLY—to disturbances—
MAX—to disturbances—
POLLY—in the plane of symmetry—
MAX—in the plane of symmetry—
POLLY—and is effected—
MAX—and is effected
POLLY—by the stabilizer elevator combination.
MAX—by the stabilizer elevator combination.
POLLY (*triumphantly*)—*That's right!* (*Slapping* MAX *on the shoulder.*) Question number two: What is the difference between the—
The curtain falls.

ACT III

Three weeks later the living room at 26-D Palmetto Court is in a state of disorder, indicating plainly enough that the Whartons are leaving. Polly's Vuitton suitcase and hat box have been joined by a new Gladstone bag. Vuitton wardrobe and steamer trunks are packed and practically ready. The upper doors of the kitchenette are open, revealing empty shelves.

Polly is at the telephone and someone is being given a swell account of what happened at Max's graduation. "Oh, God, he was wonderful," Polly is saying. "You can imagine the way he looked, of course. And you know when they gave him the citation or diploma or whatever you call it, he gave a little bow, nothing much, just terrific. I am telling you I thought my heart was going to stop. . . . Well, all right, Lamby, I knew you'd want to know right away . . . I'll write you, darling. The minute I know where we're stationed. G'by!"

Polly is happily singing "Cuddle Up a Little Closer, Lovey Mine" as she collects her hat and gloves. She has barely time to complete this chore when the phone calls her back. This is a long distance call from Washington. From a person named Felix, no less. And now Felix is given a wife's eye report of the graduation. Not only had Max graduated, terrifically, but in a class of 353 he graduated 271. And is that good? Polly will say it is. And anybody who doesn't think so is just crazy!

She finishes with Felix. There is just one more call expected. That would be from Bar Harbor. Polly goes back to cuddling up a little closer while she waits. "Cuddle up a little closer, lovey mine, Cuddle up a little closer, you're dee-vine—" And then the call comes.

"Hello? . . . Hello, Angel, it's me, Polly . . . What are you doing? . . . Now, don't be coarse . . . Have you heard? . . . Max . . . Yes!!! . . . This afternoon . . . I just came from there . . . Where's Laura? . . . Oh, God. Well, have her call me the minute she comes in . . . Honestly, it would have broken your heart. Max was so wonderful. Just calm and smiling and . . . Oh, that darling smile of his . . . And honestly, you won't believe this, you'll say I just imagined it, but when the General handed him his . . . Why, General . . . uh, you know . . . but anyway, what I'm telling you, when he handed Max this thing, he smiled at him so wonderfully you knew just how much he thought of Max. And he looked simply glorious. And did I tell you? . . . Two hundred and seventy-

first. No, darling, there were three hundred and fifty-three in
the class. That's what makes it so terrific . . . And listen,
these boys are all brainy. They're special. They're twenty-one.
Honestly, it is the most wonderful triumph."

Finished with Bar Harbor, Polly goes back to her packing and
tidying up. She has switched tunes and is singing confidently
the one that goes "Soldier Boy, Soldier Boy, where are you going?" "To fight for my country, the red, white and blue—"

Coming upon a half gallon bottle of Poland water Polly leaves
her Soldier Boy long enough to drink the one drink left, and
tosses the bottle into the waste basket. In the near distance
someone can be heard whistling the Air Corps Song. It turns
out to be Max. He is wearing his new officer's uniform of a
Second Lieutenant and is carrying a folded newspaper. Polly
can hardly wait to hear his report. Where are they going?

Max doesn't know. The orders were being handed out, but
he won't get his until later. A lot of the fellows, he had noticed, were being sent to Mitchell Field. And wouldn't that be
great? Max is a little worried about a copy of his old paper
he has picked up—but hell, no—he isn't going to worry about
that—or anything—today—

"Say, is it too early for a drink?"

"What's early about it?" demands Polly, fishing a bottle out
of one of the bags. "It's tomorrow in Europe and yesterday in
China."

There is an embrace before the drink and then a toast. Polly
raises her glass: "To the very greatest feller that ever graduated two hundred and seventy-first," says she—and promptly
bursts into tears.

"Baby—darling, what are you crying for? Didn't you think
that was good?"

"*Good!* Max, you're wonderful. There's nobody like you.
Nobody in this whole entire gorgeous stinking world!"

"Then don't cry, baby, *please!*" He has his arm around her
now. "You know I could have been three hundred and fifty-
third."

"Oh, darling, this is the very best Graduation Day of my
whole life."

A feminine "Yoo-hoo" announces the arrival of Colonel and
Mrs. Foley and Mrs. Gates. They have come bearing the
Colonel's congratulations and, in a manner of speaking, a gift.
Col. Foley has stopped on the way over and picked up Max's
orders.

"I understand you finished seventy-first, Lieutenant?" says the Colonel.

"Oh—no, not exactly." Max might be blushing.

"It was—two *hundred* and seventy-first," proudly announces Polly.

"Oh!"

"Daddy graduated *thirty-ninth* in his class," recalls Mrs. Foley.

"There were forty in the class," adds Mrs. Gates, before Mrs. Foley can stop her.

Now Col. Foley has taken a long Kraft envelope from the pocket of his tunic and is dangling it before them. Polly would grab it, if she dared, but the Colonel has quite a bit to say before the ceremony is completed. He has, he explains, brought Max's orders to him because he remembers that when he graduated, a Capt. Hartley had brought his (Foley's) orders to him—

"I was sitting in my quarters just as you're sitting here—only, of course I wasn't married then—" recalls the Colonel.

"We were engaged," inserts Mrs. Foley, beaming.

"I'll never forget it," adds Mrs. Gates, also smiling at the happy recollection. "She came home to me and said, '*Who* do you think I'm going to marry?' And I said, 'Who?' And she said, 'Old Foley!' "

"Mama, I did not."

"You did so."

"Well—what I was going to say was— You thought I wasn't paying any attention that day when you talked to me about it here." The Colonel is addressing Max, across Polly. "Well, I guess I can take a hint. You wanted to go to Crocker Field, Arkansas, and that's where you're going."

"It wasn't the easiest thing in the world to fix," Mrs. Foley smilingly assures Polly, who is doing her best not to appear too glum about it. "Daddy just put his foot down and you got it."

"Well, I don't know what to say, sir," Max is saying. "Uh—thank you very much and—I wish you were going to be there, too."

"Yes . . . it was just wonderful of you . . . er . . ." chips in Polly.

"Not at all. Well, we're on our way. And some day, when the war is over, we must all get together."

"At Crocker Field," finishes Polly.

The Foleys have gone and the Wharton discussion has started.

Crocker Field, of all places! Of course, for Polly, going to
Crocker Field is out of the question, according to Max. And
Polly couldn't even consider not going, according to Polly. Max
argues and Polly pays little or no attention. Calmly she gets
a pencil and goes about writing her approved destination on all
the tags attached to the bags. "Policeman, this man is following me," she protests, when Max stays at her heels.

"Polly, listen—and Muscalong, where you'd have to live—
darling, there's no hotel—you'd have to find a room and you
couldn't—and the Field is twenty miles away—"

Polly is down on her haunches writing on a tag. ". . . No
cars, of course, only a bus line—the boys cue up for two hours
just waiting to *get on* the bus—now, how often could I do that?"

POLLY (*still writing*)—Oftener than you could cue up to come
to New York or California.

MAX—It's for *men only,* darling—the wives never go.

POLLY—Well, this wife's going. Darling, it's our last six
weeks together. After that you get sent off—you said.

MAX—But I'll be working every minute.

POLLY—And I'll be helping you. Didn't I help you here?

MAX—Yes, sweet, but not there. There we aren't reading
about flights and guns and maneuvers—we're out in the open
doing them.

POLLY—Bub, bub, bub, bub.

MAX—Angel, look at those trunks. The Savoy, London; the
Normandie; The *Queen Mary;* Paris-Ritz. (*He looks at her.*)
Next stop Muscalong, Arkansas.

POLLY—Why, you're just a great big snob.

MAX—No, I'm not. But you're special and elegant and that's
how I want to think of you. I know you can do all this and
you can wash and cook and go shopping!

POLLY—Darling, I don't want to be special and elegant, that's
old-fashioned. We've got a chance to get in with the furnished
room crowd and we can do it, too. Angel, go get our tickets.
It said proceed without delay.

MAX—You're not going, darling. I can't let you.

The discussion might easily have continued far into the night,
but at that moment Robert Drexel Gow appears in the doorway. He is dressed in the Army uniform of a Major. Max and
Polly find him rather startling.

"Robert, what have you got on your shoulder? Candy?" demands Polly.

"Are you in the Army—or are you down here in summer stock?" Max would know.

"You'll find out when you get outside and have to *salute* me," Gow promises.

"When did all this happen?"

"Oh, I went down to Washington last week and offered my services. Yesterday they accepted, so I turned in my carnation."

"Services? What services?"

"Well—er—I tell you they sent for me to come down. Department was lagging—"

"Lagging. Oh, that's your department, all right."

"Listen, Robert," says Polly, "if you're going to be lifting and carrying in Washington, who's going to be looking after the paper?"

"Well! My compliments." There's a light sneer in Gow's voice. "I thought you'd gotten so flighty you were above being interested in the facts of life—that's what I've come down here to tell you. (*He pauses a moment.*) I'm selling the paper. Frank wants it for his chain."

The results of this bombshell are immediate and devastating. It is difficult for Polly to control herself. Robert has no right to do that to Max, says she. The paper is as much Max's as it is Robert's.

Max is hit even harder. Nor can Polly comfort him. Why did Robert have to sell the paper to *Frank?* "Hasn't he got enough knives stuck in the country?" says Max.

Robert must know what such an owner will do with the paper. It took ten years to put it where it is, and it will come down in one edition. So troubled is Max that he is glad of an excuse to leave. He must go to the station.

Max is barely out of the house when Polly turns on Gow. "I just want to tell you *one* thing, Robert. Whether you're a Major or a publisher to the general public—to *me* you're a *depressing skunk.*"

"Now, calm down, Polly."

"Do you realize that you've come damn close to breaking a man's spirit?"

"Well, it was his spirit or my bank account."

"What do you want, the Midas touch? You'll have gold in your hair and eyes and ears and your belly button. Let me just tell you something, that ain't going to be a bit becoming unless you're thinking of going into the ballet."

"Well, my God, I didn't know it would be such a bombshell. I've been warning you all down the line."

"Why, you great friendly *stinkweed,* how would you like to step outside?"

"Listen, Polly—"

"Come on—" Polly is at the door. "Or do you want me to help you out?"

"All right, I'll go. But nobody below a Colonel can call me a stinkweed."

Gow has stormed out without his hat. Polly is pacing the room trying to control her anger. When the phone rings she grabs the receiver from the hook and answers the call from Bar Harbor. Certainly Max graduated, she shouts. But what is that to be happy about? "Listen, honeybunch, just crawl back into your Bar Harbor fox hole and let us sulk in peace . . ." With this she slams the receiver down and starts out. At the door she encounters the beaming face of Joel I. Nixon, a stocky man of Hebraic cast, who is followed by Miss Manley, his secretary.

"How are you, Brains?" This is the Nixon greeting.

Polly would ignore Joel if she could. Hadn't she told him back in Hollywood not to bother her—no matter what he wanted?

"Polly, I need you," pleads Joel. "It's only maybe for a few minutes, but I need you bad."

It is the Gettysburg Address sequence in the picture that is bothering Joel. Orson can't take it. Orson wants a topper. "Says he can't sit there and listen to Lincoln and not answer back," reports Joel, adding by way of explanation: "Orson gets six thousand a week—Lincoln gets seventy-five bucks a day. And we use him for two days."

"All right, then—let Orson say the Gettysburg Address and Lincoln can listen." Polly is furious. She would have Joel get the hell out of there. But Joel won't. If she won't fix the Gettysburg Address sequence, won't she please do something about the Molly Pitcher sequence?

"Well, what can I do about it?" demands Polly. "I didn't write the Molly Pitcher sequence. I lifted it straight out of history."

"*I know.* That's what's the matter with it. It may get four stars in history, but in the projection room it lays an egg."

Max is back, and in a hurry. He has come for a copy of his "Officer's Guide." Will Polly please help him find it? He pays little attention to Joel and Miss Manley, but is quite glad to hear Joel say that they are just going.

As Polly joins the search for the book, Joel trails her from bag to trunk and to bag again, trying to explain what he wishes she would do with the Molly Pitcher sequence. Parts of it are all right. Parts of it had the camera crew bawling. But a lot of it is also unbelievable. Then Polly turns on him—

"What's unbelievable? What's the matter with you, Joel? What the hell is Molly Pitcher famous for? For shooting off a cannon! So what else do you want her to do?—Bust out crying or get drunk or sing a number?—Well, she just didn't happen to, and *still* they named a hotel in New Jersey for her. What is so unbelievable about the truth?"

"You hit it!" Joel is also getting a bit excited. "The truth's no good to me, Polly! History just isn't practical. You say she shoots off a cannon—well, all right. But *how?* After all, she's a simple Colonial, not a Russian sniper. She hasn't been to West Point, you know. This is American history . . . not Abbott-Costello. Polly, don't you see what I mean?—We can't stick to history. History's *unbelievable!* And it's up to us to make it *seem real* . . .

"Honest to God, Joel, you must have a brain of solid popcorn." That amuses Joel. He snaps his fingers and motions to Miss Manley to take it down. Polly goes on: "Will you kindly tell me what is unbelievable about a woman in the midst of battle in a do-or-die situa . . . Listen, Joel, in the fell clutch of circumstance, people with gumption don't wince and turn aside and send for Madame LaZonga to give 'em six lessons in how to start punching. If they *have* to, they *do!*—So what the hell is so unbelievable about a woman in the midst of battle taking over her husband's . . . (*A full realization of how she can save the paper comes to her.*) taking over her husband's . . ."

Suddenly a new light comes to Polly's eyes. Couldn't that be the solution to her problem? "Angel!" she calls to Max in the bedroom. "Angel! Would you let *me* take over for you?"

"What?"

"The paper. Would you let me be the editor of it?"

"Editor!" Max is still a little puzzled.

"Your job, darling. Then he wouldn't have to sell the paper."

"Darling!"

"Max, I can do it if you think that I can."

"My God! Baby! Would you?"

"It's what I was born for. Would you let me?"

"Who else, darling? Who else in the world?"

"This is our day all right. Baby, admit it . . . wasn't I right to ask you to marry me?"

"I'm glad I came," mutters a completely nonplused Joel, sinking to the couch.

Robert Drexel Gow is back for his hat, and pretty mad. "Most humiliating experience of my whole life," he grumbles. "Went and left my hat here and two Military Police came up and made a public issue of it."

Gow has certainly walked into something. Polly fairly swarms upon him. "When you walked through that door you walked right into Opportunity," explodes Polly, when she has Gow seated. "You don't have to sell the paper. You got help like you never dreamed of . . . how'd you like help that's hotter than a pistol—the biggest ball of fire since Halley's Comet?"

GOW—I'd like it. Who?

POLLY—Me.—Ever hear of her?

GOW—You! Yuh, but, Polly, what makes you think you can do it?—You never done anything like it before.

POLLY—Well, you never were a *Major* before. Women never ran railroads or built airplanes or were welders before.

JOEL (*to* MISS MANLEY, *who is taking it all down*)—She's right.

POLLY—Look at the kids flying in bombers and fortresses!—Yesterday they were cutting rugs at college! Men who never even left their *home towns* before, today they're scrambling up the hills to Rome!

JOEL (*to* MISS MANLEY—*all admiration*)—Dialogue—

POLLY (*unmindful of the interruption*)—This is a world of changes. The waltz is on the wane, kiddo. You'd better oil up your joints, or you'll turn quaint.

JOEL (*to* MISS MANLEY)—Wire that to Orson. He can say it to Lincoln.

GOW—But the newspaper business, Polly— There's a lot to know.

POLLY—Lamby, it's a luxury of the *past* to be doing something that's your business to do. So, once more into the breach, dear friends, and mama'll handle the home front!

MAX—What do you say?

GOW—Not bad—not bad— (*An auto horn is heard.* MAX *runs into bedroom.*) Say, you know it really would be a stunt—

POLLY—What do you mean stunt? You talk as though I was

Joe Daniels, the Educated Ape. (*Affectionately.*)   Come on, what d'you say, Chowder Head?

GOW—How do you want me to address you—Sir or Ma'am?

JOEL (*to* MISS MANLEY)—She got the job.

POLLY—Oh, honest to God, Robert, you kind of bring out the sentimentalist in me.   Just call me Boss.

Max has come from the bedroom.   He has his hat on and is carrying both his bags.   Polly is startled.   Surely he isn't going now!   Not right this minute!

But he is.   The auto horn was the signal.   He didn't want to have a scene.   Polly couldn't have gone with him, anyway.   It's a troop train.   He'd rather Polly wouldn't even come to the station with him.   Everything's fine now.   Max isn't worried about the paper or anything.

Max and Polly are in each other's arms now, whispering their good-bys, and after a moment Max has gone.   Polly rushes out for a last sight of him as the sound of his motor fades away.

"How do you like that?" a disgusted Joel demands of Miss Manley.   "Paula Wharton says good-by to her husband and there's not a word of dialogue you can use!"

Polly is in agony when she comes back into the house.   There is a great rushing about to comfort her, but she is miserably unhappy.   Max is gone and she may never see him again.   Why didn't she go with him?   He didn't want her, but she should have gone.

That just doesn't make sense to Joel.   If she wanted to go why didn't she go?   Had she ever seen "Test Pilot?"   There's an idea!   In "Test Pilot" Spencer Tracy and Clark Gable are both nuts about Myrna Loy.   In Kansas City Spence takes Clark to the train, gives him the tickets, tells him to go to Myrna; he's the one she really loves.   Then Spence hops a plane, and when Clark gets to Myrna, Spence and Myrna meet him.   They're married!

"You mean that I take a plane and get there and surprise Max?"   The idea finally has landed.

"That's it!   That's it!" screams Joel.

"Well—er—how *could* I?   I mean, would it work?"

"Would it work?   The picture grossed eight million dollars!   Would it work!!"

Miss Manley is at the phone, taking a report of box office receipts at the leading picture theatres of the country.   Joel turns quickly to her.   "Miss Manley, tell Danny to get transportation to get Mrs. Wharton on a plane to— Where'd he go?"

"Crocker Field, Arkansas."

Joel repeats the destination to Miss Manley and Miss Manley asks California to put Shapiro, in transportation, on the wire.

Polly, in spite of herself, "is caught up with the magnificence of the thing," but is still a little bewildered. "What are you doing, Joel?" she asks. "She's calling up California and California is calling Florida to get me transportation to Arkansas!"

"Certainly. No use trying to get a connection from this end. They wouldn't know who you were."

It's done. The reservation is made. The plane leaves in twenty minutes. Can Polly make it? She can. And will, if Miss Manley will help her pack.

"Yuh, she *will make* it," Joel reports back to California. "You have the seat there in her name . . . don't ask me *how* . . . just do it . . . Listen, if people weren't peculiar, how much would you be getting a week?" And he hangs up.

The rush continues. Joel drops a roll of bills in Polly's pocketbook. Miss Manley will see that her things are sent after her. Gow is the only one who is not sharing in the fun of the adventure.

"Where the hell are you going?" the Publisher demands, roughly. "Are you Quentin Reynolds or are you going to run the paper?"

"I'm going to run the paper—but I'm starting with a six weeks' vacation," gaily answers Polly.

She has rushed into the bedroom and out again, grabbed her pocketbook and is ready to start.

"But Max is going to Crocker Field, Arkansas," repeats Gow, in complete befuddlement. "Why did you just say good-by to him?"

"Because, Stupid—did you ever see 'Test Pilot'?"

"No."

"Well, neither did I. But *I'm* Spencer Tracy!"

As she disappears through the door, an angry Gow grabs his hat and is ready to start after her.

"Miss Manley, get me the studio," orders Joel, crisply. Miss Manley is calling long distance when—

THE CURTAIN FALLS

OUTRAGEOUS FORTUNE

A Drama in Three Acts

By Rose Franken

THERE was, according to press confessions current at the time, considerable trouble connected with the staging of Rose Franken's "Outrageous Fortune." It happened to be a favorite drama of the author's. She had already scored outstanding successes with "Another Language" and "Claudia," so she was in an admirable position to be a bit independent when independence suited her mood. During the try-out period Gilbert Miller was interested with William Brown Meloney in the production. Later Mr. Miller withdrew from the enterprise and the Meloneys (Mr. Meloney being Miss Franken's husband) decided to go ahead on their own.

The play was brought into New York in early November. It was practically the first thoughtful drama of the new theatre season. The reviewers fell upon it with enthusiasm, freely admitting its virtues. It was well written and of honest boldness in exposition, but they found it somewhat lacking in coherency in both subject and character development. "Her [Miss Franken's] play will be violently denounced, violently upheld, loathed, liked and discussed with heat—which will attest to its vitality and to its interest as sheer entertainment," Burton Rascoe wrote in the New York *World-Telegram*. "It is a play people will be talking about, and therefore one which everyone will want to see."

As it turned out, enough people wanted to see "Outrageous Fortune" to keep it playing for ten weeks and it did excite a good deal of honest controversy.

This is a drama of case histories associated with a family of wealthy Jews living near New York. Its story covers the adventures of a week-end during which a certain strange and glamorous lady, with decidedly mystic leanings, tries with better than fair success to resolve a few of the problems with which the family is beset.

This character proved sufficiently attractive to Elsie Ferguson, a farmer-neighbor of the Meloneys, to lure her back to the stage after a retirement of some fourteen years. Miss Ferguson was credited with a commanding personal success in playing the role of Crystal Grainger, but she re-embraced retirement when the Franken play was withdrawn.

The living room of the Harris shore home is "flushed with the afternoon sun" on the particular Friday in the summer of 1941 on which we enter it. "The proportions of the room are palatial" and the rather rich furnishings are largely Chippendale and Queen Mary. There are a grand piano, a small love seat with ottoman, and various armchairs conveniently grouped. "There is no mark of poor taste, neither is there a striking evidence of originality. The atmosphere is one of affluence, and there is an aura of unremitting upkeep. . . . Everything stands just as it fell from the hands of the decorator. The room might be the lobby of an opulent country club."

As we enter, Mrs. Harris is seated in an armchair and Dr. Andy Goldsmith is about to take her blood pressure. "The relationship is more friendly than professional, and she submits to him with a fractious but winning impatience." Mrs. Harris is over seventy. "Age has descended upon her suddenly and swiftly. Her work in life has come abruptly to an end, and within her resides neither bitterness nor complaints."

Dr. Goldsmith is in his early forties, "short, slight and sandy-haired. The suavity and studied bedside manner of the physician are missing entirely. He is spontaneous, eager, penetrating— burning up with his own inner fire."

"The world is dying and you waste your time with an old lady's blood pressure," Mrs. Harris is protesting. The doctor will have none of her interference. He finds her condition very good. She may live to be a hundred, he assures her. The picture does not please her. Bert, her married son, and Madeleine, his wife, no longer need her; Julian, her younger son, is about to get married. So, why should she linger?

A moment later Madeleine Harris has arrived, a little nervously, fearing she is late for expected company. "Madeleine is in her middle thirties and possesses a somber, luminous beauty . . . Although there is about her an untouchable and untouched quality . . . there is nothing in her bearing to indicate a lack of emotional stability. To the casual observer she is a patrician young woman several octaves higher in breeding than her forebears."

A mention of the company that is coming reminds Mrs. Harris that she had fixed some herring and would like to give Dr. Goldsmith some. Which is good news to the doctor, seeing that his wife refuses to have anything to do with herring. "The smell gets her down."

Barry Hamilton, one of Madeleine's expected guests, has telephoned that Mrs. Grainger, who is coming with him, is also bringing her maid. The news is a bit startling, because of the shortage of room, but Mary, the maid, relieves the situation by suggesting that Mrs. Grainger's maid sleep in her room, seeing she has twin beds.

As for Mrs. Grainger, to appease Dr. Goldsmith's curiosity Madeleine explains that she is Crystal Grainger, a very good friend of Barry's. Madeleine has never met her. "I imagine she is quite a lot older than he is," says Madeleine, adding, with a short laugh: "I am, too, for that matter."

"Women will always be older than Barry—he's that kind of a lad," ventures the doctor.

"He's not so young. Twenty-six next month."

It is further recounted that Dr. Goldsmith likes Barry. So does Bert—probably because Barry is a musician and music is almost a religion with Bert. Yet Bert cannot play a note—

"Clear up his gall bladder if he could," declares Dr. Goldsmith.

"Andy, you're so right, really," agrees Madeleine. "Sometimes when he sits at the piano, fumbling over the keys or holding Doris' violin under his chin, it almost breaks my heart. He's like a dumb person, trying to talk.—It's a crime that all the chance to study went to Julian. (*Adds a little bitterly.*) For all he's done with it."

Bert's brother, Julian, it appears, is at the moment writing an operetta with Russel Train, a young man of some reputation whom Madeleine frankly does not like. Perhaps she's jealous. Bert idolizes Julian. But if she is jealous she is glad—it shows that she is at least alive.

Mrs. Harris has come from the kitchen with the jar of herring for Andy and gone on upstairs, after announcing with amusing firmness that she is going to have dinner in her room. Now Madeleine and Andy have turned abruptly to the subject of themselves.

"How long have Gertrude and you been married, Andy?" asks Madeleine.

ANDY—Twelve years next October.

MADELEINE (*thinking back*)—Was it only one month after Bert and I were married—?

ANDY (*bending to tie his shoe-lace*)—That's right. When Bert got you, I said what the hell—

MADELEINE—Oh, yes.

ANDY (*with a shade of changing emphasis*)—Oh, yes— (*Straightens.*) You know I've never seen you looking better. What have you done that's different?

MADELEINE—Hair. And make-up. Bert can't get used to me. He likes me better the old way. (*She wears her attractiveness like an unaccustomed mantle.*)

ANDY (*speculatively*)—I think it does you good, having a protégé.

MADELEINE—Protégé— That's a terrible word. It makes me feel like a dowager, with a big bust, a shelf behind, and a lot of money.

ANDY—Well, so far, you've got one of the requirements, anyway.

MADELEINE—I hope you're talking about the money— (*Breaks, and continues with small jerky pauses.*) Andy, you don't think Barry's the kind who would accept anything, do you? He didn't even want Bert to pay him in advance for Doris' lessons, and he was down to his last penny when I met him. Met him? I picked him up. Just like that, walking out of a concert. I often look back and wonder where I got the courage. It must have been the latent something or other in me. (*She seems wound up into a kind of defiant exaltation.*) Do you think there's the latent something or other in all women?

ANDY—More something than other in most.

MADELEINE—Anyway, it's all worked out beautifully. Now he's got a dozen pupils at ten dollars an hour. Not bad.

ANDY—Not bad? I wouldn't mind having you for my manager.

MADELEINE—I didn't have to do a thing but start the ball rolling. You know how our crowd is. Read the same books, use the same caterer, go to the same dentist—

ANDY—And the same doctor, thank heaven. It's our security, moving with the clan.

MADELEINE (*with sudden passion*)—I'm tired of the clan.

ANDY (*after an elliptical pause*)—You'll get hurt—

MADELEINE (*a little desperately*)—All right, I'll get hurt.

ANDY—Don't.

MADELEINE—Why not?

ANDY—It hurts too much.

MADELEINE (*arrested by his tone*)—How do you know, Andy?

Andy—I've been there.

Madeleine—I wonder if we're talking about the same thing.

Andy—We're talking about a sick world.

Madeleine—Maybe it isn't the world that's sick.   Maybe it's us.

Andy—We're part of the world.

Madeleine—(*haltingly*)—You said a little while ago that if Bert could play some instrument, he wouldn't have any more trouble with his liver.—I wonder what could cure me.

Andy—What ails you?

Madeleine—You're the doctor. Don't you know?

Andy—Sure. I know. But do you know?

Madeleine—Yes. The same as ails all of us.

Andy (*taking her by the shoulders*)—Look. Relax. You're riding for a fall.

For an instant Andy seems about to launch into a serious talk with Madeleine, but suddenly he changes his mind, picks up his bag and starts upstairs. He will have a look at Madeleine's mother, too, while he is there. Madeleine would stop him. She needs desperately to talk to him.

"Andy, listen to me. Help me. If a woman loves her husband—and he's the most marvelous husband in the world—he is, Andy—and she has a child and everything to make her happy and alive—only she's not alive, she doesn't feel—(*On a breath.*) That isn't normal, is it?"

"First you tell me what the normal is."

"I wish I knew."

Madeleine thinks probably that her husband is normal. Not because he is happy, but because he doesn't know he's not happy. True, Bert worries. "He worries about everything. Strikes, labor, the war in Europe. But I can't worry about anything but myself." She laughs nervously. "What do you call that? A neurosis?"

"We'll find a nicer name for it."

"There isn't a nice name for what ails me.—Why don't you try to jolt me to my senses, make me see that my puny little problems aren't important?"

"Because they are important. If each one of us swept up his own door-step, the world would be clean. But we won't sweep. Raises too much dirt."

Bert Harris appears just in time to take a hand in helping Madeleine decide whether or not they should send the station wagon or the Rolls for Barry and Mrs. Grainger. The Rolls it is. "Bert is perhaps a little more recognizable than the others. . . . No description fits him so well as that he 'has a heart of gold.' . . . With Bert there is no middle course. Good is good and bad is bad. . . . But his middle class morality is neither apparent nor obnoxious, for he is too intensely human for anyone to mistake his virtue for a pedestal. He is robustly normal."

When Madeleine has gone upstairs to dress, Bert turns with something resembling beaming satisfaction to Dr. Goldsmith. Mrs. Harris' blood pressure is better. That's great. Madeleine is looking well, too, isn't she? And the enlarged snapshot of daughter Doris in camp, which he is proud to show Andy, indicates the improvement that two added pounds has made in the child's appearance.

"Your small kingdom's all in order, isn't it?" suggests Andy.

"Couldn't be better.—Except the news is pretty rotten tonight. . . . By God, it makes a man feel he has no right to contentment."

"Nice work, though, if we can get it—"

Andy, too, should be feeling pretty good, Bert figures. "What do they call it? Attending Physician or Hospital Attending?"

"They call it in a pig's eye," answers Andy, with a short laugh. "The board meeting was this morning . . . I got a package of neat regrets tied up in blue ribbon. It's not a question of competence, you understand—" he adds mockingly; "Nothing personal—"

"What the hell, then—"

"My name should have been Smith—without the Gold in front of it. . . . Oh, I can see their point, all right."

"I'll be damned if I can!"

"Sure, I'm a good doctor. I breathe it, eat it, sleep it. And what does it get me? A kick in the pants.—Oh, well, we all meet it. The only thing makes me sick, they gave it to a jackass."

Julian Harris and Kitty Fields have come from the tennis court. Julian, ten or twelve years his brother Bert's junior, "is handsome and well set up, full of a smoldering animal magnetism which passes for an impressive masculinity. . . . He has advanced beyond his family and knows it." "Kitty is young and would like to be brittle and worldly. She is the . . . victim of a social existence that confines her, rather than irks her."

Julian and Kitty have been spatting about Julian's having discovered another "important conference in town" which is go-

ing to take him away after dinner. Julian isn't sure. He'll
phone and see what can be done about it.

It is while Julian is at the phone that Kitty nicks Bert for a
twelve hundred and fifty dollar donation for her China Relief
fund. She finishes this successful campaign in time to hear
Julian saying over the phone: ". . . Oh, well, if that is the way
it is going to be, I will. . . . Why didn't you say so in the beginning? . . . I don't like the way you're coughing. Take care
of that cold."

"Aren't you jealous, Kitty?" Bert wants to know. "Who's
that he's talking to?"

"Russel Train," Kitty answers, shortly.

"For a minute I thought it was a lady friend. Russel Train.
That's the boy he's writing his musical with."

"Yep," answers Julian, before Kitty can speak. Turning to
her he adds: "I won't go until ten. Does that satisfy you?"

"Always thankful for small favors," says Kitty.

Madeleine has reappeared on the stairs wearing a charming
dinner gown. Kitty is of a mind to admire the gown and also
to tease Madeleine a little about the care she is taking to please
her company, including "a nice young man with rosy cheeks."

"You seem to forget Barry's ten years younger than I am,"
Madeleine reminds them, as their teasing continues. And Bert
adds: "I only hope when you two are married as long as we are,
you'll be as happy, eh, Madeleine?"

"What's happiness got to do with it?" demands Kitty. "It's
just Nature, taking her own sweet course."

"I'm afraid whatever you find so amusing is over my head,"
admits Madeleine.

"That's all right, baby; what you don't know won't hurt you."
This from Julian.

"Which," puts in Kitty, "is the very principle I'm beginning
married life on."

A moment later there is an explosion of surprise. Kitty and
Julian have discovered that the extra guest Barry is bringing is
not a man, but a woman—a woman, moreover, whom Madeleine
has never met.

"That's a new one, isn't it? Having week-end company we
don't even know?" demands Bert.

KITTY—What do you want to know them for? (*To* MADE-
LEINE.) What's her name? Do you know that?

MADELEINE (*frugally*)—She's a Mrs. Grainger.

BERT (*with mounting disapproval*)—Mrs.? I thought it was "Miss." What's Barry doing, running around with married women?

MADELEINE—This sounds like an inquisition.

JULIAN (*suddenly*)—Did you say Grainger?

MADELEINE—Yes.

JULIAN—Her first name wouldn't be Crystal by any chance?

KITTY (*pooh-poohing it*)—Ass.

MADELEINE—But it is. What about it?

KITTY (*on a bleat of disbelief*)—What *about* it! Julian, do you actually believe it. *Crystal Grainger!* Here? Tonight? To visit Madeleine and Bert? I could die!

BERT (*a trifle distrustfully*)—What's so funny about it?

MADELEINE (*stiffening*)—Yes, what?

KITTY (*with relish*)—What's funny about it is that Julian's been trying to wangle an introduction to Crystal Grainger for a year!

JULIAN (*scowling*)—I know her, what are you talking about?

KITTY (*derisively*)—Oh, yes, once we met her at an opening and you said "Hello, Mrs. Grainger," and she said "Hello" back, but she didn't recognize you from Adam . . . How'd you get her to come, Madeleine? She never goes places, except a concert or a first night once in a blue moon—

MADELEINE (*unimpressed*)—Barry said he'd like to bring her.

KITTY—And she said yes?

MADELEINE—Apparently.

BERT—I still don't see what's so remarkable about it.

KITTY (*elaborately*)—Oh, she just happens to be the most talked of woman in America—

JULIAN (*ironically*)—Why stop with America?

ANDY (*who has been telephoning a patient*)—She sounds mysterious. What kind of a person is she?

JULIAN—All kinds. She stops at nothing.

KITTY—And gets away with it. She has a little colored maid. She took her to an opening night last winter.—Everybody died.

BERT—What's to die about? The girl might have wanted to see the show.

KITTY—*Darling*, she's just odd, that's all. But fascinating. You wouldn't understand.

BERT (*bluntly*)—Who's she married to?

JULIAN (*enjoying* BERT's *discomfiture*)—She doesn't bother with it any more.

KITTY—She hasn't had a husband in years.

BERT (*with finality*)—I don't like the sound of her.

JULIAN—Bert likes his women in wives. With a dash of bigotry thrown in.

KITTY—You mean he just likes wives. Bless his baby heart.

Dr. Andy takes Kitty and Julian along with him, but something to Madeleine's dismay they insist that they must come back after dinner. "Having guests in this house is like having them in Grand Central Station," she mutters.

When she and Bert are alone, Madeleine would continue the protest. Has it ever occurred to Bert that she would like to have her own friends for once, without the family spoiling everything? As for the gossip about Mrs. Grainger, she doesn't believe any of it.

When Bert suggests that neither Mrs. Grainger—nor Barry, either, for that matter—are their kind, Madeleine is mad enough to throw things at him. Why should he always be so intolerant of everything he doesn't understand? Furthermore, if he must know it, she has come to hate the whole damn life they lead—

"And what's the matter with the life we lead?" demands Bert, with mounting spirit.

MADELEINE—It's perfect for you, isn't it? Your wife, your child, your mother, your brother, your friends. Dozens of friends. Hundreds of friends. All cut out of the same mold, thinking the same thoughts, doing the same things—

BERT (*in slow realization*)—Maybe you're ashamed to be what you are. Is that it?

MADELEINE—Not ashamed, no. But not proud of it either, the way you are, carrying your pride around like a challenge— like an eternal chip on your shoulder! That's what's wrong with us, every last one of us. We can't act normal, we can't act natural. We either cringe or we strut—

BERT (*incredulously*)—I think you've taken leave of your senses—

MADELEINE (*wearily*)—I suppose you do. You don't really understand what I'm saying, do you?

BERT—I understand this much: You stay in your own back yard where you belong. And stop running around with people that are only going with you for what they can get out of you.

MADELEINE—You mean—Barry?

BERT (*flaring*)—Yes, Barry, and all the rest of them—!

MADELEINE (*haltingly*)—When you talk like that I feel as if you'd put me in a cage and locked the door.

BERT—The sooner we all lock the door the happier we'll be.

MADELEINE—But you're making your own prison! You're asking for it!

BERT (*harshly*)—And you're asking to be hurt. Look at Andy, isn't that enough for you?

MADELEINE (*swiftly*)—Andy? Andy proves my point exactly. He hasn't let religion interfere with his marriage or his profession.

BERT (*staring at her*)—Then he didn't tell you—

MADELEINE—Tell me what?

BERT (*in pity*)—It makes me sick to do this to you, Madeleine. (*As* MADELEINE *looks at him in puzzled questioning, he continues without triumph.*) I suppose you meant by Andy's proving your point—that appointment in the hospital?

MADELEINE—It's the beginning. Yes.

BERT—And it means a lot to him—?

MADELEINE—Yes—

BERT—And he deserves it—

MADELEINE—Of course he deserves it. It's as good as promised to him—

BERT (*starkly*)—Only he didn't get it.

MADELEINE (*stunned*)—Didn't get it? How do you know?

BERT—The board meeting was today.

MADELEINE—Oh, no! It can't be! I don't believe it!— (*Numbly.*) He never said a word.

BERT—I guess the poor devil couldn't talk about it.

MADELEINE—(*her lips dry*)—I think—he tried to—but I didn't understand him.

It's a rotten world, Bert is agreed. It's a sick world they are living in, as Andy had said, and somebody has got to start to make it well. But he doesn't want Madeleine to undertake the job. Such things have been going on for centuries—didn't she know?

"Does it have to go on for centuries more?" demands Madeleine, in simple despair.

Bert has gone to shave. Mary, the maid, appears suddenly in the dining-room door. She has come to announce that she and Katie are giving notice. Madeleine is at a loss to understand. Mary has been with them a long time—almost two years—

"Yes," Mary admits, "and it was all right too, until lately.

You're as nice a lady as anyone could wish for, no matter what. You and Mr. Harris both is all right, but things have changed, and Katie and me would rather be in another kind of place now."

Presently it appears that it is old Mrs. Harris to whom the help mostly object. She (Mrs. H.) is in the kitchen all the time, messin' around with awful-smelling fish, putting yeast dough to raise, and so on. "It's foreign ways, that's what it is," says Mary.

With that Madeleine bristles. Mary and Katie can both leave directly after dinner. Nor need the fact that there is no night train deter them. Mr. Julian is driving in and won't mind taking them. With this Madeleine walks smartly out of the room.

Mary is a little stunned at this turn of affairs, but takes it defiantly. She is getting out cushions for the terrace furniture when the doorbell announces the arrival of Barry Hamilton and Crystal Grainger. Barry is in his middle twenties—"tall, slender and good to look at. If he were a woman he would exude a kind of inherent fragrance. In a male it must be marked against him as . . . a sensitivity easily mistaken for a lack of virility. . . . It is easy to understand a woman falling in love with him, for he has tenderness, intuition and polish."

Crystal Grainger "is a woman whose face is naked and ageless, and whose body tells no tales." They are followed into the room by Cynthia, "probably the skinniest little colored girl in all of Harlem."

Cynthia is sent to join the chauffeur, who is taking the rest of the bags in the back way. She will sleep on a cot in her room, Mrs. Grainger tells her, a suggestion that irritates Barry. He still can't understand why Cynthia was dragged along at the last minute. In fact by now Barry is sorry he even brought Crystal.

"It won't be so much strain if you stop trying to show me off like a little boy bringing his mother to school," Crystal tells him. This is also upsetting to Barry.

"I was a fool to beg you to come," he says. "I should have known better. This isn't your milieu— You don't know anything about people like this—"

CRYSTAL—Oh, but I do. Didn't I ever tell you? Some of my best lovers were Jews. (*Dreamily.*) One was very poor—a poet. Another was very rich—a banker. And a poet, too, in his way. Your Bert's a banker, isn't he?

BARRY—Don't call him "my" Bert.—No, he's a stockbroker—

Listen, Crystal, I like him. I like Madeleine. They've both been wonderful to me. I don't want to see them hurt. Please.

CRYSTAL—There are nice things in you, boy. I could wring your neck for all the cheap little posing you do, but there are nice things in you.—No, I won't hurt your Bert and Madeleine. Maybe I don't want them to be hurt. Maybe that's why I let you talk me into coming.—She's in love with you, you know.

BARRY—You're out of your mind!

CRYSTAL—Don't be so frightened at the thought of a woman being in love with you. (*He starts to protest.*) Oh, but you are. That's one of the things that's wrong with you. For a while you were frightened that I was in love with you, too.

BARRY (*humbly*)—I wouldn't have the nerve.

CRYSTAL—Have the nerve to believe that Madeleine is.

BARRY—Crystal, listen to me. You don't understand. There aren't any murky corners in this household. It's made up of good simple people.

CRYSTAL—And you don't think I'm good simple people?

BARRY—I don't know what you are. I don't know anything about you. Nobody does, really. You're an enigma. (*His voice deepens almost to tragedy.*) But I wish I did know the secret of you, Crystal. I wish to God I could be in love with you—

CRYSTAL (*broodingly*)—I like you enough—to wish you could—

Madeleine has come hurrying in from the dining room to greet them. The introductions are friendly and informal. Crystal thinks it good of Madeleine to let her come and she knows, just from the smell of food and a sight of the terrace, that she is going to have a fine time.

Bert has come to add his greeting, and though the discovery that Crystal has brought her colored maid along is something of a poser, he manages to absorb the news with more or less grace. Barry and Crystal have no more than gone to their rooms, however, than Bert would like to know a few things—

What does Barry see in a woman like that? Crystal may have a fascination that grows on people, but it will have to grow a hell of a lot on him. And why is Crystal running around with a boy Barry's age? She must be near fifty, a suggestion that is not altogether displeasing to Madeleine.

Neither is Bert pleased by the news that Mary and Katie are leaving. Why not raise their salaries if that's the trouble? But

Madeleine will not listen. Mary was insolent and they will have to go—

"I guess coming after Andy's experience with the hospital I'm a little sensitive," admits Madeleine. To which she quickly adds: "Oh, it wasn't anything Mary said, I just read between the lines."

Bert has gone to get his check book when Barry joins Madeleine. He has a gift for her, a small and lovely Old Bristol vase which he had picked up in a funny little shop on Third Avenue. Madeleine is delighted with it, though she would chide him for his extravagance.

It is apparent to Barry that Madeleine doesn't want to talk about Crystal, but he rather forces her to. She admits a curiosity as to how Barry ever met Crystal— "I rather took your knowing her for granted," she says, "until—well, until I saw her."

"Funny how it happened. She rented a tiny apartment across the gardens from mine. I was practicing one morning and she came to my door. She wore a man's old black overcoat over her shoulders. She said, 'Play some more. It's good for what ails me.' "

"What ailed her, Barry?"

"I never knew."

"But you've been playing for her ever since?"

"I swear I think you're jealous—!"

"That's ridiculous—" But Madeleine quickly changes the subject.

Now Crystal has appeared on the stairway, "statuesque as a Grecian figure in a white gown draped in large, simple lines." It is a gown to inspire comment. To Barry it looks like something Crystal has wrapped around her like a towel. It is, Crystal explains, a gown she made from an old window drapery. The old gold fringe is still on it. To Madeleine it is as striking as a Paris model. To Barry it looks like a shroud. Bert, joining the group, finds it beautiful. He always has liked white.

Bert and Crystal also discover other likes in common. Especially the herring Mrs. Harris has fixed for Andy. Crystal discovers the herring when Bert accidentally tips over the jar. The others may have canapes if they like, but, if they don't mind, Crystal will gorge on the herring.

Bert has brought a silver plate and fork from the table and Crystal has helped herself generously to the herring. Now she is following Bert into the kitchen to find rye bread to go with it, and also to escape from the disapproving glances of Barry and Madeleine. "These two fastidious onlookers spoil my appetite," says Crystal. . . .

Barry is disappointed. He had hoped that Madeleine would like Crystal and it is apparent that she doesn't.

"I resent her," Madeleine admits. "She's so secure. And her security brings out all my weaknesses like a magnifying glass." Madeleine is quite unhappy and in no mood to be comforted by Barry.

In the kitchen Crystal has found "the little artist who made the herring," Mrs. Harris herself. Already as they return to the living room they are great friends. The idea of Mrs. Harris thinking she is going to have a tray in her room—

"Mamma's got some lovely recipes," Bert is saying, proudly.

"I bet she has," says Crystal. "I can see them in her eyes."

"My eyes are old."

"Young. Young as the sun."

"The sun is old."

"It's both," agrees Crystal.

Madeleine orders an extra place, and Mother Harris is carried away to the terrace with no chance "to fix up a little," as she is sure she should.

Crystal stops in the doorway to the terrace, from where she can literally taste the ocean in every deep breath she draws. She can imagine the syringa, and the "little new green smell of tomato plants." Bert is delighted.

"Funny. I love that smell, too— Never knew anybody else noticed it though," says Bert.

"Only toward evening—"

"Yes—"

"When the frogs sound like sleighbells in the distance—"

Bert nods. Crystal has turned back into the room and is reaching for the cigarette box on the table.

"Don't take one of those, I've got some special ones for you," he says, laying a restraining hand on top of hers.

The curtain falls.

ACT II

Later that evening Julian, slouched in an armchair in the living room, would have the news of the family's present whereabouts from Cynthia, who is passing through.

"Where is everyone, dead?"

"No, sir, nobody's dead," answers Cynthia, slipping back into her rich native dialect. "Mistah Barry is havin' a walk over the garden with Miss Madeleine, and Mistah Harris, he's settin' out with his Mammy. But I don't know where Miss Crystal is—" Her brow is puckered with anxiety as she hurries out.

Kitty has come to plead again with Julian not to go into town tonight. She admits that she was eager to have him do a musical with Russel Train—until she heard more of Train's reputation. Now she is quite unhappy about it.

Julian, for his part, refuses to get the least excited over Kitty's state of mind about anything. He isn't even sufficiently interested to fight back. Sometimes he doubts if Kitty is really in love with him.

"You're not a romantic and neither am I," says Julian. "You're marrying me because I am the stepping stone to what you want out of life."

"What do I want out of life?"

"Security and glamour. You're part of a social order that gripes you but you don't want to break away from it."

"Maybe— But what will you get out of it?"

"The two major requisites to my particular scheme of domesticity. Money and brains."

"By the conspicuous absence of the word 'love' I gather that I'd better make up a nice single bed and be prepared to lie on it most of the time."

Julian considers that remark a little crude, but is content to let it pass. He really is extremely fond of Kitty. She had told him once that she didn't want children, but if she should change her mind it would be quite all right with Julian, so long as she did not expect him to act the role of a loving father. So far as their marriage is concerned, it still is not too late for her to back out.

Kitty admits that she is scared, but she is not that scared. "Don't worry, darling," she says. "I'm smart enough not to ever really get in your hair. You'll have the name and not the nuisance. It's a promise."

"You're a funny girl."

"I know. You thought I was an open book and now you find a couple of pages you can't make head or tail of." She has lifted her lips to his. "That's all right, darling. At least I won't be dull. You could never stand a dull woman."

"The point is, can I stand *any* woman?"

"That's my problem. Are you going to kiss me, or do I have to go on hanging here in mid-air?"

"OUTRAGEOUS FORTUNE"

"Now Crystal has appeared on the stairway, 'statuesque as a Grecian figure in a white gown draped in large, simple lines.'"

(*Elsie Ferguson*)

Julian bends a little awkwardly to touch Kitty's lips. Bert and Mrs. Harris come from the terrace. That "the children" are there is a bit of a surprise to Mrs. Harris, but she is pleased to see them.

Knowing that the maids are leaving, Mrs. Harris' present interest is centered in doing what she can to fill the gap. Right now she thinks she will put some lentils to soak for tomorrow's lunch. Mrs. Grainger, being a plain woman, will love lentil soup.

"Mother Harris, listen to me," protests a startled Kitty. "Crystal Grainger is not a very plain woman. She's about the fanciest woman in America. I can't explain it, but she's—well, she's a celebrity. You know what a celebrity is? Somebody people talk about because they're famous writers, or actors. Well, Crystal Grainger is famous, but not because of what she does, but because of what she is—

So determined is Kitty that Mrs. Grainger shall not be subjected to lentil soup that she is prepared to go to Madeleine about it. Or perhaps she can bring over a maid—

Kitty has no sooner disappeared on the terrace than Crystal emerges from the library. She stands for a moment in the doorway. "There is about her a repressed voltage, as if she were using only a part of herself."

"I heard someone say I couldn't have lentil soup— Why not?"

Mrs. Harris explains the situation to Crystal. The maids are leaving. That has upset Kitty. The maids are leaving because of her (Mrs. Harris) fussing around in the kitchen with the herring. But she is going to ask them to stay and tell them that it is she who will be leaving shortly. It would be better for Madeleine and Bert and it would be better for her if she were to go. Crystal would challenge that idea, but Mrs. Harris is firm—

"My body is tired. Seventy-eight years it has been going around with me."

"It's been in good company," says Crystal, softly.

"Not so good. I say to myself: *Don't* go in the kitchen and make herring. But I do it. I can feel myself getting to be a child again. I fight against it. But I cannot help it."

"I think we're meant to become like children," observes Crystal, slowly. "Tonight, sitting there in Bert's study by myself, I was a child again, too. I wanted my mother. She died when I was six years old. But suddenly I wanted her. I needed her. And now, all at once I see that it doesn't make any difference.

The part is the whole. One mother is all mothers. You are my mother. Perhaps that's why I came here. So that we could find each other, and for an instant let our hands touch."

"You are right. It does not matter if they stay or go. (*With a little sigh.*) But it is a trouble for Madeleine to make a change in the middle of the summer. (*With a comical return to her old self.*) Do you think it would be all right if I talked to them? If I told them that I promise to stay out of the kitchen?"

"Tell them you're going to take up tennis instead—"

"Or music, maybe."

Mrs. Harris has moved over to the piano. Now she is playing, "with great punctiliousness," a few bars of an old-fashioned polka. "Now you see where Julian gets it from," she says, complacently. A moment later her mood has deserted her abruptly. She sighs as she rises from the piano, her thought still on Julian— "He is so different from Bert," she says. "So different."

Cynthia has come looking for her mistress. She is greatly worried. Crystal might have been having an attack. She had, admits Crystal—a peach of an attack—while Cynthia was having her supper. But she is better now.

"You ain't over it yet, no, sir," announces Cynthia. "Your face is cold as death, an' wet—" She has delved for something in the pocket underneath her apron. "You shouldn't ought to take this long trip after the way you was this morning, Mis' Crystal, you oughtn't should. Why you did it?"

"I don't know."

"You don't even like visiting."

"God knows I don't."

Mis' Crystal is a puzzle to Cynthia. Why did she sell all her lovely furniture and move into two little rooms? It may be "putting your house in order," as Crystal says, but it doesn't sound good to Cynthia. If anything should happen to Mis' Crystal, Cynthia's heart is just "gone bust in two."

"Nonsense. When I pop off, don't you dare cry. You just lift your voice and sing!" says Crystal, and adds, matter-of-factly: "And then get busy and sweep up the pieces as fast as you can."

"I wish you'd let me tell Mr. Barry how sick you are."

"If I ever catch you telling Mr. Barry, or anyone else, I'll wring your neck."

Cynthia has found a box of pills. Crystal should take one of these, though Cynthia is convinced her mistress should first have one of those little things she breaks and sniffs. Crystal will have two pills now and take a credit on the ampule. In the exchange one pill is dropped and rolls away. That doesn't worry Cynthia. They got lots of those little jiggers, and they taste so nasty nobody would be wanting to eat one.

Cynthia has gone to the kitchen for water. Crystal has thrown her head back against the love seat and is relaxing with her eyes closed. Presently Julian comes down the stairs carrying a small overnight bag. Seeing Crystal, he continues quietly into the room and is standing directly within her line of vision when she opens her eyes. For a moment she stares at him without moving her head. It is a disconcerting gaze and Julian loses something of his usual poise and cocksureness. As Crystal continues to gaze at him, quietly and steadily, he becomes increasingly uncomfortable. She suggests a zombie to him, "only zombies aren't beautiful."

She thanks him for that, but goes calmly on "taking off his outer skin" as he describes it.

"Are you ashamed of what's underneath?" she would know.

"Why should I be?" he parries, defiantly.

Cynthia brings the water and is sent on to bed. Crystal unobtrusively swallows the pills. Julian would resume the duel.

"Look here, let's begin all over again," he is saying, straddling a chair in front of her. "What plays have you seen?" Crystal shakes her head a little wearily. "All right, here's another start: What has Barry got that I haven't?"

"So many things."

"In case you've been looking for him, he's walking in the garden with my sister-in-law."

"I'm glad. They're good for each other."

"They complement each other's insecurity, if that's what you mean."

"That's true. In a way."

"Now we're beginning to talk a common language."

"I don't deny you've an excellent mind. Why don't you use it?"

"What makes you think I don't?"

"Because, if I were to ask you a certain question, I know that you would give me a certain answer." Crystal has weighed her words carefully.

"You intrigue me. What's the question?"

"It's not my business to ask it?"

"At least tell me the answer, and I can work backwards."

"The answer would be: 'What have you got to offer that's better?'"

"Well—what have you?"

"I could weep for you," says Crystal, simply.

"That, from you," declares Julian, with deliberate insolence, "is very amusing."

For seconds "his eyes lock hers in a bold challenge, then his gaze shifts before her clear scrutiny."

Bert has come down the stairs to join them. He is surprised and pleased to discover that Julian and Crystal know each other. Shortly Julian has drifted out to the terrace, and Bert is staring after him—

"It's hard to believe you're brothers," Crystal is saying.

"I'm the rough diamond in the family," Bert explains. "Never got to college. Glad Julian got a whack at education, though. Brilliant boy. D'you get a chance to talk to him?"

"Interesting."

"Wait'll he settles down. Marriage'll do a lot for him.—Too bad he couldn't find a girl like Madeleine, but Kitty's a nice youngster. She'll grow up to be a fine woman one of these days."

Bert is at the piano, fumbling awkwardly with the keys, wondering why it is he can't play a note and any tune that is hummed to Julian "comes out of his fingertips." He picks up Doris' small violin and holds it caressingly under his chin, reporting, a little proudly, that from this toy-like instrument Doris can drawn beautifully a Brahms lullaby that Barry has taught her. There's another lad with talent—Barry—

"Barry's had a tragic childhood," says Crystal, abruptly. "I'd like to see him give up his music and settle down to some regular job."

"You like the lad, don't you?"

"I love the lad," admits Crystal, with a smile. "All women love Barry."

BERT—I guess I come of an upbringing where one woman loves one man.

CRYSTAL—And one man loves one woman.

BERT—You bet.

CRYSTAL—That isn't love. It's possession.

BERT—Whatever name you call it, it's good enough for me.

CRYSTAL—The way you see it, good is good, and bad is bad.

BERT (*argumentatively*)—What's wrong with that?

CRYSTAL—It has no mind behind it.

BERT—What doctrine are you preaching, anyway?

CRYSTAL—Purity.

BERT—Maybe you don't know there's mud in the world.

CRYSTAL—I've waded through it.

BERT—And came out clean?

CRYSTAL—I feel clean.

BERT—You certainly make vice sound damned attractive.

CRYSTAL—On the contrary. My theory does away with vice.

BERT—This talk's above my head. I don't like abstractions, I'm no mystic.

CRYSTAL (*derisively*)—Ha!

BERT (*protesting too much*)—I'm a down-to-earth business man.

CRYSTAL—With a couple of thousand years of persecution churning in your blood.

BERT—Yes, and I'm proud of it!

CRYSTAL—That's a pity.—(*Curiously.*) Why should you be proud of it?

BERT (*belligerently*)—Why not? Should I be ashamed of it?

CRYSTAL—Neither. If you must be proud, be proud of what you are, not what you were born. Birth is an accident. Once the damn thing's happened to us, we have to go through with it.

BERT (*suddenly hostile*)—You don't like Jews?

CRYSTAL (*undramatically*)—I love them.

BERT (*still disgruntled*)—You seem to love everybody.

CRYSTAL (*lightly*)—That's my reputation—

Mrs. Harris has come from the dining room and started upstairs. She has won the battle of the lentil soup. They're going to have sausage in it, too. Crystal is pleased with the victory.

"Sounds like a conspiracy between you two," suggests a suspicious Bert.

"It is," admits Crystal. "Your mother illustrates my point. One-tenth, race. Nine-tenths, person."

"You certainly like the old lady, don't you?"

"I love her—"

Kitty and Madeleine are in from the garden. Madeleine, "enveloped in a luminous glow of happiness," carries a freshly picked rose which she puts in the vase that Barry gave her.

The maids are getting ready to go and Bert would know what time Julian is expecting to leave. Kitty wouldn't know. At that moment Julian is in the garden with Barry, talking music. Perhaps Kitty had better take up music, Bert suggests. Perhaps she had, Kitty admits—music or something.

Bert has taken Crystal for a walk around the garden, that she may see the ocean with the moonlight on it.

Dr. Goldsmith is back, having forgot his bag. "Shows where your subconscious wants to be," accuses Kitty.

"Listen, youngster—the trouble with you is you've read too many books.—Too much information; not enough significance."

"Could be," admits Kitty.

"Where is everybody?"

"Different places, doing different things."

"Why aren't you doing it with them?"

"Me? I'm waiting at the church." There is a degree of poignancy beneath this flip retort.

Julian and Barry are in from the garden. Julian has decided that it won't be necessary for him to go back to town, and Kitty is grateful enough to drop a kiss upon his hair as he opens the piano and begins to play.

Barry has wandered over to the piano and is quickly charmed by Julian's playing. Suddenly Kitty feels herself something of an intruder. She is in no mood for serious music; something to dance to is what she wants. Julian switches to a slow, insinuating waltz and she quickly pulls Barry out onto the floor. "They both have youth, grace and rhythm" but Julian, as he plays, watches them indifferently. Kitty's dancing is an old story to him.

As Barry and Kitty waltz they talk. Barry can forgive Kitty a lot for her dancing; being "hard and sometimes cruel" among other things.

"Women don't get under your skin," Kitty says accusingly. "If they did you wouldn't act the way you do. . . . I saw you in the garden with Madeleine—before Julian came out."

"It's no crime to kiss a woman," answers Barry, with no sense of guilt.

"It is if it doesn't mean anything to you, and it happens to mean a lot to the woman.—Poor Madeleine, she was walking on air when she came in."

"Why do you always fight with everybody?" Barry would know.

"Maybe it's because I'm lost before I begin, and I don't want to admit it," suggests Kitty. "I just found it out. Over there at the piano. Like that." She snaps her fingers.

"What do you mean?"

"I thought Julian was staying over tonight because of me. But he isn't."

A moment later she has a little abruptly brought the subject back to Madeleine. "Madeleine is riding for an awful fall," she says, "but who am I to blame her? If you're in love, you're in love, and that's all there is to it." All the harshness has gone from her voice. Barry is plainly moved.

"It's a slushy waltz," Kitty suddenly explains. "Julian! Stop that funeral march."

Julian plunges into jazz, accelerating the piece to a high emotional peak and watching with seeming satisfaction its effect upon the dancers. A moment later the music ends on a crashing chord. . . .

Mary has appeared with a tray of drinks, causing a minor sensation. Bert has discovered that Dr. Goldsmith has left Gertrude, his wife, out in his car, and insists that she shall be brought in.

"Gertrude is thirty-odd, looks forty-odd and acts twenty. She is thoroughly lovable, and as ingratiating as a clumsy Newfoundland pup. . . . Of the entire group her appearance, along with her preoccupation with money and food, might seem to stem from a racial inheritance, but her name, before she married Andy, was McDougal, and she was a student nurse at the hospital when he first met her."

Gertrude breezes into the party and for the next few minutes is the life of it. Her subjects run from that of a broken tooth that is going to deny her the joy of eating corn on the cob all summer, through that of the quantities of food and drink she consumes, to the girdle that is killing her that very minute. Reminded of Andy, she is free to confess to Crystal that she did not marry the doctor, she just grabbed him, and he had proved the grandest husband woman ever had. That's what makes her so sick about the hospital mess.

"What hospital mess?" Crystal inquires, innocently.

"Do you mean to say nobody mentioned it? (CRYSTAL *shakes her head.*) Is that decent of them—or isn't it? If that was me, I'd have blabbed it all over the place. Don't let on I told you. You say one word, I'll call you a liar—Andy was due for the post of Attending Physician at the hospital, and didn't get it. I tell you I'm sick about it. Just sick."

"What a shame. Why?"

"Jew.—Isn't that the limit?"

"Oh—"

"Honestly, it makes me so furious. And it's just ignorance and blind, stupid prejudice."

"It's amazing to find one of you so objective," murmurs Crystal.

"One of us?" cries Gertrude, staring at her. "Good heavens, didn't they tell you that either?"

"What?"

"Andy married an Irishman. That's me."

"And she's as much like one of us as we are," Andy adds. He has just come from a ping-pong game and is looking for a substitute. With some urging Gertrude agrees to take Andy's place, though she had much rather play bridge.

Dr. Goldsmith has picked from the floor the pellet that Cynthia had dropped. He would like to know why Crystal is taking them. With some little fencing she finally confesses. It is her heart. She knows she is finished; knows infinitely more about herself than the doctors know. She is hoping she will go painlessly when it happens. She feels that she has earned that much.

"You wouldn't like me to call you gallant, would you?" asks Andy.

"Just try it."

"That's what I figured."

"Look here," Crystal quickly adds. "I keep this to myself because it's nobody's business. They're coming back. Will you tell them I've gone up to bed and say good-night for me?"

Andy has walked with her to the stairs and is holding the hand she offers him in both of his. "If we don't meet again—" she says. He is standing watching her disappear up the stairs when Kitty comes in.

"Has Julian come back?" Kitty pours herself a drink.

"Not yet."

"I didn't expect he would." There is a desperate note in her voice. "Oh, what's the use? If it isn't Russel Train it's Barry— if it isn't Barry it'd be somebody else. I'm licked."

"Listen, bach-fish, you're drinking too much—"

"What of it?"

The others are back. All but Julian. Suddenly Kitty decides that she will go home. Not with the Goldsmiths, however. She prefers to have Barry take her. "You've never seen our place, have you?" she calls to him in a high, clear voice. "We've got the most divine pool, with real waves. Too bad you don't swim. There ought to be a saying: Graceful in dancing, clumsy in sports—"

"A violinist can't afford to take chances with his hands," protests Madeleine, sensing Kitty's intent.

"Even if he wasn't a violinist he's not the type." She turns on Barry cruelly. "I bet you played with dolls when you were little, didn't you, darling?"

"No, Kitty, I didn't play with dolls. But I did housework and cooking, because after my father died there wasn't any money, and my mother, who had never worked before, had to get a job. The boys on the block used to call me sissy. Maybe I was. Maybe I am, according to the way you see things."

A moment later a contrite Kitty is making her apologies. She knows she's a louse. There must be a reason why. The doctor, she insists, should know why. "I'm awfully sorry, Madeleine. I've spoiled your party," Kitty is saying in a muffled voice. "It was a nice party, too. And you can tell Julian for me when he turns up that I hate his guts! I hate him! I hate him! And I never want to see him again as long as I live!" She is sobbing as she goes out across the terrace. . . .

Bert and Madeleine are alone. Their talk has run on the party and its unexpected developments; on Barry, whom both Madeleine and Crystal have admitted liking; on Crystal, in whom Bert has found much to interest him. Crystal, Bert says, is "a catalytic agent." Madeleine would not know about a catalytic agent, except that it has something to do with chemistry; something about one substance acting on another—

"Only there's a little trick in it," explains Bert. "The original substance doesn't change."

"I like that dress on you," says Bert, a moment later.

"You said it was too low before," Madeleine reminds him.

"I was wrong before." As Madeleine shrinks a little from his touch he adds: "You're a funny girl. A perpetual bride. Remember on our honeymoon, the way you always used to run to cover? Remember I used to tease you that a married lady didn't have to be so modest? Twelve years, and there's still something of the virgin about you. But I wouldn't want you any different. I just want you to love me and I want to hear you say it."

"I love you, Bert."

Julian has come in. He looks quizzically upon this love scene. Julian has been in the garden, thinking. He is not at all upset about Barry's having taken Kitty home. "Don't worry," he advises Madeleine. "Barry's not interested in girls his own age."

Crystal has come down. Not being very sleepy she thought

she could read here without disturbing Cynthia. Nor will she let Bert get her a glass of beer to make her sleep.

Bert has an idea. He thinks a picnic for the next day would be fine for the four of them. Let Julian stay home and make it up with Kitty.

Madeleine and Crystal are receptive and Madeleine will see about the picnic lunch. Julian goes back to the garden. Bert, turning to Crystal, can't understand why she is not at all concerned about the return of Barry. In fact Bert is quite evidently "disturbed by new and strange undercurrents in his orderly life."

"I wish to hell things didn't have a way of getting so damned complicated all at once," says Bert.

"Maybe it's because you make things complicated," suggests Crystal.

"In short, I should mind my own business."

"It's a good course to follow—"

"That's where I disagree with you. When our time's up our story'll be told in terms of others—not ourselves. . . . It's our code. A good husband, a good father, a good son. It's born and bred in us."

"And very often you die of it."

Bert is puzzled. Why, with a good, clear mind, should Crystal say such crazy things? Why, among other things, did she come there?

Crystal wouldn't know, exactly, but she expects sometime she will know. Perhaps it was because Barry had spoken of them so often and she wanted to meet them. She likes being there.

Bert is glad Crystal came, but there are still things he doesn't understand. Why, for one, is she interested in a boy Barry's age? Matter? Certainly it matters, because it isn't right.

Who's to say it is wrong? Crystal would know. Before Bert can answer, Cynthia has come again anxiously in search of her mistress. Crystal finally succeeds in shooing Cynthia off to bed, and then goes to rest in the library.

Julian, coming from the terrace, pours himself a drink. Madeleine, back from the kitchen, would not stop, but bid him goodnight and go on upstairs. Julian, however, wants to talk. "It's too bad we can't be friends," he says, as Madeleine hesitates—

"I've tried to be," she says.

JULIAN—If it's such an effort, why try?

MADELEINE (*in bitter reproach*)—Because you're Bert's

younger brother and he adores you. He thinks you're perfect.

JULIAN—And you put up with me as a form of penance because you're not everything to him that a wife ought to be—? (MADELEINE *winces*.) I'm sorry—I had no right to say that.

MADELEINE—No, Julian. You had no right to say that.

JULIAN—There's something awfully pathetic about you, Madeleine. You're so unsure of yourself—always trembling inside. Spinsters have those feelings. But you're not a spinster—you're a married woman with a child—

MADELEINE—Stop it, Julian!

JULIAN—Face it, Madeleine. We're both misfits, only you're afraid to admit it.

MADELEINE (*bloodlessly*)—Perhaps you're right.

JULIAN—But God damn it, why suffer about it! What's so rotten about loving or not loving that you're all ashamed of it? You make love rotten—you dam it back into a half light that distorts it and makes it ugly. There isn't one of you who's fit to throw the first stone at me. No—not even Bert—

MADELEINE—Leave Bert out of this—!

JULIAN—Why should I? He's gone up to bed, carrying the thought of Crystal with him, and you're taking with you the image of a Barry in that rose. And you'll make love and call yourselves happy.—Christ, I'd rather be what I am—and know it!

MADELEINE (*slowly*)—I never thought I'd live to thank you for anything, Julian. But I do.

Madeleine has left him. Julian is at the piano improvising when Barry appears. He is on his way to bed. Julian would have him stop for a drink, but Barry is not interested.

"Perhaps I should have gone back to town," Julian suggests. He leaves the piano and goes to Barry.

BARRY (*making conversation*)—I wouldn't want to be in New York on a hot night like this—

JULIAN—I don't.

BARRY (*embarrassed*)—Look here—I know it's none of my business, but why don't you go over and see Kitty for a minute? I just left her. She's upset.

JULIAN—I'm not interested in Kitty. She knows it. And you know it.

BARRY—That's a damn funny thing to say when you're engaged to a girl!

JULIAN—Kitty called that off tonight. I was outside. I heard her.

BARRY—She didn't mean it. She thinks you're coming over. She's in love with you.

JULIAN (*with implication*)—That's why she'd be a fool to go through with it. So would I.

BARRY (*stiffening*)—What are you trying to say?

JULIAN (*gently*)—I'll explain it to you in the garden.

As Julian puts his hand on Barry's arm Barry "finally gets the full significance of the overture." As he steps back he knocks over a bronze ashtray which falls to the floor with a heavy thud. Crystal has come from the library and is standing in the doorway. Hearing the click of the door Julian, "after a moment's conflict," turns back to Barry—

"In the future keep your hands off me!" he says, grinding out the words.

For a moment Barry stands stunned by the accusation. He is picking up the ashtray when he looks up and sees Crystal. He would pass her now with a quick "Good-night," and go on upstairs, but she calls to him. Let him come back and calm down. Suppose she had believed what she had heard? Everybody else is going to believe it. Julian will have the story around like wildfire before Monday. He'll have to, in self-defense. And what is Barry going to do about it?

There is nothing that he can do, so far as Barry can see, if he is to let Bert keep his illusions about Julian. Why should Crystal be afraid of nobility?

CRYSTAL—I'm not afraid of it, I distrust it.—(*Levelly.*) Why do you hide behind it?

BARRY—I'm not!

CRYSTAL—You are.

BARRY (*in hoarse protest*)—Crystal, for God's sake don't— (*He takes a few distracted steps away from her and then wheels to face her.*) All right, maybe Kitty was right in what she said tonight! If she isn't, why should these things happen to me?

CRYSTAL (*unemotionally*)—No mystery about it. You were born with too many F cells in your body.

BARRY—I didn't ask to be made that way!

CRYSTAL—Do any of us? Did Bert ask to be born a Jew? Or Cynthia, a negress?—Or me—what I am? It's the thing that brings us together, I wouldn't be surprised. We all have to beat our stars.

BARRY—What happens if we don't?

CRYSTAL—Julian.—And maybe Madeleine.

BARRY—Don't say that!

CRYSTAL—I must. She's half-way between an ism and a street corner, and you're the trigger for whichever way she blows.

BARRY—But I'm not in love with her!

CRYSTAL—That's her protection. And her torture.

BARRY (*muffled*)—It's my torture, too. (*He sinks to a low ottoman beside the love seat.*)

CRYSTAL (*simply*)—Was there ever a woman, Barry?

BARRY (*with his lips*)—Once.

CRYSTAL—Go through with it?

BARRY—Yes.

CRYSTAL (*gently*)—Tell me about it.

BARRY (*falteringly*)—It was a violin teacher I used to have when I was a youngster.—Years later, I met her again, right after my mother died. I was lonesome, I guess— She wore a brown dress. There were marks of perspiration beneath her arms—(*He stops.*)

CRYSTAL (*broodingly*)—There was no one in your life you really loved—

BARRY—My father.

CRYSTAL—And no one else—ever?

BARRY (*with increasing difficulty*)—Yes—a boy who lived on our block. In one of those big private houses. He went to France the second summer I knew him. My mother found a letter I was writing him. She thought it was to a girl.—I never finished that letter. I never wanted to see him again. (*With suppressed intensity.*) And I hated my mother for what she did to me. She made me ashamed for no reason. She frightened me about myself.

CRYSTAL—Be glad. If you didn't feel the pain of conflict, you'd be like all the poor young men, who wouldn't help themselves if they could. Boys of twenty and twenty-five without a ground tone in their voices, poor darlings. There's hope for all of them—while they suffer.—There's even hope for Julian now.

BARRY—You're strange, Crystal. One minute you're hard as nails, and the next minute you're like a Madonna—

CRYSTAL—You've got your metaphors slightly mixed.

BARRY (*awkwardly*)—It's the only way I can say the feeling that I have about you—

CRYSTAL (*softly*)—It's a sweet feeling, Barry—and somewhere, beyond the farthest star, we'll all find peace and oneness.

BARRY (*in humility*)—I told Madeleine tonight that it took a certain greatness to be your lover—I wish I had that greatness.

CRYSTAL (*She bends to lay her cheek against his head for a fleeting instant.*)—You have.

"Barry, motionless, watches her as she moves across the room to the stairs. He rises slowly to follow her." The curtain falls.

ACT III

It is evening of the following day. "The last rays of the sun are dragging the Harris living room to dimness." Mrs. Harris is sitting in the big armchair darning. She has had her supper. The tray is still on the small table beside her.

With an inquiring "Yoo-hoo!" the Goldsmiths have arrived. Dr. Andy has come to have another peek at Madeleine's mother. Afterward they are going on to the club dance.

Bert's picnic, it appears, is still going on. At least no one is back from it. Which gives Gertrude a chance to release a few personal views on related subjects. She is sorry to have missed Mrs. Grainger. "I like that woman, no matter what anybody says about her," declares Gertrude. "I wish I had a reputation. Good or bad, it gives you something to fall back on, like an annuity."

Julian? He had gone to New York late the night before for a conference, Mrs. Harris reports. Kitty? Kitty must be busy getting ready for her wedding.

Kitty isn't going to be the daughter-in-law that Madeleine is, Gertrude is convinced, but Barry's very sweet.

"I must say I like men who aren't so blasted masculine," admits Gertrude. "Honestly, I think you can carry being a man to an extreme."

Gertrude goes upstairs to see Madeleine's mother as soon as the doctor comes down, which gives Mrs. Harris a chance to do a little probing of Andy. She has sensed that there is something wrong in the house, but she doesn't know just what it is. Something is wrong between Julian and Kitty, she thinks.

"You certainly are imagining things, Mother Harris."

"No, Andy. Julian was always a strange boy—I could see it more than Bert."

"If Bert loves a person he's blind."

"But I'm not blind. I do not know what it is in Julian, but I know he cannot make a woman happy."

"That's a brave thing for a mother to say."

"I have gotten to an age where I have stopped being the mother of my children. I wish I could have done better for them. I wish I knew where I made my mistakes. But it is too late now. They will have to make their own lives with what they have." She has risen from her chair. "I think I will go to bed before they come home. I talk very big. But I am upset. I am upset."

The arrival of the returning picnic party is heralded by Bert's singing. "With formless eloquence" his deep bass is giving out "There's a Tavern in the Town." Shortly Bert and Crystal, Barry and Madeleine appear, "carrying the aftermath of a day in the wind and sun, full of healthy tiredness and well being."

They are happy over the day's adventures and have soon scattered—Bert and Madeleine to see how their respective mamas are doing, Barry to carry the picnic baskets back to the kitchen. Only Crystal lingers.

"It wasn't too smart to go on a jaunt like that," Dr. Andy tells her.

Perhaps not, Crystal is willing to admit. But just now she is eager to hear if there had been fireworks while they were gone. Yes, there had been fireworks. Julian had started his story, as Crystal suspected he would, but Andy doesn't believe Julian would have done that if Kitty had not "gone off the deep end."

"Her father called me in the middle of the night. He heard the motor going in the garage.—Then of course, Julian had to justify himself."

"I see.—How is she?"

Gertrude, coming into the room, hears and answers for him. "Now that she's got suicide out of her system, she'll be all right. It's a phase—I went through it myself once."

The adventures of the night have brought things pretty much to a head. Gertrude seriously doubts if Barry will have a violin pupil left by the beginning of the week.

"Don't worry about Barry," Gertrude advises. "Bert offered him a job in his office today."

"That was before this mess." Gertrude is skeptical. "He's not going to believe Barry against his own brother."

"I'm afraid Gertrude's right," agrees Andy. "Bert thinks Jews were born with morals in place of sex."

"And it's silly. Jews are just like anybody else—they can be wonderful and they can be louses—"

"Sad but true," admits Andy.

Julian is supposed to be on his way out from town. Andy had located him at Russel Train's. Gertrude can hardly stand that. Nor will she be shut up by her worried husband—

"Listen, I was a trained nurse—I know a thing or two. Anyway, Barry's no more that kind than the man in the moon. Andy says he's a borderline case—why push him in all the way? . . . This is a serious business and it's going to kill Bert when he finds out."

"We don't die so easily," says Andy, grimly.

"You bet we don't," adds Crystal. "And you've been married to Andy long enough, Gertrude, to know that the suffering of a Jew has strength and dignity—great dignity."

The Goldsmiths are barely out of the house before Cynthia appears. She has been waiting outside the door. All day she has had funny feelings about her mistress. Isn't there something she can do for Crystal? Can't she get her some medicine?

When Barry comes bounding down the stairs looking for his jacket Cynthia carries her plea to him. "Mis' Crystal don't feel good, Mistah Barry," she cries, despairingly.

"Cynthia, would you care to have your neck wrung?" snaps Crystal.

"She don't feel good anyway, Mistah Barry," repeats Cynthia, defiantly, as she dodges out of the way.

Crystal's dizziness could be due to too much sun, Barry thinks. He also had felt a little dizzy. But his dizziness wasn't due to the sun. Or maybe it was! "It seems to me today was the first day in all my life I could *see* the sun. Crystal—do you know what I mean—?"

"I think I do."

Madeleine, dressed for the evening, comes downstairs, and Crystal goes back to continue her rest in the library. Madeleine, too, has noticed that Crystal is looking pale, but agrees with Barry that probably the picnic was a little too much for her.

"Barry, I'm awfully happy about the job Bert offered you," Madeleine is saying. "And I'm so glad you took it."

"I've always wanted a real job—but I couldn't get one," says Barry. "Had no training. Oh, I know I'm no great shakes as a musician. My father was. I guess that's why I went into it. But I'm through with it, except to play 'Souvenir' for my grandchildren some day."

"Do you know what that means?"

"What?"

"It means that I've stopped having a protégé. And the funny part of it is I don't need one any more."

If Madeleine hasn't planned anything for the evening, Barry thinks he will take a run over to see Kitty.

"I think it's a beautiful idea, Barry.—And my plans for tonight had nothing to do with you."

Crystal is feeling better and ready to go to her room. Cynthia, appearing with the medicine, would help her up the stairs.

"Oh, stop babying me!" impatiently orders Crystal.

"You're all the baby I got to baby—" protests Cynthia.

At the foot of the stairs they have met Bert, and Bert has a plan. He thinks it would be fine if Cynthia would induce Mis' Crystal to stay on for a couple of weeks, after the others go. He likes Cynthia—likes the way she takes care of Mis' Crystal. In token of which he would like her to buy herself a pair of stockings. The bill he hands Cynthia startles her—

"You give me five dollahs, Mistah Bert!"

"Did I? Give it back. I made a mistake.—Thought it was ten. Sorry—" Bert's pretended annoyance, as he fishes out a ten-dollar bill and hands it to her, leaves Cynthia gasping. And when he adds the original five to the ten she is completely overwhelmed.

"You is a wonderful man, Mistah Bert—"

Bert's spirits are high. He would have Crystal put on "the white thing" she had worn the night before, and is greatly crestfallen when she tells him that she doesn't think she will be coming down again. He had been looking forward all day to having another talk with her.

"You don't talk much," she says.

"I don't have to when I'm with you. The whole point is it's just nice knowing you. Being with you. I think today was pretty near perfect."

"So do I."

"I even forgot there was a war going on in Europe."

"We have to forget. In order to remember."

"That takes a little thinking. If I were ten years younger I'd be over there now, fighting to keep what I've got—over here.— Oh, it isn't just freedom. Or tolerance. Or any of those high-sounding words. It's something else. Maybe it's got to do with the soul I never knew I had.—I used to be ashamed, mentioning the word 'soul.'"

"I suppose you thought it was sissy to have one."

"Especially if it was a nice one." Bert grins his admission, then quickly adds: "I'm behaving like an adolescent."

"Adolescence is the hope of the world."

"That takes a little thinking, too." He is abruptly suspicious. "You're not an intellectual, are you?"

"Good God, am I?"

"You are not. You're too sane."

"Sanity is another of your little gods, isn't it?"

"You bet. There's no mystic in me."

When Crystal has gone upstairs Bert repeats to Madeleine that he thinks it would be nice if Crystal would stay on for a couple of weeks. Do them all good. Madeleine thinks that is just like Bert—with the world camping on his doorstep again. But, curiously, this time she doesn't mind—even though she suspects that Bert is in love with Crystal.

That, to Bert, is a crazy thing to say. He's in love with his wife—and he would like to have her shut up. Madeleine understands that, too. She knows Bert loves his wife, but there's a difference. That's why men have mistresses. That's why women have lovers.

"A fine way for a respectable married woman to talk," snorts Bert. Over his protest Madeleine goes on—

MADELEINE—I wonder if there isn't a short-cut— If a husband and wife couldn't do double-duty, like a—well, like a station wagon that you can use for pleasure and business at the same time.

BERT—Look, darling. Talk sense. Please.

MADELEINE (*steadily*)—All right. Does this make sense?—I could fall in love with you.

BERT (*covering his emotion with bombast*)—Well, you immoral hussy!

MADELEINE (*steadily*)—Yes, Bert, for the first time in many years, I've forgotten you're the man I'm tied to by law—a man who can be so big in big things, and so little in little things that sometimes I can only think of weeds choking up a garden.

BERT (*vulnerable*)—You hit hard when you do hit, don't you?

MADELEINE—It's the only way. All at once I've got a lot of courage. I don't know where it came from, but I'm thankful for it, and I'm going to use it.—You've got limitations, Bert, that have been like a wall between us. False loyalties and a strange intolerance of anything outside your middle-class morality.

You're even moral with your wife. Considerate. Timid—

BERT—Madeleine, for God's sake—stop it—

MADELEINE—Please let me finish. What I'm going to tell you now takes more courage than saying the other things I've just said. Suddenly, Bert, I don't see you as my husband. I don't see you as part of a race or a social order. I see only a man, that I, as a woman, want to be one with.—I think you're quite handsome, all at once. It might be the sunburn, it might be something that comes from inside you—a left-over of the emotion that made you want Crystal to wear a certain dress. Anyway, I'm not proud, I'll take the left-overs.—Because you're probably going to have to take my left-overs, too.—I had a beautiful day with Barry. It was as if I put a lovely velvet cloak over the gingham apron of my real self. I'd like to keep that cloak on— It's becoming to me. It makes me feel young, and very important as a woman—(*With stark tragedy.*) Bert, you don't understand a word I'm saying. You think I'm crazy.

BERT—I don't know what to think. You've always been so—(*Falteringly.*) I've always known there was something missing. I've tried to fool myself that it was there. Even last night—

MADELEINE (*undramatically*)—I'll tell you about last night. Last night as I went upstairs to you I had a horrible fear of ending up in a sanitarium—one of these neurotic, unexpressed women who have lovers in the astral. I knew a woman like that once, Bert. She went to a medium twice a week and spoke to an Arabian who was supposed to have been her husband a thousand lives ago.—I never forgot that woman, because I knew how she felt, I knew what was missing in her life. I don't want that to happen to me. I want to be married to a man on this earth, a full man with the capacity to love me—even if he has to love another woman first to learn the art of love.

BERT (*hoarsely*)—Don't talk that way. There can't ever be another woman but you! Don't you know that?—Do you realize I've never even kissed another woman as long as we've been married?

MADELEINE—That's no compliment to me.

BERT—Madeleine. Listen to me. What you say might make sense for others, but not for us. It isn't our inheritance or our upbringing.—We're not that kind of people.

MADELEINE (*pleading*)—Must we be a kind of people? Can't we be just—people?

BERT (*hopelessly*)—We're going to get right back to where

we were—last night.

MADELEINE (*low*)—I'm afraid so—

Bert seems undecided as to whether or not he should follow Madeleine—"but he is not clear enough to face her clarity. Confused and baffled, he finds himself alone with new thoughts and sensations crowding up in him." He moves restlessly about the room, picking up Doris' picture, sinking down on the piano bench, suddenly banging the keys in a heavy discord. . . . The front door opens and Julian comes in. "Bert greets him with relief. Julian is an escape from his own problems, a welcome return to the familiarity of his everyday life. He does not register Julian's strained, defiant attitude—"

Julian has just come from seeing Kitty. He is startled to discover that Bert knows nothing of what has happened. Where are the others? He makes slurring allusions to Barry and Crystal and their relations. And to Bert's blindness, when it comes to Madeleine's making a fool of herself over Barry.

Bert's savage demand that Julian stop these accusations serves only to turn his brother's thoughts back to Kitty. Kitty had tried to commit suicide because she was jealous of Barry.

"By God, I ought to throw you out of the house, coming with stuff like this in your mind," shouts Bert.

"Believe what you want," snaps Julian, reaching for his hat, "but anything I've said you can check up on."

The engagement with Kitty is off, reports Julian. What of it? Broken engagements are common occurrences.

Not in the Harris family, Bert reminds him. "I'm proud of this family. It's never done anything rotten, anything to be ashamed of. You can't let Kitty down."

"Why the hell have I let Kitty down? Maybe she's let me down!"

"She said last night she hated your guts. I didn't like the way she said that, Julian. That wasn't a lovers' quarrel. If it was a lovers' quarrel she'd have just hated you. And it wouldn't have been much different than loving you. Because that's the way love is."

"What do you know about love, Bert?" There is the trace of a sneer in Julian's voice, but as he sees Bert recoil he is suddenly contrite, almost tender. "Look. I'm sorry I said that. I don't want to hurt you, you poor old bastard. Let me get out of here before I say any more things I'll regret."

"This is your home. We're all in this thing together," says

Bert. "What do you want to run away for?"

Julian is going to the coast—with Russel Train. This is a new blow to Bert. "It's not what you've done to me," he says, as Julian repeats his regret at hurting him. "It's what you've done to yourself. To your race."

"I've got no obligation to my race. What's it ever done for me, except be a millstone around my neck—"

"It should have raised you up."

"Look, old man, you're talking about God, not religion. We've been getting these two names mixed up for quite a while."

"It's time we stopped."

Mrs. Harris comes from the kitchen. She thought she had heard Julian's voice. Finding him, she is not surprised that he is going away again. Julian is always coming back or going away. Sometime he must come home to stay. . . . Julian has kissed her and gone. Mother Harris would not have Bert close the door on him.

"This time, when he comes back, I will not be here," she says.

"Nonsense!"

"Always, ever since you were a little boy, you did not like to think about things you did not want to happen," is her answer. "That does not keep them from happening— You are still a little boy."

"And this is the first real spanking you ever gave me."

"And it hurts me—as much as it hurts you—"

"Look, Mom! Don't!" Bert is near breaking.

"Shh! It does not hurt us to be hurt," she says gently.

"It gives a pretty good imitation."

"Pretty good," she agrees, as Bert takes her in his arms.

Crystal is coming down the stairs in her white gown. Cynthia is following close upon her heels, muttering that she will be in the kitchen if she is needed.

Mrs. Harris would explain that her eyes are red because she has been in the kitchen fixing herring for Crystal to take home, but Crystal is not fooled. She knows that Julian has been there.

"I'm sorry he made your universe come tumbling down," she says to Bert, when Mrs. Harris has left them. "But that's what universes are for, I suppose. So that they can be built up again. Stronger. On more solid ground.—It happens to nations, too. And whole races of people. Surely you know that."

"Sometime you can't build up," says Bert, as if each word were an effort.

"We always have."

Julian had said some ugly things about Barry, Bert tells Crystal. He wouldn't like Madeleine to know. It would hurt her. "She's in love with him. She admitted it tonight—I didn't understand her when she told me. I do now."

CRYSTAL—I'm glad you understand her. Try to understand Barry, too. He's a poor lost lad, looking for the mother he never had in the woman he wants to love.—And Madeleine? She doesn't know what she's looking for. Perhaps it's you.

BERT (*a little stolidly, a little resentfully*)—I've been here.

CRYSTAL—She couldn't find you. Your soul was too shrouded in virtue.

BERT—What are you preaching now? The value of sin?

CRYSTAL—Some of us need to sin—to become sinless.

BERT—Those are words! Fancy words!

CRYSTAL—Then look into yourself and find the truth of them. Have the courage to realize that your goodness holds the seed of all the Barrys and the Julians in the world.

BERT (*numb*)—Julian?

CRYSTAL—A part of you has known about Julian for a long time. A part of you is responsible for Julian.

BERT (*rousing to violence*)—That isn't true! He's my own brother but I'd rather see him dead than the thing that he's become. He's betrayed his race at a time when we need all our strength and honor!

CRYSTAL—He's betrayed himself. That's the real pity of it. He needs you, Bert, and your answer to his need is your salvation.

BERT—I tell you, I'd rather see him dead!

CRYSTAL (*austerely*)—If he were ill or crippled, would you turn against him? (BERT *does not answer. He walks to the terrace and stands looking out, his back to* CRYSTAL. BARRY *comes downstairs in high spirits.*)

BARRY (*defensively*)—I wasn't dressing all this time, I was having a pow-wow with Madeleine's mother—(*His gaiety vanishes as he feels the tension in the room.* BERT *turns from the terrace.*)

BERT—Julian was here. If there's anything you want to say, I'll try to understand. (*There is a short silence in which* BARRY *realizes that he has the chance to clear himself of* JULIAN'S *implications. He makes his choice.*)

BARRY—No, Bert, there isn't anything.

BERT (*with an effort that leaves him drained*)—Madeleine and

I were talking about Crystal staying on for a couple of weeks. It would be nice if you could commute with me—from the office.

BARRY (*in full significance*)—Thank you, Bert.

Barry has gone out on the terrace. Bert and Crystal are again alone. "Only her lips, tender with a gentle exultance, testify to the great wave of emotion that sweeps her." Bert, evading Crystal's eyes, has sunk down on the piano stool and is staring at the keys. Crystal goes to him, and as he looks up she places her lips on his.

"Why did you do that?"

"Because I wanted to." She has moved away from him. "I'm going to your study. It's quiet in there. And very peaceful—"

She goes through the foyer into the room beyond, as his eyes follow her. The next moment Cynthia has come hurriedly through the dining room. "I thought Mis' Crystal called me," she says, anxiously. "Where is she?"

"She's in the other room."

"I better go to her."

"No, Cynthia, stay here. I'll go," says Bert.

But Cynthia, filled with apprehension, discovers "the small, crumpled ball of Crystal's handkerchief on the floor." She picks it up and holds it in her hand as Madeleine comes from the terrace.

"Mis' Madeleine, this hanchicuff is wet with pain."

Bert's voice, on a rising cry, is heard from the study. "Cynthia! Cynthia! Come quickly!"

"No, God, no! You mustn't, God, you mustn't," mutters Cynthia, stumbling blindly toward the study.

Madeleine remains motionless, "stunned with the impact of something too vast to encompass."

Bert is standing in the doorway. "She knew I'd follow her and she was smiling," he says. His words come slowly, "at once a confession and a prayer." He turns to Madeleine, "like a child in need of comfort."

"Oh, my darling!"

Suddenly, "from the quiet room beyond, Cynthia lifts her voice in song. At first the simple melody is choked with sobbing, but it grows braver."

THE CURTAIN SLOWLY FALLS

JACOBOWSKY AND THE COLONEL

A Comedy in Three Acts

BASED BY S. N. BEHRMAN ON AN ORIGINAL PLAY BY FRANZ WERFEL

THE Theatre Guild directors, reduced now to Lawrence Langner and Theresa Helburn from the original six (Lee Simonson, Maurice Wertheim, Helen Westley and Philip Moeller were their former associates), if not exactly puffed with pride over the success of the now far-famed "Oklahoma!" and the Paul Robeson "Othello," which were the Guild's first smash hits in many months, admitted that their collective ego had been nicely expanded.

Probably the watchful gods decided that they should be taken down a peg in the cause of avoiding a further inflation. Their second production following "Othello" was that of Paul Osborn's fanciful comedy, "The Innocent Voyage," which he had chiseled out of Richard Hughes' novel, "A High Wind in Jamaica." It was a comedy of considerable charm and imagination, but a bit too fine for the crowd, and was withdrawn after forty performances.

This was in December, and the Guild directors went back to chuckling and counting standees at the performances of their two established hits. In March, however, they got around to the staging of Franz Werfel's and S. N. Behrman's "Jacobowsky and the Colonel." By the program record this is an original play by Mr. Werfel which Mr. Behrman pulled into its present shape after Clifford Odets had put in several unsatisfactory weeks on the job and turned it back.

"Jacobowsky" was no more than moderately successful during its trial weeks out of New York, but it was greatly favored by the mid-season situation on Broadway. First it had been a poor season for comedies up to that time and, second, there was a comedy-starved public of war victims of one class and another that was naturally sensitive to the appeal of racial comedy of the "Jacobowsky" pattern. Something like 26 theatre parties, each of them taking over the capacity of the Martin Beck Theatre, had been organized before the comedy opened. This naturally gave "Jacobowsky" a most helpful preliminary impetus, which, it should be added, was sustained by equally sizable audiences following in the wake of the theatre parties.

Another favoring feature was the expert casting suggestions contributed by Miss Helburn, Mr. Langner and their stage director, Elia Kazan. Oscar Karlweiss, a popular Viennese comedian, had just finished a hugely popular engagement playing the Prince in "Rosalinda." He was chosen to play Jacobowsky. The physically dominant and frankly assured Louis Calhern was available for the role of the Colonel, and Annabella, popular both as a cinema heroine of French origin and as the wife of young Tyrone Power, romantic hero of the screen, filled in pictorially as the Marianne.

Swept along by these favoring currents, "Jacobowsky and the Colonel" was soon counted with the season's few outstanding hits, and had no difficulty playing through the remainder of the season.

Facing one of the quiet little squares of Paris, on the left bank of the Seine, stands the Hotel Mon Repos et de la Rose. Our introduction to this slightly ancient hostelry is through the laundry, serving now as an air-raid shelter. It is nearing midnight on the 13th of June, 1940. Those guests who have come to the laundry and are still awake are, as we meet them, listening to the voice of Prime Minister Reynaud as it is relayed to them by radio—

". . . The situation is serious but not desperate. On the Somme our valiant troops are defending every inch of their native soil with the greatest bravery. However, the superiority of the enemy in men and materials is so great that we must be prepared to expect—"

An Old Lady from Arras who has tried to knit her way through the broadcast finds that her occupation has not entirely settled her nerves. "Dear God, dear God, M. Paul Reynaud is very far to the left," she is protesting, shrilly. "My daughter is a schoolteacher and she told me. Monsieur Léon Blum wouldn't have anyone work more than forty hours a week. And this is what it brings us to. The last war was better—I understood the last war. This war I don't understand at all. Why, my daughter says, should we die for Danzig? (*Very militant.*) She's right! Why should we?"

The proprietress of the Hotel Mon Repos et de la Rose is Madame Bouffier, a large, somewhat disheveled lady, who arrives now with a lantern, a small notebook and a pencil. She has come to check her guests, and she would have the protesting Old Lady know that the morale of her hotel is high.

"I am captain of the ship here," warns Madame Bouffier, "and I want things to be bright and cheerful. That's our way of defying the Germans."

"But this is the fourth night that I've sat till dawn in this wretched laundry," grumbles the Old Lady.

"No hotel in Paris has a more distinguished laundry than mine," snaps Madame Bouffier. "You're lucky to be in it, safe and cozy."

The suggestion does not impress the Old Lady from Arras. Her daughter has told her that the war is nonsense and won't last a week. Schoolteachers should know.

"Some schoolteachers never learn anything they don't teach," declares Madame Bouffier, with conviction.

The checking indicates that all Madame Bouffier's little family is accounted for "except 409 and 204." These rooms are occupied respectively by a Polish Colonel and a certain M. Jacobowsky. The Colonel is probably asleep, but where is Jacobowsky? Madame Bouffier is worried. She likes Jacobowsky. "I prefer a sunny day to a cloudy day. M. Jacobowsky has a nature like a sunny day," she explains.

A "fussy and nervous little man" named Szyche has arrived, wearing a pince-nez, carrying a brief case and looking for Col. Stjerbinsky. The Colonel, Madame Bouffier tells him, is still in his room. He seldom pays any attention to air raids. The Colonel's orderly, Szabuniewicz, is sleeping in the corner and comes awake after being prodded.

Szabuniewicz is evasive. He knows nothing about the Colonel. If Szyche has anything for the Colonel he, Szabuniewicz, will take it. That, says Szyche, cannot be. The documents he has for the Colonel must be delivered directly into the Colonel's hands. Also time is getting short, declares Szyche. "The Germans will be here any minute."

Now there is something resembling an emotional outbreak. Everybody in the room heard Szyche say the Germans were coming, but some of them understood him to say the Germans were here. The Old Lady is hysterical. A Young Girl is highly excited. Madame Bouffier, desperately opposed to having a panic in her hotel, sends her servant, Solomon, to fetch a gramophone record to quiet the guests.

In the midst of the excitement S. L. Jacobowsky appears. He is a smallish, almost mousy little man, but he speaks with a calm assurance that inspires conviction. The Germans, announces M. Jacobowsky, are not in Paris.

"I have just been in the Rue Royale and I assure you there isn't a German in sight. In fact there isn't even a Parisian in sight. I was the only one in sight."

The statement startles them into a jabber of surprise and wonder. Madame Bouffier is concerned about what might have happened to Jacobowsky. The Young Girl is sure M. Jacobowsky is a very courageous man. A tragic male guest suggests sarcastically that perhaps M. Jacobowsky believes that the bomb that will hit him has not yet been cast, but it has—

"Oh, yes, I have no doubt," admits Jacobowsky. "Krupp and Skoda think of me constantly. They cast their little bomb and they think: 'This one we'll send to our nice Jacobowsky.' But even Krupp has to submit to a powerful law—the law of probability. Listen: What is the population of Paris? Four million lives? Correct? Now what chance has Krupp with all his precision work of hitting one four millionth of Paris? I tell you I feel sorry for him. So, moving under the immunity of this adorable law—I have brought you back some marrons glacés—first to our distinguished hostess."

The marrons are very popular, and M. Jacobowsky, too, because of the marrons. He certainly knows what is delicious, the Young Girl is agreed. "Why is it that the best husbands are always unmarried?" Madame Bouffier would know. Certainly M. Jacobowsky ought to get married. But Jacobowsky does not think so—

"Give me one good reason why," persists his hostess.

"You see, Madame Bouffier, myself I am a worshiper of beauty but in my own person I am not quite dazzling. The indifference of the ladies has given me leisure for reading and philosophy."

He has turned to the Old Lady. She is telling him of her flight from Arras, where she had left everything, including her daughter. Even while she was flying, to be fleeing in France itself seemed unbelievable. She can't believe it even now—

"Oh, you'll get used to flight. I did," Jacobowsky assures her. "I've spent all my life in a futile effort to become a citizen of some country. You know, I speak seven languages fluently. Wrong, but fluently. In the technique of flight I may say I am a virtuoso. Migration one: Poland to Germany. My poor mother took her five children, her candlesticks, her pillows and fled to Berlin. There I grew up. I was successful in business. I was a citizen, a patriot. I belonged. My mistake. Migration two: Berlin to Vienna! The City of Waltzes. (*He hums one or two bars.*) But I soon found out that underneath the waltzes there was a counter-melody. Less charming, more ruthless. First thing you know I was embarked on migration three. Prague. Now Prague is a lovely city. Have you ever seen the lovely baroque architecture in Prague?"

"I hate baroque!"

"I understand that, too. A lot of people very qualified don't like baroque. Still I hated to leave Prague. This time without an overcoat. It was a new experience. Very interesting. Migration four: Prague to Paris. Paris! City of Light! Here I breathed the air of freedom. I understood exactly how Heine felt when *he* got here. I said to myself: 'You are Heine—without the genius.' But now I have the feeling that there is ahead of me, still another migration. Well, I'm ready. You see, one gets used to it."

"But after all, Monsieur, between us there isn't any comparison. My family has lived in Arras for five centuries."

"Five centuries! You don't mean it!"

"And now the Boches may push us into the sea." The Old Lady pounds her pillow savagely. "My daughter is right. She always says, 'France needs a Hitler, too.'"

"Don't worry, Madame, your daughter will probably get her wish—mustache, forelock and all."

Madame Bouffier does not intend to allow that kind of talk in her hotel, but before she can do much about it a shrill police whistle is followed by the entrance of an irate air raid warden. Again it is Madame Bouffier's place that is violating regulations; two windows on the fourth floor, street side, are lit up like a Christmas tree!

Madame Bouffier knows those two windows. That would be the room of the Polish Colonel. You just can't do a thing with the Colonel. The more you tell him the louder he laughs.

"He laughs, does he?" The warden has started angrily for the stairs. "He laughs! I'll teach him! I'll teach him to laugh! This is Paris, not Warsaw! . . . I'll wipe up the floor with him."

The warden's promise is exciting to Madame Bouffier and Solly, the porter, who follow him out, and interesting to Szabuniewicz, the orderly, who wonders what is going to happen to the warden.

"Colonel not alone," Szabuniewicz mutters; "and when he's not alone he wants strictly to be alone."

"So that's what he's doing . . ." muses Szyche.

"Colonel has always time for romance."

"At a time like this?"

"Any time good for romance."

Presently the warden returns, rather hurriedly. No, he had not wiped up the floor with the Colonel. The Colonel's crazy! "What's the matter with him? He's dangerous!" insists the warden.

Now the Colonel, gay in the regimentals of the Polish Army, follows Madame Bouffier into the room. To her somewhat excited protest, that even if he did fight for France, his behavior has been unpardonable, the Colonel makes no direct reply. He, too, is measurably excited and very determined—

"Szabuniewicz, prepare our departure from Paris—"

"Yes, Colonel."

COLONEL (*turning to indicate a pretty young French woman who follows him into the room*)—And, oh—Szabuniewicz, I part from this lovely creature who follows me. Disengages me from her—but—very gracious—

COSETTE—Tadeusz, if you leave Paris, I go, too—

COLONEL—This I tell you. Our roads part—perhaps forever—but the memory of your sweet face . . .

MADAME BOUFFIER—It's all very well for you to be romantic but on account of you the police will padlock my hotel tomorrow.

COLONEL—They will not. They will lack the time. Tomorrow the police of Paris will be running errands for the Huns!

MADAME BOUFFIER—Do you mean, Colonel, that the Germans will meet with no further resistance?

COLONEL—Dis I know. The regiment I command is force of three t'ousand men. On the Somme we defend a bridge and for every gun is only eight cartridges . . .

TRAGIC GENTLEMAN—Where was the French Army?

MADAME BOUFFIER—What happened to our Army?

COLONEL (*pouring himself a drink at the bar*)—The German Stukas make black the sky and not one French plane to help us. That I know . . . On my right an' on my left I see the French divisions—fine soldiers—want to fight—have nothing with which to fight—so they run—and of my own three t'ousand Polish boys only is left fifteen. I am their father and I lose my children—three t'ousand of them. This I know. This I see. This I feel . . . here . . . (*Slaps his heart.*) Rather I would be with them, with my children that are gone.

TRAGIC GENTLEMAN (*in earnest*)—Then, Colonel, it is your

considered opinion that France is lost!

COLONEL—She is not lost, monsieur. She is gift to the German. Charming gift to the German.

TRAGIC GENTLEMAN—Farewell, Paris!

OLD LADY—I don't feel very well. I don't feel . . .

JACOBOWSKY (*going quickly to the* OLD LADY's *aid*)—Courage. My poor mother, wise woman that she was, always used to say that no matter what happens in life there are always two possibilities. It is true. For example, right now it is a dark moment and yet, even now there are two possibilities. The Germans— either they'll come to Paris or they'll jump to England. If they don't come to Paris, that's good. But if they should come to Paris, again there are two possibilities. Either we succeed in escaping or we don't succeed. If we succeed, that's good but if we don't, there are two possibilities. The Germans, either they'll put us in a good concentration camp or in a bad concentration camp. If in a good concentration camp that's fine, but if they put us in a bad one, there are still two possibilities—

TRAGIC GENTLEMAN—Two fine possibilities. Jump in the river or be shot by the Boches. Paris, farewell!

The Old Lady from Arras has fainted. The guests gather around, trying to revive her. Cosette would take advantage of the others' preoccupation to have a final word with the Colonel. Why cannot there be any further possibility for them?

"My lovely friend . . . since last I saw you I have fallen in love. . . . And for you my feeling is so tender, so precious, that I cannot give you less than myself, for you deserve all." The Colonel is very tender.

Cosette would continue her protest, but at the moment the mission of the messenger, Szyche, obtrudes. Szyche has come with the documents for which the Colonel waits. They are all there, in a large wallet which he now hands over—"Addresses of our men in Warsaw, Lodz and Cracow. Every plan and communication is there. You must get it to our government in London."

"I bring it to London," announces the Colonel.

"In the Café of Papa Clairon in St. Jean de Luz you meet the Man with the Gray Gloves. He will give you passage on corvette with other of our people to London."

The papers, warns Szyche, are to be in the hands of the Man with the Gray Gloves not later than the afternoon of the 18th. Till then it is but six days. The Colonel is not worried.

"I must impress upon you, my dear bureaucrat, that you speak to one of Pilsudski's Colonels. I deliver these papers my own method, my own way, my own time."

"The corvette won't wait for you. If you're not there on the afternoon of the 18th, it sails without you."

"Then let him sail. If necessary I swim to London."

"I have obeyed my orders. The papers are in your hands."

"You go back to your bureau. Give orders to your office boy, not to Tadeusz Boleslav Stjerbinsky. Szabuniewicz, we leave Paris now."

But the leaving, as Szabuniewicz points out, will not be so easy. The last plane had left the night before. The Vice Consul had also gone off the night before, taking with him all four embassy cars. Then, announces the Colonel, they will go by horse. Let Szabuniewicz see to the packing. Let him also see to it that he doesn't forget the Colonel's rosary.

Jacobowsky, from the side, has been observing what has gone on. Now he would, if the Colonel will permit, take a hand in the arrangements. His name, he explains, is S. L. Jacobowsky. He, too, was born in Poland. And from what he has heard, it appears to be important that the Colonel should be leaving Paris. No, he has not been eavesdropping. That wasn't necessary. And he has a suggestion: It might be possible for them to get a car in which to leave Paris. The good Madame Bouffier has, in fact, spoken of a car that is for sale—

"This no doubt very convenient for you, but how does it concern me?" demands the Colonel.

"If the car were available we might take it together."

"You persist in this intimate pronoun 'we.' When I travel, I travel alone. When I travel with company it is company that I choose."

"An admirable way to travel. And from my side, I would choose you gladly . . . because you are a strong man . . . you are a chivalrous man. Now I have to provide you with a reason why you should choose me. If you will forgive me for saying say, I am a resourceful man; strength plus resourcefulness. Is not this a good combination for an emergency like this? Tell me frankly, sir, your opinion."

"I do not understand your mentality."

The Colonel turns to Cosette. Soon the alarm will stop, he tells her, and then Szabuniewicz will take her home. No, it would not be possible for her to stay with him.

"In the cathedral of my soul a candle burns for you, a flame that will never go out," promises the Colonel. And Cosette passes out of his life.

Jacobowsky would now renew their conversation. Let them assume, for the sake of argument, that they acquire the car—

"Again you assume that we are engaged in a joint enterprise," repeats the Colonel. "This is an exaggeration. I do not know you."

"I must tell you, sir, that this may be the last chance to get a car in Paris—"

"Then I go on horseback."

"You will never be in St. Jean de Luz on the 18th if you travel on horseback."

"Psiav krev—you overhear this, too! . . . Szabuniewicz, disengage me from this fellow."

At that moment the sirens howl. The alarm is over. The relieved guests find their way out of the laundry. Jacobowsky is being swept along with the current, which he would stem if he could. "Please, one moment—I am not quite ready yet—I have to negotiate for the car." But he has disappeared with the crowd.

"Szabuniewicz, the effrontery of this fellow," ejaculates the Colonel. "Every rebuff he takes for an invitation."

"Still, if he should get a comfortable car—"

"Out of the question, Szabuniewicz. I travel alone."

"Yes, I know—I know."

"Well—what are you waiting for"

"I am formulating my plans."

"Marianne is waiting at St. Cyrille."

"St. Cyrille?" Szabuniewicz is aghast.

"St. Cyrille."

"But that is North!"

"Of course it's North. Did you think that I thought it was East, or West or South?"

"But that is where the Germans are."

"Since when I fear the Germans? To this sweet lady I pledge my word—this word I keep. No obstacle stops me. . . . No German—no Germans, Marianne, I come—I—"

The Colonel has started up the stairs. Szabuniewicz follows wildly. "But, Colonel—St. Cyrille! Colonel."

The curtain falls.

It is early dawn two hours later. In front of the Hotel Mon Repos et de la Rose "a venerable but once splendid limousine" stands before the entrance. And before the limousine Jacobow-

"JACOBOWSKY AND THE COLONEL"

Jacobowsky—Our route is by the main boulevards. Place de la Bastille, Ivry, and down the Route Nationale to West-South-West.
Colonel—You are wrong, Jacobowsky. Our way go down the Champs-Elysee, Neuilly, Saint-Cloud an' Route Nationale to West-*North*-West.

(Oscar Karlweis, Louis Calhern, J. Edward Bromberg)

sky and a liveried Chauffeur are carrying on a conversation having to do with Jacobowsky's interest as a possible purchaser. With "indefatigable eloquence" the Chauffeur continues to build up his price.

Facts are facts, the Chauffeur would point out. The Germans are at Meux! They are marching this way and by evening they will be marching up the Champs Elysées!

"The Germans will enter Paris from west-north-west. Whereas, here before you stands one of the most faithful autos in France, ready to drive you west-south-west."

"Come to the point, if you please . . ."

"The point is you should thank your lucky stars I came along like this. There's not another car left in Paris! Even the few taxis that are left are hiding away since yesterday. Try to get a cab—just try, Monsieur, and see what happens. And suppose you found another car—where would you get the gasoline? Where would that blood of life come from to fill the hungry tank? (*Abruptly.*) Are you sick? You know, you look sick, Monsieur."

"Who looks well at six o'clock in the morning?"

The buildup continues. This car, the Chauffeur is proud to relate, comes from the stable of none other than the Baron Rothschild. Just before he left the Baron said, "Philbert—"

But Jacobowsky is losing patience. "Come to the point!" he repeats. "What do you want? I have been listening to you talk for twenty minutes. Your wife and children are as familiar to me as my own face. I know what you like to eat and drink, what paper you read! *But what do you want for this car?*"

Again the Chauffeur would enumerate the high points in the bargain: the tires, gas in the tank, the extra gas in the back, and finally, the price—

"This superb vehicle will cost you a mere fleabite—forty thousand francs."

Jacobowsky is threatened with a fainting spell. "Don't lift me till I fall . . ." he admonishes. But there are no counter proposals. Jacobowsky would thank the Chauffeur for his trouble and bid him a very good day.

The Chauffeur is disturbed. Did he say forty? He meant thirty thousand francs. Jacobowsky turns on him—

"I want to buy this car. You want to sell it. Fact?"

"Fact . . ."

"In a few hours the Germans will be in Paris. They will requisition this car. Fact? Fact! You have to sell it or dump it

in the river. Fact? Fact! Does it have a spare tire? No!
And look at the tires on the wheels—"

Five minutes later Jacobowsky has bought the car for seventeen thousand francs, but with the handing over of the ignition
key he suddenly remembers that he doesn't know how to drive.
Could the Chauffeur arrange with his wife to leave Paris for a
few days, for a good price? The Chauffeur could not. Besides
he has two more cars to sell before the Germans arrive.

The Tragic Gentleman comes from the hotel. Whether he
can or cannot drive a car he does not say, but he prefers to walk
—like everyone else. He calls their attention to the confused
tramping of footsteps in the near distance—

"That's the Parisians," he says, as if he were singing a
pensively tender aria. "Walking, walking, walking. They are
marching to the stations but the stations are dead—no trains
move out—so they turn about and walk through the suburbs—a
thousand, ten thousand, one hundred thousand—with bag and
baggage. Life animates the legs and they walk and walk. Where
we shall be when the Boches arrive only God and St. Denis know!
. . . When the Boches march in, Paris will be a dirty coffin, a
coffin without a corpse—but I was born in Paris and to Paris I
belong and I'm moving with the people of Paris out of Paris and
I want to walk not drive—walk with all the others—with the
moving boulevards, day after day—hour after hour—because
when your legs ache, your heart doesn't ache so much."

The Tragic Gentleman has gone on, "walking off with long
stiff strides." A distressed Madame Bouffier appears. Her house
has been deserted by everything except the "mice, the water bugs
and those two Poles." She is glad Jacobowsky has bought the
car.

Col. Stjerbinsky and Szabuniewicz have appeared, the Colonel
soundly berating his servant because no transportation has been
provided to take them away from Paris. Why is this? Szabuniewicz cannot answer. He has done his best. He has thought
his head off. But that, allows the Colonel, is not enough thinking.

It is, decides Jacobowsky, a proper time to resume negotiations.
With some confidence he indicates the car. The Colonel is not
interested. Is he an automobilist? No. He is a cavalryist.
Can he drive a car? When the road is straight he can. Curves
he does not care to see.

Suddenly the Colonel recalls Jacobowsky. Remembers that he
was born in Poland. He would know more of this. Jacobowsky
is pleased to oblige. Yes, he was born in the village of Studno,

near Kasimisz. His father had taught children Biblical history.
The Colonel seems interested.

"I think it might be interesting, sir, for us to travel together,"
ventures Jacobowsky, eager to press the point home.

"Interesting? How interesting?"

JACOBOWSKY—Psychologically. You are—if I may make so
bold—cast suddenly in a new role. Instead of being in the
enviable position of persecuting other people, you are persecuted
yourself. Now I'm used to it. I'll help you get used to it.

COLONEL—I don't need no assistance from you, Monsieur.

JACOBOWSKY—Probably not—but if you should want it, there
I'd be.

COLONEL—If I consent drive your car, it is because it help me
bring out from danger vital documents of our Polish Mother-
land's fight for freedom.

JACOBOWSKY—Do not deny me the privilege of assisting in a
patriotic act.

COLONEL (*struck by the idea*)—Ah! You want to be good
patriot?

JACOBOWSKY (*firm*)—That is my deepest ambition.

COLONEL—I cannot deny man right to be patriot.

SZABUNIEWICZ (*piously*)—That would be a sin.

COLONEL (*decides—turns to* JACOBOWSKY)—I will drive your
car!

JACOBOWSKY (*overcome*)—Colonel—if it weren't for your
rank, I'd embrace you.

COLONEL (*turning his attention to the car*)—First, get out
from this car these rugs.

JACOBOWSKY—Excuse me, Colonel, these rugs mean very much
to me.

COLONEL—Excuse me, please. I am one of Pilsudski's Colonels! I not used to voyage in furniture truck. No, the backside must remain empty.

JACOBOWSKY—And why must the backside remain empty?

COLONEL—I am not used to give reasons.

SZABUNIEWICZ (*explaining*)—He always travels light.

MADAME BOUFFIER (*intervenes*)—But it's his car—

COLONEL—Monsieur . . . (*To* SZABUNIEWICZ.) What's his
name?

MADAME BOUFFIER (*shouting*)—Jacobowsky!

COLONEL—Monsieur Jacobowsky. In this car you bring out
not only your small self but you serve a high purpose—maybe

for the first time in your life—not—no?

SZABUNIEWICZ—You help Poland, too.

JACOBOWSKY—Can't I help Poland and take my rugs too?

SZABUNIEWICZ (*in a whisper*)—Be careful—you'll irritate him.

COLONEL—You see, Szabuniewicz, what it means to take favor from certain people.

SZABUNIEWICZ—You did irritate him.

JACOBOWSKY (*after a mournful pause*)—Take the rugs out of the car, Solly. (SOLOMAN *obeys in mute protest.*) Madame Bouffier, please keep these rugs as a further souvenir of some very pleasant hours.

MADAME BOUFFIER (*hissing*)—My dear, why do you stand for it?

JACOBOWSKY—There are two things a man shouldn't be angry at—what he can help and what he can't help.

The car is ready, the time for departure has come. Jacobowsky has come with the road map. "Our route is by the main boulevards," he is saying; "Place de la Bastille, Ivry, and down the Route Nationale to west-south-west."

"You are wrong, Jacobowsky," corrects the Colonel. "Our way go down the Champs Elysées, Nuilly, Saint-Cloud an' Route Nationale to west-*north*-west."

"I am sure the Colonel means west-*south*-west."

"No. Colonel means west-*north*-west," puts in Szabuniewicz, with a malicious grin.

But—*north*-west, protests an excited Jacobowsky, there are the German divisions; to go that way is to go right into their arms. And, after all, it is his car, isn't it?

"My car, what means that?" demands the Colonel. "On a stormy sea you say 'this lifeboat is my lifeboat?' Now the devil take you—to hell you go. Szabuniewicz—horses—"

"I told you to be careful—when he says north-west, it's north-west." Szabuniewicz speaks from experience.

Jacobowsky is beaten. So, they are to go first, Szabuniewicz explains, to pick up a lady-love. That would put another complexion on the matter. "Any lady who would interest the Colonel to such an extent—where he risks his life and documents, I mean—she must be a rare person," agrees Jacobowsky. A moment later his capitulation is complete—

"Colonel, I see you're right. You are a strategist. You have some plan in mind. When you say west-*north*-west you have an idea in it—and I agree. Which direction you like, I agree. I agree. I agree."

They are in the car now, waving their good-bys to Madame Bouffier and to Solly, the porter. The Colonel steps savagely on the accelerator. The car does not move. Once, twice— Now he begins to swear—

"Psiav krev! What dirty thing is this? I give spurs to the villain but she don't move."

"The motor is a fake!" shouts Jacobowsky.

"Would I be standing here if the motor was a fake?" asks the Chauffeur. "The battery needs recharging, that's all. There is a garage twenty meters away. Everybody out and push—"

"Now, you see, Jacobowsky, what complications come with you?"

"An' is only now the beginning," moans Szabuniewicz.

The Chauffeur has got behind the car, his sleeves rolled up. "Push, gentlemen, push!"

"Stop! Nobody knows what waits before us!" The Colonel has risen and is standing in the car. "I think therefore is wise to call on the Heaven before we start on the undertaking." He is looking severely at Jacobowsky. "This means also for you, Jacobowsky."

"For me? *Twice* for me! I wept when I was born and every day shows why—"

The Colonel has crossed himself and taken a Polish prayer book from his pocket. Slowly, he begins to read: "I, Tadeusz Boleslav Stjerbinsky, I go from Paris not to fly from the Boches but them to overthrow! All right, push!"

There is a good deal of straining, but the car does not move. They have forgotten to release the brake. This being attended to the pushing is resumed and the car begins to roll slowly forward.

"God save Jacobowsky! . . ." prays Madame Bouffier.

The curtain falls.

ACT II

Twelve hours later, on a lonely road leading to a cottage at St. Cyrille, Marianne, an attractive young French woman in her early twenties, is discussing with Serouille, her lawyer, the situation that is facing her. The summer dusk is fading gradually into a brilliant moonlit night. Overhead there is the almost constant, breath-taking roar of German planes.

Marianne, by the argument of Serouille, is young and strong.

Certainly she should run away before the Germans come. But
Marianne is not interested in the Germans. She has sent for
her lawyer to settle a boundary dispute. There is a matter of
what Serouille calls "six feet of pasture, and all rocky" that
Marianne contends belongs to her and not to her thieving neighbor, and she intends to have it.

As for the Germans—Marianne cannot think of the time
when France will no longer be France. The whole world loves
France. Especially America and Poland. Look how the Poles
have fought!

"But what good was it?" wheezes Serouille, who is old and
fading. "The Poles were done for six months ago. The Germans are a very few miles to the north. What are you waiting
for?"

"Right now I am waiting for the return of my lover—a noble
Pole—Col. Tadeusz Stjerbinsky. Is not that a lovely name?"

"He will not return."

"He will! Moreover he will return with men, with planes,
with guns. He did not go to Paris for nothing."

Serouille can do no more. In forty-eight hours, he figures,
both Marianne's land and that of her hated neighbor will be in
the hands of the Germans. He has done what he could.

"Tell Vauclain if she goes to court it is she who will have to
pay the costs," Marianne calls after him, when he leaves "That'll
stop her—the penny pincher."

For a moment after Serouille has gone Marianne "stands looking out at her beloved fields, whitening in the bright moonlight."
She is deeply stirred as she mutters the name of the lover who
shall also be her deliverer. But the bark of her dog, Coco, dis-
tracts her and she disappears in the garden.

For a little the scene is empty. Then from the near distance
the "reluctant pounding and thrashing of an exhausted automobile motor" is heard, followed a moment later by Jacobowsky's
limousine, mud-bespattered and rattling. When it runs into a
heap of stones put up to serve as a tank obstruction, the car
comes to a sudden stop. Its doors fly open. Jacobowsky tum-
bles out. Szabuniewicz runs around to check the damage to the
mudguard, and Colonel Stjirbinsky arises calmly in his seat to
announce that they have arrived. This is the object of his heart's
desire.

"Are we running away from the Germans, or do we have a
rendezvous with them?" Jacobowsky would know. "You will
never know, Colonel, what these twelve hours have cost me."

"Cost you?" exclaims the Colonel, fixing Jacobowsky with a blue-eyed military stare. "Polish Government pay you back everything. Szabuniewicz, child, write down everything what we owe this *merchant*. Myself, I have no head for figures."

With a proper concentration, Szabuniewicz is searching his memory for the details of the Jacobowsky account when Jacobowsky seeks to aid him: "Write down in your head the Polish Government owes me for the following: Replacement One: a heart which has begun to flutter like a wounded bird— Replacement Two: One wrecked nervous system—and body ditto. And, if the Germans catch me, one entire Jacobowsky."

The Colonel ignores Jacobowsky and concentrates on a proper account. It amounts, as he figures it with Szabuniewicz's aid, to thirty-five thousand francs. For this amount he would toss the coin, double or nothing.

"Give me coin! Top I win! Bottom you win!"

Taking a coin from the smoldering Jacobowsky the Colonel flips it and slaps it into his palm.

"Polish Government owe him now seventy thousand francs," announces Szabuniewicz, retrieving the coin.

This is all very amusing, but it does not alter the fact that they are getting nearer and nearer to the Germans, Jacobowsky would remind them. Is Jacobowsky in a hurry? Certainly he is in a hurry.

"And you—you are not in a hurry?" Jacobowsky demands of the Colonel. "This Messiah in the gray gloves who is waiting to save you in St. Jean de Luz—he is not in a hurry? That corvette filled with Czechs and Poles—she is not in a hurry?"

"Dis corvette for us—not for you."

"I know. But I want a sight of the ocean. Perhaps for me, too, a Moses will appear who will divide the Channel and let me walk across to England."

They still have seventy-two hours. The Colonel considers that ample. Delays will take care of themselves and Jacobowsky will find the gasoline. Now they stop for ladies—

"Life of man is short," recites the Colonel adding what touches he can to the set of his tunic. "Always time to think of ladies. For my spirit—this is the fuel. Wit' out this fuel I cannot run— no more than this car, without gasoline."

JACOBOWSKY (*throwing up his hands*)—Reason rebels!

COLONEL—Reason always rebel against life. What is reason? A dried-up little bureaucrat with a green eye-shade. . . . (*Point-*

ing to MARIANNE'S *house*.) To dat lady the Colonel give his
word to return. I am return! Of equal importance my mission
an' my word. But you don't see dat. The concept of honor you
have not got.

SZABUNIEWICZ (*putting perfume in the* COLONEL'S *palm*)—
Promise of Spring.

JACOBOWSKY—Isn't your concept of honor a little exclusive?
Like a private park with a "No Trespass Sign," don't you think?

COLONEL (*grandly*)—I do not think. I feel. I act. Food—
I eat. Gun—I shoot. Horse—I ride. Woman—I love. Honor
—I defend.

JACOBOWSKY—Admirable! A renaissance figure as sure as the
world is round.

COLONEL (*truculent*)—Who say that?

JACOBOWSKY—Who says what?

COLONEL (*ready to make a fight for it*)—That she's round?

JACOBOWSKY—I don't insist—there is no doubt, Colonel, you
have one of the finest minds of the fifteenth century. I unfortunately live in the twentieth. I implore you, see your lady and
let's go.

SZABUNIEWICZ—Windows is dark. . . .

COLONEL—Madame is sleeping, probably.

SZABUNIEWICZ—I go knock.

JACOBOWSKY—Blow the horn.

COLONEL—You wake lady with automobile horn?! Psiav
krev! I break your hands for that! Szabuniewicz, child, my
violin. She is in de car. Madame is asleep. We wake her sweet.

Szabuniewicz recovers the Colonel's violin from the car. For
himself he takes a mouth-organ from his pocket and runs a few
scales. Jacobowsky, unable to believe what he sees, stands by,
fascinated.

Now the Colonel beats time for Szabuniewicz, who starts to
vamp. Soon the Colonel has begun "to squeak out a jolly, popular tune, with much double-fingering. Szabuniewicz follows on
his mouth-organ when and where he can."

"Is this real?" Jacobowsky is asking himself, pressing his
knuckles to his temples. "The air is filled with the thunder of
the German planes. The earth of Europe is crimson. Poland
lies slain—and this last of her dead stands there fiddling in the
moonlight. And I, the only son of Reba Jacobowsky, am lost,
far from home, motoring to the guillotine in Rothschild's car. It
is a grotesque dream that I dream . . ."

In the misty distance Marianne appears. The music stops. The Colonel calls, "as if over an insuperable distance"—

"Marianne!"

"Tadeusz!"

"I am return . . ."

"I am here . . ."

"My arms wait to receive you . . ."

Marianne runs through the garden gate. "I knew you would come back. I never faltered."

"My journey is over." He has taken her in his arms. "I begin my journey."

"Tadeusz!"

"My loved one!"

The Colonel no longer fights the Boches, he explains. Now he runs from them. And Marianne is to run with him.

If he would give up, then it must be true that France is defeated, Marianne sadly admits.

She sees and recognizes Szabuniewicz. Now she would know about the other. Who would that be?

"Fear not," the Colonel advises. "Only S. L. Jacobowsky—"

"The modest owner of this car, which bears us all to safety," adds Jacobowsky.

The Colonel is quick to remind Jacobowsky that his car has been requisitioned by the Polish Government, which is to pay well for it. But he also would have Marianne know that Jacobowsky is helpful.

"Very obliging person, my love. Takes care of everything— car, hotel rooms, marron glacés, gasoline. What you will, Jacobowsky supplies." And then, as one giving an order: "Jacobowsky, gasoline!" It is an order Jacobowsky has no reasonable hope of filling.

Now Marianne has decided that she cannot go with them. She never has left France, and never will. But, reasons the Colonel, with him she must leave. Again it is Jacobowsky who resolves the crisis.

"If I may make so bold, my dear lady," he says, "there are times when in order to advance one must retreat—this is one of those times."

"I cannot run away."

"Right now the shortest distance between this gate—and that house—is Bordeaux, London and back. Please believe me, Madame."

"Is it so hopeless?"

"For the moment. I am a subtle man, and I have read much but the Colonel here has a faculty worth more than all my subtleties. He will escape with you, but he will also return with you, he will fight for you."

"I do not need you to speak for me, Monsieur."

"It will save time. You have the same idea I have but it takes you too long to gather your thoughts."

There is a good deal of argument. The Colonel adds a promise that he will bring Marianne back and fight for France again. Then Marianne agrees to go with them. Now she must get her two dogs and their baskets and other things. The Colonel and Szabuniewicz will go to help her. So, too, would Jacobowsky, but the Colonel objects—

"Madame has protector. You get gasoline." That is the Colonel's order.

"If he gets gasoline, that is wonderful help," says Marianne, sweetly, turning to smile at Jacobowsky. "Good luck!" she calls, as she hurries through the gate.

Jacobowsky is quietly pondering the problem of the gas when the German plane that has been hovering overhead returns with a roar and begins spitting machine-gun bullets. Jacobowsky ducks into the back of the car and stays there until the plane recedes. When he comes timidly forth again, feeling himself all over for possible wounds, he is made conscious of the presence of a Brigadier of the Gendarmerie, wearing a red cap and carrying a service pouch, who has arrived by bicycle. The Brigadier would have a report from Jacobowsky.

"As a foreigner you have no right to fluctuate freely without the proper authorization," the Brigadier explains.

"I'm fluctuating under compulsion, not freely," Jacobowsky answers. "For that matter, all of France is fluctuating."

"To be more specific, what are your personal plans, Monsieur?"

"My personal plans are so fluid I'm apt to drown in them," answers Jacobowsky.

Even a casual investigation of such papers as Jacobowsky is able to show reveals to the Brigadier that Jacobowsky has no legal right to be where he is. Before leaving Paris he should have filed an application that would have in due time been examined and approved by the Commissariat of Police, submitted to the Prefecture and then to the Bureau Centrale Militaire of Circulation. Therefore it will be necessary for Jacobowsky to return forthwith to Paris and follow the outlined procedure.

"Otherwise," concludes the Brigadier, "you are illegally, illicitly and surreptitiously standing on this highway. You are standing before me only *de facto,* not *de jure.*"

"That means arrest and shipping me off to Paris?"

"In accordance with the regulations. . . ."

"You know what the Boches will do with me if they catch me?"

"They won't eat you."

"Especially me," answers Jacobowsky. "I am caviar for them."

In any event, if they do execute him, the Brigadier would point out, Jacobowsky will have the satisfaction of knowing that he died without having broken any of the regulations of France. It is good to die with a clear conscience.

As to further unofficial advice, the Brigadier is powerless to speak unofficially before 9 o'clock, when he will be off duty. Jacobowsky glances quickly at his watch. It is three minutes to nine—

"What I was going to ask was . . . Officer, I have an irresistible compulsion to leave the soil of France? How should I go about it?"

BRIGADIER—For the purpose of leaving France you require a a Visa de Sortie. For this purpose you must apply to the nearest Sous-Prefecture, at Sable d'Olonnes, for such a Visa de Sortie, first executing three questionnaires, each with one photograph, profile, showing right ear, and paying a fee of twenty-seven francs, seventy-five centimes. The Sous-Prefecture will communicate with the Prefecture of your basic place of residence, Paris, and will, by extended correspondence, compile a dossier of your case, which after a few weeks goes to the Ministry of the Interior for further action. (*They consult watches.*) The Ministry of the Interior instructs a special commission to investigate whether you are worthy to set foot on French soil, and whether you are worthy to leave it. That takes a certain amount of time, but goes through with the greatest smoothness. There is, however, difficulty in your problem. You must first return to Paris, and await your safe conduct pass, permitting you to come here. Is that clear?

JACOBOWSKY—Crystal!

BRIGADIER—Monsieur is very intelligent. But I must frankly tell you that even if you fulfill all the requirements I have just enumerated, your prospects are nil. After all, what can you expect from a Government which you have caused so much clerical work? You'd better come along with me right now.

JACOBOWSKY (*looking at his watch*)—Nine o'clock.

BRIGADIER—Nine? Then I'm off duty. (*Sits on bench with* JACOBOWSKY.) Now I can talk to you unofficially.

JACOBOWSKY—What would you do if you were me? . . .

BRIGADIER—You want to go down the coast to Bayonne and beyond. Right?

JACOBOWSKY—Right.

BRIGADIER—Keep away from the shore roads to begin with. They are advancing fast along the coast.

JACOBOWSKY—Thank you, but I am unable to follow your counsel.

BRIGADIER—Why?

. JACOBOWSKY—I have no gasoline—not a drop.

Marianne comes from the house, carrying her two dogs, Coco and Mignon, in their baskets. Jacobowsky springs to help her. The dogs are safely, even sympathetically stowed in the car. Jacobowsky, too, loves animals.

The appearance and explanations of Marianne—that she is being taken away by Jacobowsky and the Colonel—a noble Polish officer who will return one day to fight again for France—puts a new complexion on the gasoline problem. It is good that Marianne can go, the Brigadier agrees, as he promptly produces a paper and puts his stamp upon it—

"Take this stamped document. My colleagues in St. Cyrille will furnish you with thirty gallons at the standard price," he tells Jacobowsky, who is profusely grateful. "Carry the greetings of the Brigadier Jouet to England and to America." He has turned to Marianne. "Mamselle Roualet— I bless you. I bless your journey. I bless your mission—"

"Amen!" "Amen!" echo Jacobowsky and Marianne as one.

"If I were younger, I would go with you. But all I can do is put stamps on papers. Monsieur, I am happy to have given you what may be my last stamp for France."

The Brigadier has mounted his wheel and pedaled off into the dark.

Jacobowsky is greatly moved. "You are good fortune, Mamselle," he says as he turns back to Marianne. "You are mercy. You are hope!"

Nor would he have her grieve because she is leaving her beloved fields. She will return to them. Her country will be reborn. "There will be a new France, a new world," promises

Jacobowsky, "because the old one is sick of its own ineptitude."

"You are a comfort, Monsieur."

"You make me wish for youth that I might return here and fight too."

"Thank you, Monsieur."

"I shall dedicate myself to you."

"Thank you, Monsieur."

"To Coco and Mignon, also. Have you any other pets?"

"Only the Colonel."

"To him I am already dedicated," says Jacobowsky.

"So am I," admits Marianne.

They are laughing heartily when the Colonel appears at the gate. He eyes them suspiciously. Why are they laughing? For no reason, Jacobowsky admits. Did he gets the gasoline? Yes.

"A warm rain came down from Heaven and behold—it was gasoline."

"Pipe-line from the sky!" adds Marianne, sensing his mood. They are laughing again. But at what? Nothing! The Colonel is plainly irritated.

"Less and less I like dis Jacobowsky," he confesses to Szabuniewicz.

It will be impossible, the Colonel insists, to take all of Marianne's packages. Jacobowsky disagrees. Jacobowsky wouldn't hear of leaving even one bandbox behind. The Colonel turns on him with a roar—

"Who you not to hear of anything?"

JACOBOWSKY—Let me explain, Colonel. You are a great man but as a refugee I am more experienced—let me tell you nothing is so warming to morale in difficult hours as to have a few precious, familiar knickknacks with you. It restores your identity —gives you a link with the past, a bridge to what you were. It's important, believe me, it's important, and especially for a lady.

MARIANNE—M. Jacobowsky, you are so *understanding*.

JACOBOWSKY—It's experience, mademoiselle, simple experience.

COLONEL—All right! Take whole damn things and let's go. Make of this car a moving van.

MARIANNE—We'll compromise. I'll give up this hat box.

COLONEL—This will be great help.

SZABUNIEWICZ—Colonel—sew papers in that little hat.

COLONEL (*assimilating the idea slowly*)—What you say?

SZABUNIEWICZ—Hide documents in that hat.

COLONEL (*straightening up. Announces*)—Attention! I have

important idea! We take this bandbox, Marianne. In your little hat you sew my documents. Germans will never look there
for them.

JACOBOWSKY—It is an inspiration.

MARIANNE (*bubbling*)—And it will make me feel so important.

COLONEL—Now at last we go! Marianne, the back seat. (*He
gets in—sits at the wheel*) Szabuniewicz—beside me.

MARIANNE (*peering in—to* JACOBOWSKY)—It's so crowded—
where will you sit?

JACOBOWSKY—With great happiness—at your feet. (*Sits on
floor.*)

COLONEL (*turning from the wheel*)—Szabuniewicz—changing
places with him.

MARIANNE (*patting* JACOBOWSKY)—No. I like him here. He
comforts me.

COLONEL—Psiav krev! Less and less I like dis Jacobowsky.

SZABUNIEWICZ—Less and less.

MARIANNE (*consoling* JACOBOWSKY)—Never mind!

"She smiles down at a ravished Jacobowsky who looks up at
her adoringly."

The curtain falls.

Next day Jacobowsky, the Colonel and their party are camped
in an open spot in the woods near the city of Bayonne. The sky
is overcast, but friendly. The car, more battered than ever, has
been drawn up under a tree alongside a brook.

A peaceful scene, but still the Colonel is greatly depressed.
While Marianne sits on the bank mending his coat, he sits alongside in trousers and shirt protesting the misfortune that for the
first time in his life has reduced him to second-hand civvies.

In the Colonel's memory the Stjerbinskys have always been in
uniform. His father was a cavalry officer, his grandfather was
a cavalry officer, and even as a boy he had dressed himself up
in uniform. "In my dreams I am always in uniform," protests
the Colonel. Nor is he pleased when Marianne would quote
Jacobowsky to prove that there is a time to advance and a time
to retreat, and that therefore what he is wearing now is also a
kind of uniform—a uniform of retreat.

"If I have to govern myself by his mentality I rather die,"
snorts the Colonel.

"M. Jacobowsky says it is easy to die," calmly continues

Marianne. "But to live requires ingenuity. . . . This uniform is a part of the ingenuity." As she hands him back the mended coat Marianne sees it symbolically as a wonderful garment in which he could dream of the most heroic exploits.

"We used to have a picture in our bedroom when I was a little girl," Marianne is saying; "the Grand Armee returning through the snows of Russia. They were in rags, poor things. I used to shiver for them. Compared to what they wore—this battle-scarred coat—(*She holds up the poor garment.*) is quite grand. In your uniform you were a symbol, darling. Wonderful, but a symbol. But in this you are a human being. I'm glad for once to have seen you in it. I love you in it."

"This, too, sounds like M. Jacobowsky."

"It's not very flattering of you to assume that I am an echo of M. Jacobowsky. Am I so stupid?"

"When I first know you, you do not talk like dis."

"When I first knew you, it was so close and thrilling that, as I recall it, we didn't talk at all. There was no time between kisses."

"But now dere is plenty of time." The Colonel is bitter.

Yes, Marianne admits, now there is plenty of time. The roads are crowded, the waits are long. To talk with Jacobowsky passes the time. What do they talk about? Oh, all sorts of things. And why do they stop, suddenly, whenever he, the Colonel, appears?

Marianne wouldn't know. Probably because both she and Jacobowsky are afraid the Colonel might not be either sympathetic or interested.

That is all the Colonel wants to know. It is as he suspected. Marianne no longer feels toward him as she did. Now she feels toward Jacobowsky—

"He loves you, this M. Jacobowsky?"

"No, ridiculous! What an idea!" But as Marianne sits beside the brook a new thought assails her. "Do you think so?" she ponders. "Perhaps he does—a little bit. Oh! It's touching!"

COLONEL—You love him, too.

MARIANNE—Now, Tadeusz, don't be silly.

COLONEL—Then what you see in him? Why you like him?

MARIANNE—Why I like him?

COLONEL—You like him better than me.

MARIANNE—In one way perhaps.

COLONEL—Ah, you admit—why? Why?

MARIANNE (*thinking it out*)—I will tell you why. He makes me more—you make me less.

COLONEL (*scientifically*)—I think it necessary I kill this M. Jacobowsky. I fight him.

MARIANNE—You're so absent-minded. You forget it's the Germans you're fighting.

COLONEL—Den what you want I do with him? Engage in arguments with him?

MARIANNE—Why not? Good for you.

COLONEL—I do not argue with people like Jacobowsky over the woman I love.

MARIANNE (*teasing him*)—Oh, it doesn't have to be about me. You can argue with him over all sorts of subjects—abstract subjects.

COLONEL—You make fun of me. Dis I do not tolerate.

MARIANNE—What shall I do with you!

COLONEL—Never did I believe that I, Stjerbinsky, would wear costume like dis and have for rival, M. S. L. Jacobowsky.

MARIANNE—Both good for you!

COLONEL—Ah! You admit!

MARIANNE—Admit what?

COLONEL—He *is* my rival.

MARIANNE—Not so much your rival, darling, as—

COLONEL—As what?

MARIANNE—As your antidote. . . . The odd thing is, darling —M. Jacobowsky adores you. He's constantly telling me how wonderful you are. (*She keeps stealing glances at him but so far no change.*) He envies you. He wants you to love him. He wants the whole world to love him.

COLONEL—In this he will never succeed.

MARIANNE—He knows that. Don't you find it touching? How cheerful he is. How gentle he is. Don't you find it—appealing? He wants so to be loved. I find it very—very—

COLONEL—Obvious you do!

MARIANNE—What shall I do then? Not speak to him? Ignore him? It's his car after all. We're his guests.

COLONEL—Polish Government pay him in full—with profit.

MARIANNE—Then we're all guests of the Polish Government. Shall I be rude to a fellow-guest?

The Colonel stares at Marianne, but he does not answer. Then he tries a new attack. Perhaps if he and she were to talk about trivial things, and laugh together, that would help. Marianne is willing. The Colonel introduces the subject of ballistics. An interesting science, ballistics. But Marianne does not react as sympathetically as he had hoped. So he trades science for reminiscence. His great great-great-grandmother had danced with Napoleon! She was very beautiful. Yes, he has her picture in his home in Poland—if there is any home left!

But this subject, the Colonel decides, is too tragic. It does not make Marianne laugh as M. Jacobowsky makes her laugh. So there is nothing left to do. He must fight M. Jacobowsky. Marianne is disgusted. If only the Colonel could have a little less honor and a little more humor.

"When I love I do not laugh," announces the Colonel, solemnly.

"We French do. We manage both very well. Please, Tadeusz, be a darling and get off your high horse. Shake out of the stiff corset of your code. Relax a bit and admit the human race."

"Dis idea you also get from M. Jacobowsky."

"Don't keep saying that!" shouts Marianne, stamping her foot furiously. "I knew the alphabet before I met you *or* M. Jacobowsky. You don't know me at all. What makes you think you know anything about me?"

"I realize now dis ignorance. Mr. Jacobowsky—he make me realize—"

"Then you should be grateful to him."

"I am. I will show my gratitude by allowing him to engage me on the field of honor."

"The field of honor. It's quite true—you're a medieval man, Tadeusz."

Before he can accuse her, she beats him to the answer: "Yes, that idea I got from M. Jacobowsky!" They are glaring at each other, openly hostile, when Szabuniewicz wanders wearily into the picture.

Szabuniewicz had started upon a foraging expedition with Jacobowsky, but had lost him. They had found the city of Bayonne crowded. No room to walk, no food to buy, no gasoline, no nothing.

An old man and boy come down the road, help themselves to a drink of water from the brook and move on, the old man singing. The sight saddens Marianne. The Colonel is already sad, but determined.

"Anything I endure, but dat you do not love me. Dis I cannot," he wails.

"Oh, darling, I love you," answers Marianne, impulsively kneeling beside him. "It is only for you and with you that I would leave France for even an hour."

"Den I am able for anything," declares a reviving Colonel, taking Marianne in his arms and kissing her ardently. "My *melancholy* vanish like mist before the sun."

He is cheered Colonel now, ready to promise Marianne anything, even that for her he will like Jacobowsky. She is again in his arms, thankful for the change, when Jacobowsky hurries in from the road, "bursting with excitement and lugging a bulging straw shopping bag."

Presently the cause of Jacobowsky's excitement is told. He had miraculously met his brother-in-law's cousin in Bayonne, "He used to be conductor of the Gewandhaus Orchestra in Leipsig. Now he's a waiter in the leading café in Bayonne. He introduced me to the proprietor—and the proprietor—for a price—let me have some very interesting commodities."

As Jacobowsky begins to empty the bag of its food the interest of Marianne and the Colonel steadily mounts. The adventure that goes with the food is retailed in Jacobowsky's best vein. For the food he has acquired—including a chop for Coco—and a huge loaf of fresh bread, and many crisp Brioches—for these blessings Jacobowsky is willing to forgive his brother-in-law's cousin's whole programs badly conducted.

"Ah, Marianne, the war—it transmutes a bad conductor into a perfect head waiter. Mars has a knack for vocational guidance," enthusiastically declaims Jacobowsky. The Colonel has gone back to the car.

"And you, M. Jacobowsky, what has Mars done for you?"

"He has introduced me to you. Without him I should never have known you."

"That's a high price!"

"It's a bargain counter. I'd rather be in France escaping with you than getting a big welcome home reception any where else."

The Colonel is again upon them. Again he would know why they suddenly stop talking. Nor is he willing to accept as satisfactory Jacobowsky's explanation that they had not wished to appear trivial. The Colonel is still growling when Jacobowsky generously hands over to him a bottle of 1912 cognac. It was a bad year, 1912, the Colonel recalls, but he drinks the cognac and is a little irritated because both Jacobowsky and Marianne stick to water.

The more cognac he drinks the more resentful the Colonel becomes. Presently he is again in fighting mood. Let Szabuniewicz get the pistols.

Instinctively Marianne and Jacobowsky draw closer together. This also adds to the Colonel's irritation. Now Marianne's temper flares. She stamps her foot, again repeating that she will have no more of such foolishness. This time the Colonel is beyond listening. Cognac, he insists, makes a man see more clearly.

"Jacobowsky, you afraid from me?" he demands, as the preparations for the duel proceed.

"Yes," answers Jacobowsky, frankly, edging a little closer to Marianne. "I heard in Bayonne the armistice has been signed in Wiesbaden. The Germans are going to occupy most of France. We should be thinking of gasoline—how to get to the Coast. Instead—"

"He say, dis Jacobowsky, he is afraid from me," says the Colonel, turning to a frightened and fascinated Marianne. "I tell you truth—I am afraid from him."

"Thanks for the compliment!"

"Yes. I, Stjerbinsky, who have fought the Nazis on the Pruth and on the Somme and on the Vistula, I who have never known fear—I now know fear. I fear you, Jacobowsky. I fear the thoughts you have that you make her share, the laughter that dries up when I approach. I fear the silence you have make between me and Marianne. Talk against you I cannot. But fight you, I can. Fight you, I must. To prove to myself dat I do not fear I fight you. Because if I fear, I die."

Jacobowsky admits a dilemma. If he should happen to kill the Colonel, who would drive the car? He is much too practical. The Colonel is a fifteenth century man. He lives in the twentieth. There is nothing they can do about it.

The Colonel grows more restive. "I forgive but I do not forget. Get the pistols," he is roaring. "Between us, Jacobowsky, stands a woman. Marianne, please go to the car."

"And what if I kill you?" demands Jacobowsky, suddenly filled with a new determination. "Why not? In my veins flows the blood of great fighters—David, Saul—and the truth is—yes—the truth is you are right, Colonel—I do love her! I am in love with her—I am happy to say it for once—I am happy to hear the words for once—I love her—I love her—I love her—pistols!!"

Preparations continue. The duelists are ready to take their places. If Szabuniewicz is to act as the Colonel's second, then

Marianne will serve for Jacobowsky. Now she is shielding Jacobowsky as he surreptitiously empties his pistol of its bullets.

The Colonel is helping himself to another drink. Jacobowsky doesn't like that. He would prefer to fight his challenger at his best. Also as the challenged party, he would like to protest the pistols. He would have preferred swords.

"My dear man, I am the best swordsman in Poland," boasts the Colonel. "I cut you to pieces with swords. With pistols you have a chance."

At any rate Jacobowsky doesn't like his pistol. He prefers the Colonel's pistol and takes it. Again Marianne has thrown herself between them. She will force them to shoot through her. And, as she shields him, Jacobowsky also extracts the bullets from the Colonel's pistol.

Now they stand back to back, ready to count off the five paces each. They have begun to count when a German patrol appears on the highway. It consists of a First Lieutenant, a Gestapo Official who has not yet found time to change his tourist's garb for a uniform, and two soldiers.

The Germans are greatly interested in the duel scene. The soldiers, on the Lieutenant's orders, quickly disarm the antagonists. The Lieutenant would also have an explanation.

The duel, Jacobowsky is ready to explain, is due to an obsession. The Gestapo Officer, "a rosy-faced pig with a lisp," quickly indicates interest. "Obsthethion? What sort of obsthethion?"

The Colonel, poor man, Jacobowsky explains, had been freed from the insane asylum at Nantes when the Germans bombed that institution. He had been found later by his wife and the expert with her (Szabuniewicz) half buried in a swamp.

"What is your obsthethion?" the Gestapo demands of the Colonel.

"He can't speak. He believes every man—in this instance me —to have betrayed him with her. He insists on dueling. In the last four days, he has killed me six times. It's the only way to get him quietly back to the asylum. The guns are empty as you can see."

"Thith could only happen in France. Typically French!" announces the Gestapo.

The Lieutenant would have their identifications. His action, he assures Marianne, is not directed at peaceable citizens of France, but rather at political evil-doers and certain members of the armed forces—particularly members of the so-called Czechish and Polish armies in France.

Jacobowsky is the first to be examined. By the Gestapo Officer he is discovered to be a former member of the German Reich, now denaturalized, and "a parathite on the body of humanity." Otherwise his papers are in order. For the present they will be kept by the Gestapo.

Szabuniewicz, as a Pole, is immediately suspect, but as his name is not on the Gestapo list he is released as a "trained foot surgeon, masseur, barber and assistant asylum attendant."

Marianne gives her name as Marianne Deloupe, the Deloupe accounted for by her husband, the Colonel.

"In our country, which ith a virile civilization we sterilize fellows like that," sneers the Gestapo. "I want to see this Delupeth paperth—"

"Papers!" exclaims Marianne. "Didn't you read what happened? When I found my husband he was lying in the mud in his hospital pajamas. In the town I washed him like a baby, bought him that suit. I'm going to nurse him myself in the Sanatorium at St. Jean de Luz."

"I affirm to it as an expert," choruses Szabuniewicz.

The Gestapo Officer has started tauntingly toward the Colonel, who backs away step by step, looking very much like a madman. With a scream Marianne is between them, embracing Stjerbinsky and assuring him that nothing can hurt him as long as his Marianne is with him.

"He hasn't spoken in fifteen years," puts in Szabuniewicz. "But he is very strong. Last year he nearly killed the head official of the asylum."

The Gestapo Officer and the Lieutenant confer as to what they had best do with the Colonel. There is something about the Colonel's face that is familiar to the Gestapo man, but he can't say what it is. They might take him along but, as the Lieutenant suggests, it might also be better to let him alone and see where he goes; release him on a leash, as it were.

"Get this dangerous patient of yours to the nearest clinic at once," orders the Lieutenant.

"That's the trouble, Lieutenant," Jacobowsky explains. "Madame wants to do that but she has no gasoline. If you could only help out with a few gallons."

Certainly the Lieutenant will oblige, and does, with a five-gallon can of "gasigasol earth-crevice-exuded-oil substitute."

The intruders have gone. Jacobowsky and his friends are faint with gratitude for being saved. But another problem immediately presents itself. Without his papers Jacobowsky cannot go with them. They must hurry on and leave him to make his way as best he can.

"We'll meet again—I feel it," says Marianne, cheerfully.

"In Existence Number Five—or maybe in Existence Number Six."

"Somewhere."

"In the cathedral of my heart a candle will always burn for you," sighs Jacobowsky.

The Colonel is calm—and grateful. "M. Jacobowsky, I thank you for saving my life," he says, solemnly. "I did not request it. I will make formal request—medal in name of Polish Government in Exile."

"May I take this loaf of bread—instead?" asks Jacobowsky, recovering the loaf from Szabuniewicz's arms.

"Certainly, sirr."

The car is packed and they are ready to drive away. "Good luck! Rendezvous in Existence Five!" calls Marianne.

"I have a memory and I have a hope. Thank you for both," answers Jacobowsky.

He has waved them down the road. As he lifts his raincoat from the ground he finds Marianne's hat box underneath it. "My God, the schlemiel forgot the papers!"

He would start after the disappearing automobile, but realizes it is too late. "Passport to death!" He is apostrophizing the papers. "What a joke that I, the only son of Reba Jacobowsky, have in my hands the future of Poland!"

With a sigh he finishes his packing. Now his face lights up— "But I'll see you again, Marianne—I'll see you again."

Jacobowsky has found the little hat and put it back in the bandbox. Then, with the bandbox under one arm and the loaf of bread under the other he starts off down the road after the Colonel, whistling "Le Donne Mobile" as he goes.

The curtain falls.

ACT III

It is a quiet night at the Au Père Clairon, a waterfront café at St. Jean de Luz. Papa Clairon, the proprietor, is behind the bar, before which a Dice Player is "absorbedly shooting dice against himself." At one of the three small tables a silent man is sitting with his back to the room.

A piano is playing a twangy, banjo-like rendition of an old

waltz, to which a dancing couple, "rigid with liquor, stiff, ghastly, expressionless, a pair out of Picasso's 'Blue Period,' " is dancing.

At the back of the room are two doors, conspicuously marked "Messieurs" and "Dames." Between them is a billiard cue rack. The center of the room is occupied by a big, ungainly billiard table.

The Tragic Gentleman we met at the Hotel Mon Repos et de la Rose is there. He is about to play billiards with Senator Brisson, an old acquaintance whom he has just met.

The Tragic Gentleman is morose. He had thought to cure a heartache by walking. Now both feet and heart ache.

The Dice Player at the bar has been reported by Papa Clairon to be of the Gestapo, and the Tragic Gentleman has asked querulously: "Why do they need Gestapo when we have so many traitors of our own?"

"I beg you not to be violent against those who only are trying to accommodate themselves to the new situation. After all we—you and I—are intellectuals. We must be detached."

"Of all traitors the intellectuals are always the most logical," answers the Tragic Gentleman, bleakly. At that moment his attention is attracted to the door of he café. S. L. Jacobowsky is just coming in. "Ah! The Santa Claus from the establishment of Madame Bouffier!" heralds the Tragic Gentleman. "The purveyor of marrons glacés! What brings you to this mousetrap?"

"The green cheese of hope."

"Cheese is rationed, my friend. And as for hope—it is an extinct commodity. Let me introduce an old friend—Senator Brisson—Monsieur Jacobowsky. We were at the Sorbonne together. My friend is not only a Senator—he is also an intellectual."

"Unusual combination in any country," ventures Jacobowsky.

Over the radio rumbles the voice of Marshal Pétain. Between coughs the voice is saying: "Led to the abyss by political charlatans, feeble men and ideas, France resorted only hesitantly to arms . . . But France, though prostrate, is not defeated. . . ."

"The arch-defeatist denies defeat . . ." explodes the Tragic Gentleman, and a debate is on.

SENATOR—My dear friend— It is easy to be critical when you haven't the responsibility of power. After all, this gallant old man has to lead the nation out of our democratic chaos into the New Order.

TRAGIC GENTLEMAN—You too?

SENATOR (*looking at* DICE PLAYER)—Your pessimism is unjustified, my dear friend. Things will right themselves. The German spirit is practical as well as mystical. It will unify Europe.

TRAGIC GENTLEMAN—Say it louder. Perhaps he didn't hear you.

SENATOR—My old friend, you hurt my feelings. Please believe me—this bacillus of democracy imported from England and America—this infection—

JACOBOWSKY (*interrupting*)—Excuse me, but was the French Revolution an importation?

SENATOR—May I ask, sir, are you a citizen of France?

JACOBOWSKY—Unfortunately not.

SENATOR—On what passport do you travel?

JACOBOWSKY—I had a passport leading to nowhere but even that was confiscated by the New Order. They want to unify me out of existence.

SENATOR (*tolerantly*)—One could scarcely expect an objective opinion from a man in your position.

JACOBOWSKY—You are right, my dear Senator—I am nobody. I am a hunted man, but in this world a hunted man has one advantage. He can never be the hunter.

TRAGIC GENTLEMAN—But you, Senator—a little German tuition should make you an excellent hunter. You will soon be hunting for Jacobowsky. Perfect sport. No poaching laws. No penalties.

SENATOR—In this great convulsion of humanity what happens to Jacobowsky is none of our business. It shouldn't concern us —(*Turns to* JACOBOWSKY.) if you'll pardon my saying so—

TRAGIC GENTLEMAN—If you'll pardon my saying so—it concerns me very much. You remember when the Hitler pestilence first broke out in Germany we all of us said "what happens to Jacobowsky is none of our business" and when it spread from Vienna to Prague we said the same thing. But if instead, we and the British and the Americans and the Poles had said: "It is our business—Jacobowsky is a man too. We can't allow human beings to be treated so"—in six weeks with six divisions we could have exterminated this pestilence in Germany. In other words, my dear Senator, it was our indifference that made Hitler. We are his victory, his blitzkrieg and his world domination.—Now let's go on with the game.

Jacobowsky, noting the Dice Player is wearing gray gloves, has sidled over to the bar and is trying a little desperately to engage him in conversation.

There is no response. The Dice Player continues to order cognac, and seemingly to pay no attention to the story Jacobowsky would tell him of his recent experience with a Polish Officer and their journey together. Presently the Dice Player begs to be excused and retires to the men's room.

The Senator and the Tragic Gentleman have quit their game. As they are putting up their cues, the Tragic Gentleman is struck by the attitude of the Silent Man at the table and would awaken him. The Silent Man is dead. Has been dead for several hours. There is a half empty pill box clenched in his hand.

Before they can do anything about this discovery a town woman has burst into the room to announce that there is a raid on. The police are approaching in trucks and are taking hostages. Patrons of Au Père Clairon appear from unexpected places. There is something of a panic. In the midst of the excitement Jacobowsky can be seen clutching Marianne's bandbox, making his way through the crowd and disappearing boldly into the room marked "Dames."

The Commissaire Speciale de Police who now appears is "a fat, embarrassed man with a perspiring bald spot." He is followed into the room by two soldiers who stand guard at the door.

"No resistance from anyone and please don't make a disturbance!" commands the Commissaire, crisply. "For your own good, don't lose your heads! If your papers are in order you have nothing to fear. Come along—the quicker, the better, one after another!"

There is a good deal of confusion as the examinations proceed, and many excuses and explanations. The German Lieutenant and the Gestapo Officer return to take a hand. "This dirty sabotage has got to stop and we'll stop it" is their favorite threat.

The innkeeper is passed on the recommendation of the Commissaire. The Dice Player produces a special diplomatic passport from the Armistice Commission at Wiesbaden, which brings on a couple of "Heil Hitlers!"

Senator Brisson does not do so well. He may be a Senator of France but the institution of which he boasts no longer exists, the Lieutenant informs him.

"But you don't understand," protests the Senator. "I am sympathetic to the New Order. I am ready to collaborate."

"Good! In the concentration camp you can begin by indoctrinating the other prisoners. Take him."

The others have been pushed into the trucks, including the dead man. The washrooms are the last to be searched. The Commissaire reports nobody in the men's room. The ladies' room is passed by a frowning guard, who goes out abruptly to join his fellows.

The Dice Player drops a coin in the piano which resumes its lugubrious tune. "You might tell the anxious little man in the ladies' boudoir that he may now emerge," he says to Clairon.

Jacobowsky timidly comes from his hiding place. No, he was not lucky. Just scientific. "I have noticed that even policemen have a reluctance to investigate a place reserved for ladies," he says.

The Dice Player is willing to talk now. What about the Colonel? What happened to him? Probably ran out of gasoline, Jacobowsky thinks. He will be along.

The Dice Player cannot wait. There has been a change in plans. The Germans are watching the water front. The corvette will pick the Colonel up at the Mole in Hendaye, five miles south. No, there will not be room for Jacobowsky.

There is a loud knocking at the door. Jacobowsky flies back into the ladies' room. Papa Clairon starts for the door. At the other side of the room the Gestapo Officer appears with a gun leveled at Clairon. "Don't bother with them," he orders. "I know who they are. Come in and chat with me."

The Colonel, followed by Marianne, and later by Szabuniewicz, comes stealthily into the room.

Apparently they have missed the Man in the Gray Gloves. The Colonel is depressed. "First I leave behind the papers. I go back for them. Too late. And then the car break down. I cannot move him—this cursed mechanical thing."

"The papers are in my hat box. It's my fault as well as yours. Anybody can make a mistake," comforts Marianne.

"But not I."

"Mistakes is human—even angels slip." This from Szabuniewicz, who has taken over the bar.

"I am officer. These papers my responsibility. I too late everywhere just as in Poland we too late when Germans come.

History of my people is that we who rule them have failed them."

The Colonel, spurning Marianne's pity, continues to brood. "That little Jacobowsky—if he were here—what would he tell us to do?" he mumbles.

"I wonder what's become of him?" wonders Marianne.

SZABUNIEWICZ—Probably he borrow from Germans passage money to America.

COLONEL (*brooding*)—In every situation—no matter how dark —two possibilities.

MARIANNE (*laughing*)—This idea you got from M. Jacobowsky.

COLONEL—Why not?

MARIANNE (*delighted*)—Why not!

COLONEL (*still brooding it out in his mind*)—The Germans— either they find the papers or they don't find the papers.

SZABUNIEWICZ—Right.

COLONEL—If they don't find them, that's good. . . . But if they do find them . . .

MARIANNE (*helping him along*)—Yes, Tadeusz.

COLONEL—If they find them—

SZABUNIEWICZ—Yes, Colonel?

COLONEL—That's terrible. (*His flight collapses.*)

MARIANNE—You don't talk quite like M. Jacobowsky—not quite.

COLONEL—I myself now live like this Jacobowsky—hunted! When someone knocks, I startle. When the Nazis march across the Square, I tremble. I hang on to life with one hand. I live like Jacobowsky except he know what to do and I don't.

The door of the ladies' room opens and out pops Jacobowsky. The reunion is exciting. When he produces Marianne's hat and the papers they are so delighted all three insist on embracing him. For a moment they are wildly happy. Then, just as Jacobowsky is about to tell them of the new rendezvous at Hendaye, the inner door opens and the Gestapo Man appears.

The Gestapo looks them over accusingly. They may be on their way to the asylum, as Marianne says, but this meeting is certainly a happy coincidence.

The German Lieutenant appears, pushing Papa Clairon before him. Two German soldiers are standing guard at the door.

Catlike, the Gestapo Man would play with his captives. After

Clairon has adjusted the player piano he sits at the instrument and begins to play. He misses his music a lot, he says, when the Fuehrer sends him touring. He is playing softly as he questions Jacobowsky. Why had he not come to headquarters for his papers?

"You must be aware that without your papers you have no identity at all," says the Gestapo man.

"In my case that's an advantage," counters Jacobowsky.

The Gestapo turns tauntingly to the Colonel. Is he still jealous? When Marianne pleads that her husband be not excited, the Gestapo would advise her to get herself a man.

"One of my boys here would oblige you, though our Fuehrer has well said you French are white niggers. In your case, I'd overlook it— As I say, I'm a liberal . . ."

The Colonel can stand no more. "This is not to endure!" he shouts, turning to Marianne.

"Ah! He speaks!" The Gestapo is triumphant.

"Yes. I speak!" cries the Colonel, seizing the Gestapo man and turning him to face the soldiers, who have raised their guns. "Shoot!" the Colonel dares them. "Shoot! I die—but he dies!" . . . "Get behind me, Jacobowsky."

They are still maneuvering to keep in front of the German guns when the Lieutenant appears. A quick blow from Szabuniewicz takes care of the Lieutenant, knocking him out the door he entered.

"Marianne, get his gun. Put it in his back!" calls the Colonel, as the thud of the Lieutenant's body is heard.

"Lower your guns," the German Officer commands. He turns to the Colonel—"I'll let you go!" he promises, laying his own gun on the billiard table.

"You are a lie and your words are a lie! . . . Szabuniewicz! Put him in the ladies' room."

"I put!" gleefully answers Szabuniewicz—and he does.

Now the Gestapo would make terms. "You have the gun and I am unarmed," he says. "Shall we negotiate?"

COLONEL—Not with you.

LISPER—I know you, Col. Stjerbinsky. You are a survival from a dead past. Your code won't permit you to shoot an unarmed man.

COLONEL—You Nazis do it.

LISPER—Ah! That's different. We are not diseased by codes. We have abolished conscience. That's why your victories over us don't last—because when you win you are drugged by sense of guilt. Now my boys—Wilhelm, Max—they don't understand chivalry but they do know how to kill. (*His voice rises.*)

COLONEL—Keep your voice down.

LISPER—All you have is your code. If you break your code you are nothing—you are destroyed—(*As if addressing two men behind the* COLONEL.) Wilhelm—Max—in here quick. (*Obeying a reflex action, the* COLONEL *and* SZABUNIEWICZ *turn around to defend themselves against* WILHELM *and* MAX. *Immediately they turn the German bolts for the door to the street. The* COLONEL *swings around just in time and shoots him. The Gestapo falls dead.*)

COLONEL—I have broken my code and it feels wonderful.

JACOBOWSKY—Now, Colonel, we are lost.

COLONEL (*intoxicated with himself*)—On the contrary this brings back the old days when I am in uniform. I am myself again. I am new found.

JACOBOWSKY—I think I am mislaid. I have a message for you from the Messiah in the Gray Gloves.

COLONEL—What he say?

JACOBOWSKY—The corvette that takes you to England—sails from Hendaye.

COLONEL—Hendaye. Good—we go! You come with us.

JACOBOWSKY—No use—I asked him—he said "out of the question."

COLONEL—You come with us. From now on you take orders from me. I take you under my wing—Jacobowsky, child, I adopts you.

They go out. The curtain falls.

On the mole at Hendaye that night Marianne is comforting a small boy she had rescued from the confusion and the Germans at the Au Père Clairon. It is dark. At the edge of the shadows Szabuniewicz is keeping guard. He can see the Germans on the hunt everywhere. There is no sign yet of the Man with the Gray Gloves.

Marianne would have Szabuniewicz leave her, but the Colonel had told him to stay and guard her and there he will stay. Besides he has heard a new edict over the radio. Because someone killed the Gestapo man, all aliens and Jews are to be shot on sight.

Jacobowsky slides into the scene. He is pretty trembly. He had been close to discovery by a platoon of German soldiers. He, too, has heard the edict. "No more than two persons allowed together in the streets. Should they detect a group of three, the third one will be shot. I, of course, am always the third."

"When the Colonel comes back, we'll be four," Marianne reminds him, smiling. "That will confuse them."

"You love the Colonel?" Jacobowsky asks, kneeling beside Marianne.

"Yes."

"One day you will marry him."

"I'm not sure I'll marry him."

"But—you'll always be in love with him. Of that you are sure."

"Yes—" she says. Jacobowsky receives the *coup de grâce*, straightening up. "But until he learns a little of what you know —I cannot marry him," she adds.

"What *I* know! Useless knowledge."

"He must learn that the world is not made for him, he must learn to suffer, to imagine, to endure. He is learning."

"I am learning, too," and Jacobowsky taps a pistol he has borrowed from Szabuniewicz.

"The world needs you both—why can't it use you both?"

"Yes— Between us—we're a hero!" he agrees.

The Colonel has come, but they have stopped laughing, which he finds amusing. The Colonel has been thinking. Of this he would tell Marianne. Just now he had been lying in a ditch to escape a German searching party. It had made him think—

"I think—I think—formerly other people lie in ditch, I ride by proud. I think: 'Well, they belong in ditch. It is right they lie here. It is right I ride by them.' "

"And now?"

"But now I know: all over the world people lie in ditch because I, aristocrat Stjerbinsky, did not give damn. Now I know—I know what it is to be Jacobowsky."

"Then I feel sorry for you."

"What you say?" demands the Colonel, truculently.

"You think because you've been lying in a ditch for fifteen minutes you know what it is to be me! You have to lie much longer, my dear Colonel. And the difference is this: when you get up you are still Colonel Stjerbinsky. When I get up—I am still S. L. Jacobowsky, the ditch follows me."

Quickly the Colonel remounts his high horse. "I don't know if I care to travel with this fellow!" he says.

"Tadeusz! You know you won't sail without him," chides Marianne.

"Well. . . ." The Colonel gives way reluctantly. "I want him near me so I can dislike him." To Jacobowsky he adds: "Jacobowsky, I warn you, our duel is postponed."

"My dear friend and opposite, our duel is for all eternity," says Jacobowsky.

The Dice Player has been found. He appears to tell them that the time of sailing has been advanced. The boat will be there in eight minutes. The Colonel begins to bustle.

"Ready, Marianne— Ready, Jacobowsky—ready?"

But there will be room for only one. "It's very difficult, but we're full," the Dice Player announces.

"Without my wife I don't go."

"Very well. For her I'll stretch a point. Two places."

There will be no room for Jacobowsky. There will be no room for Szabuniewicz. For Jacobowsky the Colonel would make a special plea.

"Damn all to hell. Listen to me. This Jacobowsky soldier like me. For days now we are in flight. He devote his property an' life to cause of my people who bring him only bad before. Two times now, by turn of mind he rescue my life and papers. I ask you, as officer, can I leave this man to the Boches?"

"That may indeed be a problem, but it is not mine," answers the Dice Player.

Jacobowsky is agreed, but the Colonel is not. Finally Marianne must have her say. "Tadeusz, I am what you said—I am your wife. In my soul and body. Forever. I will wait for you, Tadeusz . . . Take M. Jacobowsky in my place! When you return I shall be waiting."

"Marianne, without you I don't go."

"Tadeusz, here I stand at the outermost tip of my Country. I cannot tear myself away. Behind me I feel the country's grief —the horrible silence of the oppressed . . . how can I forsake my people to go into a foreign land, even for love? You'll soon be fighting again. Shall I sit before your picture in a hotel room in London and do nothing? I must stay here and work for my people. . . . I know you understand me."

The Colonel is convinced. "For days my heart tell me dis—as we get closer to the sea I feel it more and more—that you would never leave France."

She has taken his head in her hands and kissed him. From the near distance a low whistle, which the Dice Player answers.

Again he would know the two who are to go. Jacobowsky, says the Colonel, is to go in his wife's place.

"I cannot leave this man, Jacobowsky, here. There is no place for him any more on earth. Ten steps forward is the sea and ten steps back is death."

Again Jacobowsky would insist that they stop worrying about him. "Colonel, I beg you. I am not afraid to die but I am also not afraid to live. Marianne, look, my headache pills—I throw them away. Now are you convinced?"

"But if they catch you?"

"I promise you I will live as long as the circumstances permit. Now you are endangering your mission. Go, Colonel, and take these."

"What are these?"

"Sea-sick pills. I traded them yesterday for my French Grammar."

"This Jacobowsky—he don't change," says the Colonel.

"Very well—the second place is his."

"His?"

"Yes. I'm not convinced by your arguments, Colonel, but by his tenacity for life. Jacobowsky, England can use in the Ministry of Propaganda."

"You'll even find him useful on the boat."

"I prayed for Moses to open the channel for me. You are Moses!"

Marianne and the Colonel are in each other's arms. "Between St. Cyrille and here we have gone through much," Marianne is saying.

"It's strange, I leave you but now for the first time I feel sure of you."

"Be sure."

"Will you kindly curtail this grand opera before the Gestapo tunes in?" pleads the Dice Player.

"Come back soon—I'll be waiting . . ." calls Marianne, as their embrace is broken and the Colonel gets into the boat.

"I come back!"

"Madame La France! Farewell and hail!" Jacobowsky's voice comes up from the boat.

Szabuniewicz is playing La Marseillaise on his mouth-organ.

"Softly . . ." cautions Marianne.

THE CURTAIN FALLS

STORM OPERATION

A Drama in Two Acts

By Maxwell Anderson

THERE was a good deal of talk of the trouble to which Maxwell Anderson had gone in his preparation of the script of "Storm Operation" previous to the play's production in January, 1944.

He first had to gain permission from Army authorities to make a trip into North Africa to study invasion results at first hand. He must travel as an accredited correspondent and have the approval of no less an Army personage than Gen. Dwight D. Eisenhower.

After a good deal of persistent effort Mr. Anderson was duly accepted as such a correspondent and flown in an Army ferry plane to Algiers. There, at Allied Headquarters, he met and talked with Gen. Eisenhower.

"I want to write a play about Anglo-American military co-operation in this area," the dramatist told the General.

"Now, there you've got something," responded the General, slapping his knees in his enthusiasm, as we have it from Mr. Anderson's report of the interview. "Why don't you write a play about the entire storm operation?"

"What's the storm operation?" asked Mr. Anderson, quite naturally.

"This North African campaign," replied Gen. Eisenhower. "That's the code name we gave it when we started laying the plans back in London a year ago. Storm operation. You could tell the whole story—the planning, the landing, the junction of the armies, the victory—you'll never get a better climax than that victory."

Immediately following his adventures at the front, Mr. Anderson began the writing of his play. The fact that "Storm Operation" proved a box office failure, and was quite generously criticized by the reviewers, does not alter the fact that it was the only play of the season produced on Broadway that was concerned seriously with America's first and greatest act of participation in the greatest war of her history up to that time. Record of this production should, therefore, your editor believes, be made in this year book of the American theatre, both for the information of American theatre followers of today and the aid of theatre historians in the future.

By critical estimate "Storm Operation" is really two plays in one. The first and better drama tells with factual fidelity of the invasion of Africa and certain common reactions registered by the American troops involved. The second and weaker drama is one of those sops to playwrighting tradition that calls for the inclusion of a love interest and so much romantic motivation as the dramatist believes his story and his audiences can absorb. Many another dramatist has missed an effective proportioning of two themes in the construction of one play. But the result is never entirely excusable.

Our introduction to "Storm Operation" is the sight of an invasion barge against the side of a transport that towers above it. The scene is in the deep shadows of early morning. "Men with full packs and wearing helmets stand with their backs to the audience quietly waiting for a signal." One or two others, climbing down the rope ladders hanging from the ship, are joining their mates.

At the head of the barge a First Sergeant is facing the men in the barge, his face silhouetted in the light of a partly opened porthole. He is a man of medium build, probably in his middle or late twenties.

"How long are we going to wait here, Sarge?" a husky voice from the barge inquires.

"That's a bright, intelligent question," answers the Sergeant. "We're going to wait here until they tell us to go." He looks carefully, calmly around the group. "Gen. Eisenhower didn't take me in on the over-all planning of this operation, but looking at the way the barges are lined up, I judge we'll be the last to cast off. Capt. Johnson's in the lead, then the three lieutenants— and we're fifth with a lousy first sergeant commanding."

"O.K., O.K., we know you're lousy," calls a soldier named Simeon.

Before they start moving the Sergeant wants every man to check his ammunition, to be sure he can reach it quickly. There is a stir as they do this. He would next have them loosen the slings on all packs and guns. "If we're fired on before we land, we may find ourselves in the water, and you may have to get rid of your stuff in a hurry."

Anything might happen. They might miss the beach, but it isn't likely that they will. The Captain has a French fisherman with him and the chances are that they will follow the two of them right up on the beach at Oran.

"If we're going to be sitting here awhile, I'd better go over the whole set-up," decides the Sergeant, as they shoot other questions at him. "We're landing on the beach just east of Oran. If anybody gets lost from the outfit he can follow the coast-line west and he'll get to the city docks—and they're going to be damn soon held by Americans. We're going to be met at the beach by a Frenchman who'll know the pass-word. If one of us happens to be the first to see him, say 'Whiskey' to him and he'll respond with the same sacred word. He'll have some Arabs with him and donkeys and camels to carry our heavy stuff, and they won't know the password or any English at all. Don't get excited and shoot 'em before you know who they are. On the other hand, if we meet with opposition—that is, if there is any enemy action—have your arms ready for trouble. Don't get yourself killed because the other fellow fired first."

"Are you scared, Sarge?" comes from the barge.

"Hell, yes. Who isn't? My guts are sticking to my backbone. On the other hand, what the hell would I be scared of? If you're dead you never know it, and if you're alive you're lucky. This is the real thing. A lot of people never get a chance to see the real thing, and we're seeing it." *Type?*

There's another thing he wants them to remember. They're a company of infantry, and despite how some people feel, the infantry is still the "queen of battles." "When the artillery gets stuck, it sends for us," the Sergeant reminds them, with some warmth. "When the air force gets all through bombing we have to march in. When the Navy gets to the edge of the water that's as far as it goes. That's where we take over. The infantry is it. We've got the toughest job and the least spectacular and the most important."

There is also time for a little vocabulary practice. They go over the Arabic words they have learned. "Izek," meaning, "How are you?" "Hamdulala?"—"Allah with you." "Aywa?" —"Yes." And so on. They can count up to three—"Wahad— Etnin—Telata." "Telata beera—Three Beers."

"Suppose four of you wanted to order beer?" asks the Sergeant, who has now been identified as Peter.

"You could order two beers twice," suggests Simeon.

"Or three or four times," adds a fellow called Dougie.

"As a matter of fact there won't be any beer. And no whiskey,

either," warns the Sergeant.   Also if they don't want to get a
knife in the back or something worse, let them stay away from
the Arab women.

"Did you leave a girl behind anywhere, Sarge?" asks Dougie.

PETER—I left so many girls behind me if they all got together
it would look like the heavenly host on Christmas Day.

DOUGIE—As beautiful as that?

PETER—I like 'em beautiful.

DOUGIE—Don't you ever go steady with one?

PETER—When it comes to girls a soldier has to live off the
country.

SIMEON—I had a dream once about a place called Detroit.

DOUGIE—Was there a girl in it?

SIMEON—You bet your Chooley Macalley there was a girl
in it.

PETER—It's no time to be thinking about girls, when you're
pretty soon going to be creeping up a beach with a bayonet stuck
out four feet in front of you.

SIMEON—How the hell did I get into this situation?

PETER—I know how I got here.   I got drafted, the same as the
rest of you.   I didn't want to be a soldier.   Nobody did, only
we knew the job had to be done, and we had to do it.   And the
only way to fight a war is to make the other fellow so Goddam
sorry he picked on us that he'll never want to do it again.   And
the only kind of soldier to be is the best there is.   That's why
we went through all that infiltration hell.   We've got to be so
good they'll never want to see us again.   (*There is a distant explosion, then a breathless pause, and another explosion nearer.
A far-away burst of machine-gun fire is heard.*)

DOUGIE—Are they shooting at us?

PETER—It doesn't sound exactly like a twenty-gun salute, does
it?   (*Calling off.*)   That's right, you sons-of-bitches!   Shoot
your friends down as fast as they come in!

ABE (*at porthole*)—Try to keep wide to port, out of reach of
those harbor guns.   (*The motor starts.*)

PETER—You hear that, Chellie?

CHELLIE—I heard it.

ABE—We're all set to turn you loose, Pete.   Griffin and Captain are under way.

PETER—Swing those gun butts over to fend us off when we
let go.   (*The men obey.*)   Any time, Li'l Abner.   Give it the

gun, Chellie. (*The muffled engine turns up a bit louder. The men lean outward as the boat starts.*)

The curtain falls.

ACT I

Outside the village of Maknassy an officers' tent has been pitched. Two other smaller tents flank it on either side. There is a passage between the tents. Near at hand is a field telephone attached to two G.I. packing boxes. A teletype machine is standing in front of the center tent, before which a private (Dougie MacDougal) is standing guard. At one side there is a crude table and two chairs.

A faint glimpse of the "round, brown, hive-like, thatched native huts and a few white-washed square houses" of the village can be seen in the distance. It is an early morning in April and the sky is blue and cloudless. In the distance a muezzin can be heard chanting a prayer, and just beyond the tents an Arab man and an Arab woman wearing a yakmish are kneeling in prayer.

The telephone rings persistently. Private MacDougal decides finally to answer it, although the job belongs to a Technical Sergeant called Mart, who presently arrives and takes over. "Sycamore talking," announces Mart. "That you, Kelly? This is Mart. . . . Yeah, the sun's out this morning, but it looks like it's going to be another scorcher today. I can read the report . . . We lost twenty-one men and a lieutenant in the landing and fourteen two months later at Constantine. Mostly from mines. Yeah, Peter's around with his arm in a sling. The captain's up at the forward command post and one of the louies is with him. The other louie went back to Gafsa for mail. . . . Well, I'll try to give you a rough idea. About thirty of the regular outfit—the rest scattered up and down the road moving stuff. And seven or eight crazy bastards belonging to some Signal Installation Company, with Simeon riding herd. . . . No, he's one of our own, but he's just as crazy. . . . Only seven wounded just now. Then we've got a crazy French paratroop officer—that took an oath he wouldn't smile till Hitler was dead, and a couple of crazy American nurses, one of whom has been jumping off the tops of tanks lately. Because she thinks maybe she's . . . And she thinks maybe that'll cure it."

A group of Arab women go through back of the tents. Mart thinks Dougie should stop them. "I got orders not to stop 'em," says Dougie, "because when we set up the tents we thought this was a sort of vacant lot but it turns out there's a kind of local

Knights of Columbus hall over on that side and this is the way to it."

"It's a mosque, you dope . . . It's where the muezzin appears on the mezzanine and orders general prayers. Five times a day he comes out like a cuckoo out of a clock, and every time every Mussulman has to flop in the dust and talk to Allah."

A bread-seller with an armful of long loaves which he carries like cord wood would like to sell his supply and the Army would like to buy. But the bread seller would have "Doos franc" and the soldiers would pay "Un franc for un," and there the matter rests through a mess of Arabic arguments and a bewildering assortment of American double talk from the soldier Simeon that leaves the Arab gasping. He is, however, still able to mutter "Doos franc!"

"Ah, well," reasons Simeon, "maybe we better work it down a little from doos franc, mon ami, we can't go completely solsimate in the Army, see, we gotta remember Uncle Sam isn't all glut-gobbles—"

"Uncle Sammy got plenty money," insists the bread seller.

"What? Uncle Sammy! He's pouvre. No money! No souvenir! His pants wear out, his nose wears out, no kovran on the stalet! No kovran, no stalet—ashtabula—absolutely—"

A bargain is finally struck by which the load of bread is acquired for ten francs and a mess of used tea leaves.

When Peter arrives he is carrying a sheaf of papers in his right hand and has his left hand in a sling. There is also a wide bandage across his chest, indicating that he might have got a bullet through the left shoulder.

Peter is looking for Simeon. The line between the camp and the Sened C.P. has been cut. It is up to Simeon to get it patched up before lunch. Simeon's protest is strong. That's bad country to work in. "There's mines all along the road and booby-traps at every pole. I'm losing half my men on those pioneer jobs."

"All right, don't fix it," snaps Peter.

"Hell, Peter, I ain't no moisenflay; we'll fix it; but if we lose the war don't blame me. I didn't send in signal corps to do sappers' work."

"You go out there and blow up those booby-traps and miss those mines. And if you get yourself killed, I'll hold it against you, because I need you for something else tonight."

Simeon has been going pretty strong and he hasn't had any sleep to speak off. Besides, he has got himself into a bit of a fix he'd like to talk over with Peter.

"Look," says Simeon, leading Peter a little away from the others. "We're driving along the Gafsa road last night and we see a celebration going on—"

"What do you mean?"

"You know, a lot of Arabs yif-yiffing in the desert, around a fire—a kind of horse-thieves' convention—and we get out and go over to it, and there's a kind of auctioneer moisenflaying around, getting the crowd all Chooley Macalleyed, and pretty soon he's selling some girls—"

"Girls?"

"Shhhh!"

"I told you to lay off that white wine."

"Honest to God."

"They don't sell girls. They might hire out bond servants for a year. That's different."

"I don't know which it was, but—"

"If you want to talk about native customs you better pick someone else. Dougie, over there. He'll listen. He can't go away."

"But, look, Pete—I bought one."

"Never mind."

Peter starts to walk away when the full import of what Simeon is trying to tell him suddenly strikes him. "What!" he all but screams. "Did you say you bought one?"

"Eight hundred francs."

"Don't let him fool you, Pete," warns Mart, who has just come in and caught up with the story. "He paid exactly ten francs for that broad."

"The most beautiful hunk of morale in all Africa," beams Simeon.

"Where is it?"

"Out in the weapons carrier."

"You're crazy."

"I certainly am. I'm crazy about morale."

Peter has turned away with an expression of mixed anxiety and disgust. Mart has brought a sheaf of orders and there is no more time to waste on a crazy Technical Sergeant.

Mart starts reading his notes. There's a radar coming up. It will weigh about 1,600 pounds and is to be installed, probably on a hill. Looks like another job for Simeon. Also the whole line is moving up that night toward Mazzouna and Sekhira. Also two nurses are being sent back to Gafsa and two replacements are coming up. Also there is an English liaison officer

coming to travel with the company. Probably from the Eighth
Army—

"If we break through toward Sekhira we'll meet the Eighth
coming up the coast, and he's here to cushion the shock," figures
Peter.

"He's expert on this region, too," says Mart. "You're supposed to consult with him about the positions we take up."

"O.K. If he'll talk to a sergeant."

Peter would get on with his work. Capt. Johnson is with the
French and hopes to rejoin his company in the morning. Mean-
time there is this juicy bunch of assignments to take care of.
Also there is Simeon and his hunk of morale to be considered.
Peter turns abruptly to the worried Simeon.

"First of all, you didn't buy anybody. Slavery is abolished."

SIMEON—No, but just the same I gave them the money and
they gave me the girl.

PETER—Simeon, if anybody could turn this war into a traveling circus you'd do it. In the middle of a black night, raining
like Tophet, you came into camp with a baby camel lost from
its mother. You didn't see any reason why you couldn't keep
it. You came back from a day's leave in Tabessa with three
baby chimpanzees you adopted. Thought they'd be nice for
mascots. Now you pick up a dirty female Moslem wearing a
yakmish and with no education which she can use standing up.
Huh-uh.

SIMEON—Look, Peter—be human, will you?

PETER—You've been away from the States too long, boy.
Anything female looks good to you. I've seen a lot of these
Arab girls, too, you know. Mostly they're homely as sin, as dirty
as the ground they walk on, and probably highly infectious in
more ways than one. What's more they're circumcised.

SIMEON—The girls?

PETER—Yes, the girls.

SIMEON—Who told you?

PETER—It's common knowledge. You take her back where
she comes from and fix that telephone.

SIMEON—Look, Chooley Macalley—I can't take her back because the camp's gone—there's nobody there—and what's more
she says she belongs to me and she wants to go where I go. She's
moisenflay about me.

PETER—What do you talk to her—Arabic or double-talk or

the language of love? Suppose you really wanted to say something to the girl.

SIMEON—What would I want to say?

PETER—It might come down to that after a while.

SIMEON—She can parley a little French.—Look, Peter, what
can I do? Set her down in the desert with a canteen and a can
of K rations? She's got no place to go.

PETER—Well, for God's sake, where could you put her here?
I don't know what you can do. Give her a hundred francs and
tell her she's on her own.

SIMEON—O.K. (*He turns.*) Who told you that about the
girls?

PETER—God damn it—I read it! If she's Arab she's circumcised.

SIMEON—That's a funny custom.

PETER—I've heard of funnier.—That's about enough about it.
I've got plenty to do, and so have you. (SIMEON *starts out.*)
Fill the truck with sand, and then if you run over a mine maybe
it won't kill you. I've got to have you tonight.

SIMEON—I've been hauling a load of sand for two months now,
Chooley Macalley—but thanks for the thought.

PETER—Get back before dark, moisenflay, and stay out of the
Garden of Allah.

An English captain and two nurses are reported in the village.
Peter sends word to them that if they would have their breakfast
hot they had better be coming along.

Turning from the phone, Mart reports that an order from the
old man directs if the Captain doesn't get back Peter is to be
in charge of taking the company forward that night. . . .

The two nurses are first to arrive in camp. Lieut. Thomasina
Gray, the Australian, is smallish, snobnosed, and attractive.
Lieut. Kathleen Byrne, the American, is of a fairer complexion
and rather more solid physically. Tech. Sergeant Mart is the
first to greet them. Yes, he assures them, they are expected and,
when they want to wash up, directs them to "it," which is right
over there, with plenty of water and plenty of soap.

Peter is back when Kathy reappears. She remembers him
from hospital days, but he doesn't look quite natural without
his crutch. She is pleased to tell him, too, that her companion
nurse is Thomasina, his little Australian. "I'll be damned," ejaculates Peter. "She will, too," predicts Kathleen.

Kathy's right. Tommy is startled when she first sees Peter.

And it may be, a little disappointed. After all, she didn't have
to volunteer for this particular job, and, if she had any sense,
wouldn't have done so if she had known it was Peter's outfit she
was joining.

"I won't bother you," promises Peter.

"No, I'm sure you won't. Well—"

"Were you with the Eighth?"

"For a few weeks. They needed everybody they could get.
It's better there now."

"Going to get worse around here maybe."

"I don't know. I just do as I'm told."

Capt. Sutton has been preceded by an English Corporal named
Ticker, a large khaki bag and a folding armchair. He arrives now
in person, a fairly dirty, generously bandaged but quite self-con-
tained blond Englishman. He is glad to meet the group assembled, particularly Lieut. Dammartin of the Fighting French.

"I'm reporting for liaison duty from the British Eighth," announces the Captain. "Where is the company C.P.?"

PETER—This is it, sir, but there's no officer about at the moment. Captain Johnson is at Kebili—asked me to apologize for
him, and one of our lieutenants is up near the line with supplies and one's in the rear bringing up the mail. Matter of fact,
I've had word I may have to take the company forward tonight.

SUTTON—You're in command here now?

PETER—At the moment.

SUTTON—Hell, I seem to be reporting to you, Sergeant. (*They
salute.*) I've heard it said the English aren't adjustable, but I'm
learning to adjust damn fast. (MART *enters.*)

PETER—I'd better explain, sir, that when the officers are all
away, I usually eat here at the Captain's table. The breakfast
has just been dished out—or, if you'd rather take over the table—

SUTTON—Not at all—invitation accepted. Ticker!

TICKER (*entering*)—Yes, sir.

SUTTON—You'd better move the car around where we can see
it from here. The Arabs'll take it apart if it stays there.

TICKER—I'll watch it, sir.

SUTTON—No, don't watch it. Bring it around. And find
something to eat and then get started on these slit trenches. I'm
gun-shy and I want my burrow quick and I want it handy.
Where can I have it dug?

PETER (*exchanging glances with* MART)—I beg your pardon,
sir, the slit trenches are behind this tent, but we have a com-

pany regulation that every man and officer digs his own.

SUTTON—Well, I'll be a son-of-a-bitch. Who made that regulation.

PETER—Captain Johnson, sir.

SUTTON—Don't get the impression I couldn't dig my own if I had to. I've done it. But I have other things on my mind this morning, and I intend to have a slit trench at once and I'm not going to dig it personally.

PETER—The regulation exists, sir, and I thought it was my duty to inform you of it.

SUTTON—What happens to me if Ticker does my excavating?

PETER—I couldn't say, sir.

SUTTON—Ticker, you will bring the entrenching tools and set to work.

TICKER—Yes, sir. (*He salutes and exits.*)

PETER—You won't really need one of your own. The officers dug theirs right behind the tent and you can use any one of them.

SUTTON—I'd rather have my own, if you don't mind. I've tried jumping in with friends, and it often leaves the rear exposed. I'll be court-martialed, naturally, and thrown out of the mucking Army for disobeying rules, but the trial will be damned amusing. Damned amusing people, you Americans, anyway. That regulation, for example. Your Captain wasn't joking, by any chance?

PETER—No, sir. He was quite serious.

SUTTON—Yes, he would be. You're a very serious people, and it does you credit. The Army, however, is not a democratic institution, no matter what you do with it.

PETER—You're telling me . . . sir!

Capt. Sutton has a look at the trenches and finds them good and deep. He is also amused when Mart slyly slips Peter a hand-book entitled "How to Get Along with the English."

Very well, if that is the way it is going to be, the Captain will also be prepared. He calls to Corp. Ticker to fetch him his pistols, loaded, and his Book of Common Prayer.

"I read a little squib the other day about the first meeting of American and English soldiers in Africa," says Capt. Sutton. "One of them, according to the story, said, 'Hi, Yank.' The other said, 'Hi, Limey,' and they sat down to share their rations. But if you have a handbook I'll have a handbook."

PETER—That's only fair, sir.

SUTTON—I hope you're not a hero.

PETER—No, sir. I'm a retired steel worker that met up with a couple of slugs crossing a mine-field. You appear to be wounded yourself.

SUTTON—Bitten, Sergeant. Bitten by parasites. And we ran out of sulfa where I was. No, I'm no hero. But I'm covered with desert sores and I itch.

PETER—You came along the coast with the Eighth, sir?

SUTTON—Right. Before that I was at Freetown. Before that I was—at Dunkirk, for instance. I've soldiered all over Europe and Africa—with stubborn Yorkshiremen and cursing New Zealanders and dour Scotsmen and the singing Welsh and the mucking Canadians. And just when I begin to know what to expect from all those quaint specimens, they send me here to take orders from an American Sergeant who acquired most of his military experience on a drill-field in—New Jersey!

PETER—Pennsylvania.

SUTTON—Pennsylvania.

PETER—And I'm not giving you any orders.

SUTTON—Wonderful. (TICKER *enters with prayer book and pistols.*) Ah, now we're on even terms. You look up answers in your manual and I'll look up answers in the Anglican Book of Common Prayer. We can eat breakfast with our reference books on the table?

PETER—It looks as if I was going to need mine.

SUTTON—I'm going to need mine—we'll keep the pistols in reserve, Ticker.

Simeon is on the phone to report, according to Mart, that there are a couple of sheiks who want telephones in their tents. One lives at Maknassy and one at Sened. Simeon, Mart adds, seems discontented in the Army and has some thought of going in the business of supplying telephones to his wife's relatives.

"Is Simeon married?" asks Mart.

"He's involved," admits Peter. "I ought to send somebody after him—but I wouldn't know where to send. Hell, he always took care of himself before, and he'll have to keep on."

The question of whether or not they should wait for the girls and let their breakfast cool brings up the subject of girls in general. Capt. Sutton favors giving the nurses rope, seeing white women are scarce.

"There's something about an American girl—I don't know—" muses Mart.

"She's an American, perhaps," fills in Capt. Sutton.

"There's something kind of unsatisfactory about other girls. You don't notice it until you get your arms around them."

"Maybe it's her religion shows up?" ventures the Captain.

"I wouldn't say it was religion."

"We have a saying, in the dark all cats are gray," puts in Lieut. Dammartin.

"Well, American girls, they're another breed of cats," insists Mart.

"How about Australians?"

"I wouldn't know about Australians. Nope, after the war I think I'll settle down and get married to an American girl—"

Peter, too, is letting his imagination run on what could happen after the war, when Capt. Sutton breaks in with—

"You've met Tommy before."

"In the hospital at Constantine," explains Peter. "I got this since then. I'm supposed to take this sling off after the Doctor looks at it, but the Doctor never shows up."

They have gone to their maps and are working out plans for the forward movement. The situation is a little awkward. Here's Lieut. Dammartin, he's liaison for the Fighting French. And Capt. Sutton, he's liaison for the English. That means they're both staff. Still, Peter, the Sergeant, is their O.C.

"That's something new in the history of warfare," protests Capt. Sutton.

"It's temporary," Peter points out.

"You give orders and we give advice. Correct?"

"I guess that's the way it has to be," agrees Peter.

A flight of planes is heard approaching overhead and the officers are on their feet, headed for the trenches, in an instant. The planes, however, turn out to be P-40's and the men quickly conquer their jitters.

Kathy and Tommy are back from their baths, looking smartly refreshed. They had pooled their rations of water and reveled in the experience of pouring it over each other.

"A blissful picture," admits Capt. Sutton.

"It felt blissful. Cold water running right down the middle of your back. Imagine!"

"I am imagining."

"Think about the water, Captain. Water is really scarce."

"Not as scarce as beautiful white women pouring water over

each other in the middle of Tunisia."

"Is he always like that?" Kathy asks Tommy.

"He has a dirty mind I guess," guesses Tommy. "Good, clean dirt, though."

"Would anybody discern, looking at me, that I was educated to be a priest in the Church of England? The answer is no. Nobody."

Capt. Sutton would try driving on to Sened, to get in touch with his Colonel, but he decides to stay on until the telephone line's fixed. That will give him a chance for a bath. Are there any volunteers to pour water over "an aging English captain, covered with festering sores and very dirty?" There are no volunteers for that job, but Kathy is ready to change the Captain's bandages, if he'll let her.

Mart is again jotting down orders at the telephone. "The radar will be here this morning," he reports to Peter. "It is coming on the train—and Corps Headquarters wants it set on Djebel Djeladin. That's a hill. Corps Headquarters wants it up there, and working, today."

"The dirty bastards," explodes Peter. "That's the highest peak on the ridge. How do you get 1,600 pounds up there?"

"It comes apart in four sections. About 400 pounds each."

"And no road!" interjects the Captain. "Who's going to carry 400 pounds up a mountain?"

The answer to this comes over the wire. Simeon has called in to report that the Sened wire is fixed. The next minute Peter is on the wire. "Look, Simeon," he calls excitedly, "every time I think the war is lost and everybody's gone crazy, you fix something—and we can go on for a few minutes. A miracle man. . . . That's all right. . . . I don't mean it. I just want to get you to do something else. . . . I want you to set the radar on a hill called Djebel Djeladin and have it working before dark. . . . I don't know. . . . I don't know . . . I don't know . . . The radar will be here as soon as you are and the hill is on the map. Over . . . What? . . . Same to you, boy, same to you."

Kathy has gone on a search for gauze to fix the Captain's bandages. The Captain is getting in touch with his Colonel at Sened on the phone. Tommy has come in and is being officially consulted by Peter as to the advisability of his taking his arm out of the sling. It can be done if he will be careful, Tommy reports, after an examination, but he will have to wear the bandages a few days longer. Capt. Sutton has disappeared into the tent.

"That's the first British officer I've seen," confesses Peter.

"Are they all like that?"

"No—he's a lord," explains Tommy.

"A what?"

"He's Capt. Sutton down here, but in England he's Lord Sutton, Marquis of Something."

It occurs to Peter that perhaps Capt. Sutton is the reason he has never heard from Tommy. "He's in love with me if that's what you want to know. Or says, so," Tommy answers. "Did you expect to hear from me?"

Yes, Peter had. Even though Tommy had told him he wouldn't Also Peter would like to know why, just as he had found out that he wasn't going to be a cripple, and had begun to think that if the war would let them alone what a wonderful world it would be, Tommy had checked out of Constantine and never let him know why or where she went.

"Jesus, I wish you'd said something before you picked up and went away," says Peter.

Tommy—You weren't really in love with me, Peter, and I wanted you to love me. Only you didn't. So I got out of there.

Peter—I did love you. But if you're in a war you're married to the war. You can't promise anything, not if you're honest. Because you never know where you're going to be, or how long you'll be gone, or whether you'll come back, and you haven't got a thing in the world except what's in your pack and what you get at the end of the month. You don't belong to yourself and you don't know about tomorrow. That goes for men and for women too.

Tommy—I know. And there are a lot of girls who get to be —part of the Army. A man dies—and they go with another. And then he's killed. And there's another. And pretty soon they don't expect anybody to come back and it doesn't matter so much who it is. And that happened to me. I'd been in love with a boy in Australia, and he was killed. There was a lieutenant here in North Africa. I was in love with him, just for a week. And he was killed. . . . I didn't want to love any more. He'd be killed. So I went with the others, from one hospital to another, and the wounded poured in—and nothing mattered except that men had such a little time to live.—But I'm not like that. I know I'm not. I'm not made that way. It's all wrong for me. I want—

Peter—What, Tommy?

TOMMY—Something to hold to. So everything won't be swept away and lost.—Everything goes by in a great rush of blood and bandages—and I'm lost. And there's nothing to believe, and nobody to believe. And it won't stop—forever.

PETER—Do you think it would do any good for two people to stand up before somebody and have words said over them? Would things last any longer?

TOMMY—They might. Never mind. It was just my bad luck we happened to stop here. I shouldn't have said anything. I never meant to see you again.

PETER—What good did it do to leave me and take up with somebody else?

TOMMY—He doesn't matter.

PETER (*his arms around her*)—You certainly matter to me, so for God's sake, Tommy—

TOMMY (*pushing him away*)—No! No! No! Oh, darling, I'm sorry! I forgot!

PETER (*holding her*)—Why not, Tommy?

TOMMY—Because—with you—it had to be more than that—or nothing—so it's nothing—and I meant—never to see you again—

PETER—How was I to know?

TOMMY—You knew. (*They break.*)

PETER—Does Sutton want you to marry him?

TOMMY—There's a Lady Sutton. He's just lost. Even more lost than I am—so he hangs on to me. It was just bad luck—stopping here.

PETER—The hell of it is I feel the same damn way about you—only—

TOMMY—No.—Don't try to fix it up. It can't be fixed. And why should it be? What's it all good for, anyway?

PETER—No, I mean it. I'm not much to talk about it, Tommy, but it's true—only—

TOMMY—Only what?

PETER—Only you're looking for something that'll last forever—and things don't last forever in this war, you know that.

TOMMY—No, I guess not.

Capt. Sutton has had his bath and is ready to have Kathy make good on her promise to change the bandages. There is, however, no chance of privacy for them. Outside the camp a caravan is arriving—camels, donkeys, drivers and Simeon.

A confused racket follows Peter's orders that the crowd be held back. Finally the happy Simeon forces his way through to explain. "Peter, my boy, come to papa's arms," he calls; "kiss me. Chooley Macalley, I'm an Arab. I've got everything fixed for the Army—we're all set and moisenflay—"

When Simeon's report is finally worked out it appears that the line to Sened is working; that it had been cut by the Arabs; that when Simeon's girl, Mabroukha, heard about it she took a hand.

"She talked to the Sheik for me and she found out he was miramar about telephones," Simeon explains. "All his life he'd heard telephones and he thought if you had a telephone you were really globious. So every once in a while he stole one of ours, but he couldn't make it work. He wanted a telephone so he could talk to his cousin, who is a Sheik at Sened. So we hooked telephones on for him and his cousin, and they're probably sitting over there now, spilling each other the Chooley Macalley over the phone. We're hooked into the same wire on another circuit and now we've got wire to Sened. What's more, it can't be cut without cutting the Sheik's communications, and he'll have the living gobelias out of anybody that touches his line. Who's burmashawn now? Does it sound like hep?"

Capt. Sutton must interrupt Kathy's bandaging long enough for him to have a good look at Simeon. "What language does this man talk?" he wants to know.

"It's code," explains Peter. "He's signal corps."

"I see. It bothered me because sometimes I seemed to understand it."

So far Peter understands. Simeon had got the wire into Sened and had given the Arabs a vested interest in it so it wouldn't be cut—but what in hell is he doing with the fifty camels?

That's simple: Simeon had explained to his good friend, Sheik Kalipha, about the problem of getting the radar up on the mountain. The Sheik agreed that it could be done with camels and here they are, the whole burping lot of 'em. And when the radar is on the mountain, who is it will deserve the credit for getting it there? No, not Simeon, the magician, but Mabroukha—

"It was my idea to give 'em the telephones," admits Simeon. "But it was her idea to talk to 'em. She said, Look—only it was in French—Voila, when the Arabs steal from you, you shoot them, but you shouldn't shoot them; you should arrange matters. This is their country you fight over. They steal from you because they are hungry and you are rich and you are here without permission. That's a rough translation. Fact is, she'd been stealing from the U. S. Army herself; she had two cans of C rations and a can of coffee under her shawl when I bought her."

Mabroukha, insists Simeon, is now the Army's liaison with the Arabs. "You need Mabroukha, Peter," he pleads. "Look, yesterday we didn't have Mabroukha and the service of supply was snafu. Today she's on our side and it all gets ironed out."

"Look," says Peter, "maybe she'd be useful to the Army, but no soldier can take a woman along, you know that. Where is she?"

"Out there holding the camel drivers together."

"What do you want me to do?"

"You've got to see her, Chooley Macalley. I told her you had to decide and she's all ready to come in and talk to you. I'll tell her you're here——"

"I can't decide anything—it's all down in the Army regulations."

"Do you want that radar on the mountain, big boy, or not?— Mabroukha! Entrez-vous."

Mabroukha comes in, hesitantly, wearing a yakmish and native costume. "She looks around timidly at the assembly, then turns to run out. Simeon grabs her arm. 'Non, non, Mabroukha —vous avez parlé—parlé le piece d'occasion—' "

After further urging, and with Lieut. Dammartin serving as interpreter, Mabroukha tells Peter her story. She had, as the Lieutenant puts it, been indiscreet with a young man of her acquaintance. For this she was sentenced by the tribal authorities to the Kasbah, a house of corruption from which by the law she can escape only by earning her way out.

"Now Mabroukha, how shall I say, she had taken her pleasure with one young man, but that did not mean that she wished to take on mankind in general," reports Dammartin. "Therefore she ran away. She was seized by strangers. She was sold, fortunately, to Sergeant Simeon here. She loves him and is extravagantly happy to be his. And now she prays you on her knees to save her from the Kasbah."

Peter, after hurriedly getting Mabroukha off her knees, makes his decision. "Look, Simeon," he says, "I guess you win. Speaking for the Army I have to say stay away from native women or I'll restrict you to quarters. Officially if I catch you with Mabroukha again I'll have to put you under arrest. On the other hand you're in charge of signal installation. If you need co-operation from the natives you have to manage that for yourself. If Mabroukha rode a camel as far as Djebel Djeladin I wouldn't know her from any other camel driver. What does she look like? Is she going to take off that domino?"

Peter has started toward Mabroukha, but Simeon gets in the way. "Uh-uh! We Arabs, we don't allow any monkey business with our women."

"Then you can get the hell out, you Arabs, and hamdulala to both of you. Allez!"

"Checka!" chirps Mabroukha.

Kathy has finished with Capt. Sutton's bandages and the Captain is eager to get started for Sened. Peter can see no reason why they should all four—Tommy, Kathy, the Captain and Ticker—crowd into one little jeep with all their baggage and equipment. There are other modes of travel. The native train for one, and a lot of carriers. Peter is himself taking the Captain's station wagon. Of course if it should happen there is not sufficient room on the train, Tommy, the Captain sarcastically suggests, could ride with Peter.

"In this man's army you leave your girl for a few minutes and when you come back she's occupied," laments the Captain.

"The word is busy, my dear," corrects Kathy.

The problem of transportation takes on new interest as Capt. Sutton argues that Tommy should go with him so that she may get to her assignment of setting up a new medical center as quickly as possible. Peter, on the other hand, contends that there is no such rush.

"Tommy, I happen to know the place," protests Capt. Sutton. "You'll be taking over an old wreck of a building the Germans used as a field hospital and just evacuated. It's filthy from end to end—bloody mattresses and stale bandages lying around. You ought to get there as soon as possible."

The Captain's argument is impressive. "I guess it does matter, Tommy," Peter reluctantly admits. "I don't like to let you go, but if that's true we'd be taking a chance if that station wasn't open. So I was wrong."

Capt. Sutton has gone to fetch Ticker and his equipment. Kathy and Tommy start for theirs. Peter stops Tommy. Putting his hands on her shoulders he kisses her. "So long, Tommy. See you at Mazzouna."

"It won't do any good. Nothing will do any good," mutters Tommy, hurrying out.

"See you anyway," calls the more cheerful Peter.

The curtain falls.

ACT II

A week later the tents are pitched against the steep sides of a rocky desert hill. It is about three o'clock in the afternoon and Sergt. Mart is again talking over the field phone. From his conversation it is apparent that there has been considerable action. Everything is fairly quiet for the moment.

"We've been here a week now," Mart is saying, "and we've stood only one pretty tough counter-attack, the second night we were here. Casualties light among the men, but we certainly had bad luck with officers. That's right—Captain Johnson's mortar squad was wiped out by a shell, all except the Captain himself, who was wounded. Griffin was hurt the next day in the mine field I told you about. Peter's running the company again. Captain Johnson is still in the field hospital here. Griffin was sent back."

There's word over the teletype that the plasma Tommy has been praying for has arrived at the dump. They send Mabroukha to get it. There has been a good deal of strafing and the strain has been hard on Tommy. The last sleep she has had was through the last strafing, curiously enough. She was out for about two hours. Capt. Johnson slept through it, too. He'll be all right now, if there is enough plasma.

"That stuff is really astonishing," reports Tommy. "A man can be dying, and you pump him full of plasma, and three minutes later he'll sit up and ask for a cigarette. It gives you a strange feeling about life and death. It's such a tiny step, one way or the other."

"Old Dr. Hylas used to say: What's a man, anyway? Just a sack of blood. Fill him up and he's fine. Empty him out and he crumbles."

Simeon is back with Mabroukha. She is carrying a heavy package on her head and dutifully following after her master. Simeon pretends he doesn't like it that way, but what can he do against native custom?

"Do you know why the man walks in front?" he demands when the girls would ride him for acting like an Arab. "She keeps him in front so she can watch him. And do you know why she carries the bundles? Because she can't trust him with anything valuable." He lifts up Mabroukha's yakmish and kisses her on the mouth. "That puts her in her place," he says, and they resume their march to the hospital.

Kathy has gone on to take care of the plasma injections so

Tommy can get a bit of sleep, and Tommy is asleep in a chair, with her head against the tent.

Back of the tents Peter has been digging an extra slit trench. He comes when Mart calls him and reads the decoded messages that have come over the wire. He will talk with Capt. Sutton and Lieut. Dammartin if Mart will find them.

Peter sees the sleeping Tommy. He stands over her for a moment and then, leaning down, he kisses her gently. That wakens Tommy with a start, but she is not displeased. However, she has not changed her mind about Peter. Nor is she greatly moved by his renewed pleading.

PETER—Look, Tommy, if you weren't around—if you'd never come along again—I'd have got over it. But seeing you here all the time—and remembering—I can't stand it. You never look at me. You're always behind a barrage of instruments and anesthetics and mops and dishes in that station. And I know it's not really that way.

TOMMY—Oh, it's not?

PETER—No. I have to look at you, and you're there all the time—and I want you, and you want me—and nothing ever comes of it. We just work.—I know you when I see you—even a long way off. I know every little thing you wear. When something's different I know. But you're always going the other way.

TOMMY—I don't believe any of it, Peter. Or not much of it—

PETER—But it's true—

TOMMY—No, what's true is that things don't last in a war, just as you said. You might as well take what you can get before it goes by. It won't be here tomorrow and you won't be either.

PETER—God knows I could wish it was different, but—

TOMMY—It would have been all right if you'd been somewhere else. I could have forgotten all about you. But you're right here, and every time I see you, I always just want you and nobody else.

PETER—That's what I was hoping . . . I love you, Tommy.

TOMMY—No, that's an entirely different matter. To you I'm just that nurse, what was her name, Tommy, the one that went by fast somewhere in Tunisia. But maybe it's better this way. It's better to know that nothing's ever forever.

PETER—That's a damn pessimistic view. When can I see you?

TOMMY—Later. Right now I'm on duty. (*She turns to go.*)

PETER—Things are happening tonight, you know.

TOMMY—This a D day? (*She turns back.*)

PETER—Something like that.

TOMMY—Do you know when things start?

PETER—There's a patrol this afternoon. Then tonight something happens. Will you give me a kiss for luck?

TOMMY—Yes. (*She comes over and kisses him lightly. They separate, then she rushes back to him, they embrace and kiss again.*) That's better.

PETER—Jeez, we have wasted a lot of time.

TOMMY—Haven't we? I must go now.

Peter has sent for Capt. Sutton. Orders have come over the teletype that should be talked over. Peter would avoid, if possible, any suggestion that he is giving the Captain orders, but the Captain does not accept the situation very gracefully. The humor of it continues to elude him. A damned Yankee noncom walks in, takes his girl, takes over his functions, gives him orders and in effect makes him out a blooming jackass, all in the name of military discipline. It may be a good joke, but—

Now Tommy steps into the situation. Did she hear the Captain say that Peter had taken his girl? She would have the Captain know that nobody takes her from anybody. "If I leave one man and take up with another it's my own doing," adds Tommy, firmly. "I do as I please. That's one thing a girl gets out of this war. She's not property any more. She's a person in her own right—as good as a man—and as much her own as a man. You two quarrel over anything you like, but don't think for a minute you're quarreling over me. The only tag I wear is a dog-tag around my neck."

Capt. Sutton feels that he should recite a little history. He remembers when a certain very competent nurse had transferred to the Eighth Army from the Americans; he remembers when he checked into her ward, with some shrapnel "embedded in my obverse." He recalls that he and the nurse became friends; that for a long time she would not talk much but that when she did talk she had a good deal to say about a certain American Sergeant named Peter who did not, as the Captain recalls, "emerge as an admirable character."

"Does that speech of yours mean that you are going back to him? And chucking me?" the Captain would know.

"Yes," answers Tommy.

"God knows, I haven't much to offer," admits Capt. Sutton,

a little dolefully. "While the war's on we're all desert rats together. I've been in it so damn long I've forgotten everything I ever knew except fighting and when it's over I think I'd bet more on the blast furnaces of Pittsburgh than on the British Aristocracy— Yes, and I have a wife somewhere—I remember that because I have a picture of her—but even so I'm certain you'll find me more dependable than Sergeant Peter here for as long as I last. I don't want to lose you, Tommy."

"I have to go with Peter. I didn't want to. But I can't help it."

"They say the test of civilization is whether the man decides or the woman. I'm not sure how civilized I am, because I'm not giving you up, and I expect you back! . . . And damn soon."

"In this war you don't know where you'll be tomorrow. Or who'll be there."

Tommy leaves them and they return to their maps and the problems of war. The Jerries, it appears, are in a certain pass. Peter thinks the plan is to bottle them up there. He is trying to find a trail to the crest of the ridge from which position his men will be able to "pour down murder on the pass."

Seeing Peter can count on no more than thirty or forty men it occurs to Capt. Sutton that, as a murder-pouring detail, this one would be pretty slim. Also he is convinced that Peter lacks the proper amount of experience to take command of such an expedition.

"There's no doubt that you've had more experience than I've had," admits Peter; "and very possibly you're more competent to be in command."

SUTTON—It's simple, then. Call the non-coms together and tell them from now on they take orders from me. They'll go along.

PETER—Of course they would, but I've no right to do it. No authority. And I don't think Captain Johnson would have the authority, either. You're a staff officer, not a line officer. You're not in the chain of command. And you're in the British Army, not the American.

SUTTON—Look, Sergeant. You're sticking to the book on this. The book says line officers command, staff officers advise, but when you get into battle things get too hot for these fine distinctions and they melt.

PETER—Well, that may be true. But right now I can't take anybody's word on a thing like that. I have to stick by my orders. I'm supposed to command here and I'll have to do it.

SUTTON—Christ, I've heard about Americans, but when you actually meet them it's worse! They're out to save the world, but only if they can run it!

PETER—Well, what in hell do you mean, coming to me and asking me to turn over a command to you? I don't make the rules. I'm not running the Army! Go to somebody that is running the Army! Talk about Americans! The British are no better than anybody else! They put on their pants one leg at a time!

SUTTON—You know what depends on holding this pass! The whole bloody line could depend on it!

PETER—I know that.

SUTTON—Do you mean to risk losing it, with inexperienced leadership, and losing men's lives, when there's an experienced man here? And do you expect me to risk my own neck under you?

PETER—You can stay here.

SUTTON—Oh, forget the bloody books and let me catch the mucking bastards on the flank! If I thought you could do it, I'd say for Christ's sake go ahead! But I doubt it—and you doubt it! I'm making a formal demand, right now, that you turn this post over to me.

PETER—I can't do it, Captain Sutton—and I won't do it.

SUTTON—You could be damn well court martialed—

PETER—I'll have to take that chance, I know. I think it's too late to do anything except try to find out about the trail.

Simeon has barged in with Mabroukha and an aging Arab guide. The old fellow, Simeon insists, knows the trail Peter is looking for. Unfortunately the Germans also know about it. This guide's brother had sold out to them.

"Maybe we've got the wrong family," suggests Peter. "I'd be happier about it if he had a more prepossessing puss. Ask him if he can lead us up the path at night."

The Arab says he can do that, even if the Germans are there. Capt. Sutton is a little suspicious. "This is a real job, Sergeant. The Germans are up there waiting for us. You'd better reconsider."

"I can't. But I would like to have you along."

"Oh, I'll go."

"Thanks."

"I think I'll be needed."

There is a hornet hum that swells to the roar of approaching planes. Mart suddenly appears with the yell: "Jerries! They're at it again!" Mart, Sutton and Peter make a dash for the trenches. The plane goes over with a terrific racket, to which the noise of a machine gun is added. Suddenly a brace holding up a camouflage net snaps and falls over a cot. After the plane has disappeared Peter and the others reappear, dusting themselves.

There is a commotion outside. Someone was hit. It was Mabroukha. Simeon carries her in in his arms, calling for a doctor. He lays Mabroukha on a cot. Tommy and Kathy take over.

"Is it bad, Tommy?" Simeon asks, anxiously. "Is it going to be serious? Can I carry her to the hospital?"

"No."

"What can I do?"

"There's a machine-gun bullet through her heart and another through her right lung. She was dead when you laid her here, Simeon."

The yakmish is off Mabroukha's face. It is a beautiful face. The Arab comes forward and gently replaces the yakmish, muttering as he does so: "La illaha il ullah. In shallah." That, Tommy thinks, means "The will of Allah be done!" She turns to a stunned Simeon.

"Come on, Simeon. I know how it is. It's better not to look too long. I'll send some of the bearers over."

Tommy puts an arm around Simeon and would lead him away, but he still stands staring at Mabroukha.

"You're coming with me, Simeon," calls Peter. "We're making a reconnaissance patrol along that trail. I'll need you."

"All right, Peter." Simeon turns to follow. The curtain falls.

Peter's patrol has got as far as the dry bed of a mountain stream. A footbridge has been blown up, the two ends resting on the floor of the gully. Distant rifle shots occasionally indicate the presence of the enemy snipers. The soldier Dougie is returning the fire whenever he sees a mark. Peter has started to set up a field radio—

"They've got us pretty well pinned down," he says as he works. "I wouldn't like to start out of here standing up. Look! Here's the situation. We can't stay in here very long, because the Germans know we're here—and it's going to be rugged when we start back. We'll have to do a lot of crawling. But if anybody can see where that mortar fire's coming from it's worth it,

because then we'll know where to find the Jerries tonight. Don't
expose yourself, but keep a look-out."

The Germans had discovered the patrol, it is revealed, when
a soldier named Hopper had stepped on a mine and had been
blown clear off the trail. His body had caught on the rocks
below, where they couldn't reach him, and his screams had
brought the snipers down on them. Probably Peter should have
shot Hopper, seeing there was no chance of saving him.

"If the Jerries hadn't heard that screaming," says Peter, "we
could have slipped up here and down again without meeting a
soul."

"You just can't do things like that," insists a soldier called
Chuck.

"In a war you do. You have to. It was one dying man's
life against a dozen healthy men. That's the logic of war and
that's one of the things we have to learn. If any of you get
killed up here it's my error—and if the Jerries block this trail
tonight and we can't relieve Joslin that's my error too."

"What happened to Hopper?"

"The Captain shot him. But too late. The Jerries had caught
on where we were. A man can make a fool of himself damn
quick in this business."

Simeon takes advantage of a quiet moment to reassure Peter
about Oujda, the Arab. He's a man of conviction, is Oujda,
whom Simeon calls George. "Last week he was working for
the Germans," relates Simeon. "They paid him off in Vichy
francs, and when he took the stuff down to the market, it
brought about half-a-cent to the nickel. Right there he began
to lose faith. He began to see there was something rotten in
the entire German way of life. Because the Americans pay off
in Tunisian francs, twenty to the dollar. Now George believes
in sound money. An old McKinley man. So out of conviction
he came over to our side."

Simeon is worried. Suddenly, without warning, he has discovered that he has lost all sense of feeling in his hand. Yet
he hasn't been hit, or anything.

Peter is sympathetic and understanding. That sort of thing
often happens. "A man's all wired up inside, you know, like
an intercom system, and if he thinks too hard about one thing
it burns out wires."

Still, Simeon is worried. Does Peter think he is losing his
mind? "Look," says Simeon, "am I a complete half-wit—or is
there sense in it? Damn it, she was an Arab, and a Moham-

medan, and I couldn't have taken her back and married her—but that's what I wanted to do."

"Well, why not?"

"Because it's crazy, Pete. And on top of it, this crazy business! What's happening to me?"

"Oh, hell, in this war anything can happen. And nearly everything does. When this is over and we get home and they begin to ask us what was it like we're going to open our traps and say something and then we're going to realize nobody at home will ever know—and we can't tell 'em—and we're going to shut our traps and keep 'em shut. Because it's impossible. Look at Mabroukha. The way she came into camp. How could you tell your mother and sisters and the folks on the next block about that? And then look at you, falling in love with her. How could you make anybody back home believe that? And now you can't feel with your left hand. Because of a very dubious Arab girl you purchased for eight hundred francs. How is anybody at home going to savvy that business?"

There is a call coming in over the radio. That would be Capt. Sutton. From where he is the Captain can see Jerries crossing the upper end of the ravine. "They'll be down on you in fifteen minutes," calls the Captain. "You never should have gone up there, and you'll have to move fast."

"The snipers have got the path covered, Captain, and we haven't found out much yet—"

There is the roar of a mortar in the distance. "For God's sake, move, and move fast—" The Captain's voice trails off.

"O.K. We'll have to make a dash for it."

Dougie, coming in from the outside, has located the probable position of the German mortar. It's on Djebel Nef on the map.

"Look, fellows," Peter is saying, "get the stuff together. We're going to have to make a break right through the sniping. There's no cover the first ten or fifteen feet. It won't do any good to crawl because they're shooting down on us, and it won't make much difference whether we go one at a time or several together. Simeon and I will go first."

Pete and Simeon duck out. There is the crack of an enemy rifle. Peter can be heard yelling: "Get back in, quick!"

Simeon has been hit in the side. He is dazed. There seems to be something wrong with his back. He knows it is serious and would have them go on and leave him. Peter won't listen.

"Look, I'm no good any more. And you guys are healthy,"

pleads Simeon, as they are getting out the sulfa and the morphine. "Don't stick around here for me and get yourselves killed. That's the logic of war, you said it yourself."

PETER—You'll be fine. (*They break out the sulfa and the needle.*)

SIMEON—Yeah? Sometimes you say things to fellows to keep 'em going. You think of the thing the sergeant ought to say, and you say it. You know God damn well I won't be all right.

PETER—You want to be left here on the mountain?

SIMEON—What difference does it make now? I used to believe you when you talked about soldiers being married to the Army and living off the country. But it's all wrong. It's not true. If you haven't got somebody to go back to, what's it all good for?

PETER (*still working with the bandage*)—You're talking to me about Tommy?

SIMEON—No, I'm talking about yourself. If you're a soldier all alone, it's just for nothing. If you're all alone you haven't got any country, and it's no use going home. I'm alone now.

PETER—You two carry him while I keep the snipers busy. I know where one of them is and maybe I can scare the others. (*They lift* SIMEON.)

SIMEON—Damn it, Peter, if you're a good soldier you'll get your men the hell out of here!

PETER—I'm taking care of you, Simeon. I need you. And don't you forget it.

SIMEON—You take care of yourself. I'm full of dope, and I'm fine.

PETER (*going to the right with a rifle*)—Now try it.

Dougie and Chuck carry Simeon out. The rifle cracks again. The curtain falls.

It is nine o'clock the same evening. The mail has just been distributed. Dougie, Chuck and Winkle have found light enough in front of the tent to read their letters. Mart isn't interested. He reads a handbook. It's Mart's idea to keep his correspondents writing each other.

For the others it is a good mail and it isn't. Chuck's wife, for one, has deliberately turned on the torture. "Look!" explodes Chuck. "She sends me a picture of herself. In a bathing suit. Showing all the curves. I've been here ten months and no chance of a furlough! And she does that to a man! Sometimes I don't know which war I'm fighting."

Winkle's girl, on the other hand, is peeved at the censor. "She says," reports Winkle, " 'At the present writing I am carrying on a correspondence more with the censor than with you. When your last arrived, your letter had been taken out and a little note was put in its place. The note said, 'For reasons of security it is necessary to delete the message entirely. However, your correspondent holds you in high esteem and expresses his affection without restraint. Kindest regards.' "

Over the phone Mart is reporting the return of Peter's patrol. The patrol had found the Germans, all right, had had a brush with an outpost and had taken some prisoners. "He's going to interrogate, but he doesn't expect to get much," Mart tells the Lieutenant.

Tommy is looking for a place for another casualty. They haven't any more cots at the hospital. Her patient is Ticker, Capt. Sutton's batman. Ticker's eyes are bandaged when the Captain brings him in. Tommy doesn't think he is going to be blind. The slug had apparently missed both eyes; just creased along above them.

Peter now has Mart's report. The Lieutenant has phoned that they've got a permanent barrage laid down at one end of the pass. The barrage is holding the Afrika Corps up to now. "When I said you were up there and had a brush with a patrol, he said tell Peter this thing's touch and go, and he'd better try to get in there and cut the bastards off. I said you'd certainly do it if you could."

Mart also reports that he has been trying to locate a padre, but the nearest one is seven miles down the valley. The chaplain is at the hospital and will try to get back.

It is mess time, but the food is not very appetizing. Camel and rice evidently, and the camel was not any too young. Only Capt. Sutton pretends to like it. "For the mess we are about to receive the Lord make us truly thankful," intones the Captain. "Why, this is exquisite," he adds, as he begins to eat.

"I've heard the English like their meat a bit dated," observes Kathy.

Mart has gone for the prisoners, with instructions from Peter to pick out a couple who can speak English. Tommy has come from looking after the wounded Ticker.

"It's awkward to have everything jammed up this way," Peter says to Tommy. "I asked the chaplain to try to get here before twenty-two to perform a marriage ceremony over a couple of un-believers."

"Arabs?"

"About as heathen as Arabs."

"I don't understand. The chaplain's coming here?" asks Kathy.

"Yes."

"Who's getting married, Peter?"

"I thought I would."

"You? Who's the unfortunate girl?"

"Tommy."

But Tommy will not have it that way. Peter, she knows, is doing this for her and he can forget it.

"Look, Tommy. Have you changed your mind about me?" Peter asks, seriously.

"Yes," she says, and quickly adds: "Oh, I wanted you to say this. I wanted you to ask me to marry you. But I don't want you to worry about me or try to take care of me. I've been here a long time. I'm an old hand and I'm useful where I am. So keep yourself free, and after this is all over you can go back and marry a sweet young thing who was never run over by a war. I wish I were a sweet young thing, and I wish to God I'd never seen a war, but there's nothing to be done about that. I've got work to do."

She turns and leaves Peter standing there. "She's trying to make you say you love her, you sad sack," chips in Kathy, as she follows Tommy. . . .

Mart has brought in the prisoners—one "Heinie and one Eytie." Peter would turn the questioning over to Capt. Sutton, but the Captain gracefully refuses the honor. Let Peter hold to his prerogatives.

The German, a stalwart, intelligent fellow, is the first to answer—or rather, to avoid answering. He cannot remember how many men the Germans had overlooking the pass. His name is Corp. Herman Geist, but he cannot recall the name of his organization. Seeing the Corporal's papers were in perfect order Peter is already in possession of that information. Will his papers be returned to him? Yes. After the war, Peter promises.

"I shall have them before that," declares Corp. Geist.

"You think so?"

GEIST—Casablanca is in German hands. You are already cut off here in the Mediterranean. You were fools to venture into the Mediterranean, you Americans, for now we have the west coast and you will never get out. I shall be recaptured.

PETER—The last I heard Casablanca was the main port of entry for American supplies.

GEIST—Yes. They fill you with propaganda and you believe it.

PETER—I see. They fill us with propaganda.

GEIST—Why not? You have no education. When those who lead are military idiots not much can be expected of the schwine who follow. (PETER *makes a move to rise.* SUTTON *stops him with a hand on his shoulder.*)

SUTTON—We were amazed at the accuracy of your fire, Corporal. You dropped those shells just where you wanted them. Did you have howitzers up on the mountain?

GEIST—No. Only mortars. Our mortars are accurate.

SUTTON—They must be. And you use them with deadly efficiency. You must be specially chosen men, all of you.

GEIST—In my division, yes. We are all specially chosen.

SUTTON—It's really hopeless to fight against such superb forces. So well equipped and in such great numbers. How a small group like yours—how many did you say were up there?

GEIST—Why . . . we were only—(*He pauses.*) No, I think you make a game of me.

SUTTON—Do you indeed?—You'll find that we don't play for fun, Corporal. Achtung! (GEIST *snaps to attention.*) Why, you poor ignorant Teutonic bastard. Put up your hands! Will you talk?

GEIST—No!

SUTTON—Get out, then! Take him out and let him sweat a while, and then bring him back!

DOUGIE—Yes, sir. (*Exits with* GEIST.)

SUTTON—To get anything out of a German you have to flatter him or else scare him to death. You can't really beat him but you can yell at him.

PETER—You should have put the questions.

SUTTON—No. This one was hopeless anyway.

The Italian prisoner is Dominico Squillini, a small man and eager to tell his story. He had learned to speak English from his brothers when they came back from Chicago, maybe twenty year ago. Now they fight, the brothers, but nota moch.

"Dey loffa d'Americano," insists Dominico, with gestures. "Dey loffa dem. Roosefelt. Teodore Roosefelt. Tom Mix.

Roberto di Taylor. Herberto Hooffer."

Sure, Dominico was up on the mountain with the Germans.
How many Italians? Maybe a hundred. "You say, 'Hallo!
Come out!' and d'Italianos put up da hands and come out. Dey
gotta brains."

"How many Germans are up there?"

"Much-a Germans. Da hundred, see, maybe da two hundred.
Much-a Germans."

"What kind of weapons are they carrying? Machine-guns?"

"Dey gotta everything. Machine-gun. Mortar. Everything."

"I guess that's all. Gracias."

Captain Sutton is surprised and a little disturbed that Peter
is not going to try to find out the enemy positions. When Peter
asks him if he thinks the Italian was telling the truth he refuses
to have anything more to do with the matter. He has had a
bellyful. As soon as he can arrange it he is asking for a transfer, and he would like Peter to know why—

"Exactly what I predicted happened," says Capt. Sutton.
"You made an error under fire and at that moment the command
passed to me. You knew it. Everybody knew it. I was conducting the patrol. But suddenly you refused to obey orders
and went rushing up on the next ridge, running unnecessary
danger and incurring unnecessary casualties."

Peter has an explanation. He and the others hadn't gone up
on the ridge just for the climb. They were trying to discover the
German positions and they were at least partly successful.
Dougie had seen a puff of smoke over the next hill. That means
the Jerries are holding the little plateau behind Djebel Nef.

"Damn your Pennsylvania soul, why couldn't you say so?"
The Captain's excitement has mounted.

"I'm telling you now; it's the first chance I've had."

There were, Peter thinks, about two hundred Germans up
there and he's all for going after them tonight. Peter will be
needing Capt. Sutton if he does.

"Do you want to get your men murdered?" demands the Captain. "Two hundred Jerries in a prepared position, and you expect to knock them out with thirty?"

PETER—I guess they'd want to go.

SUTTON—They'll go anywhere you take them, but you've got
no right to lead them into that!

PETER—If you'd heard Joslin on the phone you'd think I had.
We might manage to get behind that plateau. I don't think I

"STORM OPERATION"

"From the distance comes the first faint hornet whirr of approaching planes. . . . It is impossible to read in the darkness and Capt. Sutton is compelled to go on from memory as best he can—'In sickness and in health, to love, cherish and obey . . .'"

(*Bramwell Fletcher, Myron McCormick, Gertrude Musgrove, Dorothy Freed, Millard Mitchell*)

could do it but I think you could.

SUTTON—Let's get this thing clear. I'm taking no responsibility here till I know where I stand. I asked for the command once and you refused it. If I take it now you'll snatch it back presto the first time I disagree with you. Suppose I say no attack tonight?

PETER—Jesus. We have to go.

SUTTON—That's what I thought. You're not turning the command over to me. You're asking me to run the show as long as I run it your way! I can't work with you on those terms! I don't like your attitude, I don't like your conditions, and I won't take any more!

PETER—Don't get the idea I don't know I've made mistakes. A top sergeant is in a tough position all the time, what with trying to be just a good dog, taking orders, to the officers, and a tin god that can't be wrong in front of the men. He has to act all the time. He has to act yessir, you're right, sir, to the officers, and in front of the men he has to be like Napoleon Bonaparte and the Angel Gabriel bringing down revelations from the general staff in heaven. And when he gets stuck with too much authority the way I am, and there's a staff officer technically under him, the situation gets too damn confusing. But all I want really is for you and me and the rest of us to get together and kick the Germans out of there.

SUTTON—What I want is to find the most efficient thing to do and do it fast. And I want to say right now that unless I decide when and where we go—and whether we go—I'm not taking any responsibility. If I'm running the show, I'm running it, and if you're running the show, you're running it. That's final. Now which do you want?

PETER (*after a pause*)—All right. It's your decision. Do we go or not?

SUTTON—Do you take orders from me?

PETER—From now all orders come from you.

SUTTON—As an officer I can't justify the attack. Reckless methods don't pay off in the long run. But sometimes a thing like this has to be done, and, damme, this looks like one of those times. So I'll go. And I'll take the command.

PETER—Thanks. I might have known you'd say that.

SUTTON—Against my better judgment I'm beginning to like you—in a mild way.

PETER—Without a handbook?

SUTTON—Yes, you son-of-a-bitch! (*They shake hands.*)

We'd better start, too. The moon'll be up before long.

PETER—Mart, will you go over to the mess and tell the boys where we're going and ask how many want to come along?

If they can have a couple of minutes there is something that Peter wants to say to Tommy, and he wouldn't mind if Capt. Sutton heard. Tommy tries not to be interested, but she agrees to stop a minute.

It's only that there comes a time when the war catches up with a fellow, Peter wants Tommy to know before he goes up on the hill. He knows now what she meant when she said she wanted something to hold to. War does things to a man. He gets used to seeing others die around him, and he comes to hate war, but he comes, too, to know that he has to go on with it. And it's then a man has to know that there is something coming after—

"Simeon's dead," says Peter. "He never wanted to come back down that hill. I knew when we started up. He didn't get himself killed, mind you. It just happened. . . . He was killed because I made a mistake. And others were killed—because I made a mistake. I haven't learned how to be hard enough and ruthless enough. And I got them killed because of that. All right. I'll go ahead and learn to be ruthless and learn to be hard, and learn to be a better soldier, but I can't do it unless there's something beyond, unless there's something to come back to."

"Peter, why didn't you say it before?"

"I didn't know it. You get in the Army and they teach you it's better to be footloose. And at first it looks like a holiday with your expenses paid and no responsibilities—and you think that's a way to live. But you aren't living. You're just taking orders and eating rations and killing—and you're nothing— nothing!—unless you get a line out to that blessed place back there where there are homes and children and peace. Or a line to the future—or a hope of somebody that loves you and doesn't let go. So, it isn't silly to be married, darling, even if one of us is killed. You have to have something like that—or you're nothing—just nothing."

"And suppose we lived through the war, what then?"

"Whatever people have together, we'd have."

"Would you want me in your house, to cook for you, and live there for years—and you wouldn't mind what's happened?"

"Nothing will ever matter except not losing you or getting

lost from you."

"Are we in love, Peter? Enough to last all our lives?"

"I am. I always was if I'd let myself believe it."

"I am if you are. I always was."

Mart is back with a report from the company. All the boys want to go. There'll be about twenty-five. But there is other news, too, and that's not so good. There is a road block and the chaplain won't be able to get over.

That doesn't worry Tommy. She and Peter can say words to each other and mean them just the same. But Peter doesn't want to put his marriage off. Now he has another idea. Capt. Sutton has a prayer book. Why couldn't he read out the questions? He could, if they both want it that way.

In no time at all a wedding is arranged. Mart calls to some of the soldiers that "the top's getting married," and they begin to drift in. Kathy walks in just in time to hear Capt. Sutton saying—

"Peter, wilt thou have this woman to thy wedded wife? Wilt thou love her, comfort her, honor her and keep her, in sickness as in health, and forsaking all others, keep thee only unto her so long as ye both shall live?"

"I will."

The Captain turns to Tommy. "The page is torn here," he explains, "but, Tommy, you take Peter's right hand in your right hand—" Tommy does so, and he continues: "I, Thomasina, take thee, Peter, to my wedded husband—" She repeats after him. From the distance comes the first faint hornet whirr of approaching planes—

"For God's sake, are they strafing at night?" shouts Mart. "Get those lights!"

The men scatter to plunge the camp in darkness. Only those taking part in the ceremony stand their ground—

" 'To have and to hold from this day forward, for richer, for poorer,' " intones the Captain, and Tommy repeats the words after him.

It is impossible to read in the darkness and Capt. Sutton is compelled to go on from memory as best he can—" 'In sickness and in health, to love, cherish and obey' . . . 'According to God's holy ordinance, and thereto I give thee my troth' "—

The planes are passing overhead with a terrific roar. The machine guns are rattling. "A bomb explodes in the near distance. Everybody, except Tommy, Peter and Sutton, throws himself to the ground."

"Put your arms around me, Peter," says Tommy, as the roar of the planes begins to fade. And then she repeats—" 'According to God's holy ordinance, and thereto I give thee my troth—' "

The planes are gone. The lights are flashed on. Nobody's hurt, so far as they know. Sutton would go back to the ceremony. Where's the ring? Peter's found it. It was Mabroukha's.

"Put the ring on her finger and say—'With this ring I thee wed, and with all my worldly goods I thee endow.'" Peter repeats the words, with an amused twinkle.

"The rest of the page is gone, but—whom God hath joined together let no man put asunder—and that should be enough to marry anybody."

It is Mart's idea that this is the point at which everybody kisses the bride, but Tommy begs off. "Mart, I don't want to kiss anybody except Peter."

"O.K., Tommy."

Capt. Sutton and the others have gone to gather up the machine guns and the ammunition. With a wave and a good-by Kathy has gone back to the hospital. Tommy and Peter are again in each other's arms.

"Would you do that, Tommy? Would you cook for me and take care of the house—after the war's over?"

"Yes. If you'd want me."

"You know, that would be heaven," says Peter. "I've just been thinking about it. That would be heaven."

"Yes, it would be heaven," repeats Tommy.

There is a call for Peter from the outside. With a kiss and a "Till morning!" he is gone.

Kathy is back to report that a couple of the boys had been hit with fragments from the bomb. Will Tommy have a look at them? Tommy will.

"How is it, sweet? Being married?" Kathy would know.

"You know, Kathy, it's like an incantation, like a magic. It makes you feel entirely different. I'm not joking. Something happens."

"I'm glad. I think something does happen."

Mart is back to report that Peter's truck is leading the others out of camp. Tommy looks off in the direction the trucks are moving. Mart has gone to the phone to report.

"Sequoia? Sycamore talking. Look, Kelly, you better tell the old man we just sent off a couple of expeditions—one to the Fighting French—yeah—and one to the ridge overlooking the pass—"

Tommy has disappeared between the tents. The curtain falls.

EPILOGUE

Again an invasion barge is silhouetted against the gray sides of a transport. Peter is again in charge. Of his first company Chuck, Dougie and Winkle can be picked out of the gloom.

"There's a little change this time, as you all know," Peter is saying. "We're taking a 37-millimeter ashore with us. As soon as we hit the beach the gun-crew will unship the gun and start hauling it in through the surf. Everybody else will remain in the barge covering the landing against possible opposition. As soon as the gun's out of the way I'll give the word and we'll all hit the beach. If the crew needs a hand with the gun the nearest man will grab on and help. Only don't get caught on the damn thing and get pulled under. We lost men in Sicily that way."

Again they go through the routine of checking their ammunition and their guns. The question of language comes up and that reminds them of Mart and his handbooks. Mart isn't with them this time. He wasn't with them in Sicily, either. "He got it in Africa, remember? On Cape Bon," remembers Chuck.

"We've landed on so Goddam many beaches and lost so Goddam many men you forget who was with you when," says Winkle.

There's some satisfaction that there were also a lot of Germans who never got off Cape Bon. And the Germans never broke through that pass where they lost Simeon.

"I wonder if there's anybody that adds up?" wonders Dougie.

"Adds up?" questions Peter.

"Well, you know, Simeon didn't have to go up on that hill. Nor Sutton either. Does anybody give them credit?"

"Back in Washington maybe there's somebody. They give out Congressional medals."

"Look," says Peter. "Every once in a while I have to make a speech to you soldiers, and this looks like one of those times. You might try doing a little adding up for yourselves. Nobody will ever know those guys as well as we did—Simeon and Mart and the others. We knew what made them tick. They probably won't get any medals—but what we think about them, what you soldiers think about them, that's worth more than medals. They wanted to go home. We all want to go home. I haven't met a soldier yet that wanted to buy in on these foreign parts. America—that's for us.—It's certainly for me. I've got a wife and I hope to God I can take her back there with me some time. I remember once I told you when it comes to girls a soldier lives off the country. I know better now. The best soldier is the one that has a picture in his pocket. And every time he looks at that picture it means home to him. It means his country and what he's fighting for—and he looks at it every chance he gets.—But do you suppose we'd be allowed to keep a place like that if we weren't willing to fight for it—and run our chance of dying among these Goddam European ruins to keep it? Hell, no! The year we go soft enough to say we won't fight for it there won't be any United States. Only we haven't gone soft yet. There's Mart and Simeon and all the rest back there to prove it. And they'd rather stay there, among the ruins, than let their country down. And so would we. On the other hand, we're learning this game. Every time we land on a beach we do a better job of it. We're going to take this town so damn fast they won't know what hit it."

"You can rev up, Peter. The Captain's cast off," calls a sailor through a porthole.

"Wilco."

"What the hell's the name of this town we're taking over?"

"Why the hell would you want to know?" demands Peter. "Take the damn town and then look at the name on it." The sound of distant firing comes over the water. "Oh, oh—I guess they don't want us in there. Swing those pieces over to fend us off. . . . Pour it on, Skipper!"

The engine tunes up at the rear of the barge. The men are leaning outward as the barge starts.

THE CURTAIN FALLS

PICK-UP GIRL

A Drama in Three Acts

By Elsa Shelley

THE Second World War had no more than entered its second year before the problem of juvenile delinquency began to loom large on the police blotters and in the Children's Courtrooms of the country. In New York it quickly became so active an issue that the police admitted their alarm and something of their bafflement. Curfew laws were debated and frequently tried out, but with no more than moderate success. It was a pretty difficult assignment, that of trying to discourage the "Victory Girl" adolescents who prowled the darker side streets, or came boldly into the high-lighted sections of Broadway to make dates with servicemen. Worried social workers pleaded with both the potential delinquents and the agencies of the law that were called upon to deal with their delinquencies. It was inevitable that the subject should reach the stage in the form of a drama of fairly sordid realism sooner or later.

Elsa Shelley, who wrote "Pick-up Girl," is the actress-wife of Irving Kaye Davis, who has had several interesting adventures as a playwright. Interested in the subject of the unhappy and restless adolescent, she devoted a good deal of time to research work in the belief that she could turn her findings over to Mr. Davis and that he would write the play. Mr. Davis, however, noting the thorough job his wife had done in the preparation of her material, insisted that she should first try her own hand at putting it in play form. She finished her first script last summer and before Christmas her play was making the rounds of Broadway managers. It came finally to the offices of Michael Todd and was accepted.

Before Todd could get around to a production, however, he was called for induction into the Navy. He turned the script over to the members of his staff, assigned them shares in its ownership and told them to go ahead with the production with his blessing and his backing. "Pick-up Girl" reached production in late Spring, just a month, in fact, before the scheduled close of the season, June 1.

The newspaper reviews were more favorable than unfavorable,

315

though the critics did a good deal of regretting that such dramatic exposures had to be made, and there were frequent charges that Miss Shelley had been content merely to prepare a case history for stage presentation without offering any solution for the curbing of the evil exposed. Miss Shelley replied that exposure really was her aim, her first title having been "Elizabeth vs. You and Me." It was her hope that the story would bring home to society in general a people's responsibility for the drift of the juvenile delinquency menace.

"There is only one decent reason for writing and producing such a record as 'Pick-up Girl,'" wrote Willella Waldorf in the New York *Evening Post*, "and we prefer to believe that its sponsors were moved by a genuine feeling that such a story told on a Broadway stage, as realistically as possible, might call attention to a festering sociological condition in need of far more drastic remedies than any of the well-meaning steps so far taken to combat it."

The scene of the entire action of "Pick-up Girl" is the courtroom in a Juvenile Court now being presided over by Judge Bentley. It is simply furnished and quite evidently there has been a conspicuous effort made to get as far away from the severe legal aspect of a criminal court as possible. "There is no jury-box and the Judge sits on a low platform enclosed by a handrail." Below the Judge's platform there is a long table onto which he tosses such documents as he signs and at which sits a probation officer taking notes of the proceedings. There are several benches facing the Judge's desk and doorways leading to the Judge's chambers, just back of his desk, and at the other side of the room, to waiting rooms, in one of which detained children are held. Back of the desk, hanging on the wall, is a large American flag. A chair for witnesses has been placed on the platform to the left of the Judge's desk.

On the June day of our first visit to the courtroom the court is in session. Judge Bentley, "a keen-eyed, stern-looking man of about 55," is at his desk busily engaged in reading and signing documents while conducting his cases. Judge Bentley does not wear the usual Judge's robes, but an expensively tailored business suit instead.

Mrs. Busch, a probation officer of about 50, is at the table below the Judge and Miss Porter, the court stenographer, "a spinster lady of about 40," is sorting papers at another table on the platform back of the witness chair.

Having signed his last paper Judge Bentley is ready for the

next case. His door attendant reports that there is a lady out-side who is a friend of Judge Regan of Special Sessions. She would, if the Judge will permit, like to observe the proceedings of the Juvenile Court. The Judge will not permit. The waiting lady is not a teacher, a physician or a law-student—and what goes on in his court is not open for inspection by the public.

"I don't care whose friend she is," announces Judge Bentley, sternly. "This is a Juvenile Court and the public is not per-mitted to see or hear what goes on in this courtroom. The law is specific on that point—thank God . . . Tell this to the lady and convey my regrets. And call the next case."

The next case is that of Elizabeth Collins, announces Miss Porter. Mrs. Busch is the probation officer handling it. The door attendant goes to the door of the waiting room to summon witnesses, calling "Collins, Marti, Webster, Elliott, Lockwood—"

The Collins case is the last but one on this day's docket. There have already been thirty-eight others disposed of. Mrs. Busch can remember one day, when Judge MacGregor was sit-ting, when sixty-five children came before the court. The wit-nesses file into the room. They can, the attendant assures them, take any seat.

Elizabeth Collins is brought in by a uniformed policeman and turned over to Mrs. Busch, who guides her to a place before the platform. "Elizabeth is a golden-haired, baby-faced girl, with a beautiful maturing figure. She is wearing a summer dress and no hat. And although the day is sultry, she is wearing a red coat, collared with imitation white fox fur." Elizabeth is 15, bewildered and scared. She tries desperately to smile as she looks up at the Judge.

She answers when her name is called, as does also her mother. Elizabeth's father, Mrs. Collins explains, is likely to be late. He is coming all the way from California by bus. He doesn't live in California, but he is working there. Mrs. Collins had written him, after the preliminary hearing, about Elizabeth being in trouble and he started right back by special bus, expecting to get there in time.

Judge Bentley decides to wait a little longer for Mr. Collins. Meantime he will dispose of the case of Jack Polombo, aged 9. Jackie is shortly revealed as "a ragged and disheveled youngster; wears knickers too large for him with one trouser hanging below the knee; his shoes are torn and his shirt is dirty."

Jackie, it appears from Mrs. Busch's report, lives with his grandmother, who is too ill to be present. His mother is dead and his father is a seasonal worker who couldn't get away from his job. According to the petition in the Judge's hands Jackie is given to playing hookey and is pretty fresh to his teachers. As to these charges Jackie is quick to inform the Judge that he has "nuttin' " to say.

As to the charge of Miss Russell, his teacher, that she had had a good deal of trouble with Jackie, culminating in his blocking the door to the classroom and refusing to let the dismissed class out, Jackie informs the court that the reason he did that was because she (Miss Russell) would not give him back his harmonica. That, explains Miss Russell, was because Jackie insisted on playing during class lessons. When she had taken the harmonica from him he had bitten her hand and also used vile and abusive language, the like of which she could not possibly repeat in court.

Jackie's truancy record, according to Mrs. Busch, is also definitely against him, he having been away a good part of May and several days already in June.

The evidence complete, Judge Bentley removes his glasses and looks sternly at the culprit. "Jackie—you're a bad boy," he says. "You don't deserve a good education. You don't deserve a fine teacher."

"She's always pickin' on me, callin' me dunce and blockhead!" protests Jackie.

"Any boy who plays the harmonica when he should be paying attention to his teacher is a dunce. Any boy who plays hookey is a blockhead. Now: I can send you away to a place where they'll teach you to be a good boy. Or I can fine your father fifty dollars because *you've* been bad."

"Okay, send me away."

"Do you *want* to be sent away?"

"No. But my fahder ain't got fifty bucks."

Mrs. Busch, it appears, has had a talk with Jackie's father, who insists the boy is nervous. Also, puts in Jackie, "my tonsils hoit." This fact Mrs. Busch confirms—Jackie's tonsils are diseased—

"That's no reason why he should use foul language to his teacher," says the Judge. Turning to Jackie he adds: "Now, Jackie, I'm going to give you one more chance. I'm going to let you give *yourself* a chance. If you're brought before me once more, I'll take you away from your father and send you upstate. Now, will you show me that you can be a good boy?"

"Okay."

"All right. You may go."

Judge Bentley is in his chambers, taking a phone call from the District Attorney's office, when the detained Mr. Collins steps tentatively into the courtroom, not quite sure he is in the right place. "He is about 45, a humble-looking man, with a worry-lined face, and eyes now frantic with distraction over the misfortune of his daughter."

Presently Collins has caught sight of both his wife and his daughter, and they of him. To Mrs. Busch he explains about the bus being late. He'd like to speak to his daughter, if he could. He can, while the Judge is out, Mrs. Busch tells him.

"Well, we're in a fine peck of trouble," Mrs. Collins is saying, as she and Mr. Collins start toward Elizabeth. "I don't know *what* they're goin' to do with Elizabeth." She has paused to indicate a man among the witnesses. "See that man back there? The one in the gray suit? He was arrested with Elizabeth."

"I'll break every bone in his body. The son-of-a-bi—"

"Don't start anything!" Mrs. Collins has taken hold of her husband's arm. "It'll be bad for us before the Judge."

Elizabeth is happy to see her father, throwing her arms around his neck. "Hullo, Pa! Gee!" She is crying now. "I'm so sorry I'm givin' you all this trouble!"

"*Now* she's sorry!" sneers Mrs. Collins.

"They're gonna send me away, Pa! Will yuh get me out o' here?"

"We're goin' to do everythin' we can for you," Collins promises. And he has a surprise for her. They're movin' to California. Already he has rented a house for them with a garden in front, and another in back, with oranges growin' in it. Sounds incredible to Mrs. Collins. Where's the money comin' from? Well, for one thing the house isn't costing any more than they're paying for the flat in Fifty-eighth Street, and for another Mr. Collins has made another loan—

"Could you just give me an idea quickly what happened, so I kin put up a better fight for you . . . because I *know* you're innocent," he says to Elizabeth.

"I *can't* tell yuh!"

"That's what you'll get out of her: 'I can't tell yuh!' " puts in Mrs. Collins. "And all I know is what I wrote you. Two weeks ago last Friday a policeman broke into our flat and arrested—"

The reappearance of Judge Bentley stops the conversation. He is ready to proceed with the case, but he must first inform

them that Elizabeth is entitled to employ a lawyer if they wish
it—

"Your daughter doesn't need a lawyer here any more than
she'd need one if you were to question her in your own home.
The purpose of the Juvenile Court is purely parental. You understand that, don't you?"

"Thank you, Your Honor."

"This is the first time Elizabeth has done such a terrible thing
and we didn't know anything about it." Mrs. Collins is weeping.

"That's what I hear in this court dozens of times a day,
Madam—parents not aware of what their children are doing,
until a *calamity* happens." The Judge is plainly exasperated.
He is ready to proceed with the hearing if they wish him to and
they nod their willingness.

Police Officer Owens, who made the arrests, is the first witness
called. Being duly sworn, Officer Owens is asked to identify the
parties he had arrested. He had first seen Elizabeth, he tells the
court, in a bedroom in her parents' apartment on a Friday night
two weeks before. She was in bed with a man. The man? He
is the one in the light gray suit sitting with the witnesses. His
name is Elliott. ("Elliott is a middle-aged man, well-built, well-
dressed. He's the last person you'd expect to find involved in a
case of this kind; he's the personification of the conservative,
successful business man. Right now, when he gets up, he looks
resentful and self-conscious.")

Elliott has brought his attorney, a man named Brill, with
him and Brill is quick to begin protecting the interests of his
client.

"Is this your first case in a Children's Court?" inquires Judge
Bentley.

"Yes, Your Honor."

"I thought so. Then let me inform you, sir, that the procedure
in a Juvenile Court is strictly informal. In the child's interest,
the Court will try to learn all the facts relevant to the case, and
I'll appreciate it if you will try to waive the legal technicalities."

With an "As Your Honor pleases," Brill accepts the situation
and pulls Elliott back into his seat. The Judge turns again to
Officer Owens. How did he happen to force his way into the
Collins' apartment? Had he received a complaint?

OWENS—We got a complaint at the station house that morning. I was detailed to check up on it. The complainant stated
there was reason to believe that an act of immorality might take

place in the apartment that night. So about nine o'clock I posted myself across the street in the shadow. The complainant waited with me. At about nine-thirty, Mr. Elliott and a boy came up the street, and the complainant pointed them out to me.

JUDGE—Then what happened? Go on.

OWENS—Well, the two of them went into the house— And by the way, Your Honor, I didn't have to force an entrance into the apartment later. The door was unlocked. I just walked in. Into a little parlor.

JUDGE (*nodding*)—Proceed.

OWENS—Well, it wasn't no more'n three or four minutes after the man and boy went in, that boy came out again and went away.

JUDGE—Then you went in—

OWENS—Well, no. I thought I'd give 'em fifteen minutes or so for—well, time enough for somethin' to happen.

JUDGE (*indignant*)—But, Officer, knowing that there was a young girl involved, why didn't you go in right away, before anything could happen?

OWENS (*justifiably indignant*)—Your Honor, my superior officer ordered me to make an arrest if the complaint was true. If I'd-a walked right in and found the man just visitin' with the girl, I'd-a had no cause for arrest. It was the man we were after, not the girl.

JUDGE—Who reported the matter to the police?

OWENS—Mrs. Marti, a tenant livin' in the same house.

JUDGE—Mrs. Marti—rise, please. (MRS. MARTI *rises*. JUDGE *makes note*.) Is that the lady who made the complaint?

OWENS—Yes, Your Honor.

Mrs. Collins is on her feet, glaring at Mrs. Marti and shouting: "That noseybody! . . . She was always snoopin' around spyin' on my family!"

Collins tries to pull his wife back into her seat, but she pushes him away. It is not until Judge Bentley has warned her that another outbreak will put her out of court that Mrs. Collins agrees to be quiet.

The questioning proceeds. There were no other adults in the Collins' apartment that night, so far as the Officer knows, but there were three younger Collins children asleep in another bedroom. "The girl told me that her mother wasn't expected till morning, and the father was out of town."

"When you first entered the apartment, did Elizabeth and Mr. Elliott hear you come in?"

OWENS—I guess they did not, Your Honor, because they certainly looked surprised when I busted into the bedroom. The door to the bedroom was closed, yuh see—and there was no light in it; but I spotted the wall switch right after I swung open the door, and I turned it on.

JUDGE—What was Mr. Elliott wearing when you entered the bedroom?

OWENS (*looking at* ELLIOTT)—He was wearin' only a ribbed undershirt, Your Honor.

JUDGE—What was Elizabeth wearing?

OWENS—Nothin'. (MR. COLLINS *weeps*.)

JUDGE—What happened then, Officer? Did you take them to the police station?

OWENS—Yes, Your Honor. I ordered them to dress—and just as we were about to leave, the boy came in, carrying a bottle of Scotch. So I took the three of 'em down to the station. Elliott was arraigned and held for Felony Court, the girl was placed in the Detention Home, the boy was dismissed.

JUDGE (*with a sly look*)—And the bottle of Scotch—?

OWENS (*grinning*)—I got rid of it, Your Honor.

JUDGE (*laughing*)—All right, Officer—you may step down.

Attorney Brill would present another objection. The District Attorney is quite certain to prefer criminal charges against his client. This will be ridiculous, of course, because this is *not* an affair of *rape*, but if Mr. Elliott should have to stand trial in General Sessions, how can a man be tried in two courts for an alleged crime?

"Your client is not being 'tried' here," snaps the Judge. "We subpoenaed him because we have the right to question him in this court on the basis of his having contributed to a minor's delinquency."

Lawrence Webster is called to the stand. "He is a lad of about 16 and is nervously chewing gum." Larry's idea of the oath being a trifle vague Judge Bentley explains. "In court when you take an oath you're promising not only me but God to tell the truth. . . . If you lie you might fool me, but you'll never fool God." Larry is also induced, gently, to dispense with his gum for the time being.

Larry is in his second year of high and is majoring in athletics. He is alone in court, because his father thought he (Larry) had lip enough to speak for himself, and his mother had a lot of ironing to do.

Larry has known Elizabeth Collins about six months. Ruby Lockwood, who is in his class, introduced them at school. Yes, he had taken Mr. Elliott to the Collins apartment the Friday mentioned. "He tole me he just wanted to call around at Elizabeth's house wid me, for a few minutes, and then we'd start buzzin' the town."

"Buzzing the town?"

"Yeah, you know, hitting the spots. He said he was gonna take us both to a night club or somethin'. And then he goes and does a thing like that."

Larry had first met Mr. Elliott at Ruby Lockwood's. A lot of kids were there havin' fun. Nearly every night there were a crowd of kids at Ruby's, and there were never any other members of the family present. Ruby's father and mother were divorced and she didn't have any brothers or sisters. Nights when her mother stayed home unexpectedly Ruby always managed to let the kids know and they would stay away.

JUDGE—At what time of the night did you usually meet there?

LARRY—'Bout eight o'clock—right after Mrs. Lockwood went away to work.

JUDGE—Were the girls at these gatherings all high school girls, or were there older ones, too?

LARRY—Well, no, the *girls* were all about the same, fourteen, fifteen. I guess Ruby was the oldest.

JUDGE—How old is she?

LARRY—Sixteen.

JUDGE—Besides Mr. Elliott, were there many *men* at these— little gatherings?

LARRY—No, not many. At first there wuz only us kids. But then one time Ruby invited a man she met at a party somewhere, and then he brought another man, and so on . . . There wasn't many of 'em, but they were a pain in the neck!

JUDGE—Why?

LARRY—Aw, they were always flashin' the foldin'-money! Playin' the field and how!

JUDGE—In what way?

LARRY—Well—

JUDGE—Huh?

LARRY—Bringing the girls presents. One night a guy brought

dresses an' things for all the girls. He was in the wholesale business. Elizabeth got *that jacket* that night. (*Points to jacket.*)

MRS. COLLINS—You must be mistaken, young man!

LARRY—I ain't mistaken! I seen her get it wid my own eyes.

JUDGE (*rapping for order*)—Now, what did you all do when you got together?

LARRY—Had fun.

JUDGE—What kind of fun?

LARRY (*embarrassed*)—Well, gee, I dunno . . . Fun! . . .

JUDGE—Did you drink liquor?

LARRY—Sometimes. When some o' the older boys brought it. Mr. Elliott brought some.

BRILL (*jumping up*)—Your Honor, I object! I can't permit that boy to besmirch my client's reputation!

JUDGE—Hasn't your client done that tolerably well for himself, sir? (BRILL *sits down, angry.*) What else did you do at these parties, Larry?

LARRY (*cagey*)—We used to dance and play games.

JUDGE—What kind of games?

LARRY (*grinning*)—Like pillow-fighting; and we used to rassle—

MISS PORTER—Couldn't hear that.

LARRY—We used to rassle!

JUDGE—The older men didn't take part in these games, did they?

LARRY—Sometimes. Mostly in the dancin' though. And the rassling. . . . Then all of a sudden some guy'd turn off the lights, and zowie! Yuh didn't know *what* gawn on! Murder!

There was, Larry admits at the Judge's urging, plenty of "necking." That's what the girls wanted. But he didn't go for none of them except Elizabeth.

This statement brings a denial from Elizabeth, followed by her admission to the Judge that she doesn't like Larry. She never has, according to Larry, though why he is at a loss to understand. She was always giving Larry the brush-off—"icin'-up" —on him, even though he never had done her no harm. Then why did he go to her house with Mr. Elliott? Because she asked him. None of the other guys had ever gone to Elizabeth's house. Her mother wouldn't let them in. He had asked her if he could come because he was nuts about her and at Ruby's she wouldn't even look at him, even after he bought her a Sinatra record.

"How did you happen to take Mr. Elliott to Elizabeth's house?" the Judge asks. "Tell me all about it."

LARRY—Well, he ast me to . . . The first time he come to Ruby's house. Elizabeth hadda go home early that night. And after she went away he says to me, Mr. Elliott says, "She's a neat pigeon," and I says, "You tellin' me!" and he says, "Do you know where she lives?" and I says, "Yeah, right around de corner from me." So he says, "Is it worth a deuce to yuh to get me a date wid her? But Ruby mustn't know about it," he says—(*Explaining to the* JUDGE.)—cuz Ruby went for Mr. Elliott in a big way—so I says, "Okay, I'll try, Mr. Elliott." And he says, "That's fine, call me Alex," and he starts handin' me two bucks.

JUDGE—Did you take the two dollars?

LARRY—Naa! I says, "Keep it, Alex, I make that in one afternoon deliverin' for Renown Meats."

JUDGE—How soon after that did you arrange the date for him?

LARRY—Well, Elizabeth didn't show up at Ruby's for a couple o' days, and then Thursday night when she came, Mr. Elliott wasn't there. So I told her he wanted to come to her house and she said okay, he could come the next night, Friday. So I phoned Mr. Elliott and told him I got 'im a date at Elizabeth's house, and that she wanted me to come along too. And he ast me would her mother and father be home, and I told him no. So he says okay. When we gets there, she turns on my Sinatra record, and Mr. Elliott starts dancin' wid her.

JUDGE—And what were you doing?

LARRY (*irate*)—I jus' sat there like a dope!

JUDGE (*repressing a smile*)—Mhm . . . (*Takes drink of water.*) Go on.

LARRY—Well, we ain't there fi' minutes when he asks her, "How 'bout a drink?" and she says, "I have nothin' in the house." So he takes out a fi'-dollar bill and he writes a note on a piece of paper and he says to me, "Here, boy, take this note over to this café—I eat there, and they'll give you a bottle of Scotch."

JUDGE—Did you go?

LARRY—Well, the café was on'y on 57th Street, so I says okay and I goes out for the Scotch. When I gets back twenty minutes later a cop grabs me and takes us all away. (*Irate.*) Gee,

Your Honor, I didn't wanna get Elizabeth into trouble! When Mr. Elliott said I should get a date for him I didn't know he wanted a—a *party* wid her! She never even kissed me—and that guy, right away she tumbled for him— Just cuz he promised her a lot o' presents I bet!

BRILL (*jumping up again and moving toward platform*)— Your Honor, I—I object! That boy is making damaging statements about my client. These statements are not binding on my client. (*Indicates the* COURT STENOGRAPHER.) And they are going into the record!

JUDGE—Just what is it you mean, counsel? The fact is, your client was *arrested* at the child's house—and for a good and sufficient reason. What could be more "damaging" than that? Mr. Elliott, will you step over here, please?

As Elliott passes her on his way to the Judge's stand, Mrs. Collins would make a scene, but her husband restrains her and the Judge warns her a second time. Again she apologizes and promises to be good to escape being put out.

Attorney Brill would also again object in his client's behalf. He is promptly shut up. The Judge merely wishes to ask Mr. Elliott a few pertinent questions. For one, did Mr. Elliott ask the boy Larry to make a date for him with Elizabeth Collins at her home? He did not. He had asked Larry to tell Elizabeth that he wanted to see her, and gave Larry his business card that Elizabeth might phone if she agreed to go out with him.

How old is he? Elliott is 47. And Elizabeth is 15. But Mr. Elliott had no idea she was so young. How young did he think she was? Before he can answer this one his attorney is on his feet again protesting, so the Judge changes the form of question.

"Did you know that the girl was only in her first year in high school?"

"No, sir! I didn't inquire into that," Elliott answers, self-righteously. "Why should I? I simply wanted to give the girl an evening of entertainment at the movies or the theatre. And I would have arranged to meet her *at* the theatre. . . . But this boy told me she insisted on my coming to her *house,* and that *he* was to come along with me. Well, I had no way of reaching the girl on the phone, and I didn't want to let her down—so I thought I'd drop around for a few minutes and bow out of the whole thing without hurting the girl's feelings. When we got there, the girl was—well, she was in a night-robe . . . said she'd been preparing to go to sleep. I, of course, wanted to leave immediately, but she—begged me to stay, and—uh—well, Your Honor, *you* know how it is."

"What do you mean, *I* 'know how it is?' " snaps Judge Bentley. "Are you trying to enlist *my* sympathy, sir? . . . If your intentions were so gallant and honorable, why didn't you leave right away?"

"I would've, but this *boy* didn't want to go!"

As ridiculous as that statement may appear to the Judge, Elliott insists that Elizabeth had whispered to him that she did not want to be left alone with Larry; that after he had sent Larry on an errand he (Elliott) was ready to leave, but Elizabeth wouldn't let him go.

Attorney Brill is again protesting excitedly, but despite this Judge Bentley does get the statement from Elliott that although Elizabeth had not detained him by force she did, in fact, use a sort of compulsion.

"That girl isn't as innocent as she looks," insists Elliott. "She —well, she got amorous. . . . Well, she did! She disrobed and —well, after all, I'm only a man! I—"

"Stop right there," interrupts the Judge. " 'Only a man!' You're 'only a man' in relation to some superior being. In this instance it might be nearer the truth to say 'I am only a dog' or 'only a swine.' . . . You, sir, were posing as a benefactor with high motives, while your thoughts were in the gutter. (ELLIOTT *represses his rage.*) All right, sir. I'll want to talk to you later. Mr. Brill, will you and your client wait outside, please."

Recalled to the stand, Larry admits that he was lying when he testified that Elliott had asked him to get him a date with Elizabeth. And that he had told that same lie to Elizabeth, because it was the only way he could be with Elizabeth.

And why did Elizabeth let Larry and Mr. Elliott come to her house? Because Larry made her. Larry had threatened to write things on the door of her apartment if she didn't. He had done that once before.

What Larry had written Elizabeth doesn't want to tell, but Mrs. Busch knows. It was something quite indecent and related, as Mrs. Busch testifies, to the fact that Elizabeth had previously entertained a sailor in that same apartment.

The court attendants are forced to hold her father in his seat as he makes a lunge for Larry.

"He did it for spite!" cries Elizabeth.

"Okay, so I *did* it for spite, but it was true! And I could prove it if the sailor wasn't overseas now! Cuz he told a friend of mine."

"All right, Larry. Step down. I'll have a private talk with you later, in my chambers." The Judge has rapped the court-room into silence.

At this moment the door into the hall is opened and Ruby Lockwood steps into the room. "Ruby is a coarse-looking girl of 16, blonde, stylishly dressed, a fur around her shoulders; loud makeup, sexy, impudent in every look and gesture."

Ruby is sorry she's late. No, her mother isn't with her. Her mother is in Atlantic City. She steps smartly to the stand, toss-ing a "Hello, jerk!" at Larry as she passes him, and raises her hand to be sworn. She evidently has been in court before, Judge Bentley remarks. "Oh, sure," responds Ruby. "Mom took me along a couple o' times when she hadda go."

"What kind of work does your mother do?"

"Mother's sort of a— Oh, Mother's a sort-of-a hostess in a night club, a bar hostess sort of—"

She and her mother had not been trying to dodge a summons, Ruby insists. "Mom accepts a summons like it was an alimony check." Ruby didn't know anything about Elizabeth's trouble until Mr. Elliott wrote her. She thinks it a rotten shame get-tin' her friend, Mr. Elliott, in a spot like that. Elizabeth schemed it. Elizabeth and Larry. She knows that.

"Your Honor, the first time Elizabeth met Mr. Elliott at my house I seen she was makin' a play for him! And after I *told* her to lay off-a him! I told all the girls to lay off-a him, but *she* hadda go and double-cross me . . ."

JUDGE—What kind of talk is that from a little girl! Mr. El-liott is old enough to be your father.

RUBY—You don't understand, Your Honor. Look, Elizabeth knew he had dough, and she wanted to shake him down. Get him arrested and then shake him down. And after all the fa-vors I done for her, too!

JUDGE—What favors?

RUBY—Plenny o' them! When I first met her she looked like somethin' even the cat wouldn't bring in! Didn't know how to do her hair! Why, none o' the boys at school would even date her. *Now* she thinks she's a glamor-puss! . . . I introduced her to my crowd, so she could have a good time, and even get pres-ents. (*To* ELIZABETH.) So now she considers herself date-bait!

JUDGE—Do you accept gifts from men?

RUBY—Sure. When they offer them to me.

JUDGE—Does your mother know you do?

RUBY—Yeah. She don't mind.

JUDGE—Doesn't she ask you what *favors* you bestow for these presents?

RUBY—Favors? I don't give no favors. . . . Anyway, Mom's asleep when I'm awake and I'm asleep when she's awake, so we don't get around to quizzin' each other.

JUDGE—Does your mother know that you have parties at your apartment when she's away at night?

RUBY—She told me I could have 'em. She goes to work at eight every night, and she didn't want me to leave the house after she went. So what was I to do? Sit home alone every night? I *did* at first, when Mom first started hostessing, two years ago. And I nearly went nuts thinkin' I heard burglars, on the fire escape, at the door! Gee! I'd crawl into bed and get under the blankets and push my fingers in my ears. (*Laughs and catches herself.*) But I soon got wise to myself. I told Mom if she didn't want me to play on the streets at night, I wanted my friends to come to my house. So she said okay.

By Ruby's testimony it is established that her father and mother are divorced; that her father lives in Council Bluffs, Iowa, where they all come from, and that he comes to town every August and they all celebrate. Has she any idea of marrying Mr. Elliott some day? Certainly not. She just likes him because he takes her out and gives her a good time.

"Did Mr. Elliott or his lawyer *tell* you to say that Elizabeth tried to shake him down for money?"

"They don't have to tell me. I've got brains. Say, if the girls kin do it in Hollywood, we can do it in New York. (*Looks at* ELIZABETH.) And Elizabeth must a-thought she was the type for it. (*She laughs.*) I once heard her say she wisht she could be in the movies. And that was the way to land there, she figured: get a rich man wacky about yuh, have a drip like Larry work with her, cuz *he* was carryin' the torch for her anyway, and then trap the man in your apartment and call the police."

"You're crazy!" shouts Larry, unable to control himself. "That lady there called the police!" He is pointing at Mrs. Marti.

Ruby is dismissed and gets permission to join Mr. Elliott in the waiting room. "I'm quite sure neither of you will profit from the reunion, but you may wait out there," the Judge agrees.

Mrs. Marti is called to the stand. "She's about 45, neatly dressed, intensely in earnest and obviously nervous."

Mrs. Marti testifies that she lives in the same house as the Collins family; that there are only herself and her son; that she is a widow supporting herself and her son by dressmaking. Yes, she had registered the complaint about Elizabeth Collins. Asked to tell why she did this Mrs. Marti relates with considerable detail the story leading up to her widowhood and her discovery that her son was talented; everybody said he should become a great violinist like Heifetz. To her son's education she had devoted her life.

"My boy Peter is quiet boy," insists Mrs. Marti. "He practice hard, he read many books—he is not bozzer wiz anyone . . . But across the hall live Mr. and Mrs. Collins, and pretty soon I notice my son is fond of Elizabeth. But I do not object, Your Honor! Elizabeth was very sweet, good girl *then*."

No, Peter is not with her, Mrs. Marti explains, because he is having examinations in his school today and after school he is going for his violin lesson.

"Well—about half a year ago something happen to Elizabeth— she change!" continues Mrs. Marti. "She start going wiz Ruby. Your Honor, I not have to tell you what kind girl Ruby is. You have seen yourself. Everyone in ze neighborhood talk about her and say she is bad girl. But Elizabeth become friends wiz her . . . and *my son* is friends wiz Elizabeth. So I worry! . . . (MRS. COLLINS *nudges* COLLINS.) So one day I spoke to Mrs. Collins and I tell her about Elizabeth. Mr. Collins was already zen out of the city."

JUDGE—What did Mrs. Collins say?

MRS. MARTI—She say I should mind my own business. (MRS. COLLINS *starts to rise*—COLLINS *pulls her back*.) Well, Your Honor, that *was* my business! My son insist on being friends wiz Elizabeth no matter what I tell him. So it *is* my business if Elizabeth go wiz *bad* company! (JUDGE *nods*.) I think about moving away from the house, but I know that would not stop Peter from seeing her; and there I could at least keep an eye on them.

JUDGE—What finally decided you to complain to the police?

MRS. MARTI—It was because two weeks ago on Thursday night I overhear something Elizabeth say to zat boy Larry. (LARRY *and* ELIZABETH *look at each other*.) It was late at night and very hot then, if you remember, Your Honor. I could not sleep. So I get up and sit in parlor, by open window, wiz no light. In leetle while I see Elizabeth come, wiz Larry. They stop on stoop, and they quarrel. I hear what they say. And finally Elizabeth agree that he should come ze next night to her apartment, and he should bring Meester Elliott. . . . It was then I decide to complain to the police and ze next morning I do it!

JUDGE—How did you *know* that Mr. Elliott was coming to Elizabeth's apartment for immoral purposes?

MRS. MARTI—Monsieur, I am not baby. . . . I know zat when a man come to her apartment he not come to talk about ze climate, because I have already observed many things before which convinced me zat Elizabeth is already not respectable!

The door opens and Peter Marti comes into the room. He is a gentle lad, but obviously under a strain. He is carrying his violin case and stops to stare incredulously at his mother. Why is she there? he demands of her in French. Why has she made this cruel complaint to the police?

The Judge has rapped for order before Mrs. Marti can answer. Peter turns to the Judge to explain that he hadn't known about the trial until a boy in their block had told him. He had had to come then. He couldn't stay away. Again Judge Bentley raps for order. Advising Peter to take things easy, he calls a ten-minute recess. He will call Peter later.

Now Peter has quickly crossed the courtroom to Elizabeth. "Peter! They're gonna send me away!" wails Elizabeth, as Mrs. Busch starts toward her.

"They won't, Betty! Don't be afraid!" There is a boyish confidence in Peter's tone.

Mrs. Busch has taken Elizabeth into the detention room. Peter is still looking after her when his mother tries to speak to him. "Mother, please! Leave me alone!"

The attendant makes Larry put out the cigarette he has lighted. The Collinses settle down on their bench. The curtain falls.

ACT II

Ten minutes later in Judge Bentley's courtroom the resumption of the hearing is imminent. Peter and his mother are sitting together on a bench, but his gaze is averted from Mrs. Marti. Mrs. Busch and Miss Porter are busy with their papers.

The door into the hall is quietly opened and two young girls slip into the room. They are Jean and Mary, aged 15, and they have come hoping to be allowed to stay to hear the trial of their friend, Elizabeth. But both the attendant and Mrs. Busch soon catch sight of them, and they are shortly on their way back into the hall, disappointed but cheerful.

Larry, who has been called to the Judge's chambers, reappears. Elizabeth is brought back by Officer Owens and sits on a bench. When Peter touches her shoulder she turns and smiles at him.

The Judge has called both Mr. and Mrs. Collins to the witness stand. Mrs. Collins testifies that she is the mother of four children, Elizabeth being the oldest. The others are six, seven and nine. Both the Collinses are working, Mr. Collins in a shipyard in California, Mrs. Collins as cook for a theatrical couple. From 1929 until eight months ago Mr. Collins was without a job and the burden fell entirely on Mrs. Collins. That's what got them into debt.

Since Mr. Collins has been in California and Mrs. Collins has been obliged to work (from noon until about midnight to accommodate her theatrical couple), Elizabeth has been helping with the housework and looking after her smaller sisters and brother. That explains why she has missed so many days at school. Mrs. Collins doesn't think it should be called truancy. Lizzie wasn't playin' hookey. She just had to help at home. She got all the meals and put up the children's school lunches.

Yes, Mrs. Collins knew that the school report had said that Elizabeth's teeth were decayed. All the children had bad teeth. She and Mr. Collins, too. But what could they do about it? There was no money, and no time to take the children to the free dental clinics.

The housecleaning and washing? Well, Mrs. Collins managed to give the house a good going-over on Sundays. When Mr. Collins was idle he did the washing. Now they had a washing machine. That made it easy. So Elizabeth did it.

"Elizabeth has had too much work to do for a girl of 15," announces Judge Bentley.

Mrs. Collins—It sounds a lot, Your Honor. But after all, there were the hours from 8:30 till 3:30 when she was in school, and had nothing to do but sit. When I was her age I was working ten hours a day in a canning factory.

Judge—Mr. Collins, are you considered a good worker in your line?

Collins—I know my job all right, Your Honor; but before the war it made no difference how well you knew your work. There was no jobs.

Judge—But now that you are working, why hasn't your wife been staying at home to look properly after your family?

Collins (*apologetically*)—We're terrible in debt, Your Honor. (Mrs. Collins *nods.*) We borrowed so much when I was out of work. And now, me livin' away from home, we have a double expense.

Mrs. Collins—We owe money on the furniture, on the washing machine, and cash we loaned from my relatives and my husband's relatives.

Judge—But couldn't you have gotten another job, Madam, one that wouldn't keep you away from home so much?

Mrs. Collins—Excuse me, Your Honor, that's easy to say—"couldn't you get some other job" . . . I'm a cook. No matter what job I'd have I'd be leavin' at seven in the morning and returnin' eight, nine o'clock at night, or even later!

Judge—Mmm . . . Did you know your daughter was associating with this—Lockwood girl?

Mrs. Collins—Yes, now about Ruby: I knew that Lizzie was goin' around with her, and when I met the girl I didn't like the looks of her. So I told Lizzie not to go with her any more.

Judge—Did you make sure that she had stopped going with her?

Mrs. Collins—Lizzie usually obeyed me.

Judge—Had you heard that Ruby was kind of "wild"?

Mrs. Collins—Och, in our neighborhood they're always gossiping about everybody.

Judge—Hadn't your neighbor, Mrs. Marti, told you that Lizzie was staying out late with Ruby?

Mrs. Collins (*looking at* Mrs. Marti *and flaring up*)—Mrs. Marti was always tellin' me things that were none of her business! Half the time I couldn't make out what she was saying, and what I did understand was sure to be a squawk about someone or other. No one was good enough for her Peter! Anyway, Lizzie was always home when I got back from work.

Judge—At one in the morning—?

Mrs. Collins—Well—yes.

Mrs. Collins had allowed Elizabeth a little spending money, so the four children could have something for candy and ice cream and so on. She had never noticed that Elizabeth had spent more than she gave her. She had also bought all Elizabeth's clothes—all except the red jacket with the fur collar—and she believed Elizabeth when she said Ruby had given her that. Ruby's mother was supposed to have money, and anyway well-off people often gave practically new things away.

Had she and Elizabeth ever clashed? Certainly not. Once in a while Elizabeth was a little inconsiderate—invitin' her friends in of a Saturday morning, perhaps, and laughin' and gigglin' when Mrs. Collins was trying to sleep. Then again Elizabeth would make her mother perfectly furious by primpin' and primpin' before a mirror, fixing her hair one way and then another, when there was housework to be done.

"Your Honor—if you don't mind my sayin' it—I don't think that should count against Lizzie—I mean this primpin' in front of a mirror. All young girls do it," ventures Mr. Collins.

"That's the trouble," snaps Mrs. Collins. "You were always makin' excuses for her, spoilin' her! All young girls *don't* spend hours before a mirror! I never did. And it made me furious when she did," she adds, turning to the Judge, "and of course we'd have a row."

Mrs. Collins concludes her testimony by admitting that although she belongs to a church, she never has found time to take her children to the services. She would like to have Lizzie back home, too, if the Judge can arrange it. There's no reason why she should be held at the Detention Home.

"The Police Department took Elizabeth away, Madam. She was placed at the Detention Home until we could complete the investigation for this hearing."

"Will she be going back there?"

"We're trying to decide now, Madam, where your child should go."

Peter Marti is called. He leaves his violin on the bench and Elizabeth takes it to hold for him. Peter has been studying the violin for seven years, he tells the Judge. But right now he is more interested in finding out what the charge is against Elizabeth. The boy on the block didn't know anything except that his mother had had her arrested. Mrs. Marti, too, had refused to tell him what the charge is against Betty.

But the Judge wants to talk about Peter first. Is he studying with a good teacher? Is he planning to be a concert violinist? No. Peter is planning to get a job as soon as he can. "I don't want my mother to go blind sewing so I can play in Carnegie Hall," he says.

Peter is graduating from high school that month—he hopes.
No, he doesn't expect to go to college. Money doesn't grow on
trees, they tell him. "I don't know *where* it grows—except that
it seems to be growin' wild in the wrong places," says Peter.
And he quickly adds: "Your Honor, I want to know is there
anything I can do to help Betty!"

"That's what I'm trying to find out, my boy—in my own
clumsy way. That's why I'm asking you these questions—if you
don't mind . . . What have you been majoring in at high
school?"

"Languages. And Science, too."

"Science? And you're training to be a musician. Quite unusual."

"Fritz Kreisler was an engineer once—and William Herschel
is known as an astronomer. But *he* was a musician, an organist.
Da Vinci was an inventor—but he was a painter, of course. I
can't think of any others right now," Peter concludes, with a
laugh.

"You're also a statistician, I see."

"I learned that from some of our congressmen over the radio.
They win every argument with statistics."

Judge Bentley's manner grows increasingly confidential. He
had also studied violin as a boy, but gave it up. He didn't like
to practice. Now he's sorry. The Judge's favorite piece used
to be Bach's Air for G String. Peter knows that, too.

Yes, Peter admits, when his examination is continued, he and
Elizabeth have been very good friends. No, he doesn't know
all her other friends. Yes, he has known that Elizabeth had
been going with a pretty wild crowd, if the Judge means Ruby
and her bunch. And Peter can understand why she did that.
Why? The Judge wants to know.

"Well, for the same reason that a hungry person will steal
food. Betty was hungry for *fun*. Nobody supplied it to her so
she grabbed it where she could. Maybe it wasn't the right kind
of fun—but a hungry person grabs what he can get. (JUDGE *and*
MRS. BUSCH *exchange glances*.) Gee, I saw a bum last week
snatch a hot dog from a stand on Tenth Avenue. He rammed
it down his throat before the owner of the stand could stop him;
then he bent over the sidewalk and vomited. (*Looks around—
sees people staring*.) I advised Betty to quit going with Ruby
and her crowd—but I really had no right to lecture her. Because I understand things too well."

"What things?"

"Huh? . . . Well, the temptations a young girl is up against, Your Honor! Gosh, the papers and magazines show you pictures of—Gloria Vanderbilt and Doris Duke and even of girls fourteen, fifteen years old, at winter resorts, at summer resorts, at horse shows, on lawns of gorgeous estates. What do you think a girl like Betty or Ruby feels when she sees these pictures? . . . When you get older you understand these things, maybe—but when you're young it makes you wonder. And it makes you sore! And the first chance the girls have *they* try to have a good time too."

Peter had never taken Elizabeth out much. Too much practicing, for one thing. And when he'd ask her to go to a concert she'd never go because she said she didn't have anything to wear. But she did go to one concert in the studio of Peter's teacher. Peter played most of the program that time. And Elizabeth wore her red coat. Did Elizabeth tell him where she got the coat? No. He took it for granted that her mother had given it to her. But— If he had been told that she got it from a man—from one of Ruby's men friends—

Peter has noted the troubled look on Elizabeth's face and is quick to laugh off the suggestion. "Well, anyway, Betty enjoyed the concert," he says. "And after the concert I took her to dinner at the Automat and—we had a wonderful time! I waited on her—and I pretended I was a waiter and she was a— movie star."

He looks over at Elizabeth and she smiles back at him. They evidently enjoy this memory of their happy adventure. Soon they are all but giggling, child-like, at the recollection. The older people in the courtroom are held by their happiness, and for a moment the Judge permits the recollection to continue. Then he dismisses Peter.

"Your Honor, there's just one thing I want you to know," says Peter, as he is leaving the stand. "No matter what Betty's been doing, she's good! I *know* her and I know she's good. I only wish to God I could help her get out of this trouble, Your Honor, because—I don't just *'like'* Betty! I *love* her."

"Mhm . . . All right, son. Step down."

Elizabeth is the next one called. As Mrs. Busch shows her to the stand the Judge orders the room cleared of everyone except Mr. and Mrs. Collins, although the witnesses are not to leave the building.

"Elizabeth," begins the Judge, when the room is cleared, "I am not going to put you under oath to tell the truth. I'm going to put you on your honor to do so. If you do tell the truth, you will be the one most to benefit by it. You understand that, don't you?"

"Yes."

"All right . . . Now I want you to tell me in your own way how it happened that you, a little girl of fifteen, permitted yourself to do such wicked things."

Collins slides down on the bench. Elizabeth starts to cry. "I—I don't wanna tell yuh in front of my mother and father."

"If you had told your mother and father *before,*" says the Judge, sternly, "you wouldn't have to be doing it now, in court . . . Go on!"

So Elizabeth tells her story. She had not known, when first she began running around with Ruby, that she was going to do the things she did do. It all started in school the time she (Elizabeth) didn't have a dress to wear for the Graduation Dance. Ruby had found her crying about that and called her a fool—

" 'Honestly you're a drip—sittin' here in the can cryin' for a dress when they're so easy to get,' " Elizabeth quotes Ruby as saying. " 'Get hep, and start cookin' on the front burner!' "

Ruby loaned Elizabeth a dress for the Graduation Dance, and then, one night about a week later, she took her for a walk down Broadway to Times Square—

"What did you go there for?" Judge Bentley asks. "To pick up men—service men?"

"Well, Ruby told me we were just going there for a walk. When we got down to 'bout Forty-third Street, Ruby said, 'Let's just stand here'—And so we stood there—and pretty soon two sailors passed by. They were in the Merchant Marine. They kind-a' looked at us and Ruby kind-a' smiled to them, and so they turned back and asked us what we were doin' and Ruby said 'Nothin' ' and so one of 'em said 'We're gonna hit the Park Inn . . . would you girls like to come along?' and so Ruby said yes."

It was about 10 o'clock at night, after she had put the kids to bed, Elizabeth relates, and they had gone with the sailors to the Park Inn, which was up near Van Cortlandt Park. They had gone in a taxi and when the sailors asked them to have something to eat, Elizabeth had taken chicken à la king, because Jerry, her sailor, had said it would be all right.

Of course they had something to drink—*all* sailors drink, don't they? Elizabeth has to laugh a little at Judge Bentley's not

knowing that.   Ruby drank a lot, but Elizabeth had only one
Cuba libre, which was enough to make her cry when she remembered having slapped her little sister because she didn't want to
go to bed that night.   The Park Inn was a restaurant, but you
could get rooms upstairs if you wanted to.

Elizabeth had gone upstairs with the sailor, because her head
was dizzy.   Yes, that was the first time she had had intimate
relations with a man.   Afterward she had had an abortion.   Ruby
had taken her to a doctor and the sailor, Jerry, had paid the
bill without a squawk.

Mrs. Collins is weeping silently and Mr. Collins is crumpling
his hat in his hands.   Elizabeth has lowered her head during
most of her testimony and is fidgeting with the edge of her chair.
Mrs. Busch and Miss Porter are whispering together.   Judge
Bentley takes a drink and wipes his perspiring face.

"When you started going to Ruby's parties, didn't it seem to
you that they were pretty rough?" asks the Judge.

"It was fun," answers Elizabeth, with a shrug.

JUDGE—How about these older men who used to come there?
Did they give you money?

ELIZABETH—Sometimes.   They said we should always ask 'em
for money if we needed it.

JUDGE—Is that why you let them get familiar with you?

ELIZABETH—I didn't let them get familiar with me.   They
were fun, that's all.   They used to buy us ice cream and cake,
an' this an' that.   They were free spenders.   And Mr. Elliott
was nice.   He said I could call him Alex the first time I met
him.

JUDGE—And then he asked you for a date at your house?

ELIZABETH—Yeah.   But they all work fast when they meet up
with a military objective.

JUDGE—A "military objective"—?

ELIZABETH—Yeah . . . that means a girl they'd like to date.

JUDGE (*grunting*)—Uhuh . . . How about the young fellers
who came to the parties?—How old were they?

ELIZABETH—About my age, most of 'em.

JUDGE—Fifteen—!

ELIZABETH (*nodding*)—They get wolfish awful early.

JUDGE—And the girls—how many of you were there, usually?

ELIZABETH—About five, six.

JUDGE—Tell me the names of the other girls.   We want to get
hold of them.   (ELIZABETH *is silent.*)   They need our help.

You'd be doing them a favor.

ELIZABETH (*shaking her head*)—I wouldn't wanna tell on them.

MRS. BUSCH—Your Honor, we inspected the lockers of the boys and girls at the High School and found marijuana cigarettes in one of them. The D.A.'s office is now investigating the source of supply.

ELIZABETH—But *I* didn't smoke marijuanas! Some o' the kids did when they wanted to get high. But I didn't.

JUDGE—Did you *drink?*

ELIZABETH—Just one drink once in a while, an' this an' that.

JUDGE—Did all the girls get intimate with the young fellers and the men at these parties?

ELIZABETH (*shrugging*)—Well, I don't know. I never got intimate with them.

JUDGE (*emphatic*)—Now, getting back to that night when Larry and Elliott called on you! Was that the first time Mr. Elliott had come to your apartment?

ELIZABETH—Oh, sure.

JUDGE—Was it Larry's first visit to your house?

ELIZABETH—It certainly was! I never let him come before cuz—I didn't like him!

JUDGE—Why not?

ELIZABETH—Cuz he's rough! He's—rough.

JUDGE—Did Elliott give you money at your house that night?

ELIZABETH—No.

JUDGE—Did he *promise* you money?

ELIZABETH—Well, he said I could get it from him any time I needed it; and he asked me if I liked ear-rings. I like ear-rings. (*Flaring up again.*) But I didn't want him to come to my house, cuz my mother didn't let me bring even boys to the house. But Larry said if I didn't let them come he'd write that funny stuff on my door again. Like I told you. So I said okay. (*Looks up.*) But then, at nine o'clock, I turned out the lights so's they'd think I was sleep awreddy when they'd come. But they kept on ringin' the bell; so I hadda answer, cuz I didn't want the kids to wake up. When they came in, I turned on the dancing-record cuz I wanted to tell Mr. Elliott not to go away before Larry cuz I didn't wanna be left alone with him—he's—rough. An' so Mr. Elliott sent Larry out for Scotch. . . . I tried to stop him from sending Larry out, cuz I didn't wanna be alone with Mr. Elliott *either.* But he said he wanted a drink and I didn't have any. So Larry went, and—and Mr. Elliott started to make passes at me. So I said, "Cut it out, Mr. Elliott." And he said, "Didn't I tell you to call me Alex?" So I said, "Okay, Alex, but don't get funny!" So he started lockin' the door; so I said, "Better not, cuz Larry'll kick it in when he gets back." So he left the door unlocked. But he pushed me into the bedroom and closed the door, and he made me take off my housecoat—well, he *pulled* it off me, and—and in a little while the policeman came in.

Elizabeth admits that she likes Peter Marti, but his mother always tried to break up their friendship, even from the first. Mrs. Marti would say something nasty about Elizabeth every time Peter ever wanted to do anything nice for her, and once she had stopped Elizabeth on the street and told her she wasn't good enough to wipe Peter's shoes, and that she was spoiling his career. She had never told Peter what his mother had said, because she didn't want to start a rumpus between them.

Consulting his calendar, Judge Bentley is greatly surprised to discover that in less than two weeks after Peter had taken her to the concert she had permitted Elliott to come to her home, "and with your little brothers and sisters asleep in the next room, you dishonored that home!"

"It was the first time," mutters Elizabeth in an undertone.

"But *was* it? . . . According to Larry there *had* been a time before—when you entertained a sailor there. . . ."

"It was the sailor who took me to the Park Inn that time, Jerry," answers Elizabeth, naively. "He came to say good-by cuz he was sailing the next day. And he said his ship might be torpedoed and he'd get killed an' this an' that, and I cried, I was so sorry for 'im."

"Was this after the concert too?"

"It was before . . . It was that same day Mrs. Marti told me I wasn't good enough to wipe Peter's shoes."

No, Jerry had not given her money that night. He was broke. She had even given him his fare back to the ship.

"Now, Elizabeth," the Judge is saying, "the next question I am going to ask you is exceedingly important, and you must answer it truthfully!"

"Yuh Honor, I've been tellin' yuh the truth!"

"All right . . . Did you have intimate relations with any boy or any man, *other* than this sailor—and Mr. Elliott?"

"I didn't." Elizabeth's eyes are lowered and she mumbles inaudibly.

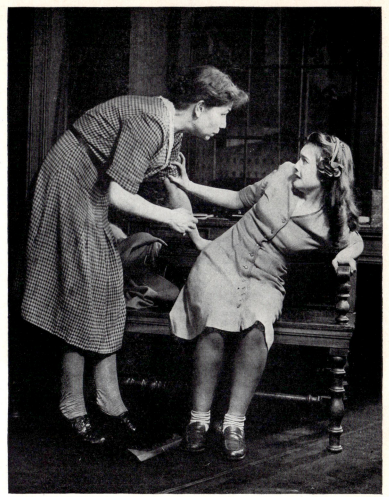

"PICK-UP GIRL"

Mrs. Collins—The Judge showed me the medical report, and you tell me I'm makin' it up. I shouldn't even be tryin' to spare your feelin's, becuz you've been a tramp and you've been sleeping with all kinds of tramps and now you've got the sickness that all tramps get!

(*Kathryn Grill, Pamela Rivers*)

"All right. You may step down."

"Your Honor, please don't send me away." Elizabeth has arisen and is leaning on the Judge's desk. "I don't wanna leave my mother an'—my father an' my little sister and brothers! Your Honor, I won't do those things any more! I promise! An' I'll keep my promise. *Please,* Y' Honor! Please—"

Judge Bentley has called for the medical and the truancy reports and retired to his chambers. He will be having another talk with Peter Marti shortly.

Left to themselves, the Collinses have a chance to consider what is happening to them. It is hard for Mr. Collins to believe that it is their Elizabeth they have been hearing tell the story she has told. To Mrs. Collins the situation is pretty hopeless. Collins might help if he would speak up to the Judge and plead with him.

But Collins doesn't know what to say. He might tell the Judge about their going to California. And the Judge, Mrs. Collins thinks, might send Elizabeth to some place in California near where they are going to be. Anyway, Collins will have to be careful to remember to deny that Elizabeth is his daughter, if the story should get out to the shipyard. It might, because of Mr. Elliott, get in the newspapers.

Mrs. Collins leaves Mr. Collins with Elizabeth, thinking maybe he can say something cheerful to his daughter. But all Collins can do is to curse the day he left New York. Things would have been different if he had stayed at home. But Elizabeth is glad he went.

"I was glad you went cuz I was sick of seein' you do the housework, sick of seein' you wear Mom's apron. And I knew you hated it! When you got the job I danced with joy! Remember, Pa? Cuz then I knew you wouldn't be ashamed any more, before the neighbors and everybody, and Mom's family couldn't throw it up to you any more that Mom was supporting you!" Mr. Collins can't understand why, if Elizabeth thought that much of him, she could ever do the things she did do. Nor can Elizabeth understand, now.

Judge Bentley has sent for Peter. Mrs. Marti would go with him, but the attendant bars her. While he is waiting in the courtroom Peter stops to speak to Elizabeth. Mr. Collins, realizing suddenly that he is in the way, leaves them together.

Elizabeth is grateful for the things Peter had said to the Judge about her. She certainly is thankful. But Peter hadn't wanted to be thanked. He said what he said because he meant it. Now what is going to happen? What had the Judge said when he sent everybody out of the room?

Elizabeth is sure the Judge is going to send her away. Peter can't understand why she hadn't let him know she was in so much trouble. Nobody on the block knew Elizabeth had been arrested. They all thought she was with her Grandmother who was sick, like her mother had told them. Peter didn't know until a boy had told him that Elizabeth had been arrested. Why had she been arrested? He wants her to tell him.

"You'll hate me for it if I do, Peter," she says to him, looking deep into his eyes for a moment. "And I don't want you to hate me."

"How could I ever hate you! . . . You heard what I told the Judge. . . . It's the first time I ever said it, right out, like that . . . but I guess you knew it all along, didn't yuh—that I'm— over my eyes in love with you? So how could I hate you?"

"But if I've been a—bad—girl . . . ?"

" 'Bad!' What's bad?" demands Peter. "They tell us not to lie—it's bad. But don't we know that *they* lie . . . a hell of a lot more than we kids do . . . ? So is it 'bad' when we do it but okay when they do it?"

"Yeah. Or when they tell yuh you mustn't kiss anybody . . . They kiss!"

"Well—maybe that's a little different," allows Peter, jealous in spite of himself.

"Why?—I can't explain it to anybody . . . I don't even understand it myself," continues Elizabeth, trying hard to be articulate. "But maybe you could, Peter—you're so brainy." They're laughing now, as Peter would disclaim the compliment. "The older people just wouldn't understand it, anyway . . . But what I mean is— Sometimes I feel like I—like I love *everybody*— everybody in the whole world—just *love* 'em—so much that you know my—my body feels too small to—to *hold* all that love in me. And—and anybody that comes near me I just—I just wanna kiss an' hug." She has thrown her arms wide. "Just *anybody*— a kid or a cat or a man or anybody! So that means I'm— I'm a bad girl, I guess. I don't know what's wrong with me."

"I know how yuh feel," agrees Peter. "But grown-ups don't understand it. They forget by the time they grow up, see?"

"Yeah . . . So—if you hear that I—that I've been—a bad girl, I—I don't know *why* I was . . . I—"

"Aw, gee, don't try to explain to me."

Peter is sure they're not going to send Elizabeth to jail—they

don't send kids to jail. But if they should send her away Peter
has an idea. Don't let her get excited or anything, but if the
Judge says he is going to send her away then they, he and Elizabeth, are going to run away.

How? Easy. Let Elizabeth ask if she can go to the ladies'
room. In the ladies' room there's a window. Below the window, about twenty feet, is a yard. In Peter's violin case is a
scarf. It is strong. It is about six feet long. By cutting it in
two the long way and tying the ends together it will be nearly
twelve feet long. Then by tying one end to the water pipe that
runs through the ladies' room Elizabeth can let herself out the
window and down to within jumping distance of the yard. Peter
will be waiting for her and before the people in the courtroom
can miss them they will be far away.

"It's a wonderful idea! . . . if we can work it," admits Elizabeth.

"We've gotta try it, Betty! It's your only way out—if the
Judge says he's gonna send you away."

Now Peter has given Elizabeth the scarf and his pocket knife
to cut it with and she has hidden them in her pocketbook. And
they have agreed upon a signal. If the Judge says he is going
to send her away, right after he says it Elizabeth is to say:
"Please, may I go to the ladies' room . . ." That will be their
high sign. Five minutes after she leaves, Peter will follow. But
there is one other thing worrying Peter—

"Look, Betty! There's something else I've been thinkin' about
—and I don't know how you're gonna take this, but—*if* we have
to run away, let's get married somewhere, right away! You
know why?"

"Why?"

"Because after we escape from here they're gonna start a hunt
for us. That's what they always do."

"Yeah. I thought about that, too. And they'll bring us back
and send me away."

"Not if we get married. Know why?"

"Why?"

"Cuz they wouldn't send a married woman to a reform school."

"So what d'yuh say? I have some money in a Savings Bank,
I'll take it out. And we'll get married in one of the States where
they give yuh a license if the husband is sixteen. Some State
in the South, I think. We'll look it up and go there, and get
married right away."

But Elizabeth says no, she doesn't want to cause any more

trouble. Besides his mother has always said Peter was never
going to marry. Concert violinists always remain bachelors—

"Like heck they do!" snorts Peter. "Heifetz is married, El-
man is married. Zimbalist is married. And Menuhin got married when he was only 19."

"But you're only 16."

"Yeah, but we've got more troubles."

"No. I wouldn't wanna spoil your career."

"Aw, heck—how would you be spoilin' my career? Can't I
practice after I'm married?" He is leaning toward her. ". . . So
what do you say?—Do we get married?"

"Okay, Peter—if you're sure you want to take a chance on
gettin' into a lot o' trouble on account o' me."

"Am I sure . . ." Peter is sitting on the stool at her feet
and looking at her adoringly. "I'm sure there's nothing on
God's earth I wouldn't do for you!"

"You're swell, Peter! I like you an awful lot, Peter, just—
such an awful lot!"

To cover their mutual excitement as their hands touch, Elizabeth recalls the day she filed the calluses on the fingers of Peter's
left hand. He remembers, too, because she filed them so much
it hurt like heck to press them on the violin strings when he
practiced. . . .

Judge Bentley has come back into court and the hearing is resumed. The Judge's first order is that Elizabeth leave the room.
This causes something of a panic. Elizabeth begins to protest
being sent away. Mr. and Mrs. Collins and Peter all would go
to her, but the Judge raps smartly for order and assures Elizabeth
that he will send for her again.

After Elizabeth has gone with the attendant Judge Bentley
calls her father and mother and Peter to the stand. He has
something very serious to say to them. In the psychiatric tests
to which Elizabeth was subjected after her arrest, in an effort to
determine the cause of her delinquency—whether it was physical,
emotional, or mental—the psychologists had decided, and the
Judge concurred, that Elizabeth was normal mentally—

"Your daughter's case is typical," the Judge is saying. "Elizabeth is typical of hundreds of other juvenile delinquents—"

"Excuse me, Your Honor, but that went through me like a
knife," interrupts Peter, his eyes flashing. "Calling Betty a
delinquent! . . . I'm studying languages. I know what 'delinquent' means! A delinquent is one who—who fails to perform
a duty. Well then, Your Honor, why don't you call the mothers

and fathers delinquents? Or the teachers and the ministers?—
Yes, sir, and even the law-makers! It's *adult* delinquency."

Mr. and Mrs. Collins are quick to protest Peter's freshness,
fearing he will do harm to Elizabeth's chances. But Judge Bentley is sympathetic and understanding. He had himself used the
term "adult delinquency" long before Peter was born—

"Peter—you're an intelligent boy, and so I'll take the trouble
to explain to you that what we call 'juvenile delinquency' is an
outgrowth of many causes—too intricate to consider here, because they're linked with a vast network of other causes, social,
economic, and even racial—I mean, of *human* race origin . . .
But this court cannot take time out to meditate on the social or
economic interpretation of the matter . . . We have here to
deal with the specific case of Elizabeth Collins . . . and promptly
. . . now . . . *before* we can find a *world-wide* cure. Understand?"

Peter does not answer, but Mr. Collins adds an earnest plea.
He knows that his little girl is not wicked. At least she didn't
mean to be. She was spoiled by bad company. She'll be different from now on, especially after the bad scare she's had.
Especially as he is moving the family to California, where Elizabeth can have a fresh start—

"Mr. Collins, I *always* send the children back to their parents
where I can. The reform school . . . the 'Home,' as we prefer to call it, is the last resort. Because I believe in the cor-
rective effect of these children just being among normal boys and
girls. But the difficulty *here* is, Mr. Collins, that for the time
being, I cannot permit Elizabeth to *mingle* with other boys and
girls."

Not mingle with them? The Judge's words shock Mrs. Collins
into an hysterical protest. There's not a girl in the lot better
than Elizabeth. They all drink. They all smoke. They all stay
out late—

"There's this one difference, Mrs. Collins—that *your* child is
very seriously ill. Elizabeth—well—Elizabeth has a venereal disease."

Peter, startled, is holding on to the Judge's desk. Mrs. Collins finds it difficult to believe what she has heard. Collins,
aghast, is protesting—"That's not possible, Your Honor—"

"Here it is on the medical report. 'L-u-e-s.' That means
syphilis."

"Oh, no! No! Charlie, NO! No-no-no— . . . that can't

be! It can't be!" screams Mrs. Collins.

Mrs. Busch has gone to Mrs. Collins and taken her by the arm, trying to quiet her.

"Take her out, Mrs. Busch," orders Judge Bentley. Collins is standing as one stricken, the medical report trembling in his hands. Peter remains below the platform as though rooted to the spot. Mrs. Busch leads the hysterical Mrs. Collins from the room.

"We'll recess until she's over it," says the Judge, taking the report from Collins. "Mr. Collins, your daughter can be cured."

He goes to his chambers. The curtain falls.

ACT III

Ten minutes later in the courtroom Miss Porter and the door attendant are loafing and waiting for the resumption of the hearing. From Judge Bentley's chambers comes the sound of a violin, Bach's Air for G String being beautifully played. That slays the attendant. The idea of the Judge's getting Peter to play for him right in the middle o' the hearing!

That's nothing. Miss Porter remembers that the week before the Judge had a girl sing for him. He's always doing things like that. Some say he helps these talented kids. The girl had said she stole money from her employer so she could take singing lessons.

"I wonder what would happen if we got a strip teaser here?" wonders the attendant. "Anyway, what are we here,—a talent bureau?"

Mrs. Busch, reappearing from the waiting room, goes to Mr. Collins, sitting dejectedly on a bench. "Your wife is all right now. I'm letting her rest till the Judge calls her again," reports Mrs. Busch.

Shortly Judge Bentley reappears and calls Mr. and Mrs. Collins. From the clerk the Judge learns that there is a bed at the Hudson shelter and orders a form made out for that.

"Well, Mr. and Mrs. Collins—the final decision of the Court is that Elizabeth must be taken away from you."

"Oh, no, no! . . . Charlie!" Mrs. Collins is in tears again.

"Madam, be reasonable. You shouldn't object to letting us take care of Elizabeth until she's straightened out. She's still young enough to readjust her life—but she needs guidance."

"Your Honor, if you'll let me take Elizabeth home, I'll look after her."

"I couldn't possibly permit that, Mrs. Collins. We must re-discipline your daughter. Another year and she might have become past redemption. Like that Lockwood girl is now, I'm afraid . . . But Elizabeth is still shy and modest, and she may turn out to be a fine woman if we take her in hand now."

"Well, why can't I do it? I'm her mother."

"You haven't done it in the past, Madam! And you've been her mother—for fifteen years . . . You've neglected your daughter. You're largely responsible for her present plight . . . You cannot neglect and overwork an adolescent girl and expect her not to revolt."

"I know dozens of girls her age who do just as much house-work, and whose mothers are away from home most of the time—some o' them playin' cards and havin' a good time—not slavin' like me; and their girls are decent . . . What happened to Liz-zie I don't know! She was just born bad, I guess."

"No, no, no. No child is born bad. No child is *born* a thief or a liar, or a sex delinquent . . . But children learn quickly, good *or* evil. And therefore they must be taught. Must be taught the right things . . . they must be taught the virtues!"

"I didn't think you had to *teach* a girl to be good. My mother didn't teach me. (*Weeping.*) Now I feel that *I'm* to blame for Lizzie's troubles! Everything is my fault."

"No, it's not your fault alone. It's the fault of all of us . : . It's our indifference, our greediness, that's at fault. We don't realize that the *real* natural wealth of the world is in children."

"That's true," murmurs Mr. Collins.

"Yes! There is the seed of divine goodness in every child. But we adults must cherish that seed, and we must nourish it! . . . If we neglect it, a young life is ruined, and we have no one to blame but ourselves."

No, it's not because they got so far in debt, as Mr. Collins timidly suggests. The debt to the children comes first, insists the Judge. Mrs. Marti is a widow who has had to work for a living, yet she has managed to supervise Peter's upbringing and his education.

Judge Bentley would like to give them another chance, but he is convinced it will be better for Elizabeth if she is sent to a training school where they know how to cope with emotional conflicts in children. He begs that when he calls Elizabeth in to tell her that her parents will help cushion the shock to their daughter by remaining calm themselves. As Mrs. Collins is again wailing and tearful he suggests they wait outside until she gets hold of herself.

In the meantime Judge Bentley will get rid of Mr. Elliott, who is summoned and reappears with his attorney, Mr. Brill. They are whispering excitedly as the door attendant motions them to a position before the Judge. Ruby Lockwood follows them into the room and sits quietly on a bench.

"Well, sir, I understand you've been indicted," says Judge Bentley, looking down at Elliott. Elliott makes no reply. "I'm not going to ask you any more questions now, Mr. Elliott. I'm not even going to ask you whether you're single or married, whether you have a little daughter of your own, perhaps, aged fifteen. . . . Your personal history interests me as little as the personal history of—a—gorilla in a Zoo. Of the two, *you* are the more dangerous to human society, and the gorilla is behind bars. I trust you will be, soon. And I want you to take this thought with you and brood on it, in your 'idle' moments: Prudence and experience are the gifts of age. It is no dishonor to a child to be without prudence. A reckless youth is to be pitied. But when a man of your years deliberately sets out to ruin his life, he is not to be pitied. It's true that man is of the animal kingdom—but even the four-legged animals have the dignity not to debauch their young. They sometimes eat them, but never defile them. (*He pauses a moment . . . then with a gesture of the hand.*) Dismissed."

As Elliott and Brill step away, the Judge calls the attorney back. He wants him to see the medical report concerning Elizabeth. Brill agrees to inform his client.

Ruby asks if she may go. She had promised her mother she'd take the 6 o'clock train back to Atlantic City and if she doesn't mother will have a blip. A "blip," Ruby explains, for the Judge's information, is very like a conniption fit.

Peter Marti is recalled. In chambers, the Judge reminds Peter, he had refused to answer a certain question. Now he will have to answer it in open court. The Judge is sending Elizabeth away immediately to a hospital. "I spoke to you as man to man," says Judge Bentley. "Even though in the eyes of the law you are still a child you're mature enough to understand the implications involved. Now answer my question."

Peter is still silent.

"Well—I wanted to spare your mother the torment, but if you won't answer me, I must inform her of the facts regarding Elizabeth, and you can tell your *mother* whether you've had intimate relations with the girl. Call Mrs. Marti."

"No!" shouts Peter, jumping to his feet.

"Then answer me!"

"How could you even ask me such a thing, Your Honor! Betty was going to be my wife some day! How could I have—" He breaks off and turns away, fighting back his tears.

"All right, Peter. You may step down—and wait outside."

The Judge sends for Elizabeth. He has signed her commitment papers to the State Training School for Girls at Hudson. "We can't have a girl like that running around contaminating everyone she contacts—not only physically but morally. I favor the idea of at least three years for her at the Training School. Maybe she'll pull herself together . . . But first . . . she's to be hospitalized. At Bellevue. And I want her to go there immediately—today."

Elizabeth, noting there is no one in the room except Judge Bentley and the two women attendants, is plainly frightened as she faces the Judge, who is leaning forward on his desk.

"Elizabeth—there's an old saying in military circles that a wise retreat is no less glorious than a courageous attack. Sometimes that holds true in civil life, too— We have to go away from the battlefield, so to speak, so that we may wisely plan the next move . . . Now you're only fifteen, but not too young to give some thought to the meaning of your life. Thus far, you know, you have been recklessly throwing it away. Haven't you? (*She shrugs—looking worried.*) Well, at your age one is naturally trustful, and you were misled. So we're not blaming you. But we don't want you to go *on* wasting your life, and therefore we're going to give you a chance to prepare yourself for a better *future*—by taking you away from the influences of your past."

"What do you mean? Are you sending me away?"

"Yes."

"When?"

"Now. Right now."

"I won't go! Where's my mother and father? Where's *Peter?*"

The Judge raps smartly for order and Mrs. Busch steps quickly to Elizabeth's side, taking a firm hold of her arm. "Here, you! Behave yourself before His Honor."

"I won't go with you! I don't wanna go with you before I— Mom! Peter! Peter!"

Mrs. Busch is shaking Elizabeth, who in her struggles has slipped down on the bench. The Judge speaks reprovingly to Mrs. Busch and calls Elizabeth before him.

"Your mother and father *are* here. And Peter is here. You'll be allowed to say good-by to them. . . . And that temper isn't going to be a bit of help to you where you're going. It's up to you to change. . . . You don't want to be a worthless person! You want to be a credit to your community, an asset to your country, to your parents who love you—" Elizabeth is trying not to cry. "And to Peter, in whose heart you fill a very large space," the Judge goes on. "*And* you want to be a credit to yourself, don't you?"

"Uhuh!"

"That's the spirit. You can be . . . All right . . . Now I'm going to let you say good-by."

A recess is called. Elizabeth and Peter are whispering together when Miss Porter and Mrs. Busch decide to give them a break by leaving the room. Now Peter, nervously, wants to know all that has happened. Yes, he knew they were sending her away.

What was he doing in the Judge's chambers? He was playing his violin. "He wanted me to play for him. Kinya beat it? . . . It was like playin' at my own funeral . . . Betty, just what did the Judge tell yuh?"

"He said I'm gonna make a retreat like a general—and plan my next battle in life. . . . He said I've been throwin' away my life and I mustn't do it any more. And he's gonna send me away from the influence of my past."

"What else?"

"Nothin' else . . . Oh, yes, he *did* say . . ." Peter is waiting breathlessly. She stops and smiles. "He said I—'fill a very large space' in your heart . . . And that's all he said."

Elizabeth would like to have Peter tell her what the Judge had said to him, but as Peter remembers it it wasn't much—about the same thing he had said to her.

A little feverishly they go over their plans. Elizabeth has the scarf cut and tied together, and in the ladies' room she had tried tying it around the waterpipe. It only took a couple of minutes. . . . Sure, she remembers the high sign, "Please may I go to the ladies' room?" Okay. After she goes out, Peter will give her four minutes— Suddenly Elizabeth feels that there is something the matter with Peter. He's getting nervous and he sounds funny. That's only because he is anxious to get started, insists Peter.

"I think it must be something else," says Elizabeth, doubtfully. "I think you're sorry you said you'd marry me."

PETER (*quickly*)—Why? What makes you think that?

ELIZABETH—I don't know. Just somethin'—tells me.

PETER—Well, you're wrong.

ELIZABETH—If you don't wanna go through with it just say so. It won't be the first time people have let me down. Everybody's always breakin' promises, anyway. Ma promised me I'd take tap-dancing and she never kept her promise. Pop once promised me he'd give me money to go to Washington with Mom to see the cherry trees, when he got a job—and he forgot all about it. So if you wanna back out now about marryin' me, it's okay. I'll just go to a reform school, that's all.

PETER (*trying to convince himself*)—Who says I wanna back out! I do *not!* I saw one of these here "reform" schools last summer. Up State—where my aunt lives. It's a great big place —for boys only. Strictly stag. My uncle knows one o' the guards there, and he took us through the joint. And I'll be darned if it didn't look like a prison—cells and everything! And the guard even told us that they have solitary confinement cells in the basement—bread and water punishment . . .

ELIZABETH—Sure! That's what a girl at the Shelter told me, too.

PETER—Well, *you're* not going to one o' those places! No, sir! . . . Come on, Your Honor, all we want now is to kiss you good-by!

ELIZABETH (*falling into his mood*)—And Mrs. Busch—I'll be glad to kiss *her* good-by! The old crumb! She'd always be after me! Pushin' me around! Pokin' her nose into everything! This morning she asked me some very personal questions and I wouldn't answer her and I said, "That's my business"; she said, "From now on everything you do is my business."

PETER—Well—she'll get a little surprise. She's not goin' to push you around!

ELIZABETH (*gratefully*)—Gee, Peter, you're a real friend, you are! It gives me such a wonderful feeling cuz you wanna help me when I'm in trouble!

PETER—Aw, what the heck—when you're in trouble, *I* am too.

Anyway my mother got you into this—I'm gonna get you out of it.

The door of the waiting room opens quietly. Collins, looking in timidly, turns back to beckon Mrs. Collins to follow. They have come to say their good-bys. They hope Elizabeth will be a good girl and mind everybody. And write often to them in Los Angeles.

"We'll be missing you—but I—I'll tell the children that you're still visitin' Grandma. I only hope that you won't be havin' hard feelin's against me, Lizzie?"

"Against *you?* Gosh, no, Mom!"

"Well, the Judge sayin' I made you work too hard. But when I was a girl I worked even harder."

"I'll bet!"

"Well—write me often, dear. And obey them, won't you? If they give you medicines, take them."

"Medicines!"

"If they put yuh to bed, stay there. You've got to do exactly as they tell you if you want to be cured."

"Cured? What are yuh talkin' about? I'm not sick. What is this? Peter askin' me if I *feel* all right, and you tellin' me to take medicines! I'm not sick!"

"Child, if you weren't, would they be sending you to a hospital?"

As the truth slowly penetrates, Elizabeth becomes openly rebellious. She lashes out viciously at her mother, who, she accuses, never really liked her. Now her mother is saying that she (Elizabeth) is sick just to get rid of her.

Mrs. Collins loses her temper, too. "The Judge showed me the medical report and you tell me I'm makin' it up," sneers Mrs. Collins. "I shouldn't even be tryin' to spare your feelin's, becuz you've been a tramp and you've been sleeping with all kinds of tramps and now you've got the sickness that all tramps get!"

Elizabeth has been a common streetwalker, yells Mrs. Collins, and she is paying the price that streetwalkers pay.

"You're a liar!" screams Elizabeth, hysterically. "I haven't got it! I haven't! You're makin' it up cuz you hate me. I haven't got it! Say I haven't! You're lying!"

She has struck her mother on the shoulder, and then thrown herself whimperingly at her feet.

"Oh, Mom, I didn't mean to hit yuh!   I didn't mean to call yuh a liar . . ."

Mrs. Collins has taken the weeping girl in her arms. "How could I lie to you about anything like that?" she pleads, consolingly. "But, listen—they can cure you. They will!"

Elizabeth raises her head hopelessly. She can't believe that. There had been a kid at school who had got the disease and he went crazy and was put in a strait-jacket.

"Mama, please!   Don't let them take me to a hospital! They'll hurt me—doctors hurt yuh. I'll die there!"

"No, no, you won't. I begged the Judge to let me take you home, but he said he can't let you mingle with other boys and girls—"

"I can't be near the kids, huh?" Elizabeth has risen slowly to her feet. "I mustn't be near Mary or Bobby or—" Suddenly the thought of Peter comes to her. A great distress is mirrored in her face. "I mustn't be near ANYBODY!"

"Only for a short time, dear!"

Guardedly Elizabeth questions her mother about who knows that she is sick. Her father knows—and, well, Mrs. Collins admits, the Judge had wanted Peter to stay when he showed them the report—so Peter knows.

"He knows and he's willing to anyway—" Elizabeth mutters to herself. She is trembling so now Mrs. Collins fears she has a chill.

Judge Bentley is back. Jovially he would know if the good-bys are all over. They are? Well, is there anything Elizabeth would like to ask him before she goes?

Peter is leaning forward anxiously. Elizabeth looks straight at him as she answers. "No."

"Take the child away." The Judge nods to Mrs. Busch.

"Betty!   There *was* something you were goin' to ask the Judge!" Peter has crossed the room to intercept Elizabeth and Mrs. Busch.

"Yes."

"Then ask it!"

Elizabeth walks over to the platform, with Peter following. "Your Honor—please—may I first—" Elizabeth hesitates. Peter is waiting anxiously for their high sign.

"May you first what, child?"

"May I first return to Peter something he gave me . . . ?"

"Of course, of course."

Elizabeth turns toward Peter, opens her pocketbook and takes out the scarf. "Here's your *scarf*, Peter," she says. "I—I won't be able to use it now."

"What are you doin'? . . . Who's breakin' a promise now?" Peter is trying wildly to give the scarf back to her.

"I am, Peter. But I— I'll make you another promise, instead . . . I promise to—to make myself . . . good enough to . . . to do what we were plannin' before and, oh . . . all the time I'll be thinkin' how you wanted to—to do *so much* for me, even when you—you knew all about me an' this an' that— . . ."

"All right, child. You must go now," says the Judge.

"This way, child." Mrs. Busch is again at her side.

"Oh! 'By now, Mom! 'By, Papa!"

" 'By."

Mrs. Busch and Elizabeth pass through the hall door. Peter stands staring after them.

THE CURTAIN FALLS

THE INNOCENT VOYAGE

A Comedy in Three Acts

By Paul Osborn

(Based on the novel, "A High Wind in Jamaica," by
Richard Hughes)

IT may be that Theresa Helburn and Lawrence Langner of
the New York Theatre Guild forgot to knock on wood before
they produced "The Innocent Voyage." They recently had had
such phenomenal success with "Oklahoma" and the Paul Robeson "Othello" that they could quite reasonably have grown a
bit boastful of their newly developed skill in popular play selection. At any rate they were temporarily humbled by this experience. With the public "The Innocent Voyage" proved one of
their less popular enterprises.

Paul Osborn made the adaptation from Richard Hughes' novel,
"A High Wind in Jamaica," originally for Dwight Deere Wiman.
Mr. Wiman kept it for many weeks and then, his war activities
interfering, he relinquished it. The Guild took over the script,
cast Oscar Homolka of the cinema in the role of the impressively
human pirate, Capt. Jonsen, and brought the comedy to production at the Belasco Theatre in November.

Critical reception was not unfavorable, but rather on the nega-
tive side, inasmuch as many of the reviewers found the play
version definitely less appealing, in both character and story values, than the Hughes novel. Audience reaction was hearty and
fairly promising, but petered out in five weeks.

"What Osborn, in both his writing and his staging, has succeeded in doing is to establish the irrational and rather fearsome
world in which aware children live," Howard Barnes wrote in the
New York *Herald Tribune*. "He has not always given his play
the continuity and dramatic accents that it might have had, but
the acid test of his chemistry is the fact that the play builds
steadily and with emotional clarity. . . . 'The Innocent Voyage'
may not be as memorable, disturbing, or what you will as 'A
High Wind in Jamaica,' but it is easy to sit in on these lean
days of playgoing."

The story of "The Innocent Voyage," in its stage version, be-

gins with a prologue. The year is 1860, and the scene is a se-
cluded place on the deck of a British gun-boat. At a table sits
Mr. Mathias, a dignified representative of the British Admiralty.
Before him stand Mr. and Mrs. Thornton, English and middle-
aged. Being in the midst of an argument with Mr. Mathias, the
Thorntons are, at the moment, as excited as middle-aged English
folk are ever likely to get.

"You see, Mr. Mathias, we want the children to forget all
about it," Mr. Thornton is saying. "When they were returned
to us in Jamaica, they were wild and unmanageable. We have
succeeded in quieting them down, but if you were to question
them it would stir them all up again."

"How would you like your children to be chained in the hold
of a pirate ship for months," chips in Mrs. Thornton; "fed only
on bread and water—with rats running all over you—with—"

"Come, Mrs. Thornton, are you positive such was the case?
Have the children ever said they were chained in the hold? Or
fed on bread and water? Or that rats ran over them? Or—?"

"They didn't have to. One has a little imagination—!"

"That's just the trouble, if I may say so," counters Mr.
Mathies, firmly. "Everyone is eager enough to tell what he
imagines might have happened—but not one single fact that can
be taken into court! I have been delegated by the Admiralty
to investigate this case and I have tried to get the evidence
against these men without bothering the children. I have not
been able to do so. We will now be docking in England shortly.
The trial is to come up. This is a sensational case and public
opinion is demanding that these men be brought to justice. If
I am not allowed to question the children, however, I will have
no case at all."

It will be possible, Mr. Mathias admits, to get a conviction
of piracy, but what he is hoping to do is to hang the pirates.
To do that it will be necessary to prove that a Swedish captain
who was found dead aboard had been murdered. All the evidence
they have is to the effect that he was bound and carried from
his ship—

"Now, there is no doubt in my mind that he was murdered
by these pirates," admits Mr. Mathias. "But such is our law
that we must have absolute proof of this fact before any jury
will convict. That is why it is imperative for me to examine
the children. They are the only ones who can tell us what happened on that boat—"

The Thorntons finally agree to having the children in. Mrs.

Thornton is remembering that she certainly had a presentiment that something dreadful was going to happen the day they sent the children away as the curtain falls.

ACT I

On the deck of the *Clorinda*, an old-fashioned English sailing vessel, anchored in Montego Bay, Jamaica, Mr. and Mrs. Thornton are standing disconsolately by as they watch the preparations for the ship's sailing. The year is 1860.

The scene is one of great activity. A variety of sailors are going about their appointed tasks of setting up shrouds, straining themselves at the creaking lanyards, etc., Capt. Marlpole, a genial but worried sea-dog in his sixties, is busy overseeing the work, issuing orders from time to time through the medium of his chief mate.

"Scattered among the sailors, watching wide-eyed everything that is happening, are five children: Emily, aged 10; Edward, 7; John, 6; Rachel, 5; and Laura, 3." Looking over the rail is a sixth, Margaret, about 14. She is taller and more mature than the others.

"Oh, I do hope we're doing the right thing, Frederick," sighs Mrs. Thornton. "I'm so terribly afraid something will happen to them."

"No, no, nothing will happen to them. She's a good ship and the Captain seems very responsible." Mr. Thornton is brusquely confident.

"But they are such *children*. When I think of them out there on the ocean all alone—"

"I know—but they'll only be alone two or three days. Their Aunt Esther will get on at Havana—she'll take good care of them."

"But the Captain says it will take three months to get to England. Frederick, it isn't too late to change our minds right now, you know. Don't let's send them away."

The Thorntons are sending their children to England, first because they do not want them to go through another West Indies hurricane, and, second, because they are satisfied Jamaica is no place in which to bring up children anyway. They are themselves planning to follow shortly.

Capt. Marlpole has come to warn the Thorntons that there are but a few minutes left. And to promise that the children will, of course, have the best of everything.

"You'll have to be patient with them," Mrs. Thornton pleads. "I don't think they really *realize* yet what it means. We've told them they're going back to England and to school and that we'll have to stay on here in Jamaica for awhile—but I don't think they *realize* it yet—not even Emily. Emily is very sensitive. When you talk to her try to talk brightly to her, Captain. As if you were terribly interested! It will stimulate her mind."

The fact that the Captain has never felt that he could afford the luxury of a wife and children is disturbing to Mrs. Thornton, but she is forced to accept it.

Mr. Thornton is more concerned with the details of the voyage. They will be putting in at the Caymans for a few hours, Capt. Marlpole tells him. After that they'll be taking the Leeward Passage around Cape San Antonio—

"Then we'll pick up your sister in Havana, ma'am. Then no other ports of call 'til England."

"Oh, my babies!! Alone on the high seas!"

"We'll watch over them, ma'am. Nothing to worry about. I've made this crossing a hundred times."

"Just one more thing, Captain. Once in a while you might speak to Margaret."

"Margaret?"

"Yes, that's Margaret." Mrs. Thornton points to the girl still looking over the rail. "She's just a half-breed, of course, and not very bright, but she might be lonesome with none of her own kind. Her family are sending her to England because she has a relative there who can support her. So you might speak to her now and then—"

"Yes, ma'am; yes, ma'am. Hello, Margaret. Really must go now—" And the Captain hurries away.

Mrs. Thornton is convinced that because Capt. Marlpole has never had a wife he can't understand children at all. But Mr. Thornton refuses to worry about that. Who, for the matter of that, does understand children?

"How can you possibly tell what goes on in the child's mind? They have a completely different way of looking at things."

"All right, Frederick. But I do wish they weren't going. They're going to miss us terribly. My heart bleeds for them."

Laura, the three-year-old, interested in the log the sailor has just placed in position, attracts her mother's attention.

"Oh, my little Laura! My baby!" Mrs. Thornton throws her arms around Laura, and is hugging her, while Laura wriggles to get away.

"I'm busy," says Laura.

"But this is good-by, Laura."

"Good-by." And Laura is free.

"You see, Frederick, even at her age! She's just fighting to keep control of herself! Just having to hold herself back."

"She's doing a good job of it," mutters Mr. Thornton.

Now the last warning and the children are gathering to chorus their good-bys. Mr. Thornton has singled out Emily. "You're the oldest, Emily," he says. "I'm depending on you to look after the liddlies."

"Yes, Father."

"We hate to let you go, Emily. We don't know when another hurricane may strike. This is a crisis. And in a crisis everybody pitches in and does everything he can. Isn't that right?"

"Yes, Father."

"You're not just a child any more—you're growing up fast—so I want you to be responsible for looking after the others. You just make it your duty to see that nothing happens to them."

"Don't worry, Father. I'll make it my duty."

"I know you will! I know you will!" He is patting her shoulder affectionately.

The chorus of "Good-bys" has started all over again. It is interspersed with cries of "Oh, my darlings!" from Mrs. Thornton. Suddenly Emily realizes that this is really a PARTING, and she begins to cry a little—

"You come with us, Mother! You come with us!"

"I can't, my darling. Not now! And just think what an adventure it will be! Much more exciting than if I came! It will be *such* an adventure."

"But I don't want any more adventures—I want to stay with you."

Mr. and Mrs. Thornton have disappeared. The last line has been cast off.

"Emily cried," says Rachel, accusingly.

"Well, what if I did?"

"But why did you?"

"You just didn't *know* enough to cry!"

"I did, too."

"Then why didn't you?"

"Why should she?"

"You don't understand—any of you. That was a PARTING! People always cry at PARTINGS!"

"Oh-h-h-!"

"They do?"

"Of course they do! If they are mannerly. Some people just don't know how to behave!"

Now Rachel starts to cry, wildly. And now they are all making the most heart-rending sounds. "Good-by! Good-by! Mummy, dear— Good-by, Daddy, dear. Good-by—Good-by— Good-by—Mummy, dear—"

The curtain falls.

It is two days later. On the deck of the *Clorinda* all the Thornton children, and Margaret as well, are grouped around Emily, who is reading to them—

" 'The boys still played in the garden, and the youngest wore the golden star on his breast, with which the tree had been adorned during the happiest evening of its existence. Now all was past; the tree's life was past, and the story also—for all stories come to an end at last.' "

The end of the story and the closing of the book bring on a discussion. To Laura it's a silly story. But Laura doesn't like fairy stories anyway. Emily thinks fairy stories are beautiful.

Edward would like to know how long it takes to get to England. John, too. Emily will pretend to ask the white mouse with an elastic tail. And does. Two years, says the mouse. But Margaret settles that. It takes only three months.

If the white mouse knows so much, Rachael has one for him. What happens to people like Margaret? Almost before Laura can ask what the white mouse says Rachael has the answer—

"They fall into the sea—and the seaweed fills them all up so they get fat—and blue—and they choke—and their eyes come out—and they die—"

"You can't scare me," shouts Margaret, being very scared. She would run away if Emily didn't stop her and convince her that Rachel has made it all up.

Now there is some excitement among the sailors. One or two are in the rigging. From somewhere a voice shouts— "Can you take some lady passengers for England?"

"We'll find out," a sailor answers.

The voice, reports Rachael, has come from a funny boat that's been watching them all day. There are women on it, standing by the rail. They're waving umbrellas. Edward decides he'll go aloft to see better. Laura, too. Before they can stop her Laura is high in the rigging.

But now the ladies from the other boat are climbing into a smaller boat and that's pretty exciting. The Mate has come in and demanded a report from the sailors.

"It's a boat that's been alongside all day," they tell him. "There's women on it, sir."

"It doesn't seem to be flying any flag, sir." . . . "They hailed us, sir. Looks like they want to board us, sir."

For a little the children's attention is diverted to Laura. The Captain's going to be angry when he sees Laura. But the Captain's asleep in his cabin.

"If she falls she'll break her neck," predicts Edward, looking anxiously up at Laura.

"She might fall in the water, then she wouldn't," corrects Rachel.

"In that case she'd drown. That's just as bad."

"I'd rather drown than break my neck," says Rachel. "It's safer."

Laura, looking down, suddenly becomes frightened and screams lustily. Immediately the Mate and the crew are in a dither. While they are getting Laura back on deck the boarding party from the other ship has come over the side. The English sailors stand amazed at what they see—

"What the devil!" . . . "My God, what are you?" . . . "They are not women!" . . .

"Of course they ain't!"

The women pirates, their male garb showing now under their skirts, are followed by their leaders, Capt. Jonsen, a burly, blustering fellow, and he by Otto, a smaller, less blustering person, who is his mate. The Mate of the *Clorinda* steps toward them with a threatening "Who the hell are you?" and is promptly floored by Capt. Jonsen.

"How many men aboard?" bellows Jonsen.

"Twenty," pipes up a sailor.

"Twenty. Round them up, Otto."

The sailors are herded into the deckhouse. The children are put in the cabin. The boarding crew begins stripping the deck of baggage. Capt. Marlpole is brought, protesting helplessly, from his cabin. He demands the return of his ship, the release of his sailors and of the children. Boarding a British ship, shouts Marlpole, is treason.

"You had better be calm, yes?" suggests Capt. Jonsen.
"Who the devil are you?"

JONSEN—Ach, dot vould be hard to explain! But at de moment, I am in need of a few stores. My fellows vill keep a tally. You shall be paid for everything I take.

MARLPOLE—You'll pay for this outrage! You'll pay a pretty tune! (*Enter two* PIRATE LADIES.) And who the devil are those, Sir?

JONSEN—Dey are not vot you tink! Ve are a respectable crew! Pable! José! (*Men step down.*) Take dem dresses off! Otto! (OTTO *repeats orders in Spanish.*) Dey is just part of my crew! You see, dot vay it makes it easier for us to come aboard.

MARLPOLE—This is piracy! You are Pirates! Bloody Pirates!

JONSEN—Ach, dat iss bad—very bad—but sometimes—ven ve meet again—I vill pay you in full—at least two thousand pounds—

MARLPOLE—You think I believe that cock and bull story?

JONSEN—And if not in money—perhaps a kindness I gif you—always one can use a kindness— (*He sees* MARLPOLE's *expression.*) No, I vill gif you money! Tree tousand pounds! Two tousand for de stores ve are taking—and one tousand for de cash you vill gif me in money—

OTTO (*coming back*)—We know you've got money aboard.

JONSEN—Our information is certain.

MARLPOLE—No—no money on board—

OTTO—Where is it hid?

MARLPOLE—I have no money— I have nothing—just some molasses and rum and—

JONSEN—If you do not tell us de hiding place, your life shall pay de forfeit. Do not expect mercy, for dis iss my profession and in it I am inured to blood.

MARLPOLE—No—no—don't shoot! My wife—my children—

JONSEN—Remember, money cannot recall life, nor at all avail you when you are dead.

There is a wail from the children in the cabin. This gives Jonsen an idea. They will do with the children as they did with the monkeys, he tells Otto. Otto doesn't like the idea, but Jonsen insists. Four of the pirate crew are ordered on deck with their muskets and lined up opposite the cabin.

"Now, where iss the money hid?" demands Jonsen.

"I have no money. I swear I have no—"

"Otto!"

The Pirates shoot. Jonsen points to three holes near the top of the cabin wall. "Three leetle holes. You see dem dere? If you refuse to tell us where the money is, next time de aim vill be a foot lower."

"You wouldn't dare!"

"Otto!"

Again the shots. "De holes are lower. Next time he gifs the signal it will be to shoot right tru der leetle bodies."

"I don't believe you! I don't believe you!" wails Marlpole. "I have no money!"

With a quick stinging blow Jonsen knocks the Captain flat. The pirates pick him up and carry him to the mast. Otto has opened the cabin door and released the children.

"God damn it, Otto, get those children out of here!"

"Don't swear like that in front of the children," chides Otto. "I'm going to get them out of here. I'll take them over to the schooner until we're finished here."

The children are filled with excitement and curiosity. "Why is this no place for children?" . . . "What have they done to Capt. Marlpole?" . . .

A sailor has found Margaret hiding in the hold, Otto reports, bringing Margaret in. "I don't give a damn where he found her. Tell him to put her in the hold with the udders," shouts Jonsen.

The pirates have lashed Marlpole to the mast and sprinkled shavings and gunpowder about his feet. Otto has taken a taper torch from the mast and lighted it.

"Ver iss de hiding place?" demands Jonsen. "Der iss gunpowder all ofer you! Der iss kindling under you. Ve vill burn de boat down—"

"I haven't any money—"

"Otto! Touch off de powder!"

Otto starts to bring his torch to the powder when Marlpole screams: "Wait! Wait! I have some money—! My freight money—nine hundred pound freight money is in my cabin—under the floor by the bunk—"

"Otto! See if he iss telling the truth."

Marlpole, who has sagged down in his ropes, suddenly rouses himself and demands to know what has been done with the children.

"Ve haf got dem all tied up. Ve iss going to chop dem up

into leetle pieces and trow dem into the sea."

Marlpole groans miserably and sags again in his bonds.

Now Otto is back from the Captain's cabin with the money—nine hundred pounds. With a chuckle Jonsen orders Marlpole's bonds cut. Again Marlpole sinks to the deck, with a groan. At the rail Jonsen has thrown one huge arm around Otto's neck, affectionately. He is beaming with good humor. "Otto, my frien'! Now ve vait for de vind and ve get ourselves goot and God-damned drunk, eh, Otto?"

Jonsen and Otto have gone over the side and disappeared. The crew of the *Clorinda*, headed by the Mate, come tumbling out of their hiding places, demanding to know what has happened.

The story they get from Capt. Marlpole is a lurid one. The pirates have taken everything. There were sixty—seventy—eighty of them. With guns and cutlasses. He was strangled, Marlpole reports. The savages had lighted torches under him.

A splash is heard. Marlpole runs excitedly to the rail. "It's the children!" he wails. "They've murdered them! They're throwing their little bodies into the sea. I can see them!" He is shouting loudly out into the night. "You scoundrels! You blackguards! You will be brought to justice! You'll pay for this! You fiends!" He turns to the crew. "Stand by to get under way." The men jump to action. "Push ahead to Havana!"

The men are working rapidly. The sail starts up. It is dark, save for the moon. Marlpole is still at the rail, shaking his fist at the night and shouting: "We'll bring these ruffians to justice!! The fiends! The wanton, murdering fiends! Fiends! Fiends!" The curtain falls.

It is just before Capt. Marlpole started screaming at the *John Dodson*, the pirate ship. Capt. Jonsen and his mate, Otto, are inspecting crates, boxes, trunks, etc., that they have taken off the *Clorinda*. The deck of the *Dodson* is in a half light and their inspection is spotty. Jonsen, however, has decided to keep a certain easy chair because it fits him so well. He would keep two or three of the trunks, too, but unhappily Marlpole has painted his name on them. To keep them, Otto points out, would be dangerous. So into the sea they should go.

"Vy vould a man put his name on a dirty old trunk?" ruminates the pirate chief. "I haf noticed dat tendency in de human race, Otto. Dey got something and right avay dey vant to put der name on it! It is bad."

The first trunk goes over with a splash. "Vy are de trunks his?" continues Jonsen, soberly. "Now dey are mine? Now dey are de sea's. Does de name count? I am very sad sometimes when I think of de greed."

As the third trunk splashes Marlpole's voice is heard hurling curses at the "fiends." Otto cannot understand that. Why, after they have taken everything Marlpole has, why should he get so angry over a few old trunks?

"Fiends! Fiends!" shouts Marlpole.

"Ach! He is a bad man, dot man," declares Jonsen. "He iss possessive. You know what he called us, Otto? He called us pirates!"

"Well?"

"It isn't de name I object to, Otto. It is de vay he said it— mit contempt! . . . You and me hass been togedder eight years, Otto—efer since I capture you off dot English merchant ship— and do you tink der iss anyting on dis business verse den being kicked around on dat filthy ship de vay you vas?"

"No, I don't."

"Vee are free men, Otto. Not slaves—working for miserable wages. Ach, you nefer knew my father, Otto. He *vas* a *real* pirate! He knew dese channels tru de reefs like no udder man. For hundreds of miles along dis coast he could make his schooner creep like a snake! Der vere many pirates and auctions in every port! It was goot! In those days there were rich hauls —not like this trash."

The moon has come out, lighting up the deck and revealing tables set for supper. The wind is coming up and they will be under way shortly. But first they must eat.

The children troop in, followed by six pirates. At table with the pirates all around them, the children proceed to eat "with a grace that would astonish their parents." The pirates, too, try to put on their best manners. When one of them starts to gobble, Emily gives him a severe look.

Turning to the sailor next to her Emily asks, with great dignity: "Could I trouble you for some salt, please?"

The sailor replies in a fluent Spanish, gesticulating wildly. Emily repeats her request. More Spanish.

"They haven't learned how to talk yet," ventures Laura. "They just make sounds, like babies."

Finally Emily decides that their friends just can't talk English. In that case it occurs to Edward that they don't even know what they (the children) are saying. What a joke!

"You! You look like a hyena!" shouts Edward, pointing at one of them. The children watch the result, frightened and breathless. Nothing happens. Then, with a loud laugh, all the children, except Emily, start pointing and shouting: "You look like a donkey; you look like a crocodile!" . . . "You're a scorpion!" . . . "You're a cray-fish!"

A small riot, with the children pounding the table with their eating implements and yelling lustily, is in progress when Jonsen and Otto break in on the scene. Otto at first is worried for fear the pirates may have done something to the children. Jonsen doesn't care a damn. Let Otto get rid of them, and quick.

Otto is herding the children for transfer back to their own ship when Jonsen discovers that the *Clorinda* has hoisted sail, taken advantage of the wind and is on her way. Excitedly he demands that Otto overtake the runaway.

"She's half a mile away already," says Otto. "We'd never catch her before daylight. She'll be in the direct trade route to Havana—and with these kids, all this stuff aboard—they'd catch us sure."

"If they catch us with them aboard—" The Captain's face is a study. What can they do? First, let Otto send the children below. Let the sailors find a place for them to sleep. Then they'll talk about getting rid of them.

Otto is worried, too. If they could put into some port tomorrow—

"And do you tink any port we put into tomorrow vouldn't know about that ship we just looted?" storms Capt. Jonsen. "No, Otto . . . If we are caught with dem kids God knows what might happen to us. They would think we kidnaped them. That's prison, Otto, for the rest of our lives."

OTTO—What can we do then?

JONSEN—Well, I've been thinking. Ve are not so far avay from the trade routes— Maybe, along towards morning, we put them in a little boat and push them away. They would be picked up and—

OTTO—No. No. What if they weren't picked up?

JONSEN—There are other ships. They would find them and—

OTTO—No, no, that's too dangerous. We've got to see that they get back to whoever owns them.

JONSEN—No, Otto. That we can't do. They would get ashore.

Otto—Then we've got to put them off somewhere where they'll be safe.

Jonsen—And where is that?

Otto—I don't know yet—but we—

Jonsen—Wait a minute, Otto. In the western end of Cuba there are many little channels—many secret little ports where my father used to take me. Maybe we go there. Maybe we can dump them off and—

Otto—No. No. They'll never be found.

Jonsen—Then what do you want? My God, we throw them overboard then. Dat is what ve should do anyway. We throw them overboard and no one would ever know.

Otto—No. No.

Jonsen—What the hell's the matter with you? It's our lives or theirs.

Otto Maybe it's a good idea to go to the western end of Cuba.

Jonsen—You go to bed! I vill take the watch.

Otto—No—I'll stay with you.

Jonsen—God damn it! You go to bed! (*As* Otto *leaves* Emily *appears.*) What do you want?

Emily—I would like to know what is happening. Why did the other boat run away? My father made me responsible for the others. I'd like to know what's happening, if you please.

Jonsen (*facing her*)—Get out of here!

Emily starts away but turns to watch him. The curtain falls.

Beds have been arranged for the children in the quarters. A half hour after they have gone to bed they are still trying to get to sleep, and practically with no success at all. Laura doesn't like her bed, principally because there isn't any bed anyway. Edward smells cockroaches. Which gives Laura an idea that there is a cockroach in her bed, too.

"Emily, what did the Captain say? Did he tell you why they changed us?" asks Rachel.

"No. Grown-ups never do tell you things. You'll learn that when you get older. Now go to sleep!"

There is a short silence. Then Edward wants to know if their captors are pirates. Of course they aren't pirates. There aren't any pirates these days. Emily is sure of that.

"When we were shut up in the other ship I heard Capt. Marlpole call them pirates," announces Rachel.

"No, you silly. He must have said 'pilots,' " ventures Emily with sudden inspiration.

"What are pilots?" Laura wants to know.

"They come on board. Don't you remember that picture in the dining room at home called 'The Pilot Comes Aboard'?"

Again a moment's silence and then someone can be heard crying. It is Margaret. Margie is probably frightened, thinks Rachel, who thereupon begins to chant: "Margie's got the bogies, the bogies, the bogies!"

EMILY—Don't, Rachel!

MARGARET (*sobbing*)—Oh, you little fools!

EDWARD—What's the matter with you then?

MARGARET—I'm older than any of you.

EDWARD—That's a funny reason to be frightened.

MARGARET—It isn't. You're all too young to know!

EDWARD—Oh, hit her, somebody.

MARGARET—You little fools!

EMILY—Now go to sleep.

LAURA—Sweet dreams, Edward.

EDWARD—Sweet dreams, Laura— Sweet dreams, John.

JOHN—Sweet dreams, Edward— Sweet dreams, Rachel.

RACHEL—Sweet dreams, John— Sweet dreams, Emily.

EMILY—Sweet dreams, *all!*

THE REST—Sweet dreams—

EMILY—Now go to sleep all of you.

JONSEN (*entering stealthily goes to the beds and begins counting*)—1-2-3-4-5-6— My God!

The curtain falls.

ACT II

Three weeks later the deck of the pirate ship is fully revealed in the bright sunshine that floods it. Sailors are busy bringing on deck the loot taken from the *Clorinda* and piling it along the rail preparatory to taking it off. There is a good deal of jabbering in Spanish.

Capt. Jonsen is moving about the deck. Suddenly he finds one of the sailors, a huge, tough-looking fellow, in his way and gives him a hearty push. The sailor staggers, rights himself, and turns angrily toward the Captain, lashing him with a string of Spanish that Jonsen finds both startling and amusing.

"Now, dot means someting! If I knew vot dot meant I vould have to put you in irons, I bet," says the Captain, grinning.

Thus encouraged the sailor redoubles his efforts and his vocabulary. "Ach, dot's bad, dot's bad!" mutters Jonsen. "You calling me terrible names! Don't you know dot's mutiny?"

Another burst and Jonsen walks over to the sailor, whacks him soundly on the back and beams in his face. A second sound whack and the sailor gives up. With a sickly grin he runs away.

"Ach, my God, sometimes I tink it vould be better if nobody could talk," sighs the Captain. "Den ve could understand each udder better."

Otto joins the Captain. He is sulky and depressed. It may be a fine day for the auction, but Otto refuses to be cheered. He has been ordered to get rid of the children in this port and he doesn't like the idea. What will become of them in this "God-forsaken, fever-ridden port—a hundred miles from everywhere?" With nobody to take care of them, without understanding the language, the children are likely to starve in a week—

"Otto! Ve von't talk about dot no more! You get rid of dem kids in dis port like ve agreed! My God, tree weeks I haf had dem kids on dis ship!"

"Well, you were afraid to put into any port before this with them aboard!"

"And whose fault iss it der still aboard?"

"All right, all right!" Otto has turned sullenly away.

"Otto, my frien', make no meestake! I vill not be so easy next time. After ve auction off de cargo—ve leaf—middout de kids!"

"All right, all right!"

The children have come quietly on deck and are watching Jonsen and Otto a little anxiously. The Captain is confiding that he has an uneasy feeling, right in the middle of his stomach, "efery minute de little bastards iss on board," when Otto sees them and quickly shushes Jonsen.

The children are all washed for the trip ashore, and proud of the job. Only Rachel is out of line. She has her arms full of a variety of things—a belaying pin, rags, chunks of odds and ends. These, announces Rachel, are her babies and she is taking them with her. When Otto would reason with her she sets up a howl that threatens to get worse. Rachel is allowed to keep her babies.

Emily detaches herself from the group and slowly approaches Capt. Jonsen. For a moment she stands regarding him gravely.

"Is this England?" Emily asks.

The Captain is uncomfortable. "Vell, no—it ain't exactly England—"

"We were supposed to get off at England."

The Captain shifts uneasily as Emily fixes him with a questioning stare. "Vell, you see—ve don't go to England. Ve only go dis far."

"Is this where you're going to get rid of us?"

"Vot you mean by dot?"

"Edward heard you tell Otto you had to get rid of us."

"Vell, it's like dis—"

"Why do you want to get rid of us? Don't you want us any more?"

"It ain't dot—! It's just dot—"

Emily is looking at him, smiling radiantly. "Don't put us ashore," she says. "I like you. I want to stay with *you*."

"Vell, you can't." The Captain is rough again. "You iss going ashore!"

Emily turns away hurt, and starts to rejoin the children. Jonsen takes a step toward her and then changes his mind. A moment later he is cursing a sailor.

Edward spies Margaret coming down the deck. She is glancing around furtively. "There is something different about her appearance. She seems less a child than she was. The children watch her fascinated."

The children are curious. "What's the matter with her?" whispers Rachel. "Why doesn't she sleep with us any more?" . . . "Why did they come and take her away that night?" . . . "She *is* silly. Look at her!"

Margaret is making up to a passing sailor. He stops to speak to her. But Capt. Jonsen will have none of that. He comes storming on deck demanding to know what Margaret is doing there.

"I thought I was to go ashore," simpers Margaret.

"You go ashore after de udders. Now you get below, you leetle—" He has pushed Margaret roughly out of sight and turned angrily to the sailor. "Vot de debil you tink you're doing?" The sailor goes into a Spanish explanation. "I gif strict orders on dis ship not to speak to dot leetle slut before de children! Vot you tink dis ship iss, hey? Dis is a respectable ship! I haf no monkeyshines on de deck. You hear dot, all of you! You go below ven you do your monkeyshines!"

He has gone over to the children to demand what it was Margaret had said to them. When they insist she had said nothing Jonsen adds, with a menacing gesture: "Vell, den! I spank you goot if I catch you with her! You inderstand?"

Otto has come hurrying to the deck to report that the Magistrate's boat is coming out from shore. The Magistrate and a couple of soldiers are on board. It is the first time that has happened to Jonsen in this port and he doesn't like the look of it.

"You better get those kids out of the way until we find out what he wants," warns Jonsen. To a pirate he adds, in Spanish: "Take them below and keep them there."

The Magistrate, "a stiff little man with a stiffer little beard, in uniform," comes on board and quietly details his guards to search the decks. His greeting is cold, but his manner is friendly in its formality. He listens patiently while Capt. Jonsen, with rather extreme obsequiousness, thanks him for the visit and reminds him that they have met on numerous occasions before.

He has come, explains the Captain, to auction off his cargo. From where? From Havana. How long from Havana? Three weeks. And why hasn't he put in at any other port between here and there?

Jonsen stumbles over that one, but Otto comes to his rescue. "We wanted to hold our auction here at Santa Lucia," explains Otto. It had been long since they had had an auction in Santa Lucia.

They had picked up their cargo at Havana, the Captain continues. It consists of molasses, chickens and a little of everything. He will, says the Magistrate, examine the cargo later.

Presently the Magistrate is ready to explain the reasons for his rather complete examination. "On the eleventh of this month, an English merchant ship, the *Clorinda*, under the command of Captain James Marlpole, left Montego Bay, Jamaica."

"Ve didn't see noting of it, your Honor," Jonsen is quick to explain.

MAGISTRATE—Three days out of port, she was fired upon by a ship bearing ten or twelve cannon and a whole broadside of artillery.

JONSEN (*in amazement*)—Cannon? Artillery?

MAGISTRATE—She was ordered to heave-to or she would be sunk.

JONSEN (*amazed*)—My God, is dot vot dot Captain Marlpole himself said?

MAGISTRATE—This is his own report.

JONSEN—Twelf cannon and artillery! Vot you know about dot!

MAGISTRATE—Although Captain Marlpole is a gallant man,

what could he do? He put up a brave resistance but he had no choice.

JONSEN—I should tink not! Twelf cannon—!

MAGISTRATE—He was then boarded by eighty Spanish ruffians—

JONSEN (*shouting*)—Vot? Vot?

MAGISTRATE—They were all armed to the teeth.

JONSEN—You hear dot, Otto! Eighty Spanish ruffians armed to de teeth! My! My!

MAGISTRATE—They took everything he had. His entire cargo and his freight money. Two thousand pounds.

JONSEN (*indignant*)—Two thousand pounds! (*He points to the paper in the* MAGISTRATE'S *hand.*) Is dot vot he says?

MAGISTRATE (*reading*)—Two thousand pounds. Why?

JONSEN (*suddenly docile*)—Noting, noting. Dot's terrible!

MAGISTRATE—Also on board were six children—passengers he was taking to England.

JONSEN (*looking at* OTTO *uneasily*)—So? Vot happened to dem?

MAGISTRATE—They were kidnaped and taken to the pirate ship.

JONSEN (*after a pause, again uneasy*)—Ach! Vot you tink of dot!

MAGISTRATE—Six innocent little children! And what followed is almost too horrible to relate!

JONSEN (*bewildered*)—So? Vot happened?

MAGISTRATE—After the children were taken onto the pirate ship, they were brutally and wantonly murdered and their little bodies were thrown into the sea!

JONSEN (*still bewildered*)—Vot?

MAGISTRATE—Captain Marlpole saw this brutality with his own eyes. He both saw and heard each little body as it went into the sea.

JONSEN (*pointing to the paper*)—Dot's vot he says?   /

MAGISTRATE (*reading*)—"—then the pirate captain took the children, one by one, and, in sheer infamous wantonness, murdered each one and threw his body into the sea. That anything so wicked could even look like a man, it was hard for me to believe. He was a creature of such hideous and vile appearance that—"

JONSEN (*unable to contain himself, roaring*)—De bastard! De dirty, snivelin'—! If I efer get my hands on dot dirty skunk—! (*Suddenly he catches* OTTO's *eye and also sees the*

"THE INNOCENT VOYAGE"

"Emily is still crying out about her leg. She puts her arms about Jonsen's neck. He would comfort her if he could. 'Der—der—don't cry. It ain't bad. We feex it in a minute. It'll be all right.'"

*(Carolyn Hummel, Mary Ellen Glass, Herbert Berghof,
Oscar Homolka, Abby Bonime)*

MAGISTRATE *watching him. He adds hurriedly.*) Dot pirate
Captain! He ought to be keeled! To murder leetle children
like dot—!

MAGISTRATE—That is the opinion of everyone! It has aroused
everyone with any human feeling. We will bring these mur-
derers to the gallows! Every ship on the sea will be on the
watch for them! They cannot escape!

While the Magistrate is speaking little Laura has suddenly put
in an appearance on deck. She is not where she can be seen by
the Magistrate and the others, but is evidently intent on approaching them. Behind Laura, on his hands and knees, is a
sailor bent on her capture. For a moment he holds the child's
attention by clowning. She, too, gets down to crawl on the deck
like the sailor.

"The ship we are to look for is one bearing twelve cannon, a
broadside of artillery and a crew of eighty. Is that right, your
Honor?"

"That is correct."

Laura has gone slowly back toward the sailor, but when he
makes a grab for her she jumps away and is starting again for
the deck.

"Ve ought to find such a ship, eh, Otto? Ve vill be on de
vatch eferywhere, your Honor. Dey vill not escape!"

"Very well! You have permission to hold your auction in
Santa Lucia. I will make you welcome to the town."

The sailor is now trying to lure Laura with an orange. She is
intrigued but not altogether certain. She goes toward him cautiously and is about to reach for the orange, just as the Magistrate is going over the rail.

"Piracy we can overlook," the Magistrate is saying. "It is not
important and it is rapidly dying out of itself. But to kidnap
and murder six innocent little children—"

The sailor has made another grab for Laura and has missed.
Now Otto has caught sight of her and is maneuvering as a shield
between Laura and the Magistrate. He manages to grab her
and clamp his hand over her mouth just as the Magistrate disappears.

Jonsen has also caught sight of the struggling, squirming Laura
in Otto's arms and is properly excited. He is ready to *keel* the
sailor for letting Laura get on deck. And if Laura ever does
such a trick again he promises to *feex* her *goot*.

With this threat Laura finally wiggles herself loose from Otto

and starts down the deck. "Lieber Gott, catch dot ting!" shouts
Jonsen. "Vot iss dis? Don't let her get to de rail! Yump on
her! Yump on her!"

The sailor and Otto corner Laura, grab her and hold her with
her mouth covered. She is kicking violently.

"Take her below! Put her in irons!" cries the Captain.

"No irons could stay on her," protests Otto, panting freely.

"Den hit her mit dem! Vot kind of business iss dis anyway?"

It is now apparent to both Jonsen and Otto that they will have
to keep the children hidden until after the auction. Then what?
Jonsen would remind Otto that he (Otto) had insisted that to
keep the trunks aboard was dangerous. How much more dangerous it would be to keep the children.

"Otto, ven those kids came aboard, our fate came with them."

The children have sneaked up back of the Captain as he is
talking. Are they going ashore, Rachel wants to know. The
Captain whirls on them angrily. Holding his voice to a hoarse
whisper he warns them to get below before anyone sees them.
Again Otto takes a hand. If they don't want to be put ashore,
he tells the children, they will have to promise him to stay below
and be very, very quiet.

John is willing to agree—if it is not too long. But Laura isn't
sure. She wants to be put ashore and doesn't care who knows it.
Emily has to take charge of Laura.

"Are you going ashore?" Rachel would know of Capt. Jonsen.

"Vot? Of course I am! Ve got to auction off the cargo!"

"The cargo you took off the other ship?"

Jonsen is embarrassed. "Vell, er—"

"The cargo that belonged to Capt. Marlpole?" puts in Edward.

"Vot you mean by dot?"

"Are you pilots or pirates?" suddenly demands Laura.

This is a poser. The children watch Jonsen eagerly as he
fumbles for an answer. Suddenly Edward senses the truth and
begins to shout at the top of his lungs:

"THEY'RE PIRATES! THEY'RE PIRATES!"

"Goody, goody! They're pirates! They're pirates!" echoes
Rachel.

The children are marching around the deck now, shouting lustily. Laura gleefully joins the procession, adding her "Pirates!
Pirates!" to the hubbub.

Edward introduces an original touch by threatening to stab
out somebody's, anybody's heart. John chimes in with a threat

to "saber" them. Laura decides she is also ready to do a job of sabering.

Jonsen is weaving excitedly among them. "Shut up! You keeds shut up dot noise! You want dem to hear you? Gott in Himmel, you shut up dot noise!"

Suddenly Otto realizes that a crisis has arisen. "We've got to get out of here!" he shouts to Jonsen, who is making frantic dives for the children as they run shouting around him.

"Vot about de auction?" shouts Jonsen.

"To hell with the auction!" Otto has turned and is yelling loud orders in Spanish. The sailors begin to appear. The children continue their mad, yelling race in and around Jonsen and the cargo.

Emily is the only one who is not excited. She sits primly and quietly at the side, watching the game. Jonsen spies her. In his excitement he does not realize that she has not been an offender. He grabs Emily.

"My God, you stop that noise!—I show you!" He turns her quickly over his knee. "I gif you a spanking you don't forget! Der!" says the Captain, suiting his action to the threat.

The sight of Emily being spanked quickly quiets the children. There is a deadly silence. They stare strangely at Emily as Jonsen puts her down. Emily, "tearless, wide-eyed with horror, stands gazing at Jonsen. She is speechless, pale and trembling."

Jonsen is mopping his brow. Suddenly he realizes the children are staring at him in horror. He looks again at Emily, who is still trembling—

"Vot's de matter? Ain't you nefer been spanked before?" As Emily starts to back away from him he adds, uneasily: "Dot didn't hurt as much as dot!"

The other children have begun to move silently toward him. "Get out of here! Get out of here! My God, one would think I—"

Emily continues to back away, the other children to move slowly. Suddenly Jonsen, puzzled and groaning, sinks to the deck, his head in his hands—

"My God, vot has happened to me? Vot has happened to me!"

The curtain falls.

Weeks later the pirate ship is drifting lazily in a calm sea. A hot sun is beating down on the deck. Otto is working over charts and maps at a table. Capt. Jonsen is sprawled out near him sleeping. John, Rachel, Edward and Laura are together, hot and listless. "They are all much dirtier than when last seen. Their hair is long and unkempt."

Rachel is rocking one of her marlin-spike babies in her arms and crooning softly. Edward is making a wooden sword. He is, admits Edward, awful lucky. "Most boys have to run away to go to sea. I just got there by myself."

Edward thinks he will always stay at sea, but Rachel is sure he'll be getting off when they get to England.

"When Capt. Jonsen gets killed the sailors are going to elect me captain, and I shall have Margaret and Laura and Emily and Rachel marooned on an island."

Rachel has dropped her baby again, and that makes clatter enough to waken Capt. Jonsen, who collects his wits slowly. It seems to the Captain that he has been awfully tired for a long time now. He hasn't any idea where they are, but it is a long way from any place he had ever been before. And for what? For a bunch of keeds—

"You know, Otto, life is a very strange thing," muses the Captain. "Ven my fodder and mutter came ofer from Holland I was only ten. I had it in my head I was going to be a preacher. Alvays I haf admired de preachers. But vun day my fodder needed some help so I vent out mit him. And den I just drifted into de business. You know how it is— And so ven he died I just took de business ofer— And now it iss too late. I vill nefer be a preacher now . . . (*He sighs.*) Dot Parson Audain vus a wonderful man. He vus de Rector of Roseau—oh, a long time back. He vas de finest preacher in de Islands. But he had bad luck. Once, ven he vas smuggling Negroes to Guadaloupe he vas captured by pirates—"

Emily comes on deck carrying a cheese. She sees Jonsen and carefully walks around him as she approaches Otto. Jonsen would stop her, asking her quite gently what it is she wants. Emily wants Otto's knife. Why Otto's? Doesn't she know Jonsen also has a knife? Can he cut the cheese for her? No.

Suddenly Jonsen is angry. He is roaring at her now. "My God, vot de matter wid you anyvay? Ain't you nefer going to forget dot spanking? I'm de Captain, ain't I? I got de right to spank anybody on dis ship!"

"Yes, sir."

"Besides, I haf explained to you dot I vas wrong about dot spanking!"

"Yes, sir."

"Den vot de matter wid you anyvay? Why don't you talk to me? Some day I gif you a *good* spanking—vun you don't nefer forget. You is a naughty girl. (*He holds out the knife and says sternly.*) Now you be careful mit dot knife, you understand?"

Emily hesitantly takes the knife. For a moment she stands as though thinking of making up with him, but he does not notice it."

"Vell, vot you waiting for?" he yells. "Go on mit you!" And she rejoins the children.

A sailor has come in excitedly with a report for Otto. Otto whips out his glasses and sweeps the horizon. There's a ship in sight—a small Swedish merchant ship . . . Otto immediately shouts an order in Spanish to give chase.

Capt. Jonsen is also excited. Will they board her? Certainly they will. They need provisions badly. Let Otto tell the men to get out their dresses. But wait! The Captain has a new idea. Why not use the children?

"They would love it! Dey is alvays playing pirate," chuckles Jonsen.

"But then they will know there are children aboard," warns Otto.

"Vot difference does it make? Dey tink de children are dead anyvay, and you yourself said the scandal would be gone. And it iss so long—and ve are so far avay . . ."

"All right. It's a good idea."

Jonsen strides over to where Emily is dividing the cheese. "Get up! All of you! I haf something to say to you . . . Iss any of you hungry?"

EDWARD (*promptly*)—Yes, sir.

JONSEN—You tink you iss hungry and you iss eating right now! Now how would you like it iff der vas no more of any-thing to eat? How would you like it if you had noting to eat for six-sefen-eight days—? Maybe longer?

EDWARD (*as the children stir uneasily*)—Aren't we going to have?

JONSEN—Dot ain't vot I ask you! I say how vould you like it?

JOHN—I wouldn't!

JONSEN (*as* OTTO *gives orders in Spanish*)—You bet you vouldn't! Now, ve haf all been eating goot on dis ship, hein?

JOHN—Yes, sir.

JONSEN (*to* EMILY)—And ve vant to eat goot all de time, no?

EMILY (*averting her eyes*)—Yes, sir.

JONSEN—Vell den, ve got to get provisions. Dot's a lesson you got to learn. You got to get provisions or go hungry.

EDWARD—Are we going to get provisions?

JONSEN—You bet ve are! Ve are going to borrow some! (*Sailor enters with dresses.*) Notrappos. You see dot ship?— (*The children look off.*) Ve are going to borrow some provisions from dot ship!!!

EDWARD—The way you borrowed them from Captain Marlpole?

JONSEN—Nebber mind about dot! Now ve are going to catch up close to dot ship. Dot vill be sometime late dis afternoon. And ven ye get close, all of you vill line up at de rail. I vill show you how. And you vill wafe your hands and shout to de ship. You understand?

JOHN—The way the "Ladies" did before?

JONSEN—Dot's right. Den you vill get into a leetle boat with five or six men and you go over to the other ship—

EDWARD—Can I have a pistol?

JONSEN—No, you can't have a pistol—what do you think this is? Now when you—

EDWARD—Then can I be the Captain?

JONSEN—You want to be Captain?

EDWARD (*shouting*)—Yes, *sir!*

JONSEN—All right, you iss de Captain!

EDWARD—Hurrah! I'm the Captain.

JOHN—And I'm the mate.

JONSEN—You two, take ofer! Gif chase!

EDWARD (*to* OTTO)—Hoist the sails! Get under way! Give chase!

The game is on and the children are happy. Edward is full of orders, including one that Rachel's baby will hereafter be a gun.

Suddenly Emily screams out in pain and falls over on the deck. Jonsen rushes to pick her up. "My God, her leg!" he cries. "It is all blood! Tar, get some tar and rags and water!"

Emily is still crying out about her leg. She puts her arms around Jonsen's neck. He would comfort her if he could. "Der —der—don't cry. It ain't bad. We feex it in a minute. It'll be all right."

"It hurts—it hurts!"

"Sure it does. Just hold on tight."

"My leg—my leg— I didn't mean to be naughty!"

"No—no—you weren't naughty."

"I *wanted* to talk to you."

"Of course you did."

"I *couldn't*."

"Of course you couldn't. You can't never talk what you feel, Emily. I was sorry I spanked you the minute I did it."

"I loved you all the time."

"Yah—yah— Now don't worry about dot no more. We got dot fixed between us once and for all. Yes?"

Otto has come with a bucket and cloths. Jonsen has gone to work on the cut.

"Der—der—hold on tight to me— Dot hurts, you know. Right to the bone! Dot hurts like hell!"

"My leg—"

"It can't hurt long. Der! Dot's better! Now ve feex it— Der—der—der—der—"

The curtain falls.

Near sunset that same day Edward, John, Rachel and Laura are lined up at the rail of the pirate ship. They have been thoroughly slicked up for the adventure. Edward's and Laura's hair has been trimmed. The children are waving and shouting greetings to a near-by ship. Five or six of the pirate crew are standing near them.

Suddenly Otto's voice booms out: "Can you take some children as passengers?"

"All right—come aboard!"

Capt. Jonsen, hidden from view of the other ship, is keeping a close watch of it with his glasses. Emily is lying on her cot, silent and watchful. A whistle is blown. Otto barks a few orders.

"Remember—ven you get on board just keep talking to dem," Jonsen calls. "Dey von't understand anyvay! And, Otto, you see dot nothing happens to dem."

"It's just a small Swedish ship. Safe enough. Here we go. Over with you."

The children clamber over the rail, Edward insisting that he is still the captain, and John echoing that he is still the mate. Otto and four of the men go with them. Jonsen and the rest of the crew are huddled out of sight near the opposite rail.

Emily smiles at the Captain. She doesn't like the idea of his going with the crew. She had rather he would stay and tell her a story. But this is business, and the Captain can't neglect it. To please her, however, he does start a story about a famous Parson Audain, a wonderful preacher, even though he had fought thirteen duels—

That is as far as he gets. Quickly he puts down his glasses and gives the crew a sweeping signal with his arm. The next minute he is following the men over the rail.

"You get to sleep and ve vill be back before you know it," Jonsen calls to Emily. He pauses to pat her head as he passes. "You iss a goot leetle keed," he says, and she smiles radiantly.

The men have gone and Emily is alone. For a little she sits smiling contentedly in the warm afternoon sun. Slowly she begins to straighten the bedclothes around her. Now she is humming a little tune, fitting the names of Captain Jonsen and Emily and Otto into it.

Suddenly she stops. She is regarding the situation with a puzzled, bewildered expression. Softly she calls her own name, "Emily Thornton!" over and over, as though to be sure she really is Emily Thornton. She feels her arms, her hands, her shoulders. Wonderingly she orders her hand to scratch her head, and, to her delight the hand does. She laughs—a gay, mocking laugh.

But just as suddenly her mood changes. She is conscious of being alone. The common noises, the wind, the creaking of a board—these sounds frighten her. Softly she calls—"Capt. Jonsen!" Now she hears heavy, plodding footsteps below decks. Her face is terror-stricken. "Capt. Jonsen!" she repeats.

The footsteps continue. They are heavy coming up the stairs and onto the deck. The girl Margaret is standing in the doorway. Emily shrinks from the sight of her. Margaret has changed. She seems dull and sluggish and moves slowly and clumsily. For a moment they stare at each other. Then Margaret begins to speak.

Shall they play fire-engine, Margaret asks. No. Emily's answer is short and frightened. Does Emily still talk to the white mouse with the elastic tail? No.

"Please, Emily, talk to him," pleads Margaret. "Ask him anything. I want to play. Please—Emily—play a game with me."

Emily shakes her head and Margaret starts to whimper. "Go away!" orders Emily. "I can't talk to you."

The noise of someone approaching is heard. Margaret hears it and runs away.

Two sailors come over the rail. They are carrying a Swedish Captain securely bound. He is struggling violently, but making no headway against his bonds. The sailors carry him to an upper part of the deck and lay him away.

"Captain— Make trouble— Leave him here until we finish— All tied up— Make no trouble here—" one sailor explains to Emily. They are back over the rail again without paying any attention to her most frightened protests.

For a moment Emily lies frozen with fear, staring wildly around her. Margaret has come back. "Can I just sit here, Emily?" pleads Margaret, dully. "I can't remember something. I never talk to anybody any more. Remember that time we played alligator? Remember that hurricane? Where was that, Emily? Where was that? I can't remember."

Suddenly the Swedish Captain is moaning. He has maneuvered himself over within sight of them. The girls rivet their eyes on him. Margaret is whimpering. Emily is stiff with fear. The Swedish Captain, a hideous-looking man, with no neck, is edging his way toward them.

As they draw back from him the bound intruder begins to talk to them in Swedish. At first plaintively, then, as they do not understand, fiercely. He keeps gesturing that they should set him free and calling: "Pliss—pliss—!"

Suddenly he sees Jonsen's knife where Emily had dropped it. The girls, following his fascinated gaze, are also staring at the knife. Emily shrinks back in her bed as far as she can. Margaret is squeezed into a corner and is making small animal, whimpering sounds.

The Swedish Captain, impatient with inching forward, has turned over and is starting to roll toward the knife. As he gets close to the knife he says something in Swedish that sounds very brutal. Margaret suddenly lets out a terrified scream—

"He's after the knife! He's going to kill us! He's going to kill us!" she yells.

Emily is staring wildly. Seeing that she is being hemmed in she screams, wildly, hysterically and throws herself off her cot. She is yelling continuously, insanely, as she grabs the knife and holds it poised high above the writhing figure before her—

The curtain falls.

Two or three hours have passed. In the rays of a cold blue

moon the Swedish Captain is lying very still on the deck. Emily is unconscious in her cot. Margaret has slumped down in her corner, staring dully before her.

Presently Jonsen, Otto and several of the crew come hurriedly over the rail. Jonsen's order is to get the crew and the kids on board as quietly and quickly as possible. The Captain has spotted a gunboat on the dim horizon. He is for slipping away in the darkness if he can. He will not stop to take any cargo from the Swedish ship.

Suddenly they have spied the body of the Swedish Captain and go quickly to him, kneeling beside him and lifting his head from the deck—

"My God, look at de blood!" murmurs Jonsen. "He iss dead— He hass been stabbed in a dozen places!"

"But—who—why?—"

Orders are quick and stern now. "Veight him down and put him oferboard. Ofer the stern avay from de gunboat—" orders Jonsen. "And see you don't spill no blood on the rail," he adds, as the men go quickly about the job of being rid of the body.

Julius and José, the sailors who had brought the Swedish Captain aboard, are called up. By now Jonsen's wrath has become terrible. He includes Otto in his menacing look as he demands to know who has done this thing without his orders—

Julius and José gesticulate wildly in their denials. Otto translates for them. They know nothing about the stabbing. Who then? There was no one on board except Emily—and—

The same thought strikes both the Captain and his mate: "Dot Margaret—!"

Slowly their eyes focus on Margaret and the unconscious Emily. They see the knife. "Yah— So many leetle stabs! Dot ain't no man—"

Jonsen has gone to Margaret and is waving the knife in front of her dull eyes—"Vy you do dis ting? Vy you do dis ting? You answer me dot, you Margaret."

Margaret does not answer. She is moaning softly to herself and mumbling: "I'm Margaret—I'm on a boat going to England—I'm Margaret—Mamma—Mamma—the wind—I'm afraid—"

"Maybe he attacked her," Otto suggests.

"He iss bound—! He iss defenseless—! Vot kind of a beast iss dis dot could keel a bound, defenseless man and den sit and watch him die!"

Margaret is still whimpering and moaning to herself. To Otto it is plain that she is out of her mind.

"Yah! No vun in his mind could do such a deed," agrees Jonsen. "Take her avay. I'll not haf such a ting on my deck."

The children have come over the rail, quietly and mysteriously. "Did we kill them all?" Edward and John want to know. They still have to be very quiet, Otto warns them, and sleep below deck. He'll be down to put them to bed.

The gunboat isn't any nearer, but that doesn't convince Jonsen that they may yet slip away.

"No, Otto, dis iss it!" The Captain is a little mournful. "Diss iss de ting I haf known vould come— Ve are doomed, Otto. Vun cannot escape his doom."

"What do you mean?"

"Efen if dis gunboat here does not stop us—vot about dot Svedish sheep? She vill put into some port—and she vill tell how her Captain was kidnaped— Dey vill make a search—a vide, vide search—and dey vill find us, Otto. De ocean ain't so beeg ven you got a guilt like dis! And ven dey say, 'Ver iss de Svedish Captain?'—vot do ve say den? Do ve say, 'None of us men did dis vicked deed. It vas dis leetle girl—dis Margaret— she did it.' Vot jury in any country vould believe dot?"

"We're not guilty! But we had nothing to do with it!"

"Otto, my frien', since ven hass de guilty been de vuns to suffer for der vickedness. Vickedness must be punished—dot iss de law—it does not so much matter ver de punishment falls— It iss a feeling I haf, Otto. Maybe for dis crime ve hang—"

Emily has been moaning in her sleep. When she wakens and is wild-eyed with fear Jonsen takes her in his arms and tries to quiet her. There is nothing for her to fear. She is safe with them. Still frightened, Emily forces herself to look over where the Swedish Captain had lain—

"Don't you tink about dot now, Emily," Jonsen advises, soothingly. "You forget all about dot."

There is something else he would also have her forget. There is a beeg gunboat coming, he tells her, and on the gunboat are cruel men who will be wanting to take them away. Emily is trembling. Will the men on the gunboat be taking them all—or just her and Margaret?

Jonsen is mystified. Why should she say that? Emily doesn't know. Of course they will be taking all of them, Jonsen explains. And Otto adds a word—

"Now, listen, Emily, if the boat out there comes and gets us—they'll ask you a lot of questions— They'll want to know how you got here."

"And, Emily, ve vant you to keep it a secret," says Jonsen, shifting uneasily. "Tell dem—you vas captured by pirates, and den—den dey put you in a leetle boat and pushes you avay—you understand?"

"They put us in a little boat and pushed us away."

"That's right. They set you adrift. And then we came along and took you aboard our schooner, to save you. You understand?"

"You took us aboard your schooner to save us."

"You'll remember to say dot—and keep de udder a secret?"

"Yes, sir."

"And do you think you could make the little ones understand too?"

"Yes, sir."

From across the water comes the boom of a cannon. Jonsen was right. There is no use to try to make a run for it. Let Otto bring the children up so Emily can tell them the story—

"Dey are coming, Emily—and der is vun more ting you can do for me," Jonsen is saying. "You listen to me close, eh, Emily? You know vot happened here tonight vile ve vas gone. Dot Svedish Captain dot vas here!"

At the mention of this Emily has drawn quickly back and is trembling violently.

"Now der iss noting for you to be afraid about, Emily. All I vant iss dot you should nefer say you saw dot Svedish Captain. If anyone should efer ask you if he was brought on board here, you are to say you don't know noting about it! Dot's all, Emily! You nefer saw him. You understand, Emily?"

Slowly Emily repeats the injunction after him. "I—never—saw him—" Then she would know why the cruel men from the gunboat will be taking him away. Because, the Captain explains, they think he has done something terribly wicked—

"What do they do to people when they've done something wicked?" Emily is watching the Captain intently. Her voice is very low. "What would they do to someone who was—*the wickedest person who had ever been born?*"

"Dey vould—ach, I don't know—"

"Would they kill him?"

"Probably—"

"And after they had killed him—would he have to go to hell, too?"

"If he vas very wicked—"

There is another boom of the cannon, much clearer than the first. Emily, startled, throws her arms around Jonsen's neck—

"Don't let them take me! Let me stay with you! I love you! Don't let them take me away! Let me stay with you always! Please! Please! Don't let them take me—"

The curtain falls.

ACT III

We are back on the deck of the gunboat we boarded in the prologue. A guard of Marines has been added. Mr. Mathias is still arguing with Mr. and Mrs. Thornton about his wish to have the children tell in their own way the story of their capture by, and experience with, the pirates. Mr. Thornton has reached the point where he is for having the children brought in and getting it over with. Mrs. Thornton has asked for a little time in which to prepare their minds for the ordeal, and has now gone to fetch them.

"So many people have talked to them in the past three weeks," Mr. Thornton is saying, "I don't think they know the difference between what really happened to them and what people have told them happened. And I still don't see why you need them. You've said you could get a conviction for piracy."

"Ah, yes, but piracy itself ceased to be a hanging offense in 1837. That is why we prefer to use it merely as a make weight along with another more serious charge. . . ."

Mr. Mathias is not at all sure they could prove kidnaping after the conflicting stories that Jonsen has told. . . . "No, we must depend solely on the killing of the Swedish Captain," says Mathias. "If we cannot find someone who saw him, after he was taken from the ship—saw him dead or alive, or wounded or something—we have no case and there is danger these men will escape with their lives. That is why it is imperative that I should examine the children."

Mathias does not propose putting all the children on the stand. He had thought of using Margaret, but Margaret's mind seems to be completely gone. The doctors say she will never regain her memory. So he has decided to use Emily. Thornton can understand this, though he is deeply sorry for Emily.

"Look here, sir," explodes Thornton, as Mathias' questions put him under pressure, "I don't understand children. But sometimes they seem—*too* damned unexplainable—too unnatural—"

MATHIAS—That is Emily, you mean?

THORNTON—Yes. Sometimes Emily—frightens me.—The others I can understand after a fashion. Rachel—has a very comfortable, smooth-working system of life. Everything is black or white. People are good or evil.—Laura, well, of course, Laura is rather an enigma. She's like a tadpole—her legs are growing but her gills haven't dropped off yet— But as for Emily— (*He pauses thoughtfully.*)

MATHIAS—Yes? Go on.

THORNTON—Emily is in a different stage altogether. She's become aware— She's really being born, in a sense. She's not a baby—she's not even a child. Sometimes she's balancing between a child and something else. She's beginning to realize there are other people in the world—and that these other people bear some relation to her— And there's a slyness— (THORNTON *suddenly turns to* MATHIAS.) I tell you, sir—before we left Kingston—her mother did mention the Swedish Captain a few times—easily, of course, not making a point of it—

MATHIAS—Yes?

THORNTON—Well, it was curious. Emily said nothing—we weren't even sure she had heard—except that she seemed to become a little too casual—over-acted a bit—and a short time later she went upstairs and was violently ill.

MATHIAS—In what way?

THORNTON—Nauseous. She retched and retched. I put her to bed and left her. But I stayed outside her door for a moment —and watched her. Suddenly she began to moan and started retching again. I ran in and she threw her arms around me and sobbed out, before she knew what she was saying, "I don't want to grow up. Why can't I always be a little girl?" It suddenly seemed to me as if she was afraid of something—afraid of growing up and facing her own life.

If this is the case, it occurs to Mathias that it might be a good plan to face the children with Capt. Jonsen and Otto, whom they haven't seen since they were taken off the schooner. With that experiment in view he orders one of the Marines to bring the prisoners to the purser's cabin and hold them there until he sends for them.

As the children file in it is noted that they are quite different than when last seen. "Carefully groomed, faultlessly dressed, they look like little ladies and gentlemen." They are also quite ill at ease and nervous.

"Now, darlings, there is nothing to be frightened of," promises Mrs. Thornton, sweetly. "We're all going to have a cozy little chat, just as if we were at home. Just Mr. Mathias and us. Now all of you sit down and relax—"

"Yes, yes, a nice little chat," echoes Mr. Mathias, also sweetly. "And then we will have some tea and cakes." The children are not impressed. Only Emily is watching him keenly. She is quite obviously frightened.

Mr. Mathias starts remembering the children with interest, mistaking John for Edward and discovering that Laura isn't Laura at all, but Abigail—according to Laura. Rachel he is sure of, but discovers, somewhat to his puzzlement that the doll she is holding is just a doll. "I had to leave all my real babies on board the schooner," explains Rachel.

When he gets to Edward there is another surprise. "I'll cut off your ears!" promises Edward, belligerently. "I'll stab out your heart!" As an added greeting Edward is also ready to burn off the Mathias hair, which distresses Mrs. Thornton greatly. "Edward, my darling! Don't!" she cautions. "He hasn't done that in weeks," she explains to Mr. Mathias. "Tear out your tongue!" adds Edward.

With Margaret he gets no place at all and orders that she, poor child, be taken to her cabin. Coming to Emily Mr. Mathias asks kindly about her leg and learns that it is improved.

"Well, now, here we are!" beams Mr. Mathias. "What shall we talk about? Shall we talk about dolls and animals maybe, or shall we talk about boats and oceans and things like that—?"

There is a dead silence. Finally Mrs. Thornton suggests that perhaps the children would like to tell Mr. Mathias about their adventures.

"Oh, yes, about your adventures!" repeats Mathias, brightly. "How stupid of me! I'd like very much to hear about them."

Another silence. "Let me see, now, you started for England on a sailing ship, months ago, didn't you?"

"Barque!" says John.

"I beg your pardon?"

"She was a barque."

"Barque? Oh! I see! The ship! Yes, to be sure! Well, then, what happened?"

There is another pause, with the children shifting about uneasily. "Tell us about the pirates, dear," prompts Mrs. Thornton. And they do. At least Edward does, with illustrations, when it comes to the actual capture.

"Bing! Bang! Bong!" shouts Edward, suiting action to his words.

"Bing-bang!" adds John.

"Bim bam!" puts in Laura.

"Oh, keep still!" orders Mr. Thornton. "Did you see them hit anybody?"

"No."

Mr. Mathias does not get much of any place with the children. When he would know whether or not they were ever chained in the hold, with rats running over them, Edward assures them they certainly were. Rats and more rats, all over the place, insist John, Rachel and Laura.

Finally Emily can take no more. "Oh, do be quiet!" she orders. "There weren't any rats! And we weren't chained in the hold. We weren't chained anywhere."

"Hadn't the pirates ever done anything to frighten them? Hadn't they ever done anything *bad?*" Mr. Mathias inquires significantly.

No one can remember anything bad—except Rachel. She remembers that once Capt. Jonsen talked about drawers. Told them that if they tobogganed about the deck on those they had they couldn't get any others. Rachel doesn't think it was *nice* to talk about drawers.

Mr. Mathias sighs deeply. "Now I want you all to think back just once more. After the pirates came aboard your boat—they locked you all in the deckhouse, is that right?"

"Yes, sir," says Emily.

"And when they let you out—did they take you onto their schooner then?"

"Oh, no, sir! They put us in a little boat and pushed us away."

"But, darling—" Mrs. Thornton is upset.

"They put you in a little boat, Emily?" Mathias prompts.

"Yes, sir. They set us adrift. We drifted and drifted—and then Capt. Jonsen came along and took us aboard his schooner and saved us."

"Then it wasn't Captain Jonsen who took you off the first boat?"

"Oh, no! Those were the wicked pirates! Captain Jonsen saved us from them."

Mathias has walked slowly across the deck and spoken to one of the marines, who promptly disappears. Mathias faces Emily and continues the examination.

"You're not telling us the truth, are you, Emily? The pirates didn't set you adrift in a little boat, did they? Because Captain Jonsen and Otto are the pirates themselves." There is a pause. Emily's eyes have shifted to her lap. Mathias goes on: "So you were never adrift in a little boat, were you, Emily?"

"Yes, sir—"

"Emily—are you telling the truth?"

"Yes, sir—"

"You are lying to us, Emily?"

"No, sir—" Emily, looking down, has begun to sob softly.

The door opens and Jonsen and Otto are brought in. They are pale and tired-looking. The children's greeting is a wild shout: "Capt. Jonsen! Capt. Jonsen!"

Jonsen, looking anxiously about, catches Emily's eye. Her sobs become louder, with tears streaming down her face. She is looking at Jonsen, not knowing what to do.

"Vot you do to her? Vy you make her cry?" Jonsen faces the others angrily.

"That's enough from you!" cautions Mathias, sharply.

"Der—der, Emily— You iss all right. No vun is going to hurt you. Blow your nose."

Emily quiets down and dutifully blows her nose.

Mathias proceeds with his examination. Emily can identify Capt. Jonsen and Otto, can't she? And these are the men who saved them when they were drifting in the little boat—

"Vot iss dot—drifting in a leetle boat? Vot haf you made her say?" Jonsen is furious.

"We have confessed that we took them off the schooner," says Otto.

"Yah, ve haf confessed dot! You know damn well ve haf!"

Emily is visibly trembling as Mathias approaches her. He is smiling but Emily regards him with terror—

"So you see, Emily, you did lie to us! Didn't you? You were never adrift in a little boat. These are the pirates who took you from the *Clorinda* in the first place, aren't they, Emily?"

"Yes, sir."

"Why did you lie to us?"

"She lied to you because we asked her to," interrupts Otto, angrily.

"Yah! Ve made dot story for her to tell you! Ve didn't get

no chance to tell her different."

"Emily—no matter what these men say—no lie is ever a good lie." Mathias has resumed his questioning. "It is sinful to lie. You know that, don't you, Emily?"

"Yes, sir."

There is a change in Mathias' tone. Suddenly he has become more cheerful. He is ready to forget that Emily has lied. Now he knows that Jonsen and Otto are the men with whom the children had spent a long time on the schooner. And that, as they all agree, they (the children) were treated nicely—

"In other words, you like these men, don't you, Emily?"

"Yes, sir. They're darlings."

The Thorntons groan. Otto and Jonsen beam. Mathias goes quickly to a table and takes a book which he holds out suddenly before Emily. Does Emily recognize the Bible? Will she put her hand on the Bible and repeat after him that she will swear to tell the truth, the whole truth, and nothing but the truth? She will. And does. Also she kisses the Bible, and agrees not to tell any more things that are not true.

"Now, Emily—while you were on the schooner with these men —there was a Swedish ship that they captured. Do you remember when they went over onto it?"

At the mention of the ship Emily becomes very frightened. Her eyes search the room for some suggestion of escape. Yes, she remembers the Swedish ship; that Jonsen and Otto went aboard her with the other children; that she (Emily) was left behind because of her hurt leg, and that she stayed on board until Jonsen and Otto came back.

"Now, Emily, a very horrid thing has been suggested," continues Mathias. "It has been said that a man was taken off the Swedish ship, the Captain of it, in fact, and that he was bound and helpless. And some people think he was taken onto the schooner where you were, and that he was murdered there!"

Emily is trembling. Her face has gone white. She is looking around frantically—

"Now what I want you to answer, honestly and loudly so we can all hear—did you see any such thing happen?"

Hemmed in like a hunted animal, Emily leaps to her feet, screaming. Otto and Jonsen and her father and mother start toward her. Her shrieks are doubled. She begins to sob hysterically. Mathias faces her relentlessly, shaking his finger in her face, his words coming clipped and sharp—

"What about that Captain? Did you see him? Was he

brought onto the schooner? Did you see anyone murdered? Did you see him murdered?"

"I never saw him!"

Emily continues to scream. The Thorntons are shouting that the examination should be stopped. The children are crying. Mathias keeps on—

"Blood! Did you see any blood? You've sworn to tell the truth. Did you see anyone murdered? Did you see—"

With a piercing shriek Emily leaps to her feet. She is sobbing hysterically—

"He was lying all in his blood! He was awful! There was blood all over him. He died! He died all bloody." Mr. Thornton has hurried to Emily, but she shrinks from him and runs frantically to Jonsen, shrieking—

"Don't let them take me! Please! Please! They want to kill me! Help me! Help me!"

Emily has fainted in Jonsen's arms. He asks that water be brought. Mr. Thornton has gone to his daughter and is chafing her hands. Mathias turns sharply on Jonsen and Otto. "So there was a body!" he shouts. And they calmly admit the charge.

"But we had nothing to do with it!" Otto insists. "The body was on the schooner when we came back. It was that girl—Margaret—who did it!"

Mathias laughs at the suggestion. How can they expect a jury to believe that a child could have done such a thing?

No, they don't expect a jury to believe it, Capt. Jonsen calmly answers him. That is why they had not told that story.

In her delirium Emily is calling for Capt. Jonsen. The Captain tries to comfort her with promises that nothing is going to hurt her. As she regains her consciousness she sees the guard back of Jonsen. Would that mean that they are going to punish her friends? Well, maybe a leetle, Jonsen admits. But they are not going to do anything to Emily. He is sure of that. Kill her? Why should she think of a thing like that?

"You don't understand, Emily. They don't kill people unless they have—*oh,* done something very, very wicked," explains Mr. Thornton.

"Like Capt. Jonsen and Otto," prompts Mathias, happily.

"Are they going to kill you?" Emily demands anxiously of Capt. Jonsen.

"Vell, you can't tell yet," Jonsen answers, slowly. "You see—vell, dot's the law. You vouldn't understand it but—but dey tink ve killed a man—dot man you saw tied up—and so maybe ve hass to pay for it."

Mathias has one more thing to clear up. When Emily was lying on the deck with her hurt leg they brought the Swedish Captain aboard. He was all tied up. And then what happened?

It takes Emily a moment to gather her thoughts, then she answers Mathias quietly—

"He rolled and rolled. He was getting the knife. He was going to kill me. I got the knife first. And I hit him and hit him and hit him—"

THORNTON—Emily, what are you saying?

EMILY (*sobbing*)—And he died! He died all bloody!

JONSEN—Emily!

OTTO—No!

MATHIAS (*angrily*)—This is preposterous! You know you never touched that knife!

EMILY—Yes, sir.

MATHIAS—It was Capt. Jonsen that had the knife.

EMILY—No, sir.

MATHIAS (*angrily*)—Captain Jonsen told you to say that!

EMILY—No, sir.

JONSEN—No—we didn't tell her to say that.

MATHIAS—Then you made it up—

EMILY—No, sir. No, sir, I didn't.

MATHIAS (*wilting and turning away angrily*)—God help me, I'd rather extract information from the devil himself than from a child.

THORNTON (*watching him*)—What does this do then?

MATHIAS (*wearily*)—Well, perhaps it doesn't matter. It's so obvious that she is lying. We have established that the body was on their schooner. That's enough to convince any jury. (*He becomes happier as he realizes this. He turns to* JONSEN.) You won't get out of this.

JONSEN—No, ve von't get out of it. (*He turns.*) Emily!

EMILY (*looking at him*)—Yes, sir.

JONSEN—No one vill nefer believe vot you haf said, Emily, No vun—nefer— I belief you iss telling de truth! And vot you did, Emily, it vos not your fault. It iss not for you to worry about. Vot you did you had to do—but it iss no sin. Never forget dot, Emily. You iss innocent. (*He looks at the others.*) I am innocent, too, of dis deed. But I am not so innocent like her. So maybe it iss all right, vot happens to me. I haf noticed de tendency in de human race to sin. Alvays dey sin vun vay or anudder. I haff sinned many times. Maybe dis hanging dot I vill haf to have—is the sum total of all the crimes I haf made in de past dot I haf not paid for. Maybe dot is justice. Anyvay ve vill all soon be dead— (*He turns back to* EMILY.) But never you forget, Emily—you iss innocent— (*Pause.*) Good-by, my little Emily. You have a beeg life ahead of you. You iss a good little kid. And remember, don't you worry, Emily. When you grow up you will understand a lot of things you don't now. You will remember what I say, that you iss innocent.

EMILY—Yes, sir.

JONSEN—Sometimes it is easier to understand things when you is grown up.

EMILY—Captain Jonsen!

JONSEN—Yes, Emily?

EMILY—How long does it *take* to grow up?

JONSEN—Not long, Emily— A few years—

EMILY—I wish—I wish it would hurry—

Mathias has motioned to the Marines to take Jonsen and Otto off. As they pass her Emily stops Jonsen and kisses him. He looks miserably at her and turns to go.

THE CURTAIN FALLS

THE PLAYS AND THEIR AUTHORS

"Winged Victory," a drama in two acts, by Moss Hart. Copyright, 1943, by the author. Copyright and published, 1944, by Random House, Inc., New York.

An account of Moss Hart and his works can be found in practically any volume of "The Best Plays," following the 1930-31 edition, when he made his first appearance as a collaborator with George S. Kaufman in the writing of the first Hollywood exposure, "Once in a Lifetime." His first solo appearance was with his highly successful "Lady in the Dark" the season of 1940-41. He accepted the assignment to write "Winged Victory" as a war job, devoted months of flying (which he heartily dislikes) to the collection of his material and was rewarded with the achievement of one of the most sensational stage successes of his or any other dramatist's career. Mr. Hart was born in New York, and was introduced to Broadway as an office boy in the offices of Augustus Pitou.

"The Searching Wind," a drama in three acts by Lillian Hellman. Copyright, 1943, by the author. Copyright and published, 1944, by Random House, Inc., New York.

Lillian Hellman's introduction to the "Best Plays" public was made in the edition of 1934-35 with "The Children's Hour." She followed this first appearance with two others equally successful, the seasons she wrote "The Little Foxes" and "Watch on the Rhine." Her present contribution is made through "The Searching Wind," which lacked but one vote of being accepted by a majority of the New York Drama Critics' Circle as the best play of American authorship produced in New York the season of 1943-44. Miss Hellman is a New Orleans girl, and had a varied literary career previous to her success as a dramatist.

"The Voice of the Turtle," a comedy in three acts by John Van Druten. Copyright, 1943, by the author. Copyright and published, 1944, by Random House, Inc., New York.

John Van Druten is London-born and was a college professor before he took to playwriting (in 1925) with "Young Woodley." He gave up teaching and lecturing pretty quickly after the success of "Young Woodley" in America, and has been a consistent contributor to our better stage fare since then. He has a fondness for small-cast plays, centering story and excitement in a few well-developed characters. "There's Always Juliet," another Van Druten success, had but four characters. "The Voice of the Turtle," getting along with three, was the outstanding comedy hit of its season. "The Distaff Side," "Old Acquaintance" and "The Damask Cheek" have been other popular Van Druten plays.

"Decision," a drama in three acts by Edward Chodorov. Copyright, 1943, by the author.

Edward Chodorov was one of those young enthusiasts who could hardly wait to get through with the dreary business of being educated before finding a job in the theatre. He was a friend of Moss Hart, whose similar ambitions gave them a hope in common. After he (Chodorov) left Brown University, Hart, who had already wormed his way into a Broadway producer's office, helped Chodorov get a job as stage manager for "Abie's Irish Rose." Later he toured South Africa as the director of "Is Zat So," in which Luther Adler and Harry Green were featured. A job as a Hollywood publicity man gave him an idea for a comedy called "Wonder Boy," which was a quick failure. His dramatization of Hugh Walpole's "Kind Lady," however, with Grace George as the star, was an overnight success, though the script had been turned down by a half dozen established Broadway managers. This season Mr. Chodorov had two plays produced, "Those Endearing Young Charms," which missed by a narrow margin, and "Decision," which made its mark. Mr. Chodorov was born in New York. He is a brother of Jerome Chodorov, whose successes include the co-authorship (with Joseph Fields) of "My Sister Eileen" and "Junior Miss." "The Doughgirls," a solo flight, is also his.

"Over 21," a comedy in three acts by Ruth Gordon. Copyright, 1943, by the author. Copyright and published, 1944, by Random House, New York.

Ruth Gordon is one who has taken both her gifts as an actress and her courage as a person in her own two hands and kept steadily marching forward with them. Her first experience as a candidate for stage honors was to be dismissed from the American Academy of Dramatic Arts, following a $400 course of study, as one "who showed little promise as an actress." She had the courage then to go back to the father who had reluctantly advanced the $400 and ask for an additional $50 to help her while she was looking for a job. She got the job playing Nibs in the Maude Adams production of "Peter Pan." That was in 1915. She headed one of the road companies playing "Fair and Warmer" after that and, after several years, came upon the series of hits that carried her through a Booth Tarkington repertory with Gregory Kelly. She scored in "Seventeen" and in "Tweedles," which Tarkington wrote for her. Her Broadway successes have included "Mrs. Partridge Presents," "The Church Mouse," "Ethan Frome," "The Country Wife," "A Doll's House" and "The Three Sisters" in the Cornell revival. Of course her most recent and most solid hit has been playing the lead she wrote for herself in this same "Over 21." This, her first play, is the work friendly gods found for her idle hands to do when she went to Washington a couple of years ago to be with her husband, Garson Kanin, who had an Army assignment to cover. She has done quite a bit of story writing for the magazines. She was born in Wollaston, Mass., which is near Quincy, and she is approaching her thirtieth year as an actress.

"Outrageous Fortune," a comedy in three acts by Rose Franken. Copyright, 1944, by Rose Franken Meloney and William Brown Meloney. Copyright and published, 1944, by Samuel French, New York.

Rose Franken's first success as a dramatist, and her first appearance in these volumes, was as the author of "Another Language," the season of 1931-32. She followed this ten years later with "Claudia," which swept the radioways as well as the stageways of the country. This season she enjoyed a new adventure, which was that of being a co-producer with her husband, William Brown Meloney, of two of her plays, "Outrageous Fortune" and "Doctors Disagree." After their adventure with "Outrageous Fortune," which they took over after Gilbert Miller withdrew his interest in it, they decided to continue the firm of Franken and Meloney as independent play producers, and their schedule already is a fairly heavy one. Miss Franken is a native of Dallas,

Texas, the mother of three children and a homebody at heart. Really likes to cook and keep house.

"Jacobowsky and the Colonel," a comedy in three acts by S. N. Behrman, based on an original play by Franz Werfel. Copyright, 1944, by S. N. Behrman; copyright, 1944, by Franz Werfel.

S. N. Behrman, a consistent contributor to the "Best Plays" series of theatre year books, took over the Franz Werfel comedy called "Jacobowsky and the Colonel" after both Mr. Werfel, whose original work it was, and Clifford Odets, who was called in to make a first adaptation, had failed to satisfy the Theatre Guild directorate with their versions. The result of the Behrman ministrations was the comedy as it ran through the New York season. Consequently "honors are easy" so far as the authorship of this popular refugee comedy are concerned.

The Behrman successes have included "Biography," "End of Summer," "Amphitryon 38" and "Rain from Heaven." He was born in Worcester, Mass., in 1893 and wrote his first play, with Kenyon Nicholson, in 1923. As a boy he had experimented with some success with vaudeville sketches. He studied at Clark, Harvard and Columbia universities and did a bit of book reviewing before he turned to playwriting.

Franz Werfel is a German refugee best known in America for his "Goat Song," produced some years back by the Theatre Guild; his "The Eternal Road," spectacularly staged in New York in 1936 by Norman Bel Geddes, and more recently for his motion picture triumph, "The Song of Bernadette."

"Storm Operation," a drama in prologue, two acts and epilogue. Copyright, 1943, by the author. Copyright and published, 1944, by Anderson House, distributed by Dodd, Mead & Co., New York.

Maxwell Anderson is another dramatist whose work has appeared in these year books practically every season since he began writing for the theatre in 1924-25. Recent contributions have included "Winterset," "High Tor," "The Star Wagon," "Key Largo," "Candle in the Wind" and "The Eve of St. Mark." The son of a preacher, Mr. Anderson was born in Atlantic, Pa. Before taking to the drama he was an editorial writer and before that did a spell of school teaching. His more successful dramas include the verse plays, "Mary of Scotland" and "Elizabeth the Queen."

"Pick-up Girl," a drama in three acts by Elsa Shelley. Copyright, 1943, by the author.

Elsa Shelley was an infant when her parents brought her to America from their native Russia. She was still a schoolgirl when she decided she wanted to be an actress, and not a musician, as her folks had planned. She didn't have sufficient funds to study at one of the high-toned dramatic schools, but she gave a sort of audition for Emanuel Reicher, father of Frank Reicher, and an actor of parts. He agreed to help with her training. She made her first appearance in a small part with Ethel Barrymore in "The Lady of the Camelias." Afterward she was selected to play Juliet to the Romeo of Walter Hampden. A long illness kept her from the stage for months. As her strength returned she took a new interest in the theatre. She tried to help her husband, Irving Kaye Davis, with certain playwriting jobs. It was for him she gathered the material that went into "Pick-up Girl," juvenile delinquency being a subject that had interested her for a long time. "Once I saw a girl go to the dogs with no one to stop her," Miss Shelley told Helen Ormsbee in a *Herald-Tribune* interview. "She was fifteen. Her mother didn't want to be bothered, didn't want to have her own concerns interfered with. So she shut her eyes. It was heartbreaking. I suppose I was thinking of that girl when I wrote my play." During the preparation of "Pick-up Girl" Miss Shelley was a privileged visitor at several Children's Courts. One Judge read her manuscript and reported that he was amazed at the accuracy of the court detail.

"The Innocent Voyage," comedy by Paul Osborn, based on a novel by Richard Hughes called "A High Wind in Jamaica." Copyright, 1929, by Richard Hughes; copyright, 1943, by Paul Osborn.

Paul Osborn's previous appearance in these volumes was made the season of 1937-38, when his "Borrowed Time" was one of the outstanding hits of the year, Dudley Digges being the star of that production. Some years ago Mary Boland helped him to another success, the comedy called "The Vinegar Tree." "Innocent Voyage" he dramatized from "A High Wind in Jamaica" at the suggestion of Dwight Deere Wiman, who was shortly afterward called to London to supervise soldier camp entertainment. The Theatre Guild took over.   Mr. Osborn has his M.A. and B.A. from the University of Michigan, and studied playwriting with George Pierce Baker at Harvard.   He was born in Evansville, Ind., 43 years ago.

PLAYS PRODUCED IN NEW YORK

June 15, 1943—June 13, 1944

(Plays marked with asterisk were still playing June 15, 1944)

THOSE ENDEARING YOUNG CHARMS

(61 performances)

A drama in three acts by Edward Chodorov. Produced by Max Gordon at the Booth Theatre, New York, June 16, 1943.

Cast of characters—

```
Mrs. Brandt.....................................Blanche Sweet
Helen.........................................Virginia Gilmore
Jerry.............................................Dean Harens
Lieut. Hank Trosper............................Zachary Scott
    Act I.—The Brandt Living Room in Apartment on the Upper
West Side of New York.  Acts II and III.—Scene 1—Brandt Liv-
ing Room.  2—Park Avenue Hotel Room.
    Staged by Edward Chodorov; settings by Frederick Fox.
```

Jerry takes his friend, Lieut. Hank Trosper, to call on the Brandts'—Helen and her mother. Lieut. Trosper, a bit of a cynic and of a mind to grab such pleasurable adventure as he may encounter before returning to the war, plays up to Helen, who is quite free to admit his fascination for her. Desperately in love, and stirred by her loyal duty to keep an Army man happy, Helen spends Hank's last two days' leave with him. She is prepared to suffer such consequences as may result. The Lieutenant discovers that he is less hard-boiled than he had imagined and moves heaven and earth to get a marriage license. They are married at the airport.

(Closed August 7, 1943)

EARLY TO BED

(382 performances)

A musical comedy in two acts by George Marion, Jr.; music by Thomas Waller; orchestration by Don Walker. Produced by Richard Kollmar at the Broadhurst Theatre, New York, June 17, 1943.

Cast of characters—

Opal	Ruth Webb
Bartender	Anthony Blair
O'Connor	John Lund
Gardener	David Bethea
Gendarme	Maurice Ellis
Lily Ann	Jeni Le Gon
Mayor	Ralph Bunker
Marcella	Louise Jarvis
Pauline	Choo Choo Johnson
Interlude	Peggy Cordrey
Jessica	Mary Small
Butch	Eleanor Boleyn
Duchess	Helen Bennett
Minerva	Honey Murray
Caddy	Harold Cromer
Madame Rowena	Muriel Angelus
Isabella	Angela Greene
Pooch	Bob Howard
Pablo	George Zoritch
El Magnifico	Richard Kollmar
Lois	Jane Deering
Wilbur	Jimmy Gardiner
Coach	George Baxter
Eileen	Jane Kean
Charlotte	Charlotte Maye
Burt	Burt Harger
Naomi	Evelyn Ward
Charles	Charles Kraft
Junior	Harrison Muller
Admiral Saint-Cassette	Franklyn Fox

Act I.—Scene 1—A Bar in New York City. 2 and 5—Villa of the Angry Pigeon, Martinique. 3—A Corridor. 4—Bedroom of Royal Suite. Act II.—Scene 1—The Bar, New York City. 2—The Corridor. 3 and 5—The Angry Pigeon. 4—Tradesmen's Entrance.

Production supervised by Alfred Bloomingdale; dialogue and dances directed by Robert Alton; music directed by Archie Bleyer; settings by George Jenkins; costumes by Miles White.

Madame Rowena is the proprietress of a bordello in pre-war Martinique called "The Angry Pigeon." For reasons known only to the librettist, all sorts of people are continually mistaking The Angry Pigeon for a girls' school. Among them are El Magnifico, a retired bullfighter who had known Madame Rowena intimately when she was a schoolteacher, and his son Pablo, who is brought in when a night club ingénue runs him down with her car. When the track team of a California University selects The Angry Pigeon Annex as their training quarters, there are complications, mostly musical.

(Closed May 13, 1944)

BOY MEETS GIRL

(15 performances)

A comedy in three acts by Bella and Samuel Spewack. Revived by Lucia Victor's New York Stock Company at the Windsor Theatre, New York, June 22, 1943.

Cast of characters—

Robert Law.....................................Lewis Charles
Larry Tom......................................Norman MacKay
J. Carlyle Benson...............................Joey Faye
Rosetti...Sanford Bickart
Mr. Friday (C.F.).............................Gordon Nelson
Peggy..Theodore Bender
Miss Crews....................................Catherine Linn
Rodney Bevan..................................Marshall Reid
Green..Bert Jeeter
Slade..Maurice Sommers
Susie..Sara Lee Harris
A Nurse..Mabel Taylor
Doctor...John Souther
Young Man.....................................Stanley Phillips
Studio Officer.................................John Souther
Major Thompson................................John Lynds

Act I.—Mr. Friday's Office, Royal Studios, Hollywood. Act II.—
Scene 1—Neighborhood Theatre. 2 and 3—Mr. Friday's Office.
Act III.—Scene 1—Hospital Corridor. 2—In Your Home. 3—Mr.
Friday's Office.

Staged by Rodney Hale; settings by Cirker and Robbins.

"Boy Meets Girl" was produced originally in November, 1935, at the Cort Theatre, New York, and ran for 669 performances. Allyn Joslyn, Joyce Arling and James McColl were the original leads. See "Best Plays of 1935-36," p. 204.

(Closed July 3, 1943)

THE VAGABOND KING

(56 performances)

A musical play in four parts, based on Justin Huntly McCarthy's "If I Were King," by Brian Hooker and Russell Janney; music by Rudolf Friml. Produced by Russell Janney at the Shubert Theatre, New York, June 29, 1943.

Cast of characters—

Rene De Montigny...............................Artells Dickson
Casin Cholet...................................Bert Stanley
Jehan Le Loup..................................George Karle
Margot...Jann Moore
Isabeau..Evelyn Wick
Jehanneton.....................................Rosalind Madison
Huguette Du Hamel.............................Arline Thomson
Guy Tabarie...................................Will H. Philbrick
Tristan L'Hermite.............................Douglas Gilmore
Louis XI.......................................José Ruben
François Villon................................John Brownlee
Katherine De Vaucelles........................Frances McCann
Thibaut D'Aussigny............................Ben Roberts
Captain of Scotch Archers....................Charles Henderson
An Astrologer.................................Franz Bendtsen
Lady Mary.....................................Teri Keane
Noel of Anjou.................................Dan Gallagher
Oliver Le Dain...............................Curtis Cooksey
Herald of Burgundy...........................Earl Ashcroft
The Queen....................................Betty Berry
The Hangman..................................Craig Newton

The Cardinal.................................Vincent Henry
The Two Dice Players......Kenneth Sonnenberg, Birger Hallderson
  Premier Dancers: Julia Harvath, Dorothee Littlefield, Peter Birch.
  Corps de Ballet: Franca Baldwin, Sally Sheppard, Carlye Ramey,
    Patricia Leith, Muriel Breunig, Anna Jacqueline, Ginee Rich-
    ardson, Davide Daniel.
  Ladies of the Ensemble: Ruth Barber, Muriel Blane, Zola Palmer,
    Helen Carlson, Claire Wells, Ann Garland, Betty Berry, Doris
    Blake, Linda Kay, Katrina VanOss, Rosalind Madison, Iris
    Howard, Helen George, Evelyn Wick, Mary David, Shirley
    Conklin, Mary Burns, Bernice Hoffman, Joan Barrie, Mary
    Ellen Bright.
  Gentlemen of the Ensemble: Frederick Langford, Vincent Henry,
    Charles Arnold, Robert Kimberly, Kenneth Sonnenberg, Chris
    Gerard, Earle Ashcoft, Al Bartolet, William Gephart, Jay Pat-
    rick, Birger Halldorson, George Walker, Norvel Campbell, Max
    Plagmann, Ernest Pavano, George Beach, Otto Simetti, Jerry
    Madden, Graham Alexander, Jerry Clayton, Harry Nordin,
    Charles Trott.
  Part I.—The Fir Cone Tavern, Old Paris. Part II.—The Court.
Part III.—The Court Garden. Part IV.—Scene 1—Gate of Old
Paris. 2—The Place de Greve.
  Staged by George Ermoloff; settings and technical direction by
Raymond Sovey; music directed by Joseph Majer; dances directed
by Igor Schwezoff; costumes by James Reynolds.

"The Vagabond King," as adapted from "If I Were King" by
Brian Hooker, who wrote the lyrics, and W. H. Post, who helped
with the book, was originally staged at the Casino Theatre, New
York, September 25, 1925. Russell Janney was the producer,
Dennis King the star, Carolyn Thomson the prima donna. It
ran for 511 performances. See "Best Plays of 1925-26."

(Closed August 14, 1943)

TRY AND GET IT

(8 performances)

A farce comedy in three acts by Sheldon Davis. Produced by
A. H. Woods at the Cort Theatre, New York, August 2, 1943.

Cast of characters—

Mignonette...Hattie Noel
Evelyn La Rue....................................Virginia Smith
Vivienne Gordon.......................................Iris Hall
Thomas Barton....................................Albert Bergh
Sarah Smith......................................Margaret Early
Barry Pickens....................................Donald Murphy
Mickey O'Toole..................................Raymond Rand
Simon Beazle.....................................Charles Knight
Grace Barton.......................................Claire Meade
  Acts I, II and III.—Vivienne Gordon's Apartment in New York
City.
  Staged by Frank Merlin; costumes by Norman Edwards.

Vivienne Gordon has been living with Thomas Barton. When
Barton goes away on a trip and asks her to be nice to an old
friend of his Vivienne agrees, with mental reservations. She will
hire innocent Sarah Smith to represent her with Barton's friend

while she has herself a time with a couple of football players and her pal, Evelyn La Rue. Barton leaves Barry, the handsome son of his old friend, substituting for his father, calls on Sarah and is puzzled but pleased to find her a good girl. Barton is killed in a train wreck. Vivienne collects handsomely from his estate and gives Sarah a bit for her help.

(Closed August 7, 1944)

THE ARMY PLAY-BY-PLAY

(40 performances)

Five one-act prize plays from the Enlisted Men's Contest, sponsored by John Golden in co-operation with Special Service Branch Headquarters, Second Service Command, Lt. Col. William R. Bolton. Presented under supervision of John Golden at the Martin Beck Theatre, New York, August 2, 1943.

WHERE E'ER WE GO
By Pfc. John B. O'Dea, Ft. Lewis, Washington
Directed by Pvt. Paul Tripp
Special Service Specialty: Pvt. Jules Munshin, Camp Upton

FIRST COUSINS
By Cpl. Kurt S. Kasznar
1204 SCSU, 2nd Service Command, New York
Directed by Sgt. Gordon B. Thomson
Special Service Specialty: Pvt. Erasmus D. Russo and Pvt. Vito
Coppola, Camp Upton

BUTTON YOUR LIP
By Pfc. Irving Gaynor Neiman
995 TSS—Unit I—Class 27A, Chicago
Directed by Sgt. Arthur O'Connell

MAIL CALL
By Former Air Cadet, Now Lieutenant, Ralph Nelson
Souther Field, Americus, Ga.
Directed by Pvt. Joseph Ross Hertz
Special Service Specialty: Pvt. Adolph Arnaut, Pvt. Henning Arnaut,
Camp Upton

PACK UP YOUR TROUBLES
By Pfc. Alfred D. Geto
1204 SCSU, 2nd Service Command, New York
Directed by Cpl. Alan Wilson

(Closed September 4, 1943)

* THE TWO MRS. CARROLLS

(370 performances)

A comedy in two acts by Martin Vale. Produced by Robert Reud and Paul Czinner at the Booth Theatre, New York, August 3, 1943.

Cast of characters—

Geoffrey	Victor Jory
Clemence	Michelette Burani
Pennington	Stiano Braggiotti
Sally	Elisabeth Bergner
Mrs. Latham	Margery Maude
Cecily Harden	Irene Worth
Dr. Tuttle	Philip Tonge
Harriet	Vera Allen

Act I.—Living Room of Villa La Vista in the South of France.
Act II.—Scene 1—Living Room.   2—Sally's Bedroom.
Staged by Reginald Denham; settings by Frederick Fox.

Sally is happily married to Geoffrey. Geoffrey is happily married to Sally—until he meets Cecily Harden. Then he thinks perhaps he can get rid of Sally and take on Cecily. Slow poison is Geoffrey's specialty when he decides to be rid of a wife. He had tried it on Harriet, who was the first Mrs. Carroll, but she caught him at it. Hearing what was going on in the second Mrs. Carroll's home the first Mrs. Carroll came to warn her endangered successor. And did. Practically in the nick of time.

THE MERRY WIDOW

(322 performances)

A musical comedy in prologue and three acts by Franz Lehar, Victor Leon and Leo Stein; new musical version by Robert Stolz, book by Sidney Sheldon and Ben Roberts; lyrics by Adrian Ross and Robert Gilbert. Revived by Yolanda Mero-Irion for the New Opera Company at the Majestic Theatre, New York, August 4, 1943.

Cast of characters—

The King	Karl Farkas
Popoff	Melville Cooper
Jolodon	Robert Field
Natalie	Ruth Matteson
Olga Bardini	Etheleyne Holt
General Bardini	Ralph Dumke
Novakovich	Gene Barry
Cascada	Alex Alexander
Khadja	Arnold Spector
Nish	David Wayne
Sonia Sadoya	Marta Eggerth
Prince Danilo	Jan Kiepura
Clo-Clo	Lisette Verea

Lo-Lo..Wana Allison
Frou-Frou..Bobbie Howell
Do-Do..Babs Heath
Premiere Danseuses........................ { Lubow Roudenko
                                            { Milada Mladova
Premier Dancer.....................................Chris Volkoff
Headwaiter...Karl Farkas
   Act I.—The Marsovian Embassy in Paris, 1906. Act II.—Grounds of Sonia's House near Paris. Act III.—Maxim's Restaurant, Paris.
    Staged by Felix Brentano; music directed by Robert Stolz; choreography by George Balanchine; settings by Howard Bay; costumes by Walter Florell.

"The Merry Widow" had its first New York production at the New Amsterdam Theatre October 21, 1907. Ethel Jackson was the Sonia, Donald Brian the Danilo, R. E. Graham the Popoff and Lois Ewell the Natalie. It ran for fifty-two weeks. There was a revival staged in 1909, when Brian had Frances Cameron as his Sonia. In 1921 at the Knickerbocker Theatre, Lydia Lipkowska sang Sonia to the Danilo of Reginald Pasch. In 1929 at the Jolson Theatre Beppe de Vries was the Sonia and Evan Thomas the Danilo. In 1931 the Civic Light Opera Company staged a revival with Donald Brian again the Danilo and Alice McKenzie the Sonia. In 1942 at Carnegie Hall Helen Gleason sang Sonia and Wilbur Evans Danilo.

(Closed May 6, 1944)

RUN, LITTLE CHILLUN

(16 performances)

A Negro folk drama with music by Hall Johnson. Revived by Lew Cooper in association with Meyer Davis and George Jessel at the Hudson Theatre, New York, August 11, 1943.

Cast of characters—

Sister Mattie Fullilove...............................Bessie Guy
Sister Flossie Lou Little............................Bertha Powell
Sister Mahalie Cockletree.............................Rosalie King
Sister Judy Ann Hicks..............................Maggie Carter
Sister Lulu Jane Hunt.............................Eloise Uggams
Sister Susie May Hunt..............................Eva Vaughan
Brother Esau Redd..................................Robert Harvey
Brother Bartholomew Little......................Wardell Saunders
Brother Goliath Simpson ....William O. Davis
Brother Jeremiah Johnson.........................Randall Steplight
Brother George W. Jenkins.........................Elijah Hodges
Ella Jones ....Helen Dowdy
Jeems Jackson......................................Edward Roche
Bessiola...Miriam Burton
Organist...Awilda Frazier
The Rev. Sister Luella Strong..........................Olive Ball
Rev. Jones...Louis Sharp
Jim..Caleb Petersen
"Charlie"..Charles Holland
Sulamai ....Edna Mae Harris

```
Mary Lou Mack.................................Violet McDowell
Elder  Tongola......................................Service  Bell
Brother Moses..................................P. Jay Sidney
Mother Kanda...................................Maude Simmons
Sister Mata .................................. Fredye Marshall
Brother Jo-Ba .................................... Walter Mosby
Mag.........................................Gertrude Saunders
Belle............................................. Viola Anderson
Mame.......................................... Myrtle Anderson
Sue Scott...........................................Lulu B. King
Sexton of the Hope Baptist Church.............Adolph Henderson
Brother Absalom Brown............................Roger Alford
Blind Man.......................................Clarence Harris
"Run, Little Chillun' "—Singer..................Charles Holland
  Scene 1—Parsonage.   2—New Day Pilgrims Meeting Place.   3—
Toomer's Bottom.  4—Hope Baptist Church.
  Staged by Clarence Muse; supervised by Lew Cooper; music di-
rected by Hall Johnson; choreography by Felicia Sorel; settings and
costumes by Perry Watkins.
```

"Run, Little Chillun" was first given in New York at the Lyric Theatre March 1, 1933, and ran for 126 performances. See "Best Plays of 1932-33," p. 471.

(Closed August 26, 1943)

CHAUVE-SOURIS 1943

(12 performances)

A new version in two acts and twenty scenes of a Russian Revue originally assembled by M. Nikita Balieff; English lyrics by Irving Florman; music by Gleb Yellin. Presented by Leon Greanin, by arrangement with Mme. Nikita Balieff at the Royale Theatre, New York, August 12, 1943.

Principals engaged—

Marusia Sava	Simeon Karavaeff
Zinaida Alvers	Michel Michon
Vera Pavlovska	Arcadi Stoyanovsky
Tatiana Pobers	Jack Gansert
Jeanne Soudeikina	Vladimir Lazarev
Dania Krupska	Leo Resnickoff
Georgiana Bannister	Arsen Tarpoff
Norma Slavina	Leo Vlassoff
Georges Doubrovsky	Nicholas Dontzoff
Michael Dalamatoff	George Yurka

Staged by Michel Michon; choreography by Vecheslav Swoboda and Boris Romanoff; comedy director, Michael Dalamatoff; settings and costumes, Serge Soudeikine.

The first "Chauve-Souris" ("The Bat Theatre of Moscow") was organized originally by members of the Moscow Art Theatre for their own diversion. During the first Russian revolution the Chauve-Souris was reorganized in Paris and London by refugees from the Stanislavsky company. It was brought to America in February, 1922; presented by Morris Gest and F. Ray Comstock at the 49th St. Theatre and continued for 520 performances. Nikita Balieff, the original organizer and conferencier, staged a new version in October, 1931. See "Best Plays of 1931-32," p. 413.

(Closed August 21, 1943)

MURDER WITHOUT CRIME

(37 performances)

A drama in three acts by J. Lee Thompson. Produced by John Howell Del Bondia, Tom Weatherly and Bretaigne Windust at the Cort Theatre, New York, August 18, 1943.

Cast of characters—

Stephen..Bretaigne Windust
Grena.. Frances Tannehill
Matthew.. Henry Daniell
Jan..Viola Keats
Acts I, II and III.—Stephen's Flat in Matthew's Home in Mayfair.
Staged by Bretaigne Windust; setting by Raymond Sovey.

Stephen has been carrying on with Grena, right in his own apartment. When he hears that his wife, Jan, with whom he had quarreled, has forgiven him and is coming home, he would send Grena away. Grena doesn't want to go. There is a bit of a struggle with a knife, and Grena is stabbed in the chest. Stephen, in panic, hides the body in the drawer of a decorative ottoman. From below stairs appears Matthew, the landlord, who is a sadist and a student of psychoanalyist Freud. Matthew proceeds to bedevil Stephen into a state of collapse by pretending that he knows all about Grena's murder. About the time Stephen's mind seems likely to crack it is made plain that Grena was not as dead as suspected.

(Closed September 18, 1943)

THE SNARK WAS A BOOJUM

(5 performances)

A comedy in three acts by Owen Davis, based on a novel by Richard Shattuck. Produced by Alex Yokel in association with Jay Faggen at the 48th Street Theatre, New York, September 1, 1943.

Cast of characters—

Rodney Shilly..Frank Lovejoy
Mrs. Wilson Wilson..Catherine Willard
Elwood.. Dickie Van Patten
Millie Smith..Joan Banks

Sidney	Ben Lackland
Sandy Gate	Jane Huszagh
Martin	Mervyn Nelson
Maybelle	Florence MacMichael
Henry	Fleming Ward
Vivian	Phyllis Adams
Ward McKay	Francis Compton
Aunt Adeline	Ann Dere
Daybreak	Harold Waldrige
Doctor Mortice	Frank Wilcox
Rosie	Grania O'Malley

Acts I, II and III.—The Old Shilly Homestead in New England.
Staged by Alexander Kirkland; setting by Frederick Fox; costumes by Michael Paul.

Old Man Shilly, a bit on the eccentric side, left a will decreeing that the first of the Shilly nieces and nephews to produce an heir that should be born in the old Shilly homestead would inherit the bulk of the Shilly estate. This brings three pregnant ladies into the action at a time when the baby race threatens to end in a dead heat. There are eccentric relatives and strange noises tying in with the escape of an inmate of a near-by sanitarium.

(Closed September 4, 1943)

TOBACCO ROAD

(66 performances)

A drama in three acts by Jack Kirkland, based on a novel by Erskine Caldwell. Revived by Jack Kirkland and H. H. Oshrin at the Ritz Theatre, New York, September 4, 1943.

Cast of characters—

Jeeter Lester	John Barton
Dude Lester	Dan Danton
Ada Lester	Sara Perry
Ellie May	Barbara Joyce
Lov Bensey	Kim Spalding
Grandma Lester	Lillian Ardell
Henry Peabody	Fred Sutton
Sister Bessie Rice	Vinnie Phillips
Pearl	Luciel Richards
Captain Tim	Michael King
George Payne	Edwin Walter

Acts I, II and III.—Farm of Jeeter Lester, on a Tobacco Road in the Back Country of Georgia.
Staged by Anthony Brown; settings by Robert Redington Sharpe.

"Tobacco Road," originally produced at the Masque Theatre, New York, in December, 1933, ran until May, 1941, a total of 3,182 performances. It was revived in September, 1942, for an additional 34 performances.

(Closed October 30, 1943)

BLOSSOM TIME

(47 performances)

A musical comedy in three acts adapted by Dorothy Donnelly
from the original of A. M. Willner and H. Reichert; music
adapted and augmented by Sigmund Romberg from melodies of
Franz Schubert and H. Berte. Revived by the Messers. Shubert
at the Ambassador Theatre, New York, September 4, 1943.

Cast of characters—

Franz Schubert	Alexander Gray
Christian Kranz	Doug Leavitt
Baron Schober	Roy Cropper
Scharntoff	Robert Chisholm
Mitzi	Barbara Scully
Fritzi	Adelaide Bishop
Kitzi	Loraine Manners
Bellabruna	Helene Arthur
Flower Girl	Helen Thompson
Mrs. Kranz	Zella Russell
Greta	Jacqueline Susann
Rosie	Helena LeBerthon
Mrs. Coburg	Pamela Dow
Vogel	Roy Barnes
Von Schwindt	George Mitchell
Kuppelweiser	Nord Cornell
Novotny	Harry K. Morton
Domeyer	Walter Johnson
Erkman	George Beach
Binder	John O'Neill
Waitress	Alice Drake
Waiter	Walter Johnson
Prima Ballerina	Monna Montes

Act I.—Domeyer's Restaurant in the Prater in Vienna. 1826.
Act II.—Drawing-Room in the House of Kranz. Act III.—Franz
Schubert's Lodgings.

Staged by J. J. Shubert; choreography by Carthay; music directed
by Pierre de Reeder; settings by Watson Barratt; costumes by Stage
Costumes, Inc.

"Blossom Time" was first sung at the Ambassador Theatre in
New York in September, 1921, continuing for 592 performances.
The original cast included Howard Marsh, Olga Cook, Roy
Cropper and William Danforth. It was revived in 1924, with
Greek Evans and Margaret Merle singing the leads; in 1926 with
Knight MacGregor and Beulah Berson; in 1931 with John
Charles Gilbert and Greta Alpeter; in 1938 with Everett Marshall
and Mary McCoy.

(Closed October 9, 1943)

BLITHE SPIRIT

(32 performances)

A farce in three acts by Noel Coward. Revived by John C.
Wilson at the Morosco Theatre, New York, September 6, 1943.

Cast of characters—

Edith .... Doreen Lang
Ruth .... Peggy Wood
Charles .... Clifton Webb
Dr. Bradman .... Philip Tonge
Mrs. Bradman .... Valerie Cossart
Madame Arcati .... Mildred Natwick
Elvira .... Haila Stoddard
    Acts I, II and III.—Living Room of the Charles Condomines' house in Kent, England.
    Staged by John C. Wilson; setting by Stewart Chaney.

"Blithe Spirit," produced in November, 1941, ran until July, 1942. After a summer rest the engagement was resumed and continued until June, 1943, for a total of 657 performances. A return engagement was begun in September, 1943, preliminary to a road tour.

(Closed October 2, 1943)

LAUGH TIME

(126 performances)

A vaudeville show. Produced by Paul Small and Fred Finklehoffe at the Shubert Theatre, New York, September 8, 1943.

Principals engaged—

Ethel Waters
Bert Wheeler
Warren Jackson
Adriana and Charly
The Bricklayers

Frank Fay
Jerri Vance
Buck and Bubbles
Jane and Adam Di Gatano
Lucienne and Ashour

The third in a series of vaudeville revivals sponsored by Fred Finklehoffe and Paul Small, the others being "Show Time" and "Big Time," all of them originating on the Pacific Coast.

(Closed November 20, 1943)

MY DEAR PUBLIC

(45 performances)

A musical revue in two acts by Irving Caesar and Chuno Gottesfeld; songs by Irving Caesar, Sam Lerner and Gerald Marks. Produced by Irving Caesar at the 46th Street Theatre, New York, September 9, 1943.

Cast of characters—

Walters .... Dave Burns
Tapps .... Georgie Tapps
Jean .... Nanette Fabray
Daphne Drew .... Ethel Shutta
Barney Short .... Willie Howard

```
Renee.............................................Renee Russell
Louise............................................. Louise Fiske
Mitzi............................................. Mitzi Perry
Byron Burns.....................................Eric Brotherson
Lulu.............................................Sherle North
Gordon............................................Gordon Gifford
Playwright.....................................William Nunn
Gus Wagner........................................Jesse White
Kelly..................................... Al Kelly
Rose Brown.......................................Rose Brown
Announcer.......................................Dave Hamilton
Ruth...........................................Janice Wallace
```
      Act I.—Scenes 1, 4 and 6—Backstage. 2—Inside Barney Short's
Office. 3 and 5—Private Room in the Crystal Hill Hospital. Act
II.—Scene 1—Pan American Airport. 2—Barney Short's Office. 3—
Backstage. 4—Jean's Dressing Room. 5—Finale.
      Staged by Edgar MacGregor; dances directed by Felicia Sorel and
Henry Le Tang; music directed by Harry Levant; settings by Albert
Johnson; costumes by Lucinda Ballard.

Barney Short is a zipper magnate. Daphne Drew Short, his
wife, a former actress, would have him back a musical, being
aided in the conspiracy by Byron Burns. The engagement, rehearsal and use of various vaudeville acts provide the entertainment.

(Closed October 16, 1943)

PORGY AND BESS

(24 performances)

An operetta in three acts by DuBose Heyward and George
Gershwin, adapted from the play "Porgy" by DuBose and Dorothy Heyward; lyrics by Mr. Heyward and Ira Gershwin. Revived by Cheryl Crawford in association with John J. Wildberg
at the 44th Street Theatre, New York, September 13, 1943.

Cast of characters—

```
Maria...........................................Georgette Harvey
Lily.............................................Catherine Ayers
Annie............................................ Musa Williams
Clara................................ .........Harriet Jackson
Jake..................................... ....... Edward Matthews
Sportin' Life.........................................Avon Long
Mingo............................................Jerry Laws
Robbins ...........................................Henry Davis
Serena........................................... Alma Hubbard
Jim...........................................William C. Smith
Peter..............................................George Randol
Porgy.............................................Todd Duncan
Crown...........................................Warren Coleman
Bess...........................................Etta Moten
Policeman.......................................Kenneth Konopka
Detective ....................................... Richard Bowler
Undertaker .....................................Coyal McMahon
Lawyer Frazier...................................Charles Welch
Nelson.........................................Charles Colman
Strawberry Woman...............................Catherine Ayers
Crab Man .........................................Edward Tyler
Coroner...........................................Don Darcy
```

Act I.—Scene 1—Catfish Row. 2—Serena's Room. Act II.—
Scenes 1 and 3—Catfish Row. 2—A Palmetto Jungle. 4—Serena's
Room. Act III.—Catfish Row.
    Staged by Robert Ross; chorus directed by Eva Jessye; settings by
Herbert Andrews; costumes by Paul du Pont.

"Porgy and Bess," having its first run under Theatre Guild
auspices in 1935, was revived in January, 1942, and continued
at popular prices until September, 1942, for a total of 286 performances. A return engagement was played in September, 1943,
prior to a road tour.

(Closed October 2, 1943)

A NEW LIFE

(70 performances)

A drama in ten scenes by Elmer Rice. Produced by The
Playwrights' Company at the Royale Theatre, New York, September 15, 1943.

Cast of characters—

Theodore Emery............................Sanford McCauley
Miss Hanson....................................Alice Thomson
Miss Devore......................................Coleen Ward
Miss Murphy....................................Ann Driscoll
Miss Weatherby..................................Sara Peyton
George Sheridan................................Kenneth Tobey
Lillian Sheridan...............................Timmie Hyler
Esther Zuckerman.............................Dorothy Darling
Mollie Kleinberger..............................Dora Weissman
Edith Charles Cleghorne..........................Betty Field
Olive Rapallo...................................Ann Thomas
Gustave Jensen..................................John Ireland
Dr. Lyman Acton...............................Blaine Cordner
Miss Kingsley...............................Frederica Going
Samuel Cleghorne...........................Walter N. Greaza
Isabelle Cleghorne.............................Merle Maddern
Millicent Prince...............................Joan Wetmore
Grover C. Charles..............................Arthur Griffin
Miss Swift......................................Terry Harris
An Anesthetist...............................Elizabeth Dewing
Captain Cleghorne.............................George Lambert
Ruth Emery..................................Helen Kingstead
Miss Woolley...................................Shirley Gale
    Scenes 1, 3, 5, 7 and 9—The Foyer on the Fifth Floor of an East
River Hospital in New York City. Scenes 2, 6, 8 and 10—Edith's
Room. 4—Twilight Zone.
    Staged by Elmer Rice; settings by Howard Bay.

Edith Charles, a radio and night club entertainer, marries
Capt. Robert Cleghorne after a wild fortnight's courtship. The
Captain is ordered into the South Pacific and later reported lost.
When Edith is about to have her baby Capt. Cleghorne's father
and mother, father being a steel magnate of Arizona, come on
to be with her at the birth of their son's child. The day a son
is born to Edith, Capt. Cleghorne arrives home. He had been

marooned on an island. The Cleghornes would then gang up on Edith and take her son back to Arizona to be brought up as they think a child of wealth and social position should be. Edith protests and eventually wins her husband over to her belief in the rights of the individual.

(Closed November 13, 1943)

BRIGHT LIGHTS OF 1944

(4 performances)

A revue in two acts by Norman Anthony and Charles Sherman; additional dialogue by Joseph Erens; lyrics by Mack David; music by Jerry Livingston. Produced by Alexander H. Cohen in association with Martin Poll and Joseph Kipness at the Forrest Theatre, New York, September 16, 1943.

Principals engaged—

James Barton	Frances Williams
Joe Smith	Charles Dale
Jayne Manners	Billie Worth
Jere McMahon	Renee Carroll
John A. Lorenz	Cece Eames
Sollen Burry	Dave Leonard
Don Roberts	Russell Morrison
Elaine Miller	Kathryn Barton
Mimi Lynne	Thomas Gleason
Arthur Barry	John Hamill
Carleton Male	Janet Joy
Betty de Elmo	Darlene Francys
Murnai Pins	Rose Marie Magrill

John Kirby's Orchestra

Staged by Dan Eckley; dances directed by Truly McGee; music directed by Max Meth and Murray Kellner; settings and costumes by Perry Watkins; lighting by Al Alloy.

Smith and Dale, veterans of vaudeville, acting as a couple of waiters in Sardi's Restaurant, a favorite haunt of professional folk in New York, undertake to back a show on Broadway. A varied vaudeville bill results.

(Closed September 18, 1944)

LAND OF FAME

(6 performances)

A drama in three acts by Albert and Mary Bein, based on an original story by Charles Paver and Albert Bein; music by Joseph Wood. Produced by Albert Bein and Frederick Fox at the Belasco Theatre, New York, September 21, 1943.

Cast of characters—

Steve	Kenneth Le Roy
Angela	Beatrice Straight
Sergeant Hauptmann	Richard Basehart
Colonel Reinicke	Hunter Gardner
Kyra Maria	Beatrice de Neergaard
Lieutenant Werner	Stefan Schnabel
General von Obermann	Ed. Begley
Major Kranz	Theo Goetz
Captain Richter	Peter von Zerneck
Sentry	George Dice
Village Elder	Lester Alden
Georgius	Royal Dana Tracy
Thanos	John Buckwalter
John	Harron Gordon
Helen	Naya Grecia
Michael	Jack W. Bittner
Peter Melinas	Norman Rose
Schoolteacher	Charles Kuhn
Wagon-Maker of Mandra	Whitford Kane
Lambros	Karl Weber
Old Villager	Harron Gordon

Act I.—Scene 1—The Shepherd's Stone. 2—German Staff Headquarters in Village of Talom, Greece. 3—A Clearing in the Forest. Act II.—Scenes 1 and 3—Staff Headquarters. 2—At Shepherd's Stone. 4—Guerrilla Camp. Act III.—Scenes 1 and 3—Staff Headquarters. 2—Shepherd's Stone. 1942.

Staged by Albert Bein; supervised by J. B. Daniels; settings by Frederick Fox; costumes by Grace Houston.

Peter Melinas, formerly a lieutenant colonel in the Greek army, turns guerrilla when the Nazis take over his country. Operating with Peter's peasant followers in the hills back of the village of Talom the guerrillas are able to harass and finally to defeat the enemy by employing an old Greek military ruse. Their supporting friends include Angela, Peter's fiancée, and Steve, her shepherd brother, as well as Lieut. Werner, a member of the Gestapo whose heart is with the Greeks. Werner is shot when he would go over bodily, as well as sentimentally, to freedom's side.

(Closed September 25, 1943)

ALL FOR ALL

(85 performances)

A new version of Aaron Hoffman's "Give and Take" in three acts, by Norman Bruce (a collective nom de plume). Produced by A. L. Berman at the Bijou Theatre, New York, September 29, 1943.

Cast of characters—

Marion Kruger	Flora Campbell
John Bauer, Jr.	Lyle Bettger
Albert Kruger	Harry Green
John Bauer, Sr.	Jack Pearl

Daniel Drum..Wyrley Birch
Thomas W. Craig...................................Loring Smith
    Acts I, II and III.—Executive Office of Bauer's K.O. Brand,
Bauerville, California.
    Staged by Harry Green; setting by A. A. Ostrander.

The original "Give and Take" from which "All for All" is taken was produced in New York January 13, 1923. The story has been altered but little. John Bauer, Sr., a successful fruit canner in California, is emotionally and financially upset when his progressive son, John Jr., comes home from college bursting with enthusiasm for the new industrial democracy idea that swept the country after the First World War. Siding with Albert Kruger, foreman of the Bauer plant and leader of the workmen, young John takes over the plant and, with the help of the men, runs it into financial difficulties. The appearance of a demented millionaire with a new selling scheme saves the day for both the Bauers and industrial democracy.

(Closed December 11, 1943)

HAIRPIN HARMONY

(3 performances)

A musical farce in two acts by Harold Orlob. Produced by Harold Orlob at the National Theatre, New York, October 1, 1943.

Cast of characters—

Bill Heller...Lennie Kent
Howard Swift.....................................Carlyle Blackwell
Chet Warren......................................Gil Johnson
Reenie Franton...................................Maureen Cannon
Jackie Stevens....................................Teri Keane
Evelyn..Karen Conrad
Betty...Gay Gaynor
June..Barbara Clawson
Ruth..Doris Clawson
Sue...Dorothy Clawson
Cobalt   }
Looseknit }......................................Smiles & Smiles
Racey Corday......................................Irene Corlett
Rev. Dr. Brown....................................Don Valentine
Buddy Roc..Ving Merlin
Mrs. Warren......................................Margaret Irving
Inspector..David Leonard
State Trooper......................................Clair Kramer
                    Hairpin Harmonettes
    Acts I and II.—Lucy Warren's Home.
    Staged by Dora Maugham; setting by Donald Oenslager; costumes by Mahieu; lighting by Jeanette Hackett; supervised by Mack Hilliard.

Howard Swift is looking for a radio feature to advertise the baby food he manufactures. Bill Heller tries to sell him a girl orchestra. Swift refuses to buy until he discovers that Heller can imitate an infant's voice, which does something to help the sale of the act but nothing for the show.

(Closed October 2, 1943)

*ONE TOUCH OF VENUS

(295 performances)

A musical comedy in two acts by S. J. Perelman and Ogden Nash, suggested by F. Anstey's story, "The Tinted Venus"; lyrics by Ogden Nash; music by Kurt Weill. Produced by Cheryl Crawford in association with John Wildberg at the Imperial Theatre, New York, October 7, 1943.

Cast of characters—

Whitelaw Savory	John Boles
Molly Grant	Paula Laurence
Taxi Black	Teddy Hart
Stanley	Harry Clark
Rodney Hatch	Kenny Baker
Venus	Mary Martin
Mrs. Moats	Florence Dunlap
Store Manager	Sam Bonnell
Bus Starter	Lou Wills, Jr.
Sam	Zachary A. Charles
Mrs. Kramer	Helen Raymond
Gloria Kramer	Ruth Bond
Police Lieutenant	Bert Freed
Rose	Jane Hoffman
Zuvelti	Harold Stone
Dr. Rook	Johnny Stearns
Anatolians	Sam Bonnell, Matthew Farrar
Premier Danseuse	Sono Osato

Singers: Misses Jane Davies, Beatrice Hudson, Rose Marie Elliot, Julie Jefferson, Willa Rollins, Betty Spain. Messrs. Lynn Alden, Arthur Davies, Matthew Farrar, Jeffrey Warren. Dancers: Nelle Fisher, Ruth Harte, Jinx Heffelfinger, Jean Houloose, Ann Hutchinson, Pearl Lang, Allyn Ann McLerie, Lavina Nielsen, Ginee Richardson, Patricia Schaeffer, Kirsten Valbor, Carle Erbele, William Garrett, Ralph Linn, Duncan Nobl, Kevin Smith, William Weber, Lou Wills, Jr. and Parker Wilson.

Act I.—Scene 1—Main Gallery of Whitelaw Savory Foundation of Modern Art. 2—Rodney's Room. 3—Arcade of N.B.C. Building, Radio City. 4—Waiting Room of Mid-City Bus Terminal. 5 and 7—Roof of Museum. 6—Rodney's Barber Shop. Act II.—Scene 1—Savory's Bedroom. 2—The Tombs. 3—A Hotel Room. 4—Main Gallery of Foundation.

Staged by Elia Kazan; dances directed by Agnes de Mille; music directed by Maurice Abravanel; settings by Howard Bay; costumes designed by Paul du Pont, Kermit Love and Mainbocher.

Rodney Hatch, an honest barber by profession, tries the ring he has bought for his fiancée on the finger of a statue of Venus, with arms, recently imported by Whitelaw Savory, an art collector. Venus, like Galatea, comes quickly and charmingly to life and falls in love with her reviver. When his fiancée gets in the way the goddess whistles her down the wind, and complications multiply. A dream motif is the only escape for the barber, who later discovers that there are more Venuses in the world than he had suspected.

ANOTHER LOVE STORY

(104 performances)

A comedy in two acts by Frederick Lonsdale. Produced by Louis Lotito at the Fulton Theatre, New York, October 12, 1943.

Cast of characters—

George Wayne	Roland Young
Mortimer	Henry Mowbray
Elsie Williams Browne	Doris Dalton
Robert Crayle	Richard Barbee
Reginald Williams Browne	Fred Irving Lewis
John Asprey	Arthur Margetson
Michael Foxx	Philip Ober
Molly Asprey	Augusta Dabney
Celia Hale	Fay Baker
Diana Flynn	Margaret Lindsay
Maggie Sykes	Jayne Cotter

Act I.—Living Room in Home of Mrs. Williams Browne. Act II.—Scenes 1 and 3—Mrs. Browne's Living Room. 2—Bedroom. Staged by Frederick Lonsdale; settings by Raymond Sovey.

Diana Flynn, who had lived tempestuously with Michael Foxx, an engaging but irresponsible litterateur, left him following a quarrel. She comes upon Michael again at the home of Mrs. Williams Browne. Michael is now engaged to a wealthy girl, Molly Asprey, and Diana, to save Molly and be even with Michael, arranges a rendezvous in her room in which she hopes to entrap Michael and start a minor scandal. Michael, too smart for Diana, not only eludes the trap but gives Diana a good spanking for luck, thus reviving her great love for him. Between the Michael-Diana scenes George Wayne, a disconsolate banker, seeks to avoid marriage with his boss' daughter and continue happily with his secretary, Maggie Sykes.

(Closed January 8, 1944)

* OTHELLO

(280 performances)

A tragedy by William Shakespeare adapted to two acts and eight scenes by Margaret Webster, with music by Tom Bennett. Revived by the Theatre Guild in association with John Haggott at the Shubert Theatre, New York, October 19, 1943.

Cast of characters—

Roderigo .... Jack Manning
Iago .... José Ferrer
Brabantio .... Averell Harris
Othello .... Paul Robeson
Cassio .... James Monks
Duke .... Robert E. Perry
Lodovico .... Philip Huston
A Messenger .... Henry Barnard
First Senator .... Jack De Shay
Second Senator .... Graham Velsey
Third Senator .... John Ireys
Desdemona .... Uta Hagen
Montano .... William Woodson
First Soldier .... Sam Banham
Second Soldier .... Eugene Stuckmann
Third Soldier .... Bruce Brighton
Emilia .... Margaret Webster
Bianca .... Edith King
Gratiano .... Robert E. Perry

Senators. Soldiers, Servants and Citizens: Martha Falconer, Timothy Lynn Kearse, David Koser, John Gerstad, Jeff Brown, Albert Hachmeister, Ronald Bishop.

Act I.—Scene 1—Street Scene in Venice. 2—The Council Chamber. 3—Seaport in Cyprus. 4—Castle in Cyprus. Act II.—Scene 1—Castle in Cyprus. 2—Room in the Castle. 3—Street in Cyprus. 4—Bedroom in Castle.

Staged by Margaret Webster; settings and lighting by Robert Edmund Jones; music directed by Milan Hartz.

"Othello" has been in the repertory of all first flight American actors. Edwin Booth played the Moor as early as 1866, later alternating the role with that of Iago in co-starring engagements with Lawrence Barrett. Edwin Forrest, E. L. Davenport and John McCullough were prominent Othellos. Louis James played Othello to Frederick Warde's Iago many times; Robert Mantell made the Moor a feature of his repertory. William Faversham made a notable revival of the tragedy in 1914, playing Iago to R. D. McLean's Iago, Pedro de Cordoba's Cassio, Cecilia Loftus' Desdemona and Constance Collier's Emelia. In 1925 Walter Hampden revived the tragedy for 57 Broadway performances, the English actor, Baliol Halloway, being his Iago. Philip Merivale tried Othello in 1935, with Kenneth McKenna as his Iago and Gladys Cooper as Desdemona. Walter Huston's revival in 1937 (following a trial in Central City, Colo., in 1934), had Brian Aherne as Iago and Nan Sunderland as Desdemona.

THE NAKED GENIUS

(36 performances)

A comedy in two acts by Gypsy Rose Lee. Produced by Michael Todd at the Plymouth Theatre, New York, October 21, 1943.

Cast of characters—

Honey Bee Carroll	Joan Blondell
Angela	Pauline Myers
Stuart Tracy	Millard Mitchell
Williams	Byron Russell
Fred-eric	Rex O'Malley
Shop Girls	{ Eleanor Prentiss { Kay Buckley
Alonzo	Marcel Rousseau
Drunk	Anton McQuade
Pansy	Phyllis Povah
Lollie Adams	Bertha Belmore
Alibassi	Georgia Sothern
Sam Hinkle	Lewis Charles
Charles Goodwin	Donald Randolph
Myrtle McGuire	Doro Merande
Mrs. Davis	Frieda Altman
Mrs. Thompson	Emily Ross
Miss Holmes	Edmonia Nolley
Emily	Rosemary Rice
Gladys	Mary Ashworth
Teddy Martin	Gil Maison
Sally Martin	Bernice Maison
First Judge	James Moore
Second Judge	William Torpey
Judge Taylor	John Souther
Mr. Goodwin	Judson Langill
Mrs. Goodwin	Marie Louise Dana
A Moving Man	George Cotton
Life Man	Tom Daly
A. P. Man	Ralph Lewis
State Trooper	Robert Downing
A Man	Ralph Glover

Act I.—Honey Bee Carroll's New York Apartment. Act II.—Honey Bee Carroll's House in the Country.

Staged by George S. Kaufman; settings by Frederick Fox; costumes by Billy Livingston.

Honey Bee Carroll, socially and literarily ambitious, is the reputed author of a ghost-written novel that has considerable success. Furnishing herself a bizarre apartment over a saloon Honey seeks further cultural progress, and has some chance of marrying the son of her publisher. The wedding is extravagantly staged, tickets selling for $5 and the coatroom privilege being let out. At the last minute there is a change in grooms.

(Closed November 20, 1943)

SLIGHTLY MARRIED

(8 performances)

A farce in three acts by Aleen Leslie. Produced by Melville Burke at the Cort Theatre, New York, October 25, 1943.

Cast of characters—

Brian Quin	Leon Ames
Stanley Quin	Scotty Beckett
Audrey Quin	Leona Maricle
Margaret Quin	Patty Pope

```
Terry Jamison.......................................Tom Seidel
Josie Dowling......................................Mona Barrie
Keith Morehouse...................................Jimmie Smith
Lisa Ward........................................Kathryn Keys
Grandma Jamison............................Isabel O'Madigan
Bella...........................................Teddi Sherman
Hortense......................................Kate Harrington
Ambulance Driver................................Bert Horton
```
Acts I, II and III.—Living Room of the Quin Home in Erie, Pennsylvania.
Staged by Melville Burke; setting by Phil Raiguel.

Margaret Quin, aged 17, and Keith Morehouse, 19, have an idea that if they get married they will be doing something to help their country and preserve their own morale. Jimmie is old enough to be in the Army, but not old enough to know that getting married legally demands more than the purchase of a license and the acquiring of a clean bill of health. Shortly Margaret is worried by her condition. The announcement of her pregnancy stirs up other Quins and their friends as well. Audrey Quin, Margaret's mother, thinks she will pretend to have the baby to save the house from scandal, which adds to both the confusion and the complications.

(Closed October 30, 1943)

VICTORY BELLES

(87 performances)

A farce-comedy in three acts by Alice Gerstenberg. Produced by Henry Adrian at the Mansfield Theatre, New York, October 26, 1943.

Cast of characters—

```
Miss Ann Stewart.................................Ellen Merrill
Miss Kathlene Stirling............................Sally Gracie
Miss Mary Breton.................................Marie Gale
Mrs. Grace Stewart.........................Mabel Taliaferro
Geejan.......................................Addison Randall
Mrs. Mildred Stirling............................Jessie Miller
Miss Flo Hilliard..............................Barbara Bennett
Lieutenant James Richardson.....................Ralph Clanton
Private Eric Stanley............................Stanley Phillips
Sergeant Joe Collier............................Walter Appler
Colonel Edward Horton...................Raymond Van Sickle
Donald Bacchus................................Philip Denman
Thomas Richardson..............................Robert Ober
June Winkle................................Margaret Eckman
Mr. Popa.......................................Burton Mallory
Two policemen...............................{ William Paul
                                            { Oscar Miller
```
Acts I, II and III.—Tarrytown, New York.
Staged by Henry Adrian; setting by Edward de Forrest.

Mrs. Grace Stewart, having read that there is certain to be a shortage of husband material after the war, decides to speed the marriage of her daughter, Ann, as much as possible. She organizes week-end parties to which the more promising soldier boys from a near-by camp are her welcome guests. When the scheme appears to be bogging down Mrs. Stewart accepts the advice of a family friend, Flo Hilliard, who knows her way about the Reno divorce courts and is artful in the practice of feminine lures. It is Flo who organizes a corps of Victory Belles to further such assaults as may be necessary.

(Closed January 22, 1944)

MANHATTAN NOCTURNE

(23 performances)

A drama in three acts by Roy Walling. Produced by Walter Drey and George W. Brandt at the Forrest Theatre, New York, October 26, 1943.

Cast of characters—

Eddie Talmo	Dehl Berti
Peter Wade	Eddie Dowling
Ann Stevens	Terry Holmes
Grace Wade	Lorraine MacMartin
Monroe Lessing	Donald Keyes
Gimbel	Tom McElhany
Helen	Julann Caffrey
Dolan	Wendell Corey
Mahoney	John Farrell
Judge Petrie	Howard Smith
Carew	Robert Toms

Acts I and II.—Room in a Hotel. Act III.—Magistrate's Chamber in Felony Court.

Staged by Stella Adler; settings by Parry Watkins.

Peter Wade, a novelist who has lost both the writing touch and a market for his wares, has agreed to the divorce his disappointed mate demands. He rents a room in a hotel that operates as a call house and engages Ann Stevens to serve as his companion in giving the wife and her attorney the evidence they require. It turns out that Ann is herself in a state of mental turmoil, suffering repeated attacks of amnesia and emotional upset. Wade becomes interested in seeing that Ann gets a break with the law when she is arrested as a prostitute. The experience helps him regain a new confidence in himself.

(Closed November 13, 1943)

THE PETRIFIED FOREST

(8 performances)

A drama in two acts by Robert E. Sherwood. Revived by Mary Elizabeth Sherwood at the New Amsterdam Roof, New York, November 1, 1943.

Cast of characters—

Gramp Maple	E. G. Marshall
Boze Hertzingler	William Forester
A Telegraph Linesman	William Marceau
Another Linesman	Frederic Cornell
Jason Maple	Grover Burgess
Gabby Maple	Barbara Joyce
Paula	Charlotte Rogers
Alan Squier	Wendell K. Phillips
Herb	Clark Poth
Mr. Chisholm	Robert J. Lance
Mrs. Chisholm	Natalie Benisch
Joseph	H. Randolph Nash
Jackie	Jack Bittner
Duke Mantee	John McQuaden
Ruby	William Toubin
Pyles	Slim Thompson
Legion Commander	George Spelvin
Another Legionnaire	Fred Spelvin

Acts I and II.—Black Mesa Bar-B-Que Gas Station and Lunch Room in the Arizona Desert.

Staged by David Alexander; setting by Cracraft.

"The Petrified Forest" was first produced at the Broadhurst Theatre, New York, January 1, 1935, with the late Leslie Howard as star and co-producer with Gilbert Miller. Humphrey Bogart and Peggy Conklin were in the cast. It ran for 197 performances. The above revival was made by Mary Elizabeth Sherwood, who had some hope of establishing a popular-priced New York stock company. Alan Squier, disillusioned novelist and intellectual, on his way to the Petrified Forest in Arizona, meets interesting people in the Bar-B-Que lunch room; has a run-in with Duke Mantee, the killer, and his gang, and finds a way to help the heroine of the lunch room, who convinces him she has possibilities, as well as ambitions, beyond her station.

(Closed November 6, 1943)

OUTRAGEOUS FORTUNE

(77 performances)

A drama in three acts by Rose Franken. Produced by William Brown Meloney at the 48th Street Theatre, New York, November 3, 1943.

Cast of characters—

Mrs. Harris	Maria Ouspenskaya
Dr. Andrew Goldsmith	Eduard Franz
Madeleine Harris	Margalo Gillmore
Mary	Mabel Taylor
Bert Harris	Frederic Tozere
Julian Harris	Brent Sargent
Kitty	Adele Longmire
Barry Hamilton	Dean Norton
Crystal Grainger	Elsie Ferguson
Cynthia	Margaret Williams
Gertrude	Margaret Hamilton

Acts I, II and III.—Living Room of the Harris' Shore Home Near New York.

Staged by Rose Franken; setting by Raymond Sovey.

See page 198.

See page 198.

(Closed January 8, 1944)

ARTISTS AND MODELS

(28 performances)

A revue in two acts assembled by Lou Walters; lyrics and music by Dan Shapiro, Milton Lascal and Phil Charig; dialogue by Lou Walters, Don Ross and Frank Luther. Produced by Lou Walters and Don Ross in association with E. M. Loew and Michael Redstone at the Broadway Theatre, New York, November 5, 1943.

Principals engaged—

Jane Froman	Jackie Gleason
Frances Faye	Marty May
Collette Lyons	Billy Newell
Barbara Bannister	Nick Long
Billy Boze	Ben Yost
Carol King	Don Saxon
Mayla	Mildred Law
Gloria Blake	Harold and Lola
Peter Sisters	Worth Sisters
Mary Raye	Naldi
Mullen Twins	Radio Aces

Christiani Troupe

Staged by Lou Walters; dialogue directed by John Kennedy; choreography by Natalie Kamarova and Laurette Jefferson; music directed by Max Meth; costumes by Kathryn Kuhn; settings by Watson Barratt.

(Closed November 27, 1943)

I'LL TAKE THE HIGH ROAD

(7 performances)

A comedy in three acts by Lucille Prumbs. Produced by Clifford Hayman and Milton Berle at the Ritz Theatre, New York, November 9, 1943.

Cast of characters—

Ma Budd	Wanda Lyon
Sam Budd	Len Doyle
Pa Budd	John McGovern
Floyd Budd	Allan Rich
Theresa Packett	Ethel Remey
Judy Budd	Jeanne Cagney
Mrs. Hale	Angela Willard
Beaver	John Bradley
Cissy	Mona Graham
Kewpie	Billy Sands
United Parcel	Lester Lonergan
MacNaughton	Betty Kelley
Western Union	James Elliott
Rafferty	Leslie MacLeod
Keenan	Ben Laughlin
Joe Kindle	Larry Hugo
Ed	Gordon Hammill
Corp. Stuart Charters	Michael Strong
V. Poniakoff	Leo Chalzel
Manager	G. Swayne Gordon

Acts I and III.—The Budd Home, Mansondale, Long Island. Act II.—Scene 1—Budd Home. 2—Stage of Mansondale Theatre.
Staged by Sanford Meisner; settings by Paul Morrison.

Judy Budd is chief telephone operator at the Manson Aircraft Factory. Elected "Miss Average Girl" to represent the workers at a party to celebrate Manson's achievement in war production, Judy remembers that she has overheard a telephone conversation between Manson and an American fascist for whom the FBI is searching. At the party Judy denounces her boss and refuses to go on with the show. With the help of a Clarkgableish movie hero who has joined the Army the fascist is apprehended and the heroine is headed for romance.

(Closed November 13, 1943)

GOODBYE AGAIN

(8 performances)

A comedy in three acts by Allan Scott and George Haight. Revived by Mary Elizabeth Sherwood at the New Amsterdam Roof, New York, November 9, 1943.

Cast of characters—

Anne Rogers	Barbara Coburn
Kenneth Bixby	Jim Boles
Bellboy	Frank Bradley
Maid	Isobel Rose
Julia Wilson	Camelia Campbell
Chauffeur	Jay Westley
Elizabeth Clochessy	David Lewis
Arthur Westlake	David Lewis
Harvey Wilson	Gordon Nelson
Mr. Clayton	John Regan
Theodore	Gerald Matthews

Acts I, II and III.—Double Bedroom in the Hotel Statler, Cleveland.
Staged by Marjorie Maynard; setting by Cracraft.

"Goodbye Again" was first produced December 28, 1932, at the Masque Theatre, New York. Osgood Perkins, Sally Bates and Leslie Adams had the leads. It had a run of 216 performances. This was the second of Miss Sherwood's stock company revivals. The story is of a touring novelist and lecturer, Kenneth Bixby, who suffers somewhat from woman trouble when an old flame in Cleveland attempts to revive their former affair to the distress of the novelist's adoring, and current, secretary.

(Closed November 14, 1943)

WHAT'S UP

(63 performances)

A musical comedy in two acts by Jay Lerner and Arthur Pierson; music by Frederick Loewe. Produced by Mark Warnow at the National Theatre, New York, November 11, 1943.

Cast of characters—

Louise	Sondra Barrett
Margaret	Lynn Gardner
May	Marjorie Beecher
Pamela	Honey Murray
Jennifer	Phyllis Hill
Susan	Pat Marshall
Eleanor	Mitzi Perry
Jayne	Mary Roche
Harriett Spinner	Claire Meade
Doctor	Frank Kreig
Sgt. Willie Klink	Larry Douglas
Captain Robert Lindsay	Rodney McLennan
Sgt. Henry Wagner	Jack Baker
1st Lt. Ed. Anderson	Don Weissmuller
2nd Lt. Murray Bacchus	Robert Bay
Sgt. Moroney	Johnny Morgan
Sgt. Dick Benham	William Tabbert
Virginia Miller	Gloria Warren
Judy	Helen Wenzel
Rawa of Tanglinia	Jimmy Savo
Sgt. Jimmy Stevenson	Kenneth Buffett

Act I.—Scene 1—The Living Room. 2—The Men's Bedroom. 3—The Girls' Bedroom. 4—The Rawa's Bedroom. 5—The Rumpus Room, Laurel House of Miss Langley's School for Girls, Crestville, Va. Act II.—Scene 1—The Boys' and Girls' Rooms. 2 and 4—The Living Room. 3—The Linen Closet.

Staged by George Balanchine and Robert H. Gordon; music directed by Will Irwin; settings by Boris Aronson; costumes by Grace Houston.

The Rawa of Tanglinia, an East Indian potentate become of some importance in the war situation, is being brought to the United States for a conference with the state department by an American Air Force crew. His interpreter, Virginia Miller, accompanies him. The Army plane crashes near Miss Langley's School for Girls in Virginia. The Rawa and crew, taking refuge in the school while awaiting help, are quarantined for eight days following an outbreak of measles. They pass the time singing, dancing and making love, which amuses and intrigues the Rawa.

(Closed January 4, 1944)

THE INNOCENT VOYAGE

(40 performances)

A comedy in three acts by Paul Osborn, from a novel by Richard Hughes. Produced by the Theatre Guild at the Belasco Theatre, New York, November 15, 1943.

Cast of characters—

Captain Marlpole	Ralph Cullinan
Mate of the *Clorinda*	Edgar Kent
Mrs. Thornton	Norah Howard
Mr. Thornton	Guy Spaull
Rachel Thornton	Carolyn Hummel
John Thornton	Dean Stockwell
Emily Thornton	Abby Bonime
Edward Thornton	Guy Stockwell
Laura Thornton	Mary Ellen Glass
Margaret	Lois Wheeler
Captain Jonsen	Oscar Homolka
Otto	Herbert Berghof
Magistrate	Boris Marshalov
Swedish Captain	Arvid Paulson
Mr. Mathias	Clarence Derwent

Clorinda Crew: James Coyle, William Foran, Don Lee, Dan Lounsberry, Philip Sheridan, Norman Scheffer, John Roche.

Dodson Crew: Alcides Briceno, Nick Dennis, Harron Gordon, Bruce Halsey, John O. Hewitt, Orin Jannings, Peter M. Kass.

Act I.—Scenes 1 and 2—Deck of the *Clorinda*, 1860. 3 and 4— Deck of the *John Dodson*. Act II.—Scenes 1, 2, 3 and 4—Deck of the *John Dodson*. Act III.—Deck of British Gunboat.

Staged by Paul Osborn; supervised by Lawrence Langner and Theresa Helburn; settings by Stewart Chaney; costumes by Aline Bernstein.

See page 355.

(Closed December 18, 1943)

LADY, BEHAVE

(23 performances)

A farce in three acts by Alfred L. Golden. Produced by High Bennett at the Cort Theatre, November 16, 1943.

Cast of characters—

George Morton	Jack Sheehan
Roland Talbert	Karl Weber
Louise Morton	Pert Kelton
Margaret Bannington	Lois Dow
Mike Rogers	Thomas Hume
Mrs. Lansing	Madge Skelly

Miss Jones...Norma Winters
Miss Shaw..Carol Stone
Dr. Baker..J. Warren Lyons
Inspector Weiskopf...Dan Niels
    Acts I, II and III.—George Morton's Apartment, New York City.
Staged by Alfred L. Golden; settings by Frederick Fox.

George Morton, a timid eccentric, egged on by an ex-wife, Louise Morton, rents the apartment of a psychoanalyst and poses as the absent consultant. His patients include a variety of erotic defectives. His advice is lowdown and bold. He recovers his confidence and takes back his wife.

(Closed November 23, 1943)

A CONNECTICUT YANKEE

(135 performances)

A musical adaptation of Mark Twain's novel in prologue, epilogue and two acts by Herbert Fields; music by Richard Rodgers, lyrics by Lorenz Hart; orchestrations by Don Walker. Produced by Richard Rodgers at the Martin Beck Theatre, New York, November 17, 1943.

Cast of characters—

IN HARTFORD

Lt. (J.G.) Kenneth Kay, U.S.N......................Robert Byrn
Judge Thurston Merrill.............................John Cherry
Admiral Arthur K. Arthur, U.S.N...............Robert Chisholm
Ensign Gerald Lake, U.S.N.......................Chester Stratton
Ensign Allan Gwynn, U.S.N.......................Jere McMahon
Lt. Martin Barrett, U.S.N...........................Dick Foran
Capt. Lawrence Lake, U.S.N..........................Stuart Casey
Lt. Fay Merrill, W.A.V.E...........................Vivienne Segal
Corp. Alice Courtleigh, W.A.C......................Julie Warren

IN CAMELOT

Sir Kay, The Seneschal............................Robert Byrn
Martin..Dick Foran
The Demoiselle (Sandy)............................Julie Warren
Arthur, King of Britain........................Robert Chisholm
Merlin..John Cherry
Queen Guinevere.............................Katherine Anderson
Sir Launcelot of the Lake..........................Stuart Casey
Sir Galahad.....................................Chester Stratton
Angela..Mimi Berry
Queen Morgan La Fay.............................Vivienne Segal
Sir Gawain.......................................Jere McMahon
Mistress Evelyn La Rondelle.........................Vera-Ellen
    Prologue and Epilogue.—Banquet Hall of Hotel in Hartford, 1943.
Act I.—Scene 1—On the Road to Camelot, 543 A.D. 2—Courtyard of King Arthur's Castle. Act II.—Scene 1—Corridor of Royal Factory. 2—On the Road from Camelot. 3—Palace of Queen Morgan La Fay.
    Staged by John C. Wilson; music directed by George Hirst, dances directed by William Holbrook and Al White; settings by Nat Karson.

"A Connecticut Yankee" was first produced November 3, 1927, at the Vanderbilt Theatre in New York. It was generally jazzed then, and is modestly jived in its rewritten form. Several of the more popular numbers, including "Thou Swell," "My Heart Stood Still" and "I Feel at Home with You," have been retained. To these others have been added, notably one entitled "To Keep My Love Alive." The role of the Yankee, played in 1927 by William Gaxton, has gone to Dick Foran of the films in the revival. The heroine, Queen Morgan La Fay, played originally by Nana Bryant, in the new version was sung by Vivienne Segal. Lorenz Hart, who wrote the lyrics, both for the original and the adapted versions, succumbed to an attack of pneumonia the second week of the revival.

(Closed March 11, 1944)

WINGED VICTORY

(212 performances)

A drama in two acts by Moss Hart; music by Sgt. David Rose. Produced by U. S. Army Air Forces for the benefit of Army Emergency Relief at the 44th Street Theatre, New York, November 20, 1943.

Cast of characters—

Allan Ross	Cpl. Mark Daniels
Frankie Davis	Pvt. Dick Hogan
Danny (Pinky) Scariano	Pvt. Don Taylor
Dorothy Ross	Phyllis Avery
Mrs. Ross	Virginia Hammond
Whitey	Pvt. Red Buttons
Fred Cassidy	Pvt. Bert Hicks
Eddie Borden	Pfc. Kenneth Forbes
Tommy Gregg	Pvt. William Nash
Ronny Meade	Sgt. Kevin McCarthy
Sergeant Casey	Pvt. Elliot Sullivan
Bobby Grills	Pvt. Barry Nelson
Irving Miller	Pfc. Edmond O'Brien
Dave Anderson	Sgt. Rune Hultman
Sergeant Everett	Sgt. Edward Reardon
Major Halper	Pvt. Alan Baxter
Lt. Jules Hudson	Pvt. Whitner Bissell
Captain Elkton	Pvt. Grant Richards
Captain Payne	Cpl. Edward Ashley
Captain Speer	Pvt. Henry Rowland
Lt. Johnson	1st Lt. William Neil
Peter Clark	Pvt. Harry Lewis
Lt. McCarthy	Pvt. Paul Kaye
Henry Larsen	Pvt. John Elliott
A. L. Simpson	Sgt. Gilbert Frye
Ed Slater	Sgt. Frank Kane
Russell Chandler	Cpl. Russell W. Drewes
Gordon Williams	Pvt. Hayes Gordon
Mark Walton	Cpl. Don Richards
Al Black	S/Sgt. Daniel Scholl
Gilbert Paxton	Pvt. John R. Kearney
Bob Chapman	Pvt. Stuart Langley

Jim Gardner...............................Sgt. Robert Willey
Mr. Gardner...............................Pfc. Anthony Ross
Mrs. Gardner..................................Laura Pierpont
Lt. Stevens..............................Pvt. Michael Harvey
Ed Ried..................................Pvt. Kent Morrison
Sally...Mary Lenhardt
Jane...Jean McCoy
Captain McIntyre..........................Cpl. Gary Merrill
Dick Talbert..............................Sgt. David Calvin
Nick Bush..................................Pvt. Cy Perkins
Gordon Cantrell.............................Cpl. Ira Cirker
Mack Hall.............................Pfc. Edward McMahon
Sid Marshall.............................Sgt. David Durston
Ralph Stevens.............................Pvt. James Engler
Leo Nadler..............................Pfc. Donald Hanmer
David Michaelson..........................Pfc. Thomas Dillon
Colonel Gibney.........................Pvt. Phillip Bourneuf
Lt. Thompson............................Sgt. George Reeves
Jerry Ellison..............................Pvt. Walter Reed
Russ Coleman.............................Sgt. Zeke Manners
George Morse..............................Pvt. Ray Merrill
Sid Green..........................Cpl. Jerry Hilliard Adler
Fred Kelly..............................Pfc. Ray McDonald
Lee......................................Sgt. Victor Young
Chaplain...................................Cpl. Fred Cotton
Lt. Reynolds...........................2nd Lt. Gilbert Herman
Colonel Ross............................Pvt. Damian O'Flynn
Lt. Sperry..............................Sgt. Ray Middleton
Lt. Rayburn...........................1st Lt. George Hoffmann
Major Burke............................Pvt. William Marshall
Charles Jordan............................Capt. Raye Bidwell
The Mayor................................Capt. Sidney Bassler
Mr. Grills...............................Sgt. Joseph Meyer
Helen.....................................Elisabeth Fraser
Mrs. Grills.............................Genevieve Frizzell
The Minister............................Pvt. Richard Beach
Barker....................................Pvt. George Petrie
Milhauser.................................Pvt. Alfred Ryder
Adams......................................Pvt. Karl Malden
O'Brien..............................S/Sgt. Peter Lind Hayes
Gleason....................................Pfc. Martin Ritt
Ruth......................................Olive Deering
Radio Announcer...........................Sgt. John Ademy
Glenn Barrows.............................Pvt. Archie Robbins
Paul Conway.............................Pvt. Jack Powell, Jr.
Miguel Lopez...........................S/Sgt. Sascha Brastoff
Sam Preston...............................Pvt. Henry Slate
Harry Preston..............................Pvt. Jack Slate
Colonel Blakely........................2nd Lt. Donald Beddoe
Corporal Regan.............................Pvt. John Tyers
Jack Browning...........................Pvt. Barry Mitchell
Miss Aldridge...............................Mary Cooper
Doctor Baker.............................Pvt. Lee J. Cobb
Milton Benson............................Pvt. Michael Duane

Act I.—Scene 1—Back Porch of Ross Home, Mapleton, Ohio.
2—Barrack Street. 3—Examination Room. 4—Washroom. 5—
Academic Board Meeting Room. 6—Classification Room. 7—Entrance Gates at Classification Center. 8—Hangar. 9—Clearing in
Desert. 10—Parade Ground. Act II.—Scene 1—Grills' Farmhouse
in Oregon. 2—Flying Field. 3—Bedroom in Barracks. 4—Hotel
Room in Oakland. 5—Island in South Pacific. 6—Landing Field.
7—Winged Victory.

Staged by Moss Hart; music directed by Sgt. David Rose; choral
direction by 2nd Lt. Leonard de Paur; settings by Sgt. Harry
Horner; costumes by Sgt. Howard Shoup; lighting by Sgt. Abe
Feder.

Executive Director Army Air Forces Show—Lt. Col. Dudley S.
Dean.

See page 32.

(Closed May 20, 1944)

GET AWAY OLD MAN

(13 performances)

A comedy in three acts by William Saroyan. Produced by George Abbott at the Cort Theatre, New York, November 24, 1943.

Cast of characters—

Patrick Hammer	Edward Begley
Ben Manheim	William Adams
Harry Bird	Richard Widmark
Rose Schornbloom	Hilda Vaughn
Sam	Glenn Anders
Correspondent of the N. Y. *Times*	Edwin Hodge
Martha Harper	Beatrice Pearson
Pianist	Sula Levitch
Bernice Fitch	Joyce Mathews
Messenger	Mason Adams
Doctor	Jerome Thor

Act I.—Office of Patrick Hammer. Acts II and III.—Harry Bird's Office, California.

Staged by George Abbott; settings by John Root.

Harry Bird has been invited to write a screen story for Patrick Hammer, Hollywood tycoon. Harry, convinced that he is the greatest story writer that America has produced, actively resents both the blandishments and the directions of his blustering employer. Harry lives his own eccentric life, on and off the lot; takes up with an inquiring and insistently naive extra girl, who would give anything to get into the movies; pals with a soused cynic, and finally goes home to San Francisco, where he feels his ideas will simmer more productively than they can in Hollywood.

(Closed December 4, 1943)

LOVERS AND FRIENDS

(168 performances)

A romantic drama in prologue, epilogue and three acts by Dodie Smith. Produced by Katharine Cornell and John C. Wilson at the Plymouth Theatre, New York, November 29, 1943.

Cast of characters—

Rodney Boswell	Raymond Massey
Stella	Katharine Cornell
Agnes	Katherine Hynes
Lennie Lorrimer	Carol Goodner
Martha Jones	Anne Burr
Edmund Alexander	Henry Daniell

Prologue.—Regent's Park, London, 1918. Acts I, II and III.—The Boswells' Drawing Room, London, 1930. Epilogue.—Regent's Park, 1942.

Staged by Guthrie McClintic; settings and costumes by Motley.

Rodney Boswell, home on leave from World War I, has a date with an actress friend in Regent's Park, London. The friend does not materialize, but sends Stella, a fellow actress, to explain. Stella and Rodney decide to fill in the date themselves. Romance follows. After they are married Rodney grows restless and stuffy and turns to Martha Jones, secretary of one of his law clients, for a new mental stimulation. Believing himself in love with Martha he asks Stella to divorce him. Stella reluctantly agrees. By degrees she fancies herself again in love with another man. Rodney discovers Martha to be a fraud and returns repentantly to Stella. Stella is seriously considering taking him back at play's end.

(Closed April 22, 1944)

* CARMEN JONES

(231 performances)

A musical play in two acts by Oscar Hammerstein, 2d, based on Meilhac and Halevy's adaptation of Prosper Merimee's "Carmen"; music by Georges Bizet; orchestral arrangements by Robert Russell Bennett. Produced by Billy Rose at the Broadway Theatre, New York, December 2, 1943.

Cast of characters—

Corporal Morrell	Napoleon Reed
Foreman	Robert Clarke
Cindy Lou	Carlotta Franzell or Elton J. Warren
Sergeant Brown	Jack Carr
Joe	Luther Saxon or Napoleon Reed
Carmen	Muriel Smith or Muriel Rahn
Sally	Sibol Cain
T-Bone	Edward Roche
Tough Kid	William Jones
Drummer	Cosy Cole
Bartender	Melvin Howard
Waiter	Edward Christopher
Frankie	June Hawkins
Myrt	Jessica Russell
Rum	Edward Lee Tyler
Dink	Dick Montgomery
Husky Miller	Glenn Bryant
Mr. Higgins	P. Jay Sidney
Miss Higgins	Fredye Marshall
Photographer	Alford Pierre
Card Players	Urylee Leonardos, Ethel White, Sibol Cain
Dancing Girl	Ruth Crumpton
Poncho	William Dillard
Dancing Boxers	Sheldon B. Hoskins, Randolph Sawyer
Bullet Head	Melvin Howard
Referee	Tony Fleming, Jr.

Soldiers: Robert Clarke, William Woolfolk, George Willis, Elijah Hodges.

Act I.—Scene 1—Outside a Parachute Factory near a Southern Town. 2—Near-by Roadside. 3—Billy Pastor's Café. Act II.—

Scene 1—Terrace, Meadowland Country Club, Southside of Chicago.
2—Outside Sport Stadium.
Staged by Hassard Short; libretto directed by Charles Friedman;
choreography by Eugene Loring; choral direction by Robert Shaw;
music directed by Joseph Littau; settings by Howard Bay; costumes
by Raoul Pene duBois.

Carmen Jones is working in a parachute factory in the South.
Joe (Don José) is a corporal M.P. in the soldier guard protecting
the factory. Carmen, getting into a muss through her flirtations,
stabs one of her jealous fellow workers, is arrested and placed
in Joe's charge. She vamps herself out, dates Joe at Billy
Pastor's café and keeps him there by fascinating him with her
swinging hips and sensuous singing. Joe goes AWOL, deserts
Cindy Lou (Micaela) and he and Carmen fly to Chicago, where
Husky Miller (Escamillo) is to fight Poncho, a Latin American
champion. In Chicago Carmen, fascinated by Husky, gives Joe
the brushoff. Joe gets his revenge with a knife, slaying Carmen
and himself.

THE WORLD'S FULL OF GIRLS

(9 performances)

A comedy in three acts by Nunnally Johnson, based on a novel
by Thomas Bell, "Till I Come Back to You." Produced by Jed
Harris at the Royale Theatre, New York, December 6, 1943.

Cast of characters—

Mr. Bridges	Thomas W. Ross
Mrs. Bridges	Eva Condon
Dave	Thomas Hume
Hannah	Julie Stevens
Florrie	Gloria Hallward
Adele	Francis Heflin
Nick	Walter Burke
Edward	Charles Lang
Miley	Berry Kroeger
Sally	Virginia Gilmore
Sergeant Snyder	Harry Bellaver
Mel Fletcher	John Conway
Mrs. Fletcher	Cora Smith

Acts I and II.—Living Room of Bridges Family in Brooklyn.
Act III.—Miley's Room in Greenwich Village.
Staged by Jed Harris; settings by Stewart Chaney.

Miley, who has just been inducted into the Marines, goes back
to Flatbush to say good-by to the Bridges, with whom he had
lived for three years. While he is at the Bridges, who are a mess,
Miley's old girl, Sally, calls and would resume the love dream
she and Miley once enjoyed, but found economically unprom-
ising. Miley thinks maybe it would be all right—after he gets
back. Sally thinks it would be all right now. The night Miley

shuts up his Greenwich Village apartment, preparatory to sailing next day, Sally appears to bid him good-by and stays till morning.

(Closed December 12, 1943)

* THE VOICE OF THE TURTLE

A comedy in three acts by John Van Druten. Produced by Alfred de Liagre, Jr. at the Morosco Theatre, New York, December 8, 1943.

Cast of characters—

Sally Middleton	Margaret Sullavan
Olive Lashbrooke	Audrey Christie
Bill Page	Elliott Nugent

Acts I, II and III.—Apartment in the East Sixties, Near Third Avenue, New York City.

Staged by John Van Druten; setting by Stewart Chaney.

See page 104.

PILLAR TO POST

(31 performances)

A comedy in three acts by Rose Simon Kohn. Produced by Brock Pemberton at the Playhouse, New York, December 10, 1943.

Cast of characters—

Mrs. Bromley	Grace MacTarnahan
Sgt. Jackson	Paul Kirk Giles
Private Corliss	Alfred Porter
Miss Dawson	Jean Mann
Frances Bass	Elaine Perry
Private Pearl Hart	Susana Garnett
Jean Howard	Perry Wilson
"Pudge" Corliss	Lorraine Pressler
Private Dixon	Bob King
Vera Marsh	Judith Cargill
Private Peters	Henry Michaels
Lt. Don Mallory	Carl Gose
Mrs. Harley	Agnes Scott Yost
Hattie Beekman	Margaret Power
Private Curley Hart	Guy Gillette
Alabama	Hamtree Harrington
Capt. Jack Ross	Richard Hart
Col. Michael Otley	Franklyn Fox
Mrs. Kate Otley	Frances Woodbury
Milly Ross	Elsie Hanover
Lt. Thompkins	Lee Parry
Dotty Thompkins	Frances McCabe
Sgt. Tommy Withers	Kip Good
Mrs. Mallory	Suzanne Jackson
Sgt. Jones	William Christal
Cab Driver	Robert Clark

Act I.—Scene 1—USO Housing Bureau, Near a Large Army Camp. 2—Colonial Auto Court. Act II.—Colonial Auto Court. Scenes 1 and 3—Jean's Cabin. 2—The Otleys' Cabin. Act III.—Jean's Cabin.

Staged by Antoinette Perry; settings by John Root.

Jean Howard is in a USO Housing Bureau looking for a place to sleep. There aren't any. Lt. Don Mallory, with a night's leave, offers to drop Jean at an auto court five miles down the road. At the auto court there is but one bungalow left. Jean and Don are mistaken for bride and groom. They meet the Colonel of Don's outfit and are forced to occupy the vacant bungalow. Also forced to accept the embarrassing congratulations of Don's military pals. Don sleeps on the floor with his bed roll. Jean tosses fitfully on the bed. The second night different arrangements are made.

(Closed January 1, 1944)

NEW YORK CITY CENTER OF MUSIC AND DRAMA

Dedicated December 11, 1943, with a concert by the Philharmonic-Symphony Society of New York, under the direction of Artur Rodzinski. Lawrence Tibbett and Bidu Sayao assisting artists.

SUSAN AND GOD

(8 performances)

A drama in three acts by Rachel Crothers. Revived by John Golden at City Center, New York, December 13, 1944.

Cast of characters—

Irene Burroughs	Jeannette C. Chinley
Michael O'Hara	Douglas Gilmore
Leeds	Earl McDonald
Charlotte Marley	Eleanor Audley
Hutchins Stubbs	Francis Compton
Leonora Stubbs	Doris Day
Clyde Rochester	William Weber
Susan Trexel	Gertrude Lawrence
Barrie Trexel	Conrad Nagel
Blossom Trexel	Jean Sampson

Act I.—The Terrace Room in Irene Burroughs' Home in the Country. Act II.—Scene 1—Guest Room. 2—Terrace Room. Act III.—Susan's Sitting Room in Her House.

Staged by Robert Burton; settings by Jo Mielziner.

First produced by John Golden at the Plymouth Theatre, New York, October 7, 1937, and ran for 288 performances.

(Closed December 18, 1943)

THE PATRIOTS

(8 performances)

A drama in a prologue and three acts by Sidney Kingsley.
Revived by Playwrights Company and Rowland Stebbins at City
Center, New York, December 20, 1943.

Cast of characters—

Captain	Matthew Ayres
Thomas Jefferson	Walter Hampden
Patsy	Julie Haydon
Martha	Marie Dow
Jupiter	Ken Renard
James Madison	Ross Matthew
Alexander Hamilton	Guy Sorel
George Washington	Cecil Humphreys
Sergeant	Peter Emery
Colonel Humphreys	John Stephen
Jacob	William C. Tubbs
Ned	Paul Ransom
Mat	Philip White
James Monroe	John P. Boyd
Mrs. Hamilton	Sonya Stokowski
Henry Knox	Joe Byron Totten
Butler	Paul Mosnar
Mr. Fenno	Freeman Hammond
Mrs. Conrad	Leslie Bingham
Frontiersman	John Stephen
Thomas Jefferson Randolph	Allen Martin, Jr.
George Washington Lafayette	Theodore Leavitt

Prologue.—Deck of a Schooner, 1790. Act I.—Scene 1—The Presidential Mansion, New York. 2—Smithy of an Inn on Outskirts of
New York. Act II.—Scene 1—Hamilton's Home, Philadelphia.
2 and 3—Jefferson's Rooms, Philadelphia. Act III.—Scene 1—
Jefferson's Rooms at Conrad's Boarding House, 1801. 2—Interior
of Capitol.

Staged by Shepard Traube; lighting by Moe Hack; costumes by
Rose Bogdanoff and Toni Ward; scenery by William Kellam.

First produced by Playwrights Company and Rowland Stebbins at the National Theatre, New York, January 29, 1943, and
ran for 173 performances. Awarded the New York Drama
Critics' Prize for the season of 1942-43.

(Closed December 25, 1943)

PAUL DRAPER AND LARRY ADLER

Paul Draper and Larry Adler, tap dancer and harmonica virtuoso, with Arthur Ferrente as piano accompanist, presented a
program New Year's Eve, December 31, 1943, and a return engagement February 3, 1944, with four performances closing
February 5, 1944.

OUR TOWN

(24 performances)

A drama in three acts by Thornton Wilder. Revived by Jed Harris at the City Center, New York, January 10, 1944.

Cast of characters—

Stage Manager	Marc Connelly
Dr. Gibbs	Curtis Cooksey
Joe Crowell	Richard Dalton
Howie Newsome	Donald Keyes
Mrs. Gibbs	Evelyn Varden
Mrs. Webb	Ethel Remey
George Gibbs	Montgomery Clift
Rebecca Gibbs	Carolyn Hummel
Wally Webb	Teddy Rose
Emily Webb	Martha Scott
Professor Willard	Arthur Allen
Mr. Webb	Parker Fennelly
Woman in the Balcony	Alice Hill
Man in the Auditorium	John Paul
Lady in the Box	Frederica Going
Simon Stimson	William Swetland
Mrs. Soames	Doro Merande
Constable Warren	Owen Coll
Si Crowell	Roy Robson
Sam Craig	Jay Velie
Joe Stoddard	John Ravold
Mr. Carter	Walter O. Hill

Acts I, II and III.—Grover's Corners, N. H., 1901 to 1913.
Staged by Wesley McKee and Jed Harris.

First produced by Jed Harris at the Henry Miller Theatre, New York, February 4, 1938, and ran for 336 performances. Awarded the Pulitzer Prize for the season of 1937-38. Frank Craven, being held in Hollywood after he had expected to be in New York, his original part of the Stage Manager in this revival was assigned to and ably played by dramatist Marc Connelly, author of "The Green Pastures," "Wisdom Tooth" and many another successful play.

(Closed January 29, 1944)

THE AMERICAN BALLAD SINGERS

(2 performances)

A program of native American music arranged by Elie Siegmeister. Presented at City Center, New York, February 6, 1944.

Principals engaged—

Helen Yorke	Earl Waldo
Ruth Fremont	Dolf Swing
Rebekah Crawford	Lester German

Directed by Elie Siegmeister.

PORGY AND BESS

(First engagement 16 performances.   Return 48.   Total 64.)

An operetta in three acts adapted by DuBose Heyward and George Gershwin from a play by DuBose and Dorothy Heyward; lyrics by Mr. Heyward and Ira Gershwin.   Revived by Cheryl Crawford and John Wildberg at City Center, New York, February 7, 1944.

Cast of characters—

Maria...Georgette Harvey
Lily...Catherine Ayres
Annie...Musa Williams
Clara...Harriett Jackson
Jake..Edward Matthews
Sportin' Life......................................Avon Long
Mingo..Jerry Laws
Robbins..Henry Davis
Serena..Alma Hubbard
Jim..William C. Smith
Peter..George Randol
Porgy..William Franklin
Crown..Warren Coleman
Bess..Etta Moten
Policeman.......................................Kenneth Konopka
Detective..Richard Bowler
Undertaker..Coyal McMahon
Lawyer Frazier....................................Charles Welch
Nelson..Charles Colman
Strawberry Woman..............................Catherine Ayres
Crab Man..Leslie Gray
Coroner..Don Darcy
    Act I.—Scene 1—Catfish Row, Charleston, S. C.   2—Serena's Room.   Act II.—Scenes 1 and 3—Catfish Row.   2—A Palmetto Jungle.   4—Serena's Room.   Act III.—Catfish Row.
    Staged by Robert Ross; choral direction by Eva Jessye; settings by Herbert Andrews; costumes by Paul du Pont.

First produced by Theatre Guild at the Alvin Theatre, October 10, 1935, and ran for 124 performances.

(Closed February 19, 1944; returned February 28 and closed April 8, 1944)

TOSCA

(4 performances)

An opera in three acts by Victorien Sardou, L. Illica and G. Giacosa; music by G. Puccini.   Presented by the City Center Opera Company at City Center, New York, February 21, 23, May 3 and 14, 1944.

Cast of characters—

Floria Tosca.................................Dusolina Giannini
Mario Cavaradossi.................Mario Berini, Norbert Ardelli
Baron Scarpia..............................George Czaplicki
Cesare Angelotti..................Ralph Leonard, Sidor Belarsky
Spoletta.......................................Hubert Norville
A Sacristan......................Stanley Carlson, Emile Renan
Sciarrone.....................................Emanuel Kazaras
Gaoler..Alexander Lorber

Act I.—Interior of Church in Rome. Act II.—Scarpia's Study in the Farnese Palace. Act III.—Citadel of San Angelo, June, 1800. Staged by Hans Wolmut; music directed by Laszlo Halasz.

MARTHA

(6 performances)

An opera in four acts by Friedrich von Flotow, adapted for the American stage by Vicki Baum and Ann Ronell. Presented by the City Center Opera Company at City Center, New York, February 22, 25, 26, 27, May 7 and 13, 1944.

Cast of characters—

Lady Harriet Durham.....Mary Martha Briney, Adelaide Abbot,
                                            Ethel Colt Barrymore
Nancy..............Alice Howland, Suzanne Sten, Martha Lipton
Lionel...Edward Kane
Plunkett ....Robert Brink, Charles Yearsley,
                                     Emile Renan, Hugh Thompson
Lord Tristram........Emile Renan, Hamilton Benz, Stanley Carlson
Sheriff of Richmond............Emanuel Kazaras, Ralph Leonard

Act I.—Scene 1—Royal Gardens Near Richmond, England, 1712. 2—Fair at Richmond. Act II.—Plunkett's Farm. Act III.—Royal Hunting Grounds. Act IV.—Richmond Square. Staged by Hans Wolmut; music directed by Laszlo Halasz and James Sample.

CARMEN

(6 performances)

An opera in four acts by Georges Bizet. Presented by the City Center Opera Company at City Center, New York, February 24, 26, 27, May 1, 9 and 12, 1944.

Cast of characters—

Carmen........................Jennie Tourel, Dusolina Giannini
Don José............................Norbert Ardelli, Mario Berini
Escamillo.......................................George Czaplicki
Micaela.........................Irma Gonzales, Regina Resnik,
                                          Mary Martha Briney
Zuniga..........................Ralph Leonard, Sidor Belarsky
Frasquita.......................Dorothy Benfield, Regina Resnik
Mercedes.......................Rosalind Nadell, Alice Howland
Remendado.......................Hubert Norville, Henry Cordy
Dancairo...Emile Renan
Morales........................Hugh Thompson, Eduardo Rael
Solo Dancers..................Pilar Gomez and Giovanni Rozzino

Act I.—Public Square in Seville. Act II.—Tavern Outside of Seville. Act III.—Ravine in Mountains. Act. IV.—Entrance of Arena. Staged by Laszlo Halasz; music directed by Hans Wolmut.

NEW YORK CITY SYMPHONY

(2 performances)

The New York City Symphony under the direction of Leopold Stokowski presented scenes from "Ivan the Terrible" by Rimsky-Korsakoff; Symphony No. 6 by Shostakovich; "Pacific Prayer" by Dai-Keong Lee; "The Afternoon of a Faun" by Debussy and Wagner's Prelude and Love Death from "Tristan and Isolde" at City Center, March 13 and 14, 1944.

BALLET RUSSE DE MONTE CARLO

(27 performances)

The Ballet Russe de Monte Carlo presented a three week's program at the City Center, New York, April 9 to April 30, 1944.

The repertory included "Les Sylphides," "The Red Poppy," "Gaite Parisienne," "Etude," "Rodeo," "Pas De Deux Classique," "The Cuckolds' Fair," "The Swan Lake," "Ancient Russia," "Le Beau Danube," "Chopin Concerto," "Scheherazade," "Serenade," "The Snow Maiden," "Prince Igor," "Carnaval," "Igrouchki," "The Bluebird" and "The Nutcracker."

Directed by Sergei J. Denham; Regisseur General, Jean Yazvinsky; Executive Assistant, Jean Cerrone.

Principals engaged—

Alexandra Danilova	Igor Youskevitch
Nathalie Krassovcka	Frederick Franklin
Ruthanna Boris	Leon Danielian
Dorothy Etheridge	Alexander Goudovitch
Maria Tallchief	James Starbuck
Tatiana Grantzeva	Alfredo Corvino
Anna Istomina	Grant Mouradoff
Anna Scarpova	Nikita Talin
Vida Brown	Nicolas Magalenes
Tatiana Semenova	Peter Deign
Mary Ellen Moylan	Jean Yasvinsky
Ruth Riekman	Michel Katcharoff
Yvonne Hill	Alan Banks
Yvonne Chouteau	Karl Shook
Nina Popova	Ivanova
Gertrude Svobodina	Serge Ismailoff
Jean Ivanoff	Casimir Kokitch

Directed by Sergei J. Denham; Regisseur General, Jean Yazvinsky.

(Closed April 30, 1944)

LA BOHEME

(3 performances)

An opera in four acts by G. Puccini. Presented by the City Center Opera Company at City Center, New York, May 4, 6 and 11, 1944.

Cast of characters—

Mimi	Irma Gonzalez
Musetta	Natalie Bodanya
Rudolpho	Mario Berini
Marcello	John DeSurra
Schaunard	Emile Renan, Eduardo Rael
Colline	Sidor Belarsky, Ralph Leonard
Benoit ⎱ Alcindoro ⎰	Hamilton Benz

Acts I and IV.—Attic Studio on Montmartre.   Act II.—Café Momus.   Act III.—At the Gate of Paris.

Staged by José Ruben; music directed by Laszlo Halasz; settings by H. A. Condell.

CAVALLERIA RUSTICANA

(3 performances)

A melodrama in one act by G. Targioni and G. Menasci; music by P. Mascagni. Presented by the City Center Opera Company at City Center, May 5, 7 and 14 (matinee), 1944.

Cast of characters—

Santuzza	Regina Resnik, Dusolina Giannini
Turiddu	Edward Kane
Alfio	Francis Row
Lola	Alice Howland
Mamma Lucia	Carol Taussig, Sura Aronovich

Scene—A Sicilian Village.

Staged by Hans Wolmut; music directed by Hans Schwieger.

Followed by

PAGLIACCI

A drama in two acts by R. Leoncavallo.

Cast of characters—

Nedda	Irma Gonzalez, Norina Greco
Canio	Eric Rowton, Norbert Ardelli
Tonio	John DeSurra
Silvio	Eduardo Rael
Beppo	Frank Murray, Henry Cordy

Acts I and II.—A Calabrian Village.

Staged by Hans Wolmut; music directed by Laszlo Halasz.

LA TRAVIATA

(3 performances)

An opera in four acts by Giuseppe Verdi. Presented by the City Center Opera Company at City Center, New York, May 8, 10 and 13, 1944.

Cast of characters—

Violetta Valery..................................Dorothy Kirsten
Alfred Germont...................................John Hamill
George Germont...................................Mack Harrell
Flora Bervoix.....................Ilona Szendy, Marjorie King
Annina..Nina Sanya
Gaston de Letorieres.................Frank Murray, Henry Cordy
Baron Douphol...................................Hamilton Benz
Marquis D'Orgibny...............................Edward Visca
Doctor Grenville...............Alexander Lorber, Ralph Leonard
Solo Dancers..................Pilar Gomez and Giovanni Rozzino
    Act I.—Terrace of Violetta's Mansion, Paris, 1700.   Act II.—
A Villa near Paris.   Act III.—Ballroom in Flora's Mansion.   Act
IV.—Violetta's Bedroom.
    Staged by José Ruben; music directed by Wolfgang Martin.

The New York City Center Opera Company had as its company manager, Richard Highley; orchestra manager, Joseph Fabroni; scenic adviser, Richard Rychterik and technical adviser, Hans Sondheimer.

* THE NEW MOON

(44 performances)

An operetta in two acts by Oscar Hammerstein, 2d, Laurence Schwab and Frank Mandel; music by Sigmund Romberg. Revived by Perry Frank for Belmont Operetta Company at New York City Center, May 17, 1944.

Cast of characters—

Julie...Elizabeth Houston
M. Beaunoir.....................................Laurence Hayes
Captain Duval...................................George Mitchell
Vicomte Ribaud..................................Harold Gordon
Fouchette.......................................Carl Nelson
Robert..Earl Wrightson
Alexander.......................................Johnny Morgan
Besac...Hamilton Benz
Jacques...Frederick Poller
Marianne Beaunoir...............................Dorothy Kirsten
Doorkeeper of Tavern............................William Sutherland
Tavern Proprietor...............................Ludlow White
A Spaniard......................................Peter Hamilton
A Dancer..Zoya Leporsky
Philippe..John Hamill
Clotilde Lombaste...............................Dorothy Ramsey
Emile...Hall Carnegie
Brunet..Vaughn Trinnier
Latouche..Ralph Sassano

```
Gervais..............................................John  Scott
A  Sailor...........................................George  Bruno
Admiral  De  Jean..................................Dick  Todd
```
Act I.—Grand Salon of Monsieur Beaunoir's Mansion in New Orleans and at the Chez Creole. Act II.—Deck of *The New Moon* and on an island.

Staged by José Ruben; choreography by Charles Weidman; settings by Oliver Smith.

FEATHERS IN A GALE

(7 performances)

A comedy in three acts by Pauline Jamerson and Reginald Lawrence. Produced by Arthur Hopkins and Martin Burton at the Music Box, New York, December 21, 1943.

Cast of characters—

```
Matilda  Phinney..............................Louise  Lorimer
Phoebe  Fuller..................................Paula  Trueman
Zeb  Hibbitt....................................John  Hamilton
Lucy  Abner................................Zamah  Cunningham
Annabella  Hallock.............................Peggy  Conklin
Reverend  David  Thatcher......................Harry  Ellerbe
Captain  Seth  Barnabas.......................Norman  MacKay
Felipe.........................................Stuart  Brody
Josiah  Abner................................Richard  Garrick
Town  Clerk........................................John  Robb
Captain  Ebenezer.........................Alexander  Campbell
Abigail............................................Aileen  Poe
Mr.  Otis....................................Cyrus  H.  Staehle
Mr.  Carey...................................Edwin  Cushman
```
Acts I, II and III.—The Great Room of Annabelle Hallock's Home in Sesuit, Cape Cod, June, 1804.

Staged by Arthur Hopkins; setting by Raymond Sovey; costumes by Aline Bernstein.

Annabelle Hallock, Matilda Phinney and Phoebe Fuller are penniless widows in the town of Sesuit, Cape Cod, in 1804. At that time it was the quaint old New England custom to auction off penniless widows to the highest bidder. Annabelle, to escape this indignity, sets her cap for Capt. Barnabas, a rough but likable sea captain. She has some difficulty landing the Captain, but he finally succumbs. Matilda is bought in by the house man for $3, and Phoebe's fortunes are looking up at play's end.

(Closed December 25, 1943)

LISTEN, PROFESSOR!

(29 performances)

A comedy in three acts by Alexander Afinegenov; adapted by Peggy Phillips. Produced by Milton Baron in association with Jean Muir and Toni Ward at the Forrest Theatre, New York, December 22, 1943.

Cast of characters—

Anya...Virginia Farmer
Professor Vassily Okayemov......................Dudley Digges
Masha...Susan Robinson
Leonid Karayev..................................Martin Blaine
Nina Alexandrovna...............................Frances Reid
Victor Tumansky.................................Peter Fernandez
Dr. Pavel Tumansky.............................Alexander Clark
Senya Marshak..................................Michael Dreyfuss
Lyolya Spirina.................................Peggy Allardice
Galya Chikova............................Anne Marie Macauley
Vera..Viola Frayne
    Acts I, II and III.—Home of Prof. Okayemov in Moscow.
    Staged by Sanford Meisner; setting by Howard Bay; costumes by
Lucinda Ballard.

Prof. Okayemov, aging and crotchety, is devoting all his thought to a written work about the seventh century. Suddenly, and without warning, his son's widow, with whom he has disagreed violently, sends her 15-year-old daughter, the old man's granddaughter, to live with him while she tries a second marriage. Masha, the 15-year-old, immediately begins worming her way into the crusty old man's heart. She joins a youth's collective (the locale being Russia) and introduces Grandpa to her associate collectivists. Shortly Grandpa is out of the seventh century and living actively in the 20th. In the end he asks Masha's mother, whose second marriage proves a mistake, to come live with him and Masha.

(Closed January 15, 1944)

DOCTORS DISAGREE

(23 performances)

A drama in three acts by Rose Franken. Produced by William Brown Meloney in association with Buford Armitage and Peter Davis at the Bijou Theatre, New York, December 28, 1943.

Cast of characters—

Celia...Eda Heinemann
Dr. Margaret Ferris............................Barbara O'Neil
Mrs. Deane......................................Dolly Haas
Pete..Jack Willett
Dr. William Lathrop............................Philip Ober
Laura...Ethel Intropidi
Dr. Stanley Bates..............................Judson Laire
Miss Kelly......................................Ann Thomas
Mr. Deane.......................................John Ireland
    Acts I and III.—Apartment and Office of Dr. Margaret Ferris.
    Act II.—Scene 1—The Deane Nursery. 2—Office of Dr. Ferris.
    Staged by Rose Franken; settings by John Root.

Dr. Margaret Ferris feels that she is "scorned as a doctor because she is a woman, and scorned as a woman because she is a doctor." The fellow medic with whom she is in love, Dr. William Lathrop, would have her give up her career for marriage and a home. She had rather live with him without marriage, but he will not agree to that arrangement. Dr. Margaret finally performs a difficult operation upon a neighbor's child, following a disagreement with consulting doctors. The child lives. This gives Dr. Margaret better standing with her male contemporaries and paves the way to her marriage.

(Closed January 15, 1944)

SOUTH PACIFIC

(5 performances)

A drama in three acts by Howard Rigsby and Dorothy Heyward; incidental music by Paul Bowles. Produced by David Lowe at the Cort Theatre, New York, December 29 1943.

Cast of characters—

Sam Johnson	Canada Lee
Captain Dunlap	Wendell K. Phillips
Ruth	Wini Johnson
Daniel	Rudolph Whitaker
Liliboi	Dan Johnson
Dr. John	Louis Sharp
The Luluai	Frank Wilson
Japanese Voice	Kaie Deei
Natives	Gordon Heath, George Fisher, Ruby Dee

Native Children: Ledia Rosa, Gloria Robinson, Emanuel Gillard, James Reason, Clyde Goines

Acts I, II and III.—Government Community House, Small Island in the South Pacific.

Staged by Lee Strasberg; supervised by W. Horace Schmidlapp; setting by Boris Aronson.

Sam Johnson, a Negro seaman, is thrown into the Pacific from the deck of a torpedoed merchant ship. On a raft he and a white United States Army Captain float to a small Jap-controlled island near Bougainville. The natives accept Sam as one of their own. For the first time in his life he is in a position to lord it over his white companion. When the Captain and a loyal native doctor take arms against the Japs, gambling their lives on the wiping out of a gun nest, Sam holds back. He sees no reason why he should fight for freedom. What has freedom ever done for him? The Captain and the doctor are taken and hanged by the Japs. Gradually the natives turn against Sam. His conscience finally spurs him into action. As the invading American forces draw near he takes a gun and goes out to fight for his soul's salvation.

(Closed January 1, 1944)

* OVER 21

(197 performances)

A comedy in three acts by Ruth Gordon. Produced by Max Gordon at the Music Box New York, January 3, 1944.

Cast of characters—

Jan Lupton......................................Beatrice Pearson
Roy Lupton...Tom Seidel
Paula Wharton......................................Ruth Gordon
Max Wharton..................................Harvey Stephens
Robert Drexel Gow...............................Loring Smith
An Elderly Gent....................................Eddie Hodge
Mrs. Armina Gates...............................Jessie Busley
Col. H. C. Foley...............................Carroll Ashburn
Mrs. Foley.......................................Dennie Moore
Joel I. Nixon.......................................Philip Loeb
Miss Manley.....................................Kay Aldridge

Acts I, II and III.—Living Room of 26D, Palmetto Court, Miami, Florida, Summer, 1943.

Staged by George S. Kaufman; setting by Raymond Sovey.

See page 164.

* RAMSHACKLE INN

(192 performances)

A melodramatic farce in three acts by George Batson. Produced by Robert Reud at the Royale Theatre, New York, January 5, 1944.

Cast of characters—

Arbothnot...Mason Curry
Joyce Rogers.......................................Ruth Holden
Patton...Joe Downing
Mame Phillips......................................Ruth Gates
Constable Small.... ....Harlan Briggs
Belinda Pryde..Zasu Pitts
Commodore Lucius Towser.....................Ralph Theadore
Gail Russell.......................................Helen Heigh
Alice Fisher................................Maurine Alexander
Dr. Russell......................................Richard Rober
Bill Phillips......................................William Blees
Mr. Temple...................................Royal Dana Tracy
Mary Temple...............................Mary Barthelmess
Gilhooley...Robert Toms
Fred Porter.......................................John Lorenz

Acts I, II and III.—Interior of Ye Olde Colonial Inn, Not Far from Gloucester.

Staged by Arthur Sircom; setting by Frederick Fox; costumes by Peggy Clark.

Belinda Pryde is a New England schoolteacher who saves her money and revels in motion pictures. When she has $3,000 she buys a ramshackle inn near Gloucester, Mass. It is supposed to be a haunted inn as well, and this intrigues Belinda. What she runs into are several mysterious murders, a couple of FBI agents and a liquor-cutting gang that had as soon shoot her as breathe. Belinda manages to outwit the evil forces with comical tricks and unexpected triumphs and collects the $5,000 reward offered for the gang.

STORM OPERATION

(23 performances)

A drama in prologue, two acts and epilogue by Maxwell Anderson. Produced by The Playwrights Company (Maxwell Anderson, S. N. Behrman, Elmer Rice, Robert E. Sherwood and John F. Wharton), at the Belasco Theatre, New York, January 11, 1944.

Cast of characters—

1st Sgt. Peter Moldau	Myron McCormick
Abe	Joseph Dorn
Winkle	Alan Schneider
Simeon, a Technical Sgt.	Cy Howard
Mart, a Technical Sgt.	Millard Mitchell
Dougie	Michael Ames
Bread Seller	Maurice Doner
The Muezzin	Nehem Simone
Stefano	Carlo Respighi
Lt. Thomasina Grey	Gertrude Musgrove
Lt. Kathryn Byrne	Dorothea Freed
Lt. Dammartin	Walter Kohler
Corp. Ticker	Bertram Tanswell
Capt. Sutton	Bramwell Fletcher
Mabroukha	Sara Anderson
Arab Guide	Maurice Doner
Chuck, a Technical Sgt.	Charles Ellis
Corp. Hermann Geist	Louis Fabien
Squillini	Nick Dennis
Arab Boy	Neil Towner

Arab Women: Marianne Bier, Julie O'Brien, Elizabeth Inglise, Lela Vanti

Prologue and Epilogue.—An Invasion Barge, Somewhere on the Mediterranean. Act I.—In Front of Officer's Tent near Maknassy. Act II.—Scenes 1 and 3—The Tent Now Pitched on a Rocky Desert Hill. 2—The Dry Bed of a Stream in Mountains Above Mazzouna. Staged by Michael Gordon; settings by Howard Bay; lighting by Moe Hack.

See page 277.

See page 277.

(Closed January 29, 1944)

SUDS IN YOUR EYE

(37 performances)

A farcical comedy in three acts by Jack Kirkland, based on a novel by Mary Lasswell. Produced by Katharine Brown and J. H. Del Bondio at the Cort Theatre, New York, January 12, 1944.

Cast of characters—

Chinatown................Chueck Ming Chin, Fredric Munn Szeto
1st Buyer.......................................Russell Morrison
Mrs. Feeley..Jane Darwell
Mr. Fitzgerald.......................................John Adair
Miss Tinkham..................................Brenda Forbes
Shipyard Worker....................................Bruno Wick
Conchita...Ruth Gilbert
Mr. Reynolds..Tom Hoier
Mrs. Rasmussen...............................Kasia Orgazewski
Mrs. Rasmussen's Daughter.....................Wanda Sponder
Elmer..John Gerard
Kate Logan...Janet Tyler
Mrs. Ferguson...............................Lujah Fonnesbeck
Mr. Wilson.......................................Robert Rhodes
Mrs. Katz...Marie Kenney
Mac...Kenneth Tobey
Mrs. Miller.....................................Cynthia Latham
Danny Feeley..Will Hare
Policeman...Bert James
Armond Hansen...............................Frank Tweddell
Pinky Kennedy................................Tom McElhany
Moe...Loy Nilson
June..Helene Young

Acts I, II and III.—Mrs. Feeley's Junk Yard, San Diego, California.

Staged by Jack Kirkland; setting by Joseph B. Platt; costumes by Kermit Love.

Mrs. Feeley has inherited a junk yard in San Diego, California, from her husband. Miss Tinkham, a spinster music teacher, and Mrs. Rasmussen, an elderly neighbor, come to live with her at her invitation. The three of them have a time of it dodging the tax collector, while they fix up the romance of a sailor nephew and an attractive ingénue who teaches Spanish between scenes. The three old pals depend a good deal on beer for their inspirations and their humor.

(Closed February 12, 1944)

JACKPOT

(69 performances)

A musical comedy in two acts by Guy Bolton, Sidney Sheldon and Ben Roberts; music and lyrics by Howard Dietz and Vernon Duke. Produced by Vinton Freedley at the Alvin Theatre, New York, January 13, 1944.

Cast of characters—

Peggy...Althea Elder
Billie..Billie Worth
Mr. Dill......................................Morton L. Stevens
Bill Bender.......................................Ben Lackland
Nancy Parker....................................Mary Wickes
Sally Madison.....................................Nanette Fabray
Dexter De Wolf................................Houston Richards
Edna..Jacqueline Susann
Hedy...Helena Goudvis

```
Hawley.............................................John  Kearny
Assistant  Bartender.............................Walter  Monroe
Jerry  Finch.......................................Jerry  Lester
Winkie  Cotter....................................Benny  Baker
Hank Trimble....................................Allan  Jones
Girl...............................................Flower  Hujer
Reporter............................................Bill  Jones
Tot  Patterson...................................Althea  Elder
Sgt.  Naylor.....................................Wendell  Corey
Sgt.  Maguire...................................Betty  Garrett
Helen  Westcott............................Frances  Robinson
Sniper.............................................Bob  Beam
1st  Marine......................................John  Hamil
2nd  Marine.......................................Bill  Jones
Edith.............................................Edith  Turgell
Accordionist...................................Eva  Barcinska
Monica.........................................Drucilla  Strain
Pat................................................Pat  Ogden
Betty.............................................Betty  Stuart
Sherry.......................................Sherry  Shadburne
Mary Lou.................................Marie  Louise  Meade
Connie.........................................Connie  Constant
Nurse............................................Billie  Worth
```

Act I.—Scene 1—Assembly Room of Duff and Dill Engine Corporation. 2—Hawley's Bar. 3—Broadcasting Studio. 4 and 6—Recreation Room, Priscilla Room, Turtle Beach, S. C. 5—A Cornfield. Act II.—Scenes 1 and 4—Garden of Priscilla Manor. 2—Bedroom of the Bridal Suite. 3—The Balcony.

Staged by Roy Hargrave; dances by Lauretta Jefferson; ballet directed by Charles Weidman; music directed by Max Meth; settings by Raymond Sovey and Robert Edmond Jones; costumes by Kiviette.

Sally Madison permits herself to be put up as the first prize in a bond-selling rally. Three Marines win her, and there is a lot of talk about the division that should, but can't reasonably, be made of the fair prize. It is Hank Trimble who wins in the end—he being the handsomest man and the best singer of the three.

(Closed March 11, 1944)

THE DUKE IN DARKNESS

(24 performances)

A drama in three acts by Patrick Hamilton. Produced by Alexander H. Cohen and Joseph Kipness at the Playhouse, New York, January 24, 1944.

Cast of characters—

```
Gribaud.........................................Edgar  Stehli
The Duke of Laterraine.........................Philip  Merivale
Voulain.........................................Raymond  Burr
Chauvet........................................Horace  Cooper
Marteau.......................................Wells  Richardson
The Duke of Lamorre............................Louis  Hector
The Count D'Aublaye...........................Albert  Carroll
Guards..........Dorman Leonard, Ralph Douglas, Joseph Vernay
```

Acts I, II and III.—Room in Château Lamorre, France, About 1580.

Staged by Robert Henderson; setting and costumes by Stewart Chaney.

About 1580, in France the Duke of Laterraine was imprisoned in the Château Lamorre for fifteen years by his ancient enemy, the Duke of Lamorre. For five years Laterraine pretended to be stone blind, hoping thus to effect his release. Imprisoned with Laterraine was his one-time valet Gribaud who became his good friend. As help was about to be given the prisoners Gribaud lost his mind and had to be sacrificed by being thrown over the wall. The escape plot succeeded and the good Duke was free to rejoin his people and again take arms against their enemies.

(Closed February 12, 1944)

THE CHERRY ORCHARD

(96 performances)

A comedy in four acts by Anton Chekhov; translated by Irina Skariatina. Revived by Carly Wharton and Margaret Webster at the National Theatre, New York, January 25, 1944.

Cast of characters—

Lopahin (Yermolay Alexeyevitch)................Stefan Schnabel
Dunyasha.......................................Virginia Campbell
Epihodov...Rex O'Malley
Firs...A. G. Andrews
Anya...Lois Hall
Varya...Katherine Emery
Lyubov Andreyevna.............................Eva Le Gallienne
Leonid Andreyevitch.......................Joseph Schildkraut
Charlotta Ivanovna.............................Leona Roberts
Semyomov-Pistchik........................Carl Benton Reid
Yasha...Stanley Phillips
Petya Trofimov...................................Eduard Franz
A Tramp...Bruce Adams
The Station Master...............................Michael Gray
A Post-Office Clerk................................Jack Lynds
Servants and Guests................Lois Holmes, Beatrice Manley,
                                    Annette Sorell, H. Etienne

Acts I and IV.—A Room in the House. The Old Nursery. Act II.—The Open Country. Act III.—The Living Room. Estate of Lyubov Andreyevna.

Staged by Eva Le Gallienne and Margaret Webster; settings by Motley.

The last previous revival of the Chekhov classic was made by Miss Le Gallienne in 1933. Produced in Russia in 1904, and played over 400 times in the repertory of the Moscow Art Theatre, the play was given in New York in 1923, during the first tour of the Moscow Art Theatre Company, with Constantin Stanislavsky, Olga Knipper-Tchekova and Vassily Katchaloff playing the leads. Miss Le Gallienne included "The Cherry Orchard" in the repertory of the Civic Repertory Theatre in 1928, with Alla Nazimova in the cast.

(Closed April 15, 1944)

* WALLFLOWER

(168 performances)

A comedy in three acts by Mary Orr and Reginald Denham. Produced by Meyer Davis at the Cort Theatre, New York, January 26, 1944.

Cast of characters—

Jessamine Linnet	Kathryn Givney
Brigitte	Vilma Kurer
Warren James	Joel Marston
Mrs. Hennicut	Ann Dere
Andrew Linnet	Walter N. Greaza
Joy Linnet	Sunnie O'Dea
Jackie Linnet	Mary Rolfe
Bruce	James McMahon
Chet	Michael King
Wardwell James	Fred I. Lewis
Dixie James	Leona Powers
Jasper	Kurt Richards
Bobbie	Charles Laffin
Ruth Hennicutt	Mary Orr
Larry Oakleaf	Frank McNellis

Acts I, II and III.—Rumpus Room in the Linnet Home, Ironville, Ohio.

Staged by Reginald Denham; setting by Samuel Leve; costumes by Bianca Stroock.

Joy Linnet is the blonde beauty of the family and the one who gets all the dates. Her sister Jackie is her brunette foil who must be content to sit back and take what falls into her lap. Comes the night that Joy imperiously refuses the proposal of young Warren James. Warren thereupon drinks a lot of liquor and suggests a ride in the moonlight to Jackie who has long been in love with him. The ride winds up at a roadhouse where Warren and Jackie are caught in a raid. Scandal threatens. It could have been pretty serious if the elopers had not been able to show a marriage certificate signed by a Massachusetts Justice of the Peace.

* MEXICAN HAYRIDE

(167 performances)

A musical comedy in two acts by Herbert and Dorothy Fields; music and lyrics by Cole Porter. Produced by Michael Todd at the Winter Garden, New York, January 28, 1944.

Cast of characters—

Lombo Campos	George Givot
Mrs. Augustus Adamson	Jean Cleveland
Eadie Johnson	Edith Meiser

Augustus, Jr. ....Eric Roberts
Mr. Augustus Adamson...........................William A. Lee
Joe Bascom (alias Humphrey Fish).................Bobby Clark
Montana...June Havoc
Picadors.......................Horton Henderson, Jerry Sylvon
Billy...Bill Callahan
Senor Martinez................................David Leonard
Miguel Correres...............................Sergio DeKarlo
David Winthrop................................Wilbur Evans
Henry A. Wallace..............................Byron Halstead
José...Paul Reyes
A. C. Blumenthal..............................Larry Martin
Tillie Leeds....................................Lois Bolton
Lydia Toddle..................................Virginia Edwards
Carol (Ex-King of Roumania)....................Arthur Gondra
Mme. Lupescu...................................Dorothy Durkee
Lolita Cantine..................................Corinna Mura
Dagmar Marshak...............................Luba Malina
Bolero...Alfonso Pedroza
Chief of Police................................Richard Bengali
Lottery Boy...................................Hank Wolff
Mrs. Molly Wincor.............................Jeanne Shelby
1st Merchant.....................................Paul Reyes
2nd Merchant...............................Horton Henderson
3rd Merchant................................Hen Hernandez
4th Merchant.................................Jerry Sylvon
5th Merchant..................................Bobby Lane
Woman Vendor...............................Claire Anderson
Lottery Girl......................................Eva Reyes
Paul...Paul Haakon
Eleanor...Eleanor Tennis
Lillian...Marjory Leach

Act I.—Scene 1—Plaza de Toros, Mexico, D.F. 2—Bedroom of
Reforma Hotel. 3—Bar at Ciro's. 4—Street in Merced Market.
5—Outdoor Corridor of National Palace. 6—Terrace of Palace of
Chepultepec. Act II.—Scene 1—Xochimilco. 2—A Gas Station
(on the Paseo do la Reforma). 3—Taxco. 4—Terrace of the Palace at Chepultepec.

Staged by Hassard Short; book directed by John Kennedy; music
by Harry Levant; choreography by Paul Haakon; sets by George
Jenkins; costumes by Mary Grant.

Joe Bascom, in Mexico hoping to dodge a pursuing FBI, takes
time out to organize a numbers racket below the border. This
forces Joe into a variety of disguises and brings him up eventually with a comic jerk. With a number of comic jerks, in
fact.

DECISION

(160 performances)

A drama in three acts by Edward Chodorov. Produced by
Edward Choate at the Belasco Theatre, New York, February 2,
1944.

Cast of characters—

Miss Baines..Jean Casto
Felix...Dickie Van Patten
Harriet Howard.................................Gwen Anderson
Riggs...Raymond Greenleaf
Anderson......................................Len D. Hollister
Brown..Homer Miles

```
Mrs. Bowen.........................................Grace Mills
Jim Morgan.......................................Herbert Junior
Bennett..............................................Rusty Lane
Fitzgerald...........................................Paul Huber
Tommy Riggs........................................Larry Hugo
Virgie............................................Georgia Burke
Mrs. May Howard..............................Merle Maddern
Masters...........................................Matt Crowley
Allen.............................................Howard Smith
Peters.............................................Lee Sanford
Sergeant Carey......................................Paul Ford
```

Act I.—Scene 1—Riggs' Office at the High School. 2—The Riggs Home. Act II.—The High School. 2—The Riggs Home. Act III.—The Riggs Home.

Staged by Edward Chodorov; settings by Frederick Fox.

See page 133.

(Closed June 17, 1944)

PEEPSHOW

(29 performances)

A comedy in three acts by Ernest Pascal. Produced by Ernest Pascal in association with Samuel Bronston at the Fulton Theatre, New York, February 3, 1944.

Cast of characters—

```
Jonathan Mallet.....................................John Emery
His Conscience....................................David Wayne
Julius..........................................Lionel Monagas
Tommy Cobbe.....................................Dwight Weist
Leonie Cobbe.....................................Tamara Geva
Jessica Broome.....................................Joan Tetzel
Waiter...........................................Dayton Lummis
Porter........................................Edward Broadley
Nurse..........................................Elizabeth Dewing
```

Act I.—Scene 1—Jonathan Mallet's Apartment, New York City. 2—Le Coquille au Citron. Act II.—Scene 1—The Treetop Inn. 2—A Room at St. Agatha's. 3—Jonathan's Apartment. Act III.—Scene 1—Brixton's Cellar. 2 and 3—Jonathan's Apartment.

Staged by David Burton; settings by Lemuel Ayers; lighted by Carl Kent.

Jonathan Mallet is a bridge expert with a passion for lovely women as well as cards. He is also troubled occasionally by his Conscience. In the play Jonathan's Conscience follows him about with interjections of good advice, which Jonathan seldom takes. Engaged to marry glamorous but dumb Jessica Broome, Jonathan indulges in one last affair with beautiful Leonie Cobbe, wife of his best friend. A motor car accident threatens to spoil everything, but they all lie generously and Jonathan's Conscience is restored temporarily to favor.

(Closed February 26, 1944)

TAKE IT AS IT COMES

(16 performances)

A comedy in three acts by E. B. Morris. Produced by Armin L. Robinson at the 48th Street Theatre, New York, February 10, 1944.

Cast of characters—

Albert D. Bliven	Frank Wilcox
Cora	Louise Lorimer
Elfreda	Angela Jacobs
Tommy	Jackie Ayers
Mary Sellers	Marylyn Monk
Emma	Sara Floyd
Kip	Richard Basehart
Anthony Pasquale	Tito Vuolo
Herb Jenkins	Grover Burgess
Andy Sellers	Harry Pedersen
Stella	Gloria Willis
Chief of Police	Curtis Cooksey
Mayor Stone	Arthur Griffin
Mr. Plummitt	John Souther
Dr. Witherspoon	Harold Moulton
Veronica	Harriet White
Wilbur Kenyon	Robert West
Vincent Davis	David Lewis
Radio Engineer	James Rawls
Photographer	Martin Leonard
Postman	George Spelvin
Mrs. Pasquale	Shaque Hampar

Acts I, II and III.—Living Room of the Blivens, in Wiltonwood, N. J.

Staged by Anthony Brown; setting by Perry Watkins.

Albert Bliven is Superintendent of Schools in Wiltonwood, N. J. His family of gentle, decent folk is voted the model family of the town and freely exploited in and out of the illustrated papers. Tommy Bliven, a model Boy Scout, is given a package by Neighbor Pasquale and asked to hide it as a surprise for Mrs. Pasquale's birthday. That night Pasquale is machine-gunned by a group of his fellow gangsters. The package is opened by the inquisitive Blivenses and found to contain $100,000 in cash. The struggles of the model family to satisfy their natural acquisitiveness and still stay within shooting distance of respectability are finally settled by Mr. Blivens getting squiffy and telling off the grafting mayor of the town. Thereupon Bliven is elected a reform mayor, and threatens himself to develop a more elastic view of graft.

(Closed February 23, 1944)

GILBERT AND SULLIVAN OPERA CO.

(54 performances)

A repertory of Gilbert and Sullivan operettas presented by R. H. Burnside at the Ambassador Theatre, New York, February 11, 1944. Musical direction by Louis Kroll.

THE MIKADO

(February 11, 1944)

(6 performances)

Cast of characters—

```
The Mikado of Japan...............................Robert Pitkin
Nanki-Poo.......................James Gerard or Allen Stewart
Ko-Ko............................................Florenz Ames
Pooh-Bah.........................................Robert Eckles
Pish-Tush......................................Bertram Peacock
Go-Go.............................................Lewis Pierce
Yum-Yum.........................................Kathleen Roche
Pitti-Sing......................................Kathryn Reece
Peep-Bo..........................................Marie Valdez
Katisha.........................................Catherine Judah
```
    Act I.—Courtyard of Ko-Ko's Palace in Titipu. Act II.—Ko-Ko's Garden.

TRIAL BY JURY

(February 14, 1944)

(7 performances)

Cast of characters—

```
Judge............................................Florenz Ames
Plaintiff.......................................Kathryn Reece
Counsel for Plaintiff..........................Bertram Peacock
Defendant........................................Frank Murray
Foreman of Jury..................................Robert Eckles
Usher............................................Robert Pitkin
```

Followed by—

H.M.S. PINAFORE

(7 performances)

Cast of characters—

```
The Rt. Hon. Sir Joseph Porter, K.C.B.............Florenz Ames
Captain Corcoran...............................Bertram Peacock
Ralph Rackstraw...................................James Gerard
Dick Deadeye.....................................Robert Pitkin
Bill Bobstay.....................................Robert Eckles
Bob Becket.......................................Frank Murray
Tommy Tucker........................Master Arthur Henderson
```

Josephine..Kathleen Roche
Cousin Hebe.......................................Marie Valdez
Little Buttercup....................................Catherine Judah
First Lord's Sisters, His Cousins and His Aunts.
Sailors and Marines.
Scene—Quarter Deck of the *H.M.S. Pinafore,* off Portsmouth.

COX AND BOX

(February 17, 1944)

(8 performances)

Book by F. C. Burmand; music by Arthur Sullivan.

Cast of characters—

James John Cox....................................Allen Stewart
John James Box....................................Florenz Ames
Sergeant Bouncer..................................Robert Eckles
Scene—Furnished Room in Bloomsbury, London.

Followed by—

THE PIRATES OF PENZANCE

(8 performances)

Cast of characters—

The Pirate King....................,...............Robert Eckles
Samuel...Bertram Peacock
Frederic...........................Allen Stewart or James Gerard
Major-General Stanley.............................Florenz Ames
Sergeant of Police.................................Robert Pitkin
Mabel..Kathleen Roche
Edith..Kathryn Reece
Kate...Marie Valdez
Isabel..Mary Lundon
Ruth...Catherine Judah
General Stanley's Wards. Pirates and Police.
Act I.—A Rocky Seashore on the Coast of Cornwall. Act II.—A Ruined Chapel by Moonlight.

THE GONDOLIERS

(February 21, 1944)

(4 performances)

Cast of characters—

The Duke of Plaza-Toro...........................Florenz Ames
Luiz...Roland Partridge
Don Alhambra Bolero.............................Robert Pitkin
Marco Palmieri...................................Allen Stewart
Giuseppe Palmieri.................................Lewis Pierce
Antonio..Frank Murray
Francesco..Edwin Marsh
Giorgio..Robert Eckles
The Duchess of Plaza-Toro.......................Catherine Judah
Casilda..Marie Valdez
Gianetta...Kathleen Roche
Tessa..Kathryn Reece
Fiametta...Virginia Tyre

Giulia...Mary Lundon
Vittoria...Jean Davis
Inez...Florence Keezel
    Act I.—The Piazetta, Venice. Act II.—The Pavilion in the Palace of Barataria.

IOLANTHE

(February 22, 1944)

(6 performances)

Cast of characters—

The Lord Chancellor...........................Florenz Ames
Earl of Mountararat...........................Robert Pitkin
Lord Tolloller................................Allen Stewart
Private Willis................................Robert Eckles
Strephon.....................................Lewis Pierce
Queen of the Fairies..........................Catherine Judah
Iolanthe.....................................Kathryn Reece
Celia..Mary Lundon
Fieta..Marie Valdez
Phyllis......................................Kathleen Roche
    Act I.—Arcadian Landscape. Act II.—Palace Yard, Westminster.

PATIENCE

(February 25, 1944)

(4 performances)

Cast of characters—

Colonel Calverley.............................Robert Pitkin
Major Murgatroyd.............................Bertram Peacock
Lieut. The Duke of Dunstable..................Roland Partridge
Reginald Bunthorne...........................Florenz Ames
Mr. Bunthorne's Solicitor.....................Frank Murray
Archibald Grosvenor..........................Allen Stewart
The Lady Angela..............................Kathryn Reece
The Lady Saphir..............................Marie Valdez
The Lady Ella................................Mary Lundon
The Lady Jane................................Catherine Judah
Patience.....................................Kathleen Roche
    Act I.—Exterior of Castle Bunthorne. Act II.—A Glade.

RUDDIGORE

(March 2, 1944)

(3 performances)

Cast of characters—

MORTALS
Sir Ruthven Murgatroyd.......................Florenz Ames
Richard Dauntless..............Allen Stewart or Roland Partridge
Sir Despart Murgatroyd.......................Robert Pitkin
Old Adam Goodheart..........................Robert Eckles
Rose Maybud.................................Kathleen Roche
Mad Margaret................................Marie Valdez
Dame Hannah................................Catherine Judah
Zorah.......................................Kathryn Reece
Ruth..Mary Lundon

GHOSTS

Sir Rupert Murgatroyd...........................Lewis Pierce
Sir Jasper Murgatroyd............................Walter George
Sir Lionel Murgatroyd...........................August Loring
Sir Conrad Murgatroyd............................Edwin Marsh
Sir Desmond Murgatroyd........................Chester MaDan
Sir Gilbert Murgatroyd............................Joseph Filos
Sir Mervin Murgatroyd...........................David Bogart
Sir Roderic Murgatroyd........................Bertram Peacock
    Act I.—The Fishing Village of Rederring, in Cornwall. Act II.—
Picture Gallery in Ruddigore Castle.
Early in the Nineteenth Century.

YEOMEN OF THE GUARD

(March 3, 1944)

(1 performance)

Cast of characters—

Sir Richard Cholomondeley......................Bertram Peacock
Colonel Fairfax....................................James Gerard
Sergeant Meryll...................................Robert Eckles
Leonard Meryll....................................Allen Stewart
Jack Point...Florenz Ames
Wilfred Shadbolt.................................Robert Pitkin
The Headsman....................................Walter George
First Yeoman.....................................Frank Murray
Second Yeoman....................................Lewis Pierce
First Citizen....................................Chester MaDan
Second Citizen......................................Gus Loring
Elsie Maynard...................................Kathleen Roche
Phoebe Meryll....................................Kathryn Reece
Dame Caruthers.................................Catherine Judah
Kate..Marie Valdez
    Chorus of Yeomen of the Guard, Gentlemen, Citizens.
    Scene—Tower Green.
    Date—16th Century.

(Closed March 26, 1944)

CAUKEY

(22 performances)

A comedy in prologue and three acts by the Rev. Thomas
McGlynn. Produced by the Blackfriars' Guild at the Blackfriars' Theatre, New York, February 17, 1944.

Cast of characters—

Ma...Ruth P. White
Forrest...John Tate
Mrs. Hatch..................................Barbara Winchester
Emma...Florence Fox
Henry..Robert Lancet
Gas Man.......................................William Johnson
Lorraine...Cathy Parsons
George..Dennis McDonald
Miss Jenkins..................................Claire R. Leyba
Officer Larkin.....................................James Slater
Ed Barton.....................................Clarence Q. Foster
Miss Stevens................................Geraldine Prillerman

```
Gloria..........................................Betty E. Haynes
Wentworth...................................Vernon Chambers
Police Captain..............................John J. McClain
Officer Thompson.............................Charles Baker
     Acts I and III.—Ma Pringle's Kitchen.  Act II.—Wentworth Real
Estate Office.
     Staged by Dennis Gurney; settings by Thomas Fabian.
```

Reversing the problems of the races, Ed Barton is a Negro, idealist who is hopeful of bringing about reforms and bettering the conditions of those white citizens whose degrading and unfair living conditions are brought under his observation. Wentworth is a Negro of wealth and the owner of a group of rundown tenements the whites, or "Caukeys," are forced to inhabit. There are also Negro storekeepers, Negro landlords, and a Negro gas company to make life miserable for the Caucasians. Also George, a white clerk, who hopes to study law and help to advance his race as well as himself.

(Closed March 12, 1944)

RIGHT NEXT TO BROADWAY

(16 performances)

A comedy in three acts by Paul K. Paley. Produced by Paul K. Paley at the Bijou Theatre, New York, February 21, 1944.

Cast of characters—

```
Sam............................................Rubin Goldberg
Adrey..........................................Gloria Mann
Marian.........................................Dorothy Eaton
Jerry..........................................Roger Sullivan
Dotty..........................................Frances Tannehill
"Poppa" Weinstein..............................Leon Schachter
Charlie........................................Joseph Leon
Lee Winston....................................Jeannette C. Chinley
Carlo Marchetti................................James Russo
Ben............................................Tom Daley
Irwin Cole.....................................John Baragrey
Gertie Smith...................................Cleo Mayfield
Danny..........................................Lee Bergere
Mr. Loucheim...................................Norman H. Miller
Raubvogel......................................Norman Rose
Charles Bradford Ramsey 3rd....................Jack Bostick
Heinz..........................................Otto Simetti
Moskin.........................................Jonathan Harris
Boskin.........................................Charles Cohan
     Acts I, II and III.—Office of Lee Winston on Seventh Avenue,
New York.
     Staged by William B. Friedlander; setting by Karl Amend.
```

Lee Winston inherits a dressmaking establishment and seeks to reorganize it along practical lines. She has trouble with manufacturers, models, unions, the OPA and love. Also with her author.

(Closed March 4, 1944)

MRS. KIMBALL PRESENTS

(7 performances)

A farce comedy by Alonzo Price. Produced by Ted Gerken and Joe Chandler at the 48th Street Theatre, New York, February 29, 1944.

Cast of characters—

Harold L. Burton	Arthur Margetson
Ambrose J. Piel, Jr.	Bruce Evans
Jim	Hall Shelton
J. G. McGuire	Jesse White
Dick Hastings	Michael Ames
Cynthia Lane	Elizabeth Inglise
Babs Sloan	Joan Cory
Connie Kimball	Vicki Cummings

Act I.—Scene 1—Dick Hastings' Dressing Room in a Broadway Theatre. 2—Dick's Penthouse Apartment in Sutton Place. Acts II and III.—The Penthouse.

Staged by Alonzo Price; settings by Cirker and Robbins.

Connie Kimball is a society dame with a theatre complex. She produces a play, scores a hit and takes after her leading man. The leading man, Dick Hastings, being engaged to a debutante, mistakes Mrs. Kimball's intentions. He also becomes embroiled in the affairs of a pal and fellow-actor, Harold Burton, who is trying to hide from a pursuing bailiff by pretending to be Hastings' butler. As it turns out Dick's love is preserved and the bailiff is discovered to be a motion picture scout with a contract for Burton.

(Closed March 4, 1944)

THANK YOU, SVOBODA

(6 performances)

A comedy by H. S. Kraft from John Pen's novel, "You Can't Do That to Svoboda." Produced by Milton Baron at the Mansfield Theatre, New York, March 1, 1944.

Cast of characters—

Colonel Fiala	Arnold Korff
Mr. Vesley	Francis Compton
Josef	Frank Conlan
Doctor Burian	John McGovern
The German Salesman	William Malten
Svoboda	Sam Jaffe
Mr. Novotny	Donald Keyes
Mr. Hanoi	Len Mence
Mary	Adrienne Gessner
The Padre	John Ravold
Hugo	Whitford Kane

Sergeant Kurtz....................................Ronald Telfer
Private Recht.....................................Louis Fabien
Private Schmatz...................................Michael Strong
Private Langheld..................................Dehl Berti
    Act I.—A Small Inn in a Village of Czechoslovakia. March 15,
1939. Act II.—Scene 1—Mary's House. 2—The Inn. 3—Cell in
Police Station. Act III.—Scene 1—The Inn. 2—Mary's House.
    Staged by H. S. Kraft and Moe Hack; settings by Samuel Leve.

Svoboda, the handyman of a Czechoslovakian village, is accused of having planted dynamite with which to blow up a bridge when the Germans occupy the country. Unable to read or write, he amiably puts his cross to a confession. The Germans send him to a concentration camp. Here he does odd jobs for other internees, buys himself a fine outfit of clothes and is finally released by the Germans as harmless. Back in the village Svoboda discovers that the invaders, in looting the town, have stolen his savings. This makes him so mad he goes out and finally does blow up the bridge he had been previously accused of destroying.

(Closed March 4, 1944)

BRIGHT BOY

(16 performances)

A comedy in three acts by Lt. John Boruff, U.S.N.R. Produced by Arthur J. Beckhard and David Merrick at the Playhouse, New York, March 2, 1944.

Cast of characters—

Tittman (Shakespeare)......................Carleton Carpenter
Willie Barnes....................................Beman Lord
Si Williams......................................Frank Jacoby
Peterson (Pete)..................................Jeff Brown
Prof. McGiffin...................................Liam Dunn
David Bennett....................................Charles Bowlby
Allen Carpenter..................................Donald Buka
Stevens (Steve)..................................John Cushman
John Wallace (Specs).............................Michael Dreyfuss
Watts (Sleepy)...................................William McGuire
Pinky Jenks......................................Eugene Ryan
Dr. Sewell.......................................Ivan Simpson
Margaret...Joyce Franklin
    Act I.—Scene 1—David and Allen's Room, Brown Hall, Boy's
Prep School. 2—Smoke Hill, Small Hill off Campus. Act II.—
Scene 1—Smoke Hill. 2—David and Allen's Room. Act III.—
Smoke Hill.
    Staged by Arthur J. Beckhard; settings by Watson Barratt.

Allen Carpenter, a tutored son of rich parents whose fortunes have slipped, finds himself at Brown Hall, a prep school in an Eastern city. Embittered and resentful, as well as intellectually the superior of his fellow students, Allen makes himself unpopular. During the hazing period he is dunked in the lake. Devoting the rest of the term to getting even, he employs the

Machiavellian tactics of first ingratiating himself with his tormentors and getting himself elected class president. As he is ready to turn on his fellows he suffers a change of heart, induced by a roommate's kindness and continued faith in him.

(Closed March 15, 1944)

* JACOBOWSKY AND THE COLONEL

(111 performances)

A comedy in three acts by S. N. Behrman, based on an original play by Franz Werfel; incidental music by Paul Bowles. Produced by the Theatre Guild in association with John H. Skirball at the Martin Beck Theatre, New York, March 14, 1944.

Cast of characters—

A Young Girl	Louise Dowdney
Sleeping Shopkeeper	Harrison Winter
The Tragic Gentleman	Herbert Yost
Old Lady from Arras	Jane Marbury
Madame Bouffier	Hilda Vaughn
Soloman	Harry Davis
Szycke	Peter Kass
Szabuniewicz	J. Edward Bromberg
S. L. Jacobowsky	Oscar Karlweis
Air Raid Warden	Philip Collier
Colonel Tadeusz Boleslav Stjerbinsky	Louis Calhern
Cosette	Kitty Mattern
A Chauffeur	Coby Ruskin
Monsieur Serouille	Donald Cameron
Marianne	Annabella
Brigadier	E. G. Marshall
Street Singer	Joseph Kallini
Child	Jules Leni
First Lieutenant	Frank Overton
Gestapo Official	Harold Vermilyea
First German Soldier	Don Lee
Second German Soldier	Bob Merritt
Papa Clarion	Harry Davis
The Dice Player	Philip Coolidge
Senator Brisson	Donald Cameron
The Commissaire	William Sanders
First French Soldier	Burton Tripp
Second French Soldier	Edward Kreisler

Act I.—Scene 1—Laundry of Hotel Mon Repos et de la Rose, Serving as Air-Raid Shelter, Paris, Midnight, June 13, 1940. 2—In Front of Hotel. Act II.—Scene 1—Lonely Road at St. Cyrille near Sables d'Ollones. 2—Open Spot in Woods near City of Bayonne. Act III.—Scene 1—The "Au Père Clairon" Waterfront Café at St. Jean de Luz. 2—Mole at Hendaye, St. Jean de Luz. Night, June 18, 1940.

Staged by Elia Kazan; settings by Stewart Chaney; production under supervision of Lawrence Langner and Theresa Helburn.

See page 236.

THE HOUSE IN PARIS

(16 performances)

A drama in prologue and three acts by Eric Mawby Green and Edward Allen Feilbert, with revisions by Caroline Francke suggested by Arthur Richman; based on a novel by Elizabeth Bowen. Produced by H. Clay Blaney at the Fulton Theatre, New York, March 20, 1944.

Cast of characters—

Naomi Fisher	Cavada Humphrey
Henrietta	Pauline Robinson
Leopold	Alastair Boyd Kyle
Two American Girls	{ Marguerete Lewis / Penelope Sack
Madame Fisher	Ludmilla Pitoeff
Max Ebhart	Michael Ingram
Karen Michaels	Lorraine Clewes
Ray Forrestier	Isham Constable

Prologue and Acts I, II and III.—Salon of Madame Fisher's Home in Paris.   Prologue and Act III.—1911.   Acts I and II.—1900.
Staged by Clarence Derwent; setting by Stewart Chaney.

Madame Fisher is a dominating and possessive proprietress of a Paris pension supported by paying guests, many of whom are English and American.   In 1900 she was passionately in love with a young painter who would have none of her, he in turn being as deeply in love with a young English girl.   The English girl goes home and becomes engaged to another man, but returns to Paris for a last visit to her artist friend.   When she leaves a second time the artist, realizing the Madame's hold upon him, commits suicide.   In England his true love becomes the mother of his illegitimate son.   Eleven years later the boy is also a guest at Madame Fisher's and she, being remorseful, seeks to start him upon life's path with a lot of good advice.

(Closed April 1, 1944)

MRS. JANUARY AND MR. X

(43 performances)

A comedy in three acts by Zoe Akins.   Produced by Richard Myers at the Belasco Theatre, New York, March 31, 1944.

Cast of characters—

Miss Belle	Helen Carew
Charley Blaine	Edward Nannary
Stevens	Phil Sheridan
Mrs. January, nee January	Billie Burke
Martin Luther Cooper	Frank Craven

```
1st Expressman.............................Roderick  Winchell
2nd Expressman............................Robert  F.  Simon
Germaine..................................Mlle.  Therese  Quadri
Wilhelmina................................Barbara  Bel  Geddes
Rolando...................................Bobby  Perez
Carey.....................................Henry  Barnard
Burdette..................................Henry  Vincent
Clancy....................................Dorothy  Lambert
John Deacon January.......................Nicholas  Joy
Miss Peck.................................Susana  Garnett
     Acts I, II and III.—Sitting Room of Small House in New Eng-
land Town.
     Staged by Elliott Nugent and Arthur Sircom; setting by Paul Mor-
rison; costumes by Adrian.
```

Mrs. January, married three times, having acquired a considerable estate, becomes worried as a well-to-do widow about the coming revolution. She decides to practice being a Communist. Going to a small town in New England, Mrs. J rents half of a two-family house and angles instinctively for the attention of her neighbor and landlord, Martin Luther Cooper, ex-president of the United States. Mr. Cooper, a canny New Englander, is always on his guard but is eventually charmed out of his shell. He not only proposes marriage to Mrs. January, but also permits himself to be drafted as a presidential candidate hoping for a return to the White House.

(Closed May 6, 1944)

ONLY THE HEART

(47 performances)

A drama in three acts by Horton Foote. Produced by The American Actors Theatre at the Bijou Theatre, New York, April 4, 1944.

Cast of characters—

```
India Hamilton............................Mildred  Dunnock
Julia  Borden.............................Eleanor  Anton
Mamie Borden..............................June  Walker
Albert  Price.............................Will  Hare
Mr. Borden................................Maurice  Wells
     Acts I, II and III.—Living Room of Mamie Borden's House in
a Small Town, Richmond, Texas.  1921.
     Staged by Mary Hunter; setting and costumes by Frederick Fox.
```

Mamie Borden, succumbing to a passion for wealth and security, seeks to bend her family to the fulfillment of her own ambitions. She lets her husband go prowling in search of companionship with other women. She tries to divert her daughter's attention from the man the daughter loves to the one mother covets. In the end she is left rich, lonely and utterly defeated.

(Closed May 13, 1944)

*CHICKEN EVERY SUNDAY

(85 performances)

A comedy in three acts by Julius J. and Philip G. Epstein, based on a book by Rosemary Taylor. Produced by Edward Gross at the Henry Miller Theatre, New York, April 5, 1944.

Cast of characters—

Mrs. Lawson	Ethel Remey
Jeffrey Lawson	Hugh Thomas
Miss Gilley	Diana Rivers
Mr. Willard	Austin Coghlan
Emily Blachman	Mary Philips
Evie May	Viola Dean
Jake	Roy Fant
Eagle	Martin Skapik
Oliver Blachman	Guy Stockwell
Ruthie Blachman	Carolyn Hummel
Carlos	Tino Valenti
Rosemary Blachman	Jean Gillespie
Clem	Raymond Van Sickle
Mrs. Lynch (Miss Sally)	Katherine Squire
Jim Blachman	Rhys Williams
Mr. Robinson	Fleming Ward
Rita Kirby	Ann Thomas
George Kirby	Frank M. Thomas
Harold	David McKay
Rev. Wilson	Wyrley Birch
Milly Moon	Hope Emerson

Acts I, II and III.—Living Room of the Blachman Home in Tucson, Arizona, 1916.

Staged by Lester Vail; setting and lighting by Howard Bay; costumes by Rose Bogdanoff.

Emily Blachman is keeping her home and her husband together by running a boarding house in Tucson. Jim Blachman, the husband, talks loud and works little; he is the big man of the community, but always in debt. The boarders are assembled for comedy purposes. One, being on the sexy side, disturbs Jim and threatens to separate the Blachmans. Reconciliation follows.

PUBLIC RELATIONS

(28 performances)

A comedy in three acts by Dale Eunson. Produced by Robert Blake at the Mansfield Theatre, New York, April 6, 1944.

Cast of characters—

Martin	Owen Coll
Sophie Sawyer	Suzanne Jackson
Nancy Mason	Frances Henderson
David Robinson	Bradford Hunt
Mr. Bartlett	James Russo
Maurice Maxwell	Michael Ames
Anita Sawyer	Ann Andrews

```
Wallace  Maxwell................................Philip  Merivale
Dolores  Maxwell.................................Yolanda  Ugarte
Girl  Reporter.......................................Joan  Beard
Madge  Torrance....................................Betty  Blythe
Eleanor  Hollis..................................Virginia  Sherry
Frank  Hollis.....................................Mason  Adams
Bubbles.........................................Lynette  Browne
```
Acts I, II and III.—Living Room of "The White House," Bev-
erly Hills, California, Summer of 1942.
Staged by Edward Childs Carpenter; setting by Stewart Chaney.

In the old days Anita Sawyer and Wallace Maxwell were the
ideal married lovers of Hollywood. Together they built and
owned "The White House," one of the show places of the movie
colony. Then they were divorced and promptly remarried. Presently they reappear at "The White House" with their new mates
and there are complications. Additional complications also when
a forgotten daughter of one of Maxwell's earlier marriages decides that she wants to have her first child born in her father's
famous home. Numerous readjustments are tried.

(Closed April 29, 1944)

* FOLLOW THE GIRLS

(81 performances)

A musical comedy in two acts by Guy Bolton and Eddie
Davis; dialogue by Fred Thompson; lyrics and music by Dan
Shapiro, Milton Pascal and Phil Charig. Produced by Dave
Wolper in association with Albert Borde at the Century Theatre,
New York, April 8, 1944.

Cast of characters—

```
Yokel  Sailor......................................Bill  Tabbert
Doorman........................................Ernest  Goodhart
1st  Girl  Fan.......................................Terry  Kelly
2nd  Girl  Fan....................................Rae  MacGregor
Bob  Monroe......................................Frank  Parker
Anna  Viskinova..................................Irina  Baranova
Goofy  Gale.....................................Jackie  Gleason
Seaman  Pennywhistle..............................Frank  Kreig
Catherine  Pepburn.............................Geraldine  Stroock
Sailor  Val.......................................Val  Valentinoff
Marine.......................................Charles  Conaway,  Jr.
Bubbles  LaMarr...............................Gertrude  Niesen
Cigarette  Girl..................................Kathryn  Lazell
Spud  Doolittle....................................Tim  Herbert
Dinky  Riley......................................Buster  West
Peggy  Baker....................................Dorothy  Keller
Phyllis  Brent......................................Toni  Gilman
Dan  Daley.......................................Robert  Tower
Petty  Officer  Banner..............................Lee  Davis
Capt.  Hawkins....................................Walter  Long
Archie  Smith.....................................Frank  Kreig
Felix  Charrel...................................Val  Valentinoff
Officer  Flanagan..............................George  Spaulding
Dance  Team  in  Canteen..........................The  Di  Gatanos
```
Act I.—Scene 1—Outside Spotlight Canteen, 1943. 2—Inside

Canteen. 3—Outside Naval Training Station, Great Neck, L. I.
4—Trophy Room. Act II.—Scene 1—Flower Garden. 2—Room in
House. 3—Navy Park, Great Neck. 4—Good Ship *Lady Luck.*
5—Inside Spotlight Canteen.
Staged by Harry Delmar; music directed by Will Irwin; dances
and ensembles by Catherine Littlefield; settings and lighting by
Howard Bay; costumes by Lou Eisele.

It would have been the story of a burlesque queen who becomes the queen of a service men's canteen, but by the time room had been found for the vaudeville specialists employed, everybody had forgotten the story, and nobody cared.

—BUT NOT GOODBYE

(23 performances)

A comedy in three acts by George Seaton. Produced by John Golden in association with Harry Joe Brown at the 48th Street Theatre, New York, April 11, 1944.

Cast of characters—

Sam Griggs	Harry Carey
Howard Baker	Wendell Corey
Amy Griggs	Elizabeth Patterson
Jennifer Griggs	Sylvia Field
Tom Carter	Frank Wilcox
Ralph Humphrey	Hal K. Dawson
Jimmie Griggs	John Conway
Dr. Wilson	Raymond Largay
Benjamin Griggs	J. Pat O'Malley
Rev. Pritchard	Harold McGee

Acts I, II and III.—Home of the Griggs Family, Somewhere
Along the Coast of New England, in Summer of 1910.
Staged by Richard Whorf; setting by Richard Whorf.

Before Sam Griggs is stricken with a heart attack he secretly invests his savings and those of his son in a real estate deal. After Sam dies his partner in the enterprise, Tom Carter, determines to keep the profits from the deal, leading the Griggs family to believe the investment was a failure. In an effort to let the family know what the rascally one is up to, Sam is earthbound for a couple of days and, with the help of his father, also a ghost, does finally manage to get the would-be villain struck by lightning before he can go through with his scheme.

(Closed April 29, 1944)

* THE SEARCHING WIND

(77 performances)

A drama in two acts by Lillian Hellman. Produced by Herman Shumlin at the Fulton Theatre, New York, April 12, 1944.

Cast of characters—

Moses Taney.....................................Dudley Digges
Emily Hazen.............................Cornelia Otis Skinner
Alexander Hazen..................................Dennis King
Catherine Bowman...........................Barbara O'Neil
2nd Italian Waiter..........................Joseph de Santis
Samuel Hazen.............................Montgomery Clift
Sophronia....................................Mercedes Gilbert
Ponette..Alfred Hesse
1st Italian Waiter.............................Edgar Andrews
Hotel Manager.................................Walter Kohler
Eppler.....................................William F. Schoeller
Capt. Heydebreck..................................John Cole
Edward Halsey..................................Eric Latham
James Sears......................................Eugene Earl
Count Max Von Stammer.........................Arnold Korff
    Italian Soldiers, Restaurant Guests, Waiters, People in Street:
    Sylvester LaMont, Joseph Martell, Jefferson Coates, George
    Brandt, George Dice, Gerard Hollman, Marshall Reid.
    Act I.—Scenes 1 and 3—Drawing Room of Hazen Home, Wash-
ington, D. C., 1944. 2—Room in Grand Hotel, Rome, October,
1922. Act II.—Scene 1—Corner of Restaurant in Berlin, Autumn,
1923. 2—Room in Hotel Meurice, Paris, September, 1938. 3—
Drawing Room in Hazen Home, 1944.
    Staged by Herman Shumlin; settings by Howard Bay; costumes
by Aline Bernstein.

See page 69.

PRETTY LITTLE PARLOR

(8 performances)

A drama in three acts by Claiborne Foster. Produced by John Moses and Ralph Bellamy at the National Theatre, New York, April 17, 1944.

Cast of characters—

Jefferson Hilyard...............................Sidney Blackmer
Anastasia.......................................Marilyn Erskine
Dora..Joan Tetzel
Henry...Mel Roberts
Clotilde..Stella Adler
Mr. Kennedy..Paul Parks
Dennis Baldwin......................................Kip Good
Mr. Jonas..Edward Begley
    Acts I, II and III.—In the Hilyards' Parlor of a Moderately
Priced Family Hotel in Small City in United States, 1905.
    Staged by Ralph Bellamy; setting by Stewart Chaney; costumes
by Paul DuPont.

Clotilde Hilyard, overtaken by a mounting ambition, drives her husband to drink, her daughter into the theft of a half-sister's fiancé, and herself into a kind of blackmailing business that promises to pay her well.

(Closed April 22, 1944)

SHEPPEY

(23 performances)

A comedy in two acts by W. Somerset Maugham. Produced by Jacques Chambrun at the Playhouse, New York, April 18, 1944.

Cast of characters—

Albert	Harry Sothern
First Customer	Wallace Widdecombe
Miss Grange	Cathleen Cordell
Sheppey	Edmund Gwenn
Second Customer	Oswald Marshall
Mr. Bolton	Alexander Clark
Bradley	Gerald Savory
A Reporter	Cledge Roberts
Miss James	Vera Fuller Mellish
Bessie Legros	Doris Patston
A Strange Woman	Catherine Anderson
Mrs. Miller	Barbara Everest
Florrie	Frances Heflin
Ernest Turner	Anthony Kemble-Cooper
Dr. Jervis	Horace Cooper
Cooper	Victor Beecroft

Act I.—Bradley's Barber Shop in Bond Street, London. Act II.—Scenes 1 and 2—Living Room of Sheppey's House at Camberwell, London.

Staged by Sir Cedric Hardwicke; settings by Watson Barratt.

Sheppey is Bond Street's favorite tonsorialist in London. After he wins a sweepstakes prize of $40,000 he determines to try spending it as he thinks Jesus Christ would have approved his doing. He would help publicans and sinners, makes friends with a street-walker and a small-time sneak thief. He greatly disappoints both his wife and his avaricious daughter, who prays for his commitment to an insane asylum before he can spend his winnings. Sheppey is finally eased out of his difficulties by a heart attack.

(Closed May 6, 1944)

ALLAH BE PRAISED!

(20 performances)

A musical comedy in two acts by George Marion, Jr.; music by Don Walker and Baldwin Bergersen. Produced by Alfred Bloomingdale at the Adelphi Theatre, New York, April 20, 1944.

Cast of characters—

Caswell	Jack Albertson
Receptionist	Helen Bennett
Tex O'Carroll	Edward Roecker
Clerk	Sheila Bond

```
Citizen..............................................Joey Faye
Abdul................................................Sid Stone
Bulbul...........................................Jack Albertson
Carol O'Carroll............................Mary Jane Walsh
Roberta...........................................Marge Ellis
Paula..............................................Lee Joyce
Doris..........................................Mary McDonnell
Tubaga.........................................Anita Alvarez
Emir............................................John Hoysradt
Zarah..........................................Milada Mladova
Youssouf...........................................Joey Faye
Nij O'Carroll...................................Pittman Corry
Dulcy Robot..................................Margie Jackson
Beatrice.......................................Beatrice Kraft
Evelyne.........................................Evelyne Kraft
Marcia Mason Moore..........................Patricia Morison
Mimi McSlump..................................Jayne Manners
Matron.........................................Helen Bennett
Merchant..........................................Tom Powers
Girls About Teheran..................Eleanor Hall, Louise Jarvis
    Trainees: Lee Joyce, Susan Scott, Marge Ellis, Mari Lynn,
    Natalie Wynn, Barbara Neal, Alice Anthony, Olga Suarez,
    Margie Jackson, Mary McDonnell, Dorothy Bird, Ila Marie Wil-
    son, Grace Crystal, Gloria Crystal, Hazel Roy, Muriel Breunig,
    Pat Welles.
    Photographers: Mischa Pompianov, Ray Arnett, Jr., Remi Martel,
    Jack Baker, Jacy McCord, Johnny Oberon, Tom Powers, Jack
    L. Nagle, William Lundy, Forrest Boncher.
    Act I.—Scene 1—Bureau of Missing Persons, New York, February
20, 1948. 2—The Minarets of Sultanbad, February 29, 1948. 3 and
5—The Emir's Palace. 4—The Palace Gardens. Act II.—Scene 1
—Minarets of Sultanbad. 2 and 4—Harem Sleeping Porch. 3—
Hollywood, California.
    Staged by Robert H. Gordon and Jack Small; choreogoraphy by
Jack Cole; music directed by Ving Merlin; settings by George Jen-
kins; costumes by Miles White.
```

Something about a Persian harem and a group of visiting night club habitués from New York. Also investigating congressmen from Washington, and curiosity-ridden women from other parts of the country.

(Closed May 6, 1944)

*HELEN GOES TO TROY

(64 performances)

An operetta in two acts by Gottfried Reinhardt and John Meehan, Jr.; lyrics by Herbert Baker; music by Erich Wolfgang Korngold; based on Max Reinhardt's version of Jacques Offenbach's "La Belle Helene." Produced by Yolanda Mero-Irion for The New Opera Company at the Alvin Theatre, New York, April 24, 1944.

Cast of characters—

```
Philocomus........................................George Rasely
Calchas............................................Ralph Dumke
Helen, Queen of Sparta........................Jarmila Novotna
Orestes............................................Donald Buka
Parthenis..........................................Doris Blake
```

```
Leila.......................................................Phyllis Hill
Paris, Prince of Troy............................William Horne
Discordia.................................................Rose Inghram
Minerva................................................Doris  Blake
Juno....................................................Rosalind Nadell
Venus..................................................Peggy Corday
Policeman.............................................Michael Mann
White Wing...............................................John Guelis
Ajax 1st, King of Small Nation....................Jesse White
Ajax 2nd................................................Alfred Porter
Menelaus, King of Sparta........................Ernest Truex
Agamemnon................................Gordon  Dilworth
Achilles.................................................Hugh Johnson
Lady-in-Waiting.........................................Jane Kiser
```

Premier Danseuses: Katia Geleznova, Kathryn Lee, Nancy Mann.
Premier Dancers: Michael Mann, John Guelis, George Chaffee.
Alternate for Jarmila Novotna on Matinee Performance: Lillian Anderson.
Alternate for William Horne: Joseph Laderoute.
Ladies of the Ensemble: Johnsie Bason, Peggy Blatherwick, Louise Fagg, Elizabeth Giacobbe, Eleanor Jones, Nancy Kenyon, Jeanne Stephens, Virginia Beeler, Anne Bolyn, Louise Newton, Maria Orelo, Matilda Strazza, Betty Tucker, Leona Vanni.
Gentlemen of the Ensemble: Sam Adams, George Crawford, William Golden, John Gould, Vincent Henry, Robert Marco, Edwin Alberian, Paul Campbell, Robert Kirland, Seymour Osborne, Gordon Richards, Irving Strull.
Ballet: Galina Razoumova, Lee Lauterbur, Rickey Soma, Edwina Seaver, Jane Kiser, Claire Pasch, Katherine Clark, Ricia Orkina, Nina Frenkin, Nicholas Beriozoff, Sviatoslav Toumine, Todd Bolender, David Ahdar, Ricardo Sarroga.
Act I.—Scenic Overture: Antiquity Awakes. Scenes 1, 3 and 5—The Temple of Jupiter in Sparta. 2—Mount Ida. 4—Street in Sparta. Act II.—Scene 1—Helen's Bath in Palace. 2—King's Private Banquet Hall. 3—Road near Sparta. 4 and 6—Helen's Boudoir. 5—Outside Palace Door. 7—Corridor in Palace. 8—Main Banquet Hall.
Staged by Herbert Graf; choreography by Leonide Massine; dialogue directed by Melville Cooper; songs directed by Irving Landau; music by Erich Korngold; settings and lighting by Robert Edmund Jones; costumes by Ladislas Czettel.

A free adaptation of the Homeric legend concerned with the days and ways of Helen of Troy, the handsome and eager Paris, her lover, and the frustrated Menelaus, her sometime husband. To be sure of one song hit, at least, the famed barcarole from "The Tales of Hoffman" is interpolated in the score.

WAR PRESIDENT

(2 performances)

A drama in three acts by Nat Sherman. Presented by the Escholiers for the Experimental Theatre, Inc., at the Shubert Theatre, New York, April 24 and 25, 1944.

Cast of characters—

```
John Hay.........................................Philip Sand
Joel Starbuck..................................Kenneth Dana
Mrs. Lincoln...................................Joanna Roos
Abraham Lincoln...............................Joel Ashley
Tad Lincoln...................................Donald Rose
Willie Lincoln................................Teddy Rose
```

Bob Lincoln...................................Harvey Marlowe
Edwin M. Stanton............................William Marceau
General George B. McClellan..................Alexander Scourby
Senator Benjamin Franklin Wade..................Russell Collins
Senator Zachariah Chandler............................Paul Ford
Mrs. Ellen McClellan............................Barbara Pond
General William F. Smith........................Morton Da Costa
Fernando Wood ....Gregory Morton
Horatio Seymour..................................Peter Gregg
General Philip Kearny...........................Kenneth Dana
General Joe Hooker.............................Joseph Leon
Horace Greeley................................Graham Velsey
Congressman Kelly................................Bruce Halsey
    Act I.—Scenes 1 and 2—President's Office, White House. 3—
General McClellan's Headquarters in Washington. Act II.—Scenes
1 and 3—President's Office. 2—General McClellan's Headquarters
Before Richmond. Act III.—Scenes 1 and 2—President's Office.
3—Portico in Front of Office.
    Staged by Wendell K. Phillips; settings and costumes supervised
by Rose Bogdanoff; lighting by Jack Landau.

President Lincoln's troubles with Gen. McClellan are, with
considerable conviction, made to appear as stemming from Mc-
Clellan's effort to bring the Civil War to a stalemate that would
have resulted in a negotiated peace, saved the South its slaves
and given him the Democratic nomination for the Presidency, as
promised. A between-the-lines suggestion that President Roose-
velt was threatened with similar trouble with Gen. MacArthur
in World War II was less easy to accept.

SAN CARLO OPERA COMPANY

(16 performances)

A season of opera presented by Fortune Gallo at the Center
Theatre, New York, April 26, 1944. Directed by G. S. Eyssell;
staged by Mario Valle; music conducted by Emerson Buckley
and Paolo Giaquinto.

CARMEN

An opera in four acts by Georges Bizet. Presented April 26
and May 3, 1944.

Cast of characters—

Carmen, a Gypsy cigarette girl.........................Coe Glade
Don José, a brigadier...........Sydney Rayner and Tandy McKenzie
Escamillo, a toreador...........................Mostyn Thomas
Micaela, a peasant girl..........................Mary Henderson
Remendado } smugglers....................... { Francesco Curci
Dancairo }   { Fausto Bozza
Zuniga, a captain............Harold Kravitt and Arthur Anderson
Morales, a brigadier..............................Francis Scott
Frasquita } Gypsy friends { Terry Welles and Frieda Bleicher
Mercedes } of Carmen.......{   Lydia Edwards
    Act I.—Public Square in Seville. Act II.—Tavern in Suburbs.
Act III.—Rocky Pass in Mountains. Act IV.—Square in Seville.
Wall of Bull Ring at Back.

LA TRAVIATA

An opera in three acts by Giuseppe Verdi. Presented April 27 and May 6, 1944.

Cast of characters—

Violetta Vallery, a courtesan..............Stella Andreva (Guest)
Alfredo Germont, her lover...........Eugene Conley and Palermo
Giorgio Germont, his father.......................Carlo Morelli
Flora Bervoix, Violetta's friend...................Lydia Edwards
Gastone de Letorieres...........................Francesco Curci
Baron Dauphol, a rival of Alfredo.................Fausto Bozza
Marquis d'Obigny.................................Jules Sassani
Doctor Grenvil.....................................Francis Scott
Annina, confidante of Violetta....................Flora Shennan
    Act I.—Salon in Violetta's house. Act II.—Scene 1—Country House near Paris. 2—Salon in Flora Bervoix' House. Act. III.—Violetta's Bedroom.

AIDA

(2 performances)

An opera in four acts by Giuseppe Verdi, with text in Italian by Antonio Chislanzoni. Presented April 28 and May 7, 1944.

Cast of characters—

Aida, an Ethiopian slave (captive princess)......Elda Ercole and
                                                Mobley Lushanya
Amneris, daughter of the Egyptian King...........Marie Powers
Rhadames, captain of the Egyptian guard.........Sydney Rayner
Amonasro, King of Ethiopia, Aida's father........Mostyn Thomas
Ramfis, High Priest of Isis.....................Harold Kravitt
The King of Egypt............................Arthur Anderson
Messenger.......................................Francesco Curci
Priestess...Frieda Bleicher
    Act I.—Scene 1—Hall in King's Palace at Memphis. 2—Temple of Isis. Act II.—Hall in Amneris' Apartment. 2—Gates of Thebes. Act III.—Shores of the Nile Near Temple of Isis. Act IV.—Scene 1—Outside the Judgment Hall. 2—Vault Beneath the Temple.

FAUST

(2 performances)

An opera in four acts by Charles Gounod. Presented April 29 and May 4, 1944.

Cast of characters—

Marguerite..Mary Henderson
Faust, learned philosopher.......................Eugene Conley
Mephistopheles, the evil one......................Harold Kravitt
Valentin, Marguerite's brother.............Stephan Ballarini and
                                                Moslyn Thomas
Siebel, youth devoted to Marguerite...................Ivy Dale
Wagner, a student................................Fausto Bozza
Martha, neighbor of Marguerite...Philine Falco and Lydia Edwards
    Act I.—Scene 1—Dr. Faust's Study. 2—Fair in Nuremberg. Act II.—Marguerite's Garden. Act III.—Street in Nuremberg. Act IV.—Marguerite's Prison.

Other operas presented during the season were "Rigoletto" April 29 and May 5, 1944, with Marinelli, Marchetto, Shennan, Tara, Palermo, Morelli Kravitt and Curci in the cast; "La Bohème" April 30, with Henderson, Osborne, Conley, Valle, Kravitt, Malatesta and Curci; "Il Trovatore" April 30 and May 7, with Ercole, Powers, Shennan, Rayner, Ballarini, Anderson, Curci and Bozza alternating with Lushanya, Mackenzie and Pandiscio; "La Tosca" with Lushanya, Shennan, Rayner, Valle, Anderson, Lassner, Curci and Bozza; "Cavalleria Rusticana" followed by "Pagliacci" with Ercole Edwards, Betty Stone, Palermo, and Shilton in "Cavalleria Rusticana" and Henderson, Tandy Mackenzie, Mostyn Thomas, Curci and Ballarini in "Pagliacci." Lydia Arlova and Lucien Prideaux were the première danseuse and premier danseur in the San Carlo ballet and the Children's Chorus from the Children's Opera Co. of New York in "Carmen" was under the direction of Eva Leoni.

(Closed May 7, 1944)

The San Carlo Opera Co. also presented a 24-performance season at the Broadway Theatre, October 7 to October 24, 1943.

EARTH JOURNEY

(16 performances)

A comedy in four episodes by Sheldon Davis. Produced by the Blackfriars' Guild at the Blackfriars' Theatre, New York, April 27, 1944.

Cast of characters—

The Property Man	Alexander Cooper
Chorus	Ian Maclaren
Shao Kung	Edward Steinmetz
Cheng Wu Ti	Robert Hayward
Tai Wan	Christina Soulias
Tchang Lo	William Monsees
Tchi Fah	Carol Dunning
Loy Din	Bernice Grant
Su Tong Po	John Rosene
Li Chien	Elizabeth Hunt
See Nan	Ann Donaldson
Mei Fah Ling	Irene Parker
A Messenger	Jack Sherry
The Executioner	Leo Herbert
First Bearer	James Alexander
Second Bearer	Hugh Thomas, Jr.
Third Bearer	Howard Berland
Fourth Bearer	Dennis McDonald
Assistant Property Man	Michael Blair
Attendant to Emperor	John E. Montgomery

Ladies of the Court........Margaret McKenna, Catherine Campbell
    Episode I.—The Temple. 2—The Highway. 3—The Palace. 4—
The Dawn.
    Staged by Dennis Gurney; settings by W. Emerton Heitland;
lighting by Leo Herbert; costumes by Hildegart Brandes.

After successive generations a temple idol held under the curse
of a wicked emperor comes to life and falls in love with the current Emperor's lovely daughter. For an episode or two their reawakened love life is ideally sustained. Then the idol again goes
back to being an idol.

(Closed May 14, 1944)

A HIGHLAND FLING

(28 performances)

A comedy in three acts by Margaret Curtis. Produced by
George Abbott at the Plymouth Theatre, New York, April 28,
1944.

Cast of characters—

Charlie MacKenzie, former Laird of Cairn
    McGorum, a ghost...............................Ralph Forbes
Jeannie MacKenzie, formerly his wife, an angel......Frances Reid
Sir Archibald MacKenzie..........................John Ireland
The Lady of Shalott............................Margaret Curtis
Rabbie MacGregor...............................Karl Swenson
Lizzie MacGregor............................Marguerite Clifton
Bessie MacGregor..................................Patti Brady
Malcolm Graham..................................Ivan Miller
Lila Graham...................................Marjorie Davies
Hamish Hamilton....................................John Robb
Alicetrina MacLean............................Gloria Hallward
Jamie MacTavish................................John McQuade
Sandy MacGill.................................Nicholas Saunders
The Reverend Douglas Stuart..................St. Clair Bayfield
Mrs. MacGill..............................Margaret Morrissey
Mora MacTavish.................................Pax Walker
Ian...James McFadden
Mrs. Ferguson................................Margaret Thomas
Mr. MacDonald....................................James Lane
    Act I.—Outside the Castle Walls in a Remote Little Village near
the Foot of Cairn McGorum in Mountains of Scotland. Act II.—
Scene 1—The Bar at "The Rose and Thistle." 2—Outside Castle
Walls. Act III.—Scene 1—"The Rose and Thistle." 2—Outside
Castle Walls.
    Staged by George Abbott; settings by John Root; costumes by
Motley.

Charlie MacKenzie, dead these hundred and fifty years, barred
out of heaven because of certain earth-bound interests in ladies fair,
is still haunting the family castle when Malcolm Graham, a de-
scendant of the clan, comes from America to recover a scone stone
the English think they are holding safely in Westminster Abbey.
Charlie's ghost can be seen and talked with only by Silly Shalott,
the town's daftie, who imagines she is the Lady of Shalott her-

self, and Bessie MacGregor, an exuberant 7-year-old. Charlie finally decides, at the bidding of his angel wife, to make one more try for heaven by saving the soul of Rabbie MacGregor, the village sinner. But he is none too pleased, or certain of the outcome, after he gets Rabbie saved.

(Closed May 20, 1944)

* PICK-UP GIRL

(53 performances)

A drama in three acts by Elsa Shelley. Presented by Michael Todd's staff at the 48th Street Theatre, New York, May 3, 1944.

Cast of characters—

Judge Bentley	William Harrigan
Miss Porter	Doro Merande
Mrs. Busch	Edmonia Nolley
Court Clerk	Douglas Keaton
Door Attendant	William Foran
Mrs. Collins	Kathryn Grill
Larry Webster	Zachary A. Charles
Mrs. Marti	Lili Valenty
Alexander Elliott	Arthur Mayberry
Mr. Brill	Bigelow Sayre
Policeman Owens	Morty Martell
Elizabeth Collins	Pamela Rivers
Jackie Polumbo	Joe Johnson
Miss Russell	Dorothy Blackburn
Mr. Collins	Frank Tweddell
Ruby Lockwood	Toni Favor
Peter Marti	Marvin Forde
Joan	Lois Wheeler
Jean	Rosemary Rice

Acts I, II and III.—A Juvenile Court.
Staged by Roy Hargrave; production supervised by James Colligan, Harry Bloomfield and Harriet Kaplan; setting by Watson Barratt; costumes by Emeline Roche.

See page 315.

HICKORY STICK

(8 performances)

A drama in three acts by Frederick Stephani and Murray Burnett. Produced by Marjorie Ewing and Marie Louise Elkins at the Mansfield Theatre, New York, May 8, 1944.

Cast of characters—

Mary Donlan	Sarah Floyd
Miss Jastrombowski	Wanda Sponder
Peter Jastrombowski	Bill Hunt
Eugene Walsh	Lawrence Fletcher
Rita Pessolano	Adrienne Bayan
John MacLemore	Jeff Brown
Tony Pessolano	Vito Christi
Mrs. Bettina Pessolano	Frieda Altman

```
Karen Lorimer.................................Adrienne Marden
Patrick MacLemore, Sr...........................Farrell Pelly
James Kirkland................................Steve Cochran
Frank Antonucci.................................Danny Leone
Steven Ames.................................Richard Basehart
Samuel Berg.........................................Ray Fry
Lionel Warner................................Albert Popwell
Calliope Oliver..............................Violet J. Kennedy
George Uhorchak...............................Johnny Croce
Paula Taliaferro..........................Lorraine Pressler
Grace Umbdenstock.................................Janet Dowd
Gladys Steele.............................Frances Thaddeus
Elizabeth O'Hare...............................Peggy Wynne
Sophie Novak..............................Marjorie Milliard
Helen Orth.....................................Celia Babcock
Lewis Rainey.................................Ross Matthew
Joe Pessolano....................................Dehl Berti
```

Act I.—Scene 1—Guidance Office, Truxton Vodational High School. 2—Kirkland's Classroom. Act II.—Scene 1—Guidance Office. 2—Kirkland's Classroom. Act III.—Kirkland's Classroom.
Staged by J. B. Daniels; settings by Frederick Fox.

James Kirkland is home from the wars after having been wounded in the hell at Guadalcanal. He takes a job as a teacher in a New York vocational high school which has a tough reputation. The toughest of the pupils is Tony Pessalano, whose brother had been a member of Kirkland's company. With the help of an older teacher, Eugene Walsh, who fights the tough lads in their own fashion, Kirkland gets through, winning the hero-worship of Tony, who finally is egged on to murder another toughie in Kirkland's defense.

(Closed May 13, 1944)

DREAM WITH MUSIC

(28 performances)

A musical fantasy in two acts by Sidney Sheldon, Dorothy Kilgallen and Ben Roberts; music by Clay Warnick; lyrics by Edward Eager. Produced by Richard Kollmar at the Majestic Theatre, New York, May 18, 1944.

Cast of characters—

```
                          (IN REALITY)
Ella..................................................Betty Allen
Marian................................................Joy Hodges
Dinah.................................................Vera Zorina
Western Union Boy.....................................Alex Rotov
Michael...........................................Ronald Graham
Robert..............................................Robert Brink
                         (IN THE DREAM)
Scheherazade.........................................Vera Zorina
Jasmin................................................Joy Hodges
Sultan..............................................Robert Brink
Wazier................................................Alex Rotov
Mispah...........................................Marcella Howard
Hispah..............................................Janie Janvier
Rispah..............................................Lois Barnes
```

Tispah...Lucille Barnes
Fispah..Jane Hetherington
Kispah...Donna Devel
Aladdin...Ronald Graham
Rug Merchant...Ray Cook
Perfume Merchant..................................Robert Beam
Fakir..Michael Kozak
Candy Salesman.......................................Bill Jones
Musical Instrument Merchant.......................John Panter
Snake Charmer..................................Byron Milligan
Sand Diviner.....................................Ralph Bunker
Sinbad.......:.................................Leonard Elliott
Mrs. Sinbad...Betty Allen
Genie...Dave Ballard
Guards: Jerry Ross, Larry Evers, Bill Weber, Parker Wilson
The Little One.................................Dorothy Babb
The Blonde One...................................Dee Turnell
1st Hot One.......................................Sunny Rice
2nd Hot One.....................................Dixie Roberts
The Slender One..................................Mavis Mims
The Tall One....................................Dolores Milan
The One with the Pug Nose.........................Tari Vance
The Twins................Lois and Lucille Barnes
Day.............:.................................Peter Birch
Night...Sunny Rice
Mrs. Panda.....................................Dixie Roberts
Mr. Panda......................................Ralph Bunker
Lion...Peter Birch
Rabbit...Donna Devel
Mr. Owl..Byron Milligan
Mrs. Owl.......................................Marcella Howard
Unicorn...Bill Jones
Mrs. Lion......................................Janie Janvier
Penguin...Bill Weber
Wolf...Ray Cook
Ermine..Lucille Barnes
Lamb..Dorothy Babb
I. J...Robert Beam
Mrs. Fox.....................................Jane Hetherington
Leopard..Lois Barnes
Monkey...Jerry Ross
Tiger...Michael Kozak
Mouse..Buddy Douglas
Aladdin's Aide.....................................Bill Weber
Chinese Masseur..................................Jerry Ross
     Act I.—Scene 1—Dinah's Apartment. 2—Palace of Shariar. 3—
Street in Bazaars of Bagdad. 4—Sinbad's Garden. 5—Corridor in
Sinbad's House. 6—Magic Carpet. 7—In the Clouds. Act II.—
Scene 1—Aladdin's Forest-China. 2—Game Preserve. 3 and 5—
Corridor-Sinbad's. 4—Aladdin's Palace. 6—Palace of Shariar.
7—Dinah's Apartment.
     Staged by Richard Kollmar; choreography by George Balanchine;
tap routines directed by Henry Le Tang; music directed by Max
Meth; settings by Stewart Chaney; costumes by Miles White.

Dinah has been writing soap operas for the radio until she
is sick to death of them. She sleeps and dreams that she is
Scheherazade, who had a thousand and one Arabian Nights tales
to tell. This brings her into contact with a harem, a Sultan, a
Wazier and a variety of other romping stooges.

(Closed June 10, 1944)

THE MAID AS MISTRESS

(*La Serva Padrona*)

(2 performances)

An operetta by Pergolesi. Produced by Felix Brentano and presented by Yolanda Mero-Irion for the New Opera Company, at the Alvin Theatre, New York, May 14 and May 21, 1944.

Cast of characters—

```
The Host, Prince Stigliano.....................Melville Cooper
Duke of Maddeloni...............................Ralph Dumke
Duchess of Maddeloni............................Lisette Verea
Princess  D'Avellino.................,..........Elisabeth  Sutherland
Messer Greco....................................Donald Gage
    Dancers in Minuet: Babs Heath, Alla Shishkina, Stan Zompakos
    and Frank Moncion.
Serpina ........................................Virginia  MacWatters
Uberto..........................................Edwin  Steffe
Vespone.........................................Norman Budd
Dancer..........................................Kathryn  Lee
    Ballerinas:  Babs  Heath,  Alla  Shishkina,  Bobbie  Howell  and
    Cyprienne Gableman.
    Prologue and Act takes place on the grounds of Prince Stigliano's
Palace in Naples, Italy.  1733.
    Staged by Felix Brentano; music directed by Isaac Van Grove.
```

Followed by—

THE SECRET OF SUZANNE

An operetta by Wolf-Ferrari.

```
Count Gil.......................................Hugh  Thompson
Suzanne.........................................Brenda  Lewis
Sante...........................................Anne MacQuarrie
    The new version of both operas devised by Felix Brentano; lyrics
and dialogue by Marion Farquhar; choreography by Joan Woodruff;
associate conductor, Dr. Otto Herz.
```

CAREER ANGEL

(22 performances)

A comedy in three acts by Gerard M. Murray. Revived by Andrew Billings and Joseph Dicks, in association with David Shay, at the National Theatre, New York, May 23, 1944.

Cast of characters—

```
Brother  Gregory................................Donald  Foster
Donnie McAdams..................................Allen  Rich
Willie Garvey...................................David  Kelly
Brother  Fidelis................................Ronald  Telfer
Kurt Rheinhold.................................Tony  Miller
Brother  Seraphim...............................Whitford  Kane
Angel Guardian..................................Glenn  Anders
Hurdles.........................................Alvin  Allen
Glinsky.........................................Robert  Ramsen
```

```
Thompson.........................................Robert Lee
Rinn...........................................Charleton Carpenter
Bruno Chevoski..............................Michael Dreyfuss
Barr...........................................Wendell Whitten
Brother Ubaldus...:..........................Mason Adams
Duval Devois..................................Dorn Alexander
Al Fuller.......................................Gerald Matthews
Billy..........................................Charles Nevil
    Acts I, II and III.—Superior's Office of Bosco Institute, Some-
where in Georgia.  Prior to Pearl Harbor.
    Staged by Don Appell; setting by Carl Kent; lighting by Frederick
Fox.
```

Brother Seraphim, his heart devoted to the rescue of a Southern orphanage for boys, has a visit from his Guardian Angel the time the orphanage is threatened with being closed out by the holders of a mortgage. The Guardian Angel, invisible and inaudible to any save Brother Seraphim, helps Seraphim bring the orphanage to national attention, which helps to attract contributions and save the last act. A German spy plot is also uncovered.

(Closed June 10, 1944)

"Career Angel" was originally produced by the Blackfriars' Guild at the Blackfriars' Theatre, New York, November 18, 1943, with the appended cast of characters. Its semi-pro showing was the more successful of the two. The cast:

```
Brother Gregory......................................Liam Dunn
Donnie McAdams..................................John Hickton
Willie Garvey........................................David Kelly
Brother Fidelis.....................................Joseph Boley
Kurt Rheinhold......................................Eric Ladd
Brother Seraphim............................Angelo Benedetto
Angel Guardian............................David Carman Jones
J. Mosely Barr.......................................Paul Pettit
Brother Ubaldus..................................John Young
Joe Hurdles........................................Jack O'Neil
Walter Glinsky..............................Howard Berland
Frank Thompson..................................Eddie Ross
Johnnie Rinn................................Gerard McLaughlin
Bruno Chevoski..................................William Russell
Dr. Volatov...................................William J. Connor
Heinrich Von Taushauer......................C. Fabian Thomas
```

ACCORDING TO LAW

(4 performances)

A drama in one act by Noel Houston. Revived by Eugene Endrey at the Mansfield Theatre, New York, June 1, 1944.

Cast of characters—

```
Jim Nailey.......................................Gregory Robbins
Henry Terry.......................................Robert Harrison
Henry Yancey.....................................Windsor Bryan
Luke............................................Burton Mallory
Senator Lawrence.............................Dayton Lummis
```

```
Charlie Teague...............................Wardell  Saunders
George  Randall...................................Henry  Wilson
Ben  Staggs.......................................Don  Appell
Mrs.  Harkness............................Lorraine  MacMartin
Harvey......................................Harvey  Marlowe
     Scene—A  Courtroom.
     Staged  by  Eugene  Endrey;  setting  by  Harry  Bennett;  lighting  by
Leo  Kerz.
```

Charlie Teague, an innocent Negro, is charged with the rape of a married white woman. The court appoints Ben Staggs, a drunken lawyer, to defend him. Staggs proves the case framed against Teague to cover her guilt with a white man. Prejudiced court and jury send the Negro to the chair. (Originally produced at the Provincetown Theatre, New York, March 19, 1940. Best Plays of 1939-40.)

Followed by—

A STRANGE PLAY

A comedy in two acts by Patti Spears. Produced by Eugene Endrey at the Mansfield Theatre, New York, June 1, 1944.

Cast of characters—

```
Dr.  Stephen  Duryea...........................Richard  Gordon
Claire...........................................Alicia  Parnahay
Paul  Cartwright.................................Herbert  Heyes
William  Douglas.................................Ralph  Clanton
James...........................................Byron  Russell
     Acts  I  and  II.—The  Duryea  Living  Room  on  Long  Island.
     Staged  by  Eugene  Endrey.
```

William Douglas, playwright, considers the possibilities of a plot that shall involve his friend, Dr. Duryea, and Claire Duryea, his wife. Knowing that Mrs. Duryea is cheating with Paul Cartwright, an actor, should the playwright tell the husband? Or shouldn't he? With the help of the cast he tries it both ways. Both results are still terrible.

(Closed June 3, 1944)

THAT OLD DEVIL

(16 performances)

A comedy in three acts by J. C. Nugent. Produced by Lodewick Vroom at The Playhouse, New York, June 5, 1944.

Cast of characters—

```
Hester............................................Ruth  Gilbert
Officer  Williamson............................David  S.  Jordan
John  Woodruff....................................Matt  Briggs
Jim  Blair........................................J. C. Nugent
```

```
Doctor Davis...................................Matthew Smith
Harry Robinson...............................Warren Lyons
Wilbur Blime.....................................J. Colvil Dunn
Lila Merrill.......................................Agnes Doyle
Martha Blair.......................................Luella Gear
Mrs. Woodruff....................................Ruth Gates
Mrs. Blime.......................................Lou McGuire
Mrs. Robinson..................................Mary Dickson
Jerry Swift.....................................Michael Ames
```
Acts I, II and III.—Living Room of Jim Blair's Home, Beechville, Conn.
Staged by J. C. Nugent; setting by Paul Morrison; costumes by Johnnie Johnstone.

Jim Blair is aging and dull. Befriending Lila Merrill, an orphaned war worker from England, he permits the scandal to spread that he is the father of Lila's expected child. The suspicion adds glamor to Blair's life in a small Connecticut town suffering from a shortage of manpower. All the bridge-playing ladies who formerly looked right through him now pause and consider. Jim fights them off successfully until Lila's young husband is in a position to announce their secret wedding.

(Closed June 17, 1944)

SLIGHTLY SCANDALOUS

(7 performances)

A comedy in three acts by Frederick Jackson; based on an idea by Roland Bottomley. Produced by Charles Leonard in association with Thomas McQuillan at the National Theatre, New York, June 13, 1944.

Cast of characters—

```
David Stuart...............................Nino Pipitone, Jr.
Walter Stuart....................................William Berens
Jane...........................................Dorothy Vaughan
Connie..........................................Elizabeth Burt
James Willoughby.................................Paul McVey
Frances Stuart....................................Janet Beecher
Millicent Stuart...............................Anne Henderson
Edward Morrow, Jr.............................Michael Meehan
Archie Campbell..............................Barry Macollum
Wareef of Farak.....................................Ben Shaw
General Georges Rigaud..........................Jean De Briac
Jan Letzaretzsko..................................Gene Gary
Sir Michael Norman................................Boyd Davis
Mrs. Henry J. Crewe...........................Frances Carson
Daphne Crewe....................................Brooke Shane
```
Acts I, II and III.—Drawing Room of Frances Stuart's Home, Westchester, New York.
Staged by Frederick Jackson; setting by Harry Dworkin; costumes by Adrian.

Frances Stuart, writer and lecturer, had fixed ideas about the hampering and confining handicaps of marriage. Therefore she never married. There were, however, three attractive men, a titled Englishman, a Polish pianist and a French soldier, to whom she bore children. For the children she invented a fictitious parent, buying a picture of him in an antique shop to hang over the mantel in the living room. When the children grew up and the two older ones became engaged, it was decided they should be reasonably legitimatized. Their mother agreed to marry the one of three fathers they should select. When the children couldn't agree their mother decides to go on pretending that they are the offspring of the fellow in the oil painting.

(Closed June 17, 1944)

*FOR KEEPS

(5 performances)

A comedy in three acts by F. Hugh Herbert. Produced by Gilbert Miller at the Henry Miller Theatre, New York, June 14, 1944.

Cast of characters—

Miss Maxwell	Zolya Talma
Anna	Ellen Mahar
Paul Vanda	Frank Conroy
Mr. Reamer	Geoffrey Lumb
Pamela Vanda	Julie Warren
June	Norma Clerc
Jimmy McCarey	Donald Murphy
Nancy Vanda	Patricia Kirkland
Charlie	Joseph R. Garry
Frank	Grover Burgess
Norma	Joan Wetmore
Terry	George Baxter

Acts I, II and III.—Paul Vanda's Studio Apartment, New York City.

Staged by Gilbert Miller; setting by Raymond Sovey.

Nancy Vanda has been living with her mother since the Vandas were divorced. Now, at 15, she comes to visit her father, Paul Vanda, who has just married a fourth wife. Nancy is a sophisticated child with a pretended fondness for rum, cigarettes and what she knows of night club life. She lets strangers believe she is 18 at least, and probably 19. A good-looking 4-F, Jimmy McCarey, one of her father's photographic models, is not averse to accepting Nancy's advances until he discovers her real age. Then he backs quickly away. Nancy's mother, with a vulgarized second husband, comes for Nancy, but her father decides she has had enough of that atmosphere. He keeps her with him. Jimmy, the model, agrees to wait until she grows up.

*TAKE A BOW

(4 performances)

A vaudeville show in two acts; music by Ted Murray and Benny Davis. Presented by Lou Walters at the Broadhurst Theatre, New York, June 15, 1944.

Principals engaged—

Jay C. Flippen	Chico Marx
Alan Cross	Henry Dunn
Mary Raye	Naldi
Gene Sheldon	Pat Rooney
Johnny Mack	Loretta Fischer
Murtah Sisters	Whitson Brothers

Think-a-Drink Hoffman
Marjery Fielding's Dancers

Staged by Wally Wanger; music directed by Ray Kavanaugh; dances by Marjery Fielding; settings by Kaj Velden; costumes by Ben Wallace.

DANCE DRAMA

The Ballet Theatre continued into the 1943-44 season at the Lewisohn Stadium with four programs starting June 24. Antal Dorati, Mois Zlatin and Robert Lawrence directed the performances. The programs included "Les Sylphides," "Petrouchka," "Princess Aurora," "Swan Lake," "Aleko," "Bluebeard," "Capriccio Espanol," "Three Virgins and the Devil," "Giselle," "Spectre de la Rose," "Pas de Deux" and "Gala Performance." The principals included Alicia Markova, Leonide Massine, Anton Dolin, Rosella Hightower, Marina Svetlova, Lucia Chase, Andre Eglevsky, Nora Kaye, Antony Tudor, Yura Lazovsky, Nicolas Orloff, Hubert Bland, Hugh Laing, Richard Reed, Simon Semenoff, Miriam Golden, Janet Reed, Jean Hunt and John Krisa.

October 10, the Ballet Theatre opened at the Metropolitan Opera House under the management of S. Hurok. Dance dramas other than those presented earlier at the Stadium included five world premieres: "Mademoiselle Angot," a comedy ballet by Leonide Massine, with music selected from operettas by Alexander Charles Lecocq, the score arranged by Efrem Kurtz, orchestrated by Richard Mohaupt and decor by Mstislav Doboujinsky; "Pictures of Goya," based on music by Enrique Granados and Goya drawings and danced by Argentinita, Pilar Lopez, Jose Greco and Manola Vargas; "Fair at Sorochinsk," by David Lichine, with musical adaptation from Moussorgsky by Antal Dorati and decor by Nicholas Remisoff; "Dim Lustre" by Antony Tudor set to music of Richard Strauss' "Burlesca" with decor by the Motleys, and "Tally-Ho," a satiric comedy by Agnes de Mille, to music of Gluck arranged by Paul Nordoff, with decor by the Motleys. Other dance dramas not included in the Stadium program were "Salonika," restaged by Yura Lazovsky and choreographed by Vania Psota to the music of Dvorak; "Romeo and Juliet," "Helen of Troy," "Apollo," "Pillar of Fire," "Pas de Quatre," "Giselle," "Judgment of Paris," "Lilac Garden," "Peter and the Wolf," "Billy the Kid" and "Romantic Age." Besides the principals above mentioned at the Stadium were Maria Karnilova, Alicia Alonsa, Jerome Robbins, Dimitri Romanoff, Michael Kidd, Albia Kavan and John Taras. Guest dancers, Agnes de Mille, Vera Zorina, Argentinita,

Roland Guerard, Alicia Alonsa, Ensign David Nillo and Igor Stravinsky. The season closed at the Metropolitan November 7, and reopened April 9, closing May 21. Premieres during this engagement were "Fancy Free," choreographed by Jerome Robbins to an original score by Leonard Bernstein, with decor by Oliver Smith and "Amor Brujo," danced by Argentinita and her company. Other dramas not previously presented during the season were "Three Cornered Rat," "Dark Elegies," and "Barn Dance." In addition to the principals previously engaged were Nana Gollner, Paul Petroff, Muriel Bentley, Virginia Wilcox, Shirley Eckl, Rex Cooper, Harold Lang, Dorothie Littlefield and Thomas Cannon.

Katherine Dunham, with a company of dancers, was presented by S. Hurok in "A Tropical Revue" at the Martin Beck Theatre, New York, September 19. Music was directed by Albert Arkus and costumes were designed by John Pratt. The company included Roger Ohardieno, Tommy Gomes, Laverne French, Lucille Ellis, Lavinia Williams, Syvilla Fort, Claude Marchant, Leonard Morris, Vanoye Aikens, André Drew, Lawaune Ingram, Marie Montiero and Ramona Erwin. The dance dramas included "Rites de Passage," "Rumba Suite," "Woman with a Cigar," "Plantation Dances," "Br'er Rabbit," "Darktown Strutters Ball," "Santos Ritual," and "Bahiana." The engagement closed November 15.

Four new choreographies were presented by the American Concert Ballet at Needle Trades High School and at Y.M.H.A., New York, in October and November. The dance dramas shown in New York for the first time were George Balanchine's "Concerto Baroco," "Sailor Bar," by Mary Jane Shea, "Five Boons of Life," by William Dollar, and "Mother Goose Suite" by Todd Bolender.

The Don Cossack Chorus and Dancers were presented in a Russian program at the Metropolitan Opera House, New York, October 1, 2 and 3, by S. Hurok. Serge Jaroff directed the music.

Asadata Dafora staged and appeared in "African Dance Festival," sponsored by African Academy of Arts and Research at Carnegie Hall, New York, December 13. The dance dramas were based on dramas previously choreographed by Dafora: "Kykundor" and "Zunguru." The principals were Alma Sutton, Pearl Primus, Abdul Assen and Mr. Dafora.

Martha Graham and her company of dancers gave two performances at the 46th Street Theatre, New York, December 26 and January 9. The music was directed by Louis Horst and decor was by Arch Lauterer. Her program included "Salem Shore," with music by Paul Nordoff, "Punch and Judy," with music by Robert McBride, and "Deaths and Entrances" with music by Hunter Johnson. Later in the season Miss Graham appeared at the National Theatre for eight performances from May 7 to May 14. Besides the dramas mentioned above the company danced "Primitive Mysteries," "El Penitente," "Every Soul Is a Circus," "American Document," "Frontier," "Lamentation," "Deep Song," and "Letter to the World." The principals were Jane Dudley, Sophie Maslow, Eric Hawkins, Merce Cunningham, Nina Fonaroff, Pearl Lang and Jane Erdman.

OFF BROADWAY

The Light Opera Theatre, under the direction of John F. Grahame, continued its Gilbert and Sullivan Repertory into the 1943-44 season with "Ruddigore," presented at the Provincetown Playhouse, June 25 and 27. Later in the season they resumed production with "The Mikado" (November 19), "Yeomen of the Guard," "Iolanthe" and "The Sorcerer."

"Bridge to the Sun," by Phyllis Carver and Burrell Smith, was produced by Burrell Smith Productions and the Provincetown Theatre, July 24. It was staged by Phyllis Carver and the cast included George Breen, Thomas Heaphy, Naomi Laurence, Edgar Russell, Barbara Kessler and Burrell Smith.

At the same theatre "Familiar Pattern," by David S. Lifson, was produced by Modern Play Productions, September 2. Sally Nusbaum designed the settings and John F. Grahame staged the production. The cast included Herbert Giffin, Robert Feyti, Anne King, Melvin Davis, Pauline Anton, Olga Novosel, Florence Saks, Genie Conrad, Joseph Di Stefano, Miriam Hilsenroth and Howard Bradler.

Another play produced by this company at the Provincetown Playhouse was "Career," a comedy in two acts by Nan Kirby. The opening date was October 27, and the cast included Melanie Hilden, John Francis, Josephine Lombardo, Peter Zube, Maurice Vankin, Adeline Bitters, Anne King, Genie Conrad, Mary Kilman, Lucille Grayson, Onda de Munoz, Louis Carmole, Robert Feyti, Joseph DiStefano and Mabel Nash.

"Spring Production" by Oskar Gens ended the season at the Provincetown Playhouse May 19. It was produced by Modern Play Productions and the cast included Blanche Rohmier, Genie Conrad, Robert Feyti, John Francis, Joseph Nathan, Josephine Lombardo, Ola Lylak, Ben Hight, Eugene Allen and Joseph Di Stefano.

The Dramatic Workshop of the New School for Social Research, under the direction of Erwin Piscator, gave a series of plays and parts of plays illustrating "The March of Time," a program arranged by John Gassner and Paolo Milano. The plays were Bernard Shaw's "Saint Joan," Georg Kaiser's "Gas," Ibsen's "A Doll's House," Shakespeare's "Macbeth" and

"Othello," and "Doctor Sganarelle," an original adaptation by Milton Levine of Moliere's "Imaginary Invalid" and "The Doctor in Spite of Himself." Philip Huston adapted the "Macbeth," streamlining the tragedy to one hour. Philip Huston was the Macbeth, Helen Waren the Lady Macbeth and William Woodson served as Narrator. In "Othello," Canada Lee was the Othello, Elena Karam the Desdemona, John Ireland Iago, Irene Vargo Amelia and William Woodson Cassio. John Haggott staged the plays. From February 21 to March 11, the Studio Theatre presented "Nathan the Wise" in the English adaptation by Ferdinand Bruckner. The 22 performances were directed by Mr. Piscator.

Paul and Virginia Gilmore presented five revivals at the Cherry Lane Theatre, New York, beginning October 1, with "The Family Upstairs," which ran for two months. Following this were "The Bishop Misbehaves," running through December and January; "As Husbands Go," during February and March; "Dracula" in April and "Girls in Uniform" in June. A new play, "The Leavenworth Case," by Basil Ring, based on a book by Anna Katherine Green was produced in May.

The "Ice Follies of 1944" was produced by Roy and Ed Shipstad and Oscar Johnson at Madison Square Garden from November 23 to December 11. The cast included Roy Shipstad, Michael Kirby, Norah McCarthy, Jeanne Sook, Frick and Frack, Betty Atkinson, Heine Brock, Bobby Blake, Ruby Maxson, Phyllis Legg, Hazel Franklin, Richard Rassmussen, Roberta Barton, Jack Millikan and Helen Brad.

"Hollywood Ice Revue" was given by Sonja Henie and Arthur Wirtz at the Madison Square Gardens from January 18 through February 4, with Sonja Henie and Freddie Trenkler heading the cast.

The American Negro Theatre presented "Three Is a Family" at the Library Theatre in West 135th street week-ends through the Spring of 1944 and gave one performance at the Longacre Theatre, New York, April 17. June 16 this group produced a new play, "Anna Lucasta," by Philip Yordan, adapted by Abram Hill and Harry Wagstaff Gribble, at the Library Theatre. The play was staged by Mr. Gribble, with settings by Richard Bolton. The cast included Lionel Monagus, Alvin Childress, Earle Hyman, Letitia Toole, Alberta Perkins, Fred O'Neal, Betty Haynes, John Proctor, Hilda Moses Simms, Alice Childress, Martin Slade, Billy Cumberbatch and Buddy Holmes. "Anna Lucasta" is promised a Broadway hearing the season of 1944-45.

The Lighthouse Players gave three one-act plays May 3. These were "Birthday of the Infanta" by Vail Motter, "Xingu" by Thomas Seller and "Tickets, Please" by Felix Fair.

"Broken Hearts of Broadway," a melodrama by Ralph Matson, opened at the New York Music Hall under the auspices of Selected Artists, Inc., in association with Alan Corelli, June 12, closing after 14 performances. It was staged by the author. Pierre de Caillaux directed the music. The cast included Bibi Osterwald, Derrick Lynn-Thomas, Natalie Hammond Core, Brian O'Mara, Louise Kelly, Margaret Linskie, Steve Cochran, Max Leavitt and the Empire State Quartet.

The Davenport Free Theatre, under the direction of Butler Davenport, started the season October 5 with "American Reasons," dramatized by Mr. Davenport from Bonaro W. Overstreet's poems-in-prose. Other productions included revivals of "The Taming of the Shrew," Chekov's "The Swan Song," "An Interview with Mark Twain," "Difference of Gods," by Davenport, "The Bells," "The Mollusc," by Herbert Davis, and "The Silent Assertion" by Davenport.

FOREIGN LANGUAGE PLAYS

"The Golden Land," by Julie Berns with music by Alexander Olshanetsky, opened the season at the Public Theatre, New York, October 11, and ran until February 7. The musical play was produced and directed by Judah Bleich, the choreography by Lillian Shapero and the settings by H. A. Condell. In the cast were Leo Fuchs, Ludwig Satz, Aaron Lebedeff, Dinah Halpern and Jack Rechtzeit.

The season was opened by the Yiddish Art Theatre October 18 at the Adelphi Theatre, New York, with the production of "The Family Carnovsky," by I. J. Singer, with music by Joseph Rumshinsky. The production was directed by Maurice Schwartz and the settings were by H. A. Condell. In the cast were Mr. Schwartz, Isadore Casher, Morris Feder, Anatole Winogradov, Michael Goldstein, Paul Leavitt, Muriel Gruber and others. The play closed January 30, after 136 performances.

STATISTICAL SUMMARY

Plays	Number Performances	
Arsenic and Old Lace..	1,444	(Closed June 17, 1944)
Corn Is Green, The...	56	(Closed June 19, 1943)
Counsellor-at-Law	258	(Closed July 10, 1943)
Dark Eyes.............	230	(Closed July 31, 1943)
Eve of St. Mark, The..	307	(Closed June 26, 1943)
Harriet	377	(Closed April 1, 1944)
Janie	642	(Closed February 26, 1944)
Junior Miss..........	710	(Closed July 24, 1943)
Milky Way, The......	16	(Closed June 20, 1943)
Patriots, The.........	173	(Closed June 26, 1943)
Rosalinda	521	(Closed January 22, 1944)
Skin of Our Teeth, The	359	(Closed September 25, 1943)
Something for the Boys	422	(Closed January 8, 1944)
Sons o' Fun	742	(Closed August 9, 1943)
Star and Garter.......	609	(Closed December 4, 1943)
Stars on Ice..........	830	(Closed April 16, 1944)
Student Prince, The...	153	(Closed October 2, 1943)
Tomorrow the World..	500	(Closed June 17, 1944)

"Stars on Ice" closed the 1942-43 season with 427 performances, vacationed from May 16 to June 24, 1943, and continued into the 1943-44 season with an added 403 performances, making a total of 830.

LONG RUNS ON BROADWAY

To June 19, 1944

(Plays marked with asterisk were still playing June 19, 1944)

Plays	Number Performances	Plays	Number Performances
Tobacco Road	3,182	A Trip to Chinatown	657
Abie's Irish Rose	2,327	Rain	648
*Life with Father	1,937	Janie	642
Arsenic and Old Lace	1,444	The Green Pastures	640
Hellzapoppin	1,404	*The Doughgirls	623
Lightnin'	1,291	Is Zat So	618
Pins and Needles	1,108	Separate Rooms	613
*Angel Street	1,071	Star and Garter	609
The Bat	867	Student Prince	608
My Sister Eileen	865	Broadway	603
White Cargo	864	Adonis	603
You Can't Take It with		Street Scene	601
You	837	Kiki	600
Three Men on a Horse	835	Blossom Time	592
Stars on Ice	830	Brother Rat	577
The Ladder	789	Show Boat	572
The First Year	760	The Show-Off	571
Sons o' Fun	742	Sally	570
The Man Who Came to		Rose Marie	557
Dinner	739	Strictly Dishonorable	557
Claudia	722	Good News	551
Junior Miss	710	Let's Face It	547
Seventh Heaven	704	Within the Law	541
Peg o' My Heart	692	The Music Master	540
The Children's Hour	691	What a Life	538
Dead End	687	*Kiss and Tell	532
East Is West	680	The Boomerang	522
Chauve Souris	673	*Oklahoma!	522
Irene	670	Rosalinda	521
Boy Meets Girl	669	Blackbirds	518
Blithe Spirit	657	Sunny	517
The Women	657	Victoria Regina	517

*Ziegfeld Follies 513   Panama Hattie 501
The Vagabond King .. 511   Bird in Hand 500
The New Moon 509   Sailor, Beware! 500
Shuffle Along 504   Room Service 500
Personal Appearance . 501   Tomorrow the World . 500

DRAMA CRITICS' CIRCLE AWARD

The New York Drama Critics' Circle also suffered somewhat as a wartime casualty, losing six of its founding members in 1943. John Anderson of the *Journal-American*, the Circle's president, died. Brooks Atkinson of the *Times*, John Mason Brown of the *World-Telegram* and Richard Lockridge of the *Sun* were called to war, Mr. Atkinson as a correspondent and the Messrs. Brown and Lockridge as naval aides. Burns Mantle of the *Daily News* retired from his post to become a critic emeritus and George Jean Nathan of the *Journal-American* and *Esquire* magazine, following certain internal disagreements, resigned from the Circle, as also did Burton Rascoe, who was serving as Mr. Brown's substitute.

In the reorganization Howard Barnes of the *Herald Tribune* was elected president. By unanimous agreement the new Circle decided to abolish the voting rule that had previously prevailed, making a two-thirds vote necessary in the selection of a prize play. It was agreed that only one vote should be taken and a straight majority was sufficient to name the prize-winning entry.

As a result of the balloting under the new rule the Circle found itself without a best play selection for the season. Of the fourteen votes cast Lillian Hellman's "The Searching Wind" received seven (lacking one of a majority), John Van Druten's "The Voice of the Turtle" was the choice of two critics and the D'Usseau-Gow "Tomorrow the World" got one vote. Four of the Circle's members voted against any award, insisting no play written by an American author and produced in New York during the season was worthy of such honor.

A citation was awarded the Franz Werfel-S. N. Behrman "Jacobowsky and the Colonel" as the best foreign play of the year, though again five critics voted against any award being made in this division.

This is the third year in which the Drama Critics' Circle has refused its endorsement of a prize American play for the season. There was no award in 1938-39 or in 1941-42. Other selections follow:

1935-36—Winterset, by Maxwell Anderson
1936-37—High Tor, by Maxwell Anderson

1937-38—Of Mice and Men, by John Steinbeck
1938-39—No award. ("The Little Foxes" and "Abe Lincoln
          in Illinois" led the voting.)
1939-40—The Time of Your Life, by William Saroyan
1940-41—Watch on the Rhine, by Lillian Hellman
1941-42—No award.
1942-43—The Patriots, by Sidney Kingsley
1943-44—No award.

PULITZER PRIZE WINNERS

"For the original American play performed in New York which shall best represent the educational value and power of the stage in raising the standard of good morals, good taste and good manners."—The Will of Joseph Pulitzer, dated April 16, 1904.

In 1929 the advisory board, which, according to the terms of the will, "shall have the power in its discretion to suspend or to change any subject or subjects . . . if in the judgment of the board such suspension, changes or substitutions shall be conducive to the public good," decided to eliminate from the above paragraph relating to the prize-winning play the words "in raising the standard of good morals, good taste and good manners."

The Pulitzer Prize Committee also decided against making an American drama award for the season of 1943-44, although in fairness it should be noted that Miss Hellman's "The Searching Wind," which had won seven of the Drama Critics' votes, was not on the Pulitzer's list of eligible candidates. This committee closes its books on April 1 and the Hellman drama was not produced until April 12. It will therefore still be a candidate for 1944 honors next Spring. Previous Pulitzer play awards have been—

1917-18—Why Marry? by Jesse Lynch Williams
1918-19—No award.
1919-20—Beyond the Horizon, by Eugene O'Neill
1920-21—Miss Lulu Bett, by Zona Gale
1921-22—Anna Christie, by Eugene O'Neill
1922-23—Icebound, by Owen Davis
1923-24—Hell-bent fer Heaven, by Hatcher Hughes
1924-25—They Knew What They Wanted, by Sidney Howard
1925-26—Craig's Wife, by George Kelly
1926-27—In Abraham's Bosom, by Paul Green
1927-28—Strange Interlude, by Eugene O'Neill
1928-29—Street Scene, by Elmer Rice
1929-30—The Green Pastures, by Marc Connelly
1930-31—Alison's House, by Susan Glaspell
1931-32—Of Thee I Sing, by George S. Kaufman, Morrie
    Ryskind, Ira and George Gershwin

1932-33—Both Your Houses, by Maxwell Anderson
1933-34—Men in White, by Sidney Kingsley
1934-35—The Old Maid, by Zoe Akins
1935-36—Idiot's Delight, by Robert E. Sherwood
1936-37—You Can't Take It with You, by Moss Hart and
          George S. Kaufman
1937-38—Our Town, by Thornton Wilder
1938-39—Abe Lincoln in Illinois, by Robert E. Sherwood
1939-40—The Time of Your Life, by William Saroyan
1940-41—There Shall Be No Night, by Robert E. Sherwood
1941-42—No award.
1942-43—The Skin of Our Teeth, by Thornton Wilder
1943-44—No award.

PREVIOUS VOLUMES OF BEST PLAYS

Plays chosen to represent the theatre seasons from 1899 to 1943 are as follows:

1899-1909

"Barbara Frietchie," by Clyde Fitch. Published by Life Publishing Company, New York.

"The Climbers," by Clyde Fitch. Published by the Macmillan Co., New York.

"If I Were King," by Justin Huntly McCarthy. Published by Samuel French, New York and London.

"The Darling of the Gods," by David Belasco. Published by Little, Brown & Co., Boston, Mass.

"The County Chairman," by George Ade. Published by Samuel French, New York and London.

"Leah Kleschna," by C. M. S. McLellan. Published by Samuel French, New York.

"The Squaw Man," by Edwin Milton Royle.

"The Great Divide," by William Vaughn Moody. Published by Samuel French, New York, London and Canada.

"The Witching Hour," by Augustus Thomas. Published by Samuel French, New York and London.

"The Man from Home," by Booth Tarkington and Harry Leon Wilson. Published by Samuel French, New York, London and Canada.

1909-1919

"The Easiest Way," by Eugene Walter. Published by G. W. Dillingham, New York; Houghton Mifflin Co., Boston.

"Mrs. Bumpstead-Leigh," by Harry James Smith. Published by Samuel French, New York.

"Disraeli," by Louis N. Parker. Published by Dodd, Mead and Co., New York.

"Romance," by Edward Sheldon. Published by the Macmillan Co., New York.

"Seven Keys to Baldpate," by George M. Cohan. Published by Bobbs-Merrill Co., Indianapolis, as a novel by Earl Derr Biggers; as a play by Samuel French, New York.

"On Trial," by Elmer Reizenstein. Published by Samuel French, New York.

"The Unchastened Woman," by Louis Kaufman Anspacher. Published by Harcourt, Brace and Howe, Inc., New York.

"Good Gracious Annabelle," by Clare Kummer. Published by Samuel French, New York.

"Why Marry?" by Jesse Lynch Williams. Published by Charles Scribner's Sons, New York.

"John Ferguson," by St. John Ervine. Published by the Macmillan Co., New York.

1919-1920

"Abraham Lincoln," by John Drinkwater. Published by Houghton Mifflin Co., Boston.

"Clarence," by Booth Tarkington. Published by Samuel French, New York.

"Beyond the Horizon," by Eugene G. O'Neill. Published by Boni & Liveright, Inc., New York.

"Déclassée," by Zoe Akins. Published by Liveright, Inc., New York.

"The Famous Mrs. Fair," by James Forbes. Published by Samuel French, New York.

"The Jest," by Sem Benelli. (American adaptation by Edward Sheldon.)

"Jane Clegg," by St. John Ervine. Published by Henry Holt & Co., New York.

"Mamma's Affair," by Rachel Barton Butler. Published by Samuel French, New York.

"Wedding Bells," by Salisbury Field. Published by Samuel French, New York.

"Adam and Eva," by George Middleton and Guy Bolton. Published by Samuel French, New York.

1920-1921

"Deburau," adapted from the French of Sacha Guitry by H. Granville Barker. Published by G. P. Putnam's Sons, New York.

"The First Year," by Frank Craven. Published by Samuel French, New York.

"Enter Madame," by Gilda Varesi and Dolly Byrne. Published by G. P. Putnam's Sons, New York.

"The Green Goddess," by William Archer. Published by Alfred A. Knopf, New York.

"Liliom," by Ferenc Molnar. Published by Boni & Liveright, New York.

"Mary Rose," by James M. Barrie. Published by Charles Scribner's Sons, New York.

"Nice People," by Rachel Crothers. Published by Charles Scribner's Sons, New York.

"The Bad Man," by Porter Emerson Browne. Published by G. P. Putnam's Sons, New York.

"The Emperor Jones," by Eugene G. O'Neill. Published by Boni & Liveright, New York.

"The Skin Game," by John Galsworthy. Published by Charles Scribner's Sons, New York.

1921-1922

"Anna Christie," by Eugene G. O'Neill. Published by Boni & Liveright, New York.

"A Bill of Divorcement," by Clemence Dane. Published by the Macmillan Company, New York.

"Dulcy," by George S. Kaufman and Marc Connelly. Published by G. P. Putnam's Sons, New York.

"He Who Gets Slapped," adapted from the Russian of Leonid Andreyev by Gregory Zilboorg. Published by Brentano's, New York.

"Six Cylinder Love," by William Anthony McGuire.

"The Hero," by Gilbert Emery.

"The Dover Road," by Alan Aelxander Milne. Published by Samuel French, New York.

"Ambush," by Arthur Richman.

"The Circle," by William Somerset Maugham.

"The Nest," by Paul Geraldy and Grace George.

1922-1923

"Rain," by John Colton and Clemence Randolph. Published by Liveright, Inc., New York.

"Loyalties," by John Galsworthy. Published by Charles Scribner's Sons, New York.

"Icebound," by Owen Davis. Published by Little, Brown & Company, Boston.

"You and I," by Philip Barry. Published by Brentano's, New York.

"The Fool," by Channing Pollock. Published by Brentano's, New York.

"Merton of the Movies," by George Kaufman and Marc Connelly, based on the novel of the same name by Harry Leon Wilson.

"Why Not?" by Jesse Lynch Williams. Published by Walter H. Baker Co., Boston.

"The Old Soak," by Don Marquis. Published by Doubleday, Page & Company, New York.

"R.U.R.," by Karel Capek. Translated by Paul Selver. Published by Doubleday, Page & Company.

"Mary the 3d," by Rachel Crothers. Published by Brentano's, New York.

1923-1924

"The Swan," translated from the Hungarian of Ferenc Molnar by Melville Baker. Published by Boni & Liveright, New York.

"Outward Bound," by Sutton Vane. Published by Boni & Liveright, New York.

"The Show-Off," by George Kelly. Published by Little, Brown & Company, Boston.

"The Changelings," by Lee Wilson Dodd. Published by E. P. Dutton & Company, New York.

"Chicken Feed," by Guy Bolton. Published by Samuel French, New York and London.

"Sun-Up," by Lula Vollmer. Published by Brentano's, New York.

"Beggar on Horseback," by George Kaufman and Marc Connelly. Published by Boni & Liveright, New York.

"Tarnish," by Gilbert Emery. Published by Brentano's, New York.

"The Goose Hangs High," by Lewis Beach. Published by Little, Brown & Company, Boston.

"Hell-bent fer Heaven," by Hatcher Hughes. Published by Harper Bros., New York.

1924-1925

"What Price Glory?" by Laurence Stallings and Maxwell Anderson. Published by Harcourt, Brace & Co., New York.

"They Knew What They Wanted," by Sidney Howard. Published by Doubleday, Page & Company, New York.

"Desire Under the Elms," by Eugene G. O'Neill. Published by Boni & Liveright, New York.

"The Firebrand," by Edwin Justus Mayer. Published by Boni & Liveright, New York.

"Dancing Mothers," by Edgar Selwyn and Edmund Goulding.

"Mrs. Partridge Presents," by Mary Kennedy and Ruth Warren. Published by Samuel French, New York.

"The Fall Guy," by James Gleason and George Abbott. Published by Samuel French, New York.

"The Youngest," by Philip Barry. Published by Samuel French, New York.

"Minick," by Edna Ferber and George S. Kaufman. Published by Doubleday, Page & Company, New York.

"Wild Birds," by Dan Totheroh. Published by Doubleday, Page & Company, New York.

1925-1926

"Craig's Wife," by George Kelly. Published by Little, Brown & Company, Boston.

"The Great God Brown," by Eugene G. O'Neill. Published by Boni & Liveright, New York.

"The Green Hat," by Michael Arlen.

"The Dybbuk," by S. Ansky, Henry G. Alsberg-Winifred Katzin translation. Published by Boni & Liveright, New York.

"The Enemy," by Channing Pollock. Published by Brentano's, New York.

"The Last of Mrs. Cheyney," by Frederick Lonsdale. Published by Samuel French, New York.

"Bride of the Lamb," by William Hurlbut. Published by Boni & Liveright, New York.

"The Wisdom Tooth," by Marc Connelly. Published by George H. Doran & Company, New York.

"The Butter and Egg Man," by George Kaufman. Published by Boni & Liveright, New York.

"Young Woodley," by John Van Druten. Published by Simon and Schuster, New York.

1926-1927

"Broadway," by Philip Dunning and George Abbott. Published by George H. Doran Company, New York.

"Saturday's Children," by Maxwell Anderson. Published by Longmans, Green & Company, New York.

"Chicago," by Maurine Watkins. Published by Alfred A. Knopf, Inc., New York.

"The Constant Wife," by William Somerset Maugham. Published by George H. Doran Company, New York.

"The Play's the Thing," by Ferenc Molnar and P. G. Wodehouse. Published by Brentano's, New York.

"The Road to Rome," by Robert Emmet Sherwood. Published by Charles Scribner's Sons, New York.

"The Silver Cord," by Sidney Howard. Published by Charles Scribner's Sons, New York.

"The Cradle Song," translated from the Spanish of G. Martinez Sierra by John Garrett Underhill. Published by E. P. Dutton & Company, New York.

"Daisy Mayme," by George Kelly. Published by Little, Brown & Company, Boston.

"In Abraham's Bosom," by Paul Green. Published by Robert M. McBride & Company, New York.

1927-1928

"Strange Interlude," by Eugene G. O'Neill. Published by Boni & Liveright, New York.

"The Royal Family," by Edna Ferber and George Kaufman. Published by Doubleday, Doran & Company, New York.

"Burlesque," by George Manker Watters. Published by Doubleday, Doran & Company, New York.

"Coquette," by George Abbott and Ann Bridgers. Published by Longmans, Green & Company, New York, London, Toronto.

"Behold the Bridegroom," by George Kelly. Published by Little, Brown & Company, Boston.

"Porgy," by DuBose Heyward. Published by Doubleday, Doran & Company, New York.

"Paris Bound," by Philip Barry. Published by Samuel French, New York.

"Escape," by John Galsworthy. Published by Charles Scribner's Sons, New York.

"The Racket," by Bartlett Cormack. Published by Samuel French, New York.

"The Plough and the Stars," by Sean O'Casey. Published by the Macmillan Company, New York.

1928-1929

"Street Scene," by Elmer Rice. Published by Samuel French, New York.

"Journey's End," by R. C. Sherriff. Published by Brentano's, New York.

"Wings Over Europe," by Robert Nichols and Maurice Browne. Published by Covici-Friede, New York.

"Holiday," by Philip Barry. Published by Samuel French, New York.

"The Front Page," by Ben Hecht and Charles MacArthur. Published by Covici-Friede, New York.

"Let Us Be Gay," by Rachel Crothers. Published by Samuel French, New York.

"Machinal," by Sophie Treadwell.

"Little Accident," by Floyd Dell and Thomas Mitchell.

"Gypsy," by Maxwell Anderson.

"The Kingdom of God," by G. Martinez Sierra; English version by Helen and Harley Granville-Barker. Published by E. P. Dutton & Company, New York.

1929-1930

"The Green Pastures," by Marc Connelly (adapted from "Ol' Man Adam and His Chillun," by Roark Bradford). Published by Farrar & Rinehart, Inc., New York.

"The Criminal Code," by Martin Flavin. Published by Horace Liveright, New York.

"Berkeley Square," by John Balderston. Published by the Macmillan Company, New York.

"Strictly Dishonorable," by Preston Sturges. Published by Horace Liveright, New York.

"The First Mrs. Fraser," by St. John Ervine. Published by the Macmillan Company, New York.

"The Last Mile," by John Wexley. Published by Samuel French, New York.

"June Moon," by Ring W. Lardner and George S. Kaufman. Published by Charles Scribner's Sons, New York.

"Michael and Mary," by A. A. Milne. Published by Chatto & Windus, London.

"Death Takes a Holiday," by Walter Ferris (adapted from the Italian of Alberto Casella). Published by Samuel French, New York.

"Rebound," by Donald Ogden Stewart. Published by Samuel French, New York.

1930-1931

"Elizabeth the Queen," by Maxwell Anderson. Published by Longmans, Green & Co., New York.

"Tomorrow and Tomorrow," by Philip Barry. Published by Samuel French, New York.

"Once in a Lifetime," by George S. Kaufman and Moss Hart. Published by Farrar and Rinehart, New York.

"Green Grow the Lilacs," by Lynn Riggs. Published by Samuel French, New York and London.

"As Husbands Go," by Rachel Crothers. Published by Samuel French, New York.

"Alison's House," by Susan Glaspell. Published by Samuel French, New York.

"Five-Star Final," by Louis Weitzenkorn. Published by Samuel French, New York.

"Overture," by William Bolitho. Published by Simon & Schuster, New York.

"The Barretts of Wimpole Street," by Rudolf Besier. Published by Little, Brown & Company, Boston.

"Grand Hotel," adapted from the German of Vicki Baum by W. A. Drake.

1931-1932

"Of Thee I Sing," by George S. Kaufman and Morrie Ryskind; music and lyrics by George and Ira Gershwin. Published by Alfred Knopf, New York.

"Mourning Becomes Electra," by Eugene G. O'Neill. Published by Horace Liveright, Inc., New York.

"Reunion in Vienna," by Robert Emmet Sherwood. Published by Charles Scribner's Sons, New York.

"The House of Connelly," by Paul Green. Published by Samuel French, New York.

"The Animal Kingdom," by Philip Barry. Published by Samuel French, New York.

"The Left Bank," by Elmer Rice. Published by Samuel French, New York.

"Another Language," by Rose Franken. Published by Samuel French, New York.

"Brief Moment," by S. N. Behrman. Published by Farrar & Rinehart, New York.

"The Devil Passes," by Benn W. Levy. Published by Martin Secker, London.

"Cynara," by H. M. Harwood and R. F. Gore-Browne. Published by Samuel French, New York.

1932-1933

"Both Your Houses," by Maxwell Anderson. Published by Samuel French, New York.

"Dinner at Eight," by George S. Kaufman and Edna Ferber. Published by Doubleday, Doran & Co., Inc., Garden City, New York.

"When Ladies Meet," by Rachel Crothers. Published by Samuel French, New York.

"Design for Living," by Noel Coward. Published by Doubleday, Doran & Co., Inc., Garden City, New York.

"Biography," by S. N. Behrman. Published by Farrar & Rinehart, Inc., New York.

"Alien Corn," by Sidney Howard. Published by Charles Scribner's Sons, New York.

"The Late Christopher Bean," adapted from the French of René Fauchois by Sidney Howard. Published by Samuel French, New York.

"We, the People," by Elmer Rice. Published by Coward-McCann, Inc., New York.

"Pigeons and People," by George M. Cohan.

"One Sunday Afternoon," by James Hagan. Published by Samuel French, New York.

1933-1934

"Mary of Scotland," by Maxwell Anderson. Published by Doubleday, Doran & Co., Inc., Garden City, N. Y.

"Men in White," by Sidney Kingsley. Published by Covici, Friede, Inc., New York.

"Dodsworth," by Sinclair Lewis and Sidney Howard. Published by Harcourt, Brace & Co., New York.

"Ah, Wilderness," by Eugene O'Neill. Published by Random House, New York.

"They Shall Not Die," by John Wexley. Published by Alfred A. Knopf, New York.

"Her Master's Voice," by Clare Kummer. Published by Samuel French, New York.

"No More Ladies," by A. E. Thomas.

"Wednesday's Child," by Leopold Atlas. Published by Samuel French, New York.

"The Shining Hour," by Keith Winter. Published by Doubleday, Doran & Co., Inc., Garden City, New York.

"The Green Bay Tree," by Mordaunt Shairp. Published by Baker International Play Bureau, Boston, Mass.

1934-1935

"The Children's Hour," by Lillian Hellman. Published by Alfred Knopf, New York.

"Valley Forge," by Maxwell Anderson. Published by Anderson House, Washington, D. C. Distributed by Dodd, Mead & Co., New York.

"The Petrified Forest," by Robert Sherwood. Published by Charles Scribner's Sons, New York.

"The Old Maid," by Zoe Akins. Published by D. Appleton-Century Co., New York.

"Accent on Youth," by Samson Raphaelson. Published by Samuel French, New York.

"Merrily We Roll Along," by George S. Kaufman and Moss Hart. Published by Random House, New York.

"Awake and Sing," by Clifford Odets. Published by Random House, New York.

"The Farmer Takes a Wife," by Frank B. Elser and Marc Connelly.

"Lost Horizons," by John Hayden.

"The Distaff Side," by John Van Druten. Published by Alfred Knopf, New York.

1935-1936

"Winterset," by Maxwell Anderson. Published by Anderson House, Washington, D. C.

"Idiot's Delight," by Robert Emmet Sherwood. Published by Charles Scribner's Sons, New York.

"End of Summer," by S. N. Behrman. Published by Random House, New York.

"First Lady," by Katharine Dayton and George S. Kaufman. Published by Random House, New York.

"Victoria Regina," by Laurence Housman. Published by Samuel French, Inc., New York and London.

"Boy Meets Girl," by Bella and Samuel Spewack. Published by Random House, New York.

"Dead End," by Sidney Kingsley. Published by Random House, New York.

"Call It a Day," by Dodie Smith. Published by Samuel French, Inc., New York and London.

"Ethan Frome," by Owen Davis and Donald Davis. Published by Charles Scribner's Sons, New York.

"Pride and Prejudice," by Helen Jerome. Published by Doubleday, Doran & Co., Garden City, New York.

1936-1937

"High Tor," by Maxwell Anderson. Published by Anderson House, Washington, D. C.

"You Can't Take It with You," by Moss Hart and George S. Kaufman. Published by Farrar & Rinehart, Inc., New York.

"Johnny Johnson," by Paul Green. Published by Samuel French, Inc., New York.

"Daughters of Atreus," by Robert Turney. Published by Alfred A. Knopf, New York.

"Stage Door," by Edna Ferber and George S. Kaufman. Published by Doubleday, Doran & Co., Garden City, New York.

"The Women," by Clare Boothe. Published by Random House, Inc., New York.

"St. Helena," by R. C. Sherriff and Jeanne de Casalis. Published by Samuel French, Inc., New York and London.

"Yes, My Darling Daughter," by Mark Reed. Published by Samuel French, Inc., New York.

"Excursion," by Victor Wolfson. Published by Random House, New York.

"Tovarich," by Jacques Deval and Robert E. Sherwood. Published by Random House, New York.

1937-1938

"Of Mice and Men," by John Steinbeck. Published by Covici-Friede, New York.

"Our Town," by Thornton Wilder. Published by Coward-McCann, Inc., New York.

"Shadow and Substance," by Paul Vincent Carroll. Published by Random House, Inc., New York.

"On Borrowed Time," by Paul Osborn. Published by Alfred A. Knopf, New York.

"The Star-Wagon," by Maxwell Anderson. Published by Anderson House, Washington, D. C. Distributed by Dodd, Mead & Co., New York.

"Susan and God," by Rachel Crothers. Published by Random House, Inc., New York.

"Prologue to Glory," by E. P. Conkle. Published by Random House, Inc., New York.

"Amphitryon 38," by S. N. Behrman. Published by Random House, Inc., New York.

"Golden Boy," by Clifford Odets. Published by Random House, Inc., New York.

"What a Life," by Clifford Goldsmith. Published by Dramatists' Play Service, Inc., New York.

1938-1939

"Abe Lincoln in Illinois," by Robert E. Sherwood. Published by Charles Scribner's Sons, New York and Charles Scribner's Sons, Ltd., London.

"The Little Foxes," by Lillian Hellman. Published by Random House, Inc., New York.

"Rocket to the Moon," by Clifford Odets. Published by Random House, Inc., New York.

"The American Way," by George S. Kaufman and Moss Hart. Published by Random House, Inc., New York.

"No Time for Comedy," by S. N. Behrman. Published by Random House, Inc., New York.

"The Philadelphia Story," by Philip Barry. Published by Coward-McCann, Inc., New York.

"The White Steed," by Paul Vincent Carroll. Published by Random House, Inc., New York.

"Here Come the Clowns," by Philip Barry. Published by Coward-McCann, Inc., New York.

"Family Portrait," by Lenore Coffee and William Joyce Cowen. Published by Random House, Inc., New York.

"Kiss the Boys Good-bye," by Clare Boothe. Published by Random House, Inc., New York.

1939-1940

"There Shall Be No Night," by Robert E. Sherwood. Published by Charles Scribner's Sons, New York.

"Key Largo," by Maxwell Anderson. Published by Anderson House, Washington, D. C.

"The World We Make," by Sidney Kingsley.

"Life with Father," by Howard Lindsay and Russel Crouse. Published by Alfred A. Knopf, New York.

"The Man Who Came to Dinner," by George S. Kaufman and Moss Hart. Published by Random House, Inc., New York.

"The Male Animal," by James Thurber and Elliott Nugent. Published by Random House, Inc., New York, and MacMillan Co., Canada.

"The Time of Your Life," by William Saroyan. Published by Harcourt, Brace and Company, Inc., New York.

"Skylark," by Samson Raphaelson. Published by Random House, Inc., New York.

"Margin for Error," by Clare Boothe. Published by Random House, Inc., New York.

"Morning's at Seven," by Paul Osborn. Published by Samuel French, New York.

1940-1941

"Native Son," by Paul Green and Richard Wright. Published by Harper & Bros., New York.

"Watch on the Rhine," by Lillian Hellman. Published by Random House, Inc., New York.

"The Corn Is Green," by Emlyn Williams. Published by Random House, Inc., New York.

"Lady in the Dark," by Moss Hart. Published by Random House, Inc., New York.

"Arsenic and Old Lace," by Joseph Kesselring. Published by Random House, Inc., New York.

"My Sister Eileen," by Joseph Fields and Jerome Chodorov. Published by Random House, Inc., New York.

"Flight to the West," by Elmer Rice. Published by Coward, McCann, Inc., New York.

"Claudia," by Rose Franken Maloney. Published by Farrar & Rinehart, Inc., New York and Toronto.

"Mr. and Mrs. North," by Owen Davis. Published by Samuel French, New York.

"George Washington Slept Here," by George S. Kaufman and Moss Hart. Published by Random House, Inc., New York.

1941-1942

"In Time to Come," by Howard Koch. Published by Dramatists' Play Service, Inc., New York.

"The Moon Is Down," by John Steinbeck. Published by The Viking Press, New York.

"Blithe Spirit," by Noel Coward. Published by Doubleday, Doran & Co., Garden City, New York.

"Junior Miss," by Jerome Chodorov and Joseph Fields. Published by Random House, Inc., New York.

"Candle in the Wind," by Maxwell Anderson. Published by Anderson House, Washington, D. C.

"Letters to Lucerne," by Fritz Rotter and Allen Vincent. Published by Samuel French, Inc., New York.

"Jason," by Samson Raphaelson. Published by Random House, Inc., New York.

"Angel Street," by Patrick Hamilton. Published by Constable & Co., Ltd., London, under the title "Gaslight."

"Uncle Harry," by Thomas Job. Published by Samuel French, Inc., New York.

"Hope for a Harvest," by Sophie Treadwell. Published by Samuel French, Inc., New York.

1942-1943

"The Patriots," by Sidney Kingsley. Published by Random House, Inc., New York.

"The Eve of St. Mark," by Maxwell Anderson. Published by Anderson House, Washington, D. C.

"The Skin of Our Teeth," by Thornton Wilder. Published by Harper & Brothers, New York and London.

"Winter Soldiers," by Dan James.

"Tomorrow the World," by James Gow and Arnaud d'Usseau. Published by Charles Scribner's Sons, New York.

"Harriet," by Florence Ryerson and Colin Clements. Published by Charles Scribner's Sons, New York.

"The Doughgirls," by Joseph Fields. Published by Random House, Inc., New York.

"The Damask Cheek," by John Van Druten and Lloyd Morris. Published by Random House, Inc., New York.

"Kiss and Tell," by F. Hugh Herbert. Published by Coward-McCann, Inc., New York.

"Oklahoma!" by Oscar Hammerstein 2nd and Richard Rodgers. Published by Random House, Inc., New York.

WHERE AND WHEN THEY WERE BORN

(Compiled from the most authentic records available.)

Abbott, George .... Hamburg, N. Y. 1895
Abel, Walter .... St. Paul, Minn. 1898
Adams, Maude .... Salt Lake City, Utah 1872
Addy, Wesley .... Omaha, Neb. 1912
Adler, Luther .... New York City 1903
Adler, Stella .... New York City 1904
Aherne, Brian .... King's Norton, England .. 1902
Akins, Zoe .... Humansville, Mo. 1886
Allgood, Sara .... Dublin, Ireland 1883
Ames, Florenz .... Rochester, N. Y. 1884
Anders, Glenn .... Los Angeles, Cal. 1890
Anderson, Gwen .... Holland, Ia. 1921
Anderson, Judith .... Australia 1898
Anderson, Mary .... Trussville, Ala. 1917
Anderson, Maxwell .... Atlantic City, Pa. 1888
Andrews, A. G. .... Buffalo, N. Y. 1861
Andrews, Ann .... Los Angeles, Cal. 1895
Angel, Heather .... Oxford, England 1909
Anglin, Margaret .... Ottawa, Canada 1876
Arden, Eve .... San Francisco, Cal. 1912
Arling, Joyce .... Memphis, Tenn. 1911
Arliss, George .... London, England 1868
Ashcroft, Peggy .... Croydon, England 1907
Astaire, Fred .... Omaha, Neb. 1899
Atwater, Edith .... Chicago, Ill. 1912
Atwell, Roy .... Syracuse, N. Y. 1880
Atwill, Lionel .... London, England 1885

Bainter, Fay .... Los Angeles, Cal. 1892
Baker, Lee .... Michigan 1880
Bankhead, Tallulah .... Huntsville, Ala. 1902
Banks, Leslie J. .... West Derby, England 1890
Barbee, Richard .... Lafayette, Ind. 1887
Barrett, Edith .... Roxbury, Mass. 1904
Barry, Philip .... Rochester, N. Y. 1896
Barrymore, Diana .... New York City 1921

Barrymore, Ethel .... Philadelphia, Pa. 1879
Barrymore, John .... Philadelphia, Pa. 1882
Barrymore, Lionel .... Philadelphia, Pa. 1878
Barton, James .... Gloucester, N. J. 1890
Baxter, Lora .... New York 1907
Behrman, S. N. .... Worcester, Mass. 1893
Bell, James .... Suffolk, Va. 1891
Bellamy, Ralph .... Chicago, Ill. 1905
Bennett, Richard .... Cass County, Ind. 1873
Bergner, Elisabeth .... Vienna 1901
Berlin, Irving .... Russia 1888
Best, Edna .... Sussex, England 1900
Binney, Constance .... Philadelphia, Pa. 1900
Boland, Mary .... Detroit, Mich. 1880
Bolger, Ray .... Dorchester, Mass. 1906
Bondi, Beulah .... Chicago, Ill. 1892
Bordoni, Irene .... Paris, France 1895
Bourneuf, Philip .... Boston, Mass. 1912
Bowman, Patricia .... Washington, D. C. 1912
Brady, William A. .... San Francisco, Cal. 1863
Braham, Horace .... London, England 1896
Brent, Romney .... Saltillo, Mex. 1902
Brian, Donald .... St. Johns, N. F. 1877
Brice, Fannie .... Brooklyn, N. Y. 1891
Broderick, Helen .... New York 1891
Bromberg, J. Edward .... Hungary 1903
Brotherson, Eric .... Chicago, Ill. 1911
Brown, Anne Wiggins .... Baltimore, Md. 1916
Bruce, Nigel .... San Diego, Cal. 1895
Bryant, Charles .... England 1879
Buchanan, Jack .... England 1892
Burke, Billie .... Washington, D. C. 1885
Burr, Ann .... Boston, Mass. 1920
Byington, Spring .... Colorado Springs, Colo. .. 1898

Cabot, Eliot .... Boston, Mass. 1899
Cagney, James .... New York 1904
Cahill, Lily .... Texas 1891
Calhern, Louis .... New York 1895
Cantor, Eddie .... New York 1894
Carlisle, Kitty .... New Orleans, La. 1912
Carnovsky, Morris .... St. Louis, Mo. 1898
Carpenter, Edward Childs .... Philadelphia, Pa. 1871

Carroll, Earl ....Pittsburgh, Pa. 1892
Carroll, Leo G. ....Weedon, England 1892
Carroll, Nancy ....New York City 1906
Catlett, Walter ....San Francisco, Cal. 1889
Caulfield, Joan ....New York City 1924
Chandler, Helen ....Charleston, N. C. 1906
Chaplin, Charles Spencer .....London 1889
Chase, Ilka ....New York 1900
Chatterton, Ruth ....New York 1893
Christians, Mady ....Vienna, Austria 1907
Churchill, Berton ....Toronto, Can. 1876
Claire, Helen ....Union Springs, Ala. 1908
Claire, Ina ....Washington, D. C. 1892
Clark, Bobby ....Springfield, Ohio 1888
Clive, Colin ....St. Malo, France 1900
Coburn, Charles ....Macon, Ga. 1877
Cohan, George M. ....Providence, R. I. 1878
Cohan, Georgette ....Los Angeles, Cal. 1900
Colbert, Claudette ....Paris 1905
Collier, Constance ....Windsor, England 1882
Collier, William ....New York 1866
Collinge, Patricia ....Dublin, Ireland 1894
Collins, Russell ....New Orleans, La. 1901
Colt, Ethel Barrymore ......Mamaroneck, N. Y. 1911
Colt, John Drew ....New York 1914
Conroy, Frank ....London, England 1885
Conte, Nicholas ....Jersey City, N. J. 1916
Cook, Donald ....Portland, Ore. 1902
Cook, Joe ....Evansville, Ind. 1890
Cooper, Gladys ....Lewisham, England 1888
Cooper, Violet Kemble ......London, England 1890
Corbett, Leonora ....London, England 1908
Cornell, Katharine ....Berlin, Germany 1898
Corthell, Herbert ....Boston, Mass. 1875
Cossart, Ernest ....Cheltenham, England 1876
Coulouris, George ....Manchester, England 1906
Courtleigh, Stephen ....New York City 1912
Coward, Noel ....Teddington, England 1899
Cowl, Jane ....Boston, Mass. 1887
Craig, Helen ....Mexico City 1914
Craven, Frank ....Boston, Mass. 1880
Cronyn, Hume ....Canada 1912
Crosman, Henrietta ....Wheeling, W. Va. 1865

Crothers, Rachel .... Bloomington, Ill. 1878
Cummings, Constance .... Seattle, Wash. 1911

Dale, Margaret .... Philadelphia, Pa. 1880
Davis, Owen .... Portland, Me. 1874
Davis, Owen, Jr. .... New York 1910
De Cordoba, Pedro .... New York 1881
Digges, Dudley .... Dublin, Ireland 1880
Dixon, Jean .... Waterbury, Conn. 1905
Dowling, Eddie .... Woonsocket, R. I. 1895
Drake, Alfred .... New York City 1914
Dressler, Eric .... Brooklyn, N. Y. 1900
Duncan, Augustin .... San Francisco 1873
Duncan, Todd .... Danville, Ky. 1900
Dunn, Emma .... England 1875
Dunning, Philip .... Meriden, Conn. 1890
Dupree, Minnie .... San Francisco, Cal. 1875
Durante, Jimmy .... New York City 1893

Edney, Florence .... London, England 1879
Eldridge, Florence .... Brooklyn, N. Y. 1901
Ellerbe, Harry .... Georgia 1905
Emery, Gilbert .... Naples, New York 1875
Emery, Katherine .... Birmingham, Ala. 1908
Erickson, Leif .... California 1917
Errol, Leon .... Sydney, Australia 1881
Ervine, St. John Greer ...... Belfast, Ireland 1883
Evans, Edith .... London, England 1888
Evans, Madge .... New York City 1909
Evans, Maurice .... Dorchester, England 1901

Fassett, Jay .... Elmira, N. Y. 1889
Ferber, Edna .... Kalamazoo, Mich. 1887
Ferguson, Elsie .... New York 1883
Ferrer, Jose .... Puerto Rico 1909
Field, Sylvia .... Allston, Mass. 1902
Fields, W. C. .... Philadelphia, Pa. 1883
Fischer, Alice .... Indiana 1869
Fitzgerald, Barry .... Dublin, Ireland 1888
Fitzgerald, Geraldine .... Dublin, Ireland 1914
Fletcher, Bramwell .... Bradford, Yorkshire, Eng. . 1904
Fontanne, Lynn .... London, England 1887
Forbes, Ralph .... London, England 1905

Foster, Phœbe .... New Hampshire 1897
Foy, Eddie, Jr. .... New Rochelle, N. Y. 1906
Fraser, Elizabeth .... Brooklyn, N. Y. 1920
Friganza, Trixie .... Cincinnati, Ohio 1870

Gahagan, Helen .... Boonton, N. J. 1902
Gaxton, William .... San Francisco, Cal. 1893
Geddes, Barbara Bel .... Cleveland, Ohio 1912
Geddes, Norman Bel .... Adrian, Mich. 1893
George, Grace .... New York 1879
Gerald, Ara .... New South Wales 1902
Gershwin, Ira .... New York 1896
Gielgud, John .... London, England 1904
Gillmore, Margalo .... England 1901
Gish, Dorothy .... Dayton, Ohio 1898
Gish, Lillian .... Springfield, Ohio 1896
Gleason, James .... New York 1885
Golden, John .... New York 1874
Goodner, Carol .... New York City 1904
Gordon, Ruth .... Wollaston, Mass. 1896
Gough, Lloyd .... New York City 1906
Granville, Charlotte .... London 1863
Granville, Sydney .... Bolton, England 1885
Green, Mitzi .... New York City 1920
Greenstreet, Sydney .... England 1880
Groody, Louise .... Waco, Texas 1897
Gwenn, Edmund .... Glamorgan, Wales 1875

Hall, Bettina .... North Easton, Mass. 1906
Hall, Natalie .... North Easton, Mass. 1904
Hall, Thurston .... Boston, Mass. 1882
Halliday, John .... Brooklyn, N. Y. 1880
Halliday, Robert .... Loch Lomond, Scotland .. 1893
Hampden, Walter .... Brooklyn, N. Y. 1879
Hannen, Nicholas .... London, England 1881
Hardie, Russell .... Griffin Mills, N. Y. 1906
Hardwicke, Sir Cedric .... Lye, Stourbridge, England . 1893
Hargrave, Roy .... New York City 1908
Harrigan, William .... New York 1893
Haydon, Julie .... Oak Park, Ill. 1910
Hayes, Helen .... Washington, D. C. 1900
Hector, Louis .... England 1882
Heflin, Van .... Walters, Okla. 1909

Heineman, Eda .... Japan 1891
Heming, Violet .... Leeds, England 1893
Henie, Sonja .... Oslo, Norway 1912
Hepburn, Katharine .... Hartford, Conn. 1907
Henreid, Paul .... Trieste, Italy 1905
Hobart, Rose .... New York 1906
Hoey, Dennis .... London, England 1893
Holm, Celeste .... New York City 1916
Hopkins, Arthur .... Cleveland, Ohio 1878
Hopkins, Miriam .... Bainbridge, Ga. 1904
Holmes, Taylor .... Newark, N. J. 1872
Homeier, Skippy .... Chicago, Ill. 1930
Huber, Paul .... Wilkes-Barre, Pa. 1895
Humphreys, Cecil .... Cheltenham, England 1880
Hunter, Glenn .... Highland Mills, N. Y. 1896
Huston, Walter .... Toronto 1884
Hutchinson, Josephine .... Seattle, Wash. 1898

Inescort, Frieda .... Hitchin, Scotland 1905
Ingram, Rex .. .. Dublin, Ireland 1892

Jagger, Dean .... Columbus Grove, Ohio ...1904
Jameson, House .... Austin, Texas 1902
Joel, Clara .... Jersey City, N. J. 1890
Johann, Zita .... Hungary 1904
Jolson, Al .... Washington, D. C. 1883
Johnson, Harold J. (Chic) ...Chicago, Ill. 1891
Johnson, Raymond Edward ...Kenosha, Wis. 1912
Joslyn, Allyn .... Milford, Pa. 1905
Joy, Nicholas .... Paris, France 1892

Kane, Whitford .... Larne, Ireland 1882
Karloff, Boris .... Dulwich, England 1887
Kaufman, George S. .... Pittsburgh, Pa. 1889
Kaye, A. P. .... Ringwood, England 1885
Kaye, Danny .... New York City 1914
Keith, Ian .... Boston, Mass. 1899
Keith, Robert .... Scotland 1899
Kelly, Gene .... Pittsburgh, Pa. 1912
Kerrigan, J. M. .... Dublin, Ireland 1885
Kilbride, Percy .... San Francisco, Cal. 1880
King, Dennis .... Coventry, England 1897
Kingsford, Walter .... England 1876

Kingsley, Sydney ....New York 1906
Kirkland, Alexander ....Mexico City 1904
Kirkland, Muriel ....Yonkers, N. Y. 1904
Kruger, Alma ....Pittsburgh, Pa. 1880
Kruger, Otto ....Toledo, Ohio 1895

Landi, Elissa ....Venice, Italy 1904
Landis, Jessie Royce ....Chicago, Ill. 1904
Lane, Rosemary ....Indianola, Ia. 1916
Larimore, Earl ....Portland, Oregon 1899
Larrimore, Francine ....Russia 1898
Lauder, Harry ....Portobello, Scotland 1870
Laughton, Charles ....Scarborough, England 1899
Lawford, Betty ....London, England 1904
Lawrence, Gertrude ....London 1898
Lawson, Wilfred ....London, England 1894
Lawton, Frank ....London, England 1904
Lawton, Thais ....Louisville, Ky. 1881
Lederer, Francis ....Karlin, Prague 1906
Lee, Canada ....New York City 1907
Lee, Gypsy Rose ....West Seattle, Wash. 1913
Le Gallienne, Eva ....London, England 1899
Lenihan, Winifred ....New York 1898
Leontovich, Eugenie ....Moscow, Russia 1894
Lillie, Beatrice ....Toronto, Canada 1898
Locke, Katherine ....New York 1914
Loeb, Philip ....Philadelphia, Pa. 1892
Logan, Stanley ....Earlsfield, England 1885
Lord, Pauline ,.............Hanford, Cal. 1890
Lukas, Paul ....Budapest, Hungary 1895
Lunt, Alfred ....Milwaukee, Wis. 1893

Macdonald, Donald ....Denison, Texas 1898
MacMahon, Aline ....McKeesport, Pa. 1899
March, Frederic ....Racine, Wis. 1897
Margetson, Arthur ....London, England 1897
Margo ....Mexico 1918
Marshall, Everett ....Worcester, Mass. 1902
Marshall, Herbert ....London, England 1890
Massey, Raymond ....Toronto, Canada 1896
Mature, Victor ....Louisville, Ky. 1916
May, Marty ....New York City 1900
McClintic, Guthrie ....Seattle, Wash. 1893

McCormick, Myron .... Albany, Ind. 1906
McGrath, Paul .... Chicago, Ill. 1900
McGuire, Dorothy .... Omaha, Neb. 1918
Menken, Helen .... New York 1901
Mercer, Beryl .... Seville, Spain 1882
Meredith, Burgess .... Cleveland, Ohio 1909
Merivale, Philip .... Rehutia, India 1886
Merman, Ethel .... Astoria, L. I. 1909
Merrill, Beth .... Lincoln, Neb. 1916
Mestayer, Harry .... San Francisco, Cal. 1881
Miller, Gilbert .... New York 1884
Miller, Marilyn .... Findlay, Ohio 1898
Miramova, Elena .... Tsaritsyn, Russia 1907
Miranda, Carmen .... Portugal 1912
Mitchell, Grant .... Columbus, Ohio 1874
Mitchell, Thomas .... Elizabeth, N. J. 1892
Mitzi (Hajos) .... Budapest 1891
Moore, Grace .... Del Rio, Tenn. 1901
Moore, Victor .... Hammondton, N. J. 1876
Morley, Robert .... Semley, Wiltshire, England. 1908
Morgan, Claudia .... New York 1912
Morgan, Helen .... Danville, Ill. 1900
Morgan, Ralph .... New York City 1889
Morris, Mary .... Boston 1894
Morris, McKay .... San Antonio, Texas 1890
Moss, Arnold .... Brooklyn, N. Y. 1910
Muni, Paul .... Lemberg, Austria 1895

Nagel, Conrad .... Keokuk, Iowa 1897
Natwick, Mildred .... Baltimore, Md. 1908
Nazimova, Alla .... Crimea, Russia 1879
Nolan, Lloyd .... San Francisco, Cal. 1903
Nugent, J. C. .... Miles, Ohio 1875
Nugent, Elliott .... Dover, Ohio 1900

O'Brien-Moore, Erin .... Los Angeles, Cal. 1908
Odets, Clifford .... Philadelphia 1906
Oldham, Derek .... Accrington, England 1892
Olivier, Laurence .... Dorking, Surrey, England.. 1907
Olsen, John Siguard (Ole) .... Peru, Ind. 1892
O'Malley, Rex .... London, England 1906
O'Neill, Eugene Gladstone .... New York 1888

Ouspenskaya, Maria .... Tula, Russia 1876
Overman, Lynne .... Maryville, Mo. 1887

Patterson, Elizabeth .... Savannah, Tenn. 1898
Pemberton, Brock .... Leavenworth, Kansas 1885
Pennington, Ann .... Philadelphia, Pa. 1898
Philips, Mary .... New London, Conn. 1901
Pickford, Mary .... Toronto 1893
Picon, Molly .... New York City 1898
Pollock, Channing .... Washington, D. C. 1880
Powers, Leona .... Salida, Colo. 1900
Powers, Tom .... Owensburg, Ky. 1890
Price, Vincent .... St. Louis, Mo. 1914
Pryor, Roger .... New York City 1901

Rains, Claude .... London, England 1889
Rambeau, Marjorie .... San Francisco, Cal. 1889
Rathbone, Basil .... :.... Johannesburg 1892
Raye, Martha .... Butte, Mont. 1916
Reed, Florence .... Philadelphia, Pa. 1883
Rennie, James .... Toronto, Canada 1890
Ridges, Stanley .... Southampton, England ...1891
Ring, Blanche .... Boston, Mass. 1876
Roberts, Joan .... New York City 1918
Robinson, Edward G. .... Bucharest, Roumania 1893
Robson, Flora .... South Shields, Durham, Eng.1902
Roos, Joanna .... Brooklyn, N. Y. 1901
Ross, Thomas W. .... Boston, Mass. 1875
Royle, Selena .... New York 1905
Ruben, José .... Belgium 1886

Sands, Dorothy .... Cambridge, Mass. 1900
Sarnoff, Dorothy .... Brooklyn, N. Y. 1919
Savo, Jimmy .... New York City 1895
Scheff, Fritzi .... Vienna, Austria 1879
Schildkraut, Joseph .... Bucharest, Roumania 1896
Scott, Cyril .... Ireland 1866
Scott, Martha .... Jamesport, Mo. 1914
Segal, Vivienne .... Philadelphia, Pa. 1897
Selwart, Tonio .... Munich, Germany 1906
Shannon, Effie .... Cambridge, Mass. 1867
Shean, Al .... Dornum, Germany 1868
Sherman, Hiram .... Boston, Mass. 1908

Sherwood, Robert Emmet ..... New Rochelle, N. Y. 1896
Sidney, Sylvia .... New York 1910
Skinner, Cornelia Otis .... Chicago 1902
Skinner, Otis .... Cambridgeport, Mass. 1858
Slezak, Walter .... Vienna, Austria 1902
Smith, Ben .... Waxahachie, Texas 1905
Smith, Kent .... Smithfield, Me. 1910
Sondergaard, Gale .... Minnesota 1899
Starr, Frances .... Oneonta, N. Y. 1886
Stickney, Dorothy .... Dickinson, N. D. 1903
Stoddard, Haila .... Great Falls, Mont. 1914
Stone, Ezra .... New Bedford, Mass. 1918
Stone, Fred .... Denver, Colo. 1873
Stone, Dorothy .... New York 1905
Strudwick, Sheppard .... North Carolina 1905
Sullavan, Margaret .... Norfolk, Va. 1910

Tandy, Jessica .... London, England 1909
Taylor, Laurette .... New York 1884
Tearle, Conway .... New York 1878
Tearle, Godfrey .... New York 1884
Terris, Norman .... Columbus, Kansas 1904
Thomas, Frankie .... New York 1922
Thomas, John Charles .... Baltimore, Md. 1887
Thorndike, Dame Sybil ...... Gainsborough, England ...1882
Tobin, Genevieve .... New York 1901
Tobin, Vivian .... New York 1903
Toler, Sidney .... Warrensburg, Mo. 1874
Tone, Franchot .... Niagara Falls, N. Y. 1907
Tracy, Lee .... Atlanta, Ga. 1898
Travers, Henry .... Berwick, England 1874
Truex, Ernest .... Red Hill, Mo. 1890
Tynan, Brandon .... Dublin, Ireland 1879

Ulric, Lenore .... New Ulm, Minn. 1897

Vallée, Rudy .... Island Pond, Vermont 1902
Van Patten, Joyce .... New York City 1934
Varden, Evelyn .... Venita, Okla. 1893
Venuta, Benay .... San Francisco, Cal. 1912

Walker, June .... New York 1904
Walsh, Mary Jane .... Davenport, Ia. 1915

Warfield, David .... San Francisco, Cal. 1866
Waring, Richard .... Buckinghamshire, England.1912
Warwick, Robert .... Sacramento, Cal. 1878
Waters, Ethel .... Chester, Pa. 1900
Watkins, Linda .... Boston, Mass. 1908
Watson, Lucile .... Quebec, Canada 1879
Watson, Minor .... Marianna, Ark. 1889
Webb, Clifton .... Indiana 1891
Webster, Margaret .... New York City 1905
Welles, Orson .... Kenosha, Wis. 1915
Westley, Helen .... Brooklyn, N. Y. 1879
Weston, Ruth .... Boston, Mass. 1911
White, George .... Toronto, Canada 1890
Whorf, Richard .... Winthrop, Mass. 1908
William, Warren .... Aitkin, Minn. 1896
Williams, Emlyn .... Mostyn, Wales 1905
Williams, Rhys .... Wales 1903
Wiman, Dwight Deere .... Moline, Ill. 1895
Winwood, Estelle .... England 1883
Witherspoon, Cora .... New Orleans, La. 1891
Wood, Peggy .... Brooklyn, N. Y. 1894
Worlock, Frederick .... London, England 1885
Wright, Haidee .... London, England 1868
Wycherly, Margaret .... England 1883
Wynyard, Diana .... London, England 1906
Wynn, Ed. .... Philadelphia, Pa. 1886
Wynn, Keenan .... New York City 1917

Young, Roland .... London, England 1887
Yurka, Blanche .... Bohemia 1893

NECROLOGY

June 13, 1943—June 18, 1944

Ade, George, playwright, humorist and journalist, 78. Famous for his fables in slang; wrote "The Sultan of Sulu" (1902), "Peggy from Paris," "The County Chairman," "The Sho-Gun," "The College Widow," "The Fair Co-ed," etc.; authored several motion picture scripts. Born Kentland, Indiana; died Kentland, Indiana, May 16, 1944.

Anderson, John Hargis, drama critic and author, 46. Critic of New York *Evening Post* and *Journal-American;* adapted "The Inspector General" from Nicolai Gogol's play, "The Fatal Alibi" from Michael Morton's melodrama and "Collision" from Lothar and Sebesi's comedy; wrote "Box Office," "The American Theatre" and prefaces to several plays; associate editor of *Arts Weekly* and *Town and Country;* instructor of drama at New York University; president of New York Drama Critics' Circle 1942-43. Born Pensacola, Fla.; died New York City, July 16, 1943.

Bard, Wilkie, actor, 70. English comedian famous in London music halls; came to America in 1913; appeared at Hammerstein's Victoria; headlined at Palace, New York, in 1919. Born London; died Hugden, Eng., May 5, 1944.

Barlow, Reginald, actor, 76. Made stage debut at 9 with his father's minstrel troupe, Barlow, Wilson, Primrose and West; later appeared in "The Silver King," "Monte Carlo," "Sign of the Cross," etc.; "The Silent Witness" (1931) last Broadway engagement; prominent in organization of Actors' Equity; appeared in many screen plays. Born Springfield, Mass.; died Hollywood, Calif., July 6, 1943.

Belmore, Alice (Cliffe), actress, 73. First appearance in America in "Sir Anthony"; other plays included "No More Blondes," "Paddy," "Fanny Hawthorne," "Hay Fever," "Doctor's Dilemma" and "Three Sisters." Born London, Eng.; died New York, July 31, 1943.

Bernie, Ben (Anzelevitz), actor and musician, 52. Vaudeville, radio and stage comedian and entertainer; started in vaudeville as violinist; teamed with Phil Baker; played on Broadway in "Here's How"; appeared on screen in "Stolen Har-

mony" and "Shoot the Works." Born New York City;
died Beverly Hills, Calif., October 20, 1943.

Bosworth, Hobart Van Zandt, actor, director and writer, 76.
Started with Rankin Stock Co., San Francisco, in 1885;
with Augustin Daly Stock Co., New York, in early 1900s;
leading man for Mrs. Fiske, Julia Marlowe and Henrietta
Crosman; appeared in first motion picture made in Los Angeles, "The Sultan's Power" (1909); organized Bosworth
Company, specializing in screening of Jack London stories.
Born Marietta, Ohio; died Glendale, Calif., December 30,
1943.

Brown, Clark, manager, 67. Prominent in vaudeville, theatre
management and press agentry; left newspaper work for
public relations, becoming press agent for Ringling Bros.,
Walker Whiteside and Keith-Albee circuit; ten years district manager of Shea Theatre Corporation in Ohio. Born
Mankato, Minn.; died Ashtabula, Ohio, May 5, 1944.

Campeau, Frank, actor, 79. Stage and screen actor for over half
a century; best remembered as Trampas in "The Virginian"
(1907) and as Tony in "Arizona" (1899); for 25 years
played heavies in silent screen plays. Born Detroit, Mich.;
died Hollywood, Calif., November 5, 1943.

Cobb, Irvin S., author, humorist and screen actor, 67. Nationally known wit; wrote "Judge Priest" stories, dramatized
on screen for Will Rogers; wrote "Funibashi," musical comedy (1907), "Back Home" (with Bayard Veiller), and
"Under Sentence" (with Roi Cooper Megrue). Born Padu-
cah, Ky.; died New York City, March 11, 1944.

Collier, William, actor and playwright, 77. Leading stage figure
for over sixty years; first appearance in "H.M.S. Pinafore"
(1879); other plays "On the Quiet," "Hello, Broadway,"
"The City Directory," "The Man from Mexico," "The Dic-
tator," "The Hottentot," etc.; appeared in many films.
Born New York City; died Beverly Hills, Calif., November 13, 1943.

Courteney, Fay, actress, 65. Played in "Sky Farm" ((902) for
Charles Frohman; leading woman in Empire Stock Co., Columbus, Ohio; with Vaughan Glaser as co-star in Cleveland;
many seasons in Toronto, Detroit and Rochester; on Broadway played in "She Couldn't Say No," "Saturday Night,"
"It Never Rains," etc.; prominent in radio. Born San
Francisco, Calif.; died New York, July 18, 1943.

Crummit, Frank, actor and song writer, 54. Started theatrical career in vaudeville with a ukulele and singing act; was in "Betty Be Good," "Greenwich Village Follies," "Tangerine" and other musical comedies; wrote "A Gay Caballero," "Sweet Lady" and other songs; with his wife, Julia Sanderson, had had a radio program since 1928. Born Jackson, Ohio; died New York, September 7, 1943.

Dudley, Walter Bronson (Bide), drama critic and author, 66. Reviewed plays for New York *Evening World,* Kansas City *Star,* Denver *Post,* New York *Morning Telegraph* and over Radio Station WOR; first play "Odds and Ends of 1917," co-authored with Jack Norworth; other plays "The Little Whopper," "Sue Dear," "Oh, Henry," "Borrowed Love," etc. Born Minneapolis, Minn.; died New York City, January 4, 1944.

Forrest, Sam, director, actor and author, 73. Started as actor; began directing with Booth Tarkington's "Springtime" (1909); last assignment George M. Cohan's "The Return of the Vagabond" (1940); general stage director for Cohan and Harris for more than 25 years, from 1910, in "Get-Rich-Quick Wallingford," to Cohan's death in 1942; married Mary Ryan, actress. Born Richmond, Va.; died New York City, April 30, 1944.

Gay, Maria, singer, 64. Started singing career in Barcelona, Spain; American debut in "Carmen" (1908) with Metropolitan Opera Co.; sang with Boston and Chicago Opera Companies; married Giovanni Zenatello, singer. Born Barcelona, Spain; died New York, July 29, 1943.

Grossmith, Lawrence, actor, 67. British stage and film comedian for 47 years; came to America with Lillian Langtry in 1898; first appeared in New York in "The Degenerates"; member of one of England's oldest stage families. Born London, Eng.; died Hollywood, Calif., February 21, 1944.

Guilbert, Yvette, singer and actress, 76. Toured the world with her original interpretations of songs; brought to New York by Oscar Hammerstein in 1895; appeared at Koster and Bial's in 1896; toured America in 1906 with Albert Chevalier. Born Paris, France; died France, February 2, 1944.

Hackett, Walter, playwright, producer and director, 67. Authored or collaborated on more than 50 plays produced in London and New York including "The Regeneration" (with Owen Kildare), "The White Sister" (with F. Marion Craw-

ford), "It Pays to Advertise" (with Roi Cooper Megrue),
"Good Losers" (with Michael Arlen), "Espionage" and
"Captain Applejack." Born Oakland, Calif.; died New
York City, January 20, 1944.

Hart, Lorenz, author, 47. Lyricist famous for musical comedy collaborations with Richard Rodgers from college days;
plays included "The Poor Little Ritz Girl" (1920), "A Connecticut Yankee," "Jumbo," "On Your Toes," "I'd Rather
Be Right," "I Married an Angel," "The Boys from Syracuse," "Pal Joey" and "By Jupiter." Born New York
City; died New York City, November 22, 1943.

Holland, Mildred, actress, 67. First appearance in "Superba"
(1890) with Augustin Daly Co. in New York and en tour
in early nineties; organized stock companies in New York,
Buffalo, Rochester and Cleveland. Born Chicago, Ill.; died
New York, January 27, 1944.

King, Charles, actor and singer, 52. Prominent in musical comedy and later in pictures; started in burlesque and vaudeville as blackface comedian; first stage roles in "The Mimic
World" and George M. Cohan's "A Yankee Prince"; during World War I, served in Navy and in World War II
played Army and Navy bases under USO Camp Shows;
died in United States Army Hospital. Born New York
City; died London, Eng., January 11, 1944.

Korff, Arnold, actor, 73. Internationally known actor; made
stage debut with Imperial Theatre Company, Vienna, touring Europe for 26 years; played at Irving Place Theatre,
New York, in German plays (1915); first English-speaking
part on Broadway in "The Living Mask" (1923); recent
appearances in "Thank You, Svoboda" and "The Searching
Wind," in which he was playing at the time of his death.
Born Vienna, Austria; died New York City, June 3, 1944.

Kummer, Frederic Arnold, dramatic author, 70. Wrote many
stage and screen plays and novels; first play "Mr. Buttles"
(1907); others, "The Other Woman," "The Brute," "The
Painted Woman," "The Magic Melody" (with Sigmund
Romberg) and "My Golden Girl" with Victor Herbert.
Born Catonsville, Md.; died Baltimore, Md., November 22,
1943.

Loftus, Marie Cecilia (Cissie), actress, 67. Impersonator, vaudeville entertainer, stage and screen actress in England and
America for fifty years; came to America in 1900 and appeared in "The Mascot"; was E. H. Sothern's leading lady in

"Richard Lovelace" and "If I Were King"; with Sir Henry Irving in "The Merchant of Venice"; last appearance on Broadway in "The Little Dark Horse" (1941). Born Glasgow, Scotland; died New York City, July 12, 1943.

Mapes, Victor, author, journalist, playwright and producer, 73. Was Paris correspondent of New York *Sun* (1892-96); drama critic of New York *World* under pseudonym of Sidney Sharp; wrote "Don Caesar's Return" (1901), "Captain Barrington," "The Hottentot" (with William Collier) and with Winchell Smith "The New Henrietta" and "The Boomerang." Born New York City; died Cannes, France, September 27, 1943.

Martin-Harvey, Sir John, actor and producer, 81. Widely known British romantic actor; early training under Sir Henry Irving in whose company he acted for 14 years beginning in 1882; appeared in many Shakespearian plays and toured England and the provinces in extensive repertory. Born Wyvenhoe, Essex, England; died London,, May 14, 1944.

Mayhew, Kate, actress, 91. Nearly 80 years on stage; began at 5 in "Pizarro" in Indianapolis; later appeared with Lawrence Barrett, Charlotte Cushman, Lotta Crabtree, Maggie Mitchell, E. H. Sothern and others; appeared in "Uncle Tom's Cabin" during Civil War; recently in Players' Club revivals of "Beaux' Stratagem" and "Uncle Tom's Cabin"; last stage appearance in "Alice Takat" (1936); motion picture debut in "Hazel Kirke" (1915). Born Indianapolis, Ind.; died New York, June 16, 1944.

Ralph, Jessie, actress, 79. Stage and screen character actress; appeared with Jane Cowl in "Romeo and Juliet" and "The Road to Rome"; was in George M. Cohan's musical and non-musical productions; retired in 1941 after many years in Hollywood. Born Gloucester, Mass.; died Gloucester, Mass., May 30, 1944.

Ray, Charles, actor and producer, 52. Nationally famous for portrayal of country bumpkin roles on silent screen; prior to 1912 was in musical and drama stock and in vaudeville. Born Jacksonville, Ill.; died Hollywood, Calif., November 23, 1943.

Reinhardt, Max (Goldman), actor, author, producer and director, 70. Internationally famous for productions of "The Miracle," "Everyman" and "Oedipus Rex"; first direction in America in "The Miracle" (1924); also "Midsummer's

Night's Dream" in Hollywood Bowl (1934); managed many European theatres; deprived of connection with German State Theatre (1933) after production of 425 plays; fled from Hitler persecution; was active in London; received honorary degree from Oxford University (1933). Born Baden, Austria; died New York City, October 31, 1943.

Rothe, Anita, actress, 77. First appearance in "Nero" at Niblo's Gardens, New York (1890); in original cast of "Captain Jinks of the Horse Marines" with Ethel Barrymore; last appeared in revival of "School for Scandal" (1931). Born Alexandria, Va.; died Bronx, New York, January 9, 1944.

Selwyn, Edgar, actor, author and producer, 68. First appearance in "Secret Service" (1896); with his brother Archie operated Times Square, Apollo and Selwyn Theatres in New York; produced "Why Marry?" which won first Pulitzer prize, "Within the Law" and many other successes; last production "The Wookey" (1941); wrote "A Friend in Need," "Rolling Stones," "Dancing Mothers" (with Edmund Goulding), etc.; vice-president and director of Goldwyn Pictures, Inc. Born Cincinnati, Ohio; died Hollywood, Calif., February 13, 1944.

Smith, Mark, actor, 58. Third actor of same name and family; prominent on stage and in radio; first appearance in Charles H. Hoyt comedies, "A Milk White Flag" and "A Trip to Chinatown"; played Sir Toby Belch in "Twelfth Night" with Helen Hayes. Born New York City; died New York City, May 10, 1944.

Vivian, Robert, actor, 85. Debut on London stage in "Najeeda"; with Henry Irving Company for many years; first American appearance with Mary Mannering in "Glorious Betsy"; played with Maude Adams in "A Kiss for Cinderella"; last Broadway appearance in "Distant City" (1941). Born London, Eng.; died New York City, January 31, 1944.

Ward, Hap (John O'Donnell), actor and producer, 76. Teamed with Harry Vokes in vaudeville and became famous as Ward and Vokes in blackface and tumbling tramp acts; remembered as "Harold and Percy" in "The Floor Walkers" and "A Pair of Pinks." Born Cameron, Pa., died New York City, January 3, 1944.

Westford, Susan, actress, 79. Musical comedy actress of the nineties; sister of Lillian Russell, with whom she played in "The Grand Duchess," "Widow's Might," "Queen of Diamonds," etc.; retired in 1922. Born Chicago, Ill.; died Bayshore, L. I., New York, June 13, 1944.

Woolf, Edgar Allan, actor and playwright, 62. Graduated from Columbia University varsity show (1901); wrote vaudeville sketches and playlets for Rooney and Bent, Mae Murray, Mrs. Patrick Campbell, etc.; also wrote librettos for "Mme. Champagne," "Head over Heels," "Love Birds," "Rock-a-Bye-Baby," etc. Born New York; died Hollywood, Calif., December 9, 1943.

Young, J. Arthur, actor, 63. Started in stock companies in Denver, Detroit, Washington, D. C., and Philadelphia; later appeared in "Yellow Jacket," "East Is West," "Lost Horizon," etc. Born Chicago, Ill.; died Kew Gardens, New York, September 14, 1943.

THE DECADES' TOLL

(Persons of Outstanding Prominence in the Theatre Who Have Died in Recent Years)

	Born	Died
Aborn, Milton	1864	1933
Ames, Winthrop	1871	1937
Anderson, Mary (Navarro)	1860	1940
Baker, George Pierce	1866	1935
Barrymore, John	1882	1942
Belasco, David	1856	1931
Benson, Sir Frank	1859	1939
Bernhardt, Sarah	1845	1923
Campbell, Mrs. Patrick	1865	1940
Cohan, George Michael	1878	1942
Crabtree, Charlotte (Lotta)	1847	1924
De Koven, Reginald	1861	1920
De Reszke, Jean	1850	1925
Drew, John	1853	1927
Drinkwater, John	1883	1937
Du Maurier, Sir Gerald	1873	1934
Duse, Eleanora	1859	1924
Fiske, Minnie Maddern	1865	1932
Frohman, Daniel	1851	1940
Galsworthy, John	1867	1933
Gorky, Maxim	1868	1936
Greet, Sir Philip (Ben)	1858	1936
Herbert, Victor	1859	1924
Patti, Adelina	1843	1919
Pinero, Sir Arthur Wing	1855	1934
Pirandello, Luigi	1867	1936
Rejane, Gabrielle	1857	1920
Rogers, Will	1879	1935
Russell, Annie	1864	1936
Schumann-Heink, Ernestine	1861	1936
Sembrich, Marcella	1859	1935
Shaw, Mary	1860	1929

Skinner, Otis 1858   1942
Sothern, Edwin Hugh 1859   1933
Terry, Ellen 1848   1928
Thomas, Augustus 1857   1934
Yeats, William Butler 1865   1939

INDEX OF AUTHORS

Abbott, George, 502, 503
Ade, George, 498
Afinegenov, Alexander, 11, 443
Akins, Zoe, 14, 463, 497, 499, 507
Alsberg, Henry G., 502
Anderson, Maxwell, 12, 69, 277, 397, 447, 494, 497, 501, 502, 504, 505, 506, 507, 508, 509, 511
Andreyev, Leonid, 500
Ansky, S., 502
Anspacher, Louis Kaufman, 499
Anstey, F., 417
Anthony, Norman, 414
Archer, William, 500
Arlen, Michael, 502
Atlas, Leopold, 506

Baker, Herbert, 470
Baker, Melville, 501
Balderston, John, 504
Balieff, Nikita, 5, 407
Barrie, James M., 500
Barry, Philip, 500, 502, 503, 504, 505, 509
Batson, George, 12, 446
Baum, Vicki, 11, 439, 505
Beach, Lewis, 501
Behrman, S. N., 14, 236, 397, 462, 494, 505, 506, 507, 509
Bein, Albert and Mary, 6, 414
Belasco, David, 498
Bell, Thomas, 433
Benelli, Sem, 499
Bennett, Robert Russell, 432
Bennett, Tom, 418
Bergersen, Baldwin, 469
Berlin, Irving, 9
Berte, H., 410
Besier, Rudolf, 505
Biggers, Earl Derr, 498
Bizet, Georges, 9, 432, 439, 472
Bolitho, William, 505
Bolton, Guy, 448, 466, 499, 501
Boothe, Clare, 508, 509, 510
Boruff, John, 461
Bottomley, Roland, 482

Bowen, Elizabeth, 463
Bowles, Paul, 445, 462
Bradford, Roark, 504
Brentano, Felix, 479
Bridgers, Ann, 503
Brown, George Carleton, 22
Browne, Maurice, 504
Browne, Porter Emerson, 500
Bruce, Norman, 415
Burmand, F. C., 456
Burnett, Murray, 15, 476
Butler, Rachel Barton, 499
Byrne, Dolly, 499

Caesar, Irving, 411
Caldwell, Erskine, 409
Capek, Karel, 501
Carroll, Paul Vincent, 508, 509
Casella, Alberto, 504
Charig, Phil, 424, 466
Chekhov, Anton, 12, 450
Chislanzoni, Antonio, 473
Chodorov, Edward, 4, 13, 31, 69, 133, 395, 400, 453
Chodorov, Jerome, 395, 510, 511
Clements, Colin, 511
Coffee, Lenore, 509
Cohan, George M., 498, 506
Colton, John, 500
Conkle, E. P., 509
Connelly, Marc, 496, 500, 501, 502, 504, 507
Connors, Barry, 18
Cormack, Bartlett, 503
Coward, Noel, 6, 410, 505, 510
Cowen, William Joyce, 509
Craven, Frank, 499
Crothers, Rachel, 10, 435, 500, 501, 504, 505, 506, 509
Crouse, Russell, 509
Curran, Homer, 25, 27
Curtis, Margaret, 15, 475

Dane, Clemence, 500
David, Mack, 414
Davis, Benny, 484

Davis, Donald, 508
Davis, Eddie, 466
Davis, Irving Kaye, 315, 398
Davis, Owen, 408, 496, 500, 508, 510
Davis, Sheldon, 15, 403, 474
Dayton, Katharine, 507
de Casalis, Jeanne, 508
Dell, Floyd, 504
Denham, Reginald, 12, 451
Deval, Jacques, 508
Dietz, Howard, 448
Dodd, Lee Wilson, 501
Donnelly, Dorothy, 410
Drake, W. A., 505
Drinkwater, John, 499
Duke, Vernon, 448
du Maurier, Daphne, 18, 31
Dunham, Katherine, 19
Dunning, Philip, 502
d'Usseau, Arnaud, 494, 511

Eager, Edward, 477
Eliscu, Edward, 29
Elser, Frank B., 507
Emery, Gilbert, 500, 501
Epstein, Julius J. and Philip G., 465
Erens, Joseph, 414
Ervine, St. John, 499, 504
Eunson, Dale, 465

Farquhar, Marion, 479
Fauchois, René, 506
Feilbert, Edward Allen, 463
Ferber, Edna, 502, 503, 506, 508
Ferris, Walter, 504
Field, Salisbury, 499
Fields, Dorothy, 13, 451
Fields, Herbert, 13, 428, 451
Fields, Joseph, 395, 510, 511
Fitch, Clyde, 498
Flavin, Martin, 504
Florman, Irving, 407
Flotow, Friedrich von, 439
Foote, Horton, 464
Forbes, James, 499
Forrest, George, 27
Foster, Claiborne, 15, 468
Francke, Caroline, 463
Franken, Rose, 8, 11, 69, 198, 396, 423, 444, 505, 510
Friml, Rudolf, 402

Gale, Zona, 496
Galsworthy, John, 500, 503
George, Grace, 500
Geraldy, Paul, 500
Gershwin, George, 11, 412, 438, 496, 505
Gershwin, Ira, 412, 438, 496, 505
Gerstenberg, Alice, 7, 421
Geto, Alfred D., 404
Giacosa, G., 438
Gilbert, Robert, 405
Gilbert and Sullivan, 13, 17, 19, 30, 455
Gill, Frank, 22
Glaspell, Susan, 496, 505
Gleason, James, 502
Golden, Alfred L., 427
Goldsmith, Clifford, 509
Gordon, Ruth, 12, 164, 395, 446
Gore-Brown, R. F., 506
Gorney, Jay, 29
Gottesfeld, Chuno, 411
Goulding, Edmund, 502
Gounod, Charles, 473
Gow, James, 494, 511
Granville-Barker, Helen and Harley, 499, 504
Green, Eric Mawby, 463
Green, Paul, 496, 503, 505, 508, 510
Grieg, Edvard, 25, 27, 30
Guitry, Sasha, 499

Hagan, James, 506
Haight, George, 7, 425
Hamilton, Patrick, 449, 511
Hammerstein, Oscar, 2d, 9, 432, 442, 511
Hart, Lorenz, 9, 428, 429
Hart, Moss, 9, 20, 32, 69, 394, 395, 429, 497, 505, 507, 508, 509, 510
Harwood, H. M., 506
Hayden, John, 507
Hecht, Ben, 504
Hellman, Lillian, 3, 14, 69, 394, 467, 494, 495, 496, 507, 509, 510
Herbert, F. Hugh, 16, 483, 511
Heyward, Dorothy, 11, 412, 438, 445
Heyward, Du Bose, 11, 412, 438
Hoffman, Aaron, 415
Hooker, Brian, 402, 403
Housman, Laurence, 507
Houston, Noel, 480
Howard, Sidney, 31, 496, 501, 503, 506, 509

Hughes, Hatcher, 496, 501
Hughes, Richard, 8, 236, 355, 398, 427
Hurlbut, William, 502

Illica, L., 438

Jackson, Frederick, 482
James, Dan, 6, 511
Jamerson, Pauline, 11, 443
Janney, Russell, 402
Jerome, Helen, 508
Job, Thomas, 511
Johnson, Hall, 406
Johnson, Nunnally, 9, 433

Kasznar, Kurt, 404
Katzin, Winifred, 502
Kaufman, George S., 394, 496, 497, 500, 501, 502, 503, 504, 505, 506, 507, 508, 509, 510
Kelly, George, 496, 501, 502, 503
Kennedy, Mary, 502
Kern, Jerome, 25
Kesselring, Joseph, 510
Kilgallen, Dorothy, 477
Kingsley, Sidney, 10, 436, 495, 497, 506, 507, 511
Kirkland, Jack, 6, 12, 409, 447
Koch, Howard, 510
Kohn, Rose Simon, 434
Korngold, Erich Wolfgang, 470
Kraft, H. S., 460
Kummer, Clare, 499, 506

Lardner, Ring W., 504
Lascal, Milton, 424
Lasswell, Mary, 12, 447
Lawrence, D. H., 23
Lawrence, Reginald, 11, 443
Lawrence, Vincent, 30
Lee, Gypsy Rose, 8, 419
Lehar, Franz, 405
Leon, Victor, 405
Leoncavallo, R., 441
Leontovich, Eugenie, 31
Lerner, Jay, 426
Lerner, Sam, 411
Leslie, Aleen, 22, 420
Levy, Benn W., 505
Lewis, Sinclair, 506
Lindsay, Howard, 509
Livingston, Jerry, 414
Loewe, Frederick, 426

Lonsdale, Frederick, 7, 418, 502
Luther, Frank, 424

MacArthur, Charles, 504
MacGregor, Edgar, 412
Mandel, Frank, 442
Marion, George, Jr., 4, 400, 469
Marks, Gerald, 411
Marquis, Don, 501
Martin, Thomas, 23
Mascagni, P., 441
Maugham, William Somerset, 15, 469, 500, 503
Mayer, Edwin Justus, 502
McCarthy, Justin Huntly, 402, 498
McGlynn, Thomas, 13, 458
McGuire, William Anthony, 500
McLellan, C. M. S., 498
Meehan, John, Jr., 470
Meloney, Rose Franken, see Franken
Menasci, G., 441
Merimée, Prosper, 432
Middleton, George, 499
Milne, Alan Alexander, 500, 504
Miramova, Elena, 31
Mitchell, Thomas, 504
Molnar, Ferenc, 500, 501, 503
Moody, William Vaughn, 498
Moore, Lyford, 23
Morris, E. B., 13, 454
Morris, Lloyd, 31, 511
Murray, Gerard M., 16, 479
Murray, Ted, 484
Myers, Harry, 29

Nash, Ogden, 417
Neiman, Irving Gaynor, 404
Nelson, Ralph, 404
Nichols, Robert, 504
Nicholson, Kenyon, 398
Nugent, Elliott, 510
Nugent, J. C., 16, 481

O'Casey, Sean, 503
O'Dea, John B., 404
Odets, Clifford, 236, 397, 507, 509
Offenbach, Jacques, 470
O'Neill, Eugene, 496, 499, 500, 501, 502, 503, 505, 506
Orlob, Harold, 6, 416
Orr, Mary, 12, 451
Osborn, Paul, 8, 236, 355, 398, 427, 508, 510

Paley, Paul K., 459
Parker, Louis N., 498
Pascal, Ernest, 13, 453
Pascal, Milton, 466
Paver, Charles, 414
Pen, John, 460
Perelman, S. J., 417
Pergolesi, 479
Phillips, Peggy, 443
Pierson, Arthur, 426
Pollock, Channing, 501, 502
Porter, Cole, 13, 451
Post, W. H., 403
Price, Alonzo, 460
Prumbs, Lucille, 424
Puccini, G., 438, 441

Randolph, Clemence, 500
Raphaelson, Samson, 507, 510, 511
Reed, Mark, 508
Reichert, H., 410
Reinhardt, Gottfried, 470
Reizenstein, Elmer, 499
Rice, Elmer, 6, 69, 413, 496, 503, 505, 506, 510
Richman, Arthur, 463, 500
Riggs, Lynn, 505
Rigsby, Howard, 11, 445
Roberts, Ben, 405, 448, 477
Rodgers, Richard, 8, 428, 511
Romberg, Sigmund, 410, 442
Ronell, Ann, 439
Ross, Adrian, 405
Ross, Don, 424
Rotter, Fritz, 511
Rouverol, Aurania, 31
Royle, Edwin Milton, 498
Ryerson, Florence, 511
Ryskind, Morrie, 496, 505

Sardou, Victorien, 438
Saroyan, William, 9, 31, 431, 495, 497, 510
Schubert, Franz, 410
Schwab, Laurence, 442
Scott, Allan, 7, 425
Seaton, George, 467
Self, Edwin B., 20
Selver, Paul, 501
Selwyn, Edgar, 502
Shairp, Mordaunt, 507
Shakespeare, William, 24, 31, 418

Shapiro, Dan, 424, 466
Shattuck, Richard, 408
Sheldon, Edward, 498, 499
Sheldon, Sidney, 405, 448, 477
Shelley, Elsa, 15, 315, 398, 476
Sherman, Charles, 414
Sherman, Nat, 15, 471
Sherriff, R. C., 504, 508
Sherwood, Robert E., 7, 423, 497, 503, 505, 507, 508, 509
Sierra, G. Martinez, 503, 504
Skariatina, Irina, 12, 450
Smith, Dodie, 9, 431, 508
Smith, Harry James, 498
Spears, Patti, 481
Spewack, Bella and Samuel, 401, 507
Stallings, Laurence, 501
Stein, Leo, 405
Steinbeck, John, 495, 508, 510
Stephani, Frederick, 15, 476
Stewart, Donald Ogden, 504
Stolz, Robert, 405
Strauss, Richard, 30
Sturges, Preston, 504

Targioni, G., 441
Tarkington, Booth, 31, 396, 498, 499
Taylor, Byron, 20
Taylor, Rosemary, 465
Thomas, A. E., 506
Thomas, Augustus, 498
Thompson, Fred, 466
Thompson, Harlan, 23
Thompson, J. Lee, 408
Thurber, James, 510
Totheroh, Dan, 502
Treadwell, Sophie, 504, 511
Twain, Mark, 428
Turney, Robert, 508

Underhill, John Garrett, 503

Vale, Martin, 5, 405
Van Druten, John, 9, 31, 104, 394, 434, 494, 502, 507, 511
Vane, Sutton, 501
Varesi, Gilda, 499
Verdi, Giuseppi, 442, 473
Vincent, Allen, 511
Vollmer, Lula, 501

Walker, Don, 400, 428, 469
Waller, Thomas, 4, 400

Walling, Roy, 7, 422
Walpole, Hugh, 395
Walter, Eugene, 498
Walters, Lou, 424
Warnick, Clay, 477
Warren, Ruth, 502
Watkins, Maurine, 502
Watters, George Manker, 503
Webster, Margaret, 418
Weiler, Erich, 23
Weill, Kurt, 417
Weitzenkorn, Louis, 505
Welles, Orson, 30
Werfel, Franz, 14, 236, 397, 462, 494
West, Thomas, 23
Wexley, John, 504, 506

Wilder, Thornton, 11, 437, 497, 508, 511
Williams, Emlyn, 510
Williams, Jesse Lynch, 496, 499, 501
Willner, A. M., 410
Wilson, Harry Leon, 498, 501
Winter, Keith, 507
Wodehouse, P. G., 503
Wolf-Ferrari, 479
Wolfson, Victor, 508
Wood, Joseph, 414
Wright, Richard, 510
Wright, Robert, 27

Yellin, Gleb, 407

Zilboorg, Gregory, 500

INDEX OF PLAYS AND CASTS

Abe Lincoln in Illinois, 495, 497, 509
Abie's Irish Rose, 20, 25, 28, 395, 492
Abraham Lincoln, 499
Accent on Youth, 507
According to Law, 480
Adam and Eva, 499
Adonis, 492
Ah, Wilderness, 506
Aïda, 473
Alien Corn, 506
Alison's House, 496, 505
All for All, 6, 415
Allah Be Praised, 15, 469
Ambush, 500
American Way, The, 509
Amphitryon, 38, 397, 509
Angel Street, 3, 492, 511
Animal Kingdom, The, 505
Anna Christie, 496, 500
Another Language, 198, 396, 505
Another Love Story, 7, 418
Army Play by Play, 19, 404
Arsenic and Old Lace, 3, 4, 25, 28,
    491, 492, 510
Artists and Models, 424
As Husbands Go, 505
Awake and Sing, 507

Bad Man, The, 500
Barbara Frietchie, 498
Barretts of Wimpole Street, The, 505
Bat, The, 492
Beggar on Horseback, 501
Behold the Bridegroom, 503
Belle Helene, La, 470
Berkeley Square, 504
Beyond the Horizon, 496, 499
Big Time, 23, 411
Bill of Divorcement, A, 500
Biography, 397, 505
Bird in Hand, 493
Blackbirds, 492
Blackouts, 29
Blithe Spirit, 6, 19, 24, 29, 410, 492,
    510

Blossom Time, 6, 19, 24, 27, 30, 410,
    492
Bohème, La, 441, 474
Boomerang, The, 492
Both Your Houses, 497, 506
Boy Meets Girl, 401, 492, 507
Bride of the Lamb, 502
Brief Moment, 505
Bright Boy, 13, 461
Bright Lights of 1944, 6, 414
Broadway, 492, 502
Brother Rat, 492
Burlesque, 503
But Not Goodbye, 14, 467
Butter and Egg Man, The, 502
Button Your Lip, 404

Call It a Day, 508
Candle in the Wind, 397, 511
Career Angel, 16, 479
Carmen, 9, 11, 432, 439, 472, 474
Carmen Jones, 20, 432
Caukey, 13, 458
Cavalleria Rusticana, 441, 474
Changelings, The, 501
Chauve-Souris, 5, 407, 492
Cherry Orchard, The, 12, 450
Chicago, 502
Chicken Every Sunday, 465
Chicken Feed, 501
Children's Hour, The, 69, 394, 492,
    507
Christmas Carol, A., 31
Church Mouse, The, 396
Circle, The, 500
Clarence, 499
Claudia, 23, 28, 198, 396, 492, 510
Climbers, The, 498
Connecticut Yankee, A., 9, 20, 428
Constant Wife, The, 503
Coquette, 503
Corn Is Green, The, 19, 24, 28, 491,
    510
Correspondent Unknown, 25
Counsellor-at-Law, 491
Country Wife, The, 396

County Chairman, The, 498
Cox and Box, 19, 456
Cradle Song, The, 503
Craig's Wife, 496, 502
Criminal Code, The, 504
Crosstown Bus, 7
Curtain Time, 23
Cynara, 506

Daisy Mayme, 503
Damask Cheek, The, 31, 395, 511
Dancing Mothers, 502
Dark Eyes, 18, 19, 31, 491
Darling of the Gods, The, 498
Daughters of Atreus, 508
Dead End, 492, 507
Death Takes a Holiday, 504
Deburau, 499
Decent Birth a Happy Funeral, A, 31
Decision, 13, 69, 133, 395, 452
Déclassée, 499
Design for Living, 505
Desire Under the Elms, 501
Devil Passes, The, 505
Dinner at Eight, 506
Disraeli, 498
Distaff Side, The, 395, 507
Doctors Disagree, 11, 396, 444
Dodsworth, 506
Doll's House, A., 396
Doughgirls, The, 3, 18, 24, 395, 492, 511
Dover Road, The, 500
Dream of Romance, 30
Dream with Music, 15, 477
Drunkard, The, 26, 29
Duke in Darkness, The, 12, 449
Dulcy, 500
Dybbuk, The, 502

Early to Bed, 4, 15, 400
Earth Journey, 15, 474
Easiest Way, The, 498
East Is West, 492
Easy for Zee Zee, 26
8:30 Review, 30
Elizabeth the Queen, 398, 505
Emperor Jones, The, 500
End of Summer, 397, 507
Enemy, The, 502
Enter Madame, 499
Escape, 503
Eternal Road, The, 398

Ethan Frome, 396, 508
Eve of St. Mark, The, 397, 491, 511
Excursion, 508

Face, The, 30
Fair and Warmer, 396
Fall Guy, The, 502
Family Carnovsky, The, 19
Family Portrait, 509
Famous Mrs. Fair, The, 499
Farmer Takes a Wife, The, 507
Faust, 473
Feathers in a Gale, 11, 443
Firebrand, The, 502
First Cousins, 404
First Lady, 507
First Mrs. Fraser, The, 504
First Year, The, 492, 499
Five-Star Final, 505
Fledermaus, Die, 23, 30
Flight to the West, 510
Folies Bergère, 25
Follow the Girls, 14, 466
Fool, The, 501
For Keeps, 16, 483
Front Page, The, 504

George Washington Slept Here, 510
Get Away Old Man, 9, 431
Give and Take, 6, 415
Goat Song, 398
Golden Boy, 509
Gondoliers, The, 19, 456
Goodbye Again, 7, 425
Good Gracious, Annabelle, 499
Good News, 492
Good Night, Ladies, 18, 20, 22
Goose Hangs High, The, 501
Grand Hotel, 505
Great Divide, The, 498
Great God Brown, The, 502
Great Waltz, The, 20
Green Bay Tree, The, 507
Green Goddess, The, 500
Green Grow the Lilacs, 505
Green Hat, The, 502
Green Pastures, The, 492, 496, 504
Gypsy, 504

Hairpin Harmony, 6, 416
Hamlet, 24, 31
Harriet, 491, 511
He Who Gets Slapped, 500

Helen Goes to Troy, 470
Hell-bent fer Heaven, 496, 501
Hellzapoppin, 492
Her Master's Voice, 506
Here Come the Clowns, 509
Hero, The, 500
Hickory Stick, 15, 476
High Tor, 397, 494, 508
High Wind in Jamaica, A., 236, 355, 398
Highland Fling, A, 15, 475
H.M.S. Pinafore, 19, 30, 455
Holiday, 504
Hope for a Harvest, 511
House in Paris, The, 14, 463
House of Connelly, The, 505

Icebound, 496, 500
Ice Follies, 26
Idiot's Delight, 497, 507
If I Were King, 403, 498
I'll Take the High Road, 8, 424
In Abraham's Bosom, 496, 503
In Time to Come, 510
Innocent Voyage, The, 8, 236, 355, 398, 427
Iolanthe, 19, 457
Irene, 492
Is Zat So, 395, 492
It's a Wise Child, 31

Jackpot, 12, 448
Jacobowsky and the Colonel, 14, 236, 397, 462, 494
Jane Clegg, 499
Jane Eyre, 24, 29
Janie, 20, 25, 29, 491, 492
Jason, 511
Jest, The, 499
John Ferguson, 499
Johnny Johnson, 508
Journey's End, 504
June Moon, 504
Junior Miss, 19, 23, 28, 395, 491, 492, 511

Key Largo, 397, 509
Kiki, 492
Kind Lady, 395
Kingdom of God, The, 504
Kiss and Tell, 3, 16, 17, 23, 29, 492, 511
Kiss the Boys Good-bye, 509

Ladder, The, 492
Ladies' Night in a Turkish Bath, 22
Ladies of the Jury, 31
Lady and the Clown, The, 20
Lady, Behave, 427
Lady Chatterley's Lover, 23
Lady in the Dark, 394, 510
Lady of the Camellias, 398
Land of Fame, 6, 414
Last Mile, The, 504
Last of Mrs. Cheyney, The, 502
Late Christopher Bean, The, 506
Laugh Time, 23, 30, 411
Leah Kleschna, 498
Left Bank, The, 505
Let's Face It, 7, 492
Let Us Be Gay, 504
Letters to Lucerne, 511
Life with Father, 3, 18, 23, 28, 492, 509
Lightnin', 492
Liliom, 500
Listen, Professor, 11, 443
Little Accident, 504
Little Foxes, The, 69, 394, 495, 509
Lost Horizons, 507
Lovers and Friends, 9, 17, 431
Loyalties, 500

Machinal, 504
Maid as Mistress, The, 479
Maid in the Ozarks, 16, 18, 30
Mail Call, 404
Male Animal, The, 510
Mamma's Affair, 499
Man From Home, The, 498
Man Who Came to Dinner, The, 492, 510
Manhattan Nocturne, 7, 422
Margin for Error, 510
Martha, 11, 439
Mary of Scotland, 398, 506
Mary Rose, 500
Mary the 3d, 501
Meet the People, 28
Men in White, 497, 506
Merchant of Venice, 24, 31
Mercury Wonder Show, 30
Merrily We Roll Along, 507
Merry Widow, The, 3, 4, 405
Merton of the Movies, 501
Mexican Hayride, 13, 451
Michael and Mary, 504
Midsummer Night's Dream, 28

Mikado, The, 19, 30, 455
Milky Way, The, 491
Minick, 502
Miss Lulu Bett, 496
Moon Is Down, The, 510
Morning's at Seven, 510
Mother's Day, 22, 23
Mourning Becomes Electra, 18, 505
Mr. and Mrs. North, 25, 510
Mrs. Bumpstead-Leigh, 498
Mrs. January and Mr. X, 14, 463
Mrs. Kimball Presents, 13, 460
Mrs. Partridge Presents, 396, 502
Murder in a Nunnery, 31
Murder Without Crime, 5, 408
Music Master, The, 492
My Dear Children, 18
My Dear Public, 6, 411
My Sister Eileen, 31, 395, 492, 510

Naked Genius, The, 8, 419
Native Son, 11, 510
Nest, The, 500
New Life, A., 6, 69, 413
New Moon, 25, 30, 442, 493
Nice People, 500
Night Must Fall, 29
No More Ladies, 506
No Time for Comedy, 509

Of Mice and Men, 495, 508
Of Thee I Sing, 496, 505
Oklahoma, 3, 17, 19, 236, 355, 492, 511
Ol' Man Adam an' His Chillun, 504
Old Acquaintance, 395
Old English, 25
Old Maid, The, 497, 507
Old Soak, The, 501
On Borrowed Time, 398, 508
On Trial, 499
Once in a Lifetime, 394, 505
One Sunday Afternoon, 506
One Touch of Venus, 7, 417
Only the Heart, 464
Othello, 3, 7, 24, 31, 236, 355, 418
Our Town, 10, 437, 497, 508
Outrageous Fortune, 8, 11, 69, 198, 396, 423
Outward Bound, 501
Over 21, 12, 164, 395, 446
Overture, 505

Pack Up Your Troubles, 404
Pagliacci, 441, 474
Panama Hattie, 493
Paris Bound, 503
Patience, 19, 457
Patriots, The, 10, 19, 436, 491, 495, 511
Peepshow, 453
Peg o' My Heart, 492
Personal Appearance, 25, 28, 31, 493
Peter Pan, 396
Petrified Forest, The, 7, 423, 507
Philadelphia Story, The, 509
Pick-up Girl, 15, 315, 398, 476
Pigeons and People, 506
Pillar to Post, 434
Pins and Needles, 492
Pirates of Penzance, The, 19, 456
Play's the Thing, The, 503
Plough and the Stars, The, 503
Porgy, 412, 503
Porgy and Bess, 6, 11, 412, 438
Pretty Little Parlor, 15, 468
Pride and Prejudice, 508
Prologue to Glory, 509
Public Relations, 14, 465
Pursuit of Happiness, 31

Quiet Week-End, 31

Racket, The, 503
Rain, 492, 500
Rain from Heaven, 398
Ramshackle Inn, 12, 446
Rebecca, 18, 19, 31
Rebound, 504
Reunion in Vienna, 505
Right Next to Broadway, 459
Rigoletto, 474
Road to Rome, The, 503
Rocket to the Moon, 509
Romance, 498
Romeo and Juliet, 398
Room Service, 493
Rope's End, 31
Rosalinda, 491, 492
Rose Marie, 492
Rose Masque, The, 23, 30
Royal Family, The, 503
Ruddigore, 20, 457
Run, Little Chillun, 5, 406
R.U.R., 501

Sailor, Beware, 493
St. Helena, 508
Sally, 25, 30, 492
Saturday's Children, 502
School for Brides, 20, 22
Searching Wind, The, 3, 14, 69, 394, 467, 494, 496
Secret of Suzanne, The, 479
Separate Rooms, 492
Serva Padrona, La, 479
Seven Keys to Baldpate, 498
Seventeen, 396
Seventh Heaven, 492
Shadow and Substance, 508
Shanghai Gesture, The, 18
Sheppey, 15, 469
Shining Hour, The, 507
Show Boat, 25, 30, 492
Show-Off, The, 501
Show Time, 23, 411
Shuffle Along, 493
Silk Hat Harry, 30
Silver Cord, The, 503
Six Cylinder Love, 500
Skin Game, The, 500
Skin of Our Teeth, The, 491, 497, 511
Skylark, 510
Sleep It Off, 23
Slightly Married, 23, 420
Slightly Scandalous, 482
Snark Was a Boojum, The, 408
Something for the Boys, 21, 491
Song of Norway, 25, 27, 28, 30
Sons o' Fun, 21, 24, 29, 491, 492
South Pacific, 11, 445
Springtime for Henry, 25
Squaw Man, The, 498
Stage Door, 508
Star and Garter, 491, 492
Stars on Ice, 491, 492
Star-Wagon, The, 397, 508
Storm Operation, 12, 69, 277, 397, 447
Strange Interlude, 496, 503
Strange Play, A, 481
Street Scene, 492, 496, 503
Strictly Dishonorable, 492, 504
Student Prince, The, 19, 24, 30, 491
Suds in Your Eye, 12, 447
Sunny, 492
Sun-Up, 501
Susan and God, 10, 435, 509

Swan, The, 501
Sweet 'n Hot, 30

Take a Bow, 484
Take It As It Comes, 13, 454
Tarnish, 501
Thank You, Svoboda, 13, 460
That Old Devil, 16, 30, 481
There Shall Be No Night, 497, 509
There's Always Juliet, 104, 395
They Shall Not Die, 506
They Knew What They Wanted, 496, 501
This Is the Army, 9
Those Endearing Young Charms, 4, 13, 31, 69, 133, 395, 400
Three's a Family, 3, 20
Three Men on a Horse, 492
Three Sisters, The, 19, 396
Till I Come Back to You, 433
Time of Your Life, The, 31, 495, 497, 510
Tinted Venus, The, 417
Tobacco Road, 6, 12, 409, 492
Tomorrow and Tomorrow, 505
Tomorrow the World, 3, 18, 491, 493, 494, 511
Tosca, 11, 438, 474
Tovarich, 508
Traviata, 442, 473
Trial by Jury, 19, 30, 455
Trip to Chinatown, A, 492
Tropical Review, 19
Trovatore, 474
Try and Get It, 403
Turnabout, 29
Tweedles, 396
Two in a Bed, 30
Two Mrs. Carrolls, The, 5, 405

Unchastened Woman, The, 499
Uncle Harry, 18, 511
Unexpected Honeymoon, 18
Unexpected Husband, 18

Vagabond King, The, 15, 402, 493
Valley Forge, 507
Victoria Regina, 492, 507
Victory Belles, 7, 421
Vinegar Tree, The, 398
Voice of the Turtle, The, 9, 104, 394, 434, 494

Wallflower, 12, 451
Waltz King, The, 20, 24, 30
War President, 15, 471
Watch on the Rhine, 69, 394, 495, 510
We, the People, 506
Wedding Bells, 499
Wednesday's Child, 506
What a Life, 492, 509
What Price Glory, 501
What's Up, 8, 426
When Ladies Meet, 506
Where'er We Go, 404
White Cargo, 492
White Steed, The, 509
Why Marry, 496, 499
Why Not, 501
Wild Birds, 502
Winged Victory, 9, 32, 69, 394, 429
Wings Over Europe, 504
Winter Soldiers, 6, 511

Winterset, 397, 494, 507
Wisdom Tooth, The, 502
Witching Hour, The, 498
Within the Law, 492
Without Love, 19, 24, 29
Women, The, 492, 508
Wonder Boy, 395
World We Make, The, 509
World's Full of Girls, The, 9, 433

Yeomen of the Guard, The, 19, 458
Yes, My Darling Daughter, 508
You and I, 500
You Can't Do That to Svoboda, 460
You Can't Take It With You, 19, 492, 497, 508
Young Man of Today, 31
Young Woodley, 395, 502
Youngest, The, 502
Yours for Fun, 29

Ziegfeld Follies, 3, 493

INDEX OF PRODUCERS, DIRECTORS AND DESIGNERS

Abbott, George, 431, 475
Abravanel, Maurice, 417
Adler, Stella, 422
Adrian, 464, 482
Adrian, Henry, 421
Alexander, David, 423
Alloy, Al, 414
Alton, Robert, 401
Amend, Karl, 459
American Actors Theatre, The, 464
American Opera Association, 30
Anderson, Maxwell, 447
Andrews, Herbert, 413, 438
Appell, Don, 480
Armitage, Buford, 444
Aronson, Boris, 426, 445
Ayers, Lemuel, 453

Balanchine, George, 406, 426, 478
Balieff, Nikita, 408
Ballard, Lucinda, 412, 444
Ballet Russe de Monte Carlo, 440
Baron, Milton, 443, 460
Barratt, Watson, 410, 424, 461, 469, 476
Bay, Howard, 406, 413, 417, 433, 444, 447, 465, 467, 468
Beckhard, Arthur J., 461
Behrman, S. N., 447
Bein, Albert, 414, 415
Bellamy, Ralph, 468
Belmont Opera Company, 442
Bennett, Harry, 481
Bennett, High, 427
Berle, Milton, 424
Berman, A. L., 415
Bernstein, Aline, 427, 443, 468
Billings, Andrew, 479
Bischoff, Samuel, 22
Blackfriars' Guild, The, 13, 15, 16, 458, 474, 480
Blake, Robert, 465
Bleyer, Archie, 401
Bloomfield, Harry, 476
Bloomingdale, Alfred, 15, 401, 469
Blumenfeld, Joe, 25

Bogdanoff, Rose, 436, 465, 472
Bolton, William R., 4, 404
Borde, Albert, 466
Brandes, Hildegart, 475
Brandt, George W., 422
Brentano, Felix, 406, 479
Bronston, Samuel, 453
Brown, Anthony, 409, 454
Brown, Harry Joe, 467
Brown, Katharine, 447
Buckley, Emerson, 472
Burke, Melville, 420, 421
Burnside, R. H., 13, 455
Burton, David, 453
Burton, Martin, 443
Burton, Robert, 435

Caesar, Irving, 6, 411
Carpenter, Edward Childs, 466
Carradine, John, 24, 31
Carroll, Earl, 30
Carthay, 410
Cerrone, Jean, 440
Chambrun, Jacques, 469
Chandler, Joe, 460
Chaney, Stewart, 411, 427, 433, 434, 449, 462, 463, 466, 468, 478
Children's Opera Company, 474
Choate, Edward, 133, 452
Chodorov, Edward, 133, 400, 452
Cirker and Robbins, 402, 460
City Center Opera Company, 438, 439, 441, 442
Civic Opera, 20, 406
Civic Repertory Theatre, 450
Clark, Peggy, 446
Cohen, Alexander H., 414, 449
Cole, Jack, 470
Colligan, James, 476
Comstock, F. Ray, 407
Condell, H. A., 441
Cooper, Lew, 5, 406, 407
Cooper, Melville, 471
Cornell, Katharine, 9, 17, 19, 396, 431

544

Cracraft, 423, 425
Crawford, Cheryl, 412, 417, 438
Czettel, Ladislas, 471
Czinner, Paul, 5, 405

Dalamatoff, Michael, 407
Daniels, J. B., 415, 477
David, William B., 23
Davis, Meyer, 5, 406, 451
Davis, Peter, 444
Dean, Dudley S., 430
de Forest, Edward, 421
Del Bondia, John Howell, 408, 447
de Liagre, Alfred, 104, 434
Delmar, Harry, 467
de Mille, Agnes, 417
Denham, Sergei J., 440
Denham, Reginald, 405, 451
de Paur, Leonard, 430
de Reeder, Pierre, 410
Derwent, Clarence, 463
Dicks, Joseph, 479
Drey, Walter, 422
du Bois, Raoul Pene, 433
du Pont, Paul, 413, 417, 438, 468
Dworkin, Harry, 482

Eckley, Dan, 414
Edwards, Norman, 403
Eisele, Lou, 467
Elkins, Marie Louise, 476
Endrey, Eugene, 480, 481
Ermoloff, George, 403
Escholiers, The, 471
Evans, Maurice, 24
Ewing, Marjorie, 476
Experimental Theatre, Inc., 15, 471
Eyssell, G. S., 472

Fabian, Thomas, 459
Fabroni, Joseph, 442
Faggen, Jay, 408
Feder, Abe, 430
Fielding, Marjery, 484
Finklehoffe, Fred, 23, 411
Fischer, Clifford C., 25
Florell, Walter, 406
Fox, Frederick, 400, 405, 409, 414, 415, 420, 428, 446, 453, 464, 477, 480
Frank, Perry, 442
Franken, Rose, 396, 424, 444
Friedlander, William B., 459

Freedley, Vinton, 448
Friedman, Charles, 433

Gallo, Fortune, 472
Geddes, Norman Bel, 398
Gerken, Ted, 460
Gest, Morris, 5, 407
Giaquinto, Paolo, 472
Golden, Alfred L., 428
Golden, John, 4, 404, 435, 467
Gordon, Max, 4, 133, 400, 446
Gordon, Michael, 447
Gordon, Robert H., 426, 470
Graf, Herbert, 471
Grant, Mary, 452
Greanin, Leon, 5, 407
Green, Harry, 416
Gross, Edward, 465
Gurney, Dennis, 459, 475

Haakon, Paul, 452
Hack, Moe, 436, 447, 461
Hackett, Jeanette, 416
Haggott, John, 418
Halasz, Laszlo, 11, 439, 441
Hale, Rodney, 402
Hardwicke, Cedric, 469
Hargrave, Roy, 449, 476
Harris, Jed, 433, 437
Hart, Moss, 430
Hartz, Milan, 419
Hathaway, Joan, 22
Hayman, Clifford, 424
Heitland, W. Emerton, 475
Helburn, Theresa, 236, 237, 355, 427, 462
Henderson, Robert, 449
Herbert, Leo, 475
Hertz, Joseph Ross, 404
Herz, Otto, 479
Highley, Richard, 442
Hilliard, Mack, 416
Hirst, George, 428
Holbrook, William, 428
Hopkins, Arthur, 443
Horner, Harry, 430
Houston, Grace, 415, 426
Howard, Leslie, 423
Hunter, Mary, 464

Irwin, Will, 426, 467

Jackson, Frederick, 482
Janney, Russell, 403

Jefferson, Laurette, 424, 449
Jenkins, George, 401, 452, 470
Jessel, George, 5, 406
Jessye, Eva, 413, 438
Johnson, Albert, 412
Johnson, Hall, 407
Johnstone, Johnnie, 482
Jones, Robert Edmond, 449, 471

Kamarova, Natalie, 424
Kanin, Garson, 164, 396
Kaplan, Harriet, 476
Karson, Nat, 428
Kaufman, George S., 8, 420, 446
Kavanaugh, Ray, 484
Kazan, Elia, 237, 417, 462
Keith, Ian, 23
Kellam, William, 436
Kellner, Murray, 414
Kennedy, John, 424, 452
Kent, Carl, 453, 480
Kerz, Leo, 481
Kipness, Joseph, 414, 449
Kirkland, Alexander, 409
Kirkland, Jack, 6, 409, 448
Kiviette, 449
Kollmar, Richard, 4, 15, 477, 478
Korngold, Erich Wolfgang, 471
Kraft, H. S., 461
Kroll, Louis, 455
Kuhn, Kathryn, 424

La Guardia, Fiorella H., 9
Landau, Irving, 471
Landau, Jack, 472
Lang, Howard, 22
Langner, Lawrence, 236, 237, 355, 427, 462
Le Gallienne, Eva, 450
Leonard, Charles, 482
Leoni, Eva, 474
Lester, Edwin, 27
Le Tang, Henry, 412, 478
Levant, Harry, 412, 452
Leve, Samuel, 451, 461
Linder, Jack, 23
Littau, Joseph, 433
Littlefield, Catherine, 467
Livingston, Billy, 420
Loew, E. M., 424
Lonsdale, Frederick, 418
Loring, Eugene, 433
Los Angeles Civic Light Opera Association, 23, 25, 27

Lotito, Louis, 418
Love, Kermit, 417, 448
Lowe, David, 445

Mahieu, 416
Mainbocher, 417
Majer, Joseph, 403
Martin, Wolfgang, 442
Massine, Leonide, 471
Maugham, Dora, 416
Maynard, Marjorie, 425
McClintic, Guthrie, 9, 431
McGee, Truly, 414
McKee, Wesley, 437
McQuillan, Thomas, 482
Meisner, Sanford, 425, 444
Meloney, William Brown, 8, 11, 198, 423, 444
Merlin, Frank, 403
Merlin, Ving, 470
Mero-Irion, Yolanda, 405, 470, 479
Merrick, David, 461
Meth, Max, 414, 424, 449, 478
Michon, Michel, 407
Mielziner, Jo, 435
Miller, Gilbert, 8, 198, 396, 423, 483
Moeller, Philip, 236
Morris, Newbold, 9
Morrison, Paul, 425, 464, 482
Morros, Boris, 24
Moscow Art Theatre, 407, 450
Moses, John, 468
Motley, 431, 450, 475
Muir, Jean, 443
Muse, Clarence, 407
Myers, Richard, 463

New Opera Company, 405, 470, 479
New York City Center of Music and Drama, 9, 435, 438, 439, 441, 442
New York City Symphony, 440
Nugent, Elliott, 16, 464
Nugent, J. C., 482

O'Connell, Arthur, 404
Oenslager, Donald, 416
Olsen and Johnson, 21
Orlob, Harold, 6, 416
Osborn, Paul, 427
Oshrin, H. H., 409
Ostrander, A. A., 416

Paley, Paul K., 459
Pasadena Community Playhouse, 30

Pascal, Ernest, 453
Paul, Michael, 409
Pemberton, Brock, 25, 434
Perry, Antoinette, 434
Phillips, Wendell K., 472
Pitou, Augustus, 394
Platt, Joseph B., 448
Playwrights' Company, 12, 413, 436, 447
Poll, Martin, 414
Price, Alonzo, 460

Raiguel, Phil, 421
Redstone, Michael, 424
Reinhardt, Max, 28, 470
Reud, Robert, 5, 405, 446
Reynolds, James, 403
Rice, Elmer, 413, 447
Robinson, Armin L., 454
Roche, Emeline, 476
Rodgers, Richard, 428
Romanoff, Boris, 407
Root, John, 431, 434, 444, 475
Rose, Billy, 9, 20, 432
Rose, David, 429, 430
Ross, Don, 424
Ross, Robert, 413, 438
Ruben, José, 441, 442, 443
Rychterik, Richard, 442

Sample, James, 439
San Carlo Opera Company, 472
San Francisco Light Opera Association, 23, 25
Schmidlapp, W. Horace, 445
Schunzel, Reinhold, 23
Schwezoff, Igor, 403
Schwieger, Hans, 441
Sharpe, Robert Redington, 409
Shaw, Robert, 433
Shay, David, 479
Sherwood, Mary Elizabeth, 7, 423, 425
Sherwood, Robert E., 447
Shipstads and Johnson, 26
Short, Hassard, 13, 433, 452
Shoup, Howard, 430
Shubert, Messrs., 6, 13, 14, 24, 410
Shumlin, Herman, 69, 467, 468
Siegmeister, Elie, 437
Simonson, Lee, 236
Sircom, Arthur, 446, 464
Skirball, John, 14, 462

Small, Jack, 470
Small, Paul, 23, 411
Smith, Oliver, 443
Sondheimer, Hans, 442
Sorel, Felicia, 407, 412
Soudeikine, Serge, 407
Sovey, Raymond, 403, 408, 418, 424, 443, 446, 449, 483
Stage Costumes, Inc., 410
Stebbins, Rowland, 436
Stokowski, Leopold, 440
Stolz, Robert, 406
Strasberg, Lee, 445
Stratford-upon-Avon Players, 24
Stroock, Bianca, 451
Swobodo, Vecheslay, 407

Theatre Guild, 7, 8, 13, 19, 236, 355, 397, 399, 418, 427, 438, 462
Thomson, Gordon B., 404
Todd, Michael, 8, 13, 21, 315, 419, 451, 476
Traube, Shepard, 436
Tripp, Paul, 404

United States Army Air Forces, 429

Vail, Lester, 465
Vajda, Barbara, 30
Valle, Mario, 472
Van Druten, John, 434
Van Grove, Isaac, 479
Velden, Kaj, 484
Victor, Lucia, 401
Vroom, Lodewick, 481

Wallace, Ben, 484
Walters, Lou, 424, 484
Wanger, Wally, 484
Ward, Toni, 436, 443
Warnow, Mark, 426
Watkins, Perry, 407, 414, 422, 454
Weatherly, Tom, 408
Webster, Margaret, 12, 450
Weidman, Charles, 443, 449
Welles, Orson, 30
Wertheim, Maurice, 236
Westley, Helen, 236
Wharton, Carly, 450
Wharton, John F., 447
White, Al, 428
White, Miles, 401, 470, 478

Whorf, Richard, 467
Wildberg, John J., 412, 417, 438
Wilson, Alan, 404
Wilson, John C., 410, 411, 428, 431
Wiman, Dwight Deere, 355, 399
Windust, Bretaigne, 5, 408
Wolmut, Hans, 439, 441
Wolper, Dave, 14, 466

Woodruff, Joan, 479
Woods, A. H., 403

Yazvinsky, Jean, 440
Yiddish Art Theatre, 19
Yokel, Axel, 408
Youmans, Vincent, 12
Young, Felix, 30